Cognitive Linguistics and Translation

Applications of Cognitive Linguistics

Editors
Gitte Kristiansen
Francisco J. Ruiz de Mendoza Ibáñez

Honorary editor
René Dirven

Volume 23

Cognitive Linguistics and Translation

Advances in Some Theoretical
Models and Applications

Edited by
Ana Rojo and Iraide Ibarretxe-Antuñano

DE GRUYTER
MOUTON

ISBN 978-3-11-048478-6
e-ISBN 978-3-11-030294-3
ISSN 1861–4078

Library of Congress Cataloging-in-Publication Data
A CIP Catalog record for this book has been applied for at the Library of Congress.

Bibliografische Information der Deutschen Nationalbibliothek
The Deutsche Nationalbibliothek lists this publication in the Deutsche Nationalbibliografie;
detailed bibliographic data are available in the Internet at http://dnb.dnb.de.

© 2013 Walter de Gruyter GmbH, Berlin/Boston
Typesetting: Apex CoVantage, LLC, Herndon, Virginia, USA
Printing and binding: Hubert & Co. GmbH & Co. KG, Göttingen

♾ Printed on acid-free paper
Printed in Germany
www.degruyter.com

Contents

Author index —— vii
Mona Baker
Foreword —— xi

Introduction —— 1
Ana Rojo and Iraide Ibarretxe-Antuñano
Cognitive Linguistics and Translation Studies: Past, present and future —— 3

Part I: Cognitive Linguistics and Translation Theory —— 31

Sandra L. Halverson
Implications of Cognitive Linguistics for Translation Studies —— 33
Ricardo Muñoz Martín
More than a way with words: The interface between Cognitive Linguistics and Cognitive Translatology —— 75
Celia Martín de León
Who cares if the cat is on the mat? Contributions of cognitive models of meaning to translation —— 99

Part II: Meaning and translation —— 123

Hans C. Boas
Frame Semantics and translation —— 125
Eva Samaniego Fernández
The impact of Cognitive Linguistics on Descriptive Translation Studies: Novel metaphors in English-Spanish newspaper translation as a case in point —— 159
Mario Brdar and Rita Brdar-Szabó
Translating (by means of) metonymy —— 199

Part III: Constructions and translation —— 227

Elżbieta Tabakowska
(Cognitive) grammar in translation: Form as meaning —— 229
Iraide Ibarretxe-Antuñano and Luna Filipović
Lexicalisation patterns and translation —— 251

Ana Rojo and Javier Valenzuela
Constructing meaning in translation: The role of constructions in translation problems —— 283

Part IV: **Culture and translation** —— 311

Enrique Bernárdez
A cognitive view on the role of culture in translation —— 313
Farzad Sharifian and Maryam Jamarani
Cultural conceptualisations and translating political discourse —— 339

Part V: **Beyond translation** —— 373

Michele I. Feist
Experimental lexical semantics at the crossroads between languages —— 375
Anna Hatzidaki
A cognitive approach to translation: The psycholinguistic perspective —— 395

Author and Subject Index —— 415

Language Index —— 420

Author index

Ana Rojo
Universidad de Murcia
Departamento de Traducción e Interpretación
Campus de La Merced
Plaza de la Universidad 30071 Murcia
Spain
E-Mail: anarojo@um.es

Iraide Ibarretxe-Antuñano
Universidad de Zaragoza
Facultad de Filosofía y Letras
Departamento de Lingüística General e Hispánica
Pedro Cerbuna, 12
E-50009 Zaragoza
Spain
E-Mail: iraide@unizar.es

Sandra L. Halverson
Norges Handelshøyskole / Norwegian School of Economics
Institutt for fagspråk og interkulturell kommunikasjon/ Department of Professional and Intercultural Communication
Norwegian School of Economics
Helleveien 30
NO-5045 Bergen
Norway
E-Mail: Sandra.Halverson@nhh.no

Ricardo Muñoz Martín
Universidad de Las Palmas de Gran Canaria
Facultad de Traducción e Interpretación
C/Pérez del Toro, 1
35003 Las Palmas de Gran Canaria
Spain
E-Mail: rmunoz@dfm.ulpgc.es

Celia Martín de León
Universidad de Las Palmas de Gran Canaria
Facultad de Traducción e Interpretación
C/Pérez del Toro, 1
35003 Las Palmas de Gran Canaria
Spain
E-Mail: cmartin@dfm.ulpgc.es

Hans C. Boas
The University of Texas at Austin
Department of Germanic Studies
2505 University Ave, C3300
Austin, TX 78712–1088
USA
E-Mail: hcb@mail.utexas.edu

Eva Samaniego
Dpto. de Filologías Extranjeras y sus Lingüísticas
UNED
Despacho 3, planta -2
Senda del Rey s/n
28040 Madrid
Spain
E-Mail: esamaniego@flog.uned.es

Mario Brdar
Josip Juraj Strossmayer University
Faculty of Humanities and Social Sciences
L. Jägera 9
31000 Osijek
Croatia
E-Mail: mbrdar@ffos.hr

Rita Brdar-Szabó
Eötvös Loránd University
Faculty of Arts
School of Germanic Studies
Rákóczi út. 5.
1088 Budapest
Hungary
E-Mail: ritamario@dravanet.hu

Elżbieta Tabakowska
UNESCO Chair for translation Studies and Intercultural Communication
Jagiellonian University
ul. Czapskich 4
31–110 Kraków
Poland
E-Mail: elzbieta.muskat-tabakowska@uj.edu.pl

Luna Filipović
University of East Anglia
School of Language and Communication Studies
Faculty of Arts and Humanities
Norwich Research Park
Norwich NR4 7TJ.
UK
E-Mail: L.Filipovic@uea.ac.uk

Javier Valenzuela
Universidad de Murcia
Departamento de Filología Inglesa
Campus de La Merced
Plaza de la Universidad 30071 Murcia
Spain
E-Mail: jvalen@um.es

Enrique Bernárdez
Universidad Complutense de Madrid
Facultad de Filología
Departamento de Filología Románica, Filología Eslava y Lingüística General
Ciudad Universitaria
28040 Madrid
Spain
E-Mail: ebernard@filol.ucm.es

Farzad Sharifian
Monash University
English as an International Language
School of Languages, Cultures and Linguistics
Building 11
Melbourne, Victoria, 3800
Australia
E-Mail: Farzad.Sharifian@arts.monash.edu.au

Maryam Jamarani
School of Languages & Comparative
Cultural Studies
Gordon Greenwood Building,
University of Queensland
Brisbane Q 4072
Australia
E-Mail: maryam.jamarani@monash.edu

Michelle Feist
Institute of Cognitive Science
University of Louisiana at Lafayette
P. O. Drawer 43772
Lafayette, LA 70504-3772
USA
E-Mail:feist@louisiana.edu

Anna Hatzidaki
Universitat Pompeu Fabra
Center of Brain and Cognition
Speech Production and Bilingualism
Group
Tànger, 122–140
08018 Barcelona
Spain
E-Mail: annh_22@yahoo.com

Mona Baker
University of Manchester
Centre for Translation and
Intercultural Studies
School of Languages, Linguistics and
Cultures
Oxford Road M13 9PL
UK
E-Mail: mona.baker@manchester.ac.uk

Foreword

Translation and interpreting are complex phenomena that have been examined from a variety of perspectives – linguistic, literary, political, social, and cognitive. These perspectives are not mutually exclusive; they complement each other and enrich our understanding of translation and interpreting in a variety of ways.

Translation Studies has often been described as an interdiscipline that thrives on exploring connections and synergies with other fields of enquiry. Although issues of cognition have always attracted considerable attention, especially in interpreting studies, the current volume represents one of the few sustained attempts to explore the interface between Cognitive Linguistics and Translation Studies from a range of perspectives. It brings a wide range of voices to bear on this important area of enquiry and features a series of detailed theoretical expositions and case studies.

One of the advantages of bringing insights from Cognitive Linguistics and Cognitive Psychology to bear on the study of translation is that cognitive approaches in general place the translator/interpreter – rather than the text – at the centre of enquiry. They also encourage a view of translation as a dynamic, fluid activity that involves several parties and is influenced by a wide range of environmental and other factors, as is evident in Sager's account of the phenomenon (1994: 139):

> The process of translation itself constitutes a temporary suspension, of variable duration, of an intended communication process and therefore a separation of the source text from its production environment and the pragmatic meaning that can be associated with it. To justify and sustain this suspension, we must assume a strong initial motivation to communicate or to receive information which cannot be fulfilled in the intended manner because of a language barrier. The need for communication must be considered important enough to wait for the translation to be carried out and to engage other parties, i.e. mediators, to assist. Time and cost factors introduce a certain level of formality into the proceedings and increase the complexity of the task.

Cognitive approaches share Sager's focus on the conditions under which mediation takes place, the manner in which it proceeds, and the various ways in which it is influenced by a wide range of factors – environmental, emotional, linguistic, memory-related, and so on.

Although Translation Studies is widely recognized as interdisciplinary by nature, borrowing concepts and exploiting insights from other disciplines on a regular basis, this interaction must lead to new insights to be worthwhile. Interdisciplinarity does not mean uncritical borrowing or mechanistic copying of theoretical notions. The current collection of articles demonstrates how sustained engagement with another discipline can provide a platform for innovation and productive critique and offers a glimpse of the insights that Translation Studies is capable of feeding into other disciplines.

Mona Baker
January 2012

Reference

Sager, Juan C. (1994) Language Engineering and Translation. Consequences of Automation, Amsterdam & Philadelphia: John Benjamins.

Introduction

Ana Rojo and Iraide Ibarretxe-Antuñano
Cognitive Linguistics and Translation Studies: Past, present and future[*]

1 Introduction

For more than thirty years now Cognitive Linguists have striven to drift away from generativist attempts to explain linguistic patterns as internal to language. Their endeavours to relate language structure to cognition have contributed to enrich long-established linguistic areas (e.g. lexical semantics, grammar, phonology or discourse studies) with other aspects related to cognition, such as construction grammar, conceptual metaphor and blending, conceptual organisation (e.g. metonymy, Frame Semantics, iconicity), construal and subjectivity or linguistic relativism. In their attempt to connect the study of language to the study of the mind, they have brought linguistics closer to other disciplines such as psychology, sociology, embodied philosophy and cognitive science. This volume contains a collection of papers which discuss the contributions of Cognitive Linguistics to translation, a discipline long kept at bay from structuralist approaches to language.

Before we proceed to describing the contents of the volume, we will summarise the evolution of the relationship between translation and linguistics. This evolution signals the advancements of both disciplines and constitutes the framework which motivates the elaboration of the present volume.

2 Translation and linguistics: A love-hate relationship

Translation and linguistics have always held a love-hate relationship. On the one hand, their relationship has been marked by an irresistible attraction; translation scholars have searched linguistic works for concepts and principles suitable to be applied to translation, and linguists have found in translation an excellent source of examples for language teaching and the contrastive study of language. On the other hand, this attraction has at times turned into mutual dislike; linguists have looked down on translation as a type of second-class

---

[*] This research has been funded by grant FFI2010-14903 from the Spanish Ministry of Economy and Competitiveness.

language activity which they have long considered inadequate as a language teaching method and too complex to reveal reliable data on linguistic communication. Meanwhile, translation scholars have reacted to this patronising attitude of linguists with a mutual scornful stance which has highlighted the inability of linguistics to account for the cultural and cognitive aspects of translation. In this section, we describe the evolution of this love-hate relationship in order to show that the principles of Cognitive Linguistics can provide a suitable meeting point where linguistics and translation can finally forget their differences and start working together towards a cognitive theory of language and translation.

2.1 The beginnings: The 1970s and early 1980s

At the end of the 1970s and beginning of the 1980s, translation approaches shifted from a traditionally prescriptive methodology to a descriptive one. The earliest linguistic approaches focused on the contrast of the language system overlooking questions related to language use. From Vinay and Darbelnet's *Stylistique comparée du français et de l'anglais* (1958), linguistics became the main analytical tool to systematise translation phenomena. A "bottom-up" methodology was adopted which proceeded from the level of words and covered the different linguistic levels in order to establish a list of translation procedures which helped predict translation errors. The list of procedures varied according to the perspective adopted in the study of the linguistic aspects of translation: from the classical structuralism of Vinay and Darbelnet's contrastive stylistics (1958), to Catford's (1965) Hallidayan systemic-functional grammar, Vázquez-Ayora's (1977) generative grammar or García Yebra's (1982) traditional contrastive linguistics. But irrespective of the linguistic method used, all these academic works have been highly criticised, being repeatedly accused of adopting a contrastive approach in which equivalence at word or sentence level was the central issue. Their use of decontextualised sentences and their lack of attention to communicative factors soon moved these approaches away from the focus of any translation theory.

The endeavours to put an end to the servitude of translation to the source text coincided with the move from contrastive to text linguistics by the mid-1970s and with the acknowledgment of the audience's role brought about in biblical translation (Nida 1964; Nida and Taber 1969). Both in linguistics and Translation Studies the focus of attention moved from the linguistic system to language use, from the individual sign to the text. These approaches based on text linguistics defined translation as a textual operation in which the text became the central factor in the translation process. Text-based approaches to translation are highly varied; some examples are those by Neubert 1985; Neubert and Shreve 1992; Wilss 1982; Baker 1992 or Hatim and Mason 1990, 1997. But despite the differences, all of them shared a common interest for the textual factors which take part in the translation process, and highlighted the important role context, discourse and pragmatic factors play in such process.

However, the revalued importance of context and pragmatics which was shouted from the rooftops of textual approaches was still inadequate to account for their role in the translation process. In textual approaches context and receptor were still envisioned as text-bound secondary issues, whose main functions were helping disambiguate indeterminate expressions and establish their function within the text. This prime dependency on text still undervalued the primary role of cultural context in literary translation and failed to appreciate the relevance for the translator's decisions of the effect which the function of a translated text has on a given audience. To bridge these gaps, sociocultural and function-based models of translation are developed through the 1980s and 1990s in what has been called the "cultural turn" of Translation Studies.

2.2 The distant past: The 1980s and early 1990s

Function-based models of translation took as their starting point the study of text in a given situation and emphasised the role of the receptor and the communicative situation in which the translated text is received by a given audience. They expanded Nida's concept of dynamic equivalence, contributing to change the focus of attention from equivalence of linguistic units to equivalence of the text's communicative function, which was established in relation to its audience. Among the most radical versions of this type of approach we find Vermeer's (1989) *Skopostheorie* and Holz-Mänttäri's (1984) approach. They postulate that the translator is the one who defines the purpose or *skopos* of a given translation on the basis of the receptors it is aimed at and the combination of the other factors which take part in the communicative situation. The function of a translation may differ from that of the source text, since their production processes are different and may, thus, have different communicative purposes. If the communication contexts of both source and target texts are different by nature, the similarity of value which underlies the notion of equivalence becomes obsolete. Instead, they adopt the notion of "adequacy" to the function or purpose which the translated text must fulfil in the target audience's context. Some examples of more moderate versions of functionalist models are those by J. House (1977) and C. Nord (1991, 1997), who adopt a less radical approach which looks for a compromise between functionalism and faithfulness to the source text. In Nord's opinion, the function of the text depends, on the one hand, on the function receptors decide to assign it, but also on the author's intention.

Sociocultural approaches have a more pronounced literary orientation. Two of the most renowned are Gideon Toury's (1980, 1985) "Polysystem theory" and T. Hermans' (1985) "Manipulation School".[1] In these approaches, translation is defined as a sociocultural, norm-governed activity. Toury argues for the need to establish a descriptive and systematic branch of study which at last puts an end to the prescriptive tendency of linguistic approaches to translation. They adopt Holmes' ([1972] 1988) coinage of *Translation Studies* as the flagship of this new descriptive branch of the discipline. They abandon the linguistic search for invariant meaning equivalents and they propose, instead, a more functional and relational notion of equivalence, with a predominantly dynamic and historical character, which is established between every source text and each of its translations. This concept is established on the basis of what is regarded or not as a translation in a given sociocultural context. The other key notion in these approaches is that of *norm*, which is defined as certain patterns of translational behaviour which determine what translation procedures are considered acceptable in a given historical and cultural context. In each historical period, translations follow the prevailing norms, which are ultimately determined by the reception situation. These approaches have contributed to research translation norms and describe their behaviour in a given system or society. But from a teaching perspective, there is still the need to elaborate a detailed method of description which allows us to carry out a systematic comparison of source and target text. A useful attempt to fulfil this need is that of van Leuven-Zwart (1989, 1990), who, aiming at a more dynamic concept of equivalence, proposes a system which replaces the notion of equivalence for that of *shift*. In this system, shifts are first analysed at the microstructural level (words, phrases and sentences), then their consequences are described at the macrostructural level (characters, facts, time, etc.) and finally they are categorised. In spite of the empirical value of this type of framework to determine the influence of the historical and cultural context in translation, these models exhibited a primarily literary orientation which contributed to widen the gap between literary and non-literary translation.

---

1 Other relevant names in this approach are Lambert and van Gorp (1985), Delabastita (1989), Rabadán (1991) or van Leuven-Zwart and Naaijkens (1991).

2.3 The immediate past: The 1990s

But despite the recognition of the importance of context and communicative function, translation approaches entered the 1990s with a series of important issues which still needed solving. One of most important questions revolved around the status of the notion of context. The notion of context still had a secondary status which was either tightly bound to text analysis or to the reception situation in literary translation. Something similar happened with the notions of meaning and equivalence. The search for meaning invariants which underlined the notion of equivalence in linguistic approaches implied an "objectivist" view of meaning as something which existed outside the speaker's mind and in the text, and which could be apprehended and transferred into a different language. Similarly, the notion of translational norms postulated by sociocultural approaches could still be interpreted as a certain tendency to prescriptivism which had not been completely shaken off translation approaches. Moreover, even if one assumed that the ultimate purpose of these norms was descriptive, it could still be argued that translation approaches were focused on pragmatic and sociocultural factors, but lacked explanatory capacity to account for the complexities of translation in relation to general communication and language abilities. To cap it all, the breach between linguistic and literary approaches still remained to be filled. The so-called cultural turn drifted the attention of translation approaches to the cultural context, but for both types of approaches to come together it was still necessary to adopt a common definition of context.

In the 1990s, some translation scholars started to see in the postulates of Cognitive Linguistics (see Section 3 below) a way to answer all these questions which were still pending. The relevance of Cognitive Linguistics for translation arises mainly from the "experiential" notion of meaning proposed by cognitivists, which abandons the traditional notion of referential truth and highlights the central role of human experience and understanding. This type of approach based on experience allows us to bring together thought, language and culture in the speakers' cognitive context. From such a cognitive perspective, translation is still regarded as a communicative process, although one which is part of the participants' mental life. All the pragmatic and sociocultural factors underlined by descriptive approaches can be accommodated in cognitive models as part of the interlocutors' cognitive context. In this way, the notion of context can at last get rid of its burden as a secondary concept to become the prime factor in the translation process. Furthermore, a cognitive approach to translation is provided with enough explanatory capacity to account for the role of human cognitive abilities (i.e. perception, reasoning, information processing and other cognitive mechanisms) in linguistic and translation issues.

In this regard, Gutt (1991) has illustrated the usefulness for translation of Sperber and Wilson's (1995) principle of relevance (which does not belong to Cognitive Linguistics in a strict sense, but is directly related to Cognitive Linguistics postulates). Snell-Hornby ([1988] 1995) has indicated the advantages of applying the notion of "prototype" to translation: placing the different types of texts and translation situations along a continuum which ranges from more to less literal underlies the connections between the different types of translation and contributes to bringing literary and non-literary translation closer. Another cognitive approach which helps to blur the separating line between literary and non-literary translation and between literary and linguistic approaches is Tabakowska's (1993) proposal to exploit Cognitive Grammar notions – specifically, Langacker's (1987) notion of *"imagery"* – in the analysis of literary translation. For her, Cognitive Grammar provides a suitable meeting point between semantics and stylistics, since both of them focus on the study of *construal* as the speaker's choice to conceptualise a given situation in different ways. In this sense, there is not a clear boundary between the concept of *imagery* as a function of everyday language or as creative combination and exploitation of the resources available to the writer. Kussmaul (1995) and Rojo (2000, 2002a, 2002b) have stated the applicability to translation of Fillmore's "Frame Semantics". Kussmaul (1995) has argued that Fillmore's (1982, 1985) initial notion of "scene" has a plastic or pictorial quality that makes it especially useful to help understand abstract terms and find an adequate translation. He has also illustrated the usefulness of the principles of *"foregrounding"* and *"suppression"* of semantic features for the translation of terms with complex meaning. These two principles explain the fact that during comprehension only those semantic features which are relevant in a given context get activated. Extrapolating these principles to translation, Kussmaul states that translators must keep or foreground those features which are relevant in a given context, suppressing or backgrounding the non-relevant ones. Similarly, Rojo (2000, 2002a, 2002b) has illustrated the usefulness of Frame Semantics when translating cultural terms and humour, proposing a notion of equivalence based on the activation of similar frames, which envisages the translator's goal as one of guiding the target text audience along a cognitive or conceptual route similar to that of the source text reader.

The cognitive approaches of the 1990s contributed to a new way to view translation which combined traditional findings with current cognitive notions and real data analysis. They illustrated a general turn of Translation Studies towards a more experimental approach which deviated the attention from description of the translation product to research on the translation process. A similar search for an empirical-experimental approach which could shed some light on the translation process by using real data analysis was the aim of psycholinguistic approaches to translation (e.g. Séguinot 1989, 1991; Lörscher 1991a, 1991b; Tirkkonen-Condit 1991). This type of approach has mainly provided the description of a series of translation strategies which help understand the translation process better and are useful teaching instruments. They started by following a "retrospective" methodology which established translation strategies on the basis of the comparison between source and target text. Later on, they adopted an "introspective" line of research which aimed at studying the "black box" containing the translator's mental transference processes. To access this box, they developed a method taken from cognitive psychology which consisted of verbalising the translator's mental process while translating and recording their result in protocols. This technique was named the *Thinking Aloud Protocol* (TAP) and was sometimes combined with the filming of translators' eye movements and pupils' dilation as a reflection of their mental activity. This technique has been highly criticised by many scholars (e.g. Toury 1991: 59; Hatim 2001: 157–161) who have questioned the validity of recordings as a reflection of translators' mental processes: the data obtained are, after all, indirect and could be somehow affected during the task, since mental production and verbalisation are not simultaneous processes.

2.4 The present: 21st century and beyond

Since the 1990s, translation research has continued to emphasise the cultural turn of Translation Studies (e.g. Bassnett and Lefevere 1998; Bassnett and Bush 2006; Bielsa and Bassnett 2008; Pym 2004; Pym, Schlesinger and Simeoni 2008; Tymoczko 2007) and the need for empirical and experimental methodologies based on real usage data (e.g. Hansen, Chesterman and Gerzymisch-Arbogast 2009; Olohan 2004; Baker 2003, 2004). The search for these types of methodologies has swerved the attention of translation scholars to corpus-based methods which have been used either to investigate those processes which are specific to translation (cf. Olohan 2004), to validate theoretical principles and claims (e.g. Charteris-Black and Ennis 2001; Stefanowitsch 2004), or even with teaching purposes (e.g. Zanettin, Bernardini and Stewart 2003). Moreover, the investigation of the translation process has continued to look for new experimental methodologies which can overcome the shortcomings of TAPs. For example, *Translog*, a computer programme, was developed in 2002 to allow researchers to record the translator's typing production (i.e. it records all the keystrokes, including all changes, deletions, additions, cut-and-paste operations and cursor movements). By logging information about the exact time at which each keystroke operation is made, the programme allows you to create a linear representation of an entire typing event (including changes) with a graphic and/or numerical representation of the duration of any pauses occurring during the process of typing. This method allows researchers to locate problems in the translation process by measuring speed and pauses (e.g. Sullivan and Lindgren 2006).

Translation Studies entered the new century with a past background loaded with notions to be redefined, a present full of suggestive ideas to be further developed and a future packed with challenges awaiting to be achieved. The past brought about central issues whose importance still prevails in Translation Studies, such as the practical notion of equivalence or the importance of cultural and cognitive issues, but it also brought to the attention of translation scholars the need to redefine these issues in order to account for the complexity and dynamism of translation as a communicative process with a markedly cultural character. The present has reinforced the cultural turn of Translation Studies and initiated the search for new empirical methods based on real usage data, but in its efforts to grant power to cultural approaches it has relegated linguistic models to the background. In the light of such past and present research, what are then the future challenges translation must face? A critical look at the history of translation research allows us to sketch its future around five pivotal points or needs: redefine the notion of equivalence and the process of meaning construction, revisit the notions of context and culture in order to definitely bridge the gap between linguistic and literary approaches, uncover the conceptual operations which guide the use of translation strategies in the process of recreating meaning, readdress the research methodology employed in order to give way to new empirical methods, and establish the impact of the translator's bilingual competence on the translation product.

3 Cognitive Linguistics and translation

Cognitive Linguistics is a linguistic framework that, given its epistemological and ontological bases, can address all these issues in a satisfactory manner. It is often said that Cognitive Linguistics more than a unified model is a "linguistic movement" since it subsumes under its name theories and research goals of different kind. From the theories of conceptual metaphor and metonymy, Frame Semantics and blending which are mostly focused on semantic issues to the frameworks of Cognitive Grammar and Construction Grammar which are more devoted to morphosyntactic issues (see Evans and Green 2006; Geeraerts and Cuyckens 2007; Ibarretxe-Antuñano and Valenzuela 2012; for an overview).

However, all of these models and approaches, despite their different interests and viewpoints, share the same main tenets and foundations, both epistemological and methodological. The same basic pillars that can be very useful for translation theory and that we briefly summarise next.

Perhaps the most basic principle of Cognitive Linguistics is the assumption that language is an integral part of cognition, and thus, a product of general cognitive abilities. This idea opposes the belief in the independence of general cognition processes from linguistic structures and rules, as postulated in some formal approaches. Instead, Cognitive Linguists believe that different levels of linguistic analysis do not form independent modules but that all linguistic principles must be investigated in relation with other mental faculties such as memory, attention, or reasoning. This proposal is known as the "cognitive commitment" (Lakoff 1990: 40).

Another crucial tenet is that human language is symbolic in nature because it arises from the association between a phonological representation and a semantic representation (Langacker 1987). The symbolic nature of language, naturally, goes back to Saussurian linguistics but there is a radical difference that distinguishes both approaches. While Cognitive Linguistics accepts to a certain extent that the link between form and meaning is somewhat arbitrary, it denies that language is totally structured arbitrarily. Quite on the contrary, another basic principle in this model is that language is motivated and grounded more or less directly in our bodily, physical, social, and cultural experience. In other words, we create our mental and linguistic categories under the constraints imposed by our bodies, through the culture sieve, and on the basis of our concrete experiences. In short, language is *embodied* (Johnson 1987).

The postulate that language is usage-based is also crucial in Cognitive Linguistics. It has two complementary interpretations. On the one hand, it suggests that the structural properties of language emerge from usage, that is, language is a system shaped by linguistic usage (see Barlow and Kemmer 2000 for an overview) and, on the other, that every theoretical assumption has to be based on real and substantial empirical data, and not on *ad hoc* examples.

These basic principles have consequences for how Cognitive Linguistics deals with linguistic structures. First of all, classical dichotomies in traditional linguistics disappear and become clines. For example, the distinction between semantics and pragmatics, between *langue* and *parole*, between competence and performance, between linguistic meaning and encyclopaedic meaning. Language is based on our experience as human beings in this world, in a culture and in a society, and therefore, all the knowledge that we have about the system of our language must arise from our experience. Meanings reflect the mental categories we create from our interaction with the world and our conceptual structures are invoked in language use and comprehension. This relationship between language and experience has encouraged cognitive linguists to study how conceptual structures or models are reflected in language and thus proposed analytical tools such as cognitive domains, i.e. knowledge structures, mental representations about the organisation of the world around us (Langacker 1987), and similar proposals like "idealised cognitive models" (Lakoff 1987), "mental spaces" (Fauconnier 1994, 1997) and "frames" (Fillmore 1982, 1985).

Another consequence of believing in the integration of language in our cognitive abilities is that some of these abilities can precisely help us organise our mental and linguistic structures. One of these abilities is human categorisation, i.e. the ability to judge whether a particular entity is an instance of a particular category or not. Based on Rosch and colleagues' work (Mervis and Rosch 1981; Rosch 1973, 1977, 1978, 1983) on prototype categorisation model, Cognitive Linguistics organises linguistic structures around a prototype, that is, the best, most prominent and most typical member of a category. And around this prototype the other members of the category are also organised depending on how much these members resemble the prototype, on how many characteristics they share with the best example of the category (cf. Taylor 2003). This prototypical organisation has been applied to the study of different areas in linguistics, namely phonology (Mompeán 2006; Nathan 2008), morphosyntax (cf. Goldberg's Construction Grammar [1995, 2006]) and semantics (cf. Lakoff's [1987] radial categories, polysemy and semantic fields [see Valenzuela, Ibarretxe-Antuñano, and Hilferty 2012]).

Another cognitive human ability is imagination, not understood as a nonrational, unruly and idiosyncratic play of ideas, but as a basic mechanism to create meaning and rationality. Imagination, by means of metaphor and metonymy, helps us to make sense of our less directly apprehensible experiences on the basis of more directly apprehensible experiences. In Cognitive Linguistics, metaphor and metonymy are not mere figures of speech, only available to some gifted speakers, that obscure our language. They are figures of thought that shape the conceptual structure of our language. Metaphor is a basic imaginative device that establishes mappings or projections usually from a concrete source cognitive domain onto a target abstract cognitive domain (Lakoff 1993; Kövecses 2010). Similarly, metonymy also sets up mappings but within the same experiential domain (Barcelona 2000; Kövecses and Radden 1998; Panther, Thornburg, and Barcelona 2009).

The brief overview we have just presented should help the reader foresee the type of translator, translation (product-process), and translation theory that Cognitive Linguistics would favour. The emphasis of Cognitive Linguistics on cognitive aspects gives prominence to the role of the translator, who would no longer be considered just as a specialist in two languages, but rather an intercultural mediator between source and target texts. The translation as a product would be understood as a manipulation, a retextualization guided by a mediator who knows what is functionally appropriate in the target language, and not as loyal and right transfer from a source into a target language. The translation as a process would be regarded as both a communicative and a cognitive process in which linguistic and conceptual aspects are perfectly integrated, and not as a mechanical equivalence transfer between two linguistic systems. From a Cognitive Linguistics point of view, the translational act would comprise the activation and selective use of several particular kinds of knowledge filtered through the translator's cognitive process. The search for equivalence would no longer be the search for identifiable linguistic features, but the search for a complex set of links in the translator's mind, and the aim of a translation theory would be to explain aspects related to how these links are cognitively represented or cognitively processed. Therefore, a translation theory which draws on the cognitive postulates of Cognitive Linguistics would support all these characteristics and provide a solid epistemological base that relies on the relationship between language and cognition, and on the embodied character of language.

We have drawn here a possible sketch of what a Cognitive Translation Theory could be like. This type of theory is now taking its first steps in Translation Studies and some time and work would still be needed before a full-fledged form of the theory can be developed. Such enterprise is beyond the scope of this work, but it is our intention to contribute to this endeavour by raising some questions that we consider crucial for a future framework of Cognitive Translation Studies. Thus, the questions brought up in the following section pose some of the key topics that researchers should bear in mind when defining the main tenets of a cognitively founded translation theory.

4 Cognitive Linguistics and translation: Some relevant questions

This book and the papers included herein are organised and selected in order to respond to the following basic and general questions:

- How can Cognitive Linguistics and Translation Studies be bridged together?
- What theoretical constructs and empirical mechanisms does Cognitive Linguistics have that can be successfully applied to Translation Studies? In what ways can these be useful and used?

- Are there any other unexplored (or scarcely explored) areas in translation theory in which Cognitive Linguistics can make a contribution?
- Are there any insights from Translation Studies that can be adopted and benefit Cognitive Linguistics?

Taking into account the pivotal needs in translation mentioned above and bearing in mind these general research questions, the book is organised around five main research issues or areas:

- *Theoretical aspects of Cognitive Linguistics and translation.* This part offers a theoretical background to the Cognitive Translation Studies. Several research questions are addressed here: Which impact do the epistemological and ontological assumptions in Cognitive Linguistics have on Translation Theory? And the other way round, what aspects of Translation Theory are still to be sorted out by Cognitive Linguistics? In other words, the interaction between CL and translation is introduced, focusing specifically on how both fields of study can benefit from each other.
- *Meaning in Cognitive Linguistics and translation.* Previous research in Cognitive Linguistics has already proven that cognitive mechanisms such as frames, metaphor and metonymy are powerful analytic linguistic tools, but are they really useful for translation? Can these mechanisms shed some light on how to translate meaning or on what meaning should be translated?
- *Constructions in Cognitive Linguistics and translation.* The relationship between form and meaning is problematic in translation theory. Should the author be loyal to form, to meaning or to both? Form and meaning pairings, i.e. constructions, and their constructional patterns are hot topics in Cognitive Linguistics, the question now is: can they be of any help for translators?
- *Culture in Cognitive Linguistics and translation.* This is a big issue in both areas, but can Cognitive Linguistics offer solutions to deal with the cultural component in translation? Can Cognitive Linguistics integrate cultural aspects in translation while keeping both the acceptability and the adequacy poles balanced?
- *A step beyond in Cognitive Linguistics and translation.* Psycholinguistic investigation is a fruitful empirical method in Cognitive Linguistics nowadays. It has contributed to add further support to theoretical concepts (e.g. motivation and embodiment) and cognitive mechanisms, but can this methodology be applied to translation? Is it possible to use certain cognitive principles to research translation from a psycholinguistic perspective? Is translation an adequate research field to investigate Cognitive Linguistics postulates?

The papers compiled in the present volume purport to investigate the many fruitful manners in which Cognitive Linguistics can expand further on Cognitive Translation Theory. Some papers (Muñoz Martín, Halverson, Martín de León) take a theoretical stand, since the epistemological and ontological bases of both areas (Cognitive Linguistics and Translation Studies) should be known before specific contributions of Cognitive Linguistics to translation are tackled.

The volume opens with the work by Halverson, which discusses the general implications of Cognitive Linguistics for Translation Studies, focusing on three areas: theory development, methodology, and epistemology. From the point of view of a Translation Studies scholar, the author focuses on the translational issues that are of urgency with regard to future theorising and empirical study. The following two papers which adopt a theoretical stand elaborate further on two of the areas outlined by Halverson. The contribution by Muñoz Martín expands on the area of theory development. He helps to put in perspective the interaction between linguistics and translatology within second-generation Cognitive Science. The author defends the relationship between both disciplines, arguing that if Cognitive Linguistics and Cognitive Translatology share their cognitive commitment and language has a central position in translating and interpreting processes, Cognitive Linguistics should then have a crucial role in the development of Cognitive Translatology. The paper by Martín de León elaborates on the contributions of Cognitive Linguistics to the epistemological question of meaning construction in translatology. She analyses how different cognitive models have tried to solve the problem of symbol grounding, and how they can contribute to the development of a coherent and realistic theoretical framework for translatology.

Several works in the volume attempt to illustrate how some of the notions imported from Cognitive Linguistics may contribute to enriching our understanding of the translation process in a general translation problem such as metaphor (e.g. Samaniego Fernández, Sharifian and Jamarani), the relationship between form and meaning (Tabakowska, Rojo and Valenzuela), cultural aspects (Bernárdez, Sharifian and Jamarani), as well as political discourse (Sharifian and Jamarani).

Samaniego Fernández's paper focuses on metaphor and on the positive influence that the cognitive approach to metaphor has exerted on Descriptive Translation Studies. She argues that the notion of metaphor imported from Cognitive Linguistics has led to a more realistic study of metaphor translation which has allowed researchers to explain cases traditionally disregarded for being "anomalous" or "incorrect" renderings.

This cultural embodiment of the notion of metaphor acts as a kind of bridge between the papers devoted to metaphor and the two papers which focus on cultural aspects. In this sense, Sharifian and Jamarani's work also focuses on the notion of metaphor but the authors are more interested in the sociocultural and political implications of this phenomenon. They aim at demonstrating how the notion of metaphor can be a powerful analytical tool in translation by showing how the literal translation of a metaphor can be used to disclose certain underlying mismatches in cultural conceptualisations. By focusing on the implications that these mismatches may have for a particular type of communication, in this case for political discourse, the authors also provide a significant contribution in order to deal with the translation problems that characterise a specific discourse area.

Bernárdez also uses the notion of metaphor as a starting point in his paper to illustrate the problems that arise from the cultural differences which may be found in conceptual metaphors. However, the scope of his paper is more ambitious, proposing a unified framework for the analysis of cultural elements on the basis of a form of Cognitive Linguistics which integrates culture into its overall theoretical framework. Being a connoisseur of the type of cultural problems translators are faced with, the author argues that the success of the applicability of a model for dealing with cultural problems in translation depends on its capacity to integrate cultural and linguistic aspects and to analyse linguistic elements in its real use and function.

Besides cultural aspects, another area of interest in Translation Studies has been the relationship between form and meaning. In this volume, the works by Tabakowska and Rojo and Valenzuela show how Cognitive Linguistics can contribute to throwing light on this issue. The paper by Tabakowska illustrates the applicability of a model based on the principles of Cognitive Grammar when analysing those cases, such as the translation of a poem, in which meaning and form are inseparable because grammatical elements carry some meaning relevant for the interpretation of the text and thus, for its rendering into a different language. Rojo and Valenzuela's work also contribute to enriching our view of the relationship between form and meaning by focusing on the notion of construction as another case which illustrates how changes in the syntactic form of the sentence can entail subtle variations in meaning. They show how the particular mismatch which is found in the use of the resultative construction between English and Spanish can account for the difficulties translators face when dealing with this construction and for the strategies employed to sort them out. An eye-tracker is used to measure these difficulties in terms of the higher or lower level of cognitive effort employed by the translators, which is reflected in their eye movements and in the changes in their pupil dilation.

A slightly different perspective is adopted in this volume by a set of papers which use translation as a type of empirical field to test some of the basic assumptions of Cognitive Linguistics, such as frames (Boas), metonymy (Brdar and Brdar-Szabó), and lexicalisation patterns (Ibarretxe-Antuñano and Filipović). The work by Boas uses both human and machine translation to illustrate the applicability of frames to the analysis of languages for translation purposes. He manages to demonstrate that an approach to lexical organisation based on Frame Semantics offers a unique way of capturing both generalisations and idiosyncrasies in the description of semantically related words across languages. Furthermore, he also provides evidence in favour of the value of frames to integrate linguistic and cultural information, since they allow researchers to include references to culturally significant categories in the lexicon. Brdar and Brdar-Szabó argue in their paper that Translation Studies can contribute towards a better understanding of the nature of metonymy, providing practical evidence which can be used to test and/or refine some of the claims and postulates about metonymy in Cognitive Linguistics. They demonstrate that the translation of metonymies can help uncover some conditions of their use at the token level. The type of analytical model they propose shows that the degree of the difficulty in translating utterances with metonymic expressions may be linked to the type of metonymy in question as well as to the degree of its regularity and to their complexity in terms of metonymic mappings.

Ibarretxe-Antuñano and Filipović offer an overview of how the theory of Talmy's lexicalisation patterns and Slobin's thinking for speaking hypothesis has been successfully applied to translation in motion events. Translators have to make different choices in order to accommodate the characteristics of the source language to the requirements of the target language, while keeping the content of source text as accurate and fluent as possible. The main idea is that these choices are guided by the narrative or rhetorical styles that each language has. In other words, languages offer different linguistic means to codify a motion event, and as such, languages influence the way speakers, and in this paper, translators, pay attention to different elements. These authors, by compiling a list of translation strategies, attest that, in general, translators from verb-framed into satellite-framed languages tend to omit Manner and offer few details about the trajectory, whereas translators from satellite-framed into verb-framed languages behave just the other way round. They also demonstrate that to be aware of these rhetorical styles in each language is of great importance not only from a linguistic point of view but also from an applied perspective (translators' training, forensic linguistics). By examining witness reports, they convincingly show that the rhetorical styles are crucial, and that translators should keep alert about these differences in language, especially in cases where certain pieces of information can be essential for our own judgments about events and their participants.

Finally, another set of papers (Feist, Hatzidaki) opens up new lines of investigation for experimental research, a very promising area still underdeveloped. The paper by Feist explores the contribution that experimental work in lexical semantics might make to the discussion of meaning and equivalence in translation, focusing on the recent work in Cognitive Linguistics which experimentally probes word meanings, both within and across languages (e.g. Feist 2000, 2008; Tanehashi 2005). Her review of experimental work in lexical semantics makes two potential contributions to the theory and practice of translation: firstly, by illuminating the meanings of individual lexical items, it provides a means for analysing the meaning encoded in the source-language words as used in context; and secondly, this body of work provides evidence regarding the degree of equivalence between words of the source language and matched words of the target language. Hatzidaki's paper provides an overview of a variety of experimental methods and techniques that the field of psycholinguistics has used to study the cognitive underpinnings of translation. She demonstrates that the theoretical questions that concern both Cognitive Linguistics and translation have been thoroughly examined and their assumptions tested in a number of different language pairs and conditions. But despite this available evidence, she notices that most psycholinguistic work that has been conducted employing a translation task aimed at contributing to the field of psycholinguistics and Cognitive Linguistics, and not to that of Translation Studies. However, now there are well-established psycholinguistic paradigms that allow researcher to access the translator's "black box" and investigate a set of theoretical assumptions and processes central to translation.

5 From Cognitive Linguistics towards a Cognitive Translation Theory

This book constitutes the first attempt to unify previous isolated works on Cognitive Linguistics and translation. In a century which has brought to light the central role of cognition in the study of the translation process, Cognitive Linguistics can be discerned as a suitable candidate to account for the linguistic aspects of such a process. Any cognitive theory of translation will find in the postulates of Cognitive Linguistics the adequate theoretical background to explain the role which language plays in the translation process in relation to other cognitive abilities. The research programme of Translation Studies is currently staged by the desire to describing translation as a cognitive process and the tendency towards adopting an interdisciplinary approach which can contribute to describing such process from a variety of perspectives. In the same way as research on literary translation has extensively benefited from previous literary and cultural works, research on the cognitive aspects of translation will certainly benefit from works in those disciplines which have been devoted to the study of cognition in the monolingual and the bilingual mind (e.g. psychology, neurology, bilingualism, etc.).

This book starts from the assumption that Cognitive Linguistics is one of the disciplines which can help describe translation as a cognitive process by contributing to integrate linguistic aspects with other aspects relating to cognition. The central place attributed to cognition in modern Translation Studies does not interfere with the fact that language is still the raw material translators work with; therefore, a deeper understanding of language comprehension and production and of how language fits in with the rest of human cognitive abilities will undoubtedly cast some light on the role language factors play on the translation process.

In the previous section, we raised four questions that summarise the main points that we consider crucial for a future framework of Cognitive Translation Studies. These questions are the foundations that researchers working in this area and coming from these two research worlds should bear in mind and hopefully, expand in future studies. The *first question* asks whether Cognitive Linguistics and Translation Studies could be bridged together. Our answer is yes, they can. From a theoretical point of view, Cognitive Linguistics can provide the solid theoretical framework which Translation Studies has long demanded to account for the linguistic matters involved in the translation process. Its basic assumption that language is an integrated part of cognition supports the idea that translation is not a mere interchange of linguistics structures, an applied version of the linguistics principles that rule a language and that can be judged in terms of right and wrong, depending on how faithful they can be reproduced from the source language into the target language. Quite on the contrary, Cognitive Linguistics supports the cognitive nature of translation as a mediating process between two different conceptual worlds. Moreover, its integrated view of language and cognition together with the crucial role of culture helps to reinforce the link between the translator's behaviour and the cognitive strategies which lead to such behaviour, strengthening thus the link between the product and process of translation. We should bear in mind that Cognitive Linguistics fully supports the idea that the translator is an intercultural mediator who knows the cultures in which the translation process takes place. The translator, as any other speaker and supported by concepts such as embodiment and motivation, manipulates the texts based on his own knowledge and experience about the world. The translator is no longer viewed just as a "language expert' who has to remain faithful to the source text, he can and should adapt it to the target language and audience, both conceptually – appropriate information – and linguistically – appropriate constructions – and this view is supported by Cognitive Linguistics. This model then favours a more descriptive model of TS, and its usage-based approach is particularly helpful to describing the translator's behaviour.

It also supports a more explanatory approach to the study of translation, providing the necessary theoretical explanations to account for many translation phenomena which remained unexplained or unclear such as transfer, equivalence, translation shifts and translation norms. The word "transfer" falls short when describing the translation process since it is not just a mere "relocation" of some linguistic meanings from one source language into a target language. It involves, first, a whole decoding process that unveils all the conceptual meaning contained in the concepts, the contexts and the constructions used, and second, a whole recoding process in the target language. This decoding-recoding process reflects the importance of some notions which are pivotal in CL, such as those of construal, encyclopaedic meaning and the symbolic nature of language. Applying the notion of construal to translation emphasises the dynamic aspect of meaning construction which is central to translation, and allows us to integrate linguistic and other kinds of knowledge with social, historical, and contextual influences through the cognitive processes of the translator. From this perspective, the concept of transfer acquires a more dynamic nature which entails the activation and selective use of several particular kinds of knowledge filtered through the translator's cognitive process.

As a consequence, a term like "equivalence" cannot be taken to refer to the whole process of translation. If each translation text is unique – it has a particular context, meaning and constructions – the equivalence between source and target texts is "situated", and therefore, more individualised (Samaniego Fernández 2007; see also Halverson's paper). From this perspective, the notion of "shift" in translation can no longer be seen either as a *post hoc* product category established on the basis of an identified invariant. It is rather an operation of construal which translators make on the basis of their online creative interpretation of a translation, the contextualised interpreting of the source text and their knowledge of the conventionalised construals in the languages they work with. It is precisely in this concept of conventionalised construal where the controversial notion of "norms" (cf. Schäffner 1998) best fits in this cognitive approach. From a Cognitive Linguistics perspective, norms are rejected in the form of linguistic or text-related rules which regulate the translator's behaviour in all types of situations. Following the trend established by Descriptive Translation Studies, norms are best understood as general tendencies in translators' behaviour which, being motivated and constrained by the factors mentioned above, become conventionalised construals at the service of other professionals.

Translation Studies, on the other hand, provide a complex model of language functioning since, as mentioned above, we have a double process of decoding and recoding in a different language, so we can say that it provides a good/more demanding testing field to check whether the assumptions of Cognitive Linguistics work. For instance, the question of how the translator decides what and how is to be decoded from the source text and recoded in the target text. So far, some of the answers might lie in Cognitive Linguistics (cf. motivation, embodiment, cognitive process [...]), but others can be provided by Translation Studies, which can tell us more about general factors such as genre characteristics or text types as well as particular factors such as the translators' own individual and sometimes *ad hoc* choices.

This complexity can also serve to discover or reveal new aspects of the theory which do not appear in a simple language model. Research on the cognitive process of translation has started to use research methods (linguistic analysis, corpora studies, verbal reports, reaction time, and fMRIs) which are also popular in experimental work in Cognitive Linguistics. From this perspective, as Feist's, Hatzidaki's, and Rojo and Valenzuela's papers have shown, they appear to be a suitable interface to connect both disciplines, either by using cognitive principles to research translation from a psycholinguistic perspective or by using translation as a research field to investigate Cognitive Linguistics postulates. Both disciplines are also interested in similar areas of research: communicative and cultural systems, performance domain, and neural systems, just to name a few, which opens up a whole new array of possibilities for future conjoined research.

The *second question* that we put forward was whether Cognitive Linguistics has specific tools that can be useful and therefore, implemented in Translation Studies. Once again, the answer is yes, it does. Cognitive Linguistics provides a set of methodological tools that allow Translation Studies researchers to analyse in a more rigorous and systematic manner a set of traditional translation phenomena which demanded a more unified and theoretically sound explanation. We outline here some of the main, but probably not the only, tools that have already been put into practice.

Conceptual metaphor and metonymy. In traditional Translation Studies, the "translatability" of metaphors is often a major issue with mostly negative answers (see Samaniego Fernández's paper). Vinay and Darbelnet (1958: 199) state it clearly: "La langue d'arrivée ne permet pas de traduire la metaphor littéralement" [the target language does not permit literal translation of metaphor]. The problem is that in most of these studies, metaphor (and metonymy) are considered a matter of words, a figure of speech that adds stylistic effects to the text. As Dagut (1976: 22) puts it, "when translating a metaphor, the shock effect of the created image should be maintained and that is not possible when there are linguistic and cultural factors which hinder this effect". Metaphor and metonymy in Cognitive Linguistics are not a matter of translating words from one language into another, but a matter of decoding and recoding conceptual systems from a source culture into a target culture. The distinction in Cognitive Linguistics between conceptual metaphor and metonymy – the conceptual information – and the metaphorical or metonymical expression – the linguistic structure particular to each language – is paramount to understanding the potentiality of this tool. It means that metaphor is no longer a problem for translation; all conceptual metaphors are translatable from the source into the target text. What the translator needs to do is to establish which conceptual domains are involved in the metaphorical mapping that appears in the source text, and then find either the equivalent linguistic means to codify that mapping in the target text or find alternative conceptual domains that are equivalent to those in the source text. These two solutions would cover metaphors in all "gradients" and "degrees" of translatability (Dagut 1987; Van der Broeck and Lefevere 1979). As Schäffner (2004: 1258) argues, "Translatability is no longer a question of the individual metaphorical expression, as identified in ST, but it becomes linked to the level of conceptual systems in source and target culture". In this book, Samaniego Fernández's paper on metaphor and Brdar and Brdar-Szabó's paper on metonymy clearly show this capacity. What is more, novel metaphors, Samaniego Fernández suggests, can "enlarge the target conceptual world" since translators, aware of the potentiality of a given conceptual metaphor in the source text, can adapt it and use it in the target text. Besides, as Sharifian and Jamarani's paper argues, a cognitive view of metaphor can also help us to disclose underlying mismatches in cultural conceptualisations, which lead to the misrepresentation of political discourse in translation.

The importance of grammar. The concept of grammar in Cognitive Linguistics surpasses the traditional understanding that grammar is a set of structural rules that govern the composition of sentences in a language; grammar is symbolic in nature and as such, it has meaning. As a consequence, every structure or construal that the translator chooses to include in the target text adds a meaning dimension to the text. Cognitive Linguistics offers a wide array of construal operations (see Croft and Cruse 2004: ch. 3 for a review) that, as Halverson (see p. 47 of the present volume) points out, are integral to translation processes. They not only allow "us to maintain many of the insights of previous work on translational procedures such as Vinay and Darbelnet's methodology [. . .] or

Klaudy's translational operations", but also to emphasise "the creative, non-deterministic nature of the process". Construal operations, therefore, help the translator to focus on certain aspects. Tabakowska's paper is a perfect example for their usefulness in translation. In her analysis of one of Dickinson's poems, she uses three construal operations – specificity, trajectory/landmark alignment and perspective – and demonstrates that the choice of one construal can affect the whole interpretation of the translation in the target text. This, of course, also favours the integration of linguistic and cultural approaches to translation. It helps translators to be aware of the potential consequences of grammatical shifts which may go beyond the stylistic lack of naturalness.

Frames. These are also powerful tools in translation due to their double application. On the one hand, as Boas suggests, they can be useful for the creation on translation resources such as multilingual dictionaries since they offer "finely-grained conceptual structure". On the other hand, frames, as cognitive structuring devices, allow us to shed some light on how the process of meaning construction takes place in translation (see Martín de León's paper), and to analyse semantic fields both within and across languages. They consequently provide us with a mechanism for highlighting cross-linguistic similarities and differences.

Rhetorical style. Grammar is important but equally important is to adapt the translation to the style of the target language. As Ibarretxe-Antuñano and Filipović's paper shows, translators, beyond grammatical choices, count on several strategies to translate all the information from the source into the target text. However, not only do they prefer some strategies over others, but also these seem to be motivated by the narrative style that predominates in the target language.

The role of culture. Culture is part of the conceptualisation of meaning; that is why, from a Cognitive Linguistics perspective, encyclopaedic meaning cannot be separated from linguistic meaning. This favours the integration of cultural and linguistic aspects, of the cultural and linguistic context, something which is basic in the translator's work. In this way, it can also contribute to unifying linguistic and cultural approaches to translation. Following Bernárdez's proposal, a form of Cognitive Linguistics which integrates culture into its overall theoretical framework is especially suitable for translation, where linguistic elements are necessarily analysed in linguistic use and function.

We have just seen some of the prolific areas from Cognitive Linguistics that already have some implementation in translation. However, there are still other possible candidates that, as the *third question* poses, have not been applied, or not enough, to translation. One of those areas is Construction Grammar.

The notion of "construction" is one of the basic tools in Cognitive Grammar. This is defined as follows:

> Any linguistic pattern is recognised as a construction as long as some aspect of its form or function is not strictly predictable from its component parts or from other constructions recognised to exit. In addition, patterns are stored as constructions even if they are fully predictable as long as they occur with sufficient frequency. (Goldberg 2006: 5)

In a recent book on contrastive Cognitive Grammar, Boas (2010) demonstrates that it is possible to find similar constructions in different languages, but also that this framework is useful to discover not only similarities but also differences, even between genetically-close languages (see also Boas' paper). This reinforces the idea that not only is grammar symbolic, but also that it is an important factor to bear in mind in translation. Still, constructions have not been sufficiently studied under the translation perspective. Rojo and Valenzuela's chapter is perhaps one of the first attempts to do so. They show that constructional mismatches between different languages allow us to explain differences in the translator's behaviour in terms of the higher or lower processing effort involved.

Another underdeveloped area is Experimental Lexical Semantics. It has been criticised that traditional translation is mainly concerned with translation at word-level, and although Cognitive Linguistics supports the idea that there is more to translation than just words, it also provides the study of word meaning with a wide array of basic tools that can be helpful such as prototype or basic level categories. Despite the prominent role of context in translation, research on word meaning can still throw some light on how translators establish equivalence between lexical units. Moreover, although cognitive translatology has started to focus on an experimental methodology, the lack of an experimental background of most researchers has resulted in weak experimental designs. The article by Feist shows how experimental work in lexical semantics can contribute to enlighten the role of meaning and equivalence in translation.

Finally, the *fourth question* we raised was whether there were any insights from Translation Studies that could be adopted and benefit Cognitive Linguistics. Our answer yet again is yes, there are.

Muñoz Martín argues that translation provides an excellent example of realistic language use, free from the potential biases of the researchers, where meaning may be discerned by triangulation of several languages. For example, Brdar and Brdar-Szabó's and Ibarretxe-Antuñano and Filipović's papers show us how translation is a good tool to collect objective data. Translation involves different languages; therefore, it is especially suitable to illustrate culture-specific differences in linguistic phenomena. He also suggests that many traits of the translator's behaviour (as the existence of the so-called "translation universals" or general distinctive features in the language of translation; see Halverson's paper) can be explained in terms of the process of socialisation underwent by the translators. In this sense, research on translation universals could be used to illustrate the principle of motivated linguistic behaviour. Muñoz Martín also points out that by helping to show if there are distinct tendencies associated to certain language pairs and translation directions, Translation Studies can contribute to determining, for example, whether Langacker's construal dimensions are general and motivated and to provide them with empirical support.

Translation also offers us the possibility to investigate some aspects of bilingualism and second language acquisition which may also benefit research in Cognitive Linguistics. Halverson, Hatzidaki, Ibarretxe-Antuñano and Filipović, and Muñoz Martín's papers mention this possibility. One way of exploring this research path is, as Halverson (see p. 45 of the present volume) suggests, "to look for ways in which specific linguistic items may be represented and activated in the language of a bilingual and how various representational characteristics might impact translational outcomes". Another possible way could be to analyse patterns of second language acquisition and to investigate in which way code-switching optional restrictions are related to translators' interferences and Talmy's linguistic salient features. The study of interferences of the source language in the translator's performance can certainly throw some light on issues such as the role of attention or linguistic entrenchment.

In sum, the primary focus of Translation Studies on language in use points to translation as an excellent source of information about how linguistic principles work. As Martín de León's paper suggests, translation requires a dynamic process of meaning construction which can provide interesting data on this situated process of on-line meaning elaboration.

By attempting to answer the questions posed in the previous section, we have tried not only to give a coherent overview of the papers included in this volume but also to offer a general description of the theoretical and methodological stage at which these two worlds stand at the present time. It was not our intention to elaborate a full-fledged version of a Cognitive Translation Theory, but rather to depict a thorough state-of-affairs that can provide scholars with the basic ground for future research in this area. Our discussion on the status of both disciplines and their potential interaction leads us to pose a closing question for all the researchers interested in both areas: Can we talk about a promising new research framework called Cognitive Translation Studies that bridges Cognitive Linguistics and Translation Studies together? And the concluding answer can easily be glimpsed from a volume placed at the interface of both disciplines: Translation Studies have already turned to cognition in search of answers, and Cognitive Linguistics has already seen the potential of translation as a testing field. The establishment of a common framework does not seem to require any longer a radical change in the attitude of the researchers in both areas; rather, it seems to be more a matter of time, good intentions and joint work.

References

Baker, Mona 1992 *In other words*. London: Routledge.
Baker, Mona 2003 Corpus-based translation studies in the academy. In: Heidrun Gerzymisch-Arbogast, Eva Hajicová, Petr Sgall, Zuzana Jetmarová, Annely Rothkegel and Dorothee Rothfuß-Bastian (eds.), *Textologie und Translation: Jahrbuch Übersetzen und Dolmetschen 4/II*, 7–15. Tübingen, Germany: Gunter Narr.
Baker, Mona 2004 A corpus-based view of similarity and difference in translation. *International Journal of Corpus Linguistics* 9.2: 167–193.
Barcelona, Antonio (ed.) 2000 *Metaphor and metonymy at the crossroads: Cognitive approaches*. Berlin: Mouton de Gruyter.
Barlow, Michael and Suzanne Kemmer (eds.) 2000 *Usage-based models of language*. Cambridge: Cambridge University Press.
Bassnett, Susan and Peter Bush (eds.) 2006 *The translator as writer*. London: Continuum.
Bassnett, Susan and André Lefevere (eds.) 1998 *Constructing cultures: Essays on literary translation*. Clevedon, UK: Multilingual Matters.
Bielsa, Esperanca and Susan Bassnett 2008 *Translation in the global news*. London: Routledge.
Boas, Hans C. 2010 *Contrastive construction grammar studies*. Amsterdam: John Benjamins.
Catford, John C. 1965 *A linguistic theory of translation*. London: Oxford University Press.
Charteris-Black, Johnatan and Timothy Ennis 2001 A comparative study of metaphor in Spanish and English financial reporting. *English for Specific Purposes: An International Journal* 20.3: 249–266.
Croft, William and D. Alan Cruse 2004 *Cognitive linguistics*. Cambridge: Cambridge University Press.
Dagut, Menachem B. 1976 Can metaphor be translated? *Babel: International Journal of Translation* 22.1: 21–33.
Dagut, Menachem B. 1987 More about the translatability of metaphor. *Babel: International Journal of Translation* 33.2: 77–83.
Delabastita, Dirk 1989 Translation and mass communication: Film and TV translation as evidence of cultural dynamics. *Babel: International Journal of Translation* 35.4: 193–218.
Evans, Vyvian and Melanie Green 2006 *Cognitive linguistics: An introduction*. Edinburgh: Edinburgh University Press.
Fauconnier, Gilles 1994 *Mental spaces*. Cambridge: Cambridge University Press.
Fauconnier, Gilles 1997 *Mappings in thought and language*. Cambridge: Cambridge University Press.
Feist, Michele I. 2000 *On in and on: An investigation into the linguistic encoding of spatial scenes*. PhD dissertation, Department of Linguistics, Northwestern University, Evanston, IL.
Feist, Michele I. 2008 Space between languages. *Cognitive Science* 32.7: 1177–1199.

Fillmore, Charles 1982 Frame semantics. In: Linguistics Society of Korea (ed.), *Linguistics in the morning calm*, 111–137. Seoul: Hanshin Publishing.
Fillmore, Charles 1985 Frames and the semantics of understanding. *Quaderni di Semantica* 6: 222–254.
García Yebra, Valentín 1982 *Teoría y práctica de la traducción*. Madrid: Gredos.
Geeraerts, Dirk and Hubert Cuyckens 2007 *The Oxford handbook of cognitive linguistics*. Oxford: Oxford University Press.
Goldberg, Adele E. 1995 *Constructions: A construction grammar approach to argument structure*. Chicago: University of Chicago Press.
Goldberg, Adele E. 2006 *Constructions at work: The nature of generalization in nature*. Oxford: Oxford University Press.
Gutt, Ernst-August 1991 *Translation and relevance: Cognition and context*. Oxford: Blackwell.
Hansen, Gyde, Andrew Chesterman and Heidrun Gerzymisch-Arbogast 2009 *Efforts and models in interpreting and translation research: A tribute to Daniel Gile*. Amsterdam: John Benjamins.
Hatim, Basil 2001 *Teaching and researching translation*. Harlow, England: Pearson Education.
Hatim, Basil and Ian Mason 1990 *Discourse and the translator*. London: Longman.
Hatim, Basil and Ian Mason 1997 *The translator as communicator*. London: Routledge.
Hermans, Theo (ed.) 1985 *The manipulation of literature: Studies in literary translation*. London: Croom Helm.
Holmes, James S. [1972] 1988 *Translated! Papers on literary translation and translation studies*. Amsterdam: Rodopi.
Holz-Mänttäri, Justa 1984 *Translatorisches Handeln. Theorie und Methode*. Helsinki: Suomalainen Tiedeakatemia.
House, Juliane 1977 *Translation quality assessment. A model revisited*. Tübingen, Germany: Gunter Narr.
Ibarretxe-Antuñano, Iraide and Javier Valenzuela 2012 Lingüística Cognitiva: origen, principios y tendencias. In: Iraide Ibarretxe-Antuñano and Javier Valenzuela (eds.), *Lingüística cognitiva*, 13–38. Barcelona: Anthropos.
Johnson, Mark 1987 *The body in the mind: The bodily basis of meaning, imagination, and reason*. Chicago: University of Chicago Press.
Kövecses, Zoltan 2010 *Metaphor: A practical introduction*. Oxford: Oxford University Press.
Kövecses, Zoltan and Gunter Radden 1998 Metonymy: Developing a cognitive linguistic approach. *Cognitive Linguistics* 9.1: 37–77.
Kussmaul, Paul 1995 *Training the translator*. Amsterdam: John Benjamins.
Lakoff, George 1987 *Women, fire, and dangerous things: What categories reveal about the mind*. Chicago: University of Chicago Press.
Lakoff, George 1990 The invariance hypothesis: Is abstract reason based on image–schemas? *Cognitive Linguistics* 1.1: 39–74.
Lakoff, George 1993 The contemporary theory of metaphor. In: Andrew Ortony (ed.), *Metaphor and thought*, 202–251. Cambridge: Cambridge University Press.
Lambert, Jose and Hendrik van Gorp 1985 On describing translations. In: Theo Hermans (ed.), *The manipulation of literature: Studies in literary translation*, 45–53. London: Croom Helm.
Langacker, Ronald W. 1987 *Foundations of cognitive grammar. Vol. 1, Theoretical prerequisites*. Stanford, CA: Stanford University Press.
Leuven-Zwart, Kitty M. van 1989 Translation and original: Similarities and dissimilarities, I. *Target* 1: 151–182.

Leuven-Zwart, Kitty M. van 1990 Translation and original: Similarities and dissimilarities, II. *Target* 2: 69–96.
Leuven-Zwart, Kitty M. van and Ton Naaijkens (eds.) 1991 *Translation studies: The state of the art*. Amsterdam: Rodopi.
Lörscher, Wolfgang 1991a Thinking-aloud as a method for collecting data on translation processes. In: Sonja Tirkkonen-Condit (ed.), *Empirical research in translation and intercultural studies*, 67–78. Tübingen, Germany: Gunter Narr.
Lörscher, Wolfgang 1991b *Translation performance, translation process, and translation strategies*. Tübingen, Germany: Gunter Narr.
Mervis, Carolyn B. and Eleanor Rosch 1981 Categorization of natural objects. *Annual Review of Psychology* 32: 89–115.
Mompeán, José Antonio (ed.) 2006 Cognitive phonology. Special issue. *International Journal of English Studies* 6.2.
Nathan, Geoffrey S. 2008 *Phonology: A cognitive grammar introduction*. Amsterdam: John Benjamins.
Neubert, Albrecht 1985 *Text and translation*. Leipzig, Germany: VEB Verlag Enzyklopädie.
Neubert, Albrecht and Gregory M. Shreve 1992 *Translation as text*. Kent, OH: Kent State University Press.
Nida, Eugene A. 1964 *Toward a science of translating: With special reference to principles and procedures involved in Bible translating*. Leiden: Brill.
Nida, Eugene A. and Charles R. Taber 1969 *The theory and practice of translation*. Leiden: Brill.
Nord, Christiane 1991 *Text analysis in translation*. Translated into English by Christiane Nord and Penelope Sparrow. Amsterdam: Rodopi.
Nord, Christiane 1997 *Translating as a purposeful activity: Functionalist approaches explained*. Manchester: St. Jerome.
Olohan, Maeve 2004 *Introducing corpora in translation studies*. London: Routledge.
Panther, Klaus-Uwe, Linda Thornburg and Antonio Barcelona (eds.) 2009 *Metonymy in grammar*. Amsterdam: John Benjamins.
Pym, Anthony 2004 Propositions on cross-cultural communication and translation. *Target* 16.1: 1–28.
Pym, Anthony, Miriam Schlesinger and David Simeoni (eds.) 2008 *Beyond descriptive translation studies: Investigations in homage to Gideon Toury*. Amsterdam: John Benjamins.
Rabadán, Rosa 1991 *Equivalencia y traducción. Problemática de la equivalencia translémica inglés-español*. León, Spain: Universidad de León, Secretariado de Publicaciones.
Rojo, Ana 2000 *Esquemas y Traducción: un Acercamiento Cognitivo a la Traducción de Elementos Culturales*. Published PhD dissertation, CD-ROM version. Murcia, Spain: Universidad de Murcia.
Rojo, Ana 2002a Applying frame semantics to translation. *Meta* 47: 311–350.
Rojo, Ana 2002b Frame semantics and the translation of humor. *Babel: International Journal of Translation* 48: 34–77.
Rosch, Eleanor 1973 Natural categories. *Cognitive Psychology* 4: 328–350.
Rosch, Eleanor 1977 Human categorization. In: Neil Warren (ed.) *Studies in cross-cultural psychology*, 1–49. London: Academic Press.
Rosch, Eleanor 1978 Principles of categorization. In: Eleanor Rosch and B. B. Lloyd (eds.), *Cognition and categorization*, 27–48. Hillsdale, NJ: Erlbaum.

Rosch, Eleanor 1983 Prototype classification and logical classification. In: Ellin Scholnik (ed.), *New trends in cognitive representation, challenges to Piaget's theory*, 73–86. Hillsdale, NJ: Erlbaum.

Samaniego Fernández, Eva 2007 El impacto de la Lingüística Cognitiva en los Estudios de Traducción. In: Pedro Fuertes Olivera (ed.), *Problemas lingüísticos en la traducción especializada*, 119–154. Valladolid, Spain: Servicio de Publicaciones.

Schäffner, Christina 1998 The concept of norms in translation studies. *Current Issues in Language and Society* 5.1–2: 1–9.

Schäffner, Christina 2004 Metaphor and translation: Some implications of a cognitive approach. *Journal of Pragmatics* 36.7: 1253–1269.

Séguinot, Candance (ed.) 1989 *The translation process*. Toronto: School of Translation, York University.

Séguinot, Candance 1991 A study of student translation strategies. In: Sonja Tirkkonen-Condit (ed.), *Empirical research in translation and intercultural studies*, 79–88. Tübingen, Germany: Gunter Narr.

Snell-Hornby, Mary [1988] 1995 *Translation studies: An integrated approach*. Amsterdam: John Benjamins.

Sperber, Dan and Deidre Wilson 1995 *Relevance: Communication and cognition*. Oxford: Blackwell.

Stefanowitsch, Anatol 2004 HAPPINESS in English and German: A metaphorical-pattern analysis. In: Michel Achard and Suzanne Kemmer (eds.), *Language, culture, and mind*, 137–149. Stanford, CA: CSLI.

Sullivan, Kirk P. H. and Eva Lindgren 2006 *Computer keystroke logging and writing*. Amsterdam: Elsevier.

Tabakowska, Elżbieta 1993 *Cognitive linguistics and poetics of translation*. Tübingen, Germany: Gunter Narr.

Tanehashi, Nanako 2005 *Cross-linguistic differences and the second language acquisition of spatial terms: The case of English "in" and "on"*. Master's thesis, Nagoya Gakuin University, Nagoya, Japan.

Taylor, John 2003 *Linguistic categorization*. Oxford: Oxford University Press

Tirkkonen-Condit, Sonja (ed.) 1991 *Empirical research in translation and intercultural studies*. Tübingen, Germany: Gunter Narr.

Toury, Gideon 1980 *In search of a theory of translation*. Tel Aviv, Israel: The Porter Institute for Poetics and Semiotics, Tel Aviv University.

Toury, Gideon 1985 A rationale for descriptive translation studies. In: Theo Hermans (ed.), *The manipulation of literature: Studies in literary translation*, 16–41. London: Croom Helm.

Toury, Gideon 1991 Experimentation in translation studies: Achievements, prospects and some pitfalls. In: Sonja Tirkkonen-Condit (ed.), *Empirical research in translation and intercultural studies*, 45–66. Tübingen, Germany: Gunter Narr.

Tymoczko, Maria 2007 *Enlarging translation, empowering translators*. Manchester: St. Jerome.

Valenzuela, Javier, Iraide Ibarretxe-Antuñano and Joseph Hilferty 2012 La semántica cognitiva. In: Iraide Ibarretxe-Antuñano and Javier Valenzuela (eds.), *Lingüística Cognitiva*, 41–68. Barcelona: Anthropos.

Van der Broeck, Raymond and André Lefevere 1979 *Uitnodiging tot de vertaalwetenschap*. Muiderberg, the Netherlands: Coutinho.

Vázquez-Ayora, Gerardo 1977 *Introducción a la Traductología*. Washington, DC: Georgetown University Press.

Vermeer, Hans J. 1989 Skopos and commission in translational action (translated by Andrew Chesterman). In: Andrew Chesterman (ed.), *Readings on translation theory*, 173–187. Helsinki: Oi Finn Lectura.

Vinay, Jean Paul and Jean Darbelnet 1958 *Stylistique comparée du français et de l'anglais: Méthode de traduction*. Paris: Didier. [Eng. translation: *Comparative stylistics of French and English: A methodology for translation*. 1995. Amsterdam: John Benjamins.]

Wilss, Wolfram 1982 *The science of translation: Problems and methods*. Tübingen, Germany: Gunter Narr.

Zanettin, Federico, Silvia Bernardini and Dominic Stewart (eds.) 2003 *Corpora in translation education*. Manchester: St Jerome.

Part I: Cognitive Linguistics and Translation Theory

Sandra L. Halverson
Implications of Cognitive Linguistics for Translation Studies*

1 Introduction

As outlined in the introduction to this volume, Translation Studies (TS) has reached the point at which a number of traditional questions and issues can and should be either rethought or jettisoned altogether. The situation is this: the inability of structuralist or generativist linguistic theories to adequately address some of the basic questions of translation has led many scholars to reject linguistic approaches altogether. At the same time, translation scholarship within the descriptive-empirical paradigm has been accused of being unable to generate theoretical innovation (Hermans 1999: 160; Pym 2010: 86). And finally, at the same time as new methods and types of data are being introduced by those who do advocate a linguistic approach, accusations of naïve empiricism or insufficient reflexivity threaten the position of those scholars who have not been able to fully articulate a post-positivist, empirical epistemology (see Arrojo 1998; Hermans 1999: 159–160; Pym 2010: 85).

The publication of a volume such as the present one presents an opportunity to take stock of the current situation, to highlight key areas of persistent concern for linguistic approaches to translation, and to showcase the potential of cognitive linguistic approaches in addressing translational issues. In this particular contribution, the emphasis is on the second and third of these objectives, and in discussing the implications of Cognitive Linguistics for Translation Studies, the focus will be on three specific areas: theory development, methodology, and epistemology.

The perspective taken in the following discussion is that of a scholar of Translation Studies, and this vantage point within TS has driven the selection of questions and issues. Accordingly, the focus in the second section is on those translational issues that are of urgency with regard to future theorizing and empirical study. Please note that the selection is by no means exhaustive;

---

* This paper was written during a sabbatical stay at Purdue University, West Lafayette, IN, during the 2009–10 academic year. Thanks to Purdue and the Interdepartmental Program in Linguistics for their generous hospitality during that year. Thanks are also due to the Meltzer Foundation for financial support.

a number of other issues could have also been selected. Furthermore, the breadth of Cognitive Linguistics will not be adequately represented here: the main thrust of what follows will be taken from the theory of Cognitive Grammar, as articulated by Langacker (primarily [1987] 1991, 2008) and from the accounts of Cognitive Linguistics given in Croft and Cruse (2004), Lakoff (1987), Johnson (1987, 2007), and Lakoff and Johnson ([1980] 1995, 1999). This is primarily due to limitations of scope in the current paper, and is remedied by the breadth of material in the volume as a whole.

In the remainder of the introduction, a brief sketch of a cognitive linguistic view of translation is given, and some of the requisite elements from theories of bilingualism are also singled out. In the second section, a small set of translational issues will be considered in light of cognitive linguistic theory. In the third section, the growing use of multiple methods and combinations of data in one or a set of studies is discussed as an innovation in research methodology in Translation Studies. In the fourth section, two epistemological issues are addressed: (i) the need for "embodied realism" in Translation Studies and (ii) epistemology and definitions of the object of study. The final section presents a few concluding remarks, including perspectives on evolving conceptualizations of "translation" itself.

1.1 A cognitive linguistic view of translation: Translation as usage event and dynamic meaning construal

The creation of a translation,[1] in whatever medium, is recognized by translation scholars as an instance of discourse; that is, as a communicative event situated in historical, cultural, and personal circumstances and impacted by the particulars of those very real circumstances. Different theoretical approaches put more or less emphasis on the various sources of contingency: history, culture, or personal politics, status, or position (or lack thereof). To oversimplify matters quite a bit, some sociological and cultural frameworks prioritize cultural relationships, ideology and hegemonic structures (e.g. Calzada Pérez 2003; Inghilleri 2003, 2005; Simeoni 1998; Wolf 1997, 2002; Wolf and Fukari 2007), while other postmodernist theories tend to emphasize translator status and agency (e.g. Pym 1998; Tymoczko 2006; Venuti 1995). To the extent that linguistic theories

---

1 In this paper, the term "translation" is used to cover to what Jakobson referred to as "interlingual translation", including interpreting, as well as "intersemiotic translation", involving other, non-linguistic semiotic systems (1959).

have emphasized language-internal or local contextual elements they have been limited in their ability to incorporate the broader context of history and culture, ideology and individual agency.[2] In addition, both literary theory-based and linguistics-based descriptive approaches have been criticized as being overly concerned with "texts and systems", rather than people and their actions (Pym 2010: 84). A common denominator running through much of this criticism is a call for increased focus on the role of the human translator and of translator agency. From a cognitive perspective, an emphasis on the translating individual must also involve a framework to deal with the specifics of linguistic cognition. Indeed, in order to fully understand the complex interplay of the many sources of impact in the act of translation, it is imperative to look at the human basis in translational cognition, where all of these forces are brought together and where the causal struggle is actually played out (see also Chesterman 2000).

How, then, could a cognitive linguistic theory of translation grapple with the translational act? How might it be conceived? Starting with the consensual agreement that translation is a discursive act, one might consider Langacker's outline of discourse, quoted here at some length:

> A discourse comprises a series of *usage events*: instances of language use in all their complexity and specificity. A usage event has no particular size; depending on our analytical purpose, we can segment a discourse into words, clauses, sentences, intonation groups, conversational turns, and so on. An event is bipolar, consisting in both conceptualization and means of expression. On the expressive side, it includes the full phonetic detail of an utterance, as well as any other kinds of signals, such as gestures and body language (conceivably even pheromones). Conceptually, a usage event includes the expression's full contextual understanding – not only what is said explicitly, but also what is inferred, as well as everything evoked as the basis for its apprehension. (2008: 457–458, author's emphasis)

The view of language in discourse is given in the continuation:

> *Conventional linguistic units are just one resource* exploited in usage events. In speaking and understanding, we draw on our full range of knowledge, mental abilities, and interpersonal skills. Also essential is our apprehension of the context, one facet of which is the ongoing discourse itself. The various factors contributing to usage events should not be thought of as separate and discrete. In particular the specific contributions of language cannot be segregated or precisely delimited. The linguistic meaning of a word, for example, is not a distinct and self-contained entity, divorced from other knowledge and cognitive abilities – instead it recruits and exploits them. (2008: 458, my emphasis)

---

[2] Importantly, not all linguistically oriented approaches to translation fall to this criticism. Notable exceptions include the discourse-based work of Hatim and Mason (1990) and particularly Hatim and Mason (1997).

In this view, discourse, the series of usage events, draws on a broad range of human meaning-making capacities and in the process makes use of the entire embodied knowledge of the speaker/hearer, only some of which is knowledge of conventional linguistic units (hence the emphasis above). From this perspective, discursive acts are meaningful in ways that far exceed traditional views of linguistic meaning and that allow for the incorporation of personal, ideological, cultural, contextual considerations in a new way. Discursive acts are still situated in time and space, but the parameters for the discourse are created by the knowledge (conscious and subconscious) of the human interlocutors, not solely by systems, linguistic or otherwise, texts, or structural relations between other cultural entities.

A compatible cognitive linguistic account which is particularly amenable to conceptualizing the translational act is that presented in Croft and Cruse (2004: 97) under the heading "the dynamic construal of meaning". The authors argue for a view in which

> [...] words do not really have meanings, nor do sentences have meanings: meanings are something that we construe, using the properties of linguistic elements as partial clues, alongside non-linguistic knowledge, information available from context, knowledge and conjectures regarding the state of mind of hearers and so on. (2004: 98)

This is very similar to the position outlined in Langacker, as cited above. In this view also, it is important to note the description of linguistic elements as "partial cues" in meaning making, and also the significance of knowledge of various kinds. Croft and Cruse describe the dynamic construal of meaning in terms of four key concepts: (i) contextualized interpretation, (ii) purport, (iii) constraints, and (iv) construal operations. From this perspective, an act of meaning making represents a *contextualized interpretation* (Croft and Cruse 2004: 98). Such interpretation involves *purport* or a "body of conceptual content" associated with words (Croft and Cruse 2004: 98). "Purport" is to be conceived of as the raw material of meaning, which is then transformed in specific instances of meaning making. As the authors describe it, "purport is to interpretation as egg is to omelette, or flour to bread: it is of a different ontological category. Purport is an ingredient of meaning, not a constituent" (2004: 101). In addition, the meaning making/interpretation process is subject to a number of *constraints*, including human cognitive capacities, the nature of reality, convention, and context (linguistic, physical, social, and knowledge-related) (2004: 101–103), thus grounding the act in the human cognizer in a discursive situation as s/he conceives of it. The final element of this view of dynamic meaning is the notion of *construal*, which consists of a series of cognitive processes which turn the raw material of "purport" into "fully contextualized meanings" (2004: 103), operating under the constraints listed above. Grammar reflects the operation and conventionalization of construal processes. The crucial differences between this view and other linguistic theories lie in the integrated nature of linguistic and other kinds of knowledge and the integration of social, historical, and contextual influences through their basis in the knowledge and cognitive processes of the human communicator. This view of meaning creation is not deterministic or mechanical: it is human in every regard.

If linguistic communication works through dynamic meaning construal, then how do these key concepts operate in a translational scenario? Is there anything that distinguishes a translational process from a non-translational one? If so, what could it be? Though little technical integration of theory has been accomplished, it is possible, at this stage, to tentatively adopt a view of translation that builds on the basic premises of the approaches to meaning making outlined above, while retaining the insights gained through several decades of research in TS. Thus, the starting point is this: given the theory of language sketched above, what does this imply for translation? First, it is necessary to posit an anterior[3] text, spoken or written, linguistic, signed, or expressed in some other symbolic form. (Incidentally, this is also true of other linguistic acts such as paraphrase and/or the writing of a synopsis/abstract/précis [. . .]) The anterior text is expressed (in Langacker's terms [2008: 457–458]) in a different form than the ensuing translation. The creative translation process involves, minimally, (i) an emerging and dynamic contextualized interpretation of the anterior text (including knowledge of the relevant aspects of its discursive, historical, cultural context), (ii) constraints in the translational situation itself, and (iii) in the discursive situation for which the emerging translation is destined (including rich knowledge of the sort mentioned for the anterior text), (iv) a conceptualization of the translational act itself, both generally and in the specific present, and (v) the dynamic construction of a new text. Underlying and supporting all of this is the encyclopedic knowledge base of the specific translator. In other words, the translational act is comprised by the activation and selective use of several particular kinds of knowledge, including linguistic knowledge, all of which contribute to and constrain the process.

As cited above, constraints in contextualized interpretation include "human cognitive capacities, the nature of reality, convention, and context (linguistic,

---

3 The term "anterior text" is preferred to the more traditional "source text" or the older "original". Both of the latter suggest some sort of logical primacy or inherent status that is not consistent with the view to be presented here. By referring to an "anterior" text, the chronological aspect is highlighted.

physical, social and knowledge-related)" (Croft and Cruse 2004: 101–103). Thus, in addition to knowledge-related contextual constraints such as those mentioned above, there are also contextual constraints of a more social nature. Indeed, much work within functionalist TS in the 1980s and 1990s aimed at illustrating the importance of social factors (for surveys, see Munday 2008; Nord 1997; Pym 2010; Schäffner 2009). Examples of such social constraints include the specifics of a translation brief or an assumed brief, i.e. specific instructions or guidelines provided by the translation commissioner or initiator, the status or position of the translator within an organization or in the translational situation itself (e.g. in a courtroom, in a police station, in a war zone, etc.), and the use of technology, among other things. Importantly, however, these constraints are filtered through the cognitive process of the translator, and as such are also knowledge-related. This cognitive perspective on context is not one that is unique to the cognitive linguistic theorists drawn on here, nor indeed to the field of linguistics itself. Several of the relevant perspectives with regard to translation are introduced in Baker (2006), who argues for a more dynamic perspective on the process of *contextualization*, as opposed to static delineation of contextual elements and their relations. Baker discusses both social and cognitive theories of context, and emphasizes that the two represent alternative and compatible perspectives (2006: 324). A related, though separate and larger issue, is the demarcation of mind and world in cognitive processes (Clark 1997, 2008). In short, it is argued that, in many ways, it is not feasible to draw clear and definite boundaries between a cognitive operation and the situation in which it is embedded.[4] At the very least, this suggests that cognitive and socially-oriented theories should both bring analyses to the table, and that there are currently interesting ways in which they may inform one another.

1.2 Cognitive linguistic theory and bi- or multilingualism

In its earliest days, the theoretical framework of Cognitive Linguistics primarily modeled linguistic communication among monolingual speakers of the same language. In more recent years, a growing body of work in Contrastive Cognitive Linguistics has investigated cross-linguistic differences within a cognitive framework (e.g. Valenzuela and Rojo 2003) and work within second language

---

[4] Within Translation Studies work on "situated cognition" has been done by Risku (2002). These perspectives are also integrated into the work being done by the PACTE group (2003, 2005).

acquisition is increasingly adopting cognitive linguistic perspectives. Nonetheless, there has not as yet been a systematic attempt to model the particular type of bilingual communication that is translation.

Even monolingual communication is complicated enough: as Langacker points out, the usage event experienced by the speaker is not precisely identical to that experienced by the hearer, as the knowledge base of each participant is personal and unique, allowing for variations in what is inferred and evoked (2008: 458). As he points out, however, "substantial overlap is usually enough for successful communication" (458). The conceptualizations of two speakers of the same speech community are, however, grounded in somewhat shared environments, and successful linguistic interaction over time provides a basis for achieving sufficient "overlap". It is obvious, however, that in intercultural communication, whether monolingual, bilingual, or multilingual, the assumption of shared lived environments does not hold: the knowledge bases that may be activated and evoked, as well as the conventional paths of inference, may differ widely. Thus it seems that a cognitively oriented theory of translation must in some way incorporate a theory or model of knowledge, linguistic and otherwise, in bi- and/or multilingual people.

In a recent article (Halverson 2010a), it was argued that a model of bilingual representation such as that put forward in Jarvis and Pavlenko (2008) and Pavlenko (2009) is a viable source for this purpose, as it shares both cognitive assumptions and some conceptual elements with the cognitive linguistic theories mentioned above, for example, a means of capturing prototype effects and patterns of connectivity, such as polysemy, and the knowledge-based, culturally situated view of meaning. The model includes distinctions between conceptual, semantic, and phonological representational levels, which are required for the study of translational data (see Section 2.2). A detailed discussion of these models is beyond the scope of the current paper, as much work is needed in order to bring the insights of bilingualism research and Cognitive Linguistics together in specific and testable ways. Work in that area is in progress, as witnessed by work cited above (see also Robinson and Ellis 2008 and the 2009 special issue of the *Annual Review of Cognitive Linguistics* for comparable developments in second language acquisition). For the purposes at hand, it is vital to single out the cognitive aspects of bilingualism that are of most importance to further work on translational cognition. At this stage, at the very least, cognitive theories should not violate or come into conflict with current knowledge of bilingual representation and processing. In the following three central areas of research are touched on.

The first area of investigation concerns the modeling of conceptual representations in a bilingual, more specifically, the relationship between the semantic/conceptual level[5] and the level at which linguistic forms in a bilingual's two languages are stored. One of two dominant models of bilingual conceptual representation, the so-called Revised Hierarchical Model (Kroll and Stewart 1994) posits links between a conceptual tier that is common to a bilingual's two languages, and a lexical tier, where the formal elements of the two languages are stored separately. So-called "conceptual links" run between the conceptual tier and the lexical tier, and so-called "lexical links" run between the lexical items in the two languages. According to the model, the links within this system are not all of equal strengths: there is asymmetry. This is outlined as follows:

> The revised hierarchical model makes two critical assumptions about the strength of connections between words and concepts in bilingual memory. The first is that L1 words are assumed to be more strongly connected to concepts than are L2 words. The second is that L2 words are assumed to be more strongly connected to their corresponding translation equivalents in L1 than the reverse. (Kroll and Tokowicz 2005: 546)

The developmental aspect is integral to this model, as increasing L2 proficiency is claimed to strengthen the links between L2 words and the conceptual level. According to the model, over time, proficient bilinguals will also be able to process L2 words conceptually, through stronger links to that level, though asymmetry will remain for "all but the most balanced bilinguals" (Kroll and Tokowicz 2005: 546). The authors proceed to present experimental evidence in which the assumptions of the model were tested with regard to the lexicon. The results provided support for the model, but also suggested that results are not uniform across all word types, with differences for high and low frequency words, for example (Kroll and Tokowicz 2005: 548). A similar concern for differences across word types was one of the motivations for Pavlenko's articulation of an alternative version of the model, dubbed the "Modified Hierarchical Model" (2009: 146–151). Notably, the latter model allows words in different languages to share conceptual representations to differing degrees.[6]

This model is in some ways an oversimplification of some of the relevant characteristics of bilingual conceptual representation (Pavlenko 2009: 142–146),

---

[5] The use of the terms "semantic" and "conceptual" representations is inconsistent in the bilingualism literature (see Francis 2005). The terms are sometimes used interchangeably, and sometimes one or the other is used. In this paper, the two will be used to refer to two separate levels, in line with Jarvis and Pavlenko (2008).

[6] This partial sharing is also a feature of the other main model of bilingual representation, the "Distributed Feature Model" (de Groot 1992, 1993). Though it does cater for this distinction, the model suffers from other shortcomings (see Jarvis and Pavlenko 2008: 225–226), which has repercussions for its viability for the study of translation (Halverson 2010a).

and a cognitive theory of translation must ultimately address these issues in a detailed and specific way. However, the model outlined above serves as an illustration of some of the relatively uncontroversial aspects of bilingualism that cognitive translation scholars must take on board. Even a surface level understanding of the types of models mentioned here, and the evidence on which they are based, makes it clear that translational outcomes are affected by at least the following factors: (i) the degree of language dominance in the translator and how this is related to (ii) the direction of translation (into or out of the dominant language), (iii) the developmental trajectory (order of acquisition of languages, stage of proficiency), and (iv) the specific linguistic item(s) or task(s) in question. On this account, even bilinguals sharing the same two languages may translate differently, depending on the degree of proficiency in a given language, the individual's own developmental trajectory, the direction of the translation, and the item(s) and task specifications involved in translation. All of these factors are compounded in the case of multilingual speakers, a group which probably constitutes a relatively sizable percentage of professional translators (cf. Jarvis and Pavlenko 2008: 228–229).

A second issue of current interest in the bilingualism literature is the joint activation of a bilingual's two languages in language production. There is quite compelling evidence to support the claim that both of a bilingual's languages are activated in language production (Kroll et al. 2008: 427; Hartsuiker, Costa, and Finkbeiner 2008: 413), and that this is true also for quite proficient bilinguals (Kroll et al. 2008: 427). Current work focuses on identifying and investigating the detailed control mechanisms that ultimately support selection of the appropriate target language. For a cognitive theory of translation, the issues mentioned here raise numerous questions with regard to the conceptualization of linguistic knowledge and the processes by which this knowledge is used. Some of these issues will be considered in the following section.

Finally, within translation process theories, there has been some discussion of whether the process of interpreting the anterior text and the process of creating the new translation are either serial processes, parallel processes or a hybrid of the two (see Ruiz et al. 2008 for review). With regard to the hybrid model, it has been suggested that varying degrees of experience or training would determine the type of processing favored by any individual translator (Ruiz et al. 2008: 491 and sources cited there). In their study, Ruiz et al. (2008) provided experimental evidence in support for a parallel processing model: in other words, ST comprehension and TT activation processes were found to run in parallel. Further studies will undoubtedly shed more light on this issue.

2 Implications of Cognitive Linguistics for Translation Theory

In this section, a small selection of key translational issues is in focus. In each subsection, relevant background and the current state of knowledge in TS are outlined first; then the new perspectives provided by Cognitive Linguistics are sketched out. The aim is to single out those elements of the cognitive linguistic and bilingualism frameworks that might provide the necessary grounding for more specific theorizing and empirical investigation.

2.1 Two sides of the same coin: Equivalence and shifts

2.1.1 Equivalence in Translation Studies

In its emergent and early stages in the 1960s up until the 1980s, contemporary Translation Studies was primarily identified with the study of relationships between source and target structures. The concept of translation itself was defined with reference to a concept of "equivalence", and translations were identified as texts that met the requisite equivalence criteria (Halverson 1997; Koller 1995, Munday 2008: 38ff; Pym 2010: 6ff). In many ways, early work represented a variety of ways of coping with what Jakobson referred to as "equivalence in difference" (1959), or the problem of how different languages constrain the ways in which their speakers may express "the same thing". Work within this paradigm focused both on the identification of the invariant (the *tertium comparationis*) on the basis of which equivalence was to be established, and on the elaboration of the various linguistic levels or units that might be affected. Catford (1965) was careful to distinguish between formal correspondence (between languages) and translational equivalence (between texts or textual elements). He proceeded to elaborate a detailed system for the description of translational relationships that included reference to linguistic levels and structural categories, e.g. phrase, clause, sentence, text and "shifts" between them, emphasizing variability of equivalence types within a text. Nida (1964) recognized the need for a means of capturing pragmatic elements in the relationship taxonomy and distinguished between "formal equivalence", or equivalence of form and message, and "dynamic equivalence", which catered for equivalence of response in source and target contexts. Koller provided an even more detailed taxonomy of equivalence types, including denotative, connotative, text-normative, pragmatic and formal equivalence (1989). Each type identifies the invariant on the basis of which an equivalence relationship between source and target is established: here the invariants are extralinguistic content, lexical connotations, text type, communicative effect, and linguistic form, including wordplay and typical characteristics of individual authors, respectively (1989). Evolving theories of language brought with them new approaches to defining the equivalence relationship, as discourse and pragmatic concerns entered into the analyses, while the focus remained on the identification of appropriate invariance types and units. The entire equivalence paradigm gradually fell into disfavor, due to the lingering uncertainty with regard to the appropriate "unit of translation" and the inevitable proliferation of equivalence types, as well as the concept's perceived inability to address the real concerns of TS (Snell-Hornby 1988). The various equivalence typologies also proved unable to fully capture the reality of translational data (Koller 1995).

In a review of the history of the equivalence concept in TS, Pym (2007, 2010) distinguishes between what he refers to as "natural" and "directional" concepts of equivalence. In Pym's view, the work sketched above is concerned with "natural equivalence", or relationships between textual/linguistic elements that are determined by a notion of naturalness of expression that may be achieved in spite of structural or pragmatic differences between the two involved languages. According to Pym, natural equivalence "should not be affected by directionality: it should be the same whether translated from language A into language B or the other way around" (2010: 7). "Directional equivalence", on the other hand, assumes some sort of directional asymmetry. Pym introduces the term "to refer to all those cases where an equivalent is located on one side more than the other, at least to the extent that they forget to tell us about movements that could go either way" (Pym 2010: 28). The asymmetry of the relationship is often illustrated in binary pairs of translation types where each of the members in a pair captures the tilt of the equivalence balance towards either the source or target culture/language/discourse complex, for example foreignizing versus domesticating, semantic versus communicative, documentary versus instrumental, resistant versus fluent, etc. (Pym 2010: 30–33). While these types of relationship are different from those focused on "naturalness", they share the overall emphasis on articulating the nature of the source-target relationship (cf. Pym 2010: 28).

In his review, Pym states that Toury (1995), Gutt (2000) and Pym (1992) represent a genuinely different approach to the idea of equivalence through a common focus on what he refers to as "equivalence beliefs" (2010: 37–38). These authors all posit means of investigating source-target relationships on the basis of historically contingent practices or beliefs, and they all involve some sort of *post hoc* identification process, rather than the a priori definitions posited previously. For Toury, all translations are by definition equivalent to their sources, and the scholar's task is to describe and explain how equivalence is realized. Gutt, from a relevance theoretic perspective, argues that translations are those texts which present themselves as interpretations of anterior texts, and are consequently believed to be so. Pym emphasizes the historical contingency of equivalence-making practices and beliefs. The shift from a priori definition of objective relationships to *post hoc* belief practices is the only viable approach to "equivalence" in TS, according to Pym (2010: 40–41).

To sum up: the history of the equivalence concept in TS is the story of evolution from the search for a set of relationships between objectively identifiable, "natural" linguistic structures and/or contextual features towards dynamic, changing, historically situated conceptualizations of source and target and the balance between them. Over time, "equivalence" has been reconfigured from "essential characteristic of translations, defined a priori", to "quality of all translations, to be characterized post hoc". This evolution, in fact, amounts to an epistemological recategorization. The concept is no longer locked into an essentialist epistemology; it is, in its latest version, a subjective belief concerning a text or texts, relativized in time and place (Pym 2010: 37; see also Halverson 1997).

2.1.2 Equivalence from a cognitive perspective: From correspondences to knowledge constraints

Within a dynamic meaning construal approach to translation such as that outlined in Section 1.1, there is little room for distinct and uniquely isolable entities such as the traditional, systemic source-target equivalents, of whatever size or kind. To state the obvious, the first, and in some sense the only real, place where the source and target entities involved in a specific translation task actually come together is in the mind of the translator (though analysts may attempt to reconstruct this meeting later on). And while there are, clearly, relevant interlingual links involved, these are by no means the same, either in terms of how they are cognitively represented or cognitively processed, as the kinds of binary equivalence relationships that have been posited in TS. Indeed, as mentioned above, psycholinguistic studies of bilingualism demonstrate that, from a cognitive perspective, a bilingual's two languages are not completely separate (de Groot 1992, 1993; Dong, Gui, and Macwhinney 2005; Kroll et al. 2008: note 1; Pavlenko 2009). Instead, the picture emerging from studies of bilingual representation suggests that there are complex patterns of linkage involving representational elements at conceptual, semantic and formal levels, and that the conceptual level is to some degree shared by a multilingual speaker's languages (Jarvis and Pavlenko 2008). Pavlenko (2009) also addresses the question of language/culture-specific knowledge, or knowledge that is linked to linguistic items in only one of a multilingual speaker's language, and incorporates such cases into a model that caters for varying degrees of conceptual overlap, ranging from zero to completely shared. The point to be made here is that from a cognitive perspective, the interaction of the languages that a bi- or multilingual speaker knows is much more complex than any binary correspondence (equivalence) view could ever capture.

In the cognitive view, a linguistic act is conceived of as dynamic, using conceptual raw material and construal operations, under pertinent constraints. Adopting this view does not preclude some associative linking of elements of one language with elements of another within the speaker's cognitive system; but as argued in the bilingualism literature cited above, these links are complex, involving several representational levels. As a consequence, the task of a cognitive translation scholar is to look for ways in which specific linguistic items may be represented and activated in the language of a bilingual and how various representational characteristics might impact translational outcomes. In translation, an antecedent, linguistically activated, conceptualization in the mind of a translator is an integral part of the dynamic creation of another text. Linguistic correspondences, of the type previously posited as equivalence relationships, instead must be situated within a cognitive model of linguistic knowledge, which means that their status must be reassessed. Complex, multilevel, interlingual links must be conceived of as one of the many types of knowledge that are activated and utilized in the translational act (Langacker 2008: 458; Croft and Cruse 2004: 98), and as such these links function as a constraining factor in the process. They do not constitute it.

In short, it would seem that a cognitive theory of translation does not need a concept of source-target equivalence for future theorizing. However, as mentioned in Section 1.1, in addition to linguistic knowledge, the translational act also involves a translator's conceptualization of the translational act itself, and this conceptualization, in turn, will serve as a contextual constraint on the translational act.

Studies of various "translation" concepts (Chesterman 2006 and references cited there; Halverson 1999a, 2008; Tymoczko 2007 and studies cited there; Paker 2002) provide relevant examples of different conceptualizations, even though these studies were not carried out with this in mind. Another relevant example is Toury's "initial norm", described as the translator's choice of basic orientation towards either target or source (towards either "being a text [. . .]" or "constituting a representation [. . .]") (1995: 56). As pointed out in Halverson (1999a: 22), this notion actually captures the translator's concept of translation. The conceptualization that a translator maintains of the very activity in which s/he is engaged could, then, serve as the theoretical site for what Pym referred to as "equivalence beliefs". In other words, if the idea of equivalence is to have any role at all, then it may be within the concept of "translation" that a translator has, and as such it functions as a knowledge-based constraint, on a par with a number of other such constraints. In this view, the causal force of equivalence beliefs lies in the mind of the translator. But such belief systems must also be investigated in terms of the cultural, historical, and social contexts in which the translator is embedded and in which these beliefs are shared (see Halverson 2008).

2.1.3 Shifts in translation theory

Another concept used in studying and accounting for source-target relationships is the notion of "shifts" (Molina Martínez and Hurtado Albir 2002; Chesterman 2005; Halverson 2007; Marco 2007). As these authors point out, "shift" is one of a variety of terms that are meant to capture either translational procedures, conscious or subconscious, routine or automatized, problem-oriented or not, or relationships between translation products and their sources. Terms often vary also in their scope: whether they cover global or local procedures or structures. Terms such as "procedure", "technique", "strategy", "method", "shift", etc. are used differently by different authors, and different terms are also used to refer to the same concept. In several of the analyses mentioned above, the authors argue for conceptual clarification and terminological consensus, though they disagree on the requisite distinctions. Chesterman, for example, proposes a four-way conceptual framework (2005: 26–27), distinguishing between "method", "strategy", "technique", and "shift", while Marco argues that all that is needed is a two-way conceptual and terminological distinction between translational procedures and *post hoc* relationship categories (2007: 262–263).

Cross-cutting the question of whether the source-target relationship is procedural or related to end-products is the underlying issue of change. There is a fundamental tension inherent in the notion of "shift" as used to refer to "[. . .] changes which occur or may occur in the process of translating" (Bakker, Koster, and Van Leuven-Zwart 2009: 269). As the authors point out, the notion of "shift" or "change" implies that there is an invariant, and shifts or changes are identified and characterized relative to that invariant. One well-known representative of this approach is Popovič, who defines shifts as "All that appears as new with respect to the original, or fails to appear where it may have been expected [. . .]" (1970: 79). Thus procedural approaches may suggest operations that result in changes, while product-based categories classify change types. The most well-known frameworks of the former type are Vinay and Darbelnet (1995) and Klaudy (1996), which posit such processes as, modulation, adaptation, transposition, etc., operating on linguistic structures of various sizes and type. The most well-known of the latter type are arguably Catford (1965) and Van Leuven-Zwart (1989, 1990). Catford identified shifts as "departures from formal correspondence" (1965: 73), and his framework allows for the various types of formal differences, often involving either category shifts (e.g. syntax to lexis or vice versa) or rank shifts (e.g. from clause to phrase, from phrase to lexeme, etc.). Van Leuven-Zwart's framework involved the derivation of a common semantic denominator linking ST and TT segments, and shifts were then classified in terms of extent of change from the invariant and the level and type of linguistic element affected.

Chesterman illustrates the problem of operationalizing concepts of shift or invariance by demonstrating how shift analysis often ends up with overlapping or indeterminate categories, which is related to the problem of identifying the "unit of translation" (2005: 24–25). This problem was also implicated in the increasing number of equivalence types, mentioned in Section 2.1.1. Also relevant to the issue of invariance is the fact, identified by both Chesterman (2005) and Marco (2007), that a number of the types of strategies/techniques/operations/procedures may end up in either similarity or difference. On this basis, Chesterman is able to elaborate a set of parallels between types of equivalence and types of shifts (2005: 27). Chesterman advocates the term "solution type", launched by Zabalbeascoa (2000: 122) to cover *post hoc* relationships of both similarity and difference.

To sum up: the term "shift" has traditionally been applied to translational operations or actions and to categories of source-target relationships identified after the fact, though at present some scholars are calling for a clearer distinction between the two. Similar and related terms, such as "method", "strategy", "operation", and "technique", have also been used with reference to this conceptual territory, and the term "shift" has traditionally been used to refer to cases where there is some change from an identified invariant of some kind, though this is problematic in cases where a given operational translational procedure or strategy may result in either similarity or difference. There is no obvious or agreed solution to the question of how an invariant may be established.

2.1.4 Shifts as construal operations

As mentioned in the discussion of equivalence, it is not immediately obvious what role invariance or elaboration of source-target relationships of similarity or dissimilarity should have in a cognitive linguistic theory of translation. Consequently, the notion of "shift", in the sense of *post hoc* product categories established on the basis of an identified invariant, is problematic for the same reasons as "equivalence" is. As suggested above, in a dynamic meaning construal account, interlingual relationships are much more complex than theories of equivalence or shifts have previously allowed. Moreover, linguistic cues represent only part of the raw material used in meaning making.

If the notion of shifts is considered in its procedural sense, starting with the dynamic contextualized interpretation of the anterior text and without an assumption of an invariant core, it becomes easier to situate within a cognitive theory of translation. In an earlier discussion (Halverson 2007), it was argued that many of the proposed procedural categories of shift/procedure/strategy/ etc., especially those in Vinay and Darbelnet (1995) and Klaudy (1996), may be conceived of as "construal operations", as described in cognitive theories (Croft and Cruse 2004: 40–73; see also Langacker 1987). Recall that construal operations transform the raw material of conceptual purport into contextualized meanings that are conventionally linked to specific forms. At this level, translational acts are no different from monolingual communicative acts: conceptual content is transformed and linked to linguistic form. Indeed, as pointed out earlier, in one sense translation is construal (Halverson 2007).

In a cognitive linguistic translation theory, construal operations would be implicated in three ways: (i) in the translator's contextualized interpreting of the anterior text, (ii) in the translator's knowledge of the inventories of conventionalized construals in the languages s/he knows, and (iii) in his/her online, creative generation of a translation, as mentioned above. If translation is seen as dynamic meaning construal, then (i) and (iii) are actually part of the same ongoing process, though they may represent two alternating areas of attention.[7] With regard to (ii), however, it is important to avoid the risk of returning to static source-target comparisons. There are, naturally, inventories of conventionalized linguistic structures, and translators are in some ways constrained by them. If these inventories of linguistic elements are reassessed within a cognitive framework, they are reduced to the level of one of a number of constraints in the translator's creative process, operating alongside other knowledge-based constraints. Viewing construal operations as integral to, as actually constituting the translation process, allows us to maintain many of the insights of previous work on translational procedures such as Vinay and Darbelnet's methodology (1995) or

---

[7] This issue is the subject of ongoing research into serial and parallel processing, as mentioned in Section 1.2.

Klaudy's translational operations (1996), while at the same time emphasizing the creative, non-deterministic nature of the process. Translational alternatives are seen as creatively generated, while choice is constrained by cognitive factors, convention, and context.

A view similar to the above is articulated in detail in Lewandowska-Tomaszczyk (2010). We differ in some of the particulars, but in the main, the argument for a construal-oriented approach is the same. A full comparison of the two perspectives is beyond the scope of the present discussion.

2.2 "Translation universals": From description to explanation

2.2.1 Describing patterns

One of the areas in which linguistic approaches to translation have had a recent resurgence is corpus-based Translation Studies. Starting with the development of a number of parallel corpora in the early 1990s, for example the English-Norwegian Parallel Corpus and the English-Swedish Parallel Corpus, ultimately joined under the Oslo Multilingual Corpus (http://hf.uio.no/ilos/OMC/), and the first so-called "comparable corpus", the Translational English Corpus in Manchester in the mid-1990s (http://www.monabaker.com/tsresources/TranslationalEnglishCorpus.htm), a number of translation scholars have used corpus data and corpus-based methods (see Laviosa 2002; Olohan 2004; Kenny 2009 for surveys). Many, though not all, of the studies in this paradigm involved investigation of so-called "translation universals",[8] defined by Baker as "features which typically occur in translated text rather than original utterances and which are not the result of interference from specific linguistic systems" (1993: 243). The list of candidate universals suggested by Baker included:

- simplification (the idea that translators subconsciously simplify the language or message or both)
- explicitation (the tendency to spell things out in translation, including, in its simplest form, the practice of adding background information)

---

[8] Baker's use of the term "universal" has been criticized as conceptually unclear (Pym 2008) and as inappropriate for the task it was selected to do (Malmkjær 2008). For these and other reasons, in the following the term "features of translation" (or features of translated text) used by Olohan (2004) will be adopted here also.

- normalization or conservatism (the tendency to conform to patterns and practices which are typical of the target language, even to the point of exaggerating them)
- levelling out (the tendency of translated text to gravitate around the centre of any continuum rather than move towards the fringes) (1996: 176–177)

Patterns such as these may be investigated through primarily two kinds of investigations: comparing translations with their sources, or comparing translations with non-translated texts in the same language (Chesterman 2004). It was primarily the latter kind of comparison that was advocated by Baker, through the introduction of the comparable corpus methodology (Baker 1993, 1995). While Baker's program served as an impetus to a number of studies (e.g. the collections edited by Mauranen and Kujamäki 2004; Anderman and Rogers 2008), the conceptual framework came under pressure from several directions. Malmkjær (2008) argues that patterns such as those mentioned above are better conceived of as norms, rather than universals (2008: 57). Pym (2008) argues that Baker's universals are not conceptually distinct and that they ultimately reduce to the two "laws of translation" originally put forward by Toury (1995), i.e. "the law of increasing standardization" and the "law of interference". Halverson (2003) argues that the paradigm lacks an adequate theoretical foundation from which to hypothesize about potential explanations. In later work, Halverson (2010b) picks up on an element of the earlier paper, and argues that many of the proposed universal patterns may, in fact, not be unique to translation, and that they ought to be conceived of as natural effects of bilingual language production.

In later work, Sonja Tirkkonen-Condit put forward another candidate for the status of translation universal in her work on the "unique-items hypothesis" (Tirkkonen-Condit 2004, 2005). This hypothesis states that linguistic items which "lack straightforward linguistic counterparts" (2004: 177) in the source language will be underrepresented in translated language, as opposed to non-translated language. The hypothesis is supported in both studies and by Eskola (2004) and Kujamäki (2004), and is advocated as a candidate for universal status also by Malmkjær (2008).

2.2.2 Features of translation: Towards a possible explanation

The types of patterns suggested by Baker in the 1993 article, while arguably lacking in conceptual clarity, seem to capture some recurring and recognizable features of some translational and learner data (some of which is reviewed in

Halverson [2003]). However, unless the paradigm is able to put forward an adequate explanatory model, conceptual clarity will also remain elusive. In Halverson (2003), it was argued that an appropriate explanatory framework may be found in the theory of cognitive grammar. More specifically, it was proposed that the features of normalization/conservatism (Englund-Dimitrova 1997; Kenny 2001), conventionalization and exaggeration of target language features (Baker 1993) may be the effects of a what was referred to in that paper as "gravitational pull", or the effect of the cognitive salience of high-level schemas and/or prototypes within schematic networks. The hypothesis is that linguistic forms linked to highly salient cognitive structures would be overrepresented in translated, as opposed to non-translated text (Halverson 2003: 218f).

In deriving the gravitational pull hypothesis, several studies were cited that provided evidence for effects of category structure on language production in learner language (e.g. Hasselgren 1993; Ijaz 1986; Kellerman 1978, 1979). These studies showed that learner language showed effects of both L1 category structure and what Ijaz referred to as "the semantic equivalence hypothesis" (1986: 433). In her study, Ijaz found that "ESL learners [...] approximate native speakers more closely in the meaning they ascribe to typical or central instances of semantic categories than in the meaning ascribed to noncentral ones" (433). Effects of category structure (here prototypicality) on crosslinguistic influence is also discussed in Jarvis and Pavlenko (2008: 186–188), and evidence is given for an effect of prototypicality on L2 word choice (Jarvis 1998).

The gravitational pull hypothesis, as put forward in Halverson (2003), also attempted to account for the data emerging from studies of the unique items hypothesis by suggesting that schematic networks without prototypes or highly salient schemas, or with "weak" or "distant" links within bilingual networks, may tend towards underrepresentation of TL structures. In a subsequent project, attempts to operationalize "network linkage" revealed that the model presented in Halverson (2003) did not have the distinctions needed to capture the difference between effects of network salience and effects of differences in network configuration (type or strength of the links). This was hinted at in Section 1.2 (see Halverson 2009, 2010a). The problem may be resolved through the integration of a newer model of bilingual conceptual representation, with two distinct levels to capture these two difference sources of potential effect, as suggested in Section 1.2.

The ongoing project to test the gravitational pull hypothesis (outlined in Halverson 2009, 2010b, in progress b) has emphasized the need for further work on the integration of the Cognitive Grammar and bilingualism models. If the hypothesis is supported through this and other studies, then this would be a demonstration of how cognitive theory can contribute to the explanation of the linguistic characteristics of translated text. Success in this endeavor rests, not least, on a number of important methodological issues, some of which will be addressed in Section 3.

2.3 Summing up: The implications of Cognitive Linguistics for Translation Theory

This section has been organized around a selection of well-known issues which have been central to the study of translation for the past sixty years: equivalence, shifts, and more recently, translation universals. To reiterate: this does not exhaust the list of relevant or interesting issues. These have been selected due to their historical and current status in the field and the ensuing necessity for any linguistic theory to take a stance with regard to them.

Translation scholarship has moved past the stage at which the key objective was to elaborate systemic frameworks for the identification and classification of source-target relationships on the basis of a stable invariant core, though there is still some unease about how to tackle the issue of equivalence or similarity. Pym (2010) has suggested that the answer is to consider the role of equivalence as a belief: this is entirely feasible, and indeed necessary if we adopt the cognitive approach outlined above. Every translator is constrained by his/her conceptualization of what "translation" is: in many cultures, an equivalence belief is part of this. Importantly, however, this may not be universally true. Different cultures, at different times, may have conventionalized different belief systems, as suggested by, among others Tymoczko (2006) and Chesterman (2006).

The bilingualism literature provides at least one framework that might inform cognitive linguistic theory in extending it to the investigation of bilingual cognition. Having considered some of the findings from this work, it becomes imperative to ask whether Translation Studies actually needs, or is at all served by the kind of binary relational framework that underlies the concepts of equivalence, similarity, and shifts (in its *post hoc* product sense). The sources of this mindset are relatively obvious: the TRANSFER metaphor that structures our understanding of the "translation" concept (Halverson 1999b; Tymoczko 2007), the highly visible and tangible nature of both ST and TT, as well as the analytical separability of the two involved language systems. But, if translation is a kind of dynamic meaning construal, (where linguistic and non-linguistic knowledge, only partially separable and jointly activated, is constrained by the real world), cognition itself, and a variety of contextual factors, themselves the subject of online construction, then this process is a much richer, a much more creative and organic one than a structural comparison, binary relation view could ever capture. The very basis for comparison, the *tertium comparationis*, vanishes in this view, or at the very least, is buried deep in the cognitive links, the activation patterns established between words, constructions or other kinds of knowledge in the mind of the translator. It is not needed to explain translation.⁹

The concept of translation shift, if reframed in one of its two current manifestations as a set of procedural operations, can be incorporated within a cognitive theory through its conceptual overlap with construal operations, as argued in Halverson (2007).¹⁰ The notion of translation "universal" or translational patterns or features requires further clarification, but this clarification must be relative to a theory with some explanatory power. It has been argued (Halverson 2003) that the theory of cognitive grammar has explanatory potential here, and that, if combined with the insights of current work on cross-linguistic influence such as that by Jarvis and Pavlenko (2008), could prove even more fruitful. Thus both procedural "shifts" and "universals/features" remain central to a cognitive theory of translation.

From the perspective of the cognizing human translator, rather than of, say, implicated languages or cultures, the need is for a more organic translation theory with a more unitary focus on one engaged and situated mind. From the translator's perspective, languages, cultures, situations and conventions, indeed all that s/he knows, is embodied in the personal mind. In this view of translation, there is no invariant, no movement, no transfer, no carrying over. There is one creative process, drawing on and utilizing the cues provided by the anterior text and the rich cognitive resources of the translator, subject to a set of

---

9 Tabakowska (1993) also adopted a cognitive linguistic approach to translation, and in her view, the "image" or conceptualization, could serve as the *tertium comparationis*. This was a valuable contribution to thinking in TS, as it highlighted the role of cognition in translation. In adopting a view that attempts to bridge cognitive linguistic and bilingualism research, argue that we do not need an invariant, or basis for source-target comparison, and that the continuing search for it hinders further theoretical innovation.
10 In that article, the process/product distinction was not adequately made, and the analyses actually may suggest a product-type interpretation. The operations are to be considered procedural and dynamic, while further work is needed to elaborate a means of relating these operations to a set of terms to refer to their results. Actually, this problem is itself a matter of construal, in that a change of perspective from the path to its endpoint does not change the underlying process, just the view taken of it (see also Fawcett 1997: 50–51).

constraints. While all of the constraining elements listed above, both knowledge-related and contextual, have been theorized individually, they remain to be integrated into a testable holistic theory with a cognitive base that provides for their working in a unique, real translational act. A cognitive translation theory could incorporate a number of the findings of previous functionalist work, though with a realignment of conceptual status for some of the key notions in order to integrate them into a human-driven knowledge-based causal nexus.

Some might view the above as an exercise in merely moving translation theory from outside to inside the head of the translator, and not really saying anything new in the process. Indeed, the equivalence paradigm has been declared dead several times, so yet another kick in that direction will probably not do too much damage. But this is not another kick. In reframing equivalence, in line with Pym, as a belief that some cultures and the translators within them may share, it is given the potential to exercise causal force in the only way in which it can. Similarly, shifts and universals/features have been reframed in order to begin further work at conceptual clarification and operationalization for empirical study. Both of these issues are of current and ongoing interest, and new theoretical perspectives are definitely called for.

3 Implications of Cognitive Linguistics for Translation Studies methodology

For the last fifty-odd years, empirical work in Translation Studies has often been categorized as either "process- or product-based", according to whether the specific object of study was the process itself or its textual product (cf. Holmes 1988; Toury 1995). While process-oriented studies have always been oriented towards psycholinguistic methods and models from cognitive psychology, such as think-aloud protocols (see Jääskeläinen 2009 for a review), product-oriented studies have relied heavily on case study methods (Susam-Sarajeva 2009: 37). Quantitative methodologies also became more frequent with the advent of corpus-based studies (cf. Kenny 2009; Laviosa 2002; Olohan 2004).

One of the most promising innovations in research methods in TS was the introduction of keystroke logging, most often in the form of TRANSLOG technologies (Jakobsen 2006). This technology has allowed for collection of data related to the online production of translations, including all keystroking (backspace, editing, etc), as well as indications of the duration and (textual) location of all pauses. Newer versions of the software also allow for the integration of an eye-tracker and/or a screen monitor, such that data on several process variables (e.g. gaze fixation, gaze direction) may be collated and linked to the final translated product. Keystroke logging thus represents the first and only current data collection tool that allows for the integration of process- and product-related data on one and the same production sequence.

At present, the full potential of combined methods research in TS is only beginning to be explored. The most innovative research groups with an empirical focus are those working on process-oriented research. These will be very briefly mentioned in Section 3.1. The methodologies adopted by these groups remain predominantly experimental, with the possible exception of the PACTE group, which also integrates more observational data. In other areas of Translation Studies, empirical work remains focused on either case studies or corpus-based methods. Within Cognitive Linguistics, a recent development among corpus linguists is emphasis on combining corpus-based and experimental methods. This development, and its repercussions for TS, will be briefly discussed in Section 3.2.

3.1 Experimental methods in TS: Recent developments

There are currently three major research groups working on translation process projects: The Centre for Research and Innovation on Translation and Translation Technology (CRITT) in Copenhagen, the Eye-to-IT project led from Bulgaria, and the PACTE group in Spain. All of these groups have adopted a combination of psycholinguistic methods, many involving combinations of data types. Examples include studies on textual segmentation in translation (e.g. Dragsted 2004; Jakobsen 2003), ST-TT attention (Jensen 2009), and cognitive effort and metaphor (Sjørup 2009). Among other things, Dragsted found that, with relatively easy texts, novices and professionals tended to segment texts differently, with professionals demonstrating larger units and novices smaller. These differences were somewhat neutralized given a more demanding task, however (2004: 358). Jakobsen (2003) found that concurrent think-aloud had an effect on segmentation, with concurrent think-aloud resulting in smaller segments. Jensen (2009), in ongoing work using eye-tracking,[11] has found both similarities and differences between professionals and novices in the distribution of attention between ST and TT and in the duration of gaze with regard to ST and TT segments. Also in ongoing work, Sjørup (2009) studies the gaze time involved in the translation of metaphor, using this factor as an indicator of cognitive load. Much of the Copenhagen work is published in successive issues of *Copenhagen Studies in Language*.

---

11 See also Rojo and Valenzuela, this volume, for another study with eye-tracking technology.

The Eye-to-IT project, which includes several of the Copenhagen researchers, is a primarily experimental research program, and combines data collected through eye-tracking, EEG, and keystroke logging (http://cogs.nbu.bg/eye-to-it/?home). Its primary objective is to develop technologies that enable human-computer interaction during the translation process. Numerous psycholinguistic variables have also been the subject of investigation under the auspices of this project, for example, segmentation and the coordination of reading and writing (Dragsted and Hansen 2008; Jakobsen and Jensen 2008), the effects of time pressure and text complexity on cognitive processing (Sharmin et al. 2008), correspondences in the bilingual lexicon (Stamenov, Gerganov, and Popivanov 2009), and the effect of cognate status on cognitive load (Lachaud 2009) to mention a few.

The PACTE group adopts a cognitive theoretical framework, and is engaged in the study of translation processes and the development of a model of translator competence (Muñoz Martín 2006; PACTE group 2003, 2005, 2010, 2011). This group also incorporates a range of data types and methodologies in its work, including textual material, translation protocols, direct observation, questionnaires, and retrospective interviews (PACTE group 2005: 611).

The three groups mentioned here have been selected as indicative of methodological development and innovation in TS. All of these groups work within so-called process-oriented TS; that is, the main object of investigation is the translation process. Consequently, the selection of data and analytical method is driven by process-derived variables, such as reaction time, pause length, gaze fixation, EEG patterns, etc. However, as seen even in this superficial sketch, all of the groups include textual (product) data types in their portfolios, enabling combinations of textual (product) variables and process variables. The clearest implementations of this strategy are found in the Eye-to-IT work: textual variables such as syntactic segmentation, idioms, metaphor or text complexity are linked to process variables such as cognitive load, indicated by such measures as pause length, reaction time, or gaze fixation. The full potential of this wealth of data remains to be exploited through the integration of a theoretical model that would allow both product and process variables to be brought together within one and the same paradigm.

3.2 Corpus-based Cognitive Linguistics and innovation in TS

In a recent state-of-the-art review, Gilquin and Gries (2009) review the background and current state of affairs as regards data and methods in linguistics.

They single out the rapidly emerging use of combinations of corpus-based and experimental methods as a promising development, stating:

> Because the advantages and disadvantages of corpora and experiments are largely complementary, using the two methodologies in conjunction with each other often makes it possible to (i) solve problems that would be encountered if one employed one type of data only and (ii) approach phenomena from a multiplicity of perspectives. (2009: 9)

Within Cognitive Linguistics, the need for both types of data is particularly acute, given the offline nature of corpus data and the psychological/cognitive nature of the theoretical constructs put forward to explain them. As stated by Tummers, Heylen, and Geeraerts, the problem is this: "Given the offline nature of corpus data, they are not suited to support claims about the cognitive or neurological mechanisms underlying language use" (2005: 233). This issue has been the subject of considerable debate within the Cognitive Linguistics community (Sandra and Rice 1995; Croft 1998; Sandra 1998). More recently, Tummers, Heylen, and Geeraerts (2005) and Heylen, Tummers, and Geeraerts (2008) have also addressed the issue. At present, it would seem that while there is shared recognition of the need for several types of data, there is no general consensus on how different types of data should be brought together. Heylen, Tummers, and Geeraerts (2008) summarize the situation as follows:

> Relating to the second property of corpus data that we discussed, viz. *offline usage*, there are still questions about which aspects of the language system can be fruitfully studied through corpus analysis. More generally, there is a need to integrate quantitative corpus analysis with other empirical methodologies into a coherent methodological framework for research into the cognitive aspects of language. [. . .] A division of labour could be to first identify relevant variables through quantitative corpus analysis and then investigate the online properties of variables in a more targeted way through psycholinguistic experiments. On the other hand, corpus analysis has the advantage that it relies on spontaneous naturally occurring language use, whereas psycholinguistic experiments are often forced to use constructed examples. Validating experimental results against corpus data can be a way to avoid experimental artefacts. (2008: 121)

While either of these tacks are feasible, i.e. corpus to experiment or vice versa, the questions of how the data shall be integrated or what to do with diverging results remains. As pointed out by Gilquin and Gries (2009: 17), studies that do use combined methods have ended up with both converging and diverging results. As they put it,

> Possible explanations have been offered to account for the differences between corpus and experimental data, and suggestions have been made to bring them closer to each other, but it is still true that the relation between the two types of data remains unclear and that identity cannot be taken for granted. (2009:121)

The authors continue to point out that efforts toward integration should ideally proceed through recourse to linguistic theory.

Several recent papers exemplify the trend towards combining psycholinguistic experimentation and corpus analysis (e.g. Divjak and Gries 2008; Ellis and Simpson-Vlach 2009; Mollin 2009; Wulff 2009). Only the second of these studies implemented processing variables of the sort used in translation process analysis, and all of them speak to issues of semantic representation. The studies mentioned here cover, respectively, the organization of the mental lexicon, processing of formulaic language, the relationship between corpus collocation and word association, and linguistic factors used in idiomaticity judgments.

The process-oriented TS work sketched above could represent the kind of methodological step combining experiment with corpus suggested by Heylen, Tummers, and Geeraerts (2008). One study which initiates efforts in this direction is Alves et al. (2010), in which keystroke logging and eye-tracking data are brought together with corpus annotation and alignment data in an investigation of translational units. This study is one of the first of its kind. Further work will be required to isolate the appropriate links between online and offline data, as process variables such as pause duration, location and duration of gaze, etc. are to be operationalized relative to a broad, (cognitive) linguistic theory that would also allow for corpus analysis.

As sketched in Section 2.3, corpus-based methods have represented an important addition to empirical Translation Studies since the early 1990s. It is fair to say that corpus-based approaches to the study of translation have grown alongside corpus methodologies within linguistics at large. At present, however, the implementation of combined methods in the corpust-to-experiment direction has been limited. This is probably due to the lack of pressure from cognitive theories: most corpus-based studies of translation have drawn on other discourse analytical theories. Thus, there are few examples of the opposite movement, in the corpus to experiment direction. One example is the ongoing work mentioned in Section 2.3 and outlined in Halverson (2009). In this work, the gravitational pull hypothesis is first investigated through a series of corpus studies involving the light verb *get* in the English-Norwegian Parallel Corpus (ENPC), the British National Corpus (BNC), and the Translational English Corpus (TEC). The tests comprise a series of statistical analyses, including traditional bivariate analyses to test for overrepresentation of a prototypical sense in translated (as opposed to non-translated text). Additional multivariate analysis is also introduced to look for additional factors affecting the distribution of senses across corpora. Elicitation data is then gathered using the methodology outlined in Cuyckens, Sandra, and Rice (1997), involving a word prompt and sentence generation task. At a later stage, also keystroke data will be collected.

The introduction of cognitive linguistic theory has clear and immediate consequences for Translation Studies. The most obvious consequence is the need to combine online and offline methods, a requirement that stems from the nature of the theory and the data, as mentioned above. This is the price that must be paid for the explanatory power that cognitive linguistic theory has to offer with regard to the kinds of translational patterns currently under investigation in Translation Studies.

The second consequence of Cognitive Linguistics for TS methodology is less obvious, though potentially more radical: that is the breaching of the long-standing barrier between process and product perspectives. Within Cognitive Linguistics itself, there is still a clear recognition of the difference between describing semantic or conceptual representation and studying language processing. Langacker himself is quite clear in situating Cognitive Linguistics within the former category (2008: 31). However, he also makes it clear that the theory of cognitive grammar is commensurate with certain aspects of processing (2008: 31). In the bilingualism literature, there is an increasing interest in attempting to bring together the disparate perspectives of representation and processing (Hartsuiker, Costa, and Finkbeiner 2008: 413).

Within TS itself, it would seem that product and process are currently being brought together by technological advances and the ambitious research programs that utilize them. Even so, the potential offered by keystroke logs to serve as a bridge between psycholinguistic investigation and corpus-based studies has yet to be fully explored. Cognitive linguistic theory may provide the type of grounding needed to integrate these perspectives: the onus is on TS scholars to take an active part in furthering this development.

4 Implications of Cognitive Linguistics for TS epistemology

It is common in Translation Studies today to identify two apparently conflicting and supposedly incommensurable epistemological frameworks. These have been referred to as the empirical and postmodern approaches or as empirical descriptive and postmodern cultural studies approaches (Delabastita 2003; Chesterman and Arrojo 2000). The attempt to identify "shared ground" between these two broad philosophical frameworks was the subject of an extended debate conducted in *Target* from 2000 to 2002, in which a range of scholars expressed their views, though perhaps less shared ground was identified than was initially hoped.

As was pointed out in the debate (cf. Simeoni 2000; Malmkjær 2000; Sela-Sheffy 2000; Halverson 2000a), the attempt to distinguish between the two frameworks with reference to an essentialist or non-essentialist foundation is an inappropriate tack. As Simeoni puts it:

> A good many approaches to cultural diffusion and translation are at the same time empirical, descriptive and very much aware of the dynamics of culture and language. Meaning is certainly not taken by all descriptivists to be stable, neither substantially nor even formally. Nor does every researcher who considers him/herself a postmodern culturalist reject empirical work. (2000: 337)

Tymoczko makes the same point when she describes the "postpositive" stage of contemporary TS (2007). This point is also made by Delabastita, who identifies a common platform between the two approaches in "awareness of the impossibility of constructing knowledge of cultural reality that is observer-independent and value-free" (2003: 23). In his paper, Delabastita also points out that the two approaches, while sharing this common epistemological platform, make different methodological assumptions on the basis of it. The result is opposing positions with regard to two fundamental questions: (i) Should we search for hypothetical conceptual models of reality that are as observer-independent as possible? (ii) Should we search for hypothetical conceptual models of reality that are as value-free as possible? In Delabastita's account, empirical approaches comprise a position referred to as "epistemological utopianism", in which the response to the two questions is yes and no, respectively. Postmodern approaches, on the other hand, answer no and yes, respectively, and represent a program of "ethical utopianism" (2003: 23). Thus these two basic orientations end up with diametrically opposed views regarding the objectives and actual conduct of empirical research.

Delabastita's account is particularly helpful in illuminating how, given different methodological preferences and emphases, quite diverging views and practices may develop even given a shared starting point. The contribution of Cognitive Linguistics to Translation Studies lies in its potential to further enrich this common platform through more explicit use of the philosophy of "embodied realism" (Lakoff and Johnson 1999; Johnson and Lakoff 2002).

4.1 TS and embodied realism

The philosophy of embodied realism is described by Johnson and Lakoff as follows:

> Embodied realism, as we understand it, is the view that the locus of experience, meaning, and thought is the ongoing series of embodied organism-environment interactions that constitute our understanding of the world. According to such a view, there is no ultimate separation of mind and body, and we are always in touch with our world through our embodied acts and experiences. (2002: 249)

This view is presented as the alternative to traditional epistemological oppositions. According to Harder,

> By claiming that mental function is grounded in the body and imaginatively structured, in a way that reflects specifically human experience, Cognitive Linguistics has defined a new position in the philosophical landscape. This position contrasts, on the one hand, with a belief in absolute objective foundations of knowledge and, on the other hand, with a deconstructionist rejection of any kind of foundation whatsoever. (2007: 1253)

As also pointed out by Harder (2007: 1261), a philosophically related position is Putnam's "internal realism" (1992). This position too represents an alternative to both objectivist and deconstructionist/relativist programs, and grounds this middle position in a perspective that is "internal" to the human interacting with the world around him/her.

A cognitive linguistic theory of translation must build on an epistemology of this type. Indeed, the consequences of adopting such a position are amply clear in the theoretical apparatus outlined in Section 1.1. The perspective is always that of the situated, cognizing translator, and the conceptual framework is built on current understanding of general and linguistic cognition. On the other hand, the implications of this philosophy for Translation Studies epistemology have not been sufficiently explored or articulated. For that reason, the gap, or difference of direction, that separates descriptive translation scholars and postmodern translation scholars keeps re-emerging as a false dichotomy between objectivists and relativists. In outlining the anti-descriptivist position, Pym summarizes as follows:

> This argument basically sees the descriptive paradigm as an exercise in positivism. The paradigm would require belief in a neutral, transparent, objective knowledge about translation, and that progress will come by accumulating that knowledge. A great deal of armor is built around that belief. However, the armor cracks at several of the points we have seen: in the problem of defining translations, in the problem of how to use descriptions of norms, in the possibility that the various levels of description are themselves translations of a kind [. . .] and in the general emphasis on the role of context [. . . At all these points, some attention is required to the role of the observer, the person doing the describing. The descriptive paradigm has not really been able to rise to that challenge. (2010: 85)

In a similar vein, Tymoczko describes the current situation as follows:

> Failure to understand how all the branches of Translation Studies relate to postpositivist epistemology and how they represent complementary aspects of postwar investigations of language and text has contributed to the tendency of some translation scholars to position themselves rigidly within one domain or another and to see their approaches as antithetical to those of other branches of the discipline. (2007: 52)

Both of the above are fair descriptions of the current state of affairs in Translation Studies. While there is ample empirical work being done, some scholars view this work with suspicion, as a clear alternative to a relativist epistemology has not been fully worked out or adequately articulated. The response to this criticism, the alternative to defeated positivism (objectivism) and unrestrained relativism lies in the middle ground of embodied realism. From this standpoint, there is no one objective truth, no reality that is unambiguously given. There is a world "out there", but our access to it and understanding of it is always mediated by, and subject to, the workings of our own interpretive processes. This makes it necessary for us to understand how these processes work, as well as how they ultimately are shared. In this view, scientific knowledge is fundamentally human knowledge, the realism is "internal" to, or "embodied" in us.

An epistemology of embodied or internal realism has been advocated in Translation Studies earlier in Halverson (1998, 2002). However, at present exploratory work in this area has been pursued furthest for the purposes of TS in the debate concerning the definition of "translation". For that reason, this debate will be briefly outlined in the next section in order to give an indication of the current state of affairs.

4.2 TS and approaches to defining "translation"

The most extensive discussion of the "definitional impulse" in Translation Studies is found in Tymozcko's 2007 volume. Tymoczko presents a broad investigation of the history and current cultural diversity of a concept of "translation", and uses this discussion both as an epistemological diagnostic and as support in making her case for a broader field of enquiry and a more empowered position for translators themselves. Before returning to the particulars of her approach, it is helpful to reiterate the two most important definitional traditions that preceded it within TS.

As mentioned in Section 2.1.1, some of the earliest scholars in contemporary Translation Studies approached the definition issue through adopting equivalence as the defining characteristic of translations. In other words, "translations" were defined as texts that were "equivalent to" a source text in another language, and the task of the scholar was to elaborate equivalence frameworks in order to circumscribe the translation category. As also mentioned above, this pursuit was subsequently abandoned along with its underlying objectivist philosophy, and a relativistic approach was adopted. This radical turn in the study of translation was captured in Toury's well-known notion of "assumed translation", where "translations" were identified as texts that were presented or recognized as translations in a given culture at a given time (Toury 1995). This notion has been hotly debated (see Halverson 2008 for a discussion), and there is still some disagreement regarding its utility. The point to be made here is that Toury's proposal ushers in the potential for a wholly relativistic approach, in which culturally or historically situated definitions remain isolated and incomparable. The same consequence stems from the deconstructionist approach of Arrojo (1998). The pursuant challenge remains: how should a discipline do with isolated, culturally and historically relative descriptions?

At present, there are two proposals that aim to provide a framework by which to grapple with contingent conceptualizations. These are the prototype approach (Snell-Hornby 1988; Halverson 1999a, 1999b, 2002) and Tymoczko's (2007) "cluster concept" approach. Both of these build on insights drawn from cognitive science, though they take slightly different forms. Moreover, both approaches aim to provide a framework by which historically contingent, culturally relative conceptualizations may be fruitfully brought together. In fact, it is not entirely certain what the key differences in the two approaches are,[12] given that some authors use the terms "prototype" and "cluster" concept synonymously (Armstrong, Gleitman, and Gleitman 1983). Be that as it may, both authors argue for the investigation of the conceptualizations that different cultures have for a concept of "translation", and Tymoczko presents a fascinating collection of work of this kind (2007: 68–77 and sources cited there). Halverson (2008) argues along the same lines, that the words used by different cultures or times must be the relevant starting point for conceptual analyses across cultures, which all lie within the remit of the discipline, and which jointly constitute the terrain of investigation. The conceptual analyses, using the

---

12 In her book, Tymoczko argues against the prototype view (2007: 90–100). The full response to these arguments is beyond the scope of the present paper, and some of the response is also implied in Halverson (2008), in the discussion of cross-cultural comparison. Other arguments are harder to understand, such as the claim that a prototype approach implies "requiring the exclusion of empirical data from the past or from situations that are not Eurocentric" (2007: 97). For further details see Halverson (in progress a).

framework of Cognitive Linguistics, may illuminate how different members of different cultures draw on a common cognitive apparatus, within the constraints of cultures and contexts, to create and develop different models of communication, interlingual and otherwise. Thus, the method used to elucidate relationships between foundational concepts and the philosophical framework on which that task is based, emerge from Cognitive Linguistics and embodied realism. For example, the models that have been put forward for the English *translate* (Halverson 1999b) and the Norwegian *oversettelse* (Halverson 2000b) made use of image-schematic structure and prototype effects, and are based on empirical investigations of several types of data, more specifically etymological evidence, elicitation data and corpus data.

The epistemological goals of Tymozcko and Halverson seem to coincide in a call for an informed and human-based epistemology that would provide adequate grounding for empirical work while avoiding radical relativism. The two differ most, perhaps, in their predominant allegiances to epistemological utopianism (Halverson) and ethical utopianism (Tymoczko). As a result, the former advocates more empirical investigation using cognitive linguistic tools (Halverson 2008) while the latter calls for increased reflexivity and self-awareness (Tymoczko 2007). At the same time, neither scholar has adequately addressed the complex relationship between individual conceptual knowledge and shared cultural representations, even though both are aiming at cross-linguistic sharing of scientific knowledge within a research community. A full discussion of these weaknesses in the work cited here is beyond the scope of the present paper. A detailed treatment is currently in progress (Halverson in progress a).

5 Concluding remarks

The primary objective of this paper has been to demonstrate specific ways in which Cognitive Linguistics has implications for Translation Studies in terms of theory development, methodology, and epistemology. In the domain of theory, it was suggested that traditional views of equivalence should be jettisoned, but that *equivalence beliefs* may be incorporated through the constraining force of a translator's own conceptualization of what s/he is doing. The notion of translation shift may be reframed as construal and the notion of translation universals, or features of translational language, may be more clearly conceptualized and empirically investigated by adopting a cognitive linguistic translation theory. In the discussion of methodology, it was argued that a cognitive linguistic translation theory will require increased used of combined methods, with the concomitant focus on the methodological questions that arise from this. In this area, a Cognitive Linguistic Translation Studies could make valuable contributions to ongoing debates within Cognitive Linguistics itself. With regard to epistemological issues, it was argued that a clearer articulation of embodied realism within Translation Studies would be a fruitful contribution to a rather stale and artificial anti-descriptivist stance within TS and at the same time constitute a constructive alternative to deconstructive relativism.

As was pointed out in Section 2, a cognitive linguistic theory of translation posits a view of translation that is much more organic than previous accounts, in that it takes the cognizing translator as the locus of the situated event. The individual translator is taken as the source of the translated text, and the theory must then account for the ways in which the text emerges as a contextualized interpretation of an anterior text and a re-expression of it using alternative forms. The situated translator is a permeable cognizer, however, and his/her integration and interaction with the surrounding world are also part of the picture. The specific translational usage event draws on a number of different knowledge types and is subject to a variety of constraints, as discussed in Section 1. This organic and unitary view is at odds with many traditional conceptualizations of translation based on long-standing metaphors of movement, transfer and source-target relationships. It is a different conceptualization in that the prominence of source and target diminish as the prominence of the translator grows.

In many ways, the path forward in developing a cognitive linguistic framework for TS will require, and thus open for contributions to, ongoing efforts in breaching a number of interdisciplinary divides. First of all, it is clear that considerable effort must go into developing a cognitive linguistic theory that is capable of accounting for patterns of language demonstrated by language learners and highly proficient speakers of two or more languages. As mentioned in Section 1, efforts in this direction are underway, but much work needs to be done. At present the aim must be for theory developments to at least not violate fundamental knowledge within other fields. Second, as pointed out in Section 3, developments in bilingualism and in TS seem to point towards a more unified approach to representational and processing aspects of bilingualism, areas which up until now have remained relatively separate. This could be paralleled by efforts to combine and integrate so-called product- and process-based approaches in TS. Work on identifying the relevant theoretical concepts, on operationalizing these for empirical research, and on extensive testing will require a concerted effort across disciplines in the years to come. Finally, it may also be argued that within Cognitive Linguistics and Literary Studies, the traditional divide between the study of language and the study of literature is currently being crossed by several scholars working on "cognitive poetics" (for a review see Freeman 2007; see also Turner 1991, 1996; Lakoff and Turner 1989; Stockwell

2002; Tsur 2003). This particular area has not been dealt with earlier in this paper, but there is clearly room for rapprochement within TS also, as linguistic and literary approaches often find themselves on opposite sides of the epistemological divide described in Section 4. If cognitive translation scholars are willing and able to turn their analytical lights to texts and discursive practices of all kinds, then this too would facilitate intradisciplinary discourse.

In closing, it is important to point out that perhaps the most striking consequence of adopting a cognitive perspective is that it places human cognition and human agency at the center of the causal picture. This is another area in which the present author shares the concerns of, among others, Tymoczko (2007). This may be empowering, as Tymoczko claims, but it will also be better science (in the view of a humble epistemological utopian). At the same time, it is expedient to point out that not all studies must start here. As mentioned previously, also social factors are of the utmost importance, and there are numerous ways of going about studying such things, as witnessed by the recent "sociological turn" in TS.[13] In other words, this is not a call to *reduce* Translation Studies to the study of translational cognition, but a call to *augment* Translation Studies to include cognition in a broader and more comprehensive way. A cognitive linguistic approach to translation has the potential to enrich the discipline by introducing a philosophically grounded framework to enable theoretical and methodological innovation.

References

Alves, Fabio, Adriana Pagano, Stella Neumann, Erich Steiner and Silvia Hansen-Schirra 2010 Translation units and grammatical shifts: Towards an integration of product- and process-based translation research. In: Gregory Shreve and Erik Angelone (eds.), *Translation and cognition*, 109–141. Amsterdam: John Benjamins.

Anderman, Gunilla and Margaret Rogers 2008 *Incorporating corpora: The linguist and the translator*. Clevedon, UK: Multilingual Matters.

Armstrong, Sharon Lee, Lila R. Gleitman and Henry Gleitman 1983 What some concepts might not be. *Cognition* 13: 263–308.

Arrojo, Rosemary 1998 The revision of the traditional gap between theory and practice and the empowerment of translation in postmodern times. *The Translator* 4: 25–48.

Baker, Mona 1993 Corpus linguistics and translation studies: Implications and applications. In: Mona Baker, Gill Francis and Elena Tognini-Bonelli (eds.), *Text and technology: In honour of John Sinclair*, 233–250. Amsterdam: John Benjamins.

Baker, Mona 1995 Corpora in translation studies: An overview and suggestions for future research. *Target* 7.2: 223–243.

---

13 See Chesterman (2000) and Brownlie (2003) on multiple causation in translation.

Baker, Mona 1996 Corpus-based translation studies: The challenges that lie ahead. In: Harold Somers (ed.), *Terminology, LSP and translation: Studies in language engineering*, 175–186. Amsterdam: John Benjamins.

Baker, Mona 2006 Contextualization in translator- and interpreter-mediated events. *Journal of Pragmatics* 38.3: 321–337.

Bakker, Matthijs, Cees Koster and Kitty M. Van Leuven-Zwart 2009 Shifts. In: Mona Baker and Gabriela Saldanha (eds.), *Routledge encyclopedia of translation studies*, 269–274 2nd edition. London: Routledge.

Brownlie, Siobhan 2003 Investigating explanations of translational phenomena: A case for multiple causality. *Target* 15.1: 111–152.

Calzada Pérez, María 2003 *Apropos of ideology. Translation studies on ideology – ideologies in translation studies*. Manchester: St. Jerome.

Catford, J. C 1965 *A linguistic theory of translation*. London: Oxford University Press.

Chesterman, Andrew 2000 A causal model for translation studies. In: Maeve Olahan (ed.), *Intercultural faultlines: Research models in translation studies. Textual and cognitive aspects*, 15–27. Manchester: St. Jerome.

Chesterman, Andrew 2004 Beyond the particular. In: Anna Mauranen and Pekka Kujamäki (eds.), *Translation universals: Do they exist?* 33–49. Amsterdam: John Benjamins.

Chesterman, Andrew 2005 Problems with strategies. In: Krisztina Károly and Ágota Fóris (eds.), *New trends in translation studies: In honour of Kinga Klaudy*, 17–28. Budapest: Akadémiai Kiadó.

Chesterman, Andrew 2006 Interpreting the meaning of translation. In: Mickael Suominen, Antti Arppe, Anu Airola, Orvokki Heinämäki, Matti Miestamo, Urho Määtä, Jussi Niemi, Kari K. Pitkänen and Kaius Sinnemäki (eds.), *A man of measure: Festschrift in honour of Fred Karlsson on his 60th birthday*. Special supplement, SKY Journal of Linguistics 19: 3–11.

Chesterman, Andrew and Rosemary Arrojo 2000 Shared ground in translation studies. *Target* 12.1: 151–160.

Clark, Andy 1997 *Being there: Putting brain, body and world together again*. Cambridge: Cambridge University Press.

Clark, Andy 2008 *Supersizing the mind: Embodiment, action, and cognitive extension*. Oxford: Oxford University Press.

Croft, William 1998 Linguistic evidence and mental representations. *Cognitive Linguistics* 9.2: 151–173.

Croft, William and D. Alan Cruse 2004 *Cognitive linguistics*. Cambridge: Cambridge University Press.

Cuyckens, Hubert, Dominiek Sandra and Sally Rice 1997 Towards an empirical lexical semantics. In: Birgit Smieja and Meike Tasch (eds.), *Human contact through language and linguistics*, 35–54. Frankfurt am Main: Peter Lang.

De Groot, Anette M. B. 1992 Bilingual lexical representation: A closer look at conceptual representations. In: Ram Frost and Leonard Katz (eds.), *Orthography, phonology, morphology, and meaning*, 389–412. Amsterdam: North Holland.

De Groot, Anette M. B. 1993 Word-type effects in bilingual processing tasks: Support for a mixed representational system. In: Robert Schreuder and Bert Weltens (eds.), *The bilingual lexicon*, 27–51. Amsterdam: John Benjamins.

Delabastita, Dirk 2003 Translation studies for the 21st century: Trends and perspectives. *Génesis. Revista científica do ISAI* 3: 7–24.

Divjak, Dagmar and Stefan T. Gries 2008 Clusters in the mind? Converging evidence from near synonymy in Russian. *The Mental Lexicon* 3.2: 188–213.

Dong, Yanping, Shichun Gui and Brian Macwhinney 2005 Shared and separate meanings in the bilingual mental lexicon. *Bilingualism: Language and Cognition* 8.3: 221–238.

Dragsted, Barbara 2004 *Segmentation in translation and translation memory systems.* Copenhagen Working Papers in LSP 4. Copenhagen: CBS/Handelshøjskoen i København.

Dragsted, Barbara and Gitte Hansen 2008 Comprehension and production in translation: A pilot study on segmentation and the coordination of reading and writing processes. *Copenhagen Studies in Language* 36: 9–29.

Ellis, Nick and Rita Simpson-Vlach 2009 Formulaic language in native speakers: triangulating psycholinguistics, corpus linguistics and education. *Corpus Linguistics and Linguistic Theory* 5.1: 61–78.

Englund-Dimitrova, Birgitta 1997 Translation of dialect in fictional prose – Vilhelm Moberg in Russian and English as a case in point. In: J. Falk (ed.), *Norm, variation and change in language: Proceedings of the centenary meeting of the Nyfilologiska sälskapet, Nedre Manilla, 22–23 March 1996*, 49–65. Stockholm: Almqvist and Wiksell.

Eskola, Sari 2004 Untypical frequencies in translated language: A corpus-based study on a literary corpus of translated and non-translated Finnish. In: Anna Mauranen and Pekka Kujamäki (eds.), *Translation universals: Do they exist?* 83–100. Amsterdam: John Benjamins.

Fawcett, Peter 1997 *Translation and language: Linguistic theories explained.* Manchester: St. Jerome.

Francis, Wendy 2005 Bilingual semantic and conceptual representation. In: Judith Kroll and Annette M. B. de Groot (eds.), *Handbook of bilingualism: Psycholinguistic approaches*, 251–267. Oxford: Oxford University Press.

Freeman, Margaret 2007 Cognitive linguistic approaches to literary studies: State of the art in cognitive poetics. In: Dirk Geeraerts and Hubert Cuyckens (eds.), *The Oxford handbook of cognitive linguistics*, 1175–1202. Oxford: Oxford University Press.

Gilquin, Gaëtenelle and Stefan T. Gries 2009 Corpora and experimental methods: A state-of-the-art review. *Corpus Linguistics and Linguistic Theory* 5.1: 1–26.

Gutt, Ernst-August 2000 *Translation and relevance: Cognition and context.* 2nd edition. Manchester: St. Jerome.

Halverson, Sandra L. 1997 The concept of equivalence in translation studies: Much ado about something. *Target* 9.2: 207–233.

Halverson, Sandra L. 1998 *Concepts and categories in translation studies.* Unpublished PhD dissertation, University of Bergen, Norway.

Halverson, Sandra L 1999a Conceptual work and the "translation" concept. *Target* 11.1: 1–31.

Halverson, Sandra L. 1999b Image schemas, metaphoric processes and the "translate" concept. *Metaphor and Symbol* 14.3: 199–219.

Halverson, Sandra L. 2000a The fault line in our common ground. *Target* 12.2: 356–362.

Halverson, Sandra L. 2000b Prototype effects in the "translation" category. In: Andrew Chesterman, Natividad Gallardo San Salvador and Yves Gambier (eds.), *Translation in context*, 3–16. Amsterdam: John Benjamins.

Halverson, Sandra L. 2002 Cognitive models, prototype effects and "translation": The role of cognition in translation (meta)theory. *Across Languages and Cultures* 3.1: 21–43.

Halverson, Sandra L. 2003 The cognitive basis of translation universals. *Target* 15.2: 197–241.

Halverson, Sandra L. 2007 A cognitive linguistic account of translation shifts. *Belgian Journal of Linguistics* 21: 105–119.

Halverson, Sandra L. 2008 Translations as institutional facts. An ontology for "assumed translation". In: Anthony Pym, Miriam Shlesinger and Daniel Simeoni (eds.), *Beyond descriptive translation studies: Investigations in homage to Gideon Toury*, 343–361. Amsterdam: John Benjamins.

Halverson, Sandra L. 2009 Elements of doctoral training: The dynamics of the research process. *The Interpreter and Translator Trainer* 3.1: 79–106.

Halverson, Sandra L. 2010a Cognitive translation studies: Developments in theory and method. In: Gregory Shreve and Erik Angelone (eds.), *Translation and cognition*, 349–369. Amsterdam: John Benjamins.

Halverson, Sandra L. 2010b Translation universals or cross-linguistic influence: Conceptual and methodological issues. Paper presented at the 6th EST Conference, Leuven, Belgium, September 23–25, 2010.

Halverson, Sandra L. in progress a Prototypes, stereotypes, clusters, norms, and universals: Conceptual frameworks in translation studies.

Halverson, Sandra L. in progress b Testing for gravitational pull: The case of *get*.

Harder, Peter 2007 Cognitive linguistics and philosophy. In: Dirk Geeraerts and Hubert Cuyckens (eds.), *The Oxford handbook of cognitive linguistics*, 1241–1265. Oxford: Oxford University Press.

Hartsuiker, Robert J., Albert Costa and Matthew Finkbeiner 2008 Bilingualism: Functional and neural perspectives. *Acta Psychologica* 128: 413–415.

Hasselgren, Angela 1993 *Right words, wrong words and different words: An investigation into the lexical coping of Norwegian advanced learners of English*. Unpublished master's thesis, Department of English, University of Bergen.

Hatim, Basil and Ian Mason 1990 *Discourse and the translator*. London: Routledge.

Hatim, Basil and Ian Mason 1997 *The translator as communicator*. London: Routledge.

Hermans, Theo 1999 *Translation in systems: Descriptive and system-oriented approaches explained*. Manchester: St. Jerome.

Heylen, Kris, Jose Tummers and Dirk Geeraerts 2008 Methodological issues in corpus-based cognitive linguistics. In: Gitte Kristiansen and René Dirven (eds.), *Cognitive sociolinguistics: Language variation, cultural models, social systems*, 91–128. Berlin: Mouton de Gruyter.

Holmes, James S. 1988 *Translated! Papers on literary translation and translation studies*. Amsterdam: Rodopi.

Ijaz, Helene 1986 Linguistic and cognitive determinants of lexical acquisition in a second language. *Language Learning* 36.4: 401–451.

Inghilleri, Moira 2003 Habitus, field and discourse: Interpreting as a socially situated activity. *Target* 15.2: 243–268.

Inghilleri, Moira 2005 Mediating zones of uncertainty: Translator agency, the interpreting habitus and political asylum adjudication. *The Translator* 11.1: 69–85.

Jääskeläinen, Riitta 2009 Think-aloud protocols. In: Mona Baker and Gabriela Saldanha (eds.), *Routledge encyclopedia of translation studies*, 290–293. 2nd edition. London: Routledge.

Jakobsen, Arnt Lykke 2003 Effects of think-aloud on translation speed, revision and segmentation. In: Fabio Alves (ed.), *Triangulating translation*, 69–95. Amsterdam: John Benjamins.

Jakobsen, Arnt Lykke 2006 Research methods in translation – TRANSLOG. In: Kirk P. H. Sullivan and Eva Lindgren (eds.), *Computer keystroke logging: Methods and applications*, 95–105. Oxford: Elsevier.

Jakobsen, Arnt Lykke and Kristian T. H. Jensen 2008 Eye movement behaviour across four different types of reading tasks. In: Susanne Göpferich (ed.), *Looking at eyes: Eye tracking studies of reading and translation processing*, 103–124. (Copenhagen Studies in Language 36.) Copenhagen: Samfundslitteratur.

Jakobson, Roman 1959 On linguistic aspects of translation. In: R. A. Brower (ed.), *On translation*, 232–239. Cambridge, MA: Harvard University Press.

Jarvis, Scott 1998 *Conceptual transfer in the interlingual lexicon*. Bloomington: Indiana University Linguistics Association Publications.

Jarvis, Scott and Aneta Pavlenko 2008 *Cross-linguistic influence in language and cognition*. New York: Routledge.

Jensen, Kristian T.H. 2009 Distribution of attention between source text and target text during translation. Paper presented at "Source language influence", PhD seminar, University of Bergen, Norway, November 11–14, 2009.

Johnson, Mark 1987 *The body in the mind*. Chicago: University of Chicago Press.

Johnson, Mark 2007 *The meaning of the body*. Chicago: University of Chicago Press.

Johnson, Mark and George, Lakoff 2002 Why cognitive linguistics requires embodied realism. *Cognitive Linguistics* 13.3: 245–263.

Kellerman, Eric 1978 Giving learners a break: Native language intuitions as a source of predictions about transferability. *Working Papers on Bilingualism* 15: 60–92.

Kellerman, Eric 1979 The problem with difficulty. *Interlanguage Studies Bulletin* 4: 27–48.

Kenny, Dorothy 2001 *Lexis and creativity in translation*. Manchester: St. Jerome.

Kenny, Dorothy 2009. Corpora. In: Mona Baker and Gabriela Saldanha (eds.), *Routledge encyclopedia of translation studies*, 59–62. 2nd edition. London: Routledge.

Klaudy, Kinga 1996 Concretization and generalization of meaning in translation. In: Marcel Thelen and Barbara Lewandowska-Tomaszczyk (eds.), *Translation and meaning. Part 3. Proceedings of the 2nd International Maastricht-Łódź Duo Colloquium on "Translation and Meaning", Maastricht, the Netherlands, 19–22 April 1995*, 141–163. Frankfurt am Main: Peter Lang.

Koller, Werner 1989 Equivalence in translation theory. Translated by Andrew Chesterman. In: Andrew Chesterman (ed.), *Readings in translation theory*, 99–104. Finland: Oy Finn Lectura.

Koller, Werner 1995 The concept of equivalence and the object of translation studies. *Target* 7.2: 191–222.

Kroll, Judith F., Susan C. Bobb, Maya Misra and Taomei Guo 2008 Language selection in bilingual speech: Evidence for inhibitory processes. *Acta Psychologica* 128: 416–430.

Kroll, Judith F. and Erika Stewart 1994 Category interference in translation and picture naming: Evidence for asymmetric connections between bilingual memory representations. *Journal of Memory and Language* 33: 149–174.

Kroll, Judith F. and Natasha Tokowicz 2005 Models of bilingual representation and processing: Looking back and to the future. In: Judith Kroll and Annette M. B. de Groot (eds.), *Handbook of bilingualism: Psycholinguistic approaches*, 531–553. Oxford: Oxford University Press.

Kujamäki, Pekka 2004 What happens to "unique items" in learners' translations? "Theories" and "concepts" as a challenge for novices' views on "good translation". In: Anna Mauranen and Pekka Kujamäki (eds.), *Translation universals: Do they exist?* 187–204. Amsterdam: John Benjamins.

Lachaud, Christian M. 2009 EEG, EYE and KEY: Three simultaneous streams of data for investigating the cognitive mechanisms of translation. Paper presented at the IATIS Conference, Monash University, Melbourne, Australia, July 8–10, 2009.

Lakoff, George 1987 *Women, fire and dangerous things*. Chicago: University of Chicago Press.
Lakoff, George and Mark Johnson [1980] 1995 *Metaphors we live by*. Chicago: University of Chicago Press.
Lakoff, George and Mark Johnson 1999 *Philosophy in the flesh*. New York: Basic Books.
Lakoff, George and Mark Turner 1989 *More than cool reason*. Chicago: University of Chicago Press.
Langacker, Ronald [1987] 1991 *Foundations of cognitive grammar*. Vols. 1–2. Stanford, CA: Stanford University Press.
Langacker, Ronald 2008 *Cognitive grammar: A basic introduction*. Oxford: Oxford University Press.
Laviosa, Sara 2002 *Corpus-based translation studies: Theory, findings, applications*. Amsterdam: Rodopi.
Lewandowska-Tomaszczyk, Barbara 2010 Reconceptualization and the emergence of discourse meaning as a theory of translation. In: Barbara Lewandowska-Tomaszczyk and Marcel Thelen (eds.), *Meaning in translation*, 105–147. Frankfurt am Main: Peter Lang.
Malmkjær, Kirsten 2000 Relative stability and stable relativity. *Target* 12.2: 341–344.
Malmkjær, Kirsten 2008 Norms and nature in translation studies. In: Gunilla Anderman and Margaret Rogers (eds.), *Incorporating corpora: The linguist and the translator*, 49–59. Clevedon, UK: Multilingual Matters.
Marco, Josep 2007 The terminology of translation: Epistemological, conceptual and intercultural problems and their social consequences. *Target* 19.2: 255–269.
Mauranen, Anna and Pekka Kujamäki (eds.) 2004 *Translation universals: Do they exist?* Amsterdam: John Benjamins.
Molina Martínez, Lucía and Amparo Hurtado Albir 2002 Translation techniques revisited: A dynamic and functionalist approach. *Meta* 47.4: 498–512.
Mollin, Sandra 2009 Combining corpus linguistic and psychological data on word co-occurrences: Corpus collocates versus word associations. *Corpus Linguistics and Linguistic Theory* 5.2: 175–200.
Munday, Jeremy 2008 *Introducing translation studies: Theories and applications*. 2nd edition. London: Routledge.
Muñoz Martín, Ricardo 2006 Expertise and environment in translation. Paper presented at the Second IATIS Conference, "Intervention in Translation, Interpreting and Intercultural Encounters", University of the Western Cape, South Africa, July 11–14, 2006.
Nida, Eugene 1964 *Towards a science of translating*. Leiden: Brill.
Nord, Christiane 1997 *Translating as a purposeful activity: Functionalist theories explained*. Manchester: St. Jerome.
Olohan, Maeve 2004 *Introducing corpora in translation studies*. London: Routledge.
PACTE group 2003 Building a translation competence model. In: Fabio Alves (ed.), *Triangulating translation*, 43–66. Amsterdam: John Benjamins.
PACTE group 2005 Investigating translation competence: Conceptual and methodological issues. *Meta* 50.2: 609–619.
PACTE group 2010 Results of the validation of the PACTE translation competence model: Translation project and dynamic translation index. In: Sharon O'Brien (ed.), *Cognitive explorations of translation*, 30–56. London: Continuum.
PACTE group 2011 Results of the validation of the PACTE translation competence model: translation problems and translation competence. In: Cecilia Alvstad, Adelina Hild and Elisabet Tiselius (eds.), *Methods and strategies of process research*, 317–343. Amsterdam: John Benjamins.

Paker, Salitha 2002 Translation as *terceme* and *nazire*: Culture-bound concepts and their implications for a conceptual framework for research on ottoman translation history. In: Theo Hermans (ed.), *Crosscultural transgressions: Research models in translation studies II. Historical and ideological issues*, 120–143. Manchester: St. Jerome.

Pavlenko, Aneta 2009 Conceptual representation in the bilingual lexicon and second language vocabulary learning. In: Aneta Pavlenko (ed.), *The bilingual mental lexicon: Interdisciplinary approaches*, 125–160. Bristol, UK: Multilingual Matters.

Popovič, Anton 1970 The concept of "shift of expression" in translation analysis. In: James S. Holmes (ed.), *The nature of translation: Essays on the theory and practice of literary translation*, 78–87. The Hague: Mouton.

Putnam, Hilary 1992 *Renewing philosophy*. Cambridge, MA: Harvard University Press.

Pym, Anthony 1992 *Translation and text transfer: An essay on the principles of intercultural communication*. Frankfurt am Main: Peter Lang.

Pym, Anthony 1998 *Method in translation history*. Manchester: St. Jerome.

Pym, Anthony 2007 Natural and directional equivalence in theories of translation. *Target* 19.2: 271–294.

Pym, Anthony 2008 On Toury's laws of how translators translate. In: Anthony Pym, Miriam Shlesinger and Daniel Simeoni (eds.), *Beyond descriptive translation studies: Investigations in homage to Gideon Toury*, 311–327. Amsterdam: John Benjamins.

Pym, Anthony 2010 *Exploring translation theories*. London: Routledge.

Risku, Hanne 2002 Situatedness in translation studies. *Cognitive Systems Research* 3.3: 523–533.

Robinson, Peter and Nick C. Ellis 2008 *Handbook of cognitive linguistics and second language acquisition*. New York: Routledge.

Ruiz, C., N. Paredes, P. Macizo and M. T. Bajo 2008 Activation of lexical and syntactic target language properties in translation. *Acta Psychologica* 128: 490–500.

Sandra, Dominiek 1998 What linguists can and can't tell you about the human mind: A reply to Croft. *Cognitive Linguistics* 9.4: 361–378.

Sandra, Dominiek and Sally Rice 1995 Network analyses of prepositional meaning: Mirroring whose mind – the linguist's or the language user's? *Cognitive Linguistics* 6.1: 89–130.

Schäffner, Christine 2009 Functionalist approaches. In: Mona Baker and Gabriela Saldanha (eds.), *Routledge encyclopedia of translation studies*, 115–121. 2nd edition. London: Routledge.

Sela-Sheffy, Rakafet 2000 The suspended potential of culture research in TS. *Target* 12.2: 345–355.

Sharmin, Selina, Oleg Spakov, Kari-Juoko Räihä and Arnt Lykke Jakobsen 2008 Effects of time pressure and text complexity on translators' fixations. In: Stephen N. Spencer (ed.), *Proceedings of Eye Tracking Research and Applications Symposium (ETRA08), 26–28 March, Savannah, Georgia*, 123–126. New York: ACM.

Simeoni, Daniel 1998 The pivotal status of the translator's *habitus*. *Target* 10.1: 1–39.

Simeoni, Daniel 2000 When in doubt, contextualize . . . *Target* 12.2: 337–341.

Sjørup, Annette C. 2009 Cognitive effort in metaphor translation: an eye-tracking study. Paper presented at "Source linguistic influence", PhD seminar, University of Bergen, Norway, November 11–14, 2009.

Snell-Hornby, Mary 1988 *Translation studies: An integrated approach*. Amsterdam: John Benjamins.

Stamenov, Maxim, A. Gerganov and I. D. Popivanov 2009 Shortcuts to meaning: Finding out meaning correspondences in the bilingual lexicon during a word translation task. Paper presented at Eye-to-IT Conference, Copenhagen, Denmark, April 28–29, 2009.

Stockwell, Peter 2002 *Cognitive poetics: An introduction.* London: Routledge.
Susam-Sarajeva, Şebnem 2009 The case study research method in translation studies. *The Interpreter and Translator Trainer* 3.1: 37–56.
Tabakowska, Elżbieta 1993 *Cognitive linguistics and the poetics of translation.* Tübingen, Germany: Gunter Narr.
Tirkkonen-Condit, Sonja 2004 Unique items – over- or underrepresented in translated language? In: Anna Maurane and Pekka Kujamäki (eds.), *Translation universals: Do they exist?* 177–186. Amsterdam: John Benjamins.
Tirkkonen-Condit, Sonja 2005 Do unique items make themselves scarce in translated Finnish? In: Krisztina Károly and Ágota Fóris (eds.), *New trends in translation studies: In honour of Kinga Klaudy,* 177–189. Budapest: Akadémiai Kiadó.
Toury, Gideon 1995 *Descriptive translation studies and beyond.* Amsterdam: John Benjamins.
Tsur, Reuven 2003 *On the shore of nothingness: A study in cognitive poetics.* Exeter, UK: Imprint Academic.
Tummers, Jose, Kris Heylen and Dirk Geeraerts 2005 Usage-based approaches in cognitive linguistics: A technical state of the art. *Corpus Linguistics and Linguistic Theory* 1.2: 225–261.
Turner, Mark 1991 *Reading minds: The study of English in the age of cognitive science.* Princeton, NJ: Princeton University Press.
Turner, Mark 1996 *The literary mind.* New York: Oxford University Press.
Tymoczko, Maria 2007 *Enlarging translation, empowering translators.* Manchester: St. Jerome.
Valenzuela, Javier and Ana Rojo (eds.) 2003 Contrastive cognitive linguistics. Special issue, *International Journal of English Studies* 3.2.
Van Leuven-Zwart, Kitty M. 1989 Translation and original: Similarities and dissimilarities, I. *Target* 1.2: 151–181.
Van Leuven-Zwart, Kitty M. 1990 Translation and original: Similarities and dissimilarities, II. *Target* 2.1: 69–95.
Venuti, Lawrence 1995 *The translator's invisibility.* New York: Routledge.
Vinay, Jean-Paul and Jean Darbelnet 1995 *Comparative stylistics of French and English: A methodology for translation.* Translated and edited by Juan C. Sager and M.-J. Hamel. Amsterdam: John Benjamins.
Wolf, Michaela 1997 Translation as a process of power: Aspects of cultural anthropology in translation. In: Mary Snell-Hornby, Zuzana Jettmarová and Klaus Kaindl (eds.), *Translation as intercultural communication: Selected papers from the EST Congress, Prague 1995,* 123–133. Amsterdam: John Benjamins.
Wolf, Michaela 2002 Culture as translation – and beyond: Ethnographic models of representation in translation studies. In: Theo Hermans (ed.), *Crosscultural transgressions: Research models in translation studies II. Historical and ideological issues,* 180–192. Manchester: St. Jerome.
Wolf, Michaela and Alexandra Fukari (eds.) 2007 *Constructing a sociology of translation.* Amsterdam: John Benjamins.
Wulff, Stefanie 2009 Converging evidence from corpus and experimental data to capture idiomaticity. *Corpus Linguistics and Linguistic Theory* 5.1: 131–159.
Zabalbeascoa, Patrick 2000 From techniques to types of solutions. In: Allison Beeby, Doris Ensinger and Marisa Presas (eds.), *Investigating translation,* 117–127. Amsterdam: John Benjamins.

Ricardo Muñoz Martín
More than a way with words: The interface between Cognitive Linguistics and Cognitive Translatology

The aim of this text is to contribute to mapping out the interaction between linguistics and translatology within second-generation Cognitive Science, the scientific study of mind that emphasizes the role of the body and the environment. As a consequence, "Cognitive Linguistics" and "Cognitive Translatology" are understood in ways that deserve previous elaboration. Natural language structures are taken to reflect cognitive features and mechanisms influenced both by experience and the environment. This understanding of Cognitive Linguistics (henceforth CL) does not make it a unified endeavor. Rather, several partially overlapping research programs merge into this view, whether departing from Gestalt psychology (Cognitive Grammar), phenomenology (Cognitive Semantics), or sociolinguistics (cf. Geeraerts, Kristiansen, and Peirsman 2010), or else approaching language processing and use from psycholinguistics or discourse analysis (Dirven 2005). Furthermore, CL needs to make the account of the cognitive aspects of language and language use consistent with findings in other cognitive science disciplines (Lakoff 1990: 40). In turn, and as envisioned here, *Cognitive Translatology* has two basic commitments:

- An empirical commitment, which asks for knowledge to be derived by studying reality in ways that ensure intersubjective verifiability. This commitment justifies the use of *translatology* (Harris 1973, 1988) in "Cognitive Translatology", to refer to scholarly endeavors within Translation Studies that aim to build generalizable knowledge on translation and interpreting with a variety of scientific methods, such as corpora analyses and experimental procedures.
- A cognitive commitment, parallel to that proposed for CL, which sustains the use of the term *cognitive* in "Cognitive Translatology". Consequently, notions such as "context" and "culture" are seen as embodied and situated (see Halverson, Martín de León, this volume). Also, since many translation and interpreting activities – from the translation of manuals to simultaneous interpreting in a booth – are often collaborative efforts by several persons, they can be addressed as paradigmatic examples of distributed cognition (Risku 2002, 2004; Dragsted 2006). Thus, the emerging coincidences in

second-generation Cognitive Science seem to be suitable candidates to work as referents for Cognitive Translatology (Muñoz Martín 2010a, 2010b).

The combination of these commitments makes Cognitive Translatology a budding, interdisciplinary applied science (Mayoral Asensio 2001; Muñoz Martín 2010a) within second-generation Cognitive Science. Since CL and Cognitive Translatology share their cognitive commitment and language has a central position in translating and interpreting processes, CL should have a pivotal role in the development of Cognitive Translatology. Let us have a look at what CL has done for translatology so far.

1 Contributions of Cognitive Linguistics to Cognitive Translatology

Apart from some general calls to use CL as a referential framework for Cognitive Translatology (e.g. Tabakowska 1993; Muñoz Martín 1995; Olohan and Zähner 1996), most efforts concentrate on prototype semantics, conceptual metaphor, and Frame Semantics. Relevance Theory (Sperber and Wilson 1986) is very popular amongst translatologists as well. Major contributions within this scope include Gutt (1991, 1992) and Alves and Gonçalves (2006). However, Relevance Theory seems to belong to a different take on language and mind, for it "[. . .] represents a modern approach to pragmatics that adopts an explicitly generative view of language, and aims to provide a mentalist account of communication that can be integrated with the generative model of language" (Evans and Green 2006: 459). Tendahl and Gibbs (2008), on the other hand, think Relevance Theory and cognitive semantics approaches to metaphor are complementary, and even Evans and Green (2006) find some points in common between these frameworks. Nevertheless, generative approaches have some fundamental assumptions incompatible with those entertained by CL and thus translatological approaches derived from Relevance Theory are not included in this brief review. For a comparison of these frameworks as to their application in translatology, see McElhanon (2005). Let us now turn to CL-based contributions.

1.1 Prototype semantics

Prototype semantics is an approach to lexical meaning based on the work by Eleanor Rosch and colleagues on concepts and categorization in the 1970s. The basic tenet is that category membership is not based on necessary and sufficient conditions and may be graded. Tabakowska (1993) was probably the first translatologist to draw from Rosch's (1978) prototype theory. She used it to reject objectivist, truth-conditional, referential semantics, and several classical dichotomies such as literal vs. figurative meaning, denotation vs. connotation, grammatical vs. communicative competence, semantics and pragmatics (Tabakowska 1993: 22–24). This is a fundamental step towards Cognitive Translatology, but not all cognitive translatologists seem to have assumed the consequences.

Halverson (1998, 1999, 2002) adopted a different approach to analyze the concept of "translation" and concluded that it is prototypical, while Tymoczko (1998, 2005) proposed that it is an open concept whose members are linked by family resemblances. These stances have been seen as opposed but prototype theory (e.g. Rosch and Mervis 1975) considers that categorization may also be based on family resemblances and privileged properties of categories. Hence, there is no contradiction in thinking that the "translation" concept is prototypical and that its members are linked by family resemblances.

Chesterman (2008: 23) argues that both Halverson and Tymoczko "do not assume a universally valid, essentialist version of the concept" of "translation", and that the question is rather the problem of generalizing empirical research findings. However, the prototypical nature of the "translation" concept cannot explain the difficulties in generalizing empirical findings in translatology. Most, if not all, concepts are prototypical and fuzzy, including those used in sciences such as biology, physics, logic, and mathematics (Janicki 2006: 53–54), and also in other applied sciences, such as medicine. The concepts "life" (Yorek and Narli 2009), "death", and "health" are fuzzy, but medical researchers are nonetheless able to propose generalizations from empirical research. The difference may lie in the fact that, while translatologists try hard to set limits to fuzzy concepts, researchers in natural and exact sciences "[. . .] set research goals that do not involve having to define what appears to be undefinable" (Janicki 2006: 55). For example, research goals in Cognitive Translatology should strive to reduce variables and categorize texts and subjects so as to avoid fuzziness without necessarily defining what a beginner student, an advanced student, a semi-professional, and a professional are, and so on (Muñoz Martín 2009).

Halverson (1999, 2000) argued that the category "translation" displays prototypical effects, which include intersemiotic changes, but prototypical-concept boundaries do not naturally arise from prototype representations. They are just stipulated arbitrarily (Croft and Cruse 2004: 91–93, 97 *passim*), so Halverson's analysis still entails a decision on the part of the researcher. Hence, including intersemiotic exchanges is a laudable, inclusive move, but these activities are probably metaphorical extensions in a concept rooted in everyday language use. As an applied science, Cognitive Translatology needs to respond to the demands of society, and intersemiotic renderings do not usually constitute a part of the tasks requested from professional translators and interpreters.

In any case, Halverson's proposal to define the object of study of translatology by means of a prototypical view of the concept is a clear example of mistaking the map for the territory (Korzybski 1948). This confusion becomes obvious when Halverson (1999: 12) states that Harris (1977) claimed that natural translation was central *to the concept of translation*, because what Harris actually claimed was that it was central to *the interests of translatology*: "[. . .] the proper study of translatology is *all* translation. [. . .] If, though, we pursue the parallel with linguistics we shall find ourselves compelled not merely to *include* the humble and the everyday: we shall have to give them *priority*" (Harris 1977: 3, italics in the original). Categorizing implies generalizing experience, and often leads to folk theories – assumptions made in a particular culture by people who are not experts.[1] Folk theories are usually the point of departure for researchers to create philosophical and scientific theories, but there is a difference between the concepts of "translation" people have in their minds and the definition of, and scope on, "translation" adopted by (cognitive) translatology. The first is individual, fuzzy and often vague, and it is rooted in experience. The second is a social artifact developed to work as the basis of a coherent conceptual framework. The difference is similar to the one established by Neubert and Shreve (1992: 19, 52–53) between first-order and second-order understandings of translation, the former being often latent and not totally conscious everyday knowledge and the latter the descriptive level where translatological hypotheses and generalizations are to be devised. Of course, there must be a relationship between everyday concepts of translation and its translatological definitions (cf. Snell-Hornby 1990), but they do not need to overlap completely. Such is the case in medicine as well (Zhang 2002).[2] Thus, in Cognitive Translatology we are still in square one.

---

[1] Halverson (2000) carried out a small experiment to determine the boundaries of the "translation" concept, and found them to be fuzzy. However, Smith and Samuelson (1997) show that concepts are not stable and that their *ad hoc* structure depends on *past history, recent history, and current input*. Furthermore, Rosch et al. (1976) argued that the location and nature of basic levels may depend *on the subject's expertise*. Would a survey asking usual translation users and producers lead to the same results than those of the students Halverson surveyed?

[2] There seems to be a curious parallel between translatology and medicine in that science-theoretical considerations in the latter seem to be the forerunners of similar concerns in translatology. In 1929, Robinson argued in favor for a science-based medicine in an article that

There may be other ways to delimit Cognitive Translatology. For instance, with the set of empirical research methods which may intensionally define Cognitive Translatology. These methods include several ways of recording and measuring translators' and interpreters' activities (see Göpferich 2008), and they are related to the first commitment stated above. Cognitive Translatology may also be defined with respect to the second commitment. The object of study of Cognitive Translatology is translations and interpretations, which may be circumscribed by the special circumstances in the communicative acts where they are carried out and the peculiar behavior of translators and interpreters in intertwined linguistic reception and production.

The class of phenomena that allow Cognitive Translatology to be defined extensionally is a cluster of socially defined, complex human communicative activities, which entail the constrained and particular reception (Shreve et al. 1993; Castro Arce 2008; see also Konheim-Kalkstein and Van den Broek 2008) and production (cf. Toury 1995) of language samples. These activities are complex because, from the translators' perspective, they involve the use of at least two natural languages and at least three main agents – an author, an intermediary and an addressee (Muñoz Martín 2010b). The constraints for both reception and production are related to both preexisting language samples and the communicative intentions and expectations of other agents, *as constructed by the translator or interpreter*. These phenomena are a cluster because they are related by family resemblances. The elements that contribute to variation are, for instance, oral vs. written, dialogical vs. monological, isochrony vs. delayed delivery, etc. New communication technologies have enlarged the number of possible combinations, although many of the potential differences between the cognitive processes involved in different instances are still awaiting research (but see, for instance, Agrifoglio 2004).

Epistemological goals may also be used to define Cognitive Translatology. From a developmental point of view, translating (including interpreting) seems ingrained in the cognitive development of bilinguals, who display a more or less

---

started with the following sentence: "The practice of medicine is generally described by that time-worn phrase as being an art and a science". A few years later, Trotter (1935: 613) would state: "To the sober realist, however, it is clear that the rule of science in medicine is still not much more than strictly local and much qualified. The cases are very few in which general principles can be applied to the individual instance with the direct precision of an engineer designing a dinamo". In the 1970s and 1980s, medical researchers would still argue about "the gap between clinical research and what was actually happening in clinical practice" (Eddy 2005: 10). Translatology has gone through the same stages.

rudimentary ability to carry out the tasks – often, but not always, at quality levels below the standards expected in professionals (Muñoz Martín 2011). As an applied science, one of Cognitive Translatology's main concerns is finding out the best ways to develop this natural ability (Harris 1973) into professional expertise.[3] In brief, prototype semantics may fit the analysis of translation products and processes, but it is not interesting at the metatheoretical level, beyond the reappraisal of concepts such as science, meaning and language.

1.2 Conceptual metaphor theory

First proposed by Lakoff and Johnson (1980), conceptual metaphor theory sees metaphors as conceptual phenomena, rather than mere linguistic operations, and assumes they are basic scaffolds to our conceptual system. Central to this theory is the concept of "domain". Domains are described as sets of entities, attributes, processes and relationships that seem to be linked in the mind. In metaphors, a source domain is mapped onto a target domain, thereby structuring it in such a way that the relationships between entities, attributes and processes in the target domain are similar to those found in the source domain, although with some or many "blind spots" (Brünner 1987), i.e. mapping discontinuities. These metaphorical operations can be traced in language, for attributes and processes in the target domain may use words and expressions that belong to the source domain.

Tabakowska (1993) applied CL to tackle the purported untranslatability of metaphors. From her perspective, translating metaphors is subject to cognitive restrictions or incompatibilities (Tabakowska 1993: 69–72). This was a promising point, but she became entangled with "equivalence"[4] and simply proposed that metaphor equivalence was to be found at the level of imagery (Tabakowska

---

3 The notion of *expertise* (Ericsson and Smith 1991; Ericsson 1996) is meant to replace that of *competence,* which for Cognitive Translatology seems to be as faulty and problematic as it is for CL (C. Paradis 2003). Nevertheless, a thorough reading of translatological texts dealing with competence shows that the definition has been drifting towards that of expertise for more than one decade. See, for instance, Pym (2003: 484) on Risku (1998).
4 A remnant from the days of machine translation research and the computational-representational view of mind, most understandings of "equivalence" refer to the purported stable relationships of meaning correspondence between text segments in different languages. This view of meaning is (narrowly) linguistic, decontextualized, disembodied, reified, transcendental, and static. These understandings of equivalence, therefore, simply do not fit in Cognitive Translatology. For a discussion of the concept, see Halverson (1997, this volume).

1993: 72–74). Mandelblit (1996) took a different approach and hypothesized that when metaphoric expressions do not have a ready-made counterpart available in another language, they should take longer to translate. Tirkkonen-Condit (2002) found that, indeed, some translation difficulties might be explained by domain conflict, both at local and global (text) levels. This suggests that translating metaphors is possible even when there is no equivalent at the level of imagery, and reconciles theory with observed reality.

From a metatheoretical perspective, D'hulst (1992) argued that conceptual metaphors are helpful in the analogical development of translatological models. Martín de León (2005, 2008) applied conceptual metaphor theory to shed light on the implied epistemological and theoretical assumptions in Holz-Mänttäri (1984) and Reiß and Vermeer (1984), the two works which laid the foundations of translatological functionalism. Martín de León focused on the *blind spots* of two metaphors that stand out in these works in terms of frequency: the transfer metaphor and the target metaphor. Based on the conduit metaphor (Reddy 1979), the transfer metaphor is widespread both in everyday language and in translation theories. It portrays translating as the transfer of a reified, linguistic meaning between texts, and disregards both situational factors and the active role of translators and interpreters. The target metaphor portrays translating as a forward movement towards a physical target. In this metaphor, assumed phases and sequences of actions by the translator are envisioned as paths. According to Martín de León (2005), the target metaphor is characteristic of functionalist translatologies.

The use of the target metaphor in functionalist translatologies allows Martín de León to criticize them from a second-generation Cognitive Science perspective: Functionalist translatologies stress the translator's intentions and, in so doing, ground the notion of translating in Western traditional, folk-psychological theories of instrumental rationality. Martín de León (2005) argues that controlled, rational planning cannot explain large parts of professional translating and translator training, and that Cognitive Translatology needs a dynamic description of translation processes. Thus, she proposes the use of situated cognition instead, as a broader theoretical framework where intentional interpretations are based on learning processes and also on evolutionary and cultural history. Further work in this line is necessary, for it has promising prospects (see Martín de León, this volume).

1.3 Frame Semantics

Frame Semantics may be considered just one stop in the intellectual journey Charles Fillmore started with his Case Grammar (1968), followed by Frame

Semantics (1985) and then by [Berkeley] Construction Grammar (Fillmore and Kay 1987). The aim of Frame Semantics (e.g. Petruck 1996; see also Boas, this volume) is to relate language to experience by connecting semantic meaning in a strict sense with encyclopedic knowledge. Frames are assumed to be schematic representations of situations that include several conceptual roles, such as participants and props. Frames are also taken to be cognitive structuring devices that are necessary to understand language. Parts of the frames are indexed by words associated with it, in a relationship similar to that between *base* and *profile* in Langacker (1987).

Vannerem and Snell-Hornby (1986) applied scenes-and-frames semantics (Fillmore 1975, 1977) – an early, now obsolete version of Frame Semantics – to translating. Fillmore (1985: 232) seems to have thought of frames mainly as applying to units such as lexical items and sentences, which could be expanded to very short texts of just a few lines. Vannerem and Snell-Hornby (1986: 190) enlarged the original scope to propose the existence of whole text frames and scenes. Readers would work out the scene "behind the text" in order to understand it, and translators would perform their task by *looking for* the frames in the new language which would best accommodate the scene *from the original text*. This would not be a straightforward enterprise: "*Gleichzeitig birgt aber der Rückgriff auf das prototypische Vorwissen des Lesers/Übersetzers die Gefahr einer zu subjektiven Textinterpretation*" [At the same time, resorting to prototypical stored knowledge in the reader/translator entails the risk of interpreting originals *too* subjectively] (Vannerem and Snell-Hornby 1986: 190, my italics). In brief, in their approach, meaning is open to – but not the same as – encyclopedic content, and it is still (partially) independent from the interpreter. Apart from this surreptitiously prescriptive move, this attempt to apply Frame Semantics to translation amounts to a sort of reformulation of the deverbalization process proposed by Seleskovitch (1975), now enlarged to cover (written) translation as well, where scenes would be close to Lédérer's (1981: 66) *complements cognitifs*: "connaissances qui s'ajoutent à la compétence linguistique, les connaissances comunes à la collectivité, [. . .] les connaissances acquises à travers les lectures et le vécu" [knowledge that adds to linguistic competence, knowledge shared by the community, {. . .} knowledge gathered both by reading and by living]. The link between scenes and deverbalization is somewhat more explicit in Kussmaul (1995). Hoyle (2001) formulates a scenario theory along the same lines, where he draws from the common traits in schemas, frames, scripts, ICMs, etc. See also Hare et al. (2009).

Vermeer and Witte (1990) took this approach one step further. Concerned with the role of culture in translating, they explained differences in interpretations by postulating the existence of *channels* operating between frames and scenes. According to their proposal, the text producer would have a scene A in mind which she would turn into a reduced and fixed scene B when writing, and which seems to be equated to Frame 1. The reader would receive Frame 1 as Frame 2, and build a transient scene C, which would then crystallize as scene D under the influence of the reader's notions about the author and her goals, to be finally *extracted from the text* as scene E. As in the case of Vannerem and Snell-Hornby (1986), this proposal assumes chained, conscious, intentional choices and changes in and within the scenes depending on the specifics of the communicative interaction, but there is simply a dearth of empirical evidence that this is the actual process. Even if channels were considered part of a *model,* and not of a *representation* of the translation process, their potential psychological reality should be backed by indirect empirical data.

Rojo (2002a, 2002b) made a much more orthodox attempt to apply Frame Semantics to translation. In order to do so, she had to focus on the analysis of differences between text segments in originals and their translations. The success of the analysis relies on the analyst knowing the details involved in both languages and text segments under study. This renders the analysis pointless as a tool for practicing translators because, in the best case, it only rationalizes what they will be doing intuitively much faster. Of course, Rojo never claimed that her analysis should be understood as an addition to translators' techniques or strategies, let alone as a description of translators' actual behavior. But readers who are unaware of Cognitive Translatology/CL basics might think so, and this clarification seems in order.

1.4 Corollary for Cognitive Translatology

Time and again, straight-through applications of linguistic tools for language analysis (e.g. componential analysis, transformational syntax) have been advanced both by linguists and translatologists as break-throughs in translatology which are simply far removed from what translators do and what is really going on in their minds. That is why linguistics – whether CL or otherwise – is still mistrusted amongst translatologists and Cognitive Translatology is today closer to cognitive psychology than to CL. In translatology, "Adopting a cognitive perspective implies precisely changing the focus of attention from the text to the processes involved in its production and interpretation" (Rojo 2002b: 70). On its own, product approaches – those focusing on language or texts – tell us something about those texts, the languages involved in the translation, or even about language, but they only say very little about how people process language samples in real communicative events. Hence, applying analytical tools to translation may be interesting to CL, and it may also build a useful bridge between linguistic research and translatological research. However, their appeal to Cognitive Translatology is only superficial. Their application to translation training is certainly more promising, as a strategy to enhance metacognitive and metalinguistic awareness in trainees. Let us now see some points where Cognitive Translatology might be useful for CL.

2 What Cognitive Translatology may do for CL

Most linguists who adhere to CL will probably agree that "meaning" is a pivotal concept in their work and that the study of language should be organized around it. After all, sounds, letters, and their compounds become linguistic constituents because they are assigned meaning or are functional when distinguishing meaning. Language manifestations (speech, writing) are physical and therefore observable, so they may be subjected to empirical research, but meaning is not (except through introspection), so it is not the subject of direct empirical investigation. Perhaps because of this, CL theorizing is still largely deductive, an aspect which has been sharply criticized when evaluating generative linguistics. But

> [. . .] when linguists do try to get at meaning, they approach it as something to be inferred from the formal expressions of language themselves. Although it may be sad to acknowledge, this clearly makes the study of language inherently circular: linguistic facts are derived from something which is itself inferred from linguistic facts. [. . .] what we think we know about linguistic meaning is still mostly derived from the formal manifestations of language. So whenever we try to understand the latter on the basis of the former, we are for all intents and purposes thinking in circles. (Ritt 2007: 237–238)

One of the ways out of this circle is translation. Indeed, translations have traditionally been one of the main sources for cross-linguistic research, but linguistics has so far focused on "formal" comparisons between constructed or isolated, short language samples (usually words and sentences), as Brdar-Szabó and Brdar (2003: 93) and Bernárdez (2005: 203–209) have underscored. In contrast, real translations usually imply a positive judgment by the translator on the correspondence of contextualized language samples in different languages, always in terms of meaning, often as to their appropriateness and their acceptability as well. This is, hence, realistic language use, free from the potential biases of the researchers, where meaning may be discerned by triangulation of several languages. For example, Lakoff and Johnson (1980, 1999) suggested that the grounding of conceptual metaphors can be explained by co-occurrence of experience between the two mapped domains or by conflating experientially grounded, primary metaphors. Grady (1997, 1999) and Boers (2003) suggest that the sources make a difference, and that a distinction should be made between primary and complex conceptual metaphors. Primary metaphors would map image-schemas onto abstract experience, whereas complex metaphors combining or compounding primary metaphors should be more prone to culture-specific influences. If this were so, then translations of complex metaphors might show more variation than those of primary metaphors. While it may be argued that this example only points to translation as a good source for CL data, I would like now to forward a couple examples that are more related to Cognitive Translatology.

2.1 Translation universals

The first example deals with how to tackle the fact that the language of translations may have distinctive features that make them different from originals. Laviosa (1988) found that translations have higher proportions of grammatical words and of high frequency words, and that the most frequent words in translations were more repeated than in originals. Olohan's (2001) empirical results show significant differences in several optional syntactic structures. Baker (2004) found that lexical patterns such as *in the middle of the, from time to time, that is, once and for all* are much more usual in translations. Dayrell (2007, 2008) and Balaskó (2008) suggest that collocational patterns in translations are less diverse. Baroni and Bernardini (2006) reached 86.7% accuracy in automated discrimination of translations and originals, and Ilisei et al. (2010) reached up to 97.62% on a technical data set, so there must be something to it. But what is it?

Several translatologists have hypothesized the existence of universals in the process of translating, such as *simplification* and *explicitation* (cf. Mauranen and Kujamäki 2004) that would account for these differences. House (2008: 11) has argued, on the contrary, that this quest "is in essence futile, since there are no, and can there be no, translation universals". One of the points House (2008) does not explicitly raise is that translating and interpreting involve a large amount of learned behavior. In the case of professional – not necessarily trained – translators and translation trainees, their quality judgments on their own output have usually been conditioned by a host of readers, clients, revisers, colleagues, translation trainers and the like, whose feedback may have had a remarkable impact on their own criteria and preferences. Some translation choices have been clearly imposed upon translators to different degrees, so that many traits of their communicative behavior may be seen as the consequence of the very process of socialization they underwent. I believe that this may be the case for some candidates to universality as well. For example, the Mapuches (Chile) are keen on the aesthetic use of their language, Mapugundun, and consider oratory the supreme social skill. Does simplification hold for native interpreters into Mapugundun? According to Keenan (1976), in Madagascar information seems to be considered very valuable, and those who have it attain social prestige. Will explicitation still be at work in native translations into Malagasy? Thus far research into translation universals has covered about a dozen of Western languages, but claiming that a certain tendency is universal needs a much more substantial support. In present-day circumstances, proposing universal laws in Cognitive Translatology appears to be a little too far-fetched. Furthermore, "speakers have a tendency to convey the most amount of semantic information in the simplest syntactic form possible, given processing constraints" (Özçalıskan and Slobin 2000: 559). Assumed translation universals might just reflect the application of general communicative behavior. Tendencies such as simplifying and clarifying are probably learned behavior that might be found in the same and other subjects when engaged in monolingual activities such as editing, revising, proofreading, and even free writing. So we might want to look for explanations for language differences in translations somewhere else.

Perhaps CL may help Cognitive Translatology in this point. Fauconnier (1999: 98) argued that

> [. . .] by and large subjects engage in quite similar constructions on the basis of similar grammatical prompts, and thereby achieve a high degree of effective communication. The reason seems to be that the cultural, contextual, and cognitive substrate on which the language forms operate is sufficiently uniform across interlocutors to allow for a reasonable degree of consistency in the unfolding of the prompted meaning constructions.

This statement should also apply to translators and interpreters when at their tasks. Translating may be seen as an extreme case of register shift (Smith and Wilson 1980; see also Eviatar and Ibrahim 2000). Doherty and Perner (1998) argue that mastering the use of synonyms depends on children's insight that things can be represented in different ways, i.e. on their ability to adopt different perspectives on the same information, and translating should depend on this ability as well. Slobin (1996) forwarded the notion of "thinking for speaking", i.e. that speakers are eased by the grammatical patterns of their own languages into paying attention to features that need to be expressed in linguistic communication in these languages. Hence, beyond compulsory changes and learned behavior, beyond translation errors and interference, subjects might show distinct tendencies when they are translating and interpreting because of the influence of their own language *and the thought patterns that are prevalent in their communities* (see, e.g. Cadierno 2004). In other words, thinking for speaking might color translators' construals (see Ibarretxe-Antuñano and Filipović, this volume).

Langacker (2008: ch. 3) explains that construals vary in several dimensions, such as *specificity* (the level of precision at which a situation is characterized), *focusing* (selection and foregrounding of conceptual content), *prominence* (focusing attention on certain aspects, metonymy, etc.), and *perspective* (viewing arrangement, vantage point, etc). These concepts might be useful to pin down differences in the language of translations. Can there be distinct tendencies associated to certain language pairs and translation directions (whether into one's own language or into the foreign language)? The answer to these questions is crucial to determine whether Langacker's construal dimensions are general and motivated, and to provide them with empirical support. Furthermore, the answers might help Cognitive Translatology to redress the issue of translation universals.

2.2 The gravitational model of linguistic availability

Translationese has been defined as the "[. . .] systematic influence on target language (TL) from source language (SL)" (Gellerstam 1986: 88). It should not be misunderstood as translation errors or interference, although the limits between translationese and interference are fuzzy and depend on the research program. The issue of *translationese* should appeal to CL for other reasons as well. Francis (2005) concludes that languages in bilinguals have a shared semantic/conceptual system for both languages, i.e. that there is only one lexicon where items are also tagged for language membership. This causes a wide array of lexical priming effects, which can be extended to sentence production (Hartsuiker and Pickering 2008) and text translation (Hatzidaki and Pothos 2008). There is some neurological evidence (Abutalebi and Green 2007; Wang et al. 2009) to sustain that interference between the two languages might be avoided by an inhibitory control (Green 1998) to keep languages apart, by managing competing language systems and mappings. These competing items might depend on their level of activation to become selected (M. Paradis 2004: 29). In turn, their level of activation may depend on their saliency. In short, language differences in translations might be the consequence of the saliency of linguistic features in both the original and the developing translation.

Talmy (2007) has proposed a large list of linguistic factors that might set strength of attention. Many of these factors are still awaiting empirical study but some of them, such as differences in salience between open-class and closed-class lexical items, have already some support (e.g. Cutler 1993; Herron and Bates 1997). The importance of this distinction in Talmy's work cannot be overestimated, since he proposes that the conceptual system is divided into a *content system* and a *structuring system*, which roughly correspond to open-class and closed-class elements, respectively. Languages seem to group in distinctive types as to the way they encode meaning. There can exist typological shifts in languages, which Talmy has studied in detail, although a tendency for these systems to be stable is implied. Since many closed-class elements tend to be very frequent, it follows that many elements in the structuring system should be more stable than many others in the content system. For example, Azuma and Meier (1997) found that bilinguals often code-switch open-class items but not closed-class items, and Hustad, Dardis, and Mccourt (2007) concluded that closed-class words were more intelligible than open-class words for speakers with dysarthria. But there is also some conflicting evidence.

First, in many languages, motion verbs entail the use of certain prepositions. Purported, *and untested*, difficulties in translating motion verbs (Pascual 1999) between typologically different languages – e.g. those that encode Manner and Path, and those that do not – might not hold. Many translators simply develop strategies to code meaning perceived as relevant in different ways (Ibarretxe-Antuñano 2003). Since one of the tenets of Cognitive Translatology is that the acquisition of translating expertise includes interiorizing translation solutions for language chunks, the next question is, do expert translators and natural (untrained) translators display the same tendencies? This is not an easy question, for bilinguals seem to be able to keep their languages apart when they communicate with monolinguals while they may choose to code-switch when interacting with other bilinguals, so the inhibitory control seems to work at will, and both globally and locally (Meuter 2005). In which way are code-switching optional restrictions related to translators' interferences and Talmy's linguistic salient features?

Second, it is a well-known fact that performance in translators and interpreters tends to decline with stress, fatigue, increased processing demands and other factors. Moser-Mercer, Künzli, and Korac (1998) found a steady increase in the number of errors in interpreters' performance that, after 30 minutes, implied a significant decline in output quality. In fact, environmental factors are not exclusive to translators and interpreters (see, e.g. Hester and Garavan 2005 and Weaver and Arrington 2010). Often, translators affected by such factors will experience interference from the original language in aspects as central as the use of prepositions, articles, possessives, and other closed-class elements. And this happens in spite of bilinguals' advantage in control of attention thanks to larger working memory capacities (Yang et al. 2005). Gile's (1995) gravitational model of linguistic availability tries to capture the status of an individual's oral or written command of a language at a particular point in time and in particular circumstances by describing the relative availability of lexical units and linguistic rules. Elements in the lexicon have different frequencies of use, and the basic hypothesis in this model is that their degrees of entrenchment (irrespective of their nature, valence, type, etc.) would correlate with their resistance to interference. How can this flexibility be accommodated in Talmy's approach?

3 What lies ahead

The examples I have offered clearly do not exhaust the list of insights to be gained in CL thanks to many advances in Cognitive Translatology and, specially, due to the many problems it has to face. The status of grammatical judgments, the fact that language change seems sometimes fortuitous and unmotivated, the disruption of apparently steady patterns by attentional shifts, might have filled the previous pages as well. If CL really wants to become a usage-based theory of language, it might find it worth to have a look at how researchers interested mainly in language use try to make sense of linguistic theoretical standpoints and put them to test. For example, in his attempt to apply generative linguistics to translation, Nida (1964: 57–69) disregarded deep structures in favor of *superficial* kernels. His arguments against the notion of equivalence (Nida 1964: 166–167) may be taken as an early objection against the autonomy of syntax, and also against studying ideal communication exchanges where idealized speakers and receivers produced and understood language automatically. However, it took three more years for Mel'chuk (1967) to state that there were some semantic or cognitive levels which could not be captured by merely focusing on linguistic structures, and some more for Bellert (1970) and Bar-Hillel (1971) to conclude that acquired knowledge and textual inferences beyond the text segment played a fundamental role in translating. This might happen today again, for instance, with several approaches to the interplay between language and consciousness, some of which might simply be unable to stand a reality check by Cognitive Translatology (e.g. Zlatev 2007).

On the other hand, as an applied science, the goals of Cognitive Translatology are pretty different from those of CL, but it needs a set of basic concepts such as "language" and "meaning". These concepts should be drawn from Cognitive Science, mainly from CL, but applications of CL analytical frameworks do not seem to hold much promise beyond what we already have. Translation is not a linguistic affair, but rather an interpersonal instance of communication, and it needs to draw from other sources such as Cognitive Psychology, for other basic concepts such as "comprehension". In short, for Cognitive Translatology, CL is interesting insofar as it provides the conceptual scaffolding to develop descriptions and explanations of the cognitive aspects of translation and interpreting processes. Thus far, most contributions to Cognitive Translatology are still representational (Risku 2002: 528) and language-centered, although many papers, such as Schäffner's (2004) on metaphor and Halverson's (2007) on translation shifts, point to a wealth of valuable insights beyond linguistic analysis that can be furthered with the help of CL.

Cognitive Translatology and CL are often interested in the same topics, albeit from different angles which can be complementary. Roher (2006: 133–136) proposes to organize the levels of investigation in CL by grouping phenomena according to the relative physical sizes at which embodied phenomena can be measured. Cognitive Translatology is not (yet) very interested in neuroanatomy, neurocellular, or subcellular systems, but translatological research carried out these days can be placed in the first three levels: communicative and cultural systems, performance domain, and neural systems. Linguistic analysis, corpora studies, verbal reports, reaction time, and fMRI, which Roher places at these levels, are popular empirical methods in Cognitive Translatology. There is, then, a rich theoretical and methodological common ground where Cognitive Translatology and CL may meet. It seems that we are gathering momentum to boost Cognitive Translatology, and to invite CL rationalists to put their proposals to test because there is more than a way with words.

References

Abutalebi, Jubin and David W. Green 2007 Bilingual language production: The neurocognition of language representation and control. *Journal of Neurolinguistics* 20.3: 242–275.

Agrifoglio, Marjorie 2004 Sight translation and interpreting: A comparative analysis of constraints and failures. *Interpreting* 6.1: 43–67.

Alves, Fabio and José Luiz Gonçalves (eds.) 2006 *Relevância em Traduçao. Perspectivas teóricas e aplicadas*. Belo Horizonte (Brazil): Faculdade de Letras UFMG.

Azuma, Shoji and Richard P. Meier 1997 Open class and closed class: Sentence-imitation experiments on intrasentential code-switching. *Applied Psycholinguistics* 18: 257–276.

Baker, Mona 2004 A corpus-based view of similarity and difference in translation. *International Journal of Corpus Linguistics* 9.2: 167–193.

Balaskó, Maria 2008 What does the *Figure* show? Patterns of translationese in a Hungarian comparable corpus. *Trans-kom* 1.1: 58–73.

Bar-Hillel, Yehoshua 1971 Some reflections on the present outlook for high quality machine translation. In: Winifred P. Lehmann and Rolf Stachowitz (eds.), *Feasibility study on fully automatic high quality translation*, 73–76. New York: Rome Air Development Centre. RADC-TR-7 N295.

Baroni, Marco and Silvia Bernardini 2006 A new approach to the study of translationese: Machine-learning the difference between original and translated text. *Literary and Linguistic Computing* 21.3: 259–274.

Bellert, Irene 1970 On a condition of the coherence of texts. *Semiotica* 2: 335–363.

Bernárdez, Enrique 2005 Social cognition: Variation, language, and culture in cognitive linguistic typology. In: Francisco Ruiz de Mendoza and M. Sandra Peña (eds.), *Cognitive linguistics: Internal dynamics and interdisciplinary interaction*, 191–222. Berlin: Mouton de Gruyter.

Boers, Frank 2003 Applied linguistics perspectives on cross-cultural variation in conceptual metaphor. *Metaphor and Symbol* 18.4: 231–238.

Brdar-Szabó, Rita and Mario Brdar 2003 Referential metonymy across languages: What can Cognitive Linguistics and Contrastive Linguistics learn from each other? *International Journal of English Studies* 3.2: 85–105.

Brünner, Gisela 1987 Metaphern für Sprache und Kommunikation in Alltag und Wissenschaft. *Diskussion Deutsch* 18.94: 100–119.

Cadierno, Teresa 2004 Expressing motion events in a second language: A cognitive typological perspective. In: Michel Achard and Susanne Neimeier (eds.), *Cognitive linguistics, second language acquisition and foreign language pedagogy*, 13–49. Berlin: Mouton de Gruyter.

Castro Arce, María 2008 Procesos de lectura y comprensión al traducir. In: M. M. Fernández and R. Muñoz (eds.), *Aproximaciones cognitivas al estudio de la traducción y la interpretación*, 31–66. Granada: Comares.

Chesterman, Andrew 2008 Translation data problems. In: Jouko Lindstedt, Andrew Chesterman, Mikhail Kopotev, Aila Laamaren, Ahti Nikunlassi, Juhani Nuorluoto, Jyrki Papinnieni, Pekka Pesonen and Johanna Viimaranta (eds.). *С любовью к слову. Festschrift in honour of Professor Arto Mustajoki on the occasion of his 60th birthday*, 17–26. (Slavica Helsingiensia 35.) Helsinki: Department of Slavonic and Baltic Languages and Literatures.

Croft, William and D. Alan Cruse 2004 *Cognitive linguistics*. Cambridge: Cambridge University Press.

Cutler, Anne 1993 Phonological cues to open- and closed-class words in the processing of spoken sentences. *Journal of Psycholinguistic Research* 22.2: 109–131.

Dayrell, Carmen 2007 A quantitative approach to compare collocational patterns in translated and non-translated texts. *International Journal of Corpus Linguistics* 12.3: 375–414.

Dayrell, Carmen 2008 Investigating the preference of translators for recurrent lexical patterns: A corpus-based study. *Trans-kom* 1.1: 36–57.

D'hulst, Lieven 1992 Sur le rôle des métaphores en traductologie contemporaine. *Target* 4.1: 33–51.

Dirven, René 2005 Major strands in cognitive linguistics. In: Francisco J. Ruiz de Mendoza and M. Sandra Peña (eds.), *Cognitive linguistics: Internal dynamics and interdisciplinary interaction*, 17–68. Berlin: Mouton de Gruyter.

Doherty, Martin J. and Joseph Perner 1998 Metalinguistic awareness and theory of mind: Just two words for the same thing? *Cognitive Development* 13: 279–305.

Dragsted, Barbara 2006 Computer-aided translation as a distributed cognitive task. *Pragmatics and Cognition* 14.2: 443–464.

Eddy, David M. 2005 Evidence-based medicine: A unified approach. *Health Affairs* 24.1: 9–17.

Ericsson, K. Anders 1996 *The road to excellence*. Mahwah, NJ: Erlbaum.

Ericsson, K. Anders and Jacqui Smith (eds.) 1991 *Toward a general theory of expertise*. New York: Cambridge University Press.

Evans, Vyvyan and Melanie Green 2006 *Cognitive linguistics: An introduction*. Edinburgh: Edinburgh University Press.

Eviatar, Zohar and Raphiq Ibrahim 2000 Bilingual is as bilingual does: Metalinguistic abilities of Arabic-speaking children. *Applied Psycholinguistics* 21: 451–471.

Fauconnier, Giles 1969 Methods and Generalizations. In: Theo Janssen and Gisela Redeker (eds.) *Cognitive Linguistics. Foundations, Scope, and Methodology*, 95–128. Berlin: Mouton de Gruyter.

Fillmore, Charles J. 1968 The case for case. In: Emmon Bach and Robert T. Harms (eds.), *Universals in linguistic theory*, 1–88. New York: Holt, Rinehart and Winston.

Fillmore, Charles J. 1975 An alternative to checklist theories of meaning. *Proceedings of the First Annual Meeting of the Berkeley Linguistics Society* 1: 123–131.

Fillmore, Charles J. 1977 Scenes-and-frames semantics. In: Antonio Zampolli (ed.), *Linguistics structures processing*, 55–81. Amsterdam: North Holland.

Fillmore, Charles J. 1985 Frames and the semantics of understanding. *Quaderni di Semantica* 6.2: 222–254.

Fillmore, Charles J. and Paul Kay 1987 *The goals of construction grammar*. (Berkeley Cognitive Science Program Technical Report 50.) Berkeley: University of California.

Francis, Wendy S. 2005 Bilingual semantic and conceptual representation. In: Judith F. Kroll and Annette M. B. de Groot (eds.), *Handbook of bilingualism: Psycholinguistic approaches*, 251–267. New York: Oxford University Press.

Geeraerts, Dirk, Gitte Kristiansen and Yves Peirsman (eds.) 2010 *Advances in cognitive sociolinguistics*. Berlin: De Gruyter Mouton.

Gellerstam, Martin 1986 Translationese in Swedish novels translated from English. In: Lars Wollin and Hans Lindquist (eds.), *Translation studies in Scandinavia*, 88–95. Lund, Sweden: CWK Geerup.

Gile, Daniel 1995 *Basic Concepts and Models for Interpreter and Translator Training*. Amsterdam: John Benjamins.

Göpferich, Susanne 2008 *Translationsprozessforschung; Stand – Methoden – Perspektiven*. (Translationswissenschaft 4.) Tübingen, Germany: Gunter Narr.

Grady, Joseph E. 1997 Theories are buildings revisited. *Cognitive Linguistics* 8: 267–290.

Grady, Joseph E. 1999 A typology of motivation for conceptual metaphor: Correlation vs. resemblance. In: Raymond W. Gibbs and Gerard J. Steen (eds.), *Metaphor in cognitive linguistics*, 79–100. Amsterdam: John Benjamins.

Green, David W. 1998 Mental control of the bilingual lexico-semantic system. *Bilingualism: Language and Cognition* 1: 67–81.

Gutt, Ernst A. 1991 *Translation and relevance: Cognition and context*. Oxford: Blackwell.

Gutt, Ernst A. 1992 *Relevance theory: A guide to successful communication in translation*. Dallas, TX: Summer Institute of Linguistics.

Halverson, Sandra L. 1997 The concept of equivalence in Translation Studies: Much ado about something. *Target* 1–2: 207–233.

Halverson, Sandra L. 1998 Translation Studies and representative corpora: Establishing links between translation corpora, theoretical/descriptive categories and a conception of the object of study. *Meta* 43.4: 494–514.

Halverson, Sandra L. 1999 Conceptual work and the "translation" concept. *Target* 11.1: 1–31.

Halverson, Sandra L. 2000 Prototype effects in the "translation" category. In: Andrew Chesterman, Natividad Gallardo and Yves Gambier (eds.), *Translation in context*, 3–16. Amsterdam: John Benjamins.

Halverson, Sandra L. 2002 Cognitive models, prototype effects and "translation": The role of cognition in translation (meta)theory. *Across Languages and Cultures* 3.1: 21–43.

Halverson, Sandra L. 2007 A cognitive linguistic approach to translation shifts. *Belgian Journal of Linguistics* 21.1: 105–121.

Hare, Mary, Michael Jones, Caroline Thomson, Sarah Kelly and Ken McRae 2009 Activating event knowledge. *Cognition* 111: 151–167.

Harris, Brian 1973 La traductologie, la traduction naturelle, la traduction automatique et la sémantique. *Cahier de linguistique* 2: 133–146.

Harris, Brian 1977 The importance of Natural Translation. *Working Papers on Bilingualism* 12: 96–114.

Harris, Brian 1988 What I really meant by "Translatology". *TTR* 1.2: 91–96.

Hartsuiker, Robert J. and Martin J. Pickering 2008 Language integration in bilingual sentence production. *Acta Psychologica* 128: 479–489.

Hatzidaki, Anna and Emmanuel M. Pothos 2008 Bilingual language representation and cognitive processes in translation. *Applied Psycholinguistics* 29: 125–150.

Herron, Daniel T. and Elizabeth A. Bates 1997 Sentential and acoustic factors in the recognition of open- and closed-class words. *Journal of Memory and Language* 37.2: 217–239.

Hester, Robert and Hugh Garavan 2005 Working memory and executive function: The influence of content and load on the control of attention. *Memory and Cognition* 33.2: 221–233.

Holz-Mänttäri, Justa 1984 *Translatorisches handeln. Theorie und Methode*. Helsinki: Suomalainen Tiedeakatemia.

House, Juliane 2008 Beyond intervention: Universals in translation? *Trans-kom* 1.1: 6–19.

Hoyle, Richard A. 2001 *Scenarios, discourse, and translation*. PhD dissertation, University of Surrey Roehampton, UK.

Hustad, Katherine C., Caitlin M. Dardis and Kelly A. Mccourt 2007 Effects of visual information on intelligibility of open and closed class words in predictable sentences produced by speakers with dysarthria. *Clinical Linguistics and Phonetics* 21.5: 353–367.

Ibarretxe-Antuñano, Iraide 2003 What translation tells us about motion: A contrastive study of typologically different languages. *International Journal of English Studies* 3.2: 153–178.

Ilisei, Iustina, Diana Inkpen, Gloria Corpas Pastor and Ruslan Mitkov 2010 Identification of translationese: A machine learning approach. In: Alexander Gelbukh (ed.), *Computational linguistics and intelligent text processing*, 503–520. Berlin: Springer.

Janicki, Karol 2006 *Language misconceived: Arguing for applied cognitive sociolinguistics*. Mahwah, NJ: Erlbaum.

Keenan, Ellinor Ochs 1976 The universality of conversational postulates. *Language in Society* 5: 67–80.

Konheim-Kalkstein, Yasmine L. and Paul Van den Broek 2008 The effect of incentives on cognitive processing of text. *Discourse Processes* 45: 180–194.

Korzybski, Alfred 1948 A non-Aristotelian system and its necessity for rigour in mathematics and physics. In: Alfred Korzybski (ed.), *Science and sanity: An introduction to non-Aristotelian systems and general semantics*, Supplement III, 747–761. Lakeville, CT: International Non-Aristotelian Library Publishing Co.

Kussmaul, Paul 1995 Translation through visualization. *Meta* 50.2: 378–391.

Lakoff, George 1990 The invariance hypothesis: Is abstract reason based on image-schemas? *Cognitive Linguistics* 1.1: 39–74.

Lakoff, George and Mark Johnson 1980 *Metaphors we live by*. Chicago: University Press.

Lakoff, George and Mark Johnson 1999 *Philosophy in the flesh: The embodied mind and its challenge to Western thought*. New York: Basic Books.

Langacker, Ronald 1987 *Foundations of cognitive grammar*. Vol. 1. Stanford, CA: Stanford University Press.

Langacker, Ronald 2008 *Cognitive grammar: A basic introduction*. Oxford: Oxford University Press.

Laviosa, Sara 1988 Core patterns of lexical use in a comparable corpus of English narrative prose. *Meta* 43.4: 557–570.

Lédérer, Marianne 1981 La compréhension des textes et des discours vue par la traductologie. In: Jacques Barbizet, Maurice Pergnier and Danica Seleskovitch (eds.), *Comprendre le langage. Actes du colloque international et multidisciplinaire sur la compréhension du langage*, 63–71. Paris: Didier Erudition.

Mandelblit, Nili 1996 The cognitive view of metaphor and its implications for translation theory. In: Marcel Thelen and Barbara Lewandowska-Tomaszczyk (eds.), *Translation and meaning*, Part 3, 483–495. Maastricht, the Netherlands: Hoogeschool.

Martín de León, Celia 2005 *Contenedores, recorridos y metas. Metáforas en la traductología funcionalista*. Frankfurt am Main: Peter Lang.

Martín de León, Celia 2008 Skopos and beyond. A critical study of functionalism. *Target* 20.1: 1–28.

Mauranen, Anna and Pekka Kujamäki (eds.) 2004 *Translation universals: Do they exist?* Amsterdam: John Benjamins.

Mayoral Asensio, Roberto 2001 *Aspectos epistemológicos de la traducción*. Castellón, Spain: Jaume I.

McElhanon, Kenneth A. 2005 From word to scenario: The influence of linguistic theories upon models of translation. *Journal of Translation* 1.3: 29–67.

Mel'chuk, Igor A. 1967 Linguistics and automatic translation. *International Social Science Journal* 19.1:64–78.

Meuter, Renata F. I. 2005 Language selection in bilinguals: Mechanisms and processes. In: Judith F. Kroll and Annete M. B. de Groot (eds.), *Handbook of bilingualism: Psycholinguistic approaches*, 349–370. New York: Oxford University Press.

Moser-Mercer, Barbara, Alexander Künzli and Marina Korac 1998 Prolonged turns in interpreting: Effects on quality, physiological and psychological stress. *Interpreting* 3.1: 47–64.

Muñoz Martín, Ricardo 1995 *Lingüística para traducir*. Barcelona: Teide.

Muñoz Martín, Ricardo 2009 The way they were: Subject profiling in translation process research. In: Inger M. Mees, Fábio Alves and Susanne Göpferich (eds.), *Methodology, technology and innovation in translation process research: A tribute to Arnt Lykke Jakobsen*, 87–108. Copenhagen: Samfundslitteratur.

Muñoz Martín, Ricardo 2010a Leave no stone unturned: On the development of Cognitive Translatology. *Translation and Interpreting Studies* 2: 145–162.

Muñoz Martín, Ricardo 2010b On paradigms and Cognitive Translatology. In: Gregory Shreve and Erik Angelone (eds.), *Translation and cognition*, 169–187. Amsterdam: John Benjamins.

Muñoz Martín, Ricardo 2011 Nomen mihi Legio est: A cognitive approach to natural translation. In: María Jesus Blasco and Amparo Jiménez (eds.), *Interpreting [. . .] naturally: Essays to honor Brian Harris*, 35–66. Frankfurt am Main: Peter Lang.

Neubert, Albrecht and Gregory M. Shreve 1992 *Translation as text*. Kent, OH: Kent State University Press.
Nida, Eugene A. 1964 *Toward a science of translation*. Leiden: Brill.
Olohan, Maeve 2001 Spelling out the optionals in translation: A corpus study. *UCREL Technical Papers* 13: 423–432.
Olohan, Maeve and Christoph Zähner 1996 Translation theory and cognitive linguistics. In: Tina Hickey and Jenny Williams (eds.), *Language, education and society in a changing world*, 143–150. Clevedon, UK: Multilingual Matters.
Özçalışkan, Şeyda and Dan I. Slobin 2000 *Climb up vs. ascend climbing*: Lexicalization choices in expressing motion events with manner and path components. In: S. Catherine-Howell, Sarah A. Fish and Tea K. Lucas (eds.), *Proceedings of the 24th Annual Boston University Conference on Language Development*, Vol. 2, 558–570. Somerville, MA: Cascadilla Press.
Paradis, Carita 2003 Is the notion of *linguistic competence* relevant in cognitive linguistics? *Annual Review of Cognitive Linguistics* 1: 247–271.
Paradis, Michael 2004 *A neurolinguistic theory of bilingualism*. Amsterdam: John Benjamins.
Pascual Aransáez, Cristina 1999 A cognitive analysis of the cross-linguistic differences between English and Spanish motion verbs and the Spanish translator's task. *C.I.F.*, 25: 127–136.
Petruck, Miriam R. L. 1996 "Frame semantics". In: Jef Verschueren, Jan-O. Östman, Jan Blommaert and Chris Bulcaen (eds.), *Handbook of pragmatics*, 251–284. Amsterdam: John Benjamins.
Pym, Anthony 2003 Redefining translation competence in an electronic age: In defense of a minimalist approach. *Meta* 48.4: 481–497.
Reddy, Michael 1979 The conduit metaphor: A case of frame conflict in our language about language. In: Andrew Ortony (ed.), *Metaphor and thought*, 284–297. Cambridge: Cambridge University Press.
Reiß, Katharina and Hans Vermeer 1984 *Grundlegung einer allgemeinen Translationstheorie*. Tübingen, Germany: Niemeyer.
Risku, Hanna 1998 *Translatorische Kompetenz. Kognitive Grundlagen des Übersetzens als Expertentätigkeit*. Tübingen, Germany: Stauffenburg.
Risku, Hanna 2002 Situatedness in translation studies. *Cognitive Systems Research* 3.3: 523–533.
Risku, Hanna 2004 *Translationsmanagement. Interkulturelle Fachkommunikation im Informationszeitalter*. Tübingen, Germany: Gunter Narr.
Ritt, Nikolaus 2007 Meaning in a material world or How to find out what linguists think about meaning. In: Malgorzata Fabiszak (ed.), *Language and meaning: Cognitive and functional perspectives*, 235–267. Frankfurt am Main: Peter Lang.
Robinson, G. Canby 1929 The application of science to the practice of medicine. *Science* 69.1792: 459–462.
Roher, Tim 2006 Three dogmas of embodiment: Cognitive linguistics as a cognitive science. In: Gitte Kristiansen, Michel Achard, René Dirven and Francisco J. Ruiz de Mendoza Ibáñez (eds.), *Cognitive linguistics: Current applications and future perspectives*, 119–146. Berlin: Mouton de Gruyter.
Rojo, Ana 2002a Applying frame semantics to translation: A practical example. *Meta* 47.3: 312–350.
Rojo, Ana 2002b Frame semantics and the translation of humour. *Babel: International Journal of Translation* 48.1: 34–77.
Rosch, Eleanor 1978 Principles of categorization. In: Eleanor Rosch and Barbara B. Lloyd (eds.), *Cognition and categorization*, 27–48. Hillsdale, NJ: Erlbaum.

Rosch, Eleanor and Carolyn B. Mervis 1975 Family resemblances: Studies in the internal structure of categories. *Cognitive Psychology* 7: 573–605.
Rosch, Eleanor, Carolyn B. Mervis, Wayne D. Gray, David M. Johnson and Penny Boyes-Braem 1976 Basic objects in natural categories. *Cognitive Psychology* 8: 382–439.
Schäffner, Christine 2004 Metaphor and translation: Some implications of a cognitive approach. *Journal of Pragmatics* 36: 1253–1269.
Seleskovitch, Danica 1975 *Langage, langues et mémoire: Étude de la pris de notes en interprétation consécutive*. Paris: Minard Lettres Modernes.
Shreve, Gregory M., Christina Schäffner, Joseph H. Danks and Jennifer Griffin 1993 Is there a special kind of reading for translation? An empirical investigation of reading in the translation process. *Target* 5.1: 21–41.
Slobin, Dan I. 1996 From "thought and language" to "thinking to speaking". In: John J. Gumperz and Stephen C. Levinson (eds.), *Rethinking linguistic relativity*, 70–96. Cambridge: Cambridge University Press.
Smith, Linda B. and Larissa K. Samuelson 1997 Perceiving and remembering: Category stability, variability, and development. In: Koen Lamberts and David Shanks (eds.), *Knowledge, concepts, and categories*, 161–195. Cambridge: Cambridge University Press.
Smith, Neil V. and Deirdre Wilson 1980 *Modern linguistics: The Chomskyan revolution*. New York: Penguin.
Snell-Hornby, Mary 1990 Linguistic transcoding or cultural transfer? A critique of translation theory in Germany. In: Susan Bassnett and Andre Lefevere (eds.), *Translation, history and culture*, 79–86. London: Pinter.
Sperber, Dan and Deirdre Wilson 1986 *Relevance: Communication and cognition*. Oxford: Blackwell.
Tabakowska, Elżbieta 1993 *Cognitive linguistics and poetics of translation*. Tübingen, Germany: Gunter Narr.
Talmy, Leonard 2007 Attention phenomena. In: Dirk Geeraerts and Hubert Cuyckens (eds.), *The Oxford handbook of cognitive linguistics*, 264–293. Oxford: Oxford University Press.
Tendahl, Markus and Raymond W. Gibbs Jr. 2008 Complementary perspectives on metaphor: Cognitive linguistics and relevance theory. *Journal of Pragmatics* 40.11: 1823–1864.
Tirkkonen-Condit, Sonja 2002 Metaphoric expressions in the translation process. *Across Languages and Cultures* 3.1: 101–116.
Toury, Gideon 1995 *Descriptive translation studies and beyond*. Amsterdam: John Benjamins.
Trotter, Wilfred 1935 General ideas in medicine. *British Medical Journal* 2.3900: 609–614.
Tymoczko, Maria 1998 Computerized corpora and the future of translation studies. *Meta* 43.4: 652–659.
Tymoczko, Maria 2005 Trajectories of research in translation studies. *Meta* 50.4: 1082–1097.
Vannerem, Mia and Mary Snell-Hornby 1986 Die Szene hinter dem Text: "scenes-and-frames-semantics" in der Übersetzung. In: Mary Snell-Hornby (ed.), *Übersetzungswissenschaft – eine Neuorientierung. Zur Integrierung von Theorie und Praxis*, 184–205. Tübingen, Germany: Francke.
Vermeer, Hans J. and Heidrun Witte 1990 *Mögen Sie Zistrosen? Scenes and Frames and Channels im translatorischen Handeln*. (TEXTconTEXT. Beiheft 3.) Heidelberg, Germany: Groos.
Wang, Yapeng, Patricia K. Kuhl, Chunhui Chen and Qi Dong 2009 Sustained and transient language control in the bilingual brain. *NeuroImage* 47.1: 414–422.
Weaver, Starla M. and Catherine M. Arrington 2010 What's on your mind: The influence of the contents of working memory on choice. *Quarterly Journal of Experimental Psychology* 63.4: 726–737.

Yang, Hwajin, Sujin Yang, Stephen J. Ceci and Qi Wang 2005 Effects of bilinguals' controlled-attention on working memory and recognition. In: James Cohen, Kara McAlister, Kellie Rolstad and Jeff MacSwan (eds.), *Proceedings of the 4th International Symposium on Bilingualism*, 2401–2404. Somerville, MA: Cascadilla Press.

Yorek, Nurettin and Serkan Narli 2009 Modeling of cognitive structure of uncertain scientific concepts using fuzzy-rough sets and intuitionistic fuzzy sets: Example of the life concept. *International Journal of Uncertainty, Fuzziness and Knowledge-Based Systems* 17.5 747–769.

Zhang, Jiajie 2002 Representations of health concepts: A cognitive perspective. *Journal of Biomedical Informatics* 35: 17–24.

Zlatev, Jordan 2007 Embodiment, language, and mimesis. In: Tom Ziemke, Jordan Zlatev, and Roslyn M. Frank (eds.), *Body, language, and mind*. Vol. 1, *Embodiment*, 297–337. Berlin: Mouton de Gruyter.

Celia Martín de León
Who cares if the cat is on the mat? Contributions of cognitive models of meaning to translation

> Language does not directly carry meaning, but rather serves, along with countless other situational elements, as a powerful instrument for prompting its construction.
>
> Gilles Fauconnier

1 Introduction

Implicit or explicit models of meaning and meaning construction play a key role in the conceptualization of translation. Different cognitive approaches provide different visions of meaning, and they also lead to different theoretical frameworks for empirical translation research. When meaning is understood as transferable, invariable information units, the translator's task is prone to be seen as transferring the information codified in a source language into a target language. If meaning construction is viewed as a complex, dynamic, and situated process, then the translator's task shall appear in a very different light: it will seek to provide target readers with the tools they need to construct their own meanings in their own situation (Risku 2004).

Until the end of the 1980s, formal linguistics did not pay much attention to meaning, which was thought to be arbitrarily connected to abstract symbols. One of the difficulties that arose in this context was the so-called *symbol-grounding problem* (Harnad 1990), which basically posits that a system of abstract symbols cannot generate meaning intrinsically. To produce meaning, symbols must somehow link to the world outside the symbol system. Translation is a domain where meaning construction processes are partly artificially situated (Holz-Mänttäri 1990), so it provides a particularly interesting arena to empirically research these processes, where advantages of choosing different cognitive approaches to meaning construction can be tested.

In this text, I will analyze how different cognitive models have tried to solve the problem of symbol grounding, and how they can contribute to develop a coherent and realistic theoretical framework for translatology. Of course, this study cannot be exhaustive, so it focuses on some of the more relevant approaches to meaning construction and their possible contributions to translation. First, I will describe the classical paradigm, which depicts meaning as arising from the syntactic combination of abstract symbols. I will then turn to connectionist approaches, which view meaning construction as a dynamic process of pattern recognition and completion. In this context, I will analyze two semantic models that are coherent with this paradigm and that have been applied to translation: prototypes and scenes-and-frames. In the last sections, I will discuss some of the possible contributions of recent developments in cognitive science that do not view cognition as a process taking place in an almost isolated system – just connected with the external world through inputs and outputs – but as a process that is part of bodily action in a social environment. Embodied and situated cognition depicts meaning as shaped by bodily action and provides a framework for the development of a realistic theory of action-oriented imagination in translation. Social and distributed cognition focuses on the collaborative construction of meaning, and on the off-loading of cognitive workload on cultural artefacts, both important dimensions of professional translation.

2 Classical paradigm: The neutral manipulation of symbols

The classical paradigm describes human cognition as manipulation of symbolic representations, a process that follows the rules of a mental language (e.g. Newell and Simon 1976; Fodor 1983). This internal language of thought is viewed as independent from natural languages, which are considered as instruments of communication, not of thought. But, at the same time, natural languages are used as models for the description of the mental language, which is depicted as sequential and guided by syntactic rules. For the classical paradigm, the symbols of mental language are abstract, amodal and arbitrary, and meaning arises from the syntactic combination of these symbols (Glenberg and Roberston 2000). Mental language symbols are arbitrary because there is no formal relationship between them and their referents, and they are amodal because they are independent of sensorial modalities, that is, because there is no correspondence between their structures and the perceptual states that caused them to exist (Barsalou 1999). The syntactic rules that guide the manipulation of mental symbols are also arbitrary and amodal (de Vega 2002).

Bruner ([1991] 2006) reports how he and other researchers who took part in the cognitive revolution against conductism at the end of the 1950s tried to give the concept of *meaning* a central position in the new cognitive paradigm, and how this concept was quickly replaced by the concept of *information*. The emphasis went from *meaning construction* to *information processing*. The latter was taken from a metaphor that portrays the human mind as a computer.

Once this metaphor had been introduced, the classical paradigm adopted a functionalist perspective, by which it considered cognition a disembodied process, independent of the physical system that supports it, in the same way as software is independent of the hardware that implements it. In this metaphorical model, information is neutral to meaning. For a machine, there is no difference between a poem and a list of aleatory numbers.

The cognitive paradigm of symbol manipulation is coherent with generative grammar (Chomsky 1965), with the mathematical model of communication (Shannon and Weaver [1949] 1963), and with truth-conditional semantics, whose goal was to describe the conditions for an utterance to be considered true. In formal logics and truth-conditional semantics, decontextualized sentences were interpreted through abstract, logical operations to determine their truth conditions. The situated meaning of real language use hardly relates to this formal meaning. In a similar way, when generative linguists tried to characterize linguistic competence, they isolated their observations from their contexts and from the actions they were a part of. In brief, they eliminated anything they considered *noise*. However, what is complex for the analyst is not necessarily complex for the participant in a communicative exchange. In fact, it is more difficult and cognitively more complex to act without a meaningful context (Fillmore 1976).

One of the main difficulties related to the classical approach of symbol manipulation is what has been termed the *symbol-grounding* problem (Harnad 1987, 1990): meaning cannot emerge from the manipulation of arbitrary symbols alone, because there is no account of how amodal symbols can be mapped to entities in the world (Barsalou 1999). However, the symbol-grounding problem only arises when cognition and communication are described in terms of information processing and transfer. Symbol grounding poses no difficulty for humans, who learn language as embedded in action, but it is a real problem for artificial cognitive systems, in particular when they are based solely on symbols and rules. In order to generate meaning, the information processed by a machine needs to be interpreted by a human being. Thus, the meaning attributed to abstract symbol systems is parasitic from the external interpreter. Harnad (1990) called this problem the *hermeneutic hall of mirrors*, which is the reverse side of the symbol-grounding problem: the persons who program the machine project onto the system the grounded meanings they have constructed.

Other approaches that, like the classical paradigm, describe meaning production as a translation of a natural language into a mental language also pose the problem of symbol grounding. Kintsch's (Kintsch 1998; Kintsch and van Dijk 1978; van Dijk and Kintsch 1983) theory about discourse comprehension describes understanding a sentence as translating it into an internal language of propositions or predicate-argument structures (de Vega 2002). Although there are empirical studies that support the psychological reality of propositions as units of thought (Ratcliff and McKoon 1978), propositional codification cannot be used to explain text comprehension because it depends on text interpretation (de Vega 2002). This is again the problem of symbol grounding, which can be described as a problem of circularity of meaning (de Vega 1984): abstract, amodal, and arbitrary symbols cannot be meaningful if they are not connected with perceptive, motor, or emotional experience.

In the last decades, statistical models of language meaning have been developed, based on the mathematics of high-dimensional spaces. Theories like Hyperspace Analogue to Language (HAL; Burguess and Lund 1997) and Latent Semantic Analysis (LSA; Landauer and Dumais 1997) represent the meaning of a word as a vector in a multidimensional space. These vectors are based on the patterns of co-occurrence of pairs of words in large corpora. Comparing the vectors of two words, it is possible to predict the probability of their co-occurrence. Although these models have some merit – for instance, in predicting semantic correlations between documents, sorting words in categories or judging semantic relationships – they have failed to solve the problem of symbol grounding, i.e., of meaning construction processes. The hypothesis underlying these models is that the meaning of a symbol arises from its relations to other symbols that are also undefined (Glenberg and Roberston 2000). However, as stated above, abstract symbols need to be grounded in something else to be meaningful at all; human cognition cannot be only based on co-occurrence frequencies of words (Barsalou 1999).

A possible solution to the problem of symbol grounding is to connect the symbol system to peripheral devices in order to *perceive* the world and to map the symbols with their referents. But, as argued by Harnad (1990), this solution underestimates the difficulty of picking out the objects and events in the world that symbols refer to. Symbols might also be mapped either to specific referents or to images, but both solutions fall short to solve the problem (Glenberg and Roberston 2000). A set of abstract symbols can be mapped to many different referents with the same relations between them (Putnam 1981). As for the images, there is some evidence suggesting that a child cannot learn a language just from watching television (Pinker 1994), which would be a human implementation of this proposal. According to Hendriks-Jansen (1996), the problem of symbol grounding lies in the very conception of the symbol system, and it cannot be solved by connecting that system with the *real world* or with some perceptual input.

In translation, the symbol-grounding problem arises when the linguistic aspects of translation are studied in isolation, trying to arrive at inherent, invariable meanings. Coherent with the symbol manipulation approach are models that describe communication as transfer of information through language (Reddy [1979] 1993), and translation as code-switching, replacement, reverbalization, or substitution (Risku 2004; Snell-Hornby [1988] 1995). These models of translation, which can be seen as elaborations of the conduit metaphor (Reddy [1979] 1993), depict the translator's work as a transfer of meanings from the source text into the target text (Martín de León 2010). The translation process is represented in an idealized way, as a linear succession of steps: source text analysis, transfer or planning, and target text elaboration. Context and situation, target and assignment, motivation, emotion, and interpretation are not taken into account (Risku 2004).

The classical paradigm influenced modern translation theories developed in the 1960s and the 1970s; for instance, Nida's (1964) theory of dynamic equivalence and other theories which focused on equivalence relations, like the approaches of the *Leipziger Schule* (e.g. Kade 1968; Jäger 1975; Neubert 1973). The notion of *equivalence* is one of the most controversial in the history of modern Translation Studies, and has received many different interpretations and elaborations (Snell-Hornby [1988] 1995). The history of these interpretations can be taken as evidence for the impossibility of explaining the translation process as simple recoding of a text in a new language, understood as a system of abstract symbols. Because meaning is not something inherent to the symbol system, equivalence cannot be absolute; it can only be defined in relation to some aspect of the communication process: it can be conceived of, for instance, as formal, dynamic, denotative, connotative, pragmatic, or functional. If meaning could emerge intrinsically from a system of abstract symbols, the degree of equivalence between two texts could be determined just comparing their respective linguistic systems. But meaning depends always on the interpreter and the situation, and it cannot be objectively and completely determined nor transferred unchanged to another language.

The classical paradigm of symbol manipulation does not provide a model for meaning construction. From its perspective, predetermined meanings are passively received and translated into the language of mind. These meanings are disembodied, independent of the situation and the interpreter. The classical paradigm, whose ideal was machine translation, cannot explain the processes involved in human translation, which is always embedded in a communication situation and depends on the translator's interpretation. It cannot explain, for instance, how meaning is grounded in individual experience, or how is it possible to create and understand new meanings (Zlatev 1999). Therefore, it simply cannot account for the dynamic and situated character of human translation.

3 Connectionism

Connectionist approaches (e.g. Rumelhart, McClelland and the PDP Research Group 1986) do not view cognition as symbol manipulation, but as the creation of dynamic patterns of activity in a network of interconnected units. Meanings are not understood as invariable, discrete packets of information, but as patterns that emerge in an unpredictable way from the parallel activation of neural connections. Neural networks operate at a sub-symbolic level; in them, single units do not carry meaning; it emerges dynamically from the patterns of activation of the whole network (Bechtel and Abrahamsen [1991] 2002). Connectionist systems do not contain explicit meanings, nor do they contain rules; both, meaning and rules, emerge by the activation of the system (Hendriks-Jansen 1996).

Connectionism depicts meaning construction as a dynamic process of pattern recognition and completion. Neural networks *learn* from each new input, changing the strengths of their connections. Each instance of learning causes a slight adjustment of the connection weights between the units. For this reason, the activation patterns of the system can be seen as internal representations based on *experience*. Concepts like those of *prototype* (Rosch 1973), *schema* (Schank and Abelson 1977), and *frame* (Fillmore 1976) are coherent with connectionist approaches: they are patterns of action and thought arrived at through experience.

To solve the grounding problem posed by symbolic structures, hybrid connectionist/symbolic models and pure connectionist models have been proposed. In hybrid models (e.g. Harnad 1993), neural networks ground the abstract symbols in categorical representations acquired during category learning tasks. However, as we have seen, the problem of symbol grounding is inherent to the system of abstract symbols, and it cannot be solved just connecting them with entities in the world or with perceptual units. Such connections are not enough to transform the system into a model of human cognition (Hendriks-Jansen 1996). As for pure connectionist models, they have been criticized as to the production of meaning for objections similar to those raised to criticize the symbol manipulation paradigm: because they are disembodied (their conceptual representations are not biologically constrained), and because, like symbol processing systems, they rest on an input-output model (Hendriks-Jansen 1996), that is, they are isolated from their environment.

In any case, connectionism is not a theory of mind but only a technology, and, as such, it can be used to model different (even conflicting) approaches to cognition (Zlatev 1999). So, on one side, some neural networks function like systems of amodal and arbitrary symbols; in particular, those in which a layer of perceptual units is arbitrarily connected to a layer of conceptual units

(Barsalou 1999). On the other side, other connectionist architectures, like those proposed by Barsalou (1999), try to model a grounded meaning construction system, representing perception and knowledge in a common layer of units.

Connectionist architectures cannot provide a global solution to the problem of symbol grounding; as in the case of symbolic architectures, they need an external interpreter. The *meaning* of the patterns of activation derives from the programmer's choice of input and output units and from the meanings assigned to them (Hendriks-Jansen 1996). They can nevertheless model different aspects of meaning construction as viewed from the perspective of embodied and situated cognition. For example, Zlatev (1999) uses the connectionist system of Regier (1992) to illustrate some aspects of situated and embodied semantics. Other connectionist experiments explore how language works as a scaffold for situated action (Clowes and Morse 2005). They depart from the idea, first explored by Vygotsky (1986), that language not only serves communication, but also the development of cognitive structures. Neural networks are used to model distributed, situated and social cognition processes, either isolated or else combined with symbolic systems or robots (Cangelosi 2008). These models can function as a bridge to situated cognition, showing how meaning can emerge in human action, even though their *situatedness* is artificial and limited; they are not involved in a physical and social world (Zlatev 1999).

From the point of view of connectionism, translation cannot be viewed as a process of decoding and recoding discrete information units. Translators construct new meanings on the basis of their individual histories and experiences and they offer their readers the possibility of constructing their own ones (Risku 2004). Meaning is not predictable, because it emerges from the activation of neural networks whose disposition changes each time they are activated. German functionalist approaches (Hönig and Kussmaul 1982; Reiß and Vermeer 1984; Holz-Mänttäri 1984) are coherent in many aspects with connectionism; for instance, in their focus on creativity, context, individual experience and situation. From their point of view, the aim of translation is not transferring or reproducing meaning, but creating the structures that make the construction possible (Risku 2004). Some of the structures they explore in this context are those provided by prototype theory and scenes-and-frames semantics, which I turn to now.

3.1 Prototype theory

The Aristotelian idea that conceptual categories are defined by a set of sufficient and necessary features has been challenged at least since Wittgenstein (1953).

Empirical research on the content of categories indicates that in most cases few or no features are common to all members of a category (Rosch and Mervis 1975). Prototype theory is a model of human categorization processes in which the internal structure of a category is defined by a series of family resemblances, with some features applying to a subgroup of the category, some others applying to another subgroup, and a most representative element or prototype. As prototypes are patterns based on the recurrence of similar experiences, prototype theory is compatible with connectionist architectures. In fact, prototype effects like those described by Rosch (1975) have been modelled with neural networks (Bechtel and Abrahamsen [1991] 2002).

In its first, standard version, prototype theory (Rosch 1973, 1975) defined prototypes as experience-based mental representations that work as best examples or most central elements of a category. The internal structure of the category was described on the basis of the prototype effects observed and operationalized in the experiments (Lakoff 1987). In the revised version of prototype semantics (Rosch 1978), prototypes were no longer considered mental representations, nor were they viewed as the basis for describing the internal structure of a category. "To speak of *a prototype* at all is simply a convenient grammatical fiction, what is really referred to are judgements of degree of prototypicality. Only in some artificial categories is there by definition a single prototype" (Rosch 1978: 40).

A criticism of prototype theories argues that they tend to simplify categorization processes, because they eliminate all data not represented by the prototype (Stibel 2008). With only the information about a prototype, a neural network cannot extrapolate to other categories or to categorize the less typical members of a category, like whales or penguins (Kruschke 1992). As an alternative to prototype theories, Medin and Shaffer (1978) proposed exemplar theory, which allows for multiple prototypes in a given category. For example, Google uses exemplar models in its search and advertising systems (Stibel 2008).

Prototype theory has been applied to translation, for instance, by Vannerem and Snell-Hornby (1986), Vermeer and Witte (1990), and Kussmaul (2000, 2007). Kussmaul (2000) advocates for prototype theory, because it takes into account comprehension processes based on experience, as opposed to checklist semantics of formal logics and generative grammar. Nevertheless, he also criticizes prototype theory for its tendency to study the meanings of decontextualized words, and because it does not explain why the internal structure of a category can be described in a different way in each context and each communicative situation.

Vermeer and Witte (1990) – like Rosch (1978) – highlighted the cultural character of prototypes, and described them as culture-specific. In their description of a prototype as a *Grundform* ('basic form') or a *Urgestalt* ('original form'), Vermeer and Witte (1990) did not seem to take into account the revisions to the theory made by Rosch (1978). They viewed prototypes as mental representations specific of a given cultural group like, for instance, the dog as a prototype of pet in the European urban culture (Vermeer and Witte 1990: 25). One of the risks of adopting a static notion of prototype in translation is that meaning construction processes can be biased towards stereotypical structures. In the revised version of prototype theory (Rosch 1978), the notion of prototype as an explanatory construct is abandoned for a similar reason: prototypes had drifted towards being understood as stable entities and had become reified.

> First, the notion of prototype has tended to become reified as though it meant a specific category member or mental structure. Questions are then asked in an either-or fashion about whether something is or is not the prototype or part of the prototype in exactly the same way in which the question would previously have been asked about the category boundary. (Rosch 1978: 36)

Vermeer (e.g. 1994) has repeatedly stressed the dynamic and situated character of meaning construction. When they applied prototype theory to translation, Vermeer and Witte (1990) added a historical component to make the model more dynamic, and suggested that prototypes are not given once and for all, neither for a society nor for an individual. However, their interpretation of prototypes tended to reify this notion in the sense pointed to by Rosch (1978), as evidenced in the examples they offered (Vermeer and Witte 1990: 22–29). Meaning cannot be exclusively grounded on this kind of predetermined structures; otherwise, we would be providing the target reader with tools for constructing stereotyped meanings (which does not seem to be the case). Perhaps, as advocated by Risku (2002), translation approaches should relativize the role played by mental representations like prototypes in the processes of text comprehension. These structures can be used as initial scaffolding, but meaning needs to be grounded ultimately in the situation of reception anticipated by the translator. As she puts it:

> If Situated Cognition were taken seriously, a different role would have to be given to prototypes, cultural norms and conventions – they are initial hypotheses, but always adapt to the specifics of the anticipated situation. Thus, the readers of the text in its anticipated situation will eventually create new, more or less *a*prototypical understandings. This fact emphasizes the importance of testing translation on authentic readers [. . .]. (Risku 2002: 528)

Translators often work under time pressure, and do not always have the possibility of testing their translations with authentic readers. They produce texts for somebody else, to be read in a situation in which they are normally not present

(Holz-Mänttäri 1993). For this reason, translators may need the support of some cognitive structures that help them anticipate the meaning construction processes of their addressees. However, these structures (for instance, cultural prototypes) cannot be taken as absolute criteria, nor should they be systematically applied.

3.2 Frame Semantics

A point common to both Frame Semantics and connectionism is describing meaning construction as a process where experience is interpreted following structured patterns (frames). Fillmore (1968) developed his notion of *frame* in his case grammar, where a *case frame*, associated with a word, was thought of as the conceptualization of an event from a given perspective (Fillmore 1977). Frames are cognitive and interactional structures that help language users to interpret their environment and to communicate with others (Fillmore 1976).

Whereas formal knowledge can be formulated propositionally, Fillmore's approach was based on experiential knowledge, which is gestalt-like and depends on experience. As a clear case of experiential knowledge, Fillmore (1977) mentioned the recognition of somebody's face. This is the type of knowledge modelled by neural networks, based on the recognition of patterns. As to the symbol-grounding problem, it is interesting to analyze Fillmore's (1985) contrast of structural semantics and Frame Semantics. While the first is described in terms of *"relations among words*, existing solely within 'the linguistic system'"*, Frame Semantics "sees the need to describe the conceptual underpinnings of a linguistically coded conceptual system independently of such putative pure intra-linguistic structures" (Fillmore 1985: 225, footnote 6, author's italics). The descriptions of lexical domains offered by structural semantics did not provide an answer to the question of grounding. If words are amodal symbols, and the description of their meanings is based on their patterns of relationships, how is language connected to experience? On the other hand, frames are structures grounded on experience.

In his article of 1977, Fillmore proposed his scenes-and-frames semantics as an alternative to semantic models based on truth conditions, taking prototype theories as a point of departure. Later works dropped the distinction between scenes and frames and both concepts were fused in the notion of frame, as suggested by Fillmore's (1985) list of cognitive structures similar to frames, which included scenes. In the last decade, Frame Semantics has been implemented in the Frame-Net project (Baker, Fillmore, and Cronin 2003; see also Boas, this volume), which aims to create an on-line lexical resource for English. Many other languages have followed suit. Frame Semantics has provided a theoretical framework for many studies that explore possible applications of Cognitive Linguistics to translation. For instance, it provides Rojo (2002a, 2002b) with a method to incorporate the social context into the description of language and to study the translation of humour: as cognitive and interactional structures, frames have a social dimension. Other studies in computational lexicography are aimed at creating multilingual lexical databases using semantic frames as interlingual representations. These databases can be useful tools for human and machine translation (Boas 2005, 2009, this volume). Frame Semantics also provides a framework to analyze semantic relations between frames and to study rephrasing, which can shed light on the processes involved in interlingual translation (Hasegawa et al. 2006). Here I will focus on scenes-and-frames semantics and its application to translation by German functionalists (see also Muñoz Martín, this volume), an approach that raises interesting questions in relation with the grounding of meaning on experiential cognitive structures; in particular, on mental images.

3.2.1 Scenes and frames

Fillmore only uses the concept of *scene* in his 1977 article. This concept was introduced as a tool to analyze the temporal development of text comprehension processes. In this context, a scene was described as an image, a picture of the world activated in the mind of the interpreter that, during the comprehension process, was developed and filled out. Fillmore's (1977) scenes-and-frames model depicted text comprehension as a process with three main elements: (i) lexical and grammatical content; (ii) the frames triggered by it and (iii) the scenes activated by these frames. Fillmore (1977) underscored frames as conceptual structures that yield a perspective to organize events. They were associated with linguistic forms (or choices), but they were not linguistic forms. Some of them were provided by language, but "most of them can be said to exist independently of language" (Fillmore 1985: 229, note 12).

Scenes-and-frames semantics was formulated, in Fillmore's (1977: 61) words, in an "imprecise way", and its main concepts received different interpretations when applied to translation by German functionalists. Vannerem and Snell-Hornby (1986) described scenes-and-frames as a model with two elements: linguistic frames and the scenes evoked by them. They interpreted Fillmore's concept of frame as linguistic coding of a scene, and identified text comprehension with capturing the scenes beneath the text. Once this had been achieved, the text could be transferred into the target language. Vermeer and Witte (1990) defined frame as double coding of a scene (at object level and at a meta-level), even though they noted that Fillmore (1977) did not view a frame as a linguistic coding of a scene, but as a field of possible expressions for a scene. The problem with these definitions is that they reduce drastically the interpretation choices. If a frame was the codification of a scene, you only had to look in the corresponding code to decode it. However, as stated by Vermeer and Witte (1990), one and the same frame can evoke different scenes in different recipients, or even in the same one, and therefore the model of coding/decoding does not suffice to describe comprehension, let alone translation's cognitive processes.

The interpretation of scenes and frames semantics offered by Vermeer and Witte (1990) is reminiscent of Seleskovitch's (1968) model of deverbalization in interpretation, where sense is represented as a mental image. This model suggests a three-step process, in which internal images function as *tertia comparationis*. The task of the translator or interpreter consists in deverbalize the source text and reverbalize its meaning in the target language, a scheme that corresponds to the coding/decoding model. Vermeer and Witte (1990: 72) were aware of this problem when they stated that scenes were not *tertia comparationis* and that the translator's task was not just transcoding frames. Quite on the contrary, the scenes behind the frames must be constructed each time anew.

Kussmaul (2000) focused on the metaphorical structure of the scene/frame relation and interpreted scenes as mental images, and frames as something that surrounds and limits these images and highlights parts of them. Kussmaul (2007) considers these images the starting point to draft the target text, and sees the scenes-and-frames model as a good source of hypotheses about the processes of comprehension and reverbalization by translation. Vannerem and Snell-Hornby (1986), Vermeer and Witte (1990), and Kussmaul (2000, 2007) argued that the conscious production of mental images can help translators (in particular, during learning processes) to construct coherent meanings and to elaborate coherent translations. The cognitive patterns described by prototype theories and Frame Semantics can be useful tools by the processes of meaning construction in translation, which are normally artificially situated. But how can they contribute to the grounding of meanings without biasing the processes towards reproducing stereotypes or recoding images as *tertia comparationis*? For situated cognition, these cognitive patterns have only a relative value. In translation, this means that intercultural comparisons of prototypical and schematic meanings could have only a limited application (Risku 2004). Embodied embedded approaches to cognition provide a framework to study how these and other cognitive patterns can be dynamically applied to constructing meanings and situations in the translation process.

4 Embodied and situated cognition

The solution to the problem of symbol grounding proposed by embodied embedded cognition is to drop the assumption that meaning is based on abstract, amodal, and arbitrary symbols (Glenberg and Roberston 2000). Embodied approaches ground meaning in bodily experience, for instance, through *image schemas* (Johnson 1987; Lakoff 1987). Image schemas are simple structures recurrent in our everyday experience like containers, paths, and links, or orientations like up-down and front-back. These schemas structure our experience and are metaphorically projected to abstract domains, providing them with a perceptually based conceptual structure. The theory of conceptual metaphor (Lakoff and Johnson 1980, 1999) provides an explanation of how abstract thinking can be grounded in bodily action and experience.

Image schemas play a central role in Cognitive Linguistics as the basis for linguistic meaning, but they have divergent definitions (Zlatev 2005). Dewell (2005) argues that the dynamic character of image schemas has been underestimated in Cognitive Linguistics, and advocates for a return to Johnson's (1987) conception of image schemas as dynamic patterns, showing how an apparently static structure like container is ontogenetically preceded by dynamic schemas. This approach challenges the standard view of cognition, which conceives conceptual structures as static representations that can be activated in different contexts (Smith and Jones 1993). According to Dewell (2005), conceptual structures are dynamic patterns based on action.

Glenberg (1997) and others have proposed that language and meaning are grounded in action. "We know that brains evolved for action. Given that evolution tends to be conservative, we might suppose that other systems, for example, language, are built on a base of action" (Glenberg 2008: 72). Neuroscience offers some empirical support for this hypothesis: for instance, when people hear verbs and sentences describing different kinds of actions, they activate the corresponding motor areas of the brain (Hauk, Johnsrude, and Pulvermüller 2004; Buccino et al. 2005). Behavioural work offers some additional data showing that verbally described actions are better comprehended when subjects first form their hand into a shape adequate for the action (Morrow and Clark 1989). Research in developmental psychology provides interesting data as well: for example, reading comprehension in children improves with the manipulation of toys related to the meaning of the sentences (Glenberg et al. 2004).

The grounding of meaning in action is coherent with German functionalism, in particular with the *Skoposttheorie*, which defined translation as purposeful situated action (Vermeer 1996), and with the *theory of translatory action* (Holz-Mänttäri 1984), which defined the translator's work within a framework of cooperation with different actors (clients, addressees, designers, authors, etc.). From the point of view of functionalism, translation is always situation-specific; each target text is designed for a specific target situation. *Skopostheorie* and the *theory of translatory action* have many traits in common with situated and embodied approaches to cognition: both highlight action in situation and culture; both offer a dynamic, relativistic view of meaning construction. However, functionalist theories developed in the 1980s were not based on situated cognition (Risku 2000, 2004). They had different focuses; in some aspects they even had opposite views. In general, these approaches were more conservative than situated cognition; in their first formulations (Reiß and Vermeer 1984; Holz-Mänttäri 1984), they coincided partially with symbol manipulation and connectionist approaches, and that lead to some contradictions (Martín de León 2005, 2008).

As commented above in relation with the notions of prototype and scenes-and-frames, these and other cognitive structures do not play a very central role in situated cognition. In fact, the most radical approaches to situated cognition (e.g. Varela, Thompson, and Rosch 1991; Thelen and Smith 1994) question the very idea of representation (Clark 1997). From their point of view, intelligent behaviour does not follow any predetermined pattern. Action is opportunistic; it is situated in a complex (physical and social) world, and uses the momentary affordances (Gibson 1979) provided by the environment as scaffolding. Delegating knowledge to our environment, we reduce the need to store it in the brain. In fact, from the perspective of situated cognition, meaning is not something stored in the brain; it emerges in a dynamic system formed by brain, body, and environment (Risku 2002, 2004). The key elements for meaning construction are neither abstract, amodal symbols, as in the classical paradigm, nor mental patterns like frames or schemas, as in connectionism, but embodied action in a physical and social environment. In this context, Risku (2002: 528) criticizes the use of representational approaches like connectionism, prototype theory, and scenes-and-frames semantics in translation, because they assume the existence of internal representations.

However, human beings do use internal representations, and the ability to represent past, future, and hypothetical situations is at the core of our ability to use language. Clark (1997: 149, author's italics) advocated for maintaining the notion of internal representation, noting that "a large body of those representations will be *local* and *action-oriented* rather than objective and action independent". The concept of *action-oriented representation* seems to be especially relevant in the domain of translation, as representations constructed by translators are clearly oriented to action: to the action of translating and to the future action of target text reception, which is artificially anticipated by the translator (Holz-Mänttäri 1990). This anticipation, as a thought about future or hypothetical events and actions, must involve creating some kind of representations for the absent phenomena, in order to facilitate behavioural coordination without the guidance provided by the actual situation. So, as an offline activity, translation depends, at least partially, on the creation of internal representations. For these reason, it seems necessary to develop a theory of situated imagination in translation, in which the processes of meaning construction are modelled taking into account the support of internal representations in a dynamic way, coherent with the findings of embodied and situated cognition.

4.1 Mental images in translation

In the last decades, perceptual theories of cognition and meaning construction have been developed in Cognitive Linguistics, psychology, philosophy, and artificial intelligence. Langacker (1999: 625) found "evident similarities" between the mechanisms of construal (the ability to conceive the same situation in alternate ways) and basic aspects of visual perception, like *granularity* (the possibility of describing a situation with different levels of precision and detail) or selecting a focus of attention. Barsalou (1999) proposed a perceptual theory of knowledge based in modal, perceptual symbols. He argued that cognition is inherently perceptual, and that perceptual symbols are analogous to the perceptual states that produced them. Barsalou's model is based on the idea of mental simulation: perceptual symbols are organized in such a way that they allow cognitive systems to simulate entities or events that are not present. From a neurological viewpoint, a mental simulation is a top-down activation of a sensory-motor area in the absence of the corresponding stimulus.

In Barsalou's (1999) model, individuals have an adequate understanding of a kind of thing when they can simulate it. For instance, to understand a text, we run perceptual and motor simulations, which are in most cases unconscious. If unconscious mental processing during text comprehension has a perceptual basis, becoming aware of it can be very helpful for translators, for they can use consciously perceptual simulations to guide their processes of meaning construction and to anticipate the reactions of their addressees. In her description of professional text design (text production for somebody else's needs, which includes translation), Holz-Mänttäri (1990: 67) stated that translators cannot simply put themselves into authors' or addressees' shoes, but they must mentally build up worlds that resemble the natural worlds of authors and recipients. Building on the idea that mental simulations are part of comprehension processes, and on Holz-Mänttäri's (1990) notion of *mental construction of worlds*, it is possible to describe important parts of the translator's work in terms of mental simulations. From this perspective, the translation process calls for at least two types of simulations: those needed to comprehend the source text, and those necessary to imagine how target addressees are probably going to interpret the target text. These two kinds of simulations are not sequentially ordered; knowledge about the expectations and needs of the target audience can influence comprehension processes and their simulations from the beginning. Although translators need not to be conscious of these processes, becoming aware of them can become a learning strategy.

5 Social and distributed cognition

Social approaches to cognition have much in common with embodied embedded cognition; from their point of view, making sense is a collaborative process that occurs in discourse, not in isolated minds (Baber et al. 2008). Zlatev (2002, 2005) has proposed a biocultural model of meaning that connects the embodied and the social character of meaning production through bodily mimesis or "whole body imitation used for representational means" (Zlatev 2002: 265). Bodily mimesis is an interpersonal phenomenon, but, as language, can be internalized in the sense proposed by Vygotsky (1978). Internalized bodily mimesis corresponds, following Zlatev (2005), to mental simulations as described by Barsalou (1999). In this way, Zlatev introduces a sociocultural dimension in the scenario of mental simulation, which becomes internalized bodily mimesis, i.e., something shared by a community, like language is.

The main evidence for the biological reality of mimetic mental simulations is provided by mirror neurons. Rizzolatti and his colleagues discovered these neurons in the brain of a macaque monkey, and later a similar system of neurons was identified in humans (Di Pellegrino et al. 1992; Rizzolati and Sinigaglia 2006). Mirror neurons fire when we do something and when we see someone else doing the same thing. In both cases, we run partially identical motor programs. This is how we make sense of somebody else's actions.

Holz-Mänttäri (1984) defined translatory action as the production of texts with the aim to guide cooperation. She stressed the collaborative aspects of translation, both in relation with the translation process itself and with the superordinated structure of actions where the translated text should integrate. In her view, these two kinds of cooperation were oriented by the common goals of the participants in the translation and communication processes. This social coordination could not be possible without the ability to assign mental states to others, in order to explain and predict their behaviour. This ability – which is known as a theory of mind – has traditionally been understood as inferential; recent approaches to intersubjectivity, however, claim that this ability, in its most basic forms, is not inferential, but rather direct (Zlatev et al. 2008). Evidence from research on mirror neurons (Gallese and Goldman 1998) supports the hypothesis that human communication relies on direct forms of intersubjectivity. In face-to-face communication, we always have a perceptual understanding about what the other person feels (Gallagher and Hutto 2008). Blakemore and Decety (2001) suggest that the system of mirror neurons could be the basis for ascribing mental states to other persons through mental simulation. In a similar way, mental simulation could help to ascribe mental states to other persons during off-line communication. As stated above, being able to anticipate the addressees' expectations can be crucial for translators, who need to imagine how their audience is going to construct meanings.

Traditionally, cognitive science has located cognition in the individual. The approach of distributed cognition (Hutchins 1995) has challenged this view, defining cognitive processes as extended beyond the individual and distributed between persons and artefacts. From the point of view of distributed cognition, translations are not only done by the translator, but by complex systems which include translators with their social and physical environments and their cultural artefacts, like language and computers. Researching distributed cognition in translation amounts to studying complex real-life translation projects. Risku (2002: 530) adopted a distributed cognitive view on translation and proposed to research not only what happens in the translator's brain, but also "in the hands, in the computers, on the desks, in the languages, in the dialogs of translators". Risku (2004) carried out a field study based on participatory observation at an international translation agency in Vienna, which works with over 1,000 specialized translators and technical communicators around the world. The approach was qualitative, based on the observation and analysis of a real-life working environment.

Dragsted (2008) described the use of a translation memory system by a group of translators working in a translation project as an instance of distributed or collaborative cognition. In this project, the translators shared their cognitive resources through the common database and constructed a common understanding of the source text and a common view of their target text. Decisions about the wording of the target text were not taken by individual translators separately, but they were rather shared by the group through the memory system. This in turn influenced the way individuals understood the source text and their view of the developing target text. In this way, the meaning was implicitly "agreed on" by the group. Collaborative work made by professional translators or by students can be seen as a distributed, social cognition process in which meanings are collectively constructed and negotiated (Kiraly 2000, 2003).

6 Summary

Cognitive models of meaning based on systems of abstract symbols, predicate arguments, or truth conditions cannot explain how meaning is constructed, nor can they be useful tools for human translation. As stated by Zlatev (2002: 282, author's italics), *"meaning is co-extensional with life"*. Artificial systems cannot produce meaning, because they do not have an intrinsic value system to preserve the system's organization. Hence, meaning needs to be grounded in embodied embedded actions. Neural networks can be viewed as useful tools for modelling different aspects of situated meaning construction, and mental structures like prototypes and frames can be used as initial scaffolding in translators training. The functionalists' application to translation of prototype theory and the scenes-and-frames model showed how constructing mental images could guide the processes of meaning construction by translation. However, these and other cognitive structures have been usually understood as static representations that can be activated in different contexts (Dewell 2005). As such, they cannot explain the dynamic processes of meaning construction within situated action.

However, cognitive models of meaning construction during translation must be representational; otherwise, they cannot account for off-line processes of communication. The notion of *mental simulation* provides translatology with a dynamic model of meaning construction that is, at the same time, representational, embodied and situated. The conscious elaboration of mental images can function as a tool for translators. Mental simulations are not static schemas but rather internal actions, dynamic processes adapted to each situation. Inferences made during the translation process can be based on the affordances provided by these simulations, like on-line meaning construction is based on the affordances provided by the environment (Barsalou 1999: 605). The concept of mimetic schema (Zlatev 2005) introduces a social dimension in this framework: mimetic schemas emerge through imitation and are shared in a social community. They can also be internalized as mental simulations, providing translators with a social and embodied ground to construct meanings and to anticipate their addressees' reactions. Only within a framework that is both representational and situated can we understand translation and prepare future translators for their work, which is, at the same time, uncoupled from the source and the target situations and situated in a complex professional environment.

Future research on translation may benefit from the insights of cognitive science on the grounding of meaning in body, action, society, and cultural artefacts. Embodied embedded perspectives provide us with models to understand how our bodily action shapes our processes of meaning construction. Social and distributed approaches offer a view of meaning construction processes in social interaction, beyond the limits of the individual mind. These and other aspects of meaning construction processes should not be understood as clearly delimited fields, but as complementary perspectives that illuminate each other. From the very beginning, our embodied experiences are socially mediated; our learning processes are distributed between persons and artefacts. Cognition cannot be studied in isolation from bodily action, and neither can translation. Gaining a deeper insight on how we construct meaning during translation is very important for translatology. I hope to have contributed to this goal.

References

Baber, Chris, Paul Smith, James Cross, John Hunter and Richard McMaster 2008 Crime scene investigation as distributed cognition. In: Itiel E. Dror and Stevan Harnad (eds.), *Cognition distributed*, 159–184. Amsterdam: John Benjamins.
Baker, Collin F., Charles J. Fillmore and Beau Cronin 2003 The structure of the FrameNet database. *International Journal of Lexicography* 16.3: 281–296.
Barsalou, Lawrence D. 1999 Perceptual symbol systems. *Behavioral and Brain Sciences* 22: 577–660.
Bechtel, William and Adele Abrahamsen [1991] 2002 *Connectionism and the mind: Parallel processing, dynamics, and evolution in networks*. 2nd edition. Malden, MA: Blackwell.
Blakemore, Sarah-Jayne and Jean Decety 2001 From the perception of action to the understanding of intention. *Nature Reviews Neuroscience* 2: 561–567.
Boas, Hans C. 2005 Semantic frames as interlingual representations for multilingual lexical databases. *International Journal of Lexicography* 18.4: 445–478.
Boas, Hans C. (ed.) 2009 *Multilingual FrameNets in computational lexicography: Methods and applications*. Berlin: Mouton de Gruyter.
Bruner, Jerome [1991] 2006 *Actos de significado. Más allá de la revolución cognitiva*. Translated by J. C. Gómez Crespo and J. L. Linaza. Madrid: Alianza.
Buccino, Giovanni, Lucia Riggio, Giorgia Melli, Ferdinand Binkofski, Vittorio Gallese and Giacomo Rizzolatti 2005 Listening to action-related sentences modulates the activity of the motor system: A combined TMS and behavioral study. *Cognitive Brain Research* 24: 355–363.
Burguess, Curt and Kevin Lund 1997 Representing abstract words and emotional connotation in high-dimensional memory space. In: Michael G. Shafto and Pat Langley (eds.), *Proceedings of the Nineteenth Annual Meeting of the Cognitive Science Society*, 61–66. Hillsdale, NJ: Erlbaum.
Cangelosi, Angelo 2008 The grounding and sharing of symbols. In: Itiel E. Dror and Stevan Harnad (eds.), *Cognition distributed*, 83–92. Amsterdam: John Benjamins.
Chomsky, Noam 1965 *Aspects of the theory of syntax*. Cambridge, MA: MIT Press.
Clark, Andy 1997 *Being there: Putting brain, body, and world together again*. Cambridge, MA: MIT Press.

Clowes, Robert and Anthony F. Morse 2005 Scaffolding cognition with words. In: Luc Berthouze, Frédéric Kaplan, Hideki Kozima, Hiroyuki Yano, Jürgen Konczak, Giorgio Metta, Jacqueline Nadel, Giulio Sandini and Christina Balkenius (eds.), *Proceedings of the Fifth International Workshop on Epigenetic Robotics: Modeling Cognitive Development in Robotic Systems*, 101–105. Lund, Sweden: Lund University Cognitive Studies.

De Vega, Manuel 1984 *Introducción a la Psicología Cognitiva*. Madrid: Alianza.

De Vega, Manuel 2002 Del significado simbólico al significado corpóreo. *Estudios de Psicología* 23.2: 153–174.

Dewell, Robert 2005 Dynamic patterns of containment. In: Beate Hampe (ed.), *From perception to meaning: Image schemas in cognitive linguistics*, 369–394. The Hague: Mouton de Gruyter.

Di Pellegrino, Giuseppe, Luciano Fadiga, Leonardo Fogassi, Vittorio Gallese and Giacomo Rizzolatti 1992 Understanding motor events: A neurophysiological study. *Experimental Brain Research* 91.1: 176–180.

Dragsted, Barbara 2008 Computer-aided translation as a distributed cognitive task. In: Itiel E. Dror and Stevan Harnad (eds.), *Cognition distributed*, 237–256. Amsterdam: John Benjamins.

Fillmore, Charles J. 1968 The case for case. In: Emmon Bach and Robert T. Harms (eds.), *Universals in linguistic theory*, 1–88. New York: Holt, Rinehart and Winston.

Fillmore, Charles J. 1976 Frame semantics and the nature of language. *Annals of the New York Academy of Sciences: Conference on the Origin and Development of Language and Speech* 280: 20–32.

Fillmore, Charles J. 1977 Scenes-and-frames semantics. In: Antonio Zampolli (ed.), *Linguistic structures processing*, 55–88. Amsterdam: North Holland.

Fillmore, Charles J. 1985 Frames and the semantics of understanding. *Quaderni di Semantica* 6.2: 222–254.

Fodor, Jerry A. 1983 *The modularity of mind*. Cambridge, MA: MIT Press.

Gallagher, Shaun and Daniel D. Hutto. 2008 Understanding others through primary interaction and narrative practice. In: Jordan Zlatev, Timothy P. Racine, Chris Sinha and Esa Itkonen (eds.), *The shared mind: Perspectives on intersubjectivity*, 17–38. Amsterdam: John Benjamins.

Gallese, Vittorio and Alvin Goldman 1998 Mirror neurons and the simulation theory of mind-reading. *Trends in Cognitive Sciences* 2.12: 493–501.

Gibson, James J. 1979 *The ecological approach to visual perception*. Boston: Houghton Mifflin.

Glenberg, Arthur M. 1997 What memory is for. *Behavioral and Brain Sciences* 20: 1–55.

Glenberg, Arthur M. 2008 Radical changes in cognitive process due to technology: A jaundiced view. In: Itiel E. Dror and Stevan Harnad (eds.), *Cognition distributed*, 71–82. Amsterdam: John Benjamins.

Glenberg, Arthur M., Tiana Gutiérrez, Joel R. Levin, Sandra Japuntich and Michael P. Kaschak 2004 Activity and imagined activity can enhance young children's reading comprehension. *Journal of Educational Psychology* 96: 424–436.

Glenberg, Arthur M., and David A. Roberston 2000 Symbol grounding and meaning: A comparison of high-dimensional and embodied theories of meaning. *Journal of Memory and Language* 43: 379–401.

Harnad, Stevan 1987 Category induction and representation. In: Stevan Harnad (ed.), *Categorical perception: The groundwork of cognition*, 535–565. Cambridge: Cambridge University Press.

Harnad, Stevan 1990 The symbol grounding problem. *Physica D* 42: 335–346.
Harnad, Stevan 1993 Symbol grounding is an empirical problem: Neural nets are just a candidate component. *Proceedings of the Fifteenth Annual Meeting of the Cognitive Science Society*, 169-174. Hillsdale, NJ: Lawrence Erlbaum Associates.
Hasegawa, Yoko, Kyoko Hirose Ohara, Russell Lee-Goldman and Charles J. Fillmore 2006 Frame integration, head switching, and translation: RISK in English and Japanese. Available at: http://citeseerx.ist.psu.edu/viewdoc/versions?doi=10.1.1.130.5237.
Hauk, Olaf, Ingrid Johnsrude and Friedemann Pulvermüller 2004 Somatotopic representation of action words in human motor and pre-motor cortex. *Neuron* 41: 301–307.
Hendriks-Jansen, Horst 1996 *Catching ourselves in the act: Situated activity, interactive emergence, evolution, and human thought*. Cambridge, MA: MIT Press.
Holz-Mänttäri, Justa 1984 *Translatorisches Handeln. Theorie und Methode*. Helsinki: Suomalainen Tiedeakatemia.
Holz-Mänttäri, Justa 1990 Das Transfer-Prinzip. In: Reiner Arntz and Gisela Thome (eds.), *Übersetzungswissenschaft. Ergebnisse und Perspektiven*, 59–70. Tübingen, Germany: Gunter Narr.
Holz-Mänttäri, Justa 1993 Textdesign – verantwortlich und gehirngerecht. In: Justa Holz-Mänttäri and Christiane Nord (eds.), *Traducere Navem. Festschrift für Katharina Reiß zum 70. Geburtstag*, 301–320. Tampere, Finland: Tampereen Yliopisto.
Hönig, Hans G. and Paul Kussmaul 1982 *Strategie der Übersetzung. Ein Lehr- und Arbeitsbuch*. Tübingen, Germany: Gunter Narr.
Hutchins, Edwin 1995 *Cognition in the wild*. Cambridge, MA: MIT Press.
Jäger, Gert 1975 *Translation und Translationslinguistik*. Halle (Saale), Germany: Niemeyer.
Johnson, Mark 1987 *The body in the mind*. Chicago: University of Chicago Press.
Kade, Otto 1968 *Zufall und Gesetzmäßigkeit in der Übersetzung*. (Beiheft zur Zeitschrift Fremdsprachen I.) Leipzig, Germany: VEB Verlag Enzyklopädie.
Kintsch, Walter 1998 *Comprehension: A paradigm for cognition*. Cambridge: Cambridge University Press.
Kintsch, Walter, and Teun A. van Dijk 1978 Towards a model of text comprehension and production. *Psychological Review* 85: 363–394.
Kiraly, Donald C. 2000 *A social constructivist approach to translator education*. Manchester: St. Jerome.
Kiraly, Donald C. 2003 From instruction to collaborative construction: A passing fad or the promise of a paradigm shift in translator education? In: Brian J. Baer and Geoffrey S. Koby (eds.), *Beyond the ivory tower*, 3–32. (American Translators Association Scholarly Monograph Series XII.) Amsterdam: John Benjamins.
Kruschke, John K. 1992 ALCOVE: An exemplar based connectionist model of category learning. *Psychological Review* 99: 22–44.
Kussmaul, Paul 2000 *Kreatives Übersetzen*. Tübingen, Germany: Stauffenburg.
Kussmaul, Paul 2007 *Verstehen und Übersetzen. Ein Lehr- und Arbeitsbuch*. Tübingen, Germany: Gunter Narr.
Lakoff, George 1987 *Women, fire, and dangerous things: What categories reveal about the mind*. Chicago: University of Chicago Press.
Lakoff, George and Mark Johnson 1980 *Metaphors we live by*. Chicago: University of Chicago Press.
Lakoff, George and Mark Johnson 1999 *Philosophy in the flesh: The embodied mind and its challenge to Western thought*. New York: Basic Books.

Landauer, Thomas K. and Susan T. Dumais 1997 A solution to Plato's problem: The latent semantic analysis theory of acquisition, induction, and representation of knowledge. *Psychological Review* 104: 211–240.
Langacker, Ronald W. 1999 A view from cognitive linguistics. Commentary to Barsalou, Lawrence W. Perceptual symbol systems. *Behavioral and Brain Sciences* 22: 625.
Martín de León, Celia 2005 *Contenedores, recorridos y metas. Metáforas en la traductología funcionalista*. (Studien zur romanischen Sprachwissenschaft und interkulturellen Kommunikation 24.) Frankfurt am Main: Peter Lang.
Martín de León, Celia 2008 Skopos and beyond: A critical study of functionalism. *Target* 20.1: 1–28.
Martín de León, Celia 2010 Metaphorical models of translation: Transfer vs imitation and action. In: James St. André (ed.), *Thinking through translation with metaphors*, 75–108. Manchester: St. Jerome.
Medin, Douglas L. and Marguerite M. Shaffer 1978 A context theory of classification learning. *Psychological Review* 85: 207–238.
Morrow, Daniel G. and Herbert H. Clark 1989 Interpreting words in spatial descriptions. *Language and Cognitive Processes* 3: 275–291.
Neubert, Albrecht 1973 Theorie und Praxis für die Übersetzungswissenschaft. *Linguistische Arbeitsberichte* 7: 120–144.
Newell, Allan and Herbert A. Simon 1976 Computer science as empirical enquiry. *Communications of the ACM* 19: 113–126.
Nida, Eugene A. 1964 *Toward a science of translating*. Leiden: Brill.
Pinker, Steven 1994 *The language instinct*. New York: William Morrow.
Putnam, Hilary 1981 *Reason, truth, and history*. Cambridge: Cambridge University Press.
Ratcliff, Roger and Gail McKoon 1978 Priming in item recognition: Evidence for the propositional structure of sentences. *Journal of Verbal Learning and Verbal Behaviour* 17: 403–417.
Reddy, Michael J. [1979] 1993 The conduit metaphor: A case of frame conflict in our language about language. In: Andrew Ortony (ed.), *Metaphor and thought*, 164–201. 2nd edition, revised. Cambridge: Cambridge University Press.
Regier, Terrance P. 1992 *The acquisition of lexical semantics for spatial terms: A connectionist model of perceptual categorisation*. PhD dissertation TR-92-062, International Computer Science Institute, University of California, Berkeley.
Reiß, Katharina and Hans J. Vermeer 1984 *Grundlegung einer allgemeinen Translationstheorie*. (Linguistische Arbeiten 147.) Tübingen, Germany: Niemeyer.
Risku, Hanna 2000 *Situated Translation* und *Situated Cognition*: ungleiche Schwestern. In: Mira Kadric, Klaus Kaindl and Franz Pöchhacker (eds.), *Translationswissenschaft. Festschrift für Mary-Snell-Hornby zum 60. Geburtstag*, 81–91. Tübingen, Germany: Stauffenburg.
Risku, Hanna 2002 Situatedness in translation studies. *Cognitive Systems Research* 3: 523–533.
Risku, Hanna 2004 *Translationsmanagement: Interkulturelle Fachkommunikation im Informationszeitalter*. Tübingen, Germany: Gunter Narr.
Rizzolati, Giacomo and Corrado Sinigaglia. 2006. *Las neuronas espejo. Los mecanismos de la empatía emocional*. Translated by B. Moreno Carrillo. Barcelona: Paidós.
Rojo, Ana 2002a Applying frame semantics to translation. *Meta* 47: 311–350.
Rojo, Ana 2002b Frame semantics and the translation of humor. *Babel: International Journal of Translation* 48: 34–77.

Rosch, Eleanor 1973 Natural categories. *Cognitive Psychology* 4: 328–350.
Rosch, Eleanor 1975 Universals and cultural specifics in human categorization. In: Richard W. Brislin, Stephen Bochner and Walter J. Lonner (eds.), *Cross-cultural perspectives on learning*, 177–206. New York: Halstedt Press.
Rosch, Eleanor 1978 Principles of categorization. In: Eleanor Rosch and Barbara L. Lloyd (eds.), *Cognition and categorization*, 27–48. Hillsdale, NJ: Erlbaum.
Rosch, Eleanor and Carolyn B. Mervis 1975 Family resemblances: Studies in the internal structure of categories. *Cognitive Psychology* 7: 573–605.
Rumelhart, David E., James L. McClelland and the PDP Research Group 1986 *Parallel distributed processing, explorations in the microstructure of cognition*. Vol. 1: Foundations. Cambridge, MA: MIT Press.
Schank, Roger C. and Robert P. Abelson 1977 *Scripts, plans, goals, and understanding* Hillsdale, NJ: Erlbaum.
Seleskovitch, Danica 1968 *L'interprète dans les conférences internationales. Problèmes de langage et de communication*. Paris: Cahiers Champollion.
Shannon, Claude E. and Warren Weaver [1949] 1963 *The mathematical theory of communication*. Urbana: University of Illinois Press.
Smith, Linda and Susan S. Jones 1993 Cognition without concepts. *Cognitive Development* 8: 181–188.
Snell-Hornby, Mary [1988] 1995 *Translation studies: An integrated approach*. Revised edition. Amsterdam: John Benjamins.
Stibel, Jeffrey M. 2008 Categorization and technology innovation. In: Itiel E. Dror and Stevan Harnad (eds.), *Cognition distributed*, 145–158. Amsterdam: John Benjamins.
Thelen, Esther and Linda B. Smith 1994 *A dynamic systems approach to the development of cognition and action*. Cambridge, MA: MIT Press.
Van Dijk, Teun A. and Walter Kintsch 1983 *Strategies of discourse comprehension*. New York: Academic Press.
Vannerem, Mia and Mary Snell-Hornby 1986 Die Szene hinter dem Text: "scenes-and-frames semantics" in der Übersetzung. In: Mary Snell-Hornby (ed.), *Übersetzungswissenschaft. Eine Neuorientierung*, 184–205. Tübingen, Germany: Francke.
Varela, Francisco J., Evan Thompson and Eleanor Rosch 1991 *The embodied mind: Cognitive science and human experience*. Cambridge, MA: MIT Press.
Vermeer, Hans J. 1994 El mundo como proceso – Reflexiones traslatológicas. Translated by C. Martín de León. *Trabalhos em Lingüística Aplicada* 24: 5–18.
Vermeer, Hans J. 1996 *A skopos theory of translation (some arguments for and against)*. (Reihe Wissenschaft 1.) Heidelberg, Germany: TEXTconTEXT.
Vermeer, Hans J. and Heidrun Witte 1990 *Mögen Sie Zistrosen? Scenes & frames & channels im translatorischen Handeln*. (TEXTconTEXT Beiheft 3.) Heidelberg, Germany: Groos.
Vygotsky, Lev S. 1978 *Mind in society: The development of higher psychological processes*. Cambridge, MA: Harvard University Press.
Vygotsky, Lev S. 1986 *Thought and language*. Translated by Myshlenie i rech'. Revised and edited by Alex Kozulin. Cambridge, MA: MIT Press.
Wittgenstein, Ludwig 1953 *Philosophical investigations*. New York: Macmillan.
Zlatev, Jordan 1999 Situated embodied semantics and connectionist modeling. In: Jens Allwood and Peter Gärdenfors (eds.), *Cognitive semantics: Meaning and cognition*, 173–194. Amsterdam: John Benjamins.

Zlatev, Jordan 2002 Meaning = life (+ culture): An outline of a unified biocultural theory of meaning. *Evolution of Communication* 4.2: 255–299.
Zlatev, Jordan 2005 What's in a schema? Bodily mimesis and the grounding of language. In: Beate Hampe (ed.), *From perception to meaning: Image schemas in cognitive linguistics*, 313–342. The Hague: Mouton de Gruyter.
Zlatev, Jordan, Timothy P. Racine, Chris Sinha and Esa Itkonen 2008 Intersubjectivity. What makes us human? In: Jordan Zlatev, Timothy P. Racine, Chris Sinha and Esa Itkonen (eds.), *The shared mind: Perspectives on intersubjectivity*, 1–14. Amsterdam: John Benjamins.

Part II: **Meaning and translation**

Hans C. Boas
Frame Semantics and translation*

1 Introduction

This paper examines how insights from Frame Semantics can be applied to translation, both by humans and computers. In particular, it shows what types of semantic frames can be used for the creation of translation resources such as electronic dictionaries and whether frames differ with respect to their universal applicability across languages. A discussion of a variety of semantic frames such as Risk, Compliance, Self_Motion, and Theft illustrates the differences between frames and their applicability to the analysis of languages for translation purposes.

The paper is structured as follows. Section 2 traces the intellectual basis underlying Frame Semantics. Section 3 shows how the theoretical concepts of Frame Semantics have been implemented in the design of the FrameNet database, a large-scale corpus-based on-line lexical resource of English (Baker, Fillmore, and Lowe 1998; Fillmore and Baker 2010). Section 4 focuses on how frame-semantic concepts have been applied to translation issues since the 1990s, particularly in the construction of multilingual dictionaries. The final section provides an in-depth discussion of specific theoretical and applied issues surrounding the use of semantic frames for translation purposes: (i) re-usability of semantic frames for descriptions of other languages; (ii) universal versus culture-specific frames; (iii) profiling differences of particular frame elements across languages; (iv) syntactic valency and null instantiation; (v) choosing between frames when translating into different languages; and (vi) the compatibility of semantic frames and Wierzbicka's (2006) cultural scripts in the translation process.

---

* Many thanks to Judith Atzler and Marc Pierce for comments on an earlier version of this paper. The usual disclaimers apply. Work on this paper was supported by Title VI grant #P229A100014 (Center for Open Educational Resources and Language Learning) to the University of Texas at Austin as well as a fellowship for experienced researchers from the Alexander von Humboldt Foundation.

2 Frame Semantics[1]

During the 1970s and 1980s Charles Fillmore developed his Case Theory (1968) into a more sophisticated theory, which eventually became known as Frame Semantics, "a research program in empirical semantics and a descriptive framework for presenting the results of such research" (Fillmore 1982: 111). This approach differs from other theories of lexical meaning in that it builds on common backgrounds of knowledge (semantic frames) against which the meanings of words are interpreted.[2] A "frame is a cognitive structuring device, parts of which are indexed by words associated with it and used in the service of understanding" (Petruck 1996: 2). The central ideas underlying Frame Semantics can be characterized as follows:

> A word's meaning can be understood only with reference to a structured background of experience, beliefs, or practices, constituting a kind of conceptual prerequisite for understanding the meaning. Speakers can be said to know the meaning of the word only by first understanding the background frames that motivate the concept that the word encodes. Within such an approach, words or word senses are not related to each other directly, word to word, but only by way of their links to common background frames and indications of the manner in which their meanings highlight particular elements of such frames. (Fillmore and Atkins 1992: 76–77)[3]

To illustrate, consider the Theft frame, which involves several semantically related verbs such as *steal, snatch, shoplift, snitch, pinch, filch, purloin,* and *thieve,* among others. The Theft frame represents a scenario with different frame elements (FEs) that can be regarded as instances of broader semantic roles such as AGENT, UNDERGOER, INSTRUMENT, etc.[4] Giving precise definitions for FEs is important because the entirety of FEs comprises the frame description,

---

1 This section is based on Boas (2005a).
2 Fillmore's use of the concept of "frame" is somewhat related to work in artificial intelligence. For example, Minsky (1975: 212) describes a frame as a "data-structure representing a stereotypical situation". Work in psychology employs a similar concept that refers to knowledge structures for sequences of events; cf. Schank and Abelson's (1975) "restaurant script" (cf. Boas 2003: 164). For differences between semantic frames, scenes, and scenarios, see Schmidt (2009: 103) and Ziem (2008: 247–272). For differences between Frame Semantics and semantic field theories, see Fillmore and Atkins (1992: 76–79).
3 For a more detailed review of the main principles of Frame Semantics, see Fillmore, Johnson and Petruck (2003); Fillmore and Baker (2010); and Petruck (1996).
4 For an overview of different characterizations of semantic roles (also known as theta-roles), see, e.g. Dowty (1991); Fillmore (1968, 1975, 1985a); Jackendoff (1990); Langacker (1990); Ravin (1990); Ruppenhofer et al. (2006); and Van Valin and Wilkins (1996).

which in turn represents a schematic arrangement of the situation type that underlies the meanings of semantically related words as in the following examples.⁵

(1) a. *Nikki stole the watch from Carolyn.*
     b. *Jana nicked the book from Vaughan.*
     c. *Guido pinched the disk from the table.*
     d. *Ingrid filched the snack from Karen.*

In (1a)–(1d), the Theft frame is evoked by the verbs *steal, nick, pinch,* and *filch*. This frame represents a scenario with different core FEs such as GOODS (anything that can be taken away), PERPETRATOR (the person or other agent that takes the goods away), SOURCE (the initial location of the goods before they change location), and VICTIM (the person [or other sentient being or group] that owns the goods before they are taken away by the perpetrator). The frame description defines the relationships between FEs, in this case that a PERPETRATOR takes GOODS that belong to a VICTIM. For example, *stole* in (1a) is the target word that evokes the Theft frame. *Nikki* is the PERPETRATOR FE, *the watch* is the GOODS FE, and *from Carolyn* is the VICTIM FE. In (1c), *from the table* is the SOURCE FE. Interpreting the verbs in (1a)–(1d) as belonging to the Theft frame requires an understanding of illegal activities, property ownership, taking things, and a great deal more.⁶ Besides so-called core FEs there are other FEs that are peripheral from the perspective of the Theft frame such as MEANS (e.g. *by trickery*), TIME (e.g. *two days ago*), MANNER (e.g. *quietly*), or PLACE (e.g. *in the city*). These FEs do not belong to the set of core FEs of the Theft frame because they are also found among other frames of agentive action. The following section shows how the theoretical principles of Frame Semantics have been applied to the creation of a lexicographic database for English, namely FrameNet. Section 4 will then illustrate how frame-semantic principles have been applied to translation efforts, primarily through the creation of multi-lingual dictionaries.

---

5 Names of semantic frames are in Courier font. Names of FRAME ELEMENTS (FEs) are in small caps. Frame Elements differ from traditional universal semantic (or thematic) roles such as Agent or Patient in that they are specific to the frame in which they are used to describe participants in certain types of scenarios. "Tgt" stands for target word, which is the word that evokes the semantic frame.
6 Other parts of speech can also evoke frames. For example, nouns such as *shoplifter, snatcher, stealer, thief,* and *pickpocket* or adjectives such as *light-fingered, thieving,* and *stolen* also evoke the same Theft frame as the verbs in (1).

3 FrameNet[7]

The FrameNet project (Lowe, Baker, and Fillmore 1997; Baker, Fillmore, and Lowe 1998) applies the principles of Frame Semantics to the description and analysis of the English lexicon, thereby creating a database of lexical entries for several thousand words taken from a variety of semantic domains. Based on corpus data, FrameNet identifies and describes semantic frames and analyzes the meanings of words by appealing directly to the frames that underlie their meanings. In addition, it studies the syntactic properties of words by asking how their semantic properties are given syntactic form (Fillmore, Johnson, and Petruck 2003: 235). Between 1997 and 2010, FrameNet defined close to 9,000 lexical units (LUs) (a word in one of its senses) in more than 1,000 frames.

The workflow of FrameNet begins by defining frame descriptions (based on corpus evidence) for the words to be analyzed. Then, the following steps are taken: "(1) characterizing schematically the kind of entity or situation represented by the frame, (2) choosing mnemonics for labeling the entities or components of the frame, and (3) constructing a working list of words that appear to belong to the frame, where membership in the same frame will mean that the phrases that contain the LUs will all permit comparable semantic analyses" (Fillmore et al. 2003: 297). The next step focuses on finding corpus sentences in the British National Corpus that illustrate typical uses of the target words in specific frames. These corpus sentences are then extracted mechanically and annotated manually by tagging the FEs realized in them. Finally, lexical entries are automatically prepared and stored in the database (for more details, see Fillmore and Baker 2010).

The result of this workflow is an on-line dictionary of English that is structured in terms of semantic frames. Going to the FrameNet website, users can search – among other things – for entries of specific LUs, frame descriptions, and combinations thereof. Lexical entries in FrameNet offer a link to the definition of the frame evoked by a LU, including FE definitions, and example sentences exemplifying prototypical instances of FEs. In addition, FrameNet includes a list of all LUs evoking the same frame while also providing frame-specific information about various frame-to-frame relations, like the child-parent relation and sub-frame relation (Fillmore et al. 2003). For example, a search for the Compliance frame returns a frame description, together with a list of several semantically related words such as *adhere, adherence, comply, compliant,*

---

[7] This section is based on Boas (2009). The FrameNet data can be accessed online at http://framenet.icsi.berkeley.edu.

and *violate*, among others (Fillmore et al. 2003), all of which evoke the same frame. It represents a kind of situation in which there are ACTS and STATES_OF_AFFAIRS for which PROTAGONISTS are responsible and which violate some NCRM(s). The FE ACT identifies the act that is judged to be in or out of compliance with the norms. The FE NORM identifies the rules or norms that ought to guide a person's behavior. The FE PROTAGONIST refers to the person whose behavior is in or out of compliance with norms. Finally, the FE STATE_OF_AFFAIRS refers to the situation that may violate a law or rule (see Boas 2005a; Ruppenhofer et al. 2006).

A FrameNet entry consists of three parts. The first provides the Frame Element Table (a list of all FEs found within the frame) and corresponding annotated corpus sentences demonstrating how FEs are realized syntactically. FrameNet uses different colors to highlight each FE, making it easier to identify individual FEs. Due to formatting restrictions, FE names are not color-coded in Figures 5.1–5.3.

Figure 5.1 illustrates how words and phrases instantiating certain FEs in corpus sentences are annotated with the same FE names as in the FE table above

Num	FE/LUset(sort = FE; Compliance, *comply*, V,)
01	Act + Degree + **comply.V**+ Norm
02	Act + **comply.V**+ Norm
01	Norm + **comply.V**+ (Protagonist)
03	Protagonist+ **comply.V**+ Degree + Norm
01	Protagonist + **comply.V**+ Manner + Norm
10	Protagonist + **comply.V**+ Norm
01	Protagonist + **comply.V**+ Norm + Time
01	State_of_Affairs + **comply.V**+ Norm
01	State_of_Affairs + **comply.V**+ (Norm)
02	**comply.V**+ Norm + (Protagonist)
23	

01. : Act + Degree + **comply.V** + Norm
1. 123614: [<Act> The last minute addition of the recommendation] did not [<Degree> in any way] *comply*^{Tgt} [<Norm>with the law] and the recommendation would be quashed.
02. : Act + **comply.V** + Norm
1. 123626: The court was told that [<Act>her appearance before the registrar] was so ely to *comply*^{Tgt} [<Norm>with the formalities of Scots law].
2. 123758: [<Act>Spending by public sector organisations] has to *comply*^{Tgt} [<Norm> with complex and changing legal regulations], and is exposed to scrutiny at a number of levels.
01. : Norm + **comply.V** + (Protagonist)
1. 123932: If [<Norm>this rule] is not *complied*^{Tgt} [<Norm>with], the issuer is guilty of an offence, any subsequent contract etc entered into may be unenforceable and the issuer of the advertisement may face criminal charges and/or fines. [<Protagonist>CNI]

Figure 5.1: First part of FrameNet entry for *comply* (Boas 2009: 18)

them. This display allows users to see the variety of different FE instantiations across a broad spectrum of words and phrases. An important feature is the split of annotated corpus sentences into different groups according to different types of combinations of FEs.[8] For example, in the first annotated sentence in Figure 5.1, *comply*, which is the target ("Tgt") evoking the Compliance frame, occurs with the FEs ACT, DEGREE, and NORM, while in the second sentence it occurs only with ACT and NORM. FE names are displayed in terms of subscript notations following the first square bracket.

Figure 5.2 illustrates the second part of a lexical entry in FrameNet, namely the Realization Table of the Lexical Entry Report. Besides providing a dictionary definition of the relevant LU, in this case *comply*, it summarizes the different syntactic realizations of the FEs. The left column lists the names of different core FEs (ACT, NORM, PROTAGONIST, and STATE_OF_AFFAIRS), the middle column lists the number of annotated example sentences in FrameNet, and the right column lists the different types of syntactic realizations of the respective FEs. Consider the FE NORM, which appears 23 times, 21 of those times as a prepositional phrase headed by *with*, once as a definite null instantiation (DNI), once as an external noun phrase argument, and once as a prepositional phrase headed by *to* (for details see Boas 2005a).

Comply.v
Frame: Compliance
Definition: COD: act in accordance with a wish or command
The Frame elememts for this word sense are (with relizations):

Frame Element	Number Annotated	Realizations(s)	
Act	(3)	NP.Ext (3)	
Norm	(23)	PP[with].Dep	(21)
		DNI.–	(1)
		NP.Ext	(1)
		PP[to].Dep (1)	
Protagonist	(18)	CNI.–	(3)
		NP.Ext (15)	
State of Affairs	(2)	NP.Ext (2)	

Figure 5.2: FrameNet entry for *comply*, Realization Table (Boas 2009: 19)

---

8 Numbers in the table represent the total number of annotated example sentences in FrameNet. Numbers at the beginning of each annotated example sentence represent their location in the British National Corpus.

Valence patterns

These frame elements occur in the following syntactic patterns:

Number Annotated	Patterns		
3 TOTAL	Act	Norm	
(3)	NP	PP[with]	
	Ext	Dep	
1 TOTAL	Norm	Norm	Protagonist
(1)	NP	PP[with]	CNI
	Ext	Dep	–
16 TOTAL	Norm	Protagonist	
(2)	PP[with]	CNI	
	Dep	–	
(14)	PP[with]	NP	
	Dep	Ext	
1 TOTAL	Norm	Protagonist	Protagonist
(1)	PP[with]	NP	NP
	Dep	Ext	Ext
2 TOTAL	Norm	State_of_Affairs	
(1)	DNI	NP	
	–	Ext	
(1)	PP[to]	NP	
	Dep	Ext	

Figure 5.3: Partial FrameNet entry for *comply*, Valence Table (Boas 2009: 20)

The third part of the Lexical Entry Report summarizes the valence patterns found with a LU, that is, "the various combinations of frame elements and their syntactic realizations which might be present in a given sentence" (Fillmore, Johnson, and Petruck 2003: 330). The third column from the left in the valence table for *comply* in Figure 5.3 illustrates how the FE NORM may be realized in terms of two different types of external arguments: either as an external noun phrase argument, or as an external prepositional phrase headed by *with*. Clicking on the link (in this case "3" or "1") in the column to the left of the valence patterns leads the user to a display of annotated examples sentences illustrating the valence pattern (see Figure 5.1 above).[9]

---

9 FEs which are conceptually salient but do not occur as overt lexical or phrasal material are marked as null instantiations. There are three different types of null instantiation: Constructional Null Instantiation (CNI), Definite Null Instantiation (DNI), and Indefinite Null Instantiation (INI). See Fillmore et al. (2003: 320–321) and Ruppenhofer et al. (2006) for details.

FrameNet differs from other approaches to lexical description such as WordNet (Fellbaum 1998) in that it makes use of independent organizational units that are larger than words, i.e., semantic frames (see also Atkins [2002] 2008; Atkins and Rundell 2008; Boas [2005b] 2009; Ohara et al. 2003). As such, FrameNet facilitates a comparison of the comprehensive lexical descriptions and their manually annotated corpus-based example sentences with those of other LUs (also of other parts of speech) belonging to the same frame. Another advantage of the FrameNet architecture lies in the way lexical descriptions are related to each other. Using detailed semantic frames makes it possible to compare and contrast their numerous syntactic valence patterns systematically (see Atkins [2002] 2008 and Fillmore 2007).

4 Applying frame-semantic insights to the creation of translation resources

Following the development of FrameNet for English, researchers became interested in re-using semantic frames based on English for the description and analysis of other languages. Studies such as Heid (1996) and Fontenelle (1997) laid the groundwork for addressing systematic ways of structuring dictionaries of multiple languages using the same set of semantic frames. These studies were followed by works like Fillmore and Atkins (2000), Petruck and Boas (2003), and Boas (2002, 2003, 2005a), which showed that semantic frames are in principle useful tools for translating between languages, whether automatically or by hand.[10] These studies all share the basic idea that semantic frames based on English can in principle be re-used in order to analyze the lexicons of other languages, thereby providing an effective tool for translation purposes.

To illustrate this idea, consider the process of creating parallel lexicon fragments for German which can then be linked to their English counterparts. This process, first proposed in Boas (2002), begins by identifying a list of English LUs evoking a particular frame and to find translation equivalents. For example, the verb *argue* in the Communication_Conversation frame describes situations in which one or more parties are exchanging information about a topic with another party. The FEs include INTERLOCUTORS and TOPIC, among others. Table 5.1

---

10 Frame-semantic analysis has also been applied to languages like German (Lambrecht 1984), Hebrew (Petruck 2009), Japanese (Ohara 2009), and Chinese (Baker 1999). These analyses focused on specific organizational principles of the lexicons of single languages, but were not directly concerned with issues surrounding translation.

Table 5.1: Partial lexical entry of *argue* in Communication-Conversation (Boas 2002)

	Interlocutors	TARGET	Topic
1	NP.Ext	argue.v	INI
2	NP.Ext	argue.v	PP_over.Comp
3	NP.Ext	argue.v	PP_about.Comp
4	NP.Ext	argue.v	PPing_about.Comp
5	NP.Ext	argue.v	Swhether.Comp

Table 5.2: Semantically annotated corpus sentences (Boas 2002)

1	[<interlocutors>Mr and Mrs Popple] argued^{Tgt} once a week. [<topic>INI]
2	[<interlocutors>Auc: on houses and buyers] argue^{Tgt} [<topic>over compensation].
3	[<interlocutors>They] argued^{Tgt} [<topic>about it].
4	Anne says [<interlocutors>they] argue^{Tgt} [<topic>about drinking beer].
5	[<interlocutors>One] can argue^{Tgt} [<topic>whether pizza is healthy].

presents a part of the FrameNet lexical entry for *argue* in the Communication_Conversation frame. corresponding annotated examples are given in Table 5.2.[11]

The next step involves the use of bilingual and monolingual dictionaries as well as electronic corpora to find German translation equivalents. For each combination of semantic and syntactic information recorded for an English LU by FrameNet, a German equivalent is identified that matches its meaning as closely as possible. For example, in cases when the INTERLOCUTORS and TOPIC FEs are realized as an external argument and an indefinite null instantiation as in (1) in Tables 5.1 and 5.2, the closest translation equivalents include the two sentences in Table 5.3. Note that both reflexive and non-reflexive usages of German

---

[11] The discussion of *argue* evoking the Communication_Conversation frame reflects its status in FrameNet up to about 2005. Since then, the Communication_Conversation frame has been split up (or: re-framed) into several finer-grained communication frames, namely Quarreling, Evidence, Reasoning, and others. This finer-grained distinction is intended to reflect sub-classes of LUs sharing particular semantics that set them apart from other sub-classes (see Petruck et al. 2004 and Ruppenhofer et al. 2006 for details). At the same time, the Quarreling frame, which is evoked in the re-framed version of FrameNet by the sense of *argue* in Table 5.1, inherits information from higher-level frames such as Discussion and Communication. As such the statements made in this paper regarding the status of *argue* in the Communication_Conversation frame are still valid.

Table 5.3: German equivalents for example (1) in Table 5.2 (Boas 2002)

1a	[<interlocutors>Herr und Frau Popple] stritten^{Tgt} ein mal pro Woche [<topic> INI].
1b	[<interlocutors>Herr und Frau Popple] stritten^{Tgt} [sich] ein mal pro Woche [<topic> INI].

Table 5.4: German equivalents for examples (2) and (3) in Table 5.2 (Boas 2002)

2a	[<interlocutors>Auktionshäuser und Käufer] stritten^{Tgt} [<topic>um die Entschädigung].
2b	[<interlocutors>Auktionshäuser und Käufer] stritten^{Tgt} [sich][<topic> um die Entschädigung].
3a	[<interlocutors>Sie] stritten^{Tgt} [<topic>darüber].
3b	[<interlocutors>Sie] stritten^{Tgt} [sich] [<topic>darüber].

streiten ('to argue') are possible equivalents expressing the same type of situation as that expressed by *argue* in the context of (1) in Table 5.2.

Similarly, the meanings expressed by *argue* in examples (2) and (3) in Table 5.2 can be expressed by reflexive and non-reflexive usages of *streiten* as Table 5.4 illustrates.[12]

Once a set of German translation equivalents is identified, electronic corpora are searched to find attested usages for each syntactic frame associated with a German LU. For example, based on the data in Tables 5.3 and 5.4, a corpus search for *streiten* is conducted to see (i) whether it is possible to find corpus attestations for each of the syntactic frames listed for the verb by traditional dictionaries, and (ii) whether there are any other syntactic frames associated with *streiten* that are not mentioned by traditional dictionaries. By supporting the search for corpus-attested example sentences with native speaker intuitions, this stage of the workflow typically reveals the full range of syntactic frames associated with a LU.[13] Semantic annotation of these corpus sentences yields examples showing how individual FEs of a semantic frame are realized syntactically by the German target LUs (see, e.g. Tables 5.3 and 5.4).

The next step involves the creation of German lexical entries that parallel their English counterparts. Each entry identifies a LU, a part of speech, and a frame. This is augmented by a list with explanations of the FEs used in the annotation together with the ways in which they can be syntactically realized, and a collection of selected and annotated corpus sentences that exhibit every attested

---

12 *Sich streiten* is not a prototypical reflexive, but is only used reciprocally.
13 This stage will require a detailed analysis of the semantics associated with a verb in combination with its various prepositional complements (cf. *streiten [um/über/für/*. . .]*) as well as its English counterparts.

Table 5.5: Partial lexical entry for *streiten* (Boas 2002)

	Interlocutors	TARGET	Topic
1a	NP.Ext	streiten.v	INI
2a	NP.Ext	streiten.v	PP_um.Comp
3a	NP.Ext	streiten.v	PP_über.Comp

Table 5.6: Partial lexical entry for reflexive *streiten* (Boas 2002)

	Interlocutors	TARGET	Reflexive	Topic
1b	NP.Ext	streiten.v	sich	INI
2b	NP.Ext	streiten.v	sich	PP_um.Comp
3b	NP.Ext	streiten.v	sich	PP_über.Comp

combinatorial pattern for the lexical unit. Tables 5.5 and 5.6 are preliminary examples of the structure of lexical entries produced by German FrameNet. They contain partial summaries of the semantic and syntactic combinatorial properties for the lexical entries of the non-reflexive and reflexive usages of *streiten* in the Communication_Conversation frame. They are based on annotated examples of the type contained in Tables 5.3 and 5.4 above.

Since frames encode semantic relationships between FEs, the inventory of FEs is used to compare how a given combination of semantic and syntactic information encoded by a LU in the source language (e.g. English) is realized in the target language (e.g. German). This means that for each semantic and syntactic combinatorial property of a given LU in the source language we will ideally have a correspondence link to its counterpart in the target language that makes use of the semantic frame as a structuring device. Figure 5.4 illustrates schematically how semantic frames can be employed for linking corresponding subparts of parallel lexical entries to each other.[14]

As discussed above, lexical entries contain exhaustive listings of the semantic and syntactic combinatorial properties. Assigning each subpart of a lexical entry a number makes it possible to identify a specific syntactic frame occurring with a given LU. When establishing correspondence links between English and German lexical entries, this numerical indexing system allows us to refer

---

14 Similar proposals in favor of using semantic frames as structuring devices to link English lexical entries to German lexical entries have been made by Boas (2001, 2003, 2005a, 2009). See also Burchardt et al (2009) for a detailed description of a large-scale FrameNet-like resource for German.

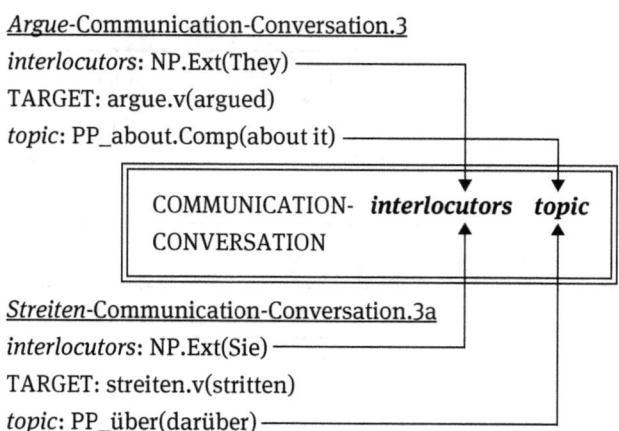

Figure 5.4: Semantic frame as a structuring device to link subparts of English and German lexical entries (Boas 2002)

precisely to a given subpart of a lexical entry in the source language when linking it to the corresponding subpart of a lexical entry in the target language. For example, index "3" in Figure 5.4 indicates that a specific syntactic frame of *argue* is used to encode the semantics of the Communication_Conversation frame (cf. Table 5.1). The German equivalent is indexed with "3a" (cf. Table 5.5), referring to a specific subpart of the lexical entry for *streiten* in the Communication_Conversation frame and thereby indicating that this is the German translation equivalent. This numerical indexing system allows for cross-referencing between subparts of multiple lexical entries across English and German lexicon fragments in combination with semantic frames. With respect to translation equivalents for *argue* in the Communication_Conversation frame in Figure 5.4, other links could be added to the Communication_Conversation frame. One such option includes a link to a subpart of the lexical entry for the reflexive version of German *streiten*. In this case, this link would be established to the syntactic frame of the reflexive (reciprocal) usage of *streiten* that is indexed with "3b" in Table 5.6.[15] Note that the linking of parallel lexicon

---

15 Using semantic frames in combination with numerical indexing mechanisms is different from the Inter-Lingual-Index (ILI) employed by EuroWordNet that aims to create a minimalized and efficient list of sense-distinctions (Vossen 1998; Peters et al. 1998). In contrast to ILI-records, GFN employs frame semantic descriptions to record lexicographically relevant corpus attestations of semantic and syntactic combinatorial properties of a lexical item without minimalizing sense distinctions.

fragments as outlined in Figure 5.4 only reflects a fraction of the entire lexicon entries. The steps described above thus need to be repeated until all subparts of an English lexical entry are linked to corresponding subparts of the parallel German lexical entry, eventually leading to a complete parallel lexical entry structured by a semantic frame.

The process for creating parallel lexicon fragments has been successfully applied to typologically diverse languages, such as French (Pitel 2009; Schmidt 2009), Hebrew (Petruck 2009; Petruck and Boas 2003), Japanese (Ohara 2009; Ohara et al. 2003), and Spanish (Subirats 2009; Subirats and Petruck 2003). While the creation of parallel lexicon fragments for other languages rely on different methodologies, tools, and resources, they all demonstrate that it is in principle possible to re-use semantic frames derived on the basis of English as an interlingual representation for the creation of parallel lexicon fragments for other languages (Boas 2005a). The advantages of this approach are the following: (i) Re-using semantic frames derived on the basis of English results in a common methodology for structuring dictionaries of different languages; (ii) When translators need to access lexical information about words in different languages, semantic frames allow for a more systematic way of searching and comparing with the help of semantic frames than traditional bi- or multi-lingual dictionaries whose lexical entries are organized alphabetically; (iii) Multilingual FrameNet dictionaries are unique resources that can aid the translation process because they provide detailed conceptual information (both generalizations and idiosyncrasies) about the types of semantic information shared by LUs across languages.[16]

5 Some issues with using semantic frames for translation purposes

Using semantic frames for structuring multilingual dictionaries for translation purposes is not always a straightforward process. For one, the procedure for

---

[16] Another advantage of this approach is its compatibility with current versions of Construction Grammar (Croft 2001; Goldberg 2006; Sag 2012), which does not assume a strict separation between syntax and the lexicon but instead views them as a continuum see Fillmore (1985b). In this view, grammatical constructions are also capable of evoking semantic frames. With respect to translation, a constructional view of language is advantageous because grammatical constructions (pairings of forms with meanings) can function as a *tertium comparationis* that make it possible to compare and contrast similar types of constructions across languages. For details, see the various contributions in Boas (2010).

creating parallel lexicon fragments can be extremely time-consuming because of the intense manual work that goes into identifying translation equivalents, finding corresponding example sentences, and annotating them. Thus, it is important to recognize that the procedure outlined above only covers a very small section of a lexical entry for *argue* in the Communication_Conversation frame. To create a full-blown parallel lexicon fragment of *argue* in another language the procedure discussed above must be repeated for every single valence pattern showing how particular FE configurations are realized syntactically (see also Boas 2005a). For example, the FE configuration INTERLOCUTOR and TOPIC in Table 5.1 may be realized in terms of five distinct valence patterns. Taking the remaining FE configurations and their valence patterns into consideration, the FrameNet entry of *argue* in the Communication_Conversation frame exhibits a total of 13 distinct valence patterns. Finding translation equivalents for each valence pattern in a FrameNet entry is not always an easy task as the following sections illustrate. Each of the issues highlighted below reflect different types of procedural and conceptual issues faced by translators when trying to find proper translation equivalents in other languages.

5.1 Differences in profiling particular aspects of semantic frames

Semantic frames offer a more finely-grained conceptual structure for multi-lingual dictionaries, thereby overcoming some of the difficulties relating to finding adequate corresponding verbs in the translation process (for some examples, see Boas 2003, 2005a; Fillmore and Atkins 2000). This methodology effectively shifts well-known issues surrounding polysemy from the level of words to the level of semantic frames and FEs, allowing us to account for both overlapping and diverging polysemy (cf. Altenberg and Granger 2002; Boas 2001; Ravin and Leacock 2000; Salkie 2002).

At the same time, however, there are instances where it is not sufficient simply to identify translation equivalents and link their parallel lexicon fragments. To provide adequate translation equivalents it sometimes becomes necessary to give more detailed information about how different aspects of a frame are realized in another language. For example, in the case of the Communication_Statement frame discussed above, I have argued that *announce* is quite flexible in how it allows the different perspectives of a communication event to be expressed (Boas 2002). This semantic flexibility is reflected by the various syntactic realizations of FEs. Table 5.7 presents an abbreviated selection of the full list of valence patterns recorded by FrameNet for *announce*.

Table 5.7: Syntactic frames highlighting different parts of the Communication_Statement frame with *announce* (Boas 2002: 1370)

1	[<speaker>They] *announced*^Tgt [<message>the birth of their child].
2	[<medium>The document] *announced*^Tgt [<message>that the war had begun].
3	[<speaker>The conductor] *announced*^Tgt [<message>the train's departure] [<medium>over the intercom].

Table 5.8: A selection of syntactic frames of *announce* and corresponding German verbs (Boas 2002: 1370)

1	speaker	TARGET	message	
	NP.Ext	announce.v	NP.Obj	
	bekanntgeben, bekanntmachen, ankündigen, anzeigen			
2	medium	TARGET	message	
	NP.Ext	announce.v	Sfin_that.Comp	
	bekanntgeben, ankündigen, anzeigen			
3	speaker	TARGET	message	medium
	NP.Ext	announce.v	NP.Obj	PP_over.Comp
	ankündigen, ansagen, durchsagen			

While *announce* is quite flexible in the types of situations it can describe, the various German translation equivalents differ significantly in the perspectives they offer of communication events. For example, Table 5.8 shows that German requires different verbs as translation equivalents for each of the three perspectives taken on the Communication_Statement frame by *announce*: when *announce* occurs with the syntactic frame [NP.Ext __ NP.Obj] to realize the SPEAKER and MESSAGE FEs, German offers several choices, such as *bekanntgeben, bekanntmachen, ankündigen,* or *anzeigen*. More specifically, the choice depends on a finely-grained distinction (including contextual background information) that formally distinguishes between the semantics of individual verbs. For example, *anzeigen* is used in a more formal sense than the other verbs, *ankündigen* is primarily used to refer to an event that will occur in the future, *bekanntmachen* refers to some way of spreading information publicly, and *bekanntgeben* implies that the information comes from an official source (perhaps due to pressure) (see also Boas 2002)

Each of these German verbs comes with their own specific syntactic frames that express the semantics of the Communication_Statement frame. The two other syntactic frames of *announce* in Table 5.7 and their German translation equivalents in Table 5.8 demonstrate how a difference in perspective on the

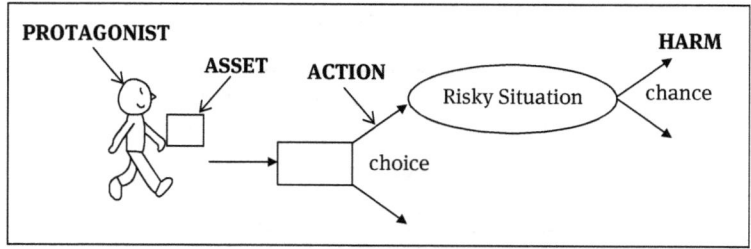

Figure 5.5: The schema for the Risk frame (Hasegawa et al. 2006)

frame is reflected by different syntactic frames in English as well as different translation equivalents in German (see also Boas 2005b for details). For example, when the communication event involves a medium such as a loudspeaker or a megaphone to transmit the message (e.g. *Joe announced the arrival of the pizza over the intercom*), German offers *ansagen* and *durchsagen* as more specific translation equivalents of *announce* besides the general *ankündigen* for describing situations in which a message is transmitted via a medium. In other words, the choice between different German translation equivalents of *announce* directly depends on subtle meaning differences of the frame and the perspective given of a situation.

Similar observations are made by Ohara (2009), who investigates the Japanese translation equivalents of the English verb *risk*.[17] Analyzing the different correspondences between English and Japanese expressions involving the concept of RISK in Figure 5.5 (cf. Fillmore and Atkins 1992; Hasegawa et al. 2006), Ohara shows that some Japanese translation equivalents of *risk* such as *kakeru* involve only one perspective on RISK-related scenes, which include the Jeopardizing frame (e.g. *He risked his life [for a man he did not know]*), the Incurring frame (e.g. *He risked losing his life savings*), and the Daring frame (e.g. *I wouldn't risk talking like that in public*). At the same time, at least one Japanese expression, namely *kiken_o_okasu*, is compatible with all three different frames associated with the English verb *risk*. When finding corresponding Japanese equivalents of the different RISK-related scenes it is thus necessary to pay close attention to the different perspectives that Japanese LUs offer of the frames and to ensure that they are in fact proper translation equivalents of the English LUs.

The procedures needed for finding adequate German and Japanese translations of English LUs evoking the Communication_Statement and Risk

---

[17] For an analysis of the Risk frame in English and Spanish, see Rojo and Valenzuela (1998).

frames show that semantic frames are helpful tools for systematically capturing adequate translation equivalents. At the same time, however, careful attention must be paid to the intricate differences in how LUs that are often thought to be translation equivalents of other differ in their profiling properties of frames. Such difficulties also represent positive aspects of semantic frames, as they are useful structuring devices for expressing subtle differences between translation equivalents, which in turn is a useful tool for translation purposes.

5.2 Differences in lexicalization patterns

When using frames as translation tools, typological differences between how languages lexicalize particular patterns (see Talmy 1985) are also important issues that need to be addressed. For example, Talmy's typology of motion events makes a broad distinction between satellite-framing languages in which the image schemas are included in verbs of motion as in English (e.g. *[find] way + in; [find] way + out*), and verb-framing languages such as Spanish, in which image schemas are indicated separately from verbs (e.g. *entrar* 'enter', *salir* 'leave') (see also Beavers, Levin, and Tham 2010; Croft et al. 2010; Ibarretxe-Antuñano and Filipović, this volume; Slobin 1996). To see how typological differences are relevant when semantic frames are used comparing languages, Ellsworth et al. (2006) discuss systematic differences between the English, Spanish, Japanese, and German versions of chapter 14 of *The Hound of the Baskervilles*. Focusing on motion and location-related verbs they show that there are a number of differences in how the various concepts of motion are associated with different types of semantic frames. Consider the following sentences.

(2) a. *The wagonette was paid off and ordered to* **return**∗Return **to**Goal *Coombe Tracey forthwith, while we started to walk to Merripit House.*

b. | *Despedimos* | *a* | *la* | *tartana* | *y* | *ordenamos* | *al* |
|---|---|---|---|---|---|---|
| said.goodbye | to | the | old.scrap | and | ordered | to.the |
| *cochero* | *que* | ***regresara***∗Return | | *a* Goal | *Coombe* | *Tracey* |
| driver | that | returned | | to | Coombe | Tracey |
| *de* | *inmediato,* | *al* | *mismo* | *tiempo* | *que* | |
| of | immediate | to.the | same | time | that | |
| *poníamos* | *en* | *camino* | *hacia* | | *la casa* | |
| put | in | path | towards | | the house | |
| *Merripit.* | | | | | | |
| Merripit | | | | | | |

c. Der Wagen wurde bezahlt und **nach**$_{Goal}$ Coombe Tracey **zurückgeschickt**$_{Sending}$, bevor wir uns zu Fuß in Richtung auf Merripit House aufmachen.
 the cart was paid and to Coombe Tracey back-sent before we us on foot in direction to Merripit House go-on

All sentences in (2) share the property that the concept of motion is incorporated into indirect causation. For example, in (2a), the LU *return to* overtly expresses the notion of motion through the preposition *to*. However, there is a difference in the types of LUs evoking different frames. While English *return* and Spanish *regresar* both evoke the Return frame, German *zurückschicken* evokes the Sending frame. This difference shows that although the concept of motion is incorporated into indirect causation, the frames expressing indirect causation may vary from language to language. Next, consider how different subparts of motion are expressed cross-linguistically.

(3) a. *The wagonette was paid off and ordered to return to Coombe Tracey forthwith, while we started to* **walk**$_{Self\_motion}$ **to**$_{Goal}$ *Merripit House.*

b. Despedimos a la tartana y ordenamos al cochero que regresara a Coombe Tracey de inmediato, al mismo tiempo que nos **poníamos en camino**$_{Setting\_out}$ **hacia**$_{Direction}$ la casa Merripit.
 said.goodbye to the old.scrap and ordered to.the driver that returned to Coombe Tracey of immediate to.the same time that we.REFL put in path towards the house Merripit

c. Der Wagen wurde bezahlt und nach Coombe Tracey zurückgeschickt, bevor wir uns **zu Fuß**$_{*Means\_of\_motion}$ **in Richtung**$_{Direction}$ auf Merripit House **aufmachten**$_{Setting\_out}$.
 the cart was paid and to Coombe Tracey back-sent before we us on Foot in direction auf Merripit House go-on

While English *walk* evokes the Self_Motion frame, its Spanish and German translations evoke the Setting_out frame, which is a subtype of the Self_Motion frame. Another difference is that while English *walk* includes the manner of walking in the verb, German *aufmachen* does not. Instead, the manner of

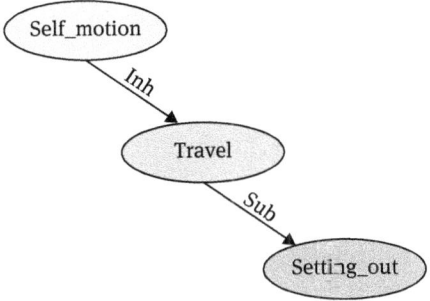

Figure 5.6: Self_Motion translated with subframes of its subtype (Ellsworth et al. 2006)

motion is expressed by a separate phrase *zu Fuss* 'on foot', which indicates the MEANS_OF_MOTION. Variations such as those in (3) show that in translation there are often subtle differences in how a particular concept is expressed in a language. The important point here is that such differences are not entirely unsystematic and that they can be captured effectively by applying frame-semantic analysis to the translation process. In the case of the Spanish and German translations in (3b) and (3c) this means that the Setting_out frame evoked by the respective LUs is a subframe of the Travel frame, which in turn inherits information from the Self_Motion frame as illustrated by Figure 5.6 (see Petruck et al. 2004 for more information on frame-to-frame relations such as inheritance). As such, differences in how an English Self_Motion LU such as *walk* is translated into Spanish or German boils down to differences in granularity of the semantic frames.[18]

Besides systematically aiding in the translation process between typologically different languages such as verb-framing and satellite-framing languages, there are also more fine-grained differences in how frames are lexicalized across languages. For example, Burchardt et al. (2009: 225) discuss cases in which the meanings of German verbs sometimes cut across frame distinctions made on the basis of English data. German *fahren* 'to drive', for example, is a translation equivalent of both *drive*, which evokes the Operate_vehicle frame with the FE DRIVER, and *ride*, which evokes the Ride_vehicle frame with the FE PASSENGER. Burchardt et al. (2009: 225) point out that in German it is often not possible to make a clear distinction between the two frames based on context as in the following example.

---

[18] See also Ohara et al. (2003) for differences in how Japanese motion verbs realize different types of paths in contrast to English motion verbs.

(4) a.

In	14	Armeefahrzeugen	**fuhren**	sie	von	dem	
In	14	army-vehicles	drove	they	from	the	
abgezäunten	Gelände,	das	der	Besatzungsmacht			28
fenced-in	area	which	the	Occupying-force			28
Jahre	lang	als	Hauptquartier	gedient		hatte.	
Years	long	as	headquarter	served		had	

b. With 14 army vehicles they **departed** from the enclosed area that had served the occupying forces as headquarters for 28 years.

In (4a), it is not clear whether *sie* 'they' refers to people as passengers or as drivers of the 14 vehicles, which in turn makes it difficult to determine which frame is evoked by *fahren*. To capture the fact that *fahren* in contexts such as (4a) is often underspecified, FrameNet includes one higher-level frame Use_vehicle, which subsumes both the Operate_vehicle frame and the Ride_vehicle frame. While the more abstract Use_vehicle frame is not lexicalized in English (where *drive* either evokes the Operate_vehicle frame or the Ride_vehicle frame), this frame is the proper level of abstraction to capture the regularly occurring underspecified meaning of *fahren*, according to Burchardt et al. (2009: 226). By including higher-level frames it thus becomes possible to systematically capture distinct lexicalization patterns exhibited by translation equivalents at different levels of granularity in the hierarchy of semantic frames. Knowledge of frame-to-frame relations and how LUs that are translation equivalents across languages evoke frames at different levels of abstraction also presents a helpful tool for translation purposes because it offers translators access to conceptual information that other translation resources do not provide.

5.3 Divergent translation equivalents and zero translations

One of the more complicated issues translators have to deal with is the divergence of translation equivalents and the issue of zero translations. In such instances, a frame-semantic analysis of the LUs in their relevant contexts may often yield helpful insights that facilitate the translation process. Consider, for example, the frame Notification_of_charges, which is part of a larger frame of Criminal_Process, and is evoked by LUs such as *accuse*, *charge*, and *indictment*. Figure 5.7 illustrates the Criminal_Process frame, with its various subframes, including Notification_of_charges in the bottom left corner.

Bertoldi (2010), in his work on contrastive legal terminology in English and Brazilian Portuguese, addresses the question of whether it is possible to find

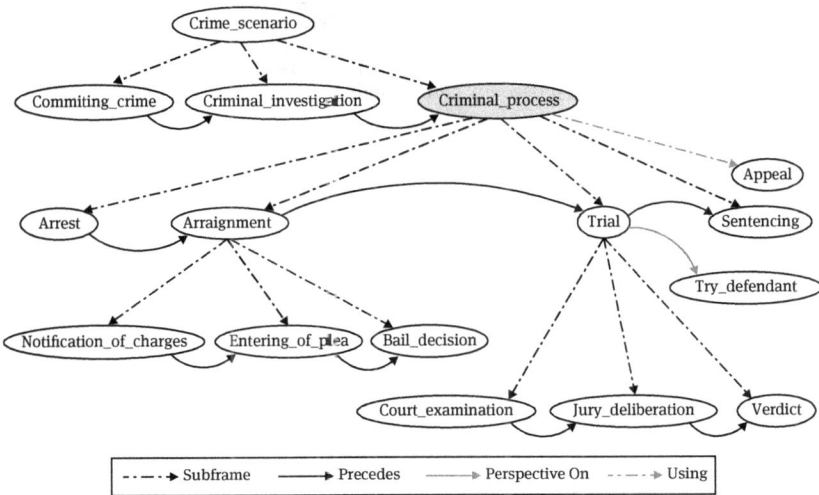

Figure 5.7: The (English) Criminal_Process frame in FrameNet (Bertoldi 2010: 1)

systematically adequate translation equivalents for these LUs in Portuguese. While he finds that there are Portuguese translation equivalents, he also shows that the polysemy and multi-faceted meaning of some of the English LUs, as shown in Figure 5.8, poses a number of issues.

The first issue is that although there are corresponding Portuguese LUs they do not evoke the same Notification_of_charges frame as the English LUs, but rather a frame that could best be characterized as Accusation. More specifically, Bertoldi points out that the six Portuguese translation equivalents of the English LUs evoking only the Notification_of_charges frame, namely *acusar* 'to accuse, to incriminate', *acusação* 'charge, complaint', *denunciar* 'to denounce', *denúncia* 'accusation', *pronunciar* 'prenounce, label, judge', and *pronúncia* 'pronunciation' potentially evoke three different frames. This leads Bertoldi to argue that the LUs *acusar*, *acusação*, *denunciar*, and *denúncia* may evoke two different Criminal_Process sub-frames, besides other general language, non-legal specific frames, as is illustrated by Figure 5.9.

Bertoldi's (2010) analysis illustrates that semantic frames are not only useful for comparing and contrasting translation equivalents, but that they are also helpful when it comes to highlighting differences in polysemy networks between languages and for showing how systematic cultural differences have direct repercussions for the organization of the conceptual system. In this case, the Brazilian legal system differs from the American legal system in that there is no exact frame that corresponds to Notification_of_charges. This difference

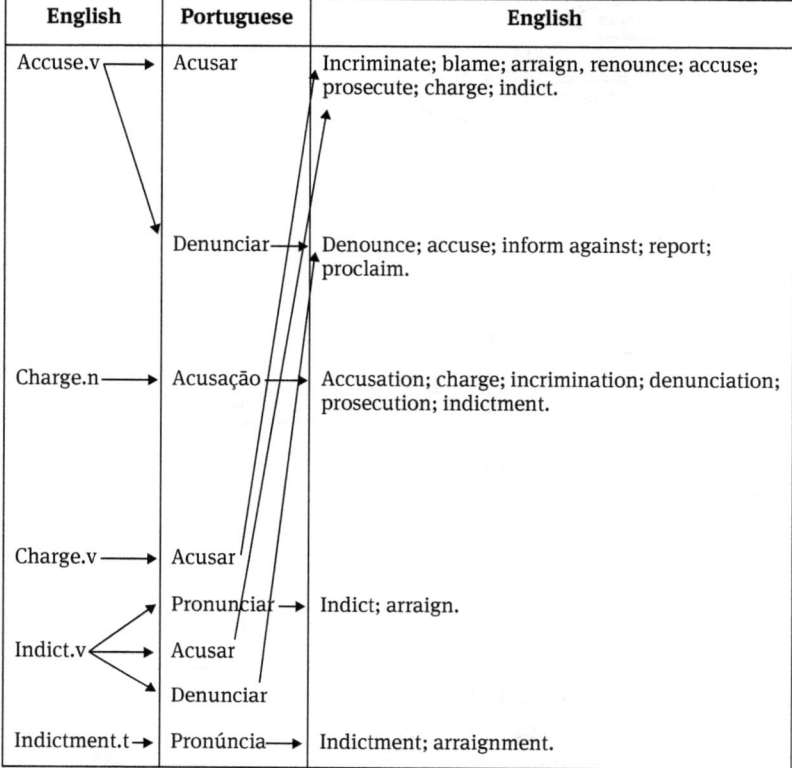

Figure 5.8: English LUs from the frame Notification_of_charges and their Portuguese translation equivalents (Bertoldi 2010: 6)

necessitates a different type of framal organization for the Brazilian Portuguese Crime_scenario frame as in Figure 5.9, which in turn serves as the organizational background for frame-evoking LUs that at first sight appear to be translation equivalents of English LUs, but in fact denote quite different situations in how the criminal process plays out in Brazil. More precisely, instead of a Notification_of_charges frame, the Brazilian legal system relies on two different frames, namely Accusation and Preliminary_hearing, as shown in Figure 5.9.[19]

---

[19] For a discussion of the role of linguistic motivation in structuring semantic frames across languages, see Petruck and Boas (2003) on Calendric_unit frames in English, German, and Hebrew.

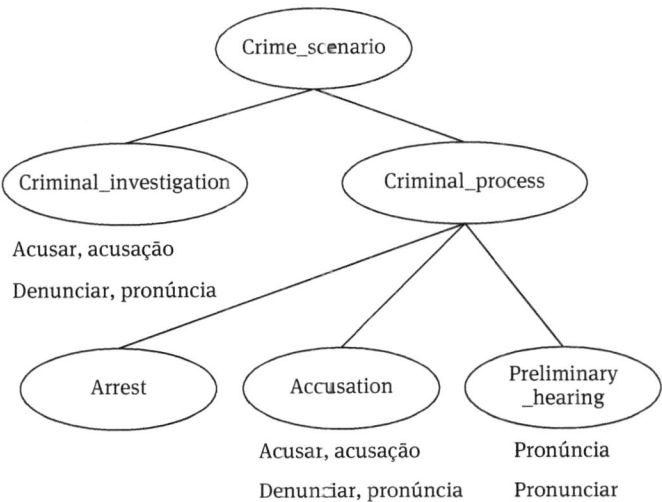

Figure 5.9: LUs evoking multiple frames in the Portuguese Crime_scenario frame (Bertoldi 2010: 7)

Another problematic area concerning divergent translation equivalents are cases in which two LUs evoke the same semantic frame but differ in their part of speech. Schmidt's (2009) parallel frame-semantic analysis of football language in German, English, and French provides an illustrative example by discussing the French translation equivalent of the English verb to *nutmeg* (e.g. *[Hector Font]*$_{PLAYER\_WITH\_BALL}$ *tried to nutmeg [Ioannis Skopelitis]*$_{OPPONENT\_PLAYER}$) in the Beat frame.[20]

(5)   *[Bastian*   *Schweinsteiger]*$_{PLAYER\_WITH\_BALL}$ *manquait*   *le*   *cadre*   *après*
     Bastian   Schweinsteiger   missed   the   target   after
     avoir   *réussi*   *un*   *petit*   *pont*   *[sur*   *William*   *Gallas]*$_{OPPONENT\_PLAYER}$.
     have   pass   a   little   bridge   to   William   Gallas
     'Bastian Schweinsteiger missed the target after having nutmegged William Gallas' (Schmidt 2009: 108)

While there appears to exist no adequate French verbal translation equivalent of the English verbal LU *nutmeg*, the nominal LU *petit pont* 'little bridge' serves this

---

[20] For more details of Schmidt's analysis of football language, see http://www.kicktionary.de and Schmidt (2009).

purpose in (5). This example shows that semantic frames are a useful tool for translators because they make it possible to recognize instantaneously how different parts of speech in two languages are capable of expressing the same concept. At the same time, semantic frames may also help translators find potential paraphrases in the target language, as in the following example, where the French nominal LU *(faire le) coup du sombrero* (lit. 'to do the coup of the sombrero' or 'to do the sombrero move') evokes the Beat frame.

(6) [Ronaldinho]$_{PLAYER\_WITH\_BALL}$ [lui]$_{OPPONENT\_PLAYER}$ *faisait le* **coup du sombrero**. (Schmidt 2009: 108)

According to Schmidt (2009), the French term *coup du sombrero* 'sombrero move' as used in (6) describes an act of getting past an opponent by lobbing the ball over them, rounding him and retrieving the ball behind his neck. Since neither English nor German have an exact translation equivalent of *coup du sombrero*, a frame-based analysis of the term may help identify potential paraphrases. More specifically, since *coup du sombrero* evokes the Beat frame, one would have to look at lexical entries in other languages to determine which English and German LUs come closest to matching the meaning of *coup du sombrero*. In this case, Schmidt (2009: 109) points out that while English *round* or German *ausspielen* 'out-play' are not an exact translation equivalent of *(faire le) coup du sombrero*, they nevertheless are fairly adequate (if less specific) translations of it.

Missing translation equivalents are other instances in which frame-based multilingual dictionaries are useful for translation purposes. This is the case when the target language does not have a translation equivalent, and it nevertheless is often possible to use another member of the corresponding frame together with an appropriate FE, according to Schmidt. An example is the missing German translation equivalent for English *side-foot*, i.e. to shoot with the side of the foot, as in the following example.

(7) [He]$_{SHOOTER}$ *calmly rounded Marshall before* **side-footing** *[the ball]*$_{BALL}$ *[into the net]*$_{TARGET}$. (Schmidt 2009: 109)

The verb *side-foot* evokes the Shot frame, which is also evoked by several other German verbal LUs whose meanings are realized with different FEs relating to PART_OF_BODY in a diverse range of contexts. When one of them, *bugsieren*, occurs with the FE PART_OF_BODY denoting the foot (or part thereof), then it is possible to arrive at an adequate translation paraphrase, as (8) shows.

(8) [Er]$_{SHOOTER}$ spielte   Marshall   aus   und   bugsierte   [den
    He   played   Marshall   out   and   steered   the
    Ball]$_{BALL}$ [mit dem Innenrist]$_{PART\_OF\_BODY}$ [ins   Netz]$_{TARGET}$.
    ball   with   the instep   into-the Net
    'He outplayed Marshall and steered the ball with his instep into the net.'

The important point in all of this is that frames facilitate the finding of appropriate translation paraphrases because they are used to structure LUs in different languages, where each LU may offer a slightly different perspective of an event while at the same time also expressing the more general idea of an LU such as *side-foot*.

5.4 "Universal" and "culture-specific" frames

Semantic frames are also helpful for translation purposes when it comes to comparing, contrasting, and highlighting cultural differences between words that either have rough translation equivalents or have no translation equivalents at all (see, e.g. Rojo 2002). Examples of the latter are culture-specific frames whose entire meanings are lexicalized by LUs in one language, but not necessarily in others. Leino (2010) discusses the case of the Finnish intransitive verb *saunoa* (literally 'to sauna') in (9) as an example of cultural differences that may lead to situations where objectively the same situation is classified as belonging to different situation types in different languages.

(9) Kalle   saunoo. (Leino 2010: 131)
    Charlie.NOM saunoa.3SG.
    Roughly: 'Charlie is in the sauna/goes to sauna/is enjoying sauna'

In discussing the conceptual underpinnings involved in interpreting the verb *saunoa* in Finnish, Leino (2010: 131) points out that

> [. . .] the fact that the sauna is an essential part of Finnish culture leads to the fact that Finns very probably experience going to the sauna as a significantly different type of event than e.g. Americans do. Correspondingly, Finnish has the intransitive verb *saunoa* which roughly expresses a situation in which the referent of the subject goes to the sauna, is in the sauna, participates in the sauna event, or something of the like. English has no corresponding verb, and, therefore, there is no one-to-one corresponding way of translating the sentence.

The rough English paraphrase of the Finnish example in (9) shows that the entire chain of events encoded by the Finnish Sauna frame and lexicalized by the Finnish verb *saunoa* has no single translation equivalent. Instead, an English paraphrase of the type in (9) needs to enumerate the different types of sauna activities by employing a number of verbs. In cases such as the Finnish Sauna frame, semantic frames are helpful for translation purposes because they combine parallel lexicon fragments that allow translators to find appropriate paraphrases consisting of a series of expressions even in cases where there is no direct translation equivalent.

Semantic frames are also useful for highlighting cultural differences between LUs that are not exact translation equivalents of each other. One such example is Bertoldi's (2010) contrastive analysis of LUs in the English and Portuguese Criminal_process frame discussed above. Another example of culturally-infused frames is the (English) Personal_Relationship frame, whose words have to do with people and the personal relationships they are or can be a part of. Some of the words in this frame denote people engaged in a particular kind of relationship, others denote the relationship, yet others denote the events bringing about or ending the relationships. Many of the words presuppose an understanding of states and events that must have occurred before another event takes place or before a person can be classified in a certain way (FrameNet definition).

Finding translation equivalents for words such as *friend, boyfriend, girlfriend, sugar daddy,* and *to date* is at times difficult because "the concept of 'friend', and the relationship linked with it, are important to Anglo culture, but it is an illusion to think that they must have their counterparts in all other cultures and that they are somehow part of human nature" (Wierzbicka 1997: 32). To determine whether it is in principle possible to apply the English Personal_Relationship frame to other languages, Atzler (2010) discusses German translation equivalents of English LUs evoking the Personal_Relationship frame. Her main finding is that the English Personal_Relationship frame cannot easily be (re-)used for the analysis of personal relationship terminology in German. For example, while some German LUs such as *Freund* 'friend' offer a reasonably close approximation of meaning of its English counterpart *friend* (e.g. *Er ist mein Freund* 'He is my friend'), this is not the case with other LUs in the same frame. To wit, German *Freundin* can imply both *girlfriend* and *female friend* in English. A more extreme example is the term *sugar daddy*, which has no exact counterpart in German, but instead requires a lengthy paraphrase such as *spendabler älterer Mann, der ein junges Mädchen aushält* 'generous older man who supports a young girl' to render the concept of this particular type of personal relationship in German (Atzler 2010: 40).

This example shows that while previous studies seem to suggest that a wide variety of frames such as Motion and Communication may in fact be found in a very broad array of languages and could hence be considered as some type of "universal frames" (with slight variations between languages), frames such as Criminal_process and Personal_Relationship are not.

One way of re-using semantic frames derived on the basis of English as translation aids for culturally-infused terms would be to expand existing (English) frame descriptions with cultural scripts from Wierzbicka's Natural Semantic Metalanguage (NSM). This approach assumes that meaning is the key to insightful and explanatory descriptions of most linguistic phenomena. To describe meanings, the NSM approach to semantic description proposes a decompositional system of meaning representation based on empirically established universal semantic primes, i.e. simple identifiable meanings which appear to be present as word-meanings in all languages (Goddard 2010: 459). Semantic primes include substantives such as I, YOU, SOMETHING/THING, PEOPLE, BODY; descriptors such as BIG and SMALL; and speech such as SAY, WORDS, and TRUE.

Besides universal combinations of semantic primes to model the meanings of words, the vocabulary of each language also contains a great deal of culture-specific items that are typically difficult to translate into other languages, such as English *reasonable, fair, right,* and *probably*. According to Wierzbicka (2006), such terms have emerged and been shaped over the last centuries in the service of a body of cultural scripts that characterize the values and habits of thought that are reflected in the use of them. To overcome this issue, Wierzbicka proposes cultural script explications consisting of formulations that use semantic atoms (primes, primitives). Such scripts are formulated in simple words and grammatical patterns which have equivalents in all languages, according to Wierzbicka. Using such cultural scripts makes it possible to articulate cultural norms, values, and practices in terms which are clear, precise, and accessible to cultural insiders and to cultural outsiders alike (Goddard and Wierzbicka 2004). An example of a cultural script is based on the idea that "individual freedom" and "personal autonomy" are among the primary ideals of mainstream Anglo culture. One script reflecting a component of the dominant "cultural ideology" in predominantly English-speaking countries like Australia, the United States and Great Britain is the following.

(10) Anglo cultural script for *"personal autonomy"*
[many people think like this:]
when someone does something,
it is good if this someone can think like this:
"I am doing this because I want to do it"

According to Goddard (2010: 482), the cultural script in (10) can inhibit speakers of mainstream English from using the bare imperative when they want someone to do something. In such cases, Anglo speakers usually prefer to frame their directives in a more elaborated (and sometimes indirect) fashion, using WH-interrogatives such as *Will you [. . .]?, Would you [. . .]?, Can you [. . .]?, Could you [. . .]?, Would you mind [. . .]?,* etc.

One way of integrating Wierzbicka's cultural scripts into frame-semantic descriptions would be to augment frame-semantic entries with cultural scripts where appropriate. For example, in cases where English LUs in the `Personal_Relationship` frame do not have an appropriate translation equivalent, such as *sugar daddy*, a lexical entry would also record the (arguably non-standard) cultural norms, values, and practices associated with an LU. When parallel lexicon fragments are linked via semantic frames, a translator would then have access to culture-specific information about a LU such as *sugar daddy* in order to arrive at an adequate paraphrase for a language such as German, which does not have a corresponding lexical equivalent. A very preliminary – and perhaps controversial – version of a cultural script for *sugar daddy*, which would be included in its FrameNet entry, would look as follows.

(11)   *Anglo cultural script for "sugar daddy"* (preliminary version)
[Some people think like this:]
It sometimes happens that older rich men enjoy the company of younger women.
It sometimes happens that younger women like to have goods or other favors from older rich men.
Because of this, when older rich men and younger women spend time together based on mutually agreed terms.
It is good that older men give goods and other favors to younger women and younger women spend time with older men.

6 Conclusions

In this paper I discussed how semantic frames are useful tools for translation purposes. In contrast to other lexical resources used for translation purposes such as traditional multi-lingual dictionaries, the frame-semantic approach to lexical organization makes it possible to relate words across languages in a systematic way. The various examples presented here show that Frame Semantics offers a unique way of capturing both generalizations and idiosyncrasies in the description of semantically related words across languages. In addition, by employing the frame as an analytic tool, it is possible to include references to culturally significant categories in the lexicon. Moreover, taking the frame as a universal cognitive structuring device provides the apparatus for analyzing semantic fields both within and across languages, thus providing a perspicuous way of characterizing cross-linguistic differences.

Future research is required to investigate extending a Frame Semantic approach by including more detailed information about culturally relevant categories. To illustrate, consider the discussion of the term *sugar daddy* and the types of problems it poses when trying to find an adequate German translation equivalent. By adopting some key insights from Wierzbicka's (2006) cultural scripts I proposed a preliminary strategy for capturing more fine-grained cultural differences between specific types of words and their possible translation paraphrases in other languages. Clearly, much more research remains to be done to combine key insights from Frame Semantics with cultural scripts, thereby refining frame-based lexical resources for translation purposes.

References

Altenberg, Bengt and Sylviane Granger 2002 Recent trends in cross-linguistic lexical studies. In: Bengt Altenberg and Sylviane Granger (eds.), *Lexis in contrast*, 3–50. Amsterdam: John Benjamins.
Atkins, B.T.S. [2002] 2008 Then and now: Competence and performance in 35 years of lexicography. In: Thierry Fontenelle (ed.), *Practical lexicography – a reader*, 31–50. Oxford: Oxford University Press.
Atkins, B.T.S. and Michael Rundell 2008 *Oxford guide to practical lexicography*. Oxford: Oxford University Press.
Atzler, Judith 2010 *Of sugar daddies and Zuckerpapas*. Unpublished PhD dissertation, the University of Texas at Austin.
Baker, Colin F. 1999 *Seeing clearly*. Unpublished PhD dissertation, University of California Berkeley.
Baker, Colin F., Charles J. Fillmore and John B. Lowe 1998 The Berkeley FrameNet Project. In: *COLING-ACL '98: Proceedings of the Conference*, 86–90. Montreal, Quebec, Canada: Université de Montréal.
Beavers, John, Beth Levin and S. Wei Tham 2010 The typology of motion expressions revisited. *Journal of Linguistics* 46: 331–772.
Bertoldi, Anderson 2010 *When translation equivalents do not find meaning equivalence: a contrastive study of the frame Criminal_Process*. Unpublished PhD dissertation, University of Texas at Austin.
Boas, Hans C. 2001 Frame semantics as a framework for describing polysemy and syntactic structures of English and German motion verbs in contrastive computational lexicography. In: Paul Rayson, Andrew Wilson, Tony McEnery, Andrew Hardie and Shereen Khoja (eds.), *Proceedings of Corpus Linguistics 2001*, 64–73. Lancaster, UK: Lancaster University Press.

Boas, Hans C. 2002 Bilingual FrameNet dictionaries for machine translation. In: Manuel González Rodríguez and Carmen Paz Suárez Araujo (eds.), *Proceedings of the Third International Conference on Language Resources and Evaluation*, Vol. 4, 1364–1371. Las Palmas, Spain. Available on-line at: http://www.lrec-conf.org/proceedings/lrec2002/.

Boas, Hans C. 2003 *A constructional approach to resultatives*. Stanford, CA: CSLI Publications.

Boas, Hans C. 2005a From theory to practice: Frame semantics and the design of FrameNet. In: Stefan Langer and Daniel Schnorbusch (eds.), *Semantik im Lexikon*, 129–160. Tübingen, Germany: Gunter Narr.

Boas, Hans C. 2005b Semantic frames as interlingual representations for multilingual lexical databases. *International Journal of Lexicography* 18.4: 445–478.

Boas, Hans C. 2009 Recent trends in multilingual lexicography. In: Hans C. Boas (ed.), *Multilingual FrameNets: Methods and applications*, 1–36. Berlin: Mouton de Gruyter.

Boas, Hans C. (ed.) 2010 *Contrastive studies in construction grammar*. Amsterdam: John Benjamins.

Burchardt, Aljoscha, Katrin Erk, Anette Frank, Andrea Kowalski, Sebastian Padó and Manfred Pinkal 2009 Using FrameNet for the semantic analysis of German: Annotation, representation, and automation. In: Hans C. Boas (ed.), *Multilingual FrameNets: Methods and applications*, 209–244. Berlin: Mouton de Gruyter.

Croft, William 2001 *Radical construction grammar*. Oxford: Oxford University Press.

Croft, William, Johanna Barðdal, Willem Hollmann, Violeta Sotirova and Chiaki Taoka 2010 Revising Talmy's typological classification of complex event constructions. In: Hans C. Boas (ed.), *Contrastive studies in construction grammar*, 201–235. Amsterdam: John Benjamins.

Dowty, David 1991 Thematic proto-roles and argument selection. *Language* 67: 547–619.

Ellsworth, Michael, Kyoko Ohara, Carlos Subirats and Thomas Schmidt 2006 Frame-semantic analysis of motion scenarios in English, German, Spanish, and Japanese. Presentation given at the 4th International Conference on Construction Grammar, Tokyo, Japan, September 1–3, 2006. Available on-line as ICSI technical report 9-2006 at: http://icsi.berkeley.edu.

Fellbaum, Christiane 1998 *WordNet: An electronic lexical database*. Cambridge, MA: MIT Press.

Fillmore, Charles J. 1968 The case for case. In: Emmon Bach and Robert T. Harms (eds.), *Universals in linguistic theory*, 1–88. New York: Holt, Rinehart, and Winston.

Fillmore, Charles J. 1970 The grammar of hitting and breaking. In: R. A. Jacobs and P. S. Rosenbaum (eds.), *Readings in English transformational grammar*, 120–133. Oxford: Ginn and Company.

Fillmore, Charles J. 1975 An alternative to checklist theories of meaning. *Proceedings of the First Annual Meeting of the Berkeley Linguistics Society* 1: 123–131.

Fillmore, Charles J. 1976 Frame semantics and the nature of language. In: Stevan R. Harnad, Horst D. Steklis and Jane Lancaster (eds.), *Origins and evolution of language and speech*, 20–32. New York: New York Academy of Sciences.

Fillmore, Charles J. 1977a Scenes-and-frames semantics. In: Antonio Zampolli (ed.), *Linguistics structures processing*, 55–81. Dordrecht, the Netherlands: North Holland.

Fillmore, Charles J. 1977b Topics in lexical semantics. In: R. W. Cole (eds.), *Current issues in linguistic theory*, 76–138. Bloomington: Indiana University Press.

Fillmore, Charles J. 1978 On the organization of semantic information in the lexicon. In: Donka Frakas, Wesley Jacobsen and Karol W. Todrys (eds.), *Papers from the parasession on the lexicon*, 148–173. Chicago: Chicago Linguistic Society.

Fillmore, Charles J. 1982 Frame semantics. In: Linguistic Society of Korea (ed.), *Linguistics in the morning calm*, 111–138. Seoul: Hanshin.

Fillmore, Charles J. 1985a Frames and the semantics of understanding. *Quadernie di Semantica* 6: 222–254.

Fillmore, Charles J. 1985b Syntactic intrusions and the notion of grammatical construction. *Proceedings of the Eleventh Annual Meeting of the Berkeley Linguistics Society* 11: 73–86.

Fillmore, Charles J. 1988 The mechanisms of construction grammar. *Proceedings of the Fourteenth Annual Meeting of the Berkeley Linguistic Society* 14: 35–55.

Fillmore, Charles J. 1994 The hard road from verbs to nouns. In: Matthew Y. Chen, Ovid J. L. Tzeng, and William S. Y. Wang (eds.), *In honor of William S.Y. Wang: Interdisciplinary studies on language and language change*, 105–129. Taipei: Pyramid Press.

Fillmore, Charles J. 2007 Valency issues in FrameNet. In: Thomas Herbst and Katrin Götz-Vetteler (eds.), *Valency: Theoretical, descriptive, and cognitive issues*, 129–160. Berlin: Mouton de Gruyter.

Fillmore, Charles J. and B.T.S. Atkins 1992 Toward a frame-based lexicon: The semantics of RISK and its neighbors. In: Adrienne Lehrer and Eva F. Kittay (eds.), *Frames, fields and contrasts: New essays in semantic and lexical organization*, 75–102. Hillsdale, NJ: Erlbaum.

Fillmore, Charles J. and B.T.S. Atkins 1994 Starting where the dictionaries stop: The challenge for computational lexicography. In: B.T.S. Atkins and Antonio Zampolli (eds.), *Computational approaches to the lexicon*, 349–393. Oxford: Oxford University Press.

Fillmore, Charles J. and B.T.S. Atkins 2000 Describing polysemy: The case of 'crawl'. In: Yael Ravin and Claudia Leacock (eds.), *Polysemy*, 91–110. Oxford: Oxford University Press.

Fillmore, Charles J. and Colin Baker 2010 A frames approach to semantic analysis. In: Bernd Heine and Heiko Narrog (eds.), *The Oxford handbook of linguistic analysis*, 313–340. Oxford: Oxford University Press.

Fillmore, Charles J., Christopher R. Johnson and Miriam R. L. Petruck 2003 Background to FrameNet. *International Journal of Lexicography* 16: 235–251.

Fillmore, Charles J. and Paul Kay 1993 *Construction grammar*. Manuscript, University of California at Berkeley.

Fillmore, Charles J., Miriam R. L. Petruck, Joseph Ruppenhofer and Abby Wright 2003 FrameNet in action: The case of attaching. *International Journal of Lexicography* 16: 297–333.

Fontenelle, Thierry 1997 Using a bilingual dictionary to create semantic networks. *International Journal of Lexicography* 10.4: 275–303.

Goddard, Cliff 2010 The semantic metalanguage approach. In: Bernd Heine and Heiko Narrog (eds.), *The Oxford handbook of linguistic analysis*, 460–485. Oxford: Oxford University Press.

Goddard, Cliff and Anna Wierzbicka (eds.) 2004 *Cultural scripts*. Special issue, *Intercultural Pragmatics* 1.2.

Goldberg, Adele 1995 *Constructions: A construction grammar approach to argument structure*. Chicago: University of Chicago Press.

Goldberg, Adele E. 2006 *Constructions at work*. Oxford: Oxford University Press.

Gross, Derek, Ute Fischer and K. J. Miller 1989 The organization of adjectival meanings. *Journal of Memory and Language* 28: 92–106.

Hasegawa, Yoko, Russell Lee-Goldman and Charles J. Fillmore 2010 *Universality of frames: Evidence from English-to-Japanese translation*. Manuscript, University of California Berkeley.

Hasegawa, Yoko, Kyoko Ohara, Russell Lee-Goldman and Charles J. Fillmore 2006 Frame integration, head switching, and translation: RISK in English and Japanese. Paper presented at the Fourth International Conference on Construction Grammar, Tokyo, Japan, September 1–3, 2006.

Heid, Ulrich 1996 Creating a multilingual data collection for bilingual lexicography from parallel monolingual lexicons. In: Martin Gellerstam, Jerker Järborg, Sven-Göran Malmgren, Kerstin Norén, Lena Rogström, Catarina Röjder Papmehl (eds.), *Euralex '96. Proceedings I–II*, 569–573. Göteborg, Sweden: Göteborg University, Department of Swedish.

Jackendoff, Ray 1990 *Semantic structures*. Cambridge, MA: MIT Press.

Lambrecht, Knud 1984 Formulaicity, frame semantics, and pragmatics in German binominal expressions. *Language* 60.4: 753–796.

Langacker, Ronald W. 1990 The rule controversy: A cognitive grammar perspective. *Center for Research in Language Newsletter* 4: 4–15.

Leacock, Claudia and Martin Chodorow 1998 Combining local context and WordNet similarity for word sense identification. In: Christiane Fellbaum (ed.), *WordNet: An electronic lexical database*, 265–284. Cambridge, MA: MIT Press.

Leino, Jakko 2010 Results, cases, and constructions: Argument structure constructions in English and Finnish. In: Hans C. Boas (ed.), *Contrastive studies in construction grammar*, 103–136. Amsterdam: John Benjamins.

Lowe, John B., Colin F. Baker and Charles J. Fillmore 1997 A frame-semantic approach to semantic annotation. In: M. Light (ed.), *Tagging text with lexical semantics. Why, what, and how?. Proceedings of the SIGLEX Workshop*, 18–24. Washington, D.C.: Association for Computational Linguistics.

Lyons, John 1977 *Semantics*. Cambridge: Cambridge University Press.

McLeod, Catherine 1998 COMLEX syntax. *Computers and the Humanities* 31: 459–481.

Miller, George A. (ed.) 1990 WordNet: An on-line lexical database. Special issue, *International Journal of Lexicography* 3.4.

Miller, George A. 1998a Foreword by George A. Miller. In: Christiane Fellbaum (ed.), *WordNet: An electronic lexical database*, xv–xxii. Cambridge, MA: MIT Press.

Miller, George A. 1998b Nouns in WordNet. In: Christiane Fellbaum (ed.), *WordNet: An electronic lexical database*, 23–46. Cambridge, MA: MIT Press.

Miller, K. J. 1998 Modifiers in WordNet. In: Christiane Fellbaum (ed.), *WordNet: An electronic lexical database*, 47–68. Cambridge, MA: MIT Press.

Minsky, Marvin 1975 A framework for representing knowledge. In: Patrick H. Winston (ed.), *The psychology of computer vision*, 211–277. New York: McGraw-Hill.

Ohara, Kyoko 2009 Frame-based contrastive lexical semantics in Japanese FrameNet: The case of risk and kakeru. In: Hans C. Boas (Ed.), *Multilingual FrameNets: Methods and applications*, 163–182. Berlin: Mouton de Gruyter.

Ohara, Kyoko, Seiko Fujii, Hiroaki Saito, Shun Ishizaki, Toshio Ohori and Ryoko Suzuki 2003 The Japanese FrameNet project: A preliminary report. In: *Proceedings of Pacific Association for Computational Linguistics (PACLING'03)*, 249–254. Halifax, Canada: Dalhousie University.

Peters, W., I. Peters, and P. Vossen. 1998. The reduction of semantic ambiguity in linguistic resources. In: A. Rubio, N. Gallardo, R. Catro, and A. Tejada (eds.), *Proceedings of the First International Conference on Language Resources and Evaluation*, 409–416. Granada, Spain.

Petruck, Miriam R. L. 1996 Frame semantics. In: Jeff Verschueren, Jan-Ola Östman, Jan Blommaert and Chris Bulcaen (eds.), *Handbook of pragmatics*, 1–13. Amsterdam: John Benjamins.

Petruck, Miriam R. L. 2009 Typological considerations in constructing a Hebrew FrameNet. In: Hans C. Boas (ed.), *Multilingual FrameNets: Methods and applications*, 183–208. Berlin: Mouton de Gruyter.

Petruck, Miriam R. L. and Hans C. Boas 2003 All in a day's week. In: E. Hajicova, A. Kotesovcova and Jiri Mirovsky (eds.), *Proceedings of CIL 17*. CD-ROM. Prague: Matfyzpress.

Petruck, Miriam R. L., Charles J. Fillmore, Colin Baker, Michael Ellsworth and Joseph Ruppenhofer 2004 Reframing FrameNet data. In: Geoffrey Williams and Sandra Vessier (eds.), *Proceedings of the eleventh EURALEX international congress. EURALEX 2004*. Lorient, France. July 6–10, 2004, 405–416. Lorient Cedex, France: Université de Bretagne-Sud.

Pitel, Guillaume 2009 Cross-lingual labeling of semantic predicates and roles: A low-resource method based on bilingual L(atent) S(emantic) A(nalysis). In: Hans C. Boas (ed.), *Multilingual FrameNets: Methods and applications*, 245–286. Berlin: Mouton de Gruyter.

Ravin, Yael 1990 *Lexical semantics without thematic roles*. Oxford: Oxford University Press.

Ravin, Yael and Claudia Leacock 2000 Polysemy: An overview. In: Yael Ravin and Claudia Leacock (eds.), *Polysemy*, 1–29. Oxford: Oxford University Press.

Rojo, Ana 2002 Frame semantics and the translation of humour. *Babel: International Journal of Translation* 48.1: 34–77.

Rojo, Ana and Javier Valenzuela 1998 Frame semantics and lexical translation: The risk frame and its translation. *Babel: International Journal of Translation* 44.2: 128–138.

Ruppenhofer, Joseph, Michael Ellsworth, Miriam R. L. Petruck, Christopher Johnson and Jan Scheffczyk 2006 *FrameNet II: Extended theory and practice*. Available at: http://framenet.icsi.berkeley.edu.

Saeed, John I. 1997 *Semantics*. Oxford: Blackwell.

Sag, Ivan 2012 Sign-based construction grammar: An informal synopsis. In: Hans C. Boas and Ivan Sag (eds.), *Sign-based construction grammar*. 69–202. Stanford, CA: CSLI Publications.

Salkie, Raf 2002 Two types of translation equivalence. In: Bengt Altenberg and Sylviane Granger (eds.), *Lexis in contrast*, 51–72. Amsterdam: John Benjamins.

Schank, Roger C. and Robert P. Abelson 1975 *Scripts, plans, goals, and understanding*. Hillsdale, NJ: Erlbaum.

Schmidt, Thomas 2009 The Kicktionary – A multilingual lexical resource of football language. In: Hans C. Boas (ed.), *Multilingual FrameNets: Methods and applications*, 101–134. Berlin: Mouton de Gruyter.

Slobin, Dan I. 1996 Two ways to travel: Verbs of motion in English and Spanish. In: Masayoshi Shibatani and Sandra A. Thompson (eds.), *Grammatical constructions: Their form and meaning*, 195–219. Oxford: Oxford University Press.

Subirats, Carlos 2009 Spanish FrameNet: A frame-semantic analysis of the Spanish lexicon. In: Hans C. Boas (ed.), *Multilingual FrameNets: Methods and applications*, 135–162. Berlin: Mouton de Gruyter.

Subirats, Carlos and Miriam R. L. Petruck 2003 Surprise: Spanish FrameNet. Paper presented at the workshop on Frame Semantics, International Congress of Linguists, July 29, 2003, Prague.

Talmy, Lepnard 1985 Lexicalization patterns: Semantic structures in lexical forms. In: Timothy Shopen (ed.), *Language typology and syntactic description*, 57–149. Cambridge: Cambridge University Press.

Tengi, R. I. 1998 Design and implementation of the WordNet lexical database and searching software. In: Christiane Fellbaum (ed.), *WordNet: An electronic lexical database*, 105–128. Cambridge, MA: MIT Press.

Van Valin, Robert D. Jr. and David P. Wilkins 1996 The case for 'effector': Case roles, agents, and agency revisited. In: Masayoshi Shibatani and Sandra Thompson (eds.), *Grammatical constructions: Their form and meaning*, 289–322. Oxford: Oxford University Press.
Vorhees, Ellen M. 1998 Using WordNet for text retrieval. In: Christiane Fellbaum (eds.), *WordNet: An electronic lexical database*, 285–304. Cambridge, MA: MIT Press.
Vossen, Piek (ed.). 1998. *EuroWordNet: A multilingual database with lexical semantic networks for European Languages*. Dordrecht: Kluwer.
Wierzbicka, Anna. 1997. *Understanding cultures through their key words: English, Russian, Polish, German, and Japanese*. New York: Oxford University Press.
Wierzbicka, Anna 2006 *English: Meaning and culture*. Oxford: Oxford University Press.
Ziem, Alexander 2008 *Frames und sprachliches Wissen*. Berlin: Mouton de Gruyter.

Eva Samaniego Fernández
The impact of Cognitive Linguistics on Descriptive Translation Studies: Novel metaphors in English-Spanish newspaper translation as a case in point*

1 Introduction

The translation of metaphor has always been of concern to Translation Studies (henceforth, TS) but, paradoxically, it is an issue that is still generally treated with a prescriptive focus, and mostly from a traditional, not a cognitive point of view. Not until very recently has a cognitive perspective been incorporated into the translational analysis of metaphor, and TS are benefiting considerably from such an approach. Apart from a few articles (Stienstra 1993; Kurth 1999; Mandelblit 1996; Barcelona Sánchez 1997; Cristofoli, Dyrberg, and Stage 1998; Saygin 2001; Al-Harrasi 2001; Tirkkonen-Condit 2001; Schäffner 2004; Dickins 2005; Al-Hasnawi 2007; Maalej 2008; and a few more), there are not many studies dealing with the translation of metaphor from a cognitive perspective and, even so, some of these papers show a prescriptive bias.

Before moving on to the sections of this paper, it seems appropriate to explain the terms *prescriptive* and *descriptive* within DTS. Prescriptive is a term used by Toury (1980, 1985) to refer to approaches to Translation Studies that are normative, that is, which impose criteria stipulating the way a translation should be made in a particular culture (Shuttleworth and Cowie 1997: 130). The term is used to refer to traditional, linguistic, static, source-oriented approaches to translation. These approaches take the ST as the model to be copied, and thus they focus, with few exceptions, on the losses or mistakes in the translation process and tend to offer closed lists of translation procedures. They are called prescriptive because they *prescribe*, that is, they say how a translation should be made in order to be as faithful to its original as possible, for the only purpose of all translations is thought to be faithfulness to their source

---

* Financial support for this research has been provided by the DGI, Spanish Ministry of Education and Science, grant FFI2008-05035-C02-01/FILO. The research has been co-financed through FEDER funds.

text. On the other hand, descriptive models say what translations are actually like (see Schäffner 2004: 1255). Descriptive Translation Studies (DTS) were defined by Holmes (1988) as one of the subdivisions of pure Translation Studies, the other being theoretical Translation Studies, but it is Gideon Toury who has developed the notion to the greatest extent and given this term the meaning that it has today for most translation scholars: a properly systematic descriptive branch of the discipline (Shuttleworth and Cowie 1997: 39). The objective of descriptive translation theory would be "the description of the phenomena of translation" (Munday 2001: 11). Among many other implications, this approach entails (Toury 1995: 36–39) situating the text within the target culture system, looking at its significance and acceptability; comparing ST and TT identifying relationships between segments and, in Munday's words (2001: 112), "attempting generalizations about the underlying concept of translation". A descriptive study of a translation would thus give us clues about the norms[1] of translation. The cumulative identification of norms would in theory bring with it the formulation of laws of translation. These methodological steps allow researchers to draw implications about how translations are actually made, not how they should be made.

Section 2 of this paper deals with metaphor in TS (translatability and translation procedures) and with CL-oriented studies on metaphor translation; Section 3 analyzes the role of novel metaphors in the translation of newspaper texts. Here we will see that many traditionally labelled "incorrect" translations of metaphors (such as literal translations) are in fact introducing new linguistic metaphors into Spanish, and there seems to be sufficient evidence that considerable cognitive innovation and changes are slowly but surely being brought into Spanish thanks to the role of metaphors in translation, regardless of the translation procedure that has been applied. Finally, Section 4 includes the conclusions and some suggestions for further research.

---

1 By *norms* Toury (1995: 55) refers to "the translation of general values or ideas shared by a community – as to what is right or wrong, adequate or inadequate – into performance instructions appropriate for and applicable to a particular situation". Thus, translational norms would be trends of translation behaviour. For example, the translation of proper nouns (both for people and places) has followed different norms in different periods, from total conversion into target language equivalents to being left in the original language. The cumulative study of translation norms would give us clues as to translation *laws* in a particular culture; a classic example of a law (also called a "universal of translation"; Munday 2001: 115) would be "the preference for clarity and avoidance of ambiguity in TTs" (Munday 2001: 118).

2 Metaphor translation in Translation Studies

There is no consensus among translators and scholars as to how to approach metaphor, since it is an area of "great unpredictability" (Menacere 1992: 568). For Dagut (1976: 21), "there is an almost grotesque disproportion between the importance and frequency of metaphor in language use and the very minor role allotted to it in translation theory". Newmark (1988b: 113) believes that metaphor is "the epitome of all translation", and for Toury (1995: 81) it is "a kind of ultimate test of any theory of translation".

In spite of metaphor's "astounding popularity" (Dobrzynska 1995: 595), it is "largely unmapped by translation theory" (Kurth 1999). Metaphor epitomizes the complexity of communication, which is highlighted when two languages are involved in the process. Hence, "metaphor presents a particularly searching test of the translator's ability" (Dagut 1987: 77). Usually, the transfer of a metaphor into another language puts it in an entirely different communicative situation: a metaphor becomes then a product of a different world of ideas (Dobrzyńska 1995: 598–599).

Although metaphor has always been a main concern in TS, little has been done to apply a far-ranging cognitive theory of metaphor and metonymy to translation. As a rule, the few authors that have tried to deal with it are eclectic in their approach. Metaphor translation theory stands on uneasy terrain: one foot stands on the ground of traditional studies of metaphor as a figure of speech, a special kind of comparison or an interaction between ideas (Van Besien and Pelsmaekers 1988: 140) whose function is to embellish the text (Vázquez Ayora 1977; Newmark 1980, 1988a & b; Dagut 1976, 1987; Van den Broeck 1981), and the other foot is starting to take a step towards a CL-oriented theory of metaphor (Mason 1982; Toury 1985; Van Besien and Pelsmaeckers 1988; Snell-Hornby 1988; Schäffner 2004; Tirkkonen-Condit 2001; Saygin 2001, etc.). In Zanotto, Cameron, and Cavalcanti's words (2008: 2), this eclecticism also applies to the methodology employed in the analysis, which seems to be typical of applied studies: "applied linguistic approaches to metaphor do not seek a linguistic theory of metaphor to apply; rather they draw together aspects of theory and methodology that serve to address research problems". Practical applications by their own nature seem to demand a combination of approaches since a single research method "is unlikely to be adequate for investigating metaphor in real world contexts" (Zanotto, Cameron, and Cavalcanti 2008: 3).

In TS most authors recognize the ubiquity and pervasiveness of metaphor, but when it comes to analyzing actual occurrences of metaphors and their translations, they resort to traditional classifications, such as the categorization of metaphors on the grounds of word number (*simplex* or one-word metaphors and *complex* or more than one word; Newmark 1988a: 85), or their function in the text (*decorative* and *creative*; Van den Broeck 1981: 76). They also tend to use traditional terminology such as *image*, *vehicle* and *tenor* (Newmark 1980, 1991, etc.). This is based both on a traditional understanding of metaphor as a figure of speech "whose main function is the stylistic embellishment of the text" (Schäffner 2004: 1254) and on a prescriptive approach to its translation; as a result, one reads in prescriptive approaches that the most important factor for the translation of metaphors is "the bilingual competence of the translator" (Dagut 1976: 24). With a descriptive focus, however, the effectiveness of metaphor translation depends as much on knowledge of the world of the target language as on cognitive skills (Menacere 1992: 568), as well as polysystemic factors. Even nowadays traditional (literalist) and cognitive (figuralist) approaches to metaphor translation coexist.

As stated by Peña Cervel and Ruiz de Mendoza, the borderline between metaphor and metonymy is not always clear, to such an extent that a metaphor-metonymy continuum has been postulated: "in practice, sometimes it is difficult to decide whether we are before a metaphor or a metonymy" (2010: 239, my translation). Unfortunately, most translation theorists "evade the question of the definition of metaphor" (Pisarska 1989: 28; see Vázquez Ayora 1977; Snell-Hornby 1988; Newmark 1988a) by arguing that "to define metaphor does not belong to the proper task of translation theory" (Van den Broeck 1981: 74). Some others study the translation problems posed by metaphor translation without hinting at what they understand by metaphors (see Mason 1982; Van Besien and Pelsmaeckers 1988), or use non-committal definitions. In none of them, with the exception of Schäffner (2004), is it possible to find a differentiation between metaphor and metonymy, since most authors take both to be different linguistic occurrences of conceptual metaphors and thus use the umbrella term "metaphor" to refer to both. Throughout this article, when I use the term *metaphor* – as is customary in TS – I will be referring to both metaphor and metonymy, since the distinction is not relevant for the purposes of my study.

2.1 The translatability of metaphor and translation procedures

In TS two of the main issues concerning metaphor are (i) the translatability of metaphor and (ii) metaphor translation procedures. Van den Broeck (1981: 76) had already established these two issues and the main concerns of TS as regards metaphors: "[TS] may content itself with the more modest task of laying bare some of the hidden mechanisms governing the translation of metaphor and their theoretic degree of translatability".

Some of the most relevant articles on metaphor translation have as a key issue "whether a metaphor can, strictly speaking, be translated as such, or whether it can only be 'reproduced' in some way" (Dagut 1976: 24), and scholars embark on collections of prescriptive rules on how to translate metaphors. Many efforts have been devoted in Translation Studies to the analysis of the variables that might have a bearing on the degree of translatability of a metaphor. Among those most often quoted one can find cultural references, communicative purpose, functional relevance, information burden, metaphor typology, cotext and context restrictions, degree of compatibility of the conceptual and formal structures of the two languages involved, synchronic translation norms, foregrounding, degree of lexicalization of the metaphor, translators' competence, connotations, degree of anisomorphism between the source and target domains in both cultures, comprehensibility of the metaphor, cognitive role, etc. However, there are many other variables which certainly have a say in the translation process but whose nature is much more elusive, such as the reference material used by translators, the time pressure, the amendments introduced in post-translation proof readings and/or revisions, the translator's mood (Newmark 1993) or affections (Jääskeläinen 1999), client-imposed terms, etc. Some of these factors have not as yet been accounted for in academic studies.

As early as 1976, Dagut had already remarked on the inadequacy of "a single generalization about the translatability of metaphor" (1976: 32), pointing out that such a generalization would fail to do justice to the great complexity of the factors determining the ontology of metaphor. Mason (1982: 140) also noticed the futility of a prescriptive approach to metaphor translation: trying to establish a theory of the translation of metaphor is not "a happy project in which to engage": each case, remarks the author, must be treated on its own merits, and thus "there cannot be a theory of the translation of metaphor; there can only be a theory of translation" (Mason 1982: 149). Toury's remark (1985) on this issue is also well-known: we cannot generalize about the translation of metaphor without being speculative. For Van den Broeck, however, who takes a more descriptive approach, to admit the inadequacy of generalizations about the translatability of metaphor would be to admit that translation theory as a whole is an absurd undertaking, "since it then should be incapable of accounting for the translation of one of the most frequent phenomena in language use" (1981: 73). The proper task of translation theory would not be to specify how metaphor should be translated, but to describe and account for actual renderings of metaphors.

For Dagut (1976: 25) there are two diametrically opposed views on the problem of translating metaphor: at one extreme it is held that there is no solution (i.e. metaphor is untranslatable) and at the other that there is no problem (i.e. metaphor can be quite simply translated word by word). Van Besien and Pelsmaeckers (1988: 144) discriminate between the traditional approach, that tends to produce normative statements about how metaphors ought to be translated, and a newer approach that sets up models for the description of actual metaphor translation. However, when all the different views on metaphor in TS are contrasted, one can observe four positions: (i) metaphors are untranslatable (Dagut 1976, 1987; Nida 1964; Vinay and Darbelnet 1958); (ii) metaphors are fully translatable, just like any other translation issue (Kloepfer 1981; Mason 1982); (iii) metaphors are translatable but pose a considerable degree of inequivalence (Van den Broeck 1981; Rabadán Álvarez 1991; Toury 1985, 1995; Newmark 1988a, 1988b; Ali 2006) and (iv) a conciliatory approach, represented by Snell-Hornby (1988) and Schäffner (2004). Snell-Hornby herself calls her approach *integrated*, and to the question of whether metaphors are translatable or untranslatable, she says (1988: 62): "[. . .] the answer lies somewhere between the two poles". For Schäffner and for Snell-Horny, the range of renderings depends on many factors.[2]

Most authors agree that the image in the ST cannot always be retained in the TT (Schäffner 2004: 1256), either because the image in the SL metaphor in unknown in the TL or because the associations that it activates in the target polysystem are meaningless and thus lost. Mason (1982: 141) highlights the fact that "any problems we may have when encountering a metaphor are located at the level of interpretation, and these have to be overcome before we can begin to consider a translation of the metaphor".

There are a few researchers who have posited generalizations about what Dagut called *gradient of translatability*[3] (1987: 82): ST metaphors would occupy a position within a hypothetical scale of translatability, depending on how

---

[2] For instance, Snell-Hornby mentions (1988: 62) "the structure and function of the metaphor within the text". She also adds that although as an abstract concept metaphor may be universal, "in its concrete realization [. . .] it is undoubtedly complicated by language specific idiosyncracies". Schäffner (2004: 1267) includes factors such as the level of conceptual systems in source and target culture, cultural specificity and metaphorical reasoning processes in different languages.

[3] "[. . .] in relation to any TL, every ST metaphor occupies a position on a gradient of translatability (ranging from completely untranslatable to literally translatable) determined by its cultural and lexical resonances and the extent to which these can be reproduced in the TL" (Dagut 1987: 82).

translatable they are, ranging from completely untranslatable to literally translatable. Most of the proposals using categorizations resort to the degree of lexicalization of the metaphor as a classifying feature. For Dagut (1976: 32, 1987: 81–82), the translatability of any given source language metaphor depends on both the particular cultural experiences and the semantic associations exploited, as well and the structural distance between the languages involved. Van Besien and Pelsmaeckers term these broad principles of translatability *speculative*, while Snell-Hornby (1988: 59) inclines to the view that translation scholars should research on metaphor singularity, and then deal with the specific contextual features involved in the process of transfer.

For Van den Broeck, it is possible to make generalizations on metaphor translation, since otherwise the applicability of translation theory would be invalidated (1981: 84):

> Translatability keeps an inverse proportion with the quantity of information manifested by the metaphor and the degree to which this information is structured in a text. The less the quantity of information conveyed by a metaphor and the less complex the structural relations into which it enters in a text, the more translatable this metaphor will be, and vice versa.

The pivotal issue for the author is whether or not metaphors are *functionally relevant* (1981: 76), that is, whether they are relevant to the communicative function of the text; this is also emphasized by Van den Broeck (1981) and Rabadán Álvarez (1991), who refer to the role played by foregrounding in metaphor translation.

In a prescriptive approach a metaphor, "once identified, should ideally be transferred intact from SL to TL" (Schäffner 2004: 1256). In fact, with such a point of view, metaphors would never be translatable as such, which is probably why Schäffner uses the word *ideally*. For Dagut (1976: 24):

> Since a metaphor in SL is, by definition, a new piece of performance, a semantic novelty, it can clearly have no existing equivalence in the TL; what is unique can have no counterpart.

Most authors divide metaphors into different types according to the degree of lexicalization or the novelty that they show. For Dagut (1976: 23) there are ephemeral metaphors, metaphors that remain as they began and metaphors that become established as part of the established stock of language; Van den Broeck (1981: 74–75) establishes three categories: lexicalized (those that have gradually lost their uniqueness and have become part of the established stock or lexicon of the language), conventional or traditional (which are more or less institutionalized in that they are common to a literary school or generation) and private (the so-called bold, innovating creations of individual poets). Dickins (2005) simplifies them to two types: lexicalized and non-lexicalized. Newmark (1988a) classified them into dead (or lexicalized) metaphors (no longer recognisable as metaphors; Snell-Hornby 1988: 57), cliché metaphors,[4] stock (or standard) metaphors[5] (traditional) and recent (or original) metaphors. In his 1988b paper, Newmark added adapted metaphors, for which he gave no definition; however, the examples he quoted were mostly idioms. Snell-Hornby brings this fine-grained classification down to two: original metaphor and dead metaphor. Between them there is a "broad and disputed" territory (1988: 57). Dobrzyńska (1995: 596) also contents herself with two: dead and live metaphors. Rabadán Álvarez (1991) prefers three categories: novel, traditional and lexicalized. However, none of these categories is clear: the borderline between the different types is blurred, which is one reason why trying to establish translation procedures for each type is mostly a fruitless endeavour.

Newmark's list of metaphor translation procedures (1988a: 88–91) is often quoted and has been used profusely, in spite of its fuzziness: reproducing the same image, replacing the SL image with a standard TL image, translation by simile, translation by simile plus sense, conversion to sense, deletion and translation by same metaphor combined with sense. This is a prescriptive list which offers very little, since none of the proposed procedures is motivated or reasoned. There seems to be no justification for its popularity: it does not consider actual translation occurrences, and it does not contemplate possibilities such as the translation of non-metaphorical expressions into metaphors or the creation of linguistic material from <Ø> ("zero into metaphor"; Toury 1985: 25), that is, the creation of a metaphor that does not exist in the ST by translators. Toury (1995) criticizes theories on the translation of metaphor which are not based on descriptive studies. For him, the traditional procedures would be: metaphor into same metaphor, metaphor into different metaphor and metaphor into non-metaphor; however, there are at least three rather common possibilities which are usually neglected: metaphor into nothing, non-metaphor into metaphor and nothing into metaphor. For Dickins (2005), ST metaphors are not necessarily

---

4 "A murky area between dead and stock metaphor. Clichés usually consist of two types of stereotyped collocations: figurative adjective plus literal noun (simplex metaphor) e.g. 'filthy lucre'; or figurative verb plus figurative noun (complex metaphor) e.g. 'explore all avenues' [. . .]" (Newmark 1980: 94).
5 Newmark initially termed them *standard metaphors*, while Van den Broeck (1981) calls them *conventional*. These are mainly metaphors coming from literature and assimilated through usage.

translated into TT metaphors and ST non-metaphors may be translated into TT metaphors or pseudo-metaphors; he does not, however get to the point of acknowledging the fact that nothing in the ST may become a metaphor in the TT. Hiraga (1991), although not referring specifically to translation but rather to comparative cultures, lists four possibilities: (i) similar metaphorical concepts and similar metaphorical expressions; (ii) similar metaphorical concepts but different metaphorical expressions; (iii) different metaphorical concepts but similar metaphorical expressions and (iv) different metaphorical concepts and different metaphorical expressions. Zabalbeascoa (2001: 860) suggests two types of translation procedures: (i) metaphor into metaphor, with different sub-types, and (ii) metaphor into no metaphor, which includes several possibilities. However, he excludes all metaphors in the TT that do not have a source text metaphor, arguing that "the absence of a metaphor in the ST cannot be considered a translation problem" (861, my translation). Van den Broeck (1981: 77), who deals with literary metaphors exclusively, lists three procedures: translation *sensu stricto*, substitution (of the vehicle) and paraphrase. Dobrzyńska (1995: 595) also refers to three categories: metaphor into exact equivalent (M→M), metaphor into metaphorical expression with a similar sense (M1→M2) and untranslatable metaphor into approximate literal paraphrase (M→P). Kurth (1995: 19) studies the translation of a literary work in the language pair English-German and ends up with nine translation procedures: "deletion, demetaphorisation, partial deletion, downtoning, adherence, enhancement, shifted image, new metaphorisation, and elaboration".

As is obvious from the above, the translation procedures that are traditionally suggested in TS for dealing with metaphors (i) are a collection of prescriptive lists of translation procedures based on theoretical hypotheses; (ii) are far from describing the true variety of actual occurrences and (iii) are not valid translation procedures inasmuch as they are not based on any real data but rather on *ad hoc* examples. More often than not, as Toury remarks (1995: 264), these generalizations, which are masked as inherently binding "downright theoretical formulations" (261), are filtered through a preconceived concept of what would constitute a better or worse translational strategy or solution. In translation, each specific situation determines what and how people communicate; situations are not universal but embedded in a cultural habitat, which in turn conditions the situation (Nord 2001: 151). Thus, every translation process is guided by the communicative purposes the target text is supposed to achieve in the target culture: the translator analyses the situation before deciding what to say and how to say it. An account of metaphor translation needs to keep this in mind.

I am not going to deal in detail with the prescriptive rules on the translatability of the different types of metaphors, firstly because these references can be easily found (see Samaniego Fernández 1996, 2000) and my approach is not prescriptive, and secondly because they do not contribute much to a cognitive-descriptive theory of metaphor translation. Suffice it to say that there is little agreement as to which metaphor would be more readily translatable or would lend itself to a more *adequate* translation.

2.2 Cognitive approaches to metaphor translation

Cognitive approaches to metaphor translation are relatively recent in time and few in number (Stienstra 1993; Kurth 1999; Mandelblit 1996; Barcelona Sánchez 1997; Cristofoli, Dyrberg, and Stage 1998; Saygin 2001; Al-Harrasi 2001; Tirkkonen-Condit 2001; Schäffner 2004; Dickins 2005; Al-Hasnawi 2007; Maalej 2008; and a few more). Conceptual metaphor theory emphasizes the embodied nature of meaning and focuses on conceptual structures which are likely to be universal and the cognitive processes involved in translation. Meaning is taken to be construed from the communicative situation and it is renegotiated and recreated in translation within culture. The main argument of the cognitive approach, then, is that metaphors are a means of understanding one domain of experience (target) in terms of another (source), by means of a mapping from the source onto the target, allowing for knowledge-based inferences, base schema and epistemic correspondences (Schäffner 2004: 1258). Metaphor is a conceptual category; therefore metaphor is not a matter of language, but of thought, and it is one of the basic principles of human cognition (Dobrovol'skij and Piirainen 2005: 122) as well as a fundamental part of everyday language, not a figure of speech designed to embellish discourse or typical of literature. In this view, metaphors are not just decorative elements, but rather, "basic resources for thought processes in human society" (Schäffner 2004: 1258). A set of conceptual metaphors structures our daily experience: emotions, abstract concepts, embodied experience, etc.

However, in spite of fact that these approaches to metaphor translation are considerably consistent in their application of cognitive metaphor theories, the same cannot be said about their approach to translation. Most of them still try to set principles of metaphor translation based on a prescriptive focus, that is, they search for a way to transfer metaphors *properly* (that is, with no loss implied). Al-Hasnawi (2007: 14), for example, states that translators' task is "to produce a TL text that bears a close resemblance to the SL text". This rings a familiar bell in the area of prescriptive debates on equivalence (see Halverson, this volume). Al-Hasnawi further assumes that the more two cultures conceptualize experience in a similar way, the more the strategy "similar mapping conditions" applies and the easier the task of translation will be. The same can be said about the studies by Barcelona Sánchez (1997), Saygin (2001), Schäffner (2004), etc.: all of them are outstanding pieces of research from a cognitive point of view, but still adhere to a source-oriented approach which detects ST metaphors (cognitive and linguistic) and judges their TT equivalent in order to find the similarities between the original and its translation. None of them start from the TT and go back to the ST without trying to establish pre-determined equivalences and/or rules on the best way to find mappings and correspondences between the SL and the TL.

From a cognitive perspective, what turns metaphor into a translation issue is that (i) SL metaphors may be approached from the TL cognitive domains and thus interpreted through the filter of the TL; (ii) SL metaphors may trigger associations in the translator that differ from the ones activated in the ST addressee and member of the source polysystem (Kurth 1999). In Lakoff and Johnson's words (1980: 142), "the meaning a metaphor will have for me will be partly culturally determined and partly tied to my past experiences". In translation, two languages are involved, each with different value systems and cultural load (Dobrzyńska 1995: 596). Language boundaries are at the same time boundaries of distinct cultural communities, and metaphor interpretation is strongly culturally conditioned: it does not consist in mere decoding of language signs. At the end of the day, what seems to be impeding the translation process is culture (Snell-Hornby 1988: 62; see also Schäffner 2004):

> As an abstract concept, metaphor might be universal [. . .]; in its concrete realization however, being closely linked with sensuous perception and culture-bound value judgement, it is undoubtedly complicated by language-specific idiosyncracies.

Cultural models are not only all-pervasive; they are also utilized in cognitive processes, such as reasoning (Kövecses 1999: 167), so culture obviously permeates translation (see Bernárdez, this volume). Comparing cultures requires a lot of knowledge by the translator on the areas of conceptual and linguistic overlap and/or dissimilarity between cultures. Different experiential realities bring about different categorizations; thus, cultural differences between the SL and the TL have often been mentioned as problems for translation in general and for the translation of metaphors in particular. In Lakoff and Turner's words (1989: 214), to study metaphor is "to be confronted with hidden aspects of one's mind and one's culture". In metaphor theory within Cognitive Linguistics (henceforth, CL), there is a long-running debate over whether metaphors constitute abstract concepts (as structured by cultural models) or whether they simply reflect them (Kövecses 1999: 167). Gibbs (1999: 162), however, in an attempt to acknowledge the culturally embodied nature of what is cognitive, suggests a new approach where there would be much less of a difference between what is cognitive and what is cultural than many of us "have been traditionally led to believe". This, to him, does not make metaphor any less cognitive.

For Snell-Hornby (1988), the extent to which a text is translatable varies with the degree to which it is embedded in its own culture. Barcelona Sánchez (1997: 84) emphasizes that English and Spanish have a basically similar worldview and that the amount of conceptual common ground shared by two languages determines to a very large extent the degree of translatability between them. Stienstra (1993) advocates for a differentiation between universal, culture-overlapping and culture-specific metaphors: human experience being largely universal, it is the linguistic realization of metaphors that would be culture-dependent. In this sense, it has been argued that if a metaphor triggers different associations in two cultures, a literal translation should be avoided, unless the culture specificity of the SL is to be emphasized, in which case the addition of an explanation is advised (Schäffner 2004).

Most of the studies dealing with metaphor translation from a cognitive perspective use very similar methodological procedures: STs are searched for linguistic metaphors of whichever type (dead, dying, original [. . .]); these are retrieved and classified into groups, so as to propose a series of conceptual metaphors that would account for them. Then the communicative value and significance of these metaphors within the specific type of discourse is assessed. There is usually also an analysis of the type of translation chosen for the linguistic metaphors, as well as an account of the match/mismatch between ST and TT conceptual metaphors. Usually this is followed by an assessment of the impact that the translations have had in the target system, nearly always in comparison with the function and impact of the ST metaphors. This approach is prescriptive in nature. Most of these papers point out the relevance of cognitive operations and abilities in translating metaphor, but use decontextualized examples to make their point. Very rarely is the role played by translator-focused factors taken into account (Chesterman 2009), such as cultural factors (values, ethics, ideologies, traditions, etc.), cognitive factors (mental processes, decision-making, text-processing and re-shaping strategies, etc.) and sociological factors (translational norms followed by translators, social status and network, professional groups, etc.). All of them, together with the overriding force of translational norms, may help to explain the decisions taken by translators as well as their creativity. Another type of study that has not been carried out as yet is the role of the *minimax strategy* suggested by Levy[6] (1987), which might account for certain unexplained (or inexplicable) shifts in the renderings of metaphors and how these may reshape the cognitive universe in the target culture.

Croft and Cruse (2004) touch very briefly on translation, and their profile-frame/domain distinction may be difficult or even unsuccessful in cases where words profile the same or similar concept domain but show differences in their frames.

Mandelblit (1996) proposed two schemes of cognitive mapping conditions: SMC (Similar Mapping Conditions) and DMC (Different Mapping Conditions). The difference in reaction time between one type and the other seems to be due to a conceptual shift that the translator is required to make between the conceptual mapping systems of the source and target languages (1995: 493). Metaphorical expressions take more time to process and are more difficult to translate if they exploit a cognitive domain different from that of the target language equivalent expression.

Barcelona Sánchez (1997) analyzes the translation of metaphorical lexemes from a lexicographic approach and concludes that the best context-free translation for metaphorical lexemes in cases where both languages have the same or a similar metaphor would in principle be expressions in the TL that, in order of importance: (i) can conventionally be used as linguistic expressions of the same metaphor; (ii) highlight in their metaphorical use the same ontological and epistemic correspondences as the original and (iii) can be used as metaphorical denotations of the same target concept. To these, two more criteria would add: that the TL equivalent is in the same position along a stylistic scale and that it should be as similar as possible in its morphosyntax (1997: 87–88). Barcelona Sánchez's approach, being cognitive, is prescriptive in its translational methodology.

Tirkkonen-Condit dealt with translators' difficulties with metaphors and in 2001 proposed, after Mandelblit (1996), the *Cognitive Translation Hypothesis*, whereby metaphorical expressions would take more time and would be more difficult to translate if they exploit a different cognitive domain than the target language equivalent expressions. In these cases, it is the search for another conceptual mapping (another cognitive domain) which causes delay, uncertainty and

---

6   The concept of *minimax strategy* was originally formulated for two-player zero-sum game theory, and it is a decision rule: minimizing the possible loss while maximizing the potential gain (Wikipedia, http://en.wikipedia.org/wiki/Minimax, consulted on May 15, 2010). As applied to TS, it refers to the possible solutions which guarantee a maximum of effect with a minimum of effort (Levy 1967).

difficulty in the translation of different domain metaphors (Tirkkonen-Condit 2001: 12).

Another cognitively focused study is carried out by Saygin (2001), who reports on metaphor comprehension and production in a multi-lingual setting using a translation task. The results obtained indicate that a significantly greater proportion of metaphors were translated literally when subjects translated from their L2 into their L1 (English into Turkish). For the author, the priming of the literal meaning of the metaphor in L2-L1 translation might activate related concepts in L1 because people make use of all the cues they can get in L2 comprehension, literal meaning being the main one in the case of figurative language. The activation of literal meaning, no matter how short, may activate related concepts in the target language, and this may aid the production of a TL metaphor and facilitate the comprehension of the original metaphor even if it does not have a counterpart in the target language. Thus, the literal meaning activation would be giving rise to analogy making.

Schäffner (2004), after giving an overview of the various theories on metaphor translation in Translation Studies, analyzes the advantages of a cognitive approach to metaphor transfer, giving illustrative examples of how some authentic metaphors from texts in political discourse have been translated from German into English. From a cognitive point of view, the first outcome of her research is that not all individual manifestations of a conceptual metaphor in a ST are accounted for in the target text using the same metaphorical expression; this confirms Stienstra's (1993) findings. Thus, from a cognitive perspective, metaphor is no longer merely a translation phenomenon of one particular text, but an intertextual phenomenon. In the examples analyzed, Schäffner identifies five cases: (i) a conceptual metaphor is identical in the ST and TT; (ii) structural components of the base conceptual schema in the ST are replaced in the TT by expressions that make entailments and knowledge-based inferences explicit; (iii) the TT metaphor is much more elaborate; (iv) ST and TT employ different metaphorical expressions (which can be brought under the same conceptual metaphor) and (v) the expression in the TT reflects a different aspect of the conceptual metaphor. All these cases give translators a much more relevant, creative and intelligent role than had traditionally been acknowledged. What is really interesting is that translations can highlight and make differences in conceptual metaphors explicit. Schäffner's is one of the first very good attempts at relating a CL theory of metaphor to DTS; it is a pity, though, that the examples she chooses merely confirm the cases illustrated rather than make up a homogeneous corpus/sample where real occurrences are studied.

Dickins (2005) carries out an in-depth study of Newmark's types of metaphors and incorporates Lakoff and Johnson's metaphor theory so as to propose two six-dimensional models of metaphor translation, full and simplified, which are then applied to Arabic-English translation. However, although the paper is a remarkable attempt at conciliating old and new theories on the translation of metaphors, it does not deal with cognitive metaphors and the examples are chosen not from a corpus, but from different text types and mostly for their representativeness and validation of the points argued in each case. It is, however, acknowledged that the paper has virtually ignored the translation from non-metaphor into metaphor, or even from Ø into metaphor.

Al-Hasnawi (2007) attempts to carry out a cognitive study of the translation of metaphors form English into Arabic. Following Mandelblit's Cognitive Translation Hypothesis, his ultimate goal is, through the study of metaphoric expressions in a given culture, "to see how the members of that culture structure or map their experience of the world and record it into their native language" (2007: 3). He studies metaphors of similar mapping conditions, metaphors of similar mapping conditions but lexically realized differently, and metaphors of different mapping conditions. However, his approach is prescriptive in nature, since he recurrently remarks that metaphors can be translated from one language to another "with a minimum degree of loss", and refers to "attempts of literal rendering" as "a noticeably bad product" (2007: 7). Metaphor translations, then, are judged once more through an a priori concept of what would be a better or worse translation according to a set of pre-established, prescriptive definition of what equivalence should be. Unfortunately, the second part of his study confirms this approach: his 23 examples are *ad hoc*, randomly selected instances chosen for their representativeness of the points argued, and the focus is not on the solutions as they really are, with no a priori criteria and value judgments.

One of the most recent studies has been carried out by Maalej (2008). His hypothesis is, following Mandelblit, that metaphoric expressions tend to be kept under the same conceptual metaphors if the two cultures share the same conceptual mappings and linguistic expressions; if, however, they do not share them, the search for a pragmatic equivalent in the TT will be very hard indeed (2008: 60). Metaphor is not a case of untranslatability, but a challenging phenomenon in terms of un-packing SL information and re-packing it in the TL and culture. Maalej points out that the criteria of understanding, using, framing and organizing experience are all crucial for translating metaphors, and argues for a three-step cognitive model of metaphor translation (65):

> Unpacking the SL/SC linguistic metaphors into their conceptual counterparts, comparing cultures by determining whether linguistic and conceptual metaphors across cultures show

a "similar mapping condition" or a "different mapping condition", and re-packing TL/TC conceptual and linguistic counterparts according to the experiential practices of the TL/TC.

Maalej's model, however, is prescriptive in nature, since it attempts to establish correspondences and refers to shifts in the translation process with a negative bias. For him, metaphor translation would work with linguistic categories that may be pragmatically equivalent in terms of semantic packaging to the knowledge carried by the TL/TC metaphor to be translated (2008: 66). Finally, he analyzes a corpus (a play written by a Tunisian playwright and translated into English), and he does find four metaphoric clusters, but (i) the examples given seem to have been chosen for their representativeness, and (ii) he still submits translation to a traditional notion of a good translation based on faithfulness: "if literal translation sounds odd, shocking, or unintelligible to English speakers, DMC [different mapping conditions] applies" (2008: 69).

Although cognitively appropriate, these proposals cannot account for cases where conceptual mappings and/or linguistic expressions may be shared but the translator decides to leave aside standard correspondences and opt for a creative translation instead. A cognitive theory of metaphor translation cannot deal with these instances without the assistance of DTS: it is, in fact, both the creativity of translators, together with other cognitive factors and translation constraints, which in certain cases seem to impede a rather straightforward transfer procedure and activate other cognitive strategies to communicate in translation (see examples 1a, 6b, 7c and 11b below, under Section 3.3). From a cognitive point of view, a lot of factors come into play when a metaphor has to be translated: issues such as the translation norm prevalent in the target universe, the translator's degree of manoeuvre and creativity, the general value system of the target universe, etc. are paramount in the translation process. Metaphor is based on people's ability to structure one conceptual domain in terms on another, generate mappings and establish conceptual correspondences (Dobrovol'skij and Piirainen 2005: 122). Thus, from the point of view of translation, the debate should not be whether to translate *image,* or *vehicle,* but rather to what extent metaphors are universal or culturally-determined, and what features – if any – will be transferred on the basis of a series of factors.

Interestingly enough, although quite a lot of researchers point out that translators often translate metaphors *incorrectly* (literally, etc.), the role of those *wrong* translations in the target system has not been studied to date. For Samaniego Fernández (2002, 2007) and Samaniego Fernández, Velasco Sacristán, and Fuertes Olivera (2005), literal translations might in fact be diffusing the distinction between culture-dependent and culture-independent subject domains. The role of English metaphors (English being a dominant language) in the creation of target conceptual scenarios in different target languages and the subsequent cognitive expansion has not been studied sufficiently. It could shed some light on the mental processes associated with translation and their effects on the cognitive potentialities of target languages. The relationship between observable data and cognition might help us understand how the human capacity for communication (translation being a type of interlinguistic communication) fits into the broader picture of social cognition. In fact, according to Halverson (2007), translation shifts may derive from so-called construal operations, and as such are fundamentally cognitive. The issue of the role played by the creativity of translators in the target cognitive world has hardly been touched upon and is an intriguing and unresolved matter in TS (Kussmaul 2000a, 2000b, 2000c); unfortunately, it is beyond the scope of this paper, but it is a very interesting issue for eager researchers.

3 The role of novel metaphors in the translation of newspaper texts

The nature of metaphor as a problem in Translation Studies has nearly always been established in the source pole, proceeding from source-text items identified as metaphors. Very often, as Toury remarks (1995: 81), the ST metaphors were given tentative TL equivalents assessed on a scale of good or bad according to some preconceived notion of equivalence and a classification of the ST metaphor in terms of meaning, constituents and metaphoricity. Thus, metaphors were judged through an *a priori* concept of what would be a better or worse translation. Only rarely has the focus been on the solutions as they really are, with no pre-established criteria and value judgments (Toury 1995: 81), which is what I aimed to do in my study. Toury's 1995 argument that Ø could be translated into metaphor seemed very attractive to us, mostly because no other author acknowledges this as a real possibility. Problematic items of this kind would go completely unnoticed "unless they are established 'in reverse'" (Toury 1995: 78), that is, starting off from the TT. This is precisely what I have done in my study, in an attempt to discover what material in the STs matches the novel metaphors chosen in the TTs, thus keeping away from traditional approaches by reversing the traditional ST-TT comparison and turning it into a TT-ST match. This is the only way for certain translational possibilities, such as the creation of novel material in the TTs from Ø textual material in the STs, or TT metaphors coming from ST non-metaphorical material, to come to light. In line with DTS methodology, I assume that the translations and their source texts are equivalent: what remains to be uncovered is the specific way this equivalence has been actually achieved in the sample.

Following this descriptive/inductive/experimental method, 389 novel metaphors were identified in the Spanish TTs, which matched 370 items (metaphorical or otherwise) in the original texts in English. The paper carries out an analysis of the results obtained, focusing in particular on cases of mismatches between ST and TT.

3.1 Novel metaphors

The adjective *novel* (Rabadán Álvarez 1991; Fraser 1993; Cristofoli, Dyrberg, and Stage 1998) has been chosen as against other terminological alternatives due to its transparency. There are a number of options, however: *recent* (Newmark 1988a), *original* (Newmark 1988a; Snell-Hornby 1988; Pisarska 1989, etc.), *similarity-creating* (Indurkhya 1992), *poetic* metaphor (Sweetser 1990; Dobrzyńska 1995: 596; Dagut 1987), *private* (Van den Broeck 1981), *creative* (Sperber and Wilson 1986), *innovative* (Pisarska 1989), *live* or *alive* (Dobrzyńska 1995: 596; Larson 1989: 331–332), *actual* (Dobrzyńska 1995: 596) or, more simply, *new* (MacCormack 1985: 136). Whichever term is used, the receiver finds novelty or communicative surprise in them; consequently, they flout addressee expectations (Rabadán Álvarez 1991: 142).

There were several reasons for choosing novel metaphors in this study: first, while stock and lexicalized metaphors have been studied profusely (particularly in literary texts), novel metaphors still lack an adequate cognitive and translational framework (Indurkhya 1992: 3; Rabadán Álvarez 1991). Second, one of my aims was to check whether novel metaphors were actually as frequent in newspaper texts as some authors believe them to be (see Newmark 1988b; Snell-Hornby 1988; Steen 1994: 73, etc.). However, I was not interested in a study on frequency of occurrence, but rather in the kind of equivalence translators ended up with. Third, it was challenging to put to test Dagut's remark that "what determines the translatability of a SL metaphor is not its 'boldness' or 'originality' but rather the extent to which the cultural experience and semantic associations on which it draws are shared by speakers of the particular TL" (1976: 28). One further aim was to take a look at the degree of creativity shown by translators and the cognitive reasons behind their choices, although this latter aim is one that goes beyond the scope of this paper and will require further research.

Novel linguistic metaphors display the following features: (i) they may manifest themselves in different linguistic forms and do not have length restrictions; (ii) they are not lexicalized (Dickins 2005), that is, standardized, and have therefore not been incorporated into common usage, having no entries as such in dictionaries or reference works; (iii) the receiver perceives them as metaphorical language and finds "novelty" or "communicative surprise" in them (they flout addressee expectations; Rabadán Álvarez 1991); (iv) they may be divided into several groups (Steen 1994; Indurkhya 1992); for this study, we have chosen four major groups: *pure* novel metaphors; novel metaphors (based on a pre-existent conceptual metaphor) showing a new combination of terms; novel metaphors that show originality of meaning even if the linguistic terms used are not original,[7] and novel metaphors that are a simultaneous exploitation of the original literal meaning and the metaphorical one (see Le Guern 1976: 123). For Dickins (2005), the distinction between a lexicalized and a non-lexicalized metaphor is not always clear-cut, but in any case from the point of view of Translation Studies the importance of the distinction is not that it should be absolutely true, but that on the whole it provides a reasonable way in the majority of cases to broadly distinguish between groups.

3.2 The sample

The study comprises 122 source newspaper texts and their translations (a total of 244), which constitute the whole of texts originally published by *The Guardian* (U.K. edition) and subsequently translated and published in *El Mundo* in a one-year period (from the 1st of January to the 31st of December). This means that the sample includes only those texts whose original *and* translation were published within the selected period. The time gap between STs and their TTs ranges from virtually Ø (text and translation published on the same day) up to 57 days (nearly 2 months) of difference between the ST and the TT.

The total number of words in the binomials studied is well above 250,000 (more specifically 285,859). This is far from being a large corpus (which is why it is called a "sample" rather than a corpus), but following Pearson (1998) and Bowker and Pearson (2002), valuable results can also be obtained from reduced studies.

It is essential to remember that, following Toury (1995), a *reverse* process of selection of the novel metaphors to be studied has been carried out: they have been detected *in the target texts*, not in the source texts, which is the only viable route to identify occurrences such as Ø into novel metaphor, or

---

[7] As shown in the study, the meaning of the metaphors belonging to this category does not correspond to what the linguistic form seems to point to. See examples 4a and 4b.

non-metaphorical material into novel metaphor. Thus I made sure that I was not looking for pre-established correspondences between the source metaphors and the target metaphors, since I was interested in looking at what I would find in the STs to match the TT novel metaphors.

The process of selection of TT novel metaphors was carried out as follows:

- Three native speakers of Spanish unrelated to English philological studies and to translation were asked to pick out any novel metaphors they could find in the TTs. The author of this paper was not one of them. They were told to use communicative surprise as a clue – as explained in Section 3.1 – and they were specifically asked not to exclude metaphors that were novel because they showed an original exploitation of a preexisting linguistic item (metaphorical or not), original meaning (but not original linguistic expression), or a simultaneous exploitation of the literal and the figurative (see examples in Section 3.3 below). The total number of TT novel metaphors chosen was 482.
- Two filters were then applied: the first one was dictionaries: if a novel metaphor was found in a dictionary, it meant that it was lexicalized and it was omitted from the candidate list. Five Spanish dictionaries were used (4 descriptive, 1 normative). The second filter was six subjects, native speakers of Spanish (unrelated to the preselectors). These subjects did not go through the texts, they were only given the candidate list. In order for a candidate metaphor to be dropped from the list, at least four of these subjects had to agree that the metaphor was not novel to them. After these two filters, 93 candidate metaphors were dropped from the list.

The result was a total of 389 novel metaphors in Spanish, which matched 370 items (metaphorical or otherwise) in English. The difference in number is due to the fact that 19 target text metaphors had as source text equivalent <Ø> and were consequently created in the TTs from zero linguistic material in the STs, thus confirming Toury's 1995 hypothesis. It is noteworthy that only 364 TT metaphors out of the total 389 correspond with metaphorical material in the source texts.

3.3 Results

Interesting as a more detailed study would be, I have chosen one parameter of analysis only, due to space restrictions: the use-related classification of the metaphors (novel as against dead, dying, etc.), which I believe can give us insight into the cognitive and linguistic impact caused by translation procedures.⁸

Once more, it is important to remember that the novel metaphors of the sample have been selected in the TTs. The possibilities of novel metaphor types for the TTs, as mentioned in Section 3.1, are:

(i) TT novel metaphors due to a simultaneous exploitation of the literal and figurative meaning (twofold exploitation):

(1) a. ST: *Dances with turkeys*
   TT: *Con el agua al cuello*⁹
   'Up to the neck in water'¹⁰
   b. ST: [. . .] *his fee can only be described as Brando-size*
   TT: [. . .] *salario de cuantía brandiana*
   'A Brandian sum salary'

(ii) TT novel metaphors due to an original exploitation of a linguistic item (metaphorical or not):

(2) a. ST: Ø
   TT: [. . .] *con su última tacada de negocios "milmillonarios"*
   'With his latest pile of multimillion business venture'
   b. ST: *Defending Spain against the English Inquisition*
   TT: *Defendiendo a España frente a la Inquisición británica*
   'Defending Spain from the English Inquisition'

(iii) TT pure novel metaphors:

(3) a. ST: [. . .] *spasm of bowing and scraping*
   TT: [. . .] *espasmo de zalemas*
   'Spasm of bowing'

---

8 For a more detailed study of other factors, see http://rua.ua.es/dspace/bitstream/10045/3989/1/Samaniego%20Fern%c3%a1ndez%2c%20Eva.pdf.
9 The double exploitation is the following: in the TT, agua 'water' refers simultaneously to the failure of the film Waterworld and to the fact that its failure put Kevin Costner in serious financial difficulties, since in Spanish to be up to the neck with water, which is a literal translation of the original, means not to be able to make both ends meet, to be in financial trouble.
10 Thanks are due to Riccardo Oprandi for the translations.

    b. ST: *Internet [. . .] the disordered, benevolent beast*
       TT: *Internet [. . .] la bestia caótica y benevolente*
       'The chaotic and benevolent beast'

(iv) TT novel metaphors with original meaning (but not an original linguistic expression):

(4) a. ST: *[. . .] bureaucratic capitalism*
       TT: *[. . .] capitalismo burocrático*[11]
       'Bureaucratic capitalism'
    b. ST: *Political suicide has been around since AD 73*
       TT: *El suicidio político ha existido desde el año 73 a.c.*[12]
       'Political suicide has existed since AD 73'

The possibilities, however, are much wider in the STs:

(i) ST Ø (absence of linguistic material):

(5) a. ST: Ø
       TT: *[. . .] convertida en un paisaje de ruinas*
       'Turned into a landscape of ruins'
    b. ST: Ø
       TT: *Entre el amasijo de hierros retorcidos, los bomberos encontraron, además de un hombre muerto, un mito roto*
       'Amongst the jumble of twisted iron, the firemen found, as well as a dead man, a broken myth'
    c. ST: Ø
       TT: *Los derechos históricos colisionan con la sed de la tierra*
       'Historic rights collide with the thirst of the land'
    d. ST: Ø
       TT: *Molotov [. . .] olvidado por un partido al que se había dedicado, a golpe de "martillazo",*[13] *toda su vida*

---

[11] The originality lies in the fact that it does not refer to a capitalist system with a lot of bureaucracy, but rather to the fact that bureaucrats in Russia are the main shareholders in private companies.
[12] The originality lies in the fact that it does not refer to the suicide of an individual politician, but to the decision by a group of population (in this case, the inhabitants of a city) to commit collective suicide rather than surrender to the enemy.
[13] Molotov in Russian means 'hammer'.

'Molotov [. . .] forgotten by the party to which he had dedicated all his life by hammer blows'

(ii) ST dead metaphors:

(6) a. ST: *Positive discrimination*
   TT: *Discriminación correcta*
   'Correct discrimination'
   b. ST: *Shotgun wedding of the year thrills beleaguered Serbia*
   TT: *La bella y el bestia*
   'Beauty and a beast'

(iii) ST non-metaphorical material:

(7) a. ST: [. . .] *a book deal*
   TT: [. . .] *ha completado su lista de honores al firmar un libro-reportaje*
   'He has completed his list of honours on signing of a book documentary'
   b. ST: *This was Bono's first interview in two years*
   TT: *Dos años de mordaza autoimpuesta*
   'Two years of self-imposed muzzling'
   c. ST: *US team finds gold-laden Japanese submarine 51 years after sinking*
   TT: *La joya hundida*
   'The sunken jewel'

(iv) ST novel metaphors due to a simultaneous exploitation of the literal and figurative meaning (twofold exploitation):

(8) a. ST: [. . .] *from the unlikely Olympus of a hotel skyscraper*
   TT: [. . .] *desde el extravagante Olimpo de un rascacielos hotelero*
   'From the extravagant Olympus of a hotel skyscraper'
   b. ST: *Island in a sea of E*
   TT: *Ibiza, una isla en un mar de éxtasis*
   'Ibiza, an island in a sea of ecstasy'

(v) ST novel metaphors due to an original exploitation of a linguistic item (metaphorical or not):

(9) a. ST: [. . .] *the much reviled lights-camel-action genre*
   TT: [. . .] *género de "luces, camello, acción"*
   'Genre of lights-camel-action'

b. ST: *The power and the Glory*[14]
TT: *El poder y la Gloria*
'The power and the Glory'

(vi) ST pure novel metaphors:

(10) a. ST: [. . .] *water has a funny way of ending in the rich man's bucket these days*
TT: [. . .] *es muy probable que el agua termine sólo en los aljibes de las villas de los ricos*
'It is likely that the water ends up in the rich people's water tanks'
b. ST: [. . .] *a computer [. . .] is an interface where the mind and the body can connect with the universe and move bits of it about*
TT: *un ordenador [. . .] es un interfaz mediante el cual la mente y el cuerpo pueden conectarse con el universo y mover partes de él*
'A computer is an interface through which the mind and the body can connect themselves to the universe and move parts of it'

(vii) ST novel metaphors with original meaning (but not an original linguistic expression):

(11) a. ST: *"interval" cancer*[15]
TT: *cáncer de "intervalo"*
'Interval cancer'
b. ST: *Window dressing*[16]
TT: *Las ventanas del telepredicador*
'The windows of the telepreacher'

(viii) ST semi-novel metaphors:

(12) a. ST: [. . .] *reverse sexism*
TT: [. . .] *sexismo a la inversa*
'Reverse sexism'
b. ST: [. . .] *she has great DNA*
TT: [. . .] *posee un estupendo DNA*
'She has a great DNA'

---

14 The originality is that it refers to Emilio Estefan, a music producer (the power), and Gloria Estefan, a singer (the Glory), who are married.
15 It refers to cancers that develop between one check-up and the next.
16 It refers to the latest version of Windows.

Table 6.1: ST-TT metaphor correspondences

	TT novel (2fold expl.)	TT novel (orig. expl. ling. item)	TT novel (pure)	TT novel mean. not form	
ST ø	0	8	7	4	Total in STs 19 (4.8%)
ST dead	1	35	48	6	Total in STs 90 (24.3%)
ST non-metaphor	0	1	5	0	Total in STs 6 (1.54%)
ST novel (2fold expl.)	20	0	4	1	Total in STs 25 (6.42%)
ST novel (orig. expl. ling. item)	0	71	30	2	Total in STs 103 (27.8%)
ST novel (pure)	0	7	90	2	Total in STs 99 (26.7%)
ST novel Mean. not form	0	1	6	19	Total in STs 26 (6.68%)
ST semi-novel	0	7	13	1	Total in STs 21 (5.39%)
					Total in STs: 370
	Total in TTs: 21 (5.6%)	Total in TTs: 130 (33.4%)	Total in TTs: 203 (52.1%)	Total in TTs: 35 (8.9%)	
	Total in TTs: 389				

Table 6.1 below shows the numbers obtained for TT-ST matching. The results obtained were the following:

Before analysing the figures obtained, let us see some illustrative examples of each of the types mentioned in the table above. The figures in Table 6.1 above can be broken down and interpreted as follows:

(i) The three most frequent types of TT novel metaphor are "pure" (52.1%; examples 3a and 3b), followed by those that show an original exploitation of a linguistic item (33.4%; examples 2a and 2b), and novel meaning (but not form) metaphors (8.9%; examples 4a and 4b). For the STs, however, the figures change significantly: the most frequent type is metaphors with an original exploitation of the linguistic items (27.8%; examples 9a and 9b), followed by novel metaphors (26.7%; examples 10a and 10b) and dead metaphors (24.3%; examples 6a and 6b).

(ii) Out of the 389 novel TT metaphors, 200 (51.41%) show the same type of metaphor as their original (examples 1a and 1b): this shows that interlinguistic anisomorphism in metaphor translation is slightly prevalent, although followed rather closely by the number of TT novel metaphors that are anisomorphic, i.e. that change the type of metaphor in the ST: 170 (43.7%; examples 6a, 6b and 11b). 19 (4.88%) have no linguistic material in the original (examples 5a, 5b, 5c and 5d).

For each of the types analysed, the most relevant features are:

- TT Novel "pure" metaphors: 203 (52.1%). 90 of them (44.3%) show anisomorphism to their original; among them it is relevant to mention that 48 (23.6%) come from dead metaphors (examples 6a and 6b), 13 (6.4%) come from seminovel (dying) metaphors (examples 12a and 12b) and 5 (2.4%) come from non-metaphorical material (examples 7a and 7b). 113 TT metaphors (55.6%) are anisomorphic, i.e., change the metaphor type in translation. Out of these 113 cases, 73 (64.6%) come from material that can be classified as non-novel, so there seems to be a relevant tendency to "enliven" non-novel material in the process of transfer, either due to literal translations that result in novel metaphors, or due to conscious choices.
- TT novel metaphors where there is an original exploitation of the linguistic items involved (examples 2a and 2b): 130.[17] 71 (54.6%) are isomorphic and 59 (45.3%) are anisomorphic; out of the latter, 51 (86.4%) come from non-novel material. Once again, where there is anisomorphism, the tendency is to create novel material in the TTs.
- TT novel metaphors that show a novelty of meaning but not so much of form (examples 4a and 4b): 35[18] (8.9%). 19 of them (54.2%) are isomorphic and 16 (45.7%) anisomorphic; out of these, 7 (43.7%) come from non-novel material.
- TT novel metaphors that exploit the literal and the figurative simultaneously (examples 1a and 1b): 21 (5.6%); in 20 the tendency is to isomorphism (95.2%).

---

17 As seen in Table 6.1, 8 of them come from Ø, 35 from ST dead metaphors, 1 from ST non-metaphorical material, 71 from ST metaphors based on the exploitation of linguistic items, 7 from ST pure novel metaphors, 1 from ST metaphors based on originality of meaning (but not form), and 7 from ST semi-novel (dying) metaphors.

18 As seen in Table 6.1, 4 of them come from Ø, 6 from ST dead metaphors, 1 from ST metaphors with twofold exploitation, 2 from ST metaphors based on the exploitation of linguistic items, 2 from ST pure novel metaphors, 19 from ST metaphors based on originality of meaning (but not form), and 1 from ST semi-novel (dying) metaphors.

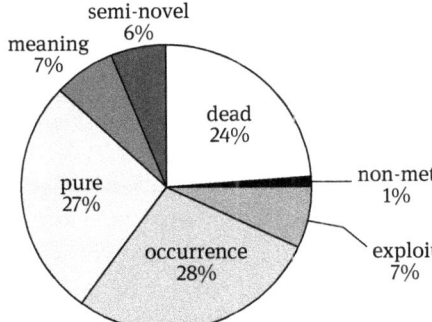

Figure 6.1: Metaphor types (STs). Key: Dead: dead metaphor; Non-met: non-metaphorical item; Exploit: simultaneous exploitation of the literal and figurative; Occurrence: original explcitation of linguistic items; Pure: pure novel metaphor; Meaning: original exploitation of meaning but not of form; Semi-novel: metaphors immersed in a process of lexicalization

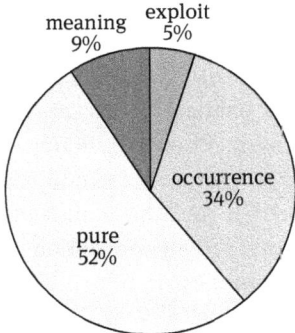

Figure 6.2: Metaphor types (TTs)

- TT novel metaphors that have no textual material in the STs (examples 5a, 5b, 5c and 5d): 19 (4.8%). These represent a spontaneous creation process by translators.

An outline, in general terms, of the results obtained from the figures in Table 6.1 and in the pie charts above would be the following:

(i) isomorphism is slightly prevalent in novel ST metaphor-novel TT metaphor translation; however, the figures for changes (anisomorphism) are shortly behind;

(ii) the most frequent type of novel metaphor in the TTs is the pure type; this is not the case with ST metaphors, where the original exploitation of linguistic items type is the most abundant;

(iii) most novel metaphors in the TTs come from novel material in the STs; there is, however, a relevant percentage of novel TT metaphors coming from non-novel material in the ST (dead metaphors, semi-novel metaphors, Ø, non-metaphorical material [. . .]). In these cases the translational tendency is to "enliven" what is dead or dying in the original;

(iv) there is also a small percentage of original creation of novel material in the TTs. This means that, as Toury had pointed out, translators *do* create their own textual material.

As Toury had observed (1995: 147), the decisions made by translators, particularly by individual translators while translating a single text, are far from erratic: in fact, they tend to be highly patterned. These regularities of behaviour can be attributed to some governing principles, the strongest of these principles originating in the target system itself, whose needs the translation is designed to satisfy.

In my opinion, case (iv) above is very interesting, particularly novel TT metaphors coming from literal translations of metaphoric material inexistent as such in the target language. This case proves that, by making intentional or unintentional use of literal translations, translators are in fact introducing new metaphorical mappings into the target culture. Basically, the immediate impact of this tendency on the target system is a remarkable contribution to intercultural terminological and conceptual standardization, and in time this develops new mechanisms of conceptual extension in the target system. Further, most of the translations of the metaphorical expressions studied are coherent with the principle of transparency: their meanings in Spanish can be guessed at because they appeal to our recognition of underlying symbolism (Fuertes Olivera and Samaniego Fernández 1998), even if the translations do not exist as common expressions in Spanish.

Let us see a few illustrative examples of creation in the TTs of novel metaphorical material through literal translation. I do not provide idiomatic translations because they are all literal translations; however, in the Spanish version I include in brackets the equivalent expression:

(13)   ST: [. . .] *to see the Chirac collapse as the mark of* [. . .] *a banana skin*
TT: [. . .] *apreciar el derrumbe de Chirac* [. . .] *como un simple resbalón sobre una piel de plátano* (un patinazo)

(14) ST: [. . .] *it was a kiss on the cheek for Murdoch*
TT: [. . .] *para Murdoch fue un beso en la mejilla* (un regalo caído del cielo; le vino de perlas)

(15) ST: [. . .] *miscalculation is an actor*
TT: [. . .] *la falta de cálculo es el principal actor* (factor, elemento)

(16) ST: [. . .] *among the media mogul's most pressing ambitions is to gain a foothold in Ted Turner's empire*
TT: [. . .] *entre las ambiciones más urgentes del magnate de los medios figura poner pie en el imperio de Turner* (meter mano/meter la cabeza)

(17) ST: [. . .] *stir the conscience of the world*
TT: [. . .] *agitar las conciencias del mundo* (sacudir)

(18) ST: [. . .] *had the dice rolled slightly differently*
TT: [. . .] *si los dados hubiesen rodado de modo distinto* (si las cosas hubieran sido distintas)

(19) ST: [. . .] *even if polls say he is the Republican frontrunner*
TT: [. . .] *pese a que los sondeos digan que será el corredor delantero de los republicanos* (candidato principal)

(20) ST: [. . .] *he had struck a deep American nerve*
TT: [. . .] *había tocado un nervio profundo de los Estados Unidos* (fibra sensible)

(21) ST: [. . .] *the tolerance of the US electorate proved its elasticity most in 1989*
TT: [. . .] *cuando más elástica resultó ser la tolerancia de los votantes estadounidenses fue en 1989* (mayor, más grande)

(22) ST: [. . .] *he saw women as gold-diggers*
TT: [. . .] *consideraba a las mujeres buscadoras de oro* (interesadas)

(23) ST: [. . .] *the Krajina was sealed like a pressure cooker yesterday*
TT: [. . .] *la región de Krajina quedó cerrada como una olla a presión* (a cal y canto)

(24)   ST: [. . .] *there is no way we are going to make that particular sum*
TT: [. . .] *no hay forma de que podamos realizar esa suma concreta* (salgan los números)

(25)   ST: [. . .] *how far the pendulum swings in the direction of autocracy*
TT: [. . .] *la distancia que llegue a recorrer el péndulo en dirección a la autocracia* (lo que se avance)

(26)   ST: [. . .] *the logic of today's profit*
TT: [. . .] *la lógica de los beneficios del día* (el aquí y ahora; pan para hoy y hambre para mañana)

(27)   ST: [. . .] *Russia had pushed its military border 384 miles to the west*
TT: [. . .] *Rusia había empujado su frontera militar 615 kilómetros al oeste* (desplazado, trasladado)

(28)   ST: [. . .] *echoes of Auschwitz* [. . .] *are still exploding in our midst*
TT: [. . .] *el eco de los gritos de Auschwitz aún estalla entre nosotros* (resuena)

A very interesting issue in the sample, apart from the role played by literal translations in the target culture, is the fact that, in line with Schäffner's (2004: 1267) conclusions, some shifts, differences or even apparently radically diverging translations can only rarely, if at all, be characterized as translation errors *from a descriptive point of view*. Linguistically, they may be errors, but culturally and cognitively they may end up being incorporated into the target universe. Even if they are errors by translators, what matters is the impact such translations may ultimately have on the target culture. Some of them show a surprising degree of creativity by translators. The analysis of metaphor translations and the metaphorical reasoning processes involved may reveal possible cultural differences in the conceptual structures. Translators may be said to operate first and foremost in the interest of the culture into which they are translating (Toury 1995: 12). Translation behaviour within a culture tends to manifest certain regularities; even if unable to account for deviations, the people belonging to that culture can tell when a translator has failed to adhere to sanctioned practice.

As the sample shows and Toury argued (1995: 57), even the most adequacy-oriented translation involves shifts from the source text. Even when no clear macro-level tendency can be shown, any micro-level decision can still be accounted for, and the reverse: where an overall choice has been made, it is not necessary that every single lower-level decision be made in accordance with it: this is because regularities are not of an absolute type. Translators' behaviour cannot be expected to be fully systematic (Toury 1995: 67); translators' decisions usually involve some *ad hoc* combination of the two extremes in the initial norm (adequacy vs. acceptability), or a compromise solution between both. Consistency is a graded notion, not a radical one. This is true to such an extent that, in Toury's words (1995: 69), "even idiosyncrasies [. . .] often manifest themselves as personal ways of realizing (more) general attitudes rather than deviations in a completely unexpected direction". To go beyond the mere establishment of check-lists of factors is the future task of TS.

Finally, it can also be pointed out that the possibility that a translator make up a metaphor from non-metaphorical material or even from "zero" material in the ST is a reality: it does happen, in a low but sufficiently relevant percentage (see Table 6.1 and examples 5a, 5b, 5c and 5d as well as examples 7a and 7b). Both Toury (1985, 1995) and Dickins (2005) had acknowledged this possibility. Other authors do not even mention this possibility because their prescriptive approach forces them to adopt a source language bias which establishes correspondences only between ST items and their equivalents, but does not look for any other occurrence. Some other authors mention this possibility, but only as an odd, infrequent case.

One remarkable aspect of this piece of research, then, is the role played by the translator's creativity. A 'creative" translation can be defined as follows (Kussmaul 2000a: 58):

> [. . .] a creative translation is a translation which (a) involves changes when compared with the source text, thereby bringing in something that is novel [. . .] and which (b) is also appropriate for the task that was set, i.e. the translation assignment (or purpose).

Some of the translations in the sample match this definition perfectly: they depart from the original considerably (example 1a), in some cases almost totally (see examples 6b, 7c and 11b), but they are still appropriate, creative, original and successful renderings. In my opinion, the role of translators' creativity in the target culture has been very seriously neglected so far, and prescriptive translation theories are to blame for that. If creative translations are brought into the arena of mainstream translational research with a cognitive focus, they could be successfully used to investigate general language processing, reasoning, information processing, knowledge representation and many other essential issues.

A cognitive view of metaphor can provide TS with valuable insights, first of all because it sheds light on the cognitive processes and reasoning behind the choice of a translation equivalent without the prejudice of a prescriptive approach which focuses on the ST as a paradigm to be followed. This descriptive approach is the only one that allows TS to account for apparently divergent translation solutions which should in justice be analyzed as selective choices or creative attempts by translators rather than as mere errors, negative shifts, undertranslations or overtranslations.

In the end, the pivotal point is the translator, which is precisely what cognitive approaches to TS are focusing on. Many disciplines, among them Translation Studies and Cognitive Linguistics, have to walk hand in hand in order to be able to account for the reasoning processes (deductive, inductive, abductive, analogical, etc.) and the re-formulating processes (problem-solving, planning, knowledge representation, etc.) carried out by translators. Chesterman's (2000: 26) remark on the role played by translator-oriented factors (see also Chesterman 2009) in the translation process is particularly applicable:

> [. . .] insofar as explanatory hypotheses appeal to situational factors such as the skopos or socio-cultural factors such as translation norms, it must be borne in mind that these only actually affect the translation via the translator's own mind. This realization places the translators themselves at the centre of a causal model.

4 Conclusion

The present study has many limitations: first of all, even though in my opinion it has rendered interesting results, it is a study of a reduced sample, and is thus restricted to a very specific genre and two languages: newspaper texts translated from English into Spanish. Any firm conclusions regarding novel metaphors and translation must await further research on larger samples and/or corpora. Many more similar experiments with more genres, text types, more subjects (informants) and other languages must obviously be carried out to test the generality and validity of the results presented here. It will take many in-depth analyses based on larger and more varied corpora before any proper hypotheses on the translation of metaphor can be formulated. Further descriptive research in the field of the translation of metaphor will no doubt yield regularities (norms) in the translation of this phenomenon, but most of all it will allow us to get a better picture both of the synchronic norms in force in the transfer of metaphors and of the cognitive processes involved. Thus, by studying the strategies and the reasoning behind the way translators deal with metaphors, and most of all, by analysing the effect and impact that specific transfers have on target cultures,[19] TS can greatly benefit from a descriptive approach to metaphor translation. This impact is analyzed in DTS, which deal with the different ways that translations ultimately influence target cultures (Toury 1995: 56–59) through norms: translation policy, operational norms, directness of translation, textual-linguistic norms, etc. At a microstructural level, the impact of the translation of metaphors on target cultures can also be analysed; for example, one can look at the way literal translations of novel metaphors may end up creating new mappings in the target culture universe.

As seen in Section 2, the translation procedures that are traditionally suggested in TS for dealing with metaphors (i) are a collection of prescriptive lists of translation techniques based on theoretical hypotheses; (ii) are far from describing the true variety of actual occurrences and (iii) are not valid translation procedures inasmuch as they are not based on any real data but rather on *ad hoc* examples. Real translation occurrences seem to validate the hypothesis that translators actually have a much more relevant, creative and intelligent role than had traditionally been acknowledged (Kussmaul 2000a; Jääskeläinen 1999).

Eventually, what is at stake in the translation of metaphor is the concept of "equivalence" to be applied. Notwithstanding the impact of functionalist, communicative, textual and most of all descriptive approaches, many scholars and translators still only use the term *translation* for binomials where an equivalence relation stands between ST and TT (Schäffner 2004: 1254–1255). However, such equivalence refers only to STs and TTs that bear a relationship of literalness and/or functional effect, (preferably both). For prescriptive studies, only when such a relationship exists can the term *translation* be used properly. Any TT that does not bear a faithfulness-based relationship of equivalence to its ST should not be called a translation but something else (adaptation, recreation, etc.). In DTS, however, equivalence is merely the relationship between an ST and a TT, of whichever type it may be; in Herman's (1998: 61) words, "it is difference, not sameness or transparency or equality, which is inscribed in the operations of translation". Unfortunately, the aforementioned prescriptive

---

[19] For example, whether a particular translation of an item catches on and in what way a collection of these individual translations may cumulatively and eventually end up changing, no matter how slowly, the cognitive universe of the target culture. As Toury remarked in 1995, it takes many studies taken together to be able to describe the translational norms that apply in a particular culture, but this is the only way for DTS to be truly scientific.

approach also applies to metaphor translation: too many pages have been written on how much is lost in their translation instead of focusing on the gains that the process of transfer may bring about, its impact on the target culture and the role of translators in the expansion of the target culture cognitive world.

In the descriptive study I have presented there are several remarkable features which I think may be a significant contribution to research on regularities prevalent in English-Spanish newspaper texts metaphor translation, although it must be borne in mind that these results are limited to the genre, text type and particular parameters under study: (i) tendency to isomorphism: in general, translations tend to "copy" the original; (ii) concomitantly, there is also a smaller but sufficiently representative tendency to "enliven" in the target texts dead or dying metaphors, as well as non-metaphorical material from the source texts (mostly through literal translations that turn ST material into novel metaphors). This may be due to the nature of newspaper texts, where the attention of the reader has to be called and kept throughout the text;[20] (iii) there is also a significant percentage of creation of novel material in the TTs from Ø in the STs. This means that translators *do* create intentionally their own novel metaphors and therefore textual material.

A relevant number of novel TT metaphors come from literal translations: by making intentional or unintentional use of literal translations, translators are in fact enlarging the target conceptual world. This, in time, could lead to intercultural standardization of culture-specific items and cognitive patterns. It is also clear that the resulting expressions in Spanish seem to have been understood correctly, and this proves their transparency: they can be interpreted precisely because they appeal to our cognitive skills.

In conclusion, the results obtained from the analysis of actual translation occurrences seem to prove what descriptive Translation Studies claim: equivalence is a formula that has to be enlarged to cover the multiplicity of translational answers given by translators, which include "unfaithfulness", creation of new material and many other options that were not formerly contemplated in more traditional approaches to translation. Translators are, after all, sharp text creators.

---

[20] A lot could also be said about the influence of the type of newspaper on translation norms, in this case a broadsheet newspaper, *The Guardian*, as against a Spanish newspaper, *El Mundo*, which is closer to a broadsheet but which makes use of some of the communicative techniques employed by tabloids. Unfortunately, this topic falls beyond the scope of this paper. For further information on this issue, see Samaniego Fernández (2001) and Samaniego Fernández and Campos Pardillos (2003).

Finally, I would like to devote a small section to some interesting issues for further research. The role of metaphor translation in the development of new cognitive domains and mappings in target languages is a field still open for descriptive studies to be carried out, as is the issue of how far literal renderings of linguistic metaphors tend to standardise conceptual metaphors across cultures and may contribute to the creation of conceptual scenarios ending up as tools for cognitive expansion in target languages. This would help us determine whether metaphors and their translations have an impact on the spread of quasi-universal conceptual domains and culturally determined ones. As a natural consequence, further research could carried out on the "intended" and "unintended" impact metaphor translations may have: change of ideologies and points of view, construction of ideas, new insights, manipulation, etc. Translational data allow us to induce metaphor translation regularities and, eventually, norms.

Another interesting question is whether, and in what sense, the analysis of texts for metaphors and metaphorical reasoning processes in different languages may reveal cultural differences/mismatches in conceptual structures, as suggested by Schäffner (2004); additionally, the relevance of Translation Studies in the research on universal, culture-overlapping and culture-specific metaphors.

Research on the topic of the translation of metaphor is still nearly unexplored: we need a specification of the constraints on metaphor translation as a norm-governed activity. The real role of cultural, textual, semiotic, pragmatic and other such constraints in metaphor translation is still to be determined, as is the relevance of the *minimax strategy* (Levy 1967: 48) as applied to metaphor translation (least effort, greatest impact) and whether it can account for some "unaccountable" renderings of metaphors. We need to know more about the type of factors that prime in the translator's mind when translating metaphors.

Another issue that is still relatively unexplored is to what extent metaphorical expressions might impede quick translations when they exploit a different cognitive domain from that of the target language equivalent expressions. Closely related is the question of whether, and in what sense, the activation of literal meaning may trigger related concepts in the target language, aiding the translation of the original metaphor even if it does not have a counterpart in the target language. We need to know if translators, as text receivers and interpreters, actually access conceptual metaphors when constructing interpretations of metaphorical expressions and how this might influence decision-making for the TT structure (see Schäffner 2004: 1258).

One could also wonder if the profile-frame/domain distinction suggested by Croft and Cruse (2004) may account for the fact that different frames for similar/

identical domains in different cultures may render difficult and often unsuccessful translations.

As for the specific collaboration between TS and CL, we could ask ourselves the following questions: To what extent is the assessment of the translations of linguistic metaphors still linguistically biased? That is, is it still too language-focused and prescriptive in approach? Could a more open-minded, descriptive approach to the translation of metaphor house translator-focused factors such as decision-making, psychological traits, etc. TS needs to know whether cognitively-focused research into creative translations (Ballard 1997; Kussmaul 2000a; Jääskeläinen 1999) can be successfully used to investigate general language processing, reasoning, information processing, knowledge representation and many other essential issues in translation.

References

Al-Harrasi, Abdulla 2001 *Metaphor in (Arabic-into-English) translation with specific reference to metaphorical concepts and expressions in political discourse.* Unpublished Ph D. thesis, Aston University, Birmingham.
Al-Hasnawi, Ali 2007 A cognitive approach to translating metaphors. *Translation Journal* 11.3. Available at: http://accurapid.com/journal/41metaphor.htm.
Ali, Abdul Sahib Mehdi 2006 On the translation of metaphor: Notions and pedagogical implications. *A International Journal of Arabic-English Studies* 7: 121–136.
Ballard, Michel 1997 Créativité et traduction. *Target* 9.1: 85–110.
Barcelona Sánchez, Antonio 1997 Metaphorical expressions in interlinguistic lexicography: A cognitive approach. In: Ricardo J. Sola, Luis A. Lázaro and José A. Gurpegui (eds.), *XVIII Congreso de AEDEAN*, 83–91. Alcalá, Spain: Servicio de Publicaciones.
Bowker, Lynne and Jennifer Pearson 2002 *Working with specialized language. A practical guide to using corpora.* London: Routledge.
Chesterman, Andrew 2000 A causal model for translation studies. In: Maeve Olohan (ed.), *Intercultural faultlines: Research models in translation studies I. Textual and cognitive aspects*, 15–27. Manchester: St. Jerome.
Chesterman, Andrew 2009 The name and nature of translator studies. *Hermes – Journal of Language and Communication Studies* 42: 13–22.
Cristofoli, Mirella, Gunhild Dyrberg and Lilian Stage 1998 Metaphor, meaning and translation. *Hermes – Journal of Linguistics* 20: 165–179.
Croft, William and Alan Cruse 2004 *Cognitive Linguistics*. Cambridge: Cambridge University Press.
Dagut, Menachem B. 1976 Can metaphor be translated? *Babel: International Journal of Translation* 12.1: 21–33.
Dagut, Menachem B. 1987 More about the translatability of metaphor. *Babel: International Journal of Translation* 33.2: 77–83.
Deignan, Alice 2008 Corpus linguistic data and conceptual metaphor theory. In: Mara Sophia Zanotto, Lynne Cameron and Marilda C. Cavalcanti (eds.), *Confronting metaphor in use: An applied linguistic approach*, 149–162. Amsterdam: John Benjamins.
Dickins, James 2005 Two models for metaphor translation. *Target* 17.2: 217–273.

Dobrynska, Teresa 1995 Translating metaphors: Problems of meaning. *Journal of Pragmatics* 24: 595–604.
Dobrovol'skij, Dimitrij and Elena Piirainen 2005 *Figurative language: Cross-cultural and cross-linguistic perspectives.* Amsterdam: Elsevier.
Fraser, Bruce 1993 The interpretation of novel metaphors. In: Andrew Ortony (ed.), *Metaphor and thought*, 329–341. Cambridge: Cambridge University Press.
Fuertes Olivera, Pedro and Eva Samaniego Fernández 1998 Metaphor and motivation: A study of English informal phraseological units. *Lexicology* 4.1: 35–59.
Gibbs, Raymond W. 1999 Taking metaphor out of our heads and putting it into the cultural world. In: Raymond W. Gibbs and Gerard J. Steen (eds.), *Metaphor in cognitive linguistics*, 145–166. Amsterdam: John Benjamins.
Halverson, Sandra 2007 A cognitive linguistic approach to translation shifts. *Belgian Journal of Linguistics* 21: 105–122.
Hatim, Basil and Ian Mason 1997 *The translator as communicator.* London: Routledge.
Hermans, Theo 1998 Translation and the representational mode. Voice, value, discourse. In P. Fernández Nistal and Jose María Bravo Gozalo (eds.), *La traducción: orientaciones lingüísticas y culturales*, 97–118. Valladolid, Spain: Servicio de Publicaciones.
Hiraga, Masako K. 1991 Metaphor and comparative cultures. In: P. G. Fendos Jr. (ed.), *Cross-cultural communication: East and west*, Vol. 3, 149–166. Taiwan: T'ai Ch'eng Publishing in Tainan.
Holmes, James (ed.) 1988 *Translated! Papers on Literary Translation and Translation Studies.* Amsterdam: Rodopi.
Indurkhya, Bipin 1992 *Metaphor and cognition: Studies in cognitive systems.* Dordrecht, the Netherlands: Kluwer Academic.
Jääskeläinen, Riitta 1999 *Tapping the process: An exploratory study of the cognitive and affective factors involved in translating.* Joensuu, Finland: Joen.
Kloepfer, Rolf 1981 Intra- and Intercultural Translation. *Poetics Today* 2.4: 29–37.
Kövecses, Zoltan 1999 Metaphor: Does it constitute or reflect cultural models? In Raymond W. Gibbs and Gerard Steen (eds.), *Metaphor in cognitive linguistics*, 167–188. Amsterdam: John Benjamins.
Kurth, Ernst-Norbert 1995 *Metaphernübersetzung.* Frankfurt am Main: Peter Lang.
Kurth, Ernst-Norbert 1999 Altered images: Cognitive and pragmatic aspects of metaphor translation. In: Jan Vandaele (ed.), *Translation and the (re)location of meaning: Selected papers of the CETRA Research Seminars in Translation Studies 1994–1996*, 97–116. Lovaina, Belgium: CETRA.
Kussmaul, Paul 2000a A cognitive framework for looking at creative mental processes. In: Maeve Olohan (ed.), *Intercultural faultlines: Research models in translation studies I. Textual and cognitive aspects*, 57–71. Manchester: St. Jerome.
Kussmaul, Paul 2000b *Kreatives Übersetzen.* Tübingen, Germany: Stauffenburg.
Kussmaul, Paul 2000c Types of creative translating. In: Andrew Chesterman, Natividad Gallardo and Yves Gambier (eds.), *Translation in context: Selected contributions from the EST Congress, Granada 1998*, 117–126. Amsterdam: John Benjamins.
Lakoff, George and Mark Johnson 1980 *Metaphors we live by.* Chicago: University of Chicago Press.
Lakoff, George and Mark Turner 1989 *More than cool reason.* Chicago: University of Chicago Press.

Larson, Milfred L. 1989 *La traducción basada en el significado*. Buenos Aires: Eudeba, translated from the 1984 edition in English.
Le Guern, Michel 1976 *La metáfora y la metonimia*. Madrid: Cátedra, translated from the 1972 edition in French.
Levy, S. 1987 Some Views on Metaphor: From Classical Rhetoric to Robbe-Grillet. *The Linguist* 26.2: 66–68.
Maalej, Zouhair 2008 Translating metaphor between unrelated cultures: A cognitive-pragmatic perspective. *Sayyab Translation Journal (STJ)* 1: 60–82.
MacCormack, Earl R. 1985 *A Cognitive Theory of Metaphor*. Cambridge (Mass.): MIT Press.
Mandelblit, Nili 1996 The cognitive view of metaphor and its implications for translation theory. In: Marcel Thelen and Barbara Lewandowska-Tomaszczyk (eds.), *Translation and meaning*, Part 3, 483–495. Maastricht, the Netherlands: Hoogeschool.
Mason, Kirsten 1982 Metaphor and translation. *Babel: International Journal of Translation* 28.3: 140–149.
Menacere, Mohammed 1992 Arabic metaphor and idiom in translation. *Meta* 37.3: 567–572.
Munday, Jeremy 2001 *Introducing translation studies: Theories and applications*. Abingdon/New York: Routledge.
Muñoz Martín, Ricardo 1995 *Lingüística para traducir*. Barcelona: Teide.
Muñoz Martín, Ricardo 2007 Traductología cognitiva y traductología empírica. In: Gerd Wotjak (ed.), *Quo Vadis, Translatologie?* 267–278. Berlin: Franck and Timme.
Newmark, Peter 1988a *Approaches to translation*. Oxford, London: Prentice Hall International (1st ed. 1981 Pergamon Institute of English).
Newmark, Peter 1988b *A textbook of translation*. London: Prentice Hall International.
Newmark, P. 1991 *About Translation*. Clevedon: Multilingual Matters Limited.
Newmark, Peter 1993 *Paragraphs on translation*. Clevedon, UK: Multilingual Matters.
Nida, Eugene A. 1964 *Toward a Science of Translating*. Leiden: E.J. Brill.
Nord, Christiane 2001 Dealing with purposes in intercultural communication: Some methodological considerations. *Revista Alicantina de Estudios Ingleses* 14: 151–166.
Pearson, Jennifer 1998 *Terms in Context*. Amsterdam/Philadelphia: John Benjamins.
Peña Cervel, Sandra and Francisco Ruiz de Mendoza 2010 Los modelos cognitivos idealizados. In: Ricardo Mairal Usón, M. Sandra Peña, Francisco Cortés and Francisco Ruiz de Mendoza, *Teoría Lingüística. Métodos, Herramientas, Paradigmas*, 231–285. Madrid, Spain: Ramón Areces/UNED.
Pisarska, Alicja 1989 *Creativity of translators: The translation of metaphorical expressions in non-literary texts*. Poznan, Poland: Uniwersytet.
Rabadán Álvarez, Rosa 1991 *Equivalencia y traducción. Problemática de la equivalencia translémica inglés-español*. León, Spain: Universidad de León.
Samaniego Fernández, Eva 1996 *La traducción de la metáfora*. Valladolid, Spain: Secretariado de Publicaciones de la Universidad de Valladolid.
Samaniego Fernández, Eva 2000 *Diseño y aplicación de un marco de análisis de la traducción de la metáfora*. Unpublished doctoral dissertation. University of Alicante, Spain. Available at: http://rua.ua.es/dspace/bitstream/10045/3989/1/Samaniego%20Fern%c3%a1ndez%2c%20Eva.pdf.
Samaniego Fernández, Eva 2001 Pragmatics and semiotics: The relevance of addressee expectations in the translation of newspaper texts. *Revista Alicantina de Estudios Ingleses* 14: 249–279.

Samaniego Fernández, Eva 2002 Translators' English-Spanish metaphorical competence: Impact on the target system. *Estudios de Lingüística Inglesa Aplicada (ELIA)* 3: 203–218.
Samaniego Fernández, Eva 2007 El impacto de la lingüística cognitiva en los estudios de traducción. In: Pedro Fuertes Clivera (ed.), *Problemas lingüísticos de la traducción especializada*, 119–154. Valladolid, Spain: Secretariado de Publicaciones, Universidad de Valladolid.
Samaniego Fernández, Eva, and Miguel Ángel Campos Pardillos 2003 El papel del anclaje en la traducción: los textos periodísticos. *Miscelánea* 27: 187–207.
Samaniego Fernández, Eva, Mariscl Velasco Sacristán and Pedro Fuertes Olivera 2005 Translations we live by: The impact of metaphor translation on target systems. In: Pedro Fuertes Olivera (ed.), *Lengua y Sociedad: Investigaciones recientes en Lingüística Aplicada*, 61–81. Valladolid, Spain: Servicio de Publicaciones.
Saygin, Ayse Pinar 2001 Processing figurative language in a multi-lingual task: Translation, transfer and metaphor. In: John A. Barden, Mark G. Lee and Katja Markert (eds.), *Proceedings of corpus-based and processing approaches to figurative language workshop*, 39–46. Lancaster University.
Schäffner, Cristine 1998 Metaphern. In: Mary Snell-Hornby, Hans G. Hönig, Paul Kussmaul and Peter A. Schmitt (eds.), *Handbuch Translation*, 280–285. Tübingen, Germany: Stauffenburg.
Schäffner, Cristine 2004 Metaphor and translation: Some implications of a cognitive approach. *Journal of Pragmatics* 36.7: 1253–1269.
Shuttleworth, Mark and Moira Cowie (eds.) 1997 *Dictionary of translation studies*. Manchester: St Jerome.
Snell-Hornby, Mary 1988 *Translation studies: An integrated approach*. Amsterdam: John Benjamins.
Sperber, Dan and Deirdre Wilson 1986 *Relevance. Communication and Cognition*. Oxford: Basil Blackwell.
Steen, Gerard J. 1994 *Understanding metaphor in literature*. London: Longman.
Steen, Gerard J. 2004b Introduction: Metaphor across languages. *Journal of Pragmatics* 36.7: 1183–1188.
Stienstra, Nelly 1993 *YHWH is the husband of is people: Analysis of a biblical metaphor with special reference to translation*. Kampen, the Netherlands: Kok Pharos.
Sweetser, Eve 1990 *From Etymology to Pragmatics. Metaphorical and Cultural Aspects of Semantic Structure*. Cambridge: Cambridge University Press.
Tirkkonen-Condit, Sonja 2001 Metaphors in translation processes and products. *Quaderns. Revista de traducció* 6: 11–15.
Toury, Gideon 1980 *In search of a theory of translation*. Tel Aviv, Israel: The Porter Institute.
Toury, Gideon 1985 A rationale for descriptive translation studies. In: Theo Hermans (ed.), *The manipulation of literature: Studies in literary translation*, 16–41. Beckenham, UK: Croom Helm.
Toury, Gideon 1995 *Descriptive translation studies and beyond*. Amsterdam: John Benjamins.
Van Besien, Fred and Katia Pelsmaeckers 1988 The translation of metaphor. In: Paul Nekeman (ed.), *Translation, our future: Proceedings of the XIth World Congress of F.I.T.*, 140–146. Maastricht, the Netherlands: Euroterm.
Van den Broeck, Raymond 1981 The limits of translatability exemplified by metaphor translation. *Poetics Today* 2.4: 73–87.

Vázquez Ayora, Gerardo 1977 *Introducción a la traductología*. Washington D.C.: Georgetown University Press.
Vinay, Jean-Paul and Jean Darbelnet 1958 *Stylistique Comparée du Français et de L'Anglais. Méthode de traduction*. Paris: Didier.
Zabalbeascoa, Patrick 2001 Un marco para el análisis de la traducción de la metáfora. In: Anne Barr, M. Rosario Martín Ruano and Jesús Torres del Rey (eds.), *Últimas corrientes teóricas en los Estudios de Traducción y sus aplicaciones*, 858–866. Salamanca, Spain: Universidad de Salamanca.
Zanotto, Mara Sophia, Lynne Cameron and Marilda C. Cavalcanti (eds.) 2008 *Confronting metaphor in use: An applied linguistic approach*. Amsterdam: John Benjamins.

Mario Brdar and Rita Brdar-Szabó
Translating (by means of) metonymy

1 Introduction

A sort of question that a naïve reader is quite likely to expect that a chapter like this one should raise is about the best way of translating metonymy, along the lines of strategies proposed by Newmark (1985: 304–311) for translating metaphor.[1] This is of course precisely what this chapter cannot provide, the most compelling reason being the fact that such an all-round recipe for the translation of metonymy is impossible. A variation on this theme might be to ask how Cognitive Linguistics can help us arrive at the most suitable translational equivalents of metonymic expressions.

Instead of trying to provide an answer to the first question, in this chapter we go part of the way towards answering the second question. Specifically, we will consider how Cognitive Linguistics can help us: (i) become more aware of possible problems, and therefore, (ii) more easily find appropriate solutions when dealing with metonymy and related phenomena in translation practice. Note that the two are, after all, very closely related. As noted by Feyaerts (2003: 7), metaphor and translation are two processes of semantic change they face the same challenge, from an onomasiological point of view, of finding co(n)textually appropriate linguistic means to express complex contents. We could also add that the same applies to metonymy.

The question can be further operationalized into two related issues indicated by the very title of the present chapter. Dealing with metonymy in translation practice can, on the one hand, mean translating metonymic expressions in a given context, but on the other hand, it can also mean translating something by means of metonymic expressions. These will be discussed in various sections in Section 3. Ideally, the two go hand in hand when we translate a metonymic expression in the source language text by a metonymic expression in the target language text. What is more, the fact that this happens so often

---

[1] Newmark actually lists eight strategies, one of them suggesting the deletion of redundant or otiose metaphors. These are in his order of preference: 1. reproducing the same image in the target language, 2. replacing the image in the source language with a standard target language image which does not clash with the target language culture, 3. translation of metaphor by simile, retaining the image, 4. translation of metaphor by simile plus sense, 5. conversion of metaphor to sense, 6. modification of metaphor, 7. deletion, 8. translation of metaphor by the same metaphor combined with sense.

without any problems is one of the reasons why metonymy is far less conspicuous in translation than, for example, metaphor (see Samaniego Fernández, this volume). In Section 3.1, we will, among other things, also be concerned with defining metonymy in contrast with metaphor because this difference, we claim, is a fairly direct consequence of the differences between the two cognitive processes producing metonymies and metaphors, respectively. This already constitutes a solid piece of evidence in support of the claim that Cognitive Linguistics should help those involved with translation practice and theorizing become more aware of metonymy.

This ideal confluence, i.e. translating metonymy by means of metonymy, discussed in Section 3.2, is, however, not necessarily always the case. A metonymic expression can for a number of reasons apparently be translated by something that is not a metonymic expression. Conversely, a non-metonymic expression can sometimes also be translated by means of a metonymic expression. These two asymmetric relations will be discussed in turn in Section 3.3.

2 Metonymy (vs. metaphor) in Cognitive Linguistics

Since we are obviously dealing in translation with lexicalized, i.e. with linguistically manifest metonymies, we take as our starting point the threefold distinction between linguistic vehicle, metonymic source and metonymic target, as proposed in Panther (2005: 358), as shown in Figure 7.1.

Within the cognitive linguistic framework, both metaphor and metonymy are considered to be cognitive operations involving domains and mappings. They have been contrasted with respect to five marked points of difference, although it has been repeatedly claimed that the borderline between the two is blurred (cf. Barcelona 2000a, 2000b; Radden 2002; Ruiz de Mendoza Ibáñez 2000).

As for the first point of difference, metonymy is in most traditional approaches usually contrasted with metaphor (and occasionally with synecdoche) concerning

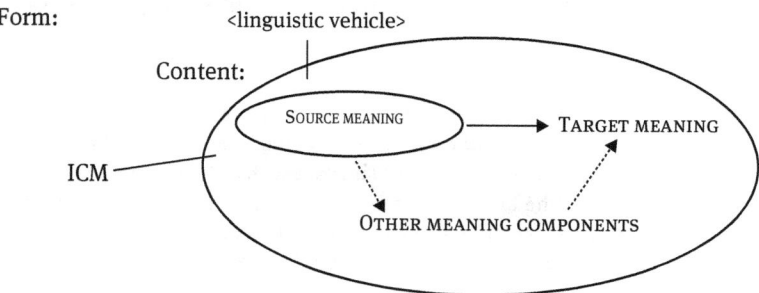

Figure 7.1: The basic metonymic relation (Panther 2005: 358)

the nature of the relationship obtaining between the vehicle and the target. Firstly, metonymy is claimed to be based on contiguity, whereas metaphor is seen as resting on similarity (cf. Ullmann 1962: 212; Taylor 1989: 122). Contiguity is here taken to cover all associative relations except similarity. This means that metonyms are expressions that are used instead of some other expressions such that the latter expressions are associated with or suggested by the former ones:

(1) He was testifying on the **Hill** earlier in the week

(2) London **is determined to** grab a share of Iraq's oil once Saddam is overthrown

In example (1), *the Hill*, short for *Capitol Hill*, is not used to denote this particular location in Washington, i.e. the hill where the Capitol building stands, or not even so much this particular building as the institution of the US Congress which meets in this building. Similarly, in (2) *London*, collocating with the adjective *determined* which presupposes an animate subject that can be attributed will/intention, is not meant to simply refer to the capital of the UK but to the government of the UK, London being its official seat.

The second important point of difference between metaphor and metonymy observed by cognitive linguists has to do with whether the mapping takes place across distinct conceptual domains or within a single domain (or idealized cognitive model, also called script, scenario, or frame in cognitive linguistic literature). The standard view is that a metonymic mapping occurs within a single domain, while metaphoric mappings take place across two discrete domains. The differences between the two types of mappings can be presented schematically as shown in Figure 7.2.

The conceptual distance between the source and target meaning is larger in the case of metaphors, as they link two more or less conceptually distinct and

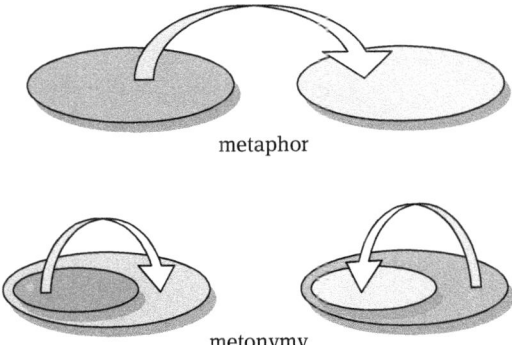

Figure 7.2: Metaphor and metonymy distinguished on the basis of domain inclusion

distant domains, the distance between metonymic source and target, which are both found within a single domain matrix, being relatively smaller.

As for the directionality of the two types of mappings as a third point of difference, metaphors typically employ a more concrete concept or domain as source in order to structure a more abstract concept or domain as target. In the majority of cases, elements from the physical world are mapped onto the social and mental world. Metaphorical mappings are thus normally unidirectional, and the source and target are not reversible. The situation with metonymies is quite different. Metonymic mappings can proceed in either direction, from the more concrete part of the domain (i.e. of the subdomain) to the more abstract one, and the other way round, as shown in Figure 7.1 above. According to Radden and Kövecses (1999: 22), "[i]n principle, either of the two conceptual entities related may stand for the other, i.e., unlike metaphor, metonymy is basically a reversible process".

Another crucial point of difference between metaphor and metonymy has to do with the number of mappings taking place. Conceptual metaphors are characterized by whole sets of systematic conceptual correspondences between certain elements of the source domain on the one hand and their counterparts which are elements of the target domain, on the other, while metonymies exhibit only a single mapping. The differences between the two types of mappings can now be presented schematically as shown in Figure 7.3.

The traditional notion of metonymy is in some recent works claimed to be a cluster of related reference point phenomena (Langacker 1999). Croft and Cruse (2004: 47), as well as Paradis (2004), thus distinguish three types of construals that are commonly referred to as metonymy in the literature. Paradis (2004) talks

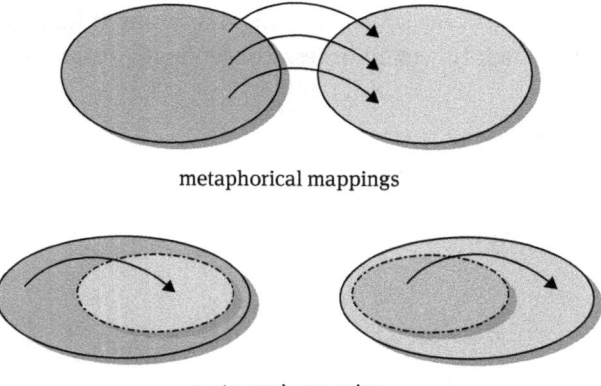

Figure 7.3: Metaphor and metonymy distinguished on the basis of the number of conceptual mappings (correspondences) involved

about metonymization, facetization, and zone activation, illustrated in the three sets of examples from Croft and Cruse (2004: 48) below.

Metonymization, i.e. the process leading to metonymies in the strictest sense of the term, involves the use of a lexical item to evoke the sense of something that is not conventionally linked to that particular lexical item. According to Croft and Cruse (2004: 48), metonymy is "the ability of a speaker to select a different contextually salient concept profile in a domain or domain matrix than the one usually symbolized by the word".

(3) **That french fries** is getting impatient (Croft and Cruse 2004: 48)

Modifying the above figure from Panther (2005: 358), we could visualize metonymy proper as shown in Figure 7.4.

Facetization, on the other hand, is the highlighting of different facets or domains in a domain matrix. Facets are readings within senses and they can be conventionally activated by one and the same lexical item, i.e. the activated meaning cannot normally be conventionally referred to by some other simple lexical item (though in some cases the concept can be expressed by means of compounds, e.g. *window pane*, in [4a]).

(4) a. The **window** is dirty (Croft and Cruse 2004: 48)
    b. *She came in through the* **window** (Croft and Cruse 2004: 48)

Assuming that one of the facets, i.e. the concept associated with one of the readings within a sense, is more basic than the rest, the facetization type of metonymy could be schematically presented as in Figure 7.5.

The facetization type of metonymy is fairly regular in a double sense. Firstly, it tends to operate on lexical items that are associated with certain types of concepts as their primary readings, e.g. the institution reading (*school, bank, court, hospital,*

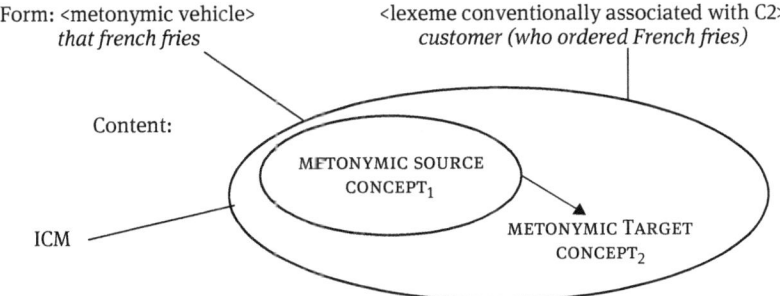

Figure 7.4: Metonymization proper

etc.). Secondly, the arrays of readings, i.e. metonymic extensions available with such lexical items are very similar ('building', 'staff', 'abstract institution', etc.)

According to Langacker (1999), (5) can be analyzed as an active zone phenomenon. In a more traditional approach to metonymy, the referential expression *the piano* would be considered to be an instance of metonymy, standing for 'the sound of piano'.

(5) She heard the **piano**

However, Langacker proposes an alternative analysis in which a relational predication, e.g. a verb, an adjective, an adverb or a preposition, adjusts its meaning to accommodate its semantic argument, and incorporates the "literal" argument as its active zone. In (5) the meaning of *heard* is claimed to shift to 'Subj **heard the sound** of Obj'. Active zone phenomena are apparently even more common than the facetization type of metonymy.

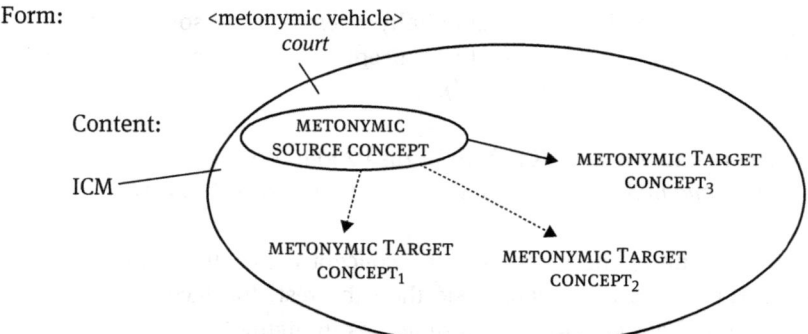

Figure 7.5: Facetization type of metonymy

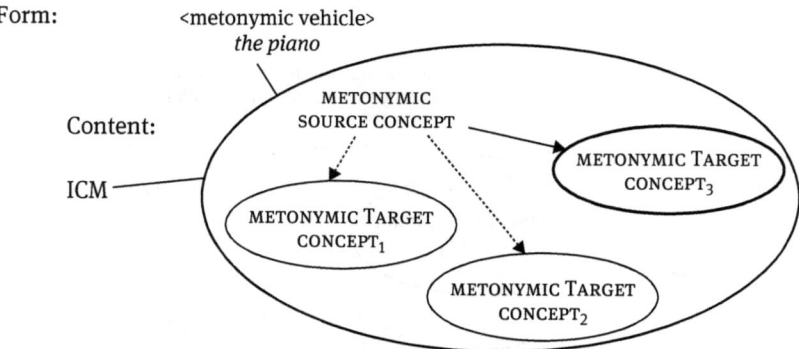

Figure 7.6: Active zone metonymy

3 Translating metonymies

3.1 Translating metonymies: What can we expect (and why)?

As outlined in the introductory part, a discussion of metonymy in translation practice can mean two things. On the one hand, we may be interested in finding out how we (can/should) translate metonymic expressions in a given context, i.e. metonymies can constitute part of the object of the translation process. On the other hand, we may also be interested in finding out how and why something could/should be translated by means of metonymic expressions. In other words, metonymy can also function as a translation tool or strategy. We also pointed out that, ideally, these two aspects mentioned above go hand in hand when we translate a metonymic expression in the source language text by a metonymic expression in the target language text. This is not the only possibility, in fact we have three possibilities here, since we are not interested in the translation of non-metonymic expressions by non-metonymic expressions. The three general possibilities are as schematized in Table 7.1.

The fact that the possibility in the lower right cell in the table often takes place without many problems is one of the reasons why metonymy is far less conspicuous in translation than, for example, metaphor. As an illustration of the magnitude of the problem of translating metaphors, we just point to an example discussed by Ahrens and Say (1999: 100; see, also, Samaniego Fernández, this volume). When Liu Tai-ying, the Chairman of the China Development Corp, called George Soros, the international financier, a "pig", it was

Table 7.1: Overview of the possibilities in translating (non-)metonymies by (non-) metonymies

source text/ language → target text/ language ↓	non-metonymic expression	metonymic expression
metonymic expression		metonymic expression
non-metonymic expression		metonymic expression

necessary for the English-language *China News* to modify the quote, adding the information that "a pig is the Mandarin equivalent of an idiot" (*China News*, October 7, 1998). Without this information, English readers would interpret the metaphorical expression to mean that Soros is a greedy person, as opposed to the intended meaning of "a stupid person", which is the entrenched meaning of this metaphor in Chinese.

We would like to submit that this inconspicuousness of metonymy in translation that we mention above is a fairly direct consequence of the differences between the two cognitive processes producing metonymies and metaphors, respectively. Note that Mandelblit's (1995) *Cognitive Translation Hypothesis* provides for two possible scenarios in the translation of metaphors. *Similar Mapping Condition* obtains if no conceptual shift occurs between languages, while in the case of *Different Mapping Condition* a conceptual shift takes place from source language to target language. In order to check the difference between the two scenarios, Mandelblit (1995: 493) used the time parameter, and concluded that "the difference in reaction time is due to a conceptual shift that the translator is required to make between the conceptual mapping systems of the source and target languages". She has found that metaphorical expressions take more time and are more difficult to translate if they exploit a cognitive domain quite different from that of the target language equivalent expression. This was also confirmed by Tirkkonen-Condit's (2002) study.

Now, if this were true, we have a piece of evidence going part of the way towards accounting for the ease with which many utterances with metonymic expressions can be translated. In addition to the fact that the conceptual distance between metonymic sources and metonymic targets is much smaller, as they are both within the same domain, the search in the target language is as a rule reduced to establishing whether there is an equivalent domain available in the target language or not.

As for the remaining two possibilities, it will be seen that what we get crucially depends on which of the two languages involved in a translation situation is the source language and which is the target language. If a metonymic expression x in a source text in language A has a non-metonymic expression y as its translation equivalent in the target text in language B, it stands to reason to expect the converse if the source text containing y in language B is translated into language A, though occasionally the picture need not be this simple.

Note, however, that these are only three general possibilities and that it would be too optimistic to expect a chapter of this size and scope to exhaustively catalogue the circumstances leading to one of these three possibilities.[2] As for the *why* part in the question in the title of the present section, we point out that the choice in specific cases depends on a number of factors. These may be structural, such as:

- the type of metonymy in question (in terms of its regularity, its complexity, the kind of relation involving parts and wholes, its cognitive and pragmatic function)
- the language pair involved in the translation situation (including their cultural background and structural givens)
- the type of (con)text

Some, of course, have to do with the translation situation itself, e.g. conventions of the specific type of translation, the translator's level of expertise, etc. Some of the linguistic, structural prerequisites for an answer to the *why* part of the question that as yet are largely missing are:

- a comprehensive typology of metonymies
- a statement about the universality of individual types of metonymy on the basis of a sizeable body of contrastive-typological studies.

3.2 Why are so many metonymies inconspicuous in translation?

As pointed out in the final paragraph in Section 3.1 above, the choice between the three basic possibilities of handling a metonymic expression in a translation situation depends on a number of factors, such as the type of metonymy in question (in terms of its regularity, its complexity, the kind of relation involving parts and wholes, its cognitive and pragmatic function), the language pair involved in the translation situation (including their cultural background and structural givens), and the type of (con)text. Far from claiming to be an exhaustive account, what follows is just a methodological exercise in the demonstration of their interplay.

A number of typologies of metonymies have been put forward in recent years in Cognitive Linguistics, some overlapping, some based on different types of criteria. Whether we base this methodological exercise on one or the

---

[2] Cf. the taxonomy of the possibilities for the translation of metaphors in Kövecses (2005: 144).

other of these, or perhaps on a combination of these, would certainly result in a more or less different picture. We have opted in this chapter for the threefold division introduced above as our starting point for two reasons. Firstly, we want to keep this methodological exercise as simple as possible, while introducing elaborate typologies with several hierarchies and intersecting criteria into a study of how metonymies behave in a translation situation might complicate things beyond the point of a reasonable overview. Secondly, this typology makes it possible to keep an eye on polysemy as one of the central problems in the translation of metonymies.

Since we use English, German, Hungarian and Croatian as members of language pairs involved in various translation situations, the sort of choices that we demonstrate below might have, of course, been different if some other languages were involved.

Considering the fact that the conceptual distance between the meaning of the metonymic vehicle and the metonymic target in the case of metonymic expressions arising through facetization as well as those of the active zone type is minimal, with hardly any noticeable shift in the direction of what we might call figurative meaning, it is no wonder that these metonymies are so common. Note some types of conceptual metaphors may be more easily translated than some other types. Maalej (2008), comparing Tunisian Arab metaphorical utterances with their English translations, argues that metaphorical expressions relying on ontological metaphors (specifically, CONTAINER metaphors) are more readily translatable as metaphors than those based on structural metaphors.

The facetization type as well as active zone metonymies are common in terms of the number of specific instances (both types and tokens) and they are also common in terms of their being wide-spread across languages. They are so common that they are virtually inconspicuous, and this also explains why they are also frequently so inconspicuous in a translation situation. Consider the following English and German examples. English is the source language, and German the target language, in (6), while the situation in (7) is reverse.

The first sentence in (6) is from Hemingway's *The Old Man and the Sea*, the second is its translation into German (*Der alte Mann und das Meer*).[3] In these

---

3 As German, Croatian, Hungarian and French examples that follow are always matched with their English translations, or translations of English examples, we only provide glosses but no idiomatic translations. The glosses contain standard abbreviations: AUX – auxiliary, DEF – definite, DAT – dative, GEN – genitive, IMPER – imperative, INDEF – indefinite, INF – infinitive, NEG – negation, PREF – prefix, REFL – reflexive.

examples both *boat* and its German counterpart, *Boot*, are used metonymically to refer to the fishermen in the boat.

(6) a. *But after forty days without a fish the boy's parents had told him that the old man was now definitely and finally salao, which is the worst form of unlucky, and the boy had gone at their orders in another **boat** which caught three good fish the first week.*

b. | Aber | nach | vierzig | fischlosen | Tagen | hatten | die | Eltern | |
| --- | --- | --- | --- | --- | --- | --- | --- | --- |
| but | after | forty | fish-less | days | had | DEF | parents | |
| des | Jungen | ihm | gesagt, | daß | der | alte | | |
| DEF.GEN | boy | him-DAT | told | that | DEF | old | | |
| Mann | jetzt | bestimmt | für | immer | salao | sei, | was | die |
| man | now | definitely | for | ever | salao | were | which | DEF |
| schlimmste | Form | von | Pechhaben | ist, | und | der | Junge | |
| worst | form | of | bad luck | is | and | DEF | boy | |
| war | auf | ihr | Geheiß | in | einem | andern | **Boot** | mitgefahren, |
| was | on | their | order | in | one | other | boat | ridden |
| das | in | der | ersten | Woche | drei | gute | Fische | gefangen |
| which | in | DEF | first | week | three | good | fish | caught |
| hatte | | | | | | | | |
| had | | | | | | | | |

In our second pair of sentences, stemming from Günter Grass' novel *Blechtrommel* and its English translation (*The Tin Drum*), we have another example of the active zone type of metonymy. What is meant by German *Flüsse* and English *rivers* is not the whole body of water but just their surface.

(7) a. | Im | Winter, | wenn | die | **Flüsse** | vereist | | waren [...] |
| --- | --- | --- | --- | --- | --- | --- | --- |
| in | winter | when | DEF | rivers | frozen-over | were | |

b. *In winter when the **rivers** were frozen over* [...]

In the source text and the target text we have two lexical items, *Flüsse* and *rivers*, which are in their literal sense associated with more or less equivalent concepts, of which only a subpart is activated in the two sentences in the same way, as indicated in Figure 7.7.

The following pairs of sentences from Grass' *Blechtrommel* and its English translation with *Schule* and *school*, respectively, illustrate some of the metonymic facets of the two. In addition to referring to an educational institution in an abstract sense, the two words can be used to refer to the building housing such an institution, as in (8–9); or to "the session of school/the set time of attendance in school", as in (10):

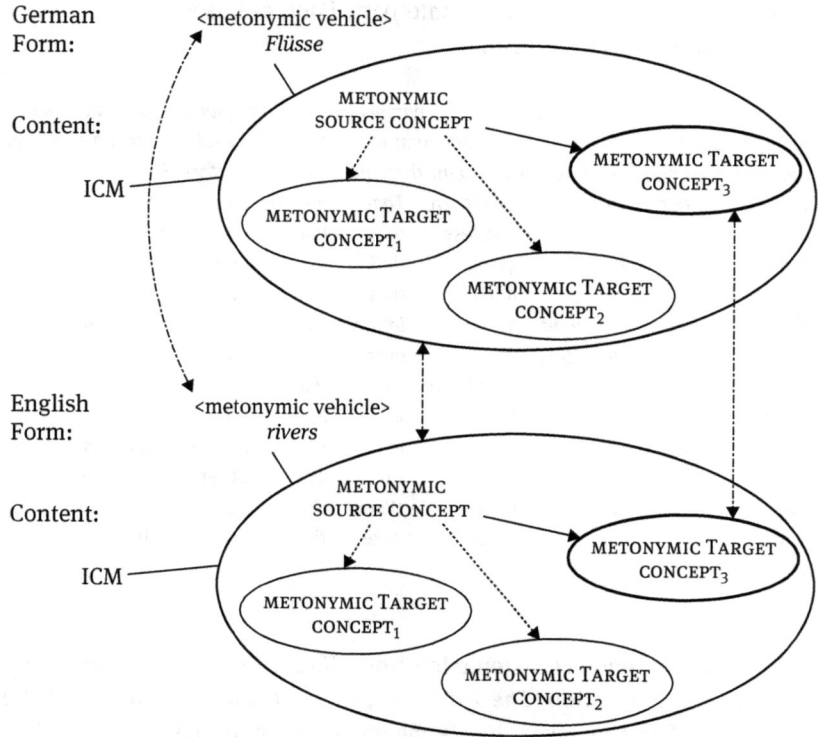

Figure 7.7: Active zone type metonymy in a translation situation

(8) a. *Dann   und   wann,   wenn   aus   der   **Schule** heimkehrende*
    then   and   now   when   from   DEF   school   returning
    Schüler   in   meiner Nähe   die   Tornister
    children   in   my   vicinity DEF   bags
    ablegten, um   Fußball oder   Völkerball zu   spielen
    down.laid down   football or   Völkerball to   play

b. *Now and then, when children on their way home from **school** laid down their bags to play football or Völkerball, I would bend down over those sponges steaming in the sun* [. . .]

(9) a. *[. . .] da   stand   mitten   im Hauptportal   der   **Schule** jener*
    There   stood   middle   in main.entrance   DEF.GEN   school that
    große   Feldherr   persönlich, [. . .]
    great   commander   personally

b. *And there, in the main entrance to the **school**, stood the great general in person;* [. . .]

(10) a. *Woraufhin   Kurtchen,   der   wechselnd   am Vormittag*
       whereupon Kurtchen   who   alternately   in morning
       oder   Nachmittag **Schule** *hatte, [. . .]*
       or   afternoon   school   had
    b. *Whereupon Kurt, who had* **school** *alternately in the morning and afternoon, [. . .]*

Again, we see that the translational situation is very similar to that observed in the case of active zone type of metonymies: generally, we can say that similar arrays of facets resulting in similar more or less regular polysemous networks, will be found in a cross-linguistic perspective, which means that, as a rule, translational equivalence will tend to hold between such metonymic vehicles and their targets in many languages.

In addition to such more or less conventional facets, we also find that *Schule* and *school* can be used, with appropriate qualification (in this case, with appropriate postmodifiers), to refer to a type of educational institution, which is a more specific reading within the reading that might be considered to be the basic reading of *school/Schule* As far as this extension seems to be regular, we do not expect to encounter any grave difficulties in translation, as corroborated by the following examples:

(11) a. *Die*   **Schule**   *der*   *Schiefertafeln war   also*
       DEF   school   DEF.GEN   slate.table   was   thus
       kaum   nach   *meinem* *Geschmack*
       hardly   in   my   taste
    b. *Certainly I had no yearning for the* **school** *of slates and sponges*

The fact that metonymies proper seem to be less regular than the other two types, does not necessarily mean that they should always pose a problem in a translation situation. Cf. another pair of sentences with *school/Schule* from the same source:

(12) a. *Das*   *war*   *eine*   *andere*   *Generation,* *und*   *meine*
       that   was   INDEF   different   generation   and   my
       Generation *hatte* *die*   **Schule**   *hinter*   *sich, [. . .]*
       generation had   DEF   school   behind   REFL
    b. *That was the new generation; my generation had school behind them [. . .]*

In both languages, the metonymic vehicles are used to refer to a period of life saliently characterized as "compulsory school age/period of compulsory formal education", i.e. here we seem to have an example of metonymy proper.

In this section, we have seen why so many metonymies can be quite easily dealt with in a translation situation. The active zone metonymies and the facetization type metonymies are so common and the metonymic extensions so regular, even from a cross-linguistic point of view, that most of them go unnoticed in a given language. The same is then true when they occur in translationally equivalent texts. They are translated by means of a lexical item that is otherwise also a translational equivalent, i.e. this equivalent item is also associated with an equivalent concept that can also serve as a metonymic source to activate an equivalent metonymic target concept. As we show in Section 3.3 below, translating a metonymy by a metonymy need not always take place in that same orderly way.

3.3 Translating a metonymy by means of a different metonymy

In this section we are concerned with variations on the first possibility, translating a metonymy by means of metonymy, but by means of another, different metonymy, which largely corresponds to Newmark's (1985) strategy no. 2 for the translation of metaphors (see note 1). We first illustrate this on some brand names that have come to function as common nouns, due to the MEMBER-OF-A-CATEGORY-FOR-THE-CATEGORY metonymy, and then turn to a metonymy-based riddle.

Discussing their MEMBER-AND-CATEGORY ICM, Radden and Kövecses (1999: 34), point out that it can be analyzed as an instance of part-whole configuration giving rise to a number of metonymies. One of them is MEMBER OF A CATEGORY FOR THE CATEGORY, which they illustrate by *aspirin* used to refer to 'any pain-relieving tablet'. Originally, the lexical item *aspirin* is a proprietary name, i.e. a brand name coined to refer to specific pain-relieving drug administered in the form of a tablet. Like many other brand names dominating their markets, it has come to be used as common noun (hence its current spelling without the initial capital letter), metonymically standing for the whole category of the drug. Translating an English sentence like

(13) Most people I know **take an** *aspirin* **or something** to get rid of their headaches daily

into German, or Croatian, or Hungarian should be no problem due to the fact that aspirin is a globally dominant pain-reliever and that therefore the metonymy in question is also available in these languages (in particular, we may as well add, it should be no problem in German, as the drug is produced by a German company and as it started its spread from Germany). However, dominating the market nowadays practically never comes to mean the same as having the 100% share of the market. In other words, other similar drugs may also be available, and some of them (particularly those locally produced and possibly having dominated the market before their opening) may also be used in the same metonymic way, in parallel with aspirin. This is actually the case with *plivadon* and *algopyrin* in Croatian and Hungarian, respectively.

While translating from English a sentence like (13) into Croatian or Hungarian, we have a choice between using the same metonymic vehicle, *aspirin*, and substituting it by another metonymic vehicle that is more specific for the linguistic community in question. We consider the latter to be a case of translating a metonymy by another metonymy, because *plivadon* and *algopyrin* as lexical items serving as metonymic vehicles are not equivalent to *aspirin* in English in the same way that *aspirin* in Croatian or *aszpirin* in Hungarian is. More specifically, we may say that this is a case of translation of a metonymy by means of another metonymy such that the two metonymic vehicles are synonyms.

If we reverse the source and the target language, this becomes even more obvious, because when translating a Croatian sentence with *plivadon* used metonymically into English, the substitution by means of *aspirin* is by far the best solution, as *plivadon* is simply utterly unfamiliar to the speakers of English as a potential lexical equivalent of *aspirin*. In other words, seen from the point of English as the target language, the two are not equivalent lexical items. The same applies to Hungarian with its *algopyrin*.

We now turn to the case of translating a metonymy-based riddle. Translating humour can occasionally be quite difficult, as shown by Rojo (2009). As is well known, there are numerous riddles in English based on a question of the general type: *What did the big X say to the little X?* The humour often stems from the homonymy or polysemy of the verb or the complement of the verb in the answer of the form: *You're too young/little to V*. The polysemy of the verb in question may be either metaphor-based, or metonymy-based. It appears to be metaphor-based in:

(14)   *What did the big maths book say to the little maths book?*
   - *You're too young* **to have so many problems***!*

(15)   *What did the big tent say to the little tent?*
   - *You're too young* **to stay up all night***!*

The humorous effect in our case study rests on the metonymy-based polysemy of the English verb *to smoke* used in the answer in the following riddle:

(16) a. *What did the big chimney say to the little chimney?*
        - You're too young **to smoke***!*

The pun is here based on the fact that *smoke* is inherently an intransitive verb meaning 'to produce or give smoke'. The verb can also be used metonymically as a transitive verb in a number of ways to refer to a complex activity whose most salient stage is the production of smoke in order to achieve various goals. As discussed in Radden and Kövecses (1999: 32), it can be used to refer to the activity of (habitually) lighting objects containing tobacco, or other suitable substance in the form of cigars, cigarettes, or of pipes, inhaling and then expelling again the fumes thus arising.

Translating this riddle into a language in which the activities in question are referred to by means of more than one verb may be a problem. *Pušiti* is the intransitively or transitively used verb in Croatian for the activity involving cigars, cigarettes, and pipes. In its reflexive variant, *pušiti se*, it is used to refer to the event of emitting or giving smoke in the case of materials that burn, or to refer to the event of giving or sending up vapour, dust, etc. Because it can be collocated only with objects that are on fire, or to substances that give up vapour, it cannot be used with the Croatian counterpart of *chimney*, i.e. *dimnjak*. Even if the reflexive variant were collocated with *dimnjak* somehow, this would effectively preclude the sense of 'smoking a cigar, etc.' getting activated. However, there is another verb, *dimiti*, derived from *dim* 'smoke', which can be used in the answer in a way that would preserve the pun:

(16) b. *Premali   si   da   **(za)dimiš**!*
        too-small are that PREF-smoke

The reflexive variant, *dimiti se*, can be used in the sense of giving or sending up smoke, or even vapour, or dust in an impersonal construction (roughly meaning something like "it smokes from X"). The non-reflexive variant can be used intransitively to refer to the event of smoke coming out of an object, e.g. a stove or a pipe emitting smoke. Further, it can be used transitively to refer to the process of curing meat. Finally, as a transitive verb it can be used in a jocular way to refer to the activity of 'smoking a cigar, etc.', as in (16b). It can be prefixed by *za-*, which would profile more clearly the onset of the activity, or its manner in the sense of 'a little/a bit'.

It will be seen that the best way of rendering the riddle in Croatian also involves a metonymy (which may in turn be based on a metaphor), but it is a different metonymy from the one employed in English. There is, first of all, no single verb that would cover all the senses involved. Secondly, the metonymic vehicle is not the transitive verb, i.e. the non-reflexive verb *pušiti*, whose only meaning is 'smoke a cigar, etc.' (so that it does not make sense to talk about its having other metonymic extensions, or its being metonymically motivated by some other meaning of this non-reflexive verb). In short, in order to translate the riddle in a satisfying way, preserving its humorous effect, we had to opt for a related, but different metonymy.

3.4 When is a metonymy not translated by metonymy, and the other way round?

As we noted in Section 3.1, if a metonymic expression *x* in a source text in language A has a non-metonymic expression *y* as its translation equivalent in the target text in language B, it stands to reason to expect the converse if the source text containing *y* in language B is translated into language A, i.e. we might end up with a metonymic expression *x* in the target text, although the equivalent concept in the source language was directly, non-metonymically associated with a given lexical item *y* that is not a straightforward equivalent of *x*. Of course, this need not always be the case. Cf. the following example from a magazine (*InterCity Magazin*) published by the Hungarian State Railways. The texts in the magazine are in Hungarian, but it also carries an English section with the translation of a selection of Hungarian articles.

(17) a. *Negyedszer*   *rugaszkodnak neki*   *a*   **Nagymező**
      for-the-fourth time   pull-their-weight   DEF   Nagymező
      utcában   *Leonard Bernstein West Side Story című*
      street-in   Leonard Bernstein West Side Story titled
      musicaljének
      musical.GEN.GEN

English metonymies of the CAPITAL-FOR-GOVERNMENT type not infrequently find their counterparts in Croatian and Hungarian in locative adverbials in impersonal constructions, and this is also true of other types of localities. Although the locative adverbial *a Nagymező utcában* might have been translated by means of a metonymy, *Nagymező utca* (or *Nagymező Street*), the name of this Budapest street with five theatres that metonymically stands for the Hungarian theatre industry (it is also known as *Budapest's Broadway*), was nevertheless rendered as a locative adverbial in the English translation, the subject being indefinite *they*:

(17) b. *They're having a fourth crack at the Leonard Bernstein musical West Side Story* **on Nagymező utca** [. . .] (*InterCity Magazin*, 2002/3: 9)

An alternative translation might have been:

(17) c. **Nagymező utca** *is having a fourth crack at the Leonard Bernstein's musical West Side Story*

where a non-metonymic expression in the source text is translated by means of a metonymic expression in the target text.

Of course, if the locative expressions in (17a, b) are not considered to be metonymic, as in most traditional accounts, this would mean that in (17b) we have a non-metonymic counterpart of a non-metonymic expression in the source text. However, as argued above, if these locatives are considered to be metonymic, we have a different constellation.

In some cases, we indeed find in a translation metonymic counterparts of non-metonymic expressions in the source text. These metonymic expressions may be chosen as more idiomatic, natural choices in the target language in a given context. Cf. the following English-Croatian translational pair, where the most natural Croatian equivalent of *have a beer/coffee*, etc. is *ići na pivo/kavu*, etc., literally 'go on beer/coffee, etc.'

(18) a. *Let's have a beer!*
 b. *Idemo   na pivo!*
    go.IMPER on beer

The Croatian translation is based on the subevent metonymy, similar to what both English and Croatian have in expressions like *go to the movies* and *ići u kino*. We may assume that an initial subevent stands for the central subevent of drinking or watching the film, or that it stands for the whole event, i.e. we have THE INITIAL PART FOR THE COMPLEX SCENARIO metonymy. Of course, one could perhaps also consider the possibility that having a beer, or getting it in English, is also a kind of precondition for its drinking, or a non-central subevent standing for the central subevent, in which case this would qualify as translating a metonymy by a metonymy of a slightly different type.

As a clear example of a non-metonymic expression translated by means of a metonymy consider also the following German-English translation pair (19) from Grass' *Blechtrommel* and its English translation, where *Werftarbeiter*, literally 'wharf workers', has been rendered as *wharf hands*. Expressions such as *farm hand, factory hand*, or *wharf hand*, etc. are well-entrenched in English as designations for various types of manual workers, clearly based on the metonymic use of *hand*, the salient body part with which work is done standing for the whole, i.e. worker. This is, of course, a case of metonymy proper.

(19) a. [. . .] *saß   er   brav   im   Troyl, wo   nur Flöβer,*
           sit   he   quietly   in   Troyl where   only raftsmen
           *Stauer   und **Werftarbeiter** wohnten* [. . .]
           longshoremen and wharf.workers   lived
      b. [. . .] *he sat quietly at home in Troyl, where only raftsmen, longshoremen, and **wharf hands** lived* [. . .]

Now that we have briefly discussed some cases where non-metonymies are rendered by metonymies in translation, let us turn to probably the most interesting issue: when (and why) metonymies are not rendered as metonymies in translation.

In the first such example, a sentence from a novel by Stephen King (*Insomnia*) we have an example of a predicational metonymy of the type POTENTIALITY FOR ACTUALITY, discussed in Panther and Thornburg (1999: 335). The utterance with the modal expression of ability in the past stands for actuality, i.e. actual performance in the past.

(20) a. *Ralph **was able to** read the bright red letters of the title: "Buckdancer's Choice"* (King, *Insomnia*, 22)

This metonymy is as good as unavailable in Croatian, and the translated sentence exhibits no metonymy, the verb used in the translation, *uspjeti* 'succeed' makes an explicit reference to the actuality, i.e. the result/success of the activity denoted by the verb in the complement clause:

(20) b. *Ralph uspije   pročitati žarko crvena slova   naslova:*
           Ralph succeeded read.INF bright red   letters title.GEN
           "Buckdancer's Choice" (20)
           "Buckdancer's Choice"

Panther and Thornburg (1999) show that this metonymy is much more productive in English than in Hungarian. The most striking contrast between the two languages emerges in the domain of sense perceptions: whereas English systematically exploits the metonymy in sentences such as *I can taste the vanilla* (for *I taste the vanilla*), Hungarian systematically excludes the metonymy and resorts to a non-modal construction in the indicative mood. Panther and Thornburg (2003) find that there is a tendency in English narrative fiction to use this metonymy, particularly with perception verbs and certain verbs denoting mental states and processes. French, on the other hand, seems to systematically avoid this metonymy with these verbs:

(21) a. *Tom **could** easily **understand** that* (*The Talented Mr. Ripley*, 8)
      b. *Tom **comprenait** très   bien* (*Le talentueux Mr. Ripley*, 11)
         Tom understood   very well

(22) a. *Tom had never seen them [drawings], but he **could see** [imagine] them now, [. . .]* (*The Talented Mr. Ripley*, 10)
      b. *Tom   ne   les   avait   jamais   vu;   mais il   **se**   les*
         Tom   NEG   them   had   never   seen   but   he   REFL   them
         Représentait très   bien   maintenant [. . .]
         imagine   very   well   at present (*Le talentueux Mr. Ripley*, 14)

Since the ability to perform an action belongs to the BEFORE component in their State-of-Affairs Scenario, i.e. it is located at its very beginning, Panther and Thornburg relate these findings with the fact that in English, in contrast to French, there is a fairly systematic exploitation of the high-level metonymy SUBEVENT FOR WHOLE EVENT.

Sometimes the reason for not rendering a metonymy in the source text by means of a metonymy in the translation may be that the metonymy in question is culturally so specific that it would be lost in translation, i.e. the translated text would be in part less intelligible because the speaker of the target language cannot be expected to be able to draw rich encyclopaedic knowledge necessary to work out the metonymy, even though we might be dealing with an example of the active zone type of metonymy. As an example of this consider the following exchange from a TV serial *The West Wing*:

(23) a. *- It's **Korematsu** all over again*

The proper name *Korematsu* is used in this SALIENT PARTICIPANT FOR THE EVENT metonymy to refer to a court case known as Korematsu vs United States. On May 19, 1942, during World War II, American citizens of Japanese descent were compelled to move into relocation camps by a Civilian Restrictive Order. Fred Korematsu, a U.S.-born Japanese American, decided to stay in San Leandro, California, and thus knowingly violate a Civilian Exclusion Order of the U.S. Army. He argued that the orders were unconstitutional and violated the Fifth Amendment to the U.S. Constitution. He was arrested and convicted. The Circuit Court of Appeals affirmed the conviction for evading internment, but it was challenged by Korematsu and finally overturned on November 10, 1983.

In the translation (actually in the subtitles) on the Croatian state television, the first mention of *Korematsu* was replaced by a phrase that can actually be seen as spelling out the metonymic target (literally 'Korematsu case'), the second was simply replaced by a lexical item *tužba* ('legal action/statement of claim, [com]plaint'):

(23) b. -Ponavlja se   slučaj Korematsu
        repeats   REFL   case   Korematsu

A related but different problem and a different solution can be seen in the German translation of Lakoff and Johnson (1980), specifically in the chapter on metonymy. This short chapter carries, all in all, 49 examples of metonymies of various types, all of them decontextualized. What we had in mind when we said that this is a related but different problem, was that we again faced some culturally very specific metonymies, but that this was language for specific purposes in which the examples had a very important role. Some of the examples lend themselves to translation into German without any difficulties:

(24) a. *I hate to read* **Heidegger**
     b. *Ich   hasse es,* **Heidegger** *zu lesen*
        I   hate   it   Heidegger   to read

(25) a. *The* **sax** *has the flu today*
     b. *Das* **Saxophon** *hat   heute die Grippe*
        DEF   sax   has   today DEF flu

While the replacement of *ham sandwich* with *Schnitzel* 'breaded veal cutlet', aka *schnitzel* in English, too, was perhaps unnecessary, it keeps the same type of conceptual metonymy, though the metonymic expressions are per se translationally non-equivalent:

(26) a. *The* **ham sandwich** *is waiting for his check*
     b. *Das* **Schnitzel** *wartet   auf seine Rechnung*
        DEF   steak   is.waiting for his   check

However, in some cases, the translator was apparently caught between the formal Scylla and functional Charybdis:

(27) a. We need a couple of **strong bodies** for our team
 b. Wir brauchen ein paar **Muskeln** für unser Team
    we need a couple muscles for our team

(28) a. We need some **new blood** in the organization
 b. Wir brauchen **frischen Wind** in der Organisation
    we need fresh wind in DEF organization

(29) a. We need a better **glove** at third base
 b. Wir brauchen einen besseren Baseball**handschuh**
    we need INDEF.ACC better baseball.glove
    an der dritten Basis
    on DEF third base

While the translation in (27b) makes use of a different metonymy, the one in (28b) is actually a replacement of a metonymy by a metaphor, possibly because *new blood* may be a metaphtonymy, i.e. a metonymy-based metaphor (cf. Ibarretxe-Antuñano 2005). In terms of conceptual meaning, this may perhaps be justified, but as an illustration of metonymy, which is its function in the text, it fails. Finally, the translation of (29a) is virtually of the word-for-word type, producing an odd effect in German. We also note that the addition of *Baseball* to *Schuh* 'glove', making it a compound, is an attempt to facilitate the activation of the appropriate ICM, prompted by the relative lack of the cultural background.

In the previous examples we have seen that the reasons for the non-translation of a metonymy by a metonymy may be differences in the entrenchment of certain high-level metonymies, or different cultural backgrounds. In the following paragraphs we show that metonymies may be lacking or be less well-entrenched in a given language due to the structural givens of the language in question. Specifically, we may end up without a metonymic expression in a translation because the target language prefers the use of certain explicit means of resolving polysemy.

Let us now consider how certain foodstuffs, specifically meat of animals, fare in this respect when used as facetization metonymies. The term "animal grinding" has been used to refer to specific cases of the phenomenon variably called logical metonymy, logical polysemy, or regular polysemy (Pustejovsky and Bouillon 1996), i.e. to those cases in which one and the same label can be used to refer holistically to the animal species or specimen as well as to the flesh of the animal in question, not necessarily always conceived of as foodstuff, i.e. as meat of that animal, as illustrated in the following English examples:

(30) a. "*I would not eat **fish**,*" he said
b. *We did not always eat **turkey** for Christmas dinner*
c. *The celebrity chef we all love to hate, Gordon Ramsay, is causing some waves. The chef is saying that the British should eat more **horse**, this on the tail-end of the Kentucky Derby* (*Telegraph*, May 7, 2007)

In Cognitive Linguistics this is treated as a subtype of WHOLE-FOR-PART metonymy, specifically OBJECT-FOR-MATERIAL-CONSTITUTING-THE-OBJECT within the *Constitution ICM* (Radden and Kövecses 1999: 32). The lexical item labelling the concept of the whole animal stands here only for a particular aspect of the whole animal, i.e. its bodily substance/flesh/meat as processed and used as foodstuff. Even literally, the substance that we use as food is only part of the whole animal's body, as animals are skinned, boned, etc., and usually it is not the whole carcass that is meant, but rather some smaller portion of it.

Although this metonymy may appear fairly productive as far as English is concerned, which is also suggested by the terms used in some unification frameworks, such as logical metonymy/polysemy, or regular polysemy, an examination of cross-linguistic data reveals a slightly different picture. While this sort of conceptual conversion is certainly more or less always available in theory as an open pattern, the fact is that it is not so regularly made use of. Of course, one of the factors diminishing the productivity of this metonymy is the well-known historical incident in the course of which a number of lexical items were borrowed from Norman French that denoted the meat of certain domestic and wild animals, thus effectively blocking the polysemy from kicking in with a series of native Anglo-Saxon items (e.g. *cow – beef, calf – veal, pig – pork, sheep – mutton, deer – venison*). In many other cases, we have a replacement by a N + N combination, with *meat* as the second noun.

As might have been expected, French exhibits regular metonymy in the case of the exceptional items listed for English above. *Mouton* is used, similarly to English *hogget*, to refer to sheep, its meat, and also to sheepskin. *Vache* in addition to functioning as the counterpart of *cow* is also used to refer to 'cowhide'; *boeuf*, on the other hand, not only means 'beef' but also 'ox/steer' (note also the use of both *viande de vache* 'meat of cow', and *viande de boeuf* 'meat of ox'). *Porc* denotes both 'pig' and 'pork' (next to *viande de porc*, 'meat of pig'). Finally, *veau* denotes both 'calf' and 'veal' (next to *viande de veau* 'meat of calf').

This pattern of the replacement of metonymy by means of N + *meat* combination, realized as a compound noun, is quite wide-spread in German (with *Fleisch* 'meat' as the second constituent, i.e. as the compound head):

(31) *Schweinefleisch* 'pig-meat', *Rindfleisch* 'cattle-meat', *Schafsfleisch* 'sheep-meat', *Ziegenfleisch* 'goat-meat'

A word for word translation of English examples in (30) into German would be decidedly odd, as the examples would convey the idea that the unprocessed animal as whole was eaten, complete with bones, skin, innards, hoofs, horns, etc., which would be more appropriate if the subject were a carnivorous animal, but it works with *Lamm* 'lamb' or *Ente* 'duck', even if *-fleisch* is ellipted.

Hungarian exhibits the same behaviour; i.e. it has compounds with *hús* 'meat' as the second constituent, i.e. as the compound head:

(32) *sertéshús* 'pig-meat', *marhahús* 'cattle-meat', *birkahús* 'sheep-meat', *kecskehús* 'goat-meat'

A language such as Croatian, which unlike Germanic languages or Hungarian, lacks compounding as a word formation process, resorts to other syntactic or morphological means. First of all, for all cases of animals that are, culturally speaking, less usual or unusual as potential foodstuffs, there is the phrasal expression *meso (od)* X$_{gen}$ 'meat of X'. However, the most important strategy is suffixation, with a cluster of related suffixes, *-ina*, *-Vtina* and *-Vvina*, used to derive names of meat of various animals:

(33) a. *govedina* 'beef'
      b. *svinjetina* 'pork', *prasetina* 'piglet-meat', *teletina* 'veal', *ovčetina* 'mutton', *koz(l)etina* 'goat-meat', *guščetina* 'goose-meat', *piletina* 'chicken-meat', *konjetina* 'horse-meat', *janjetina* 'lamb-meat', *zečetina* 'rabbit-meat'
      c. *tunjevina* 'tuna-meat', *veprovina* 'boar-meat', *kitovina* 'whale-meat', *jelenovina* 'deer-meat'

Summing up what we have seen in the case of animal grinding, we can say that the application of this metonymy is seriously constrained in a number of languages and that this also shows in translation, so that translating English utterances with items from (30) would in languages such as German, Hungarian or

Croatian (just like in many other Slavic languages; cf. Brdar 2009), result in the loss of this facetization type of metonymy. The concepts in question are expressed by means of compound nouns or suffixations.

It is important to note that these nouns can in special contexts be used as complex metonymies. It has been noted that multiple conceptual shifts are possible, breaking up "complex conceptual mappings into simple, well-motivated mappings with a strong experiential basis" (Hilpert 2007: 80). These are cases of metonymic operations stacked onto each other, producing double or even triple metonymies (Ruiz de Mendoza Ibáñez and Mairal Usón 2007). Such metonymic chains were referred to as multi-level metonymies, or as metonymic tiers in Brdar and Brdar-Szabó (2007).

The names of animals in English can be used as double metonymies, e.g. when we have an ostensive context in which a dish made out of the meat of one of these animals is contrasted with dishes made of the meat of other animals, as in:

(38) a. [. . .] *so we headed there where, yes, I ordered* **turkey** *[. . .] and loved every single bite* [. . .]

Here the name of the animal stands for the meat of that animal, which in turn stands for a dish made with that meat. Translating this into Croatian, we get, as might have been expected, the suffixation that is normally used to denote the meat of the animal, but is now used as a metonymy:

(38) b. [. . .] *da,   naručio   sam* **puretinu***, [. . .] i   uživao   u*
         yes,   ordered   AUX turkey.meat   and enjoyed in
         svakom zalogaju [. . .]
         every   bite

This means that instead of a series of two metonymies, we may get a single metonymy in the translation, which qualifies as translation by means of a different metonymy above, considering the fact that the single metonymic vehicle in the source language is matched with a metonymic vehicle in the target language, which is normally not its default translation equivalent.

Such complex metonymies may also sometimes be reduced in translation to a single metonymy, so that the metonymy that is lost is not the underlying one, as in (38), but the one on top. Consider the following example with an English-Croatian translation pair:

(39) a. *A lot of people used to think I **was** a black belt just because I was a professional athlete [. . .]*
b. Puno   ljudi   je   mislilo   da   **imam crni   pojas** samo
   many   people   AUX   thought   that   have   black   belt   just
   zato što sam   profesionalni sportaš
   because   am   professional   athlete

Black belt is considered to be a double metonymy here because we first have an object which in karate and judo stands metonymically for a certain level of expertise and skill in these martial arts. On top of that, the object can stand for its possessor. This second layer is missing in the Croatian translation, the idea is expressed by means of the verb of possession, literally 'that I have a black belt'.

4 Concluding remarks

Throughout this chapter we have sought to provide bits of answers to some of the key questions around which the present volume centres. Specifically, in Section 3, we were concerned with various ways in which Cognitive Linguistics can help those involved with translation practice and theorizing become more aware of the presence and nature of metonymy. We considered the relative ease with which metonymy can be translated by metonymy, and related it to some basic properties of metonymy as contrasted with metaphor. It was shown that the degree of the difficulty in translating utterances with metonymic expressions may be linked to the type of metonymy in question as well as to the degree of its regularity. In the present paper we could take into consideration just one of the typologies of metonymies that have been proposed recently. We are quite certain that similar findings would have resulted from taking any of these as the starting point. We have also uncovered some circumstances that may lead to complications, such as the interplay of metonymy as a cognitive process and the structural givens of a language that may constrain the application of the former, or the role of the cultural background. Last but not least, we pointed to some of the problems in translating complex metonymies involving more than one level of metonymic mappings or interplay with metaphor.

References

Ahrens, Kathleen and Alicia L. T. Say 1999 Mapping image-schemes and translating metaphors. In: Jhing-Fa Wang and Chung-Hsien Wu (eds.), *Proceedings of 13th Pacific Asia Conference on Language, Information and Computation*, 1–8. Taipei: Academia Sinica.

Barcelona, Antonio 2000a Introduction: The cognitive theory of metaphor and metonymy. In: Antonio Barcelona (ed.), *Metaphor and metonymy at the crossroads: A cognitive perspective*, 1–28. Berlin: Mouton de Gruyter.

Barcelona, Antonio 2000b On the plausibility of claiming a metonymic motivation for conceptual metaphor. In: Antonio Barcelona (ed.), *Metaphor and metonymy at the crossroads: A cognitive perspective*, 31–58. Berlin: Mouton de Gruyter.

Brdar, Mario 2009 Metonymy-induced polysemy and the role of suffixation in its resolution in some Slavic languages. *Annual Review of Cognitive Linguistics* 7: 58–88.

Brdar, Mario and Rita Brdar-Szabó 2007 When Zidane is not simply Zidane, and Bill Gates is not just Bill Gates: Or, Some thoughts on online construction of metaphtonymic meanings of proper names. In: Günter Radden, Klaus-Michael Köpcke, Thomas Berg and Peter Siemund (eds.), *Aspects of meaning construction*, 125–142. Amsterdam: John Benjamins.

Croft, William and D. Alan Cruse 2004 *Cognitive linguistics*. Cambridge: Cambridge University Press.

Feyaerts, Kurt (ed.) 2003 *The Bible through metaphor and translation: A cognitive semantic perspective*. (Religions and Discourse 15.) Oxford: Peter Lang.

Hilpert, Martin 2007 Chained metonymies in lexicon and grammar: A cross-linguistic perspective on body-part terms. In: Günter Radden, Klaus-Michael Köpcke, Thomas Berg and Peter Siemund (eds.), *Aspects of meaning construction*, 77–98. Amsterdam: John Benjamins.

Ibarretxe-Antuñano, Iraide 2005 Limitations for cross-linguistic metonymies and metaphors. In: José Luis Otal, Ignasi Navarro i Ferrando and Begoña Bellés Fortuño (eds.), *Cognitive and discourse approaches to metaphor and metonymy*, 187–200. Castelló de la Plana, Spain: Publicacions de la Universitat Jaume I, D.L.

Kövecses, Zoltán 2005 *Metaphor in culture: Universality and variation*. Cambridge: Cambridge University Press.

Lakoff, George and Mark Johnson 1980 *Metaphors we live by*. Chicago: University of Chicago Press.

Langacker, Ronald W. 1999 *Grammar and conceptualization*. Berlin: Mouton de Gruyter.

Maalej, Zouhair 2008 Translating metaphor between unrelated cultures: A cognitive perspective. *Sayyab Translation Journal* 1: 60–82.

Mandelblit, Nili 1995 The cognitive view of metaphor and its implications for translation theory. In: Marcel Thelen and Barbara Lewandowska-Tomaszczyk (eds.), *Translation and meaning*, Part 3, 483–495. Maastricht, the Netherlands: Universitaire Press.

Newmark, Peter 1985 The translation of metaphor. In: Wolf Paprotté and René Dirven (eds), *The ubiquity of metaphor: Metaphor in language and thought*, 295–326. Amsterdam: John Benjamins.

Panther, Klaus-Uwe 2005 The role of conceptual metonymy in meaning construction. In: Francisco J. Ruiz de Mendoza Ibáñez, and María Sandra Peña Cervel (eds.), *Cognitive linguistics: Internal dynamics and interdisciplinary interaction*, 353–386. Berlin: Mouton de Gruyter.

Panther, Klaus-Uwe and Linda Thornburg 1999 The potentiality for actuality metonymy in English and Hungarian. In: Klaus-Uwe Panther and Günter Radden (eds.), *Metonymy in language and thought*, 333–357. Amsterdam: John Benjamins.

Panther, Klaus-Uwe and Linda Thornburg 2003 Metonymy and lexical aspect in English and French. *Jezikoslovlje* 4: 71–101.

Paradis, Carita 2004 Where does metonymy stop? Senses, facets, and active zones? *Metaphor and Symbol* 19: 245–264.
Pustejovsky, James and Pierette Bouillon 1996 Aspectual coercion and logical polysemy. In: James Pustejovsky and Branimir Boguraev (eds.), *Lexical semantics: The problem of polysemy*, 133–162. Oxford: Clarendon Press.
Radden, Günter 2002 How metonymic are metaphors? In: René Dirven and Ralf Pörings (eds.), *Metaphor and metonymy in comparison and contrast*, 407–434. Berlin: Mouton de Gruyter.
Radden, Günter and Zoltán Kövecses 1999 Towards a theory of metonymy. In: Klaus-Uwe Panther and Günter Radden (eds.), *Metonymy in language and thought*, 17–59. Amsterdam: John Benjamins.
Rojo, Ana 2009 A cognitive approach to the translation of metonymy-based humor. *Across Languages and Cultures* 10: 63–83.
Ruiz de Mendoza Ibáñez, Francisco José 2000 The role of mappings and domains in understanding metonymy. In: Antonio Barcelona (ed.), *Metaphor and metonymy at the crossroads: A cognitive perspective*, 109–132. Berlin: Mouton de Gruyter.
Ruiz de Mendoza Ibáñez, Francisco José and Ricardo Mairal Usón 2007 High-level metaphor and metonymy in meaning construction. In: Günter Radden, Klaus-Michael Köpcke, Thomas Berg and Peter Siemund (eds.), *Aspects of meaning construction*, 33–49. Amsterdam: John Benjamins.
Taylor, John R. 1989 *Linguistic categorization: Prototypes in linguistic theory*. Oxford: Clarendon Press.
Tirkkonen-Condit, Sonja 2002 Metaphoric expressions in translation processes. *Across Languages and Cultures* 3: 101–116.
Ullmann, Stephen 1962 *Semantics: An introduction to the science of meaning*. Oxford: Blackwell.

Sources

Grass, Günter 1962 *The tin drum*. Translated by Ralph Manheim. London: Secker & Warburg.
Grass, Günter 1964 *Die Blechtrommel*. Frankfurt am Main: Fischer Bücherei.
Hemingway, Ernest 1952 *The old man and the sea*. New York: Charles Scribners Sons.
Hemingway, Ernest 1976 *Der alte Mann und das Meer*. Translated by Annemarie Horschitz-Horst. Berlin: Suhrkamp.
Hemingway, Ernest 1983 *Az öreg halász és a tenger. Elbeszélesek*. Translated by Géza Ottlik. Budapest: Europa könyvkiadó.
King, Stephen 1995 *Insomnia*. New York: Penguin.
King, Stephen 1995 *Nesanica*. Translated by Božica Jakovlev. Zagreb: Algoritam.
Lakoff, George and Mark Johnson 2004 *Leben in Metaphern: Konstruktion und Gebrauch von Sprachbildern*. Translated by Astrid Hildenbrand. Heidelberg, Germany: Carl-Auer-Systeme Verlag.

Part III: **Constructions and translation**

Elżbieta Tabakowska
(Cognitive) grammar in translation: Form as meaning

1 Preliminaries

In contemporary scholarship the difficult relation between translation theory and applied Translation Studies (TS) on one hand and linguistics on the other had not been running very smoothly; in the 20th century, fascination with generative models of language as infallible paths leading to equivalence (Nida 1964) ended in disillusion. Some of those who were (rightly) defending the autonomy of the discipline opted (wrongly) for a total ban on linguistic intrusions. As late as 2008 Routledge announced "Translation Studies, a New Journal for 2008", aimed at exploring

> promising lines of work within the discipline of Translation Studies while placing a special emphasis on existing connections with neighbouring disciplines. In addition to scholars within Translation Studies, [the editors] invite those as yet unfamiliar with or wary of Translation Studies to enter the discussion. Such scholars will include people working in *literary theory, sociology, ethnography, philosophy, semiotics, history and historiography, theology, gender studies, postcolonialism, and related fields*.(www.informaworld.com/translationstudies, emphasis added)

Linguistics was simply not there – not even among "related fields" [. . .]

Fortunately, to many people working within the field of TS it seems rather obvious that translation theory cannot exist without a theory of language and grammar – indeed so very obvious that TS are often considered to be synonymous with Applied Linguistics, where the "applied" part is supposed to provide answers to how the linguistic material is to be handled when translation is being performed, and the "linguistics" part is expected to tell the translators what the material is actually like. In recent years, the advance of the cognitive theory of language and the emergence of cognitive models of grammar have been heralding a change in the overall attitude of TS scholars towards linguistics. Out of the theories presently available, that behind Cognitive Linguistics (CL) seems the most promising: it incorporates precisely those aspects of language and grammar that have always frustrated language-oriented theorists of translation and practising translators. Indeterminacy of grammar (Langacker 2009), inherent subjectivity of meaning, the existence of motivated relationships between meaning and form, ubiquity of metaphor (Lakoff and Johnson 1980; Lakoff 1987) and conceptual integration (Fauconnier [1985] 1994; Fauconnier and Turner 2002) – all these postulates strike a sympathetic note in the hearts of translation scholars, as does the cognitivist statement that culture is embodied in grammar, which marks the "cultural turn" in linguistics, running parallel to the "cultural turn" in TS as heralded in Mary Snell-Hornby's seminal paper (1990).

Methodological consequences are pertinent: if TS is to accept the theoretical framework of CL, it also has to admit – in agreement with CL tenets – that there is no qualitative difference between "common" and "literary" language, an assumption that may be considered as the strongest pier supporting the bridge to be built over the gap which has traditionally – and unfortunately – separated linguistics from literature. According to the cognitivist stance, literature, and poetry in particular, is simply an extreme manifestation of language use. Literary (poetic) texts contain more instances of what is traditionally defined as literary (poetic) devices than ordinary everyday usage, with writers and poets pushing linguistic expressions up along the scale of linguistic creativity. Hence, ultimately, the methodological turn in TS makes "literary translation" qualitatively comparable to "translation as such".

There are at least three arguments that may be used to defend the significant role of linguistics in TS. At the first stage of the translation process, systematic reference to language, and to grammar in particular, helps to understand the original text or discourse by focusing the reader's/translator's attention on formal minutiae that ultimately decide about the overall meaning of the original. In other words, focusing on grammar underlies the necessary phase of "close reading".[1] At the second stage – that of translation proper – focus upon grammar in its traditional guise of contrastive linguistics helps to find TL counterparts of ST units. Finally, in the final phase of translation assessment and criticism, it makes it possible to judge the results of the translator's efforts in a less-than-usually impressionistic way.

All these arguments find support in the cognitivist theory of language and linguistic structure, that is, in Cognitive Grammar (CG). Underlying the cognitive theory of grammar, as developed within the framework of CL, there are some basic questions which seem relevant for TS. The first one, most significant for both disciplines, is the question concerning the nature of meaning, which cognitivist theories treat as tantamount to conceptualization. Since conceptualization is necessarily the product of an individual cognizant mind, meaning is inherently subjective. Consequently, the semantic value of an expression

---

[1] Better known to language teachers under the French name *explication du texte*.

involves not only the properties of what the expression refers to, but also the conceptualizer's individual way of looking at things. And since conceptualization results from a particular selection of a point of view and of the resulting perspective, it never covers all aspects of things perceived; hence meaning is also inherently metonymic in character.

The second basic question to be asked concerns the nature of language, which – from the cognitivist point of view – is largely motivated by perceptual abilities of the human mind. It is assumed that Gestalt principles of perception are reflected in linguistic structure. For instance, perception involves scanning of the visual field, and different types of scanning (syncretic scanning for things existing in space and sequential scanning for processes which develop in time) underlie the basic categorial opposition between nouns and verbs, found in most natural languages. The principles of similarity and proximity, whereby things that are seen as similar and close together are perceived as belonging together, account for collectivity as the grammatical property of lexemes such as the English nouns *archipelago* or *alphabet*. The principle of area, which states that the smaller of two overlapping or adjacent elements being perceived is seen as a figure against the background formed by the larger one underlies entire linguistic structure. For example, it is reflected in the choice of a lexeme for the role of the sentential subject: we tend to say *the tree near the house* rather than *the house near the tree*. Finally, since meaning is inherently metonymic, linguistic expressions of concepts are indeterminate: they only provide guidelines that lead recipients of linguistic messages towards an interpretation. This claim tallies with modern translation theories, which claim that the object of the translation process is not the original text (or discourse), but the translator's own interpretation thereof.

Although the "founding father" of CG openly rejects "uninformed commentators'" claim that all meaning is "based on space or visual perception" (Langacker 2008: 55), there are well justified (theoretically, but also empirically) proposals that some kind of visualization does indeed underlie conceptualizations. Thus perception and conception are two interconnected domains of sensorial and mental activities; taken together, they constitute a larger domain of *-ception*, which covers all cognitive processes, both conscious and subconscious (for the explanation of the notion of *-ception*, see Talmy 1996: 245–248). In reference to translation, it is not unreasonable to assume that a visualization might also arise in the translator's mind to function as the notorious *tertium comparationis* involved in the translation process (cf. e.g. Kussmaul 2005). Appeal to visualization seems particularly well grounded in the analysis presented further in this paper (in Section 3), since – like many texts – the illustrative text analyzed is predominantly descriptive.

2 Imagery – conventional and unconventional

2.1 Dimensions

Another fundamental question that underlies cognitivist models of language concerns the nature of grammar and grammatical structure. As was said in Section 1 above, the basic principle that underlies CG states that the human mind has the ability to construe the scene, that is, the situation that is *conceived*, in alternate ways. This ability is called *imagery*.

In CG the ability to create – and to choose between – alternate construals does not pertain exclusively to lexical semantics. Grammar also contributes to the meaning of expressions, and its semantic contribution resides in what is defined as *conventional imagery*: an inventory of alternate scene construals sanctioned by social conventions, which are traditionally described as grammatical rules. In this sense grammar is symbolic, since it constitutes a part of the overall semantic value of expressions: the meaning of an expression is not only its conceptual content, but also the way in which the expression is construed, that is, its grammatical construction. Obviously, such a claim undermines the traditional dichotomy between form and meaning and validates the cognitivist description of grammatical units as *cognitive routines*. In CG the status of the linguistic unit is granted to any conventional pairing of meaning with a form that has been established well enough to be "evoked as an integrated whole". Once initiated, it is carried out without much conscious reflection – very much like following a routine path (Langacker 1987: 100). Thus – unlike in other grammatical theories – a unit can be a lexeme, a bound morpheme, a complex word (for instance the plural form of a countable noun), an idiomatic phrase or, at the sentence level, a grammatical construction with a schematic meaning, e.g. *Subject-verb-object* (realized as, for instance, the sentence *The bird ate the angleworm*). Close relation between such units of language and the "units of translation" as postulated by contemporary translation theories seems fairly obvious. The early postulate by Vinay and Darbelnet ([1958] 1995) that the unit of translation should be defined as the smallest segment of the text which has to be translated as a whole has been criticized for its prescriptivism and for being "based on idealist translations" (Kenny 2008: 304). However, the definition found in a more recent presentation reads as if it were taken verbatim from a textbook of CG: "A translation unit is a segment of a text that a translator treats as a single cognitive unit for the purposes of establishing an equivalence. The translation unit may be a single word, a phrase, one or more sentences, or even a larger unit" (Banjar Yousef n.d.). Similarly, considered to be one of the key terms in translation theory, the unit of translation is defined in a glossary of computer-aided translation terms as "the smallest entity in a text that carries a discrete meaning" which "varies all the time, ranging from individual words and sentences right up to entire paragraphs" (TRANSLATUM, online). Establishing the status of cognitive routines, in the source and the target languages, could certainly be significant for the development of translation theory, practice and pedagogy. The issue deserves more detailed discussion which, however, cannot be pursued within the limits of this essay.

First defined in Langacker's programmatic article (1988), the notion of imagery has since been somewhat modified. In recent works Langacker and his followers tend to replace *mental imagery* with the term *construal*, which includes a wider array of construal operations, some of which are less easily discussed under the rubric of the imagistic dimensions of linguistic structure (cf. Langacker 2008; Croft and Cruse 2004; Taylor 2002). However, the main assumptions and definitions remain unchanged: "Cognitive Linguistics incline to [. . .] imagistic accounts" (Langacker 2008: 32). Mental images are "representations of specific, embodied experiences" (Croft and Cruse 2004: 44).

The full inventory of aspects of conventional imagery and construal phenomena has been amply discussed in the literature (for a recent account, see Langacker 2008: 55–89). The framework for the case study below is provided by those grammatical aspects of construal that are intuitively most obviously imagistic in nature, on the assumption that it is grammatical imagistic symbolism that is most relevant for TS. The dimensions, or in Langacker's terminology, *focal adjustments* (Langacker 1987: 116–138), are

- level of specificity
- figure-ground alignment
- perspective, involving point of view and subjectivity.

All these aspects are convincingly explained in terms of the visual metaphor that Langacker uses to refer to what he defines as *viewing arrangement* (2008: 73–78), or the relationship between the conceptualizer (the speaker and the hearer, metaphorized as "viewers") and the object of conceptualization (metaphorized as the "view"). The default viewing arrangement – naturally presupposed by the speaker and the hearer – is the situation in which the interlocutors are located in the same place and "view" things at the same time, like an audience in the theatre. Hence the extension of the basic viewing metaphor: whatever is located within the "visual field" of the conceptualizers, is said to be located onstage. The "visual" aspects of construal are thus seen as derivatives of the viewing arrangement.

2.2 Construal: Specificity

In Langacker's model of CG, the term *specificity* refers to the level of accuracy and precision that the conceptualizer chooses in order to characterize a given situation. Thus they can say, for instance, that *a bird came down the walk* (see the analysis of Dickinson's poem in Section 3 below), but they can also choose a more detailed account: *a small magpie ran down the narrow garden path*. In reference to the overall viewing metaphor, it can be stated that the scale running from low to high levels of specificity (i.e. from most schematic to most detailed construals) is connected with the situation (spatial and/or temporal) of the viewer and the viewed. This parameter, metaphorically referred to as "distance", finds its direct counterparts in linguistic structure. For instance, we tend to say *the bird unrolled his wings* rather than the *bird unrolled his feathers*, as the concept of "feathers" requires a reduction of the visual field to the direct scope of observation, i.e. the wings (of a bird). Conventionally, this mental (and linguistic) operation, metaphorically referred to as *zooming*, requires adherence to "what things are in the world": feathers are a part of wings, and wings are a part of a bird. As exemplified below, Dickinson's play with the level of specificity breaks the convention: the readers have to supply the missing link themselves, which makes their task more complex and at the same time justifies the classification of the expression as belonging to "the language of poetry".

In translation, shifts in levels of specificity appear as effects of translators' strategies used in dealing with cases of non-equivalence, notably those resulting from interlingual differences in the hierarchical structure of concepts (e.g. the notorious problems with culture-specific taxonomies). Such local strategies involve translation by a subordinate term (magpie vs. bird), cultural substitution, overt explanation or paraphrase, etc. (for a discussion, see, e.g. Baker 1992).

2.3 Construal: Figure-ground alignment: Trajector and landmark

As was said above (Section 1, the principle of area), the figure-ground distinction comes from Gestalt psychology. Introduced into CL by Leonard Talmy,[2] the opposition is used to account for asymmetries of linguistic structures, whereby speakers focus upon certain elements of conceived scenes by *foregrounding* them at the cost of other elements, which are *backgrounded*. Elements selected

---

[2] For an overall survey, see Talmy (2000).

for attention and consequently given more prominence are figures; the backgrounded ones serve as the ground. Thus in the sentence *A bird came down the walk* "a bird" is a figure, and "the walk" is the ground. Like in visual perception, figures tend to be smaller, more mobile, structurally simpler, more salient and more recently called upon than grounds (Talmy 2000: 315–316; cf. also Section 1 above).

In Langacker's CG the figure-ground opposition is inherent in the concepts of *trajector* and *landmark*, which will be used in the analysis in Section 3 below. In a conceptualization, the trajector is the most prominent element – the object of primary focus. The entity of secondary prominence (or secondary focus) goes by the name of landmark (Langacker 2008: 70). Two expressions might have the same semantic content, and still differ in meaning because of the difference in the trajector-landmark alignment. The semantic role of figure is found to coincide with that of the sentential subject. For instance, in *The bird glanced with rapid eyes*, also from Dickinson's poem in Section 3, it is "the bird" that is the figure (and, also, the grammatical subject) and "rapid eyes" are the landmark (the indirect object). In the almost-synonymous *The bird's rapid eyes glanced* the relationship is reversed. In traditional terms, the first sentence "is about" the bird, while the second one "is about" the bird's eyes (i.e. the sentences show the reversal of topic and comment selection).

In translation, shifts in the trajectory-landmark structure can be imposed upon the translator by systematic differences between source and target grammars, but they can also result from lack of sufficient attention to semantic nuances on the part of the translator.

2.4 Construal: Perspective

In conceptualization, perspective is closely connected with the viewing arrangement: expressions, and especially spatial descriptions, depend crucially on the speaker's position, defined as their relative point of view. The phenomenon itself is of course well known: semantic oppositions exemplified by such pairs of adverbs as *behind* vs. *in front of*, or *under* and *above*, have been amply discussed in the literature. But CG employs the term in a wider sense, to cover, for instance, also temporal and epistemic aspects. It is not only the so-called shifters (personal or demonstrative pronouns) that establish viewpoints, but also grammatical tenses, which establish temporal perspective relative to the speaker. Mental transfer, in some earlier theories of grammar discussed under the rubric of empathy (Kuno and Kaburaki 1977), accounts for shifts of perspective, which may even occur within a single expression. For instance, while the expression

A bird came down the walk establishes the viewpoint as that of the speaker, whom the bird is approaching, an alternative construal *A bird approached the poet* would bring in the point of view of an external observer, while yet another alternative, e.g. *A bird inspired the poet* would shape the conceptualizer's perspective through mental transfer.

An important parameter modifying perspective is the opposition between *subjectivity* and *objectivity* of construal. The two concepts were introduced and developed in Langacker's model of CG (Langacker 1999: 297–315). The opposition that they express refers to the way and the extent to which the speaker is present in the conceptualization. In other words, the speaker can perform – to varying extent – the role of either the *sujet parlant*, that is, the subject of the conceptualization, or – while retaining their role of the speaker – become also the object of what is being said. To come back to the viewing metaphor, in such a case the speaker is present onstage. The phenomenon can be observed in numerous manifestations of linguistic structure, and the scale ranges from high levels of objectivity of an expression, as for instance in *Mommy will give you a sweet* (said by mother to child) to high levels of subjectivity, as in *I will give you a sweet*, uttered in the same pragmatic context, with the pronoun I bringing the speaker onstage.[3]

Like other dimensions of scene construal, perspective introduces subtle, but often very significant, aspects of meaning, irrespective of the actual semantic content of utterances. And like the other dimensions, it tends to be problematic in translation, because of either systematic differences between languages (e.g. obligatory or optional presence of personal pronouns) or cultural differences (e.g. social conventions concerning the presence of the speaker onstage).

All the dimensions of construal find their way into grammatical systems through conventionalization. With particular ways of seeing the world becoming conventionalized due to repeated use, the speakers of the language begin to see things through the "optical glasses" of convention. This statement, one of the fundamental assumptions underlying the cognitive model of grammar, tallies with the principle of linguistic relativism. Banned as contradictory to algorithmic conceptions of grammar, the principle of relativism, known as the weaker version of the Sapir-Whorf hypothesis, finds its place again in contemporary linguistics. We look at the world with the eyes of a generalized (conventional) observer. But poets are different. Extending or breaking the

---

3 In Dickinson's poem there is no example to illustrate objective construals, which tallies with the interpretation proposed in Section 3.

conventions is the crux of poetry, as well as the stumbling block for poetry translators.

3 Case study

Although TS scholars who arrived from the "linguistic camp" postulate creating closer ties between theoretical assumptions and their practical applications, works devoted to the actual application of linguistics to translation (process and product) are few and far in between (Halverson 2007; O'Brien 2011; McElhanon 2005; Tabakowska 1993a, 1993b, 1993c, 1996, 1997, 2000, 2004; Wójcik-Leese 2000). The difficulty is to a large extent purely technical. Notwithstanding their claims to the contrary, grammatical descriptions made within the CL framework rarely go beyond the level of sentence as the largest unit of consideration: longer stretches of text and/or discourse used as illustration would meet theoretical requirements of the model, but at the same time become unmanageable and make high demands on the reader's time and patience. The difficulty increases when focus on translation calls for more languages – especially if one of them does not happen to be a world language – e.g. Polish, whose knowledge is still classified in job application forms as an "exotic skill".

Hence the decision taken by the present author to choose for her case study an analysis of a short poem written in English (328 by Emily Dickinson) and its Polish translation by Stanisław Barańczak (Dickinson 1990). The analysis is an attempt to substantiate two claims: firstly, that much of the meaning of a poem resides in its grammar, and secondly, that the poetry of imagery is built of the prose of grammar. I will investigate selected aspects of the grammatical structure of the original and compare them with those found in the translation, hoping to reveal (some of the) reasons why the translation – although in the opinion of Polish readership it "reads well" – prompts an interpretation different from that imposed upon the reader by the original poem.

3.1 The original poem

Emily Dickinson: 328
1   A Bird came down the Walk –
     He did not know I saw –
     He bit an Angleworm in halves
     And ate the fellow, raw,

5   And then he drank a dew
    From a convenient Grass –
    And then hopped sidewise to the Wall
    To let a Beetle pass –

9   He glanced with rapid eyes
    That hurried all around
    They looked like frightened beads, I thought –
    He stirred his Velvet Head

13 Like one in danger, Cautious,
    I offered him a Crumb
    And he unrolled his feathers
    And rowed him softer home –

17 Than Oars divide the ocean,
    Too silver for a seam –
    Or Butterflies, off banks of Noon
    Leap, plashless as they swim.

3.2 The Polish translation

1   Ptak przyskakał po Ścieżce –
    Nieświadom, że go widzę –
    Wpierw rozpołowił dziobem
    I zjadł na surowo Dżdżownicę –

5   Potem popił ją Rosą
    Z dogodnego źdźbła Trawy –
    Pod Mur uskoczył – spłoszony –
    Jakimś Żukiem niemrawym –

9   Bystre oczy strzelały
    Dookoła spojrzeniami –
    Czarne Paciorki Trwogi –
    Jego Głowy Aksamit

13 Drgał, targany przez Groźby
    Rzuciłam ostrożną Ręką
    Okruch – rozpostarł pióra
    I odpłynął tak miękko,

17 Jak Wiosła krojące Ocean –
    Zbyt srebrny, by szwy pozostały –
    Lub Motyl – co spada bez plusku
    Z Urwisk Dnia w bezdenne Upały.

3.3 The original poem and the translation: Alternate construals

3.3.1 Specificity

The original of Dickinson's 328 begins with

(1) a. *A Bird **came down** the Walk –*

which is rendered in the translation as

(1) b. *Ptak **przyskakał**   po   Ścieżce –*
    Bird *przy*.jumped.IMPERF along path
    'A/the bird approached jumping repeatedly along the path'

In (1b) the verbal prefix *przy-* – derived from the corresponding spatial preposition *przy*, and corresponding to the English prepositions *at* or *(near)by* – contributes to the meaning of the entire expression by bringing in the sense equivalent to that brought into the phrasal verb in (1a) by the element *down*: the direction of motion towards the observer. However, while the English *came down* does not specify the particular kind of this motion, its Polish counterpart does: the bird moved towards the observer (direction), jumping along the path (manner). Thus in the Polish translation the scene is "painted" in more detail. Increased specificity can thus imply a more careful observation, made possible by a shorter distance between the subject and the object.[4] The image is enhanced, in the Polish translation, by the explicit reference to the bird's beak (apparently seen in detail); compare:

(2) a. *He bit an Angleworm in halves*
    b. *Wpierw rozpołowił **dziobem** Dżdżownicę*
       At.first halved   beak.INSTR earthworm
       'At first he halved an earthworm with his beak'

---

4 For a detailed CG analysis of *przy*, see Przybylska (2002: 491–515).

The translator's choice of a higher level of specificity has yet another consequence as far as the interpretation of the poem is concerned. The translation of (1a) might have been

(1) c. *Ptak* **przyskoczył** **po** *Ścieżce*
 Bird *przy*.jumped.PERF along path
 'The bird approached by making a single jump along the path'

Przyskakał and *przyskoczył* are both perfective (in the sense of the term "perfective" commonly used in Slavic studies for aspectual oppositions, although not in the sense in which it occurs in reference to English verbs analysed in CG, where the opposition "perfective/imperfective" overlaps the distinction between simple and continuous tenses; cf. Langacker 1991: 351). However, these two Polish verb forms display a subtle semantic difference. *Przyskakał* in (1b) is rendered perfective by adding the perfectivizing prefix *przy-* to an imperfective iterative verb *skakał*, while in *przyskoczył* in (1c) the stem itself (*skoczył*) is non-iterative and perfective, and hence its lexical meaning is that of a single and completed action.[5] While both verbs focus on the aspect of completion,[6] the iterative verb in (1b) expresses a repeated action of jumping, while the non-iterative verb in (1c) relates to a single jump. By choosing (1b) over (1c) the translator "prolonged" the process, thus implying a longer lasting observation of the approaching bird on the part of the *sujet parlant*. The original construal does not carry analogous implications. But the choice seems to be a welcome decision on the part of the translator, as the iterative verb reflects the process of sequential scanning, with the act of observation extending over a period of time.

As was stated above, in visual perception the level of specificity varies relative to the distance between the observer and the object of their observation. In her readers' and critics' opinion (cf. e.g. Sewall 1963; Freeman 1997), Emily Dickinson excelled at describing minute details. However, noticing minute details implies being positioned close to the object of one's observation. Such is indeed the construal in lines 5–12 of 328. For instance, lines 5 and 6 read:

(3) a. *And then He drank **a** Dew/From **a** convenient Grass –*

---

[5] In traditional terminology used by Polish linguists, the former would be an "aspectual" and the latter a "creative" formation (cf. e.g. Janowska and Pastuchowa 2005: 150).
[6] Cf. Vendler's "accomplishment" in Vendler (1967).

which is rendered in Polish as

(3) b. *Potem   popił   ją*[7]   ***Rosą***   *z*
    Afterwards washed.down her   dew.INSTR from
    *dogodnego   **źdźbła**
    convenient   blade   *Trawy*
                               grass.GEN
    'And then he washed it down with dew from a convenient blade of grass'

In terms of prescriptive textbook rules, (3a) is ungrammatical: *dew* and *grass* designate[8] substances and as such are uncountable; their linguistic labels must not be preceded with the indefinite article. But – in perfect agreement with cognitivist principles of alternate construal (see Section 2 above) – the poet breaks the convention (twice) in order to render the two nouns countable, so that she can then make reference to individual tiny portions of each of the substances which they designate. English offers a conventional possibility of doing this by what is in CG defined as *external bounding*: a portion of substance selected for reference can be made countable by adding a notional (and linguistic) contour that provides a boundary. Thus we can (and conventionally do) talk about *drops of dew* and *blades of grass*. But Dickinson does not make use of this conventional option. Her choice of construal may be interpreted as the intention to a linguistic counterpart of what in film shooting is called zooming, that is, reduce the distance with a consequent narrowing of a visual field and focusing upon a little fragment of the scene.[9] The Polish translation fails to preserve this element of the meaning – partly due to the absence in Polish of morphological markers of countability. In the first of the two cases in (3a) the countable *a dew* changes in the translation into the unbounded substance *rosa-NOM* 'dew'. In the second case, the translator compensates for the lack of the indefinite article by adding explicit external bounding, which results in a strongly conventionalized set phrase *źdźbło trawy* – 'a blade of grass'. The result is an image inconsistent in terms of specificity and (partly) devoid of the non-conventional imagery, which in the original justifies Dickinson's famous penchant for "minute details".

---

7 The noun *rosa* 'dew' is feminine
8 In terms or, in CG terms, profile
9 A linguistic counterpart of zooming as a technique in film shooting; cf. Section 2.

3.3.2 Trajector-landmark alignment

The first four stanzas of 328 have a clear structure, enhanced both by lexical choices and by grammatical structuring. The *sujet parlant* notices a bird coming down the path and she begins to watch him. She sees him catch and eat a worm and then zooms in to watch him drink some dew off the grass close to him. She sees him look round anxiously, and zooms in again, to focus upon his frightened eyes. The fourth stanza brings a scene of a larger scope, with the observer offering the bird a crumb, and the bird flying away. However, an analysis of the Polish translation reveals a somewhat different construal.

In the original poem, the bird is the trajector – also in the grammatical sense, as he is the grammatical subject of all structures in lines 1–15: *A **bird** came down* (line 1); ***he*** *did not know* (line 2), ***he*** *bit the Angleworm* (line 3), ***he*** *drank a dew* (line 5), *[**he**] hopped to the Wall* (line 7), ***he*** *glanced* (line 9), ***he*** *stirred his Velvet Head* (line 12), ***he*** *unrolled his feathers* (line 15), ***he*** *rowed him* (line 16). In the translation the arrangement is sometimes changed:

(4) a. *He **stirred** his Velvet Head*

is rendered as:

(4) b. *Jego   Głowy   Aksamit/ **Drgał**   targany przez*
       His   head.GEN   velvet/   trembled   jerked   by
       Groźby
       threats
       'The Velvet of his Head trembled, jerked by threats'

and

(5) a. *He **glanced** with rapid eyes*

as

(5) b. ***Bystre oczy**   strzelały*
       Quick   eyes   shot
       'His quick eyes shot rapid glances'

The three metonymies (*velvet* for 'the bird's head'; *the bird's head* for 'the bird' in [4b] and *eyes of the bird* for 'the bird' in [5b]) alter the trajector/landmark alignment of the original image: in these two cases, (4b) and (5b), the function of trajectors is ascribed not to the bird itself as the overall object of observation, but to what CG refers to as *active zones,* that is, those parts of the objects which are made cognitively activated (cf. e.g. Langacker 2008: 331–334), or focused upon. In the Polish version, the observer immediately focuses upon the active zones: the velvet (of the bird's head), the quick eyes (of the bird). In the original, the observation begins with the bird as a "Gestalt" entity, and – like earlier in the poem – the eyes and the head are (gradually) focused upon through zooming in.

Similarly, where in lines 13 and 14 the original text has:

(6) a. **Cautious,**/ *I offered him a Crumb*

in the translation we read:

(6) b.   *Rzuciłam* **ostrożną**   *Ręką/*   *Okruch*
      (I) threw   cautious.INSTR   hand.INSTR/   crumb.ACC
      'I threw a crumb with a cautious hand'

Once again, the Polish phrase in (6b), retranslated into English as 'a cautious hand', makes reference to an active zone – the part of the observer's body which directly performs the action of offering a crumb to the bird. Yet the original has the "holistic" personal pronoun *I*. Lines 13–16 depict a direct confrontation between the bird and the bird-watcher, with both participants onstage. This widening of the visual field is significant because of what follows: the last stanza brings further widening of perspective, which now embraces the ocean and the "banks of Noon".

In the original poem the bird and the woman are conceptually (and syntactically) linked together by the adverb *cautiously,* which refers both "forwards" and "backwards". Both participants onstage are cautious – unlike in the Polish version, where the property is metonymically attributed to the observer alone. The interaction between the two participants of the encounter becomes in the Polish translation a rather conventional scene of a woman watching a bird and then offering it a crumb, cautious not to scare it away.

3.3.3 Perspective

As was already said, the poem reveals a clear spatial orientation: the poet begins to watch a bird, which she notices coming her way along the path. The orientation is signalled by lexical semantics (*came down, hopped sidewise to the Wall, rowed him [. . .] home*), but also, as was seen in Section 3.3.2 above, by construals implying shifts in spatial distance. The temporal orientation is marked just as clearly – again, by the time adverb *then* (line 5) and the repeated use of the sequential conjunction *and* (lines 4, 5, 7, 15, 16).[10] Perspective is shaped by the consistent use, in the original poem, of simple past tense, rendered in English by perfective verbs (iterative or non-iterative). However, there is one significant departure, in line 2:

(7) a. *He **did not know** I saw –*

rendered as

(7) b. **Nieświadom**, *że go* **widzę**
Unaware that him.ACC see.PRES
'Unaware that I see him'

The past participle *nieświadom* erases time characteristics, and the finite verb *widzę* is used in the present tense. Unlike English, Polish does not require adherence to the principle of *consecutio temporum*. The choice of present rather than the past

(7) c. *nieświadom, że go* **widziałam**
Unaware that him.ACC saw.PAST
'Unaware that I saw/had seen him'

brings in the "here and now" of the actual time of the observation, instead of the time of the poet's reporting the event. In terms of Fauconnier's theory of mental spaces,[11] the verb in the present tense becomes a *space builder*, an expression that establishes a new mental space. Evoking the mental space of the "here and now" of immediate observation makes the description more vivid, but, on the other hand, breaks the consistency of description of the English original.

Throughout the poem there are other grammatical signals shaping perspective, notably indefinite and definite articles. Thus the poem opens with

(8) a. *A Bird **came down the** Walk –*
   b. *Ptak **przyskakał** po Ścieżce*
   Bird *przy*.jumped.PERF along path
   'A/the bird approached jumping repeatedly along the path'

---

10 For the iconic sequential interpretation of *and* in natural language, see, e.g. Enkvist (1990).
11 For a detailed description, see Fauconnier ([1985] 1994).

Later on, in line 7 of the poem,

(9) a. *It hopped **sidewise** to **the** Wall.*
 b. *Pod   Mur   uskoczył –*
  Under wall *u*.jumped.PERF
  'He dodged towards the wall'

the lexical semantics of the phrasal verb *came down* in (8a) and of the adverb *sidewise* in (9a) establish the viewing arrangement relative to the positioning of the viewer (the poet) and the viewed (the bird). The situatedness of the observer relative to the things observed shapes her epistemic perspective, i.e. the knowledge that he shares – or does not share – with the reader. In languages like English, epistemic perspective is most readily expressed by the opposition between definite and indefinite articles. Thus, ***a** bird* profiles an entity new to both the observer-speaker and to the reader; ***the** Walk* and ***the** Wall*, although non-identifiable for the latter, are most probably well known to the former. The reader – especially if he knows Dickinson's biography – would interpret the walk and the wall as belonging to Emily's own garden.

In the Polish translation the bird is just this, **the** bird, identifiable (or, as Langacker would have it, mentally accessible, cf. e.g. Langacker 2008: 284); definite reference is made through the syntactic position of the noun, cf.

(8) b. *Ptak   **przyskakał**   po   Ścieżce –*
  Bird   *przy*.jumped.IMPERF   along   path
  'A/the bird approached jumping repeatedly along the path'
 c. ***Po   Ścieżce**   przyskakał   Ptak*
  Along   path   *przy*.jumped.IMPERF   Bird
  'A bird approached jumping repeatedly along the path'

The construal, most probably imposed by prosody requirements, changes the interpretation of the poem quite significantly: although "unaccessible" to the reader, the bird is known to the poet – from another occasion, or from earlier stages of the observation described. Epistemic perspective of the poem changes its value.

In the original poem the articles shape the ground relative to the speaker and position her within the viewing arrangement only in an indirect way; in this way the construal is subjective (in the sense defined in Section 2.4). Analyzed against the objectivity scale, the poem brings the *suject parlant* directly onto the stage by direct pronominal reference: *I saw* (2), *I thought* (11), *I offered* (14). In the translation, out of the three instances – each marking the "non-zoom" holistic confrontation of the bird and the observer – two (lines 2 and 14) are weakened by the grammatical convention that requires in Polish that person is morphologically marked on the verb, with the personal pronoun being verbalized only in non-neutral contexts (for semantic contrast). In the third case – the *I thought* in line 11 – the whole phrase disappears. This apparently tiny detail causes a significant shift in meaning: *I thought* is a typical space builder, and as such it signals the passage from pre- to con-ception, or from direct observation to conceptualization (making a metaphorical comparison).

In the original the bird's *rapid eyes* look *to the poet "like frightened beads"*, giving rise to a creative simile. In the translation

(10) *Czarne Paciorki Trwogi*
 Black beads fear.GEN
 'Black beads of fear'

are a "ready" metaphor rather than an *ad hoc* mapping prompted by immediate observation. It might be argued, however, that the fact that the Polish reader must himself recreate the metaphor makes mental operations more complex, whereby the description becomes "more poetical". The question whether this is an advantage or a disadvantage should be answered by a translation critic rather than a linguist.

Yet another device that may be used for establishing the point of view and perspective is word order, conforming to what CL defines as the principle of experiential iconicity, whereby the order in which constitutive elements of an expression are combined reflects the order of perception (see, e.g. Tabakowska 2005). An example is offered in lines 3–4 of the poem:

(11) a. *He **bit** an **Angleworm** in halves/And **ate** the fellow, **raw***
 b. *Wpierw rozpołowił dziobem i zjadł na*
 At.first (he)halved beak.INSTR and ate.PERF on
 *surowo **Dżdżownicę***
 raw earthworm.ACC
 'At first he halved with his beak and ate up raw an earthworm'

The thing that the observer sees the bird bite in halves is *first* identified as an "Angleworm", and only *then* she watches the bird eat the earthworm up. The image consists of two "sub-images", and the structure is reinforced by the two parts being structurally parallel: *Subject-Verb-Object-Indirect Object*. Splitting the worm in halves is actually perceived; realizing that something that was alive a second earlier must have been eaten raw, is a reflection, a mental activity. The interpretation is actually enhanced by the grammar: the adjective *raw* comes at the end of the verse, between commas, as an afterthought rather than a direct effect of visual perception. In the Polish translation the image is somewhat different. The time adverb *wpierw* (line 3, 'at first'), absent in the original, is contrasted with *potem* (a lexical equivalent of *then*, line 5). In consequence, the actions of biting and eating are less distinctly separated in time. In addition, the Polish expression *zjadł na surowo* ('[he] ate raw') is almost a unit – a cognitive routine, a set phrase, processed by the reader automatically with the semantic content being taken for granted.

4 Conclusions

With its orientation towards the text/discourse, the cognitive model of grammar seems to substantiate the claim that TS have been making all along: verbal expression is an *interpretation* rather than a *reflection* of things, and – since language is indeterminate by definition – translation becomes an interpretation of an interpretation. In this sense, the interpretation of the original version of Dickinson's 328, as proposed above, differs from that offered by her Polish translator. It does not mean that the translation analyzed above is a bad translation; it just means that the Polish reader is offered a poem somewhat different (though not necessarily worse!) than that at the disposal of the English speaking public.

It might be argued that in both versions of the poem instructions provided by the grammar prompt an interpretation whereby the poet sees a bird approaching, gets interested in its activities, some of which she watches closely, narrowing the visual field to selected salient details. Then there comes a "holistic" confrontation of the bird and the woman, which finally leads the poet to a reflection of a more general nature. But it might also be argued – which I hope I have managed to do – that painting techniques used to depict this content make the two images differ in detail, and that the differences result from construal phenomena, mostly inherent in grammatical conventions.

I hope that the analysis justifies a couple of more general conclusions. Firstly, a linguistic theory of translation is tantamount to a theory of language which is selected as its underlying set of assumptions; its shape crucially depends on this selection. Secondly, out of those presently available, the theory of CG seems best suited for the purposes of TS, because it incorporates precisely those aspects of language that have always frustrated language-oriented theorists, i.e. the subjectivity of meaning, the motivated relations between meaning and form and (some form) of language relativism. Using the CG tools makes it possible to substantiate the claim that various grammatical devices "conspire" to build up the overall meaning of expressions. And thirdly, focusing on grammar in the context of translation results in accepting a syllogism, whereby since grammar is choice and style is choice, grammar is style. This claim, however, goes beyond the problems of translation, and as such it also extends the scope of this essay.

References

Baker, Mona 1992 *In other words. A coursebook on translation*. London: Routledge.
Banjar Yousef, Shanja n.d. Unit of translation. Available at: http://www.slideshare.net/dr.shadiabanjar/translation-unit-by-dr-shadia-yousef-banjar (accessed August 29, 2011).
Croft, William and Alan D. Cruse 2004. *Cognitive Linguistics*. Cambridge: Cambridge University Press.
Dickinson, Emily 1990 *100 wierszy* [100 poems]. Translated by Stanisław Barańczak. Kraków, Poland: Arka.
Enkvist, Nils Erik 1990 Discourse comprehension, text strategies and style. *Journal of the Australasian Universities Modern Language Association* 73: 166–180.
Fauconnier, Gilles [1985] 1994 *Mental spaces*. Cambridge: Cambridge University Press.
Fauconnier, Gilles and Mark Turner 2002 *The way we think: Conceptual blending and the mind's hidden complexities*. New York: Basic Books.
Freeman, Margaret H. 1997 Grounded spaces; deictic -self anaphors in the poetry of Emily Dickinson. *Language and Literature* 6: 7–28.
Halverson, Sandra 2007 A cognitive linguistic approach to translation shifts. *Belgian Journal of Linguistics* 21.1: 105–121.
Janowska, Aleksandra and Magdalena Pastuchowa 2005 *Słowotwórstwo czasowników staropolskich*. Kraków, Poland: Universitas.
Kenny, Dorothy 2008 Unit of translation. In: Mona Baker and Gabriela Saldanha (eds.), *Routledge encyclopedia of translation studies*, 304–306. London: Routledge.
Kuno, Susumu and Etsuko Kaburaki 1977 Empathy and syntax. *Linguistic Inquiry* 8: 627–672.
Kussmaul, Paul 2005 Translation through visualisation. *Meta* 50.2: 378–391.
Lakoff, George 1987 *Women, fire and dangerous things*. Chicago: University of Chicago Press.
Lakoff, George and Mark Johnson 1980 *Metaphors we live by*. Chicago: University of Chicago Press.
Langacker, Ronald W. 1987 *Foundations of cognitive grammar. Vol. 1, Theoretical prerequisites*. Stanford, CA: Stanford University Press.
Langacker, Ronald W. 1988 An overview of cognitive grammar. In: Brygida Rudzka-Ostyn (ed.), *Topics in cognitive linguistics*, 3–48. Amsterdam: John Benjamins.
Langacker, Ronald W. 1991 *Concept, image and symbol: The cognitive basis of grammar*. Berlin: Mouton de Gruyter.
Langacker, Ronald W. 1999 *Grammar and conceptualization*. Berlin: Mouton de Gruyter.
Langacker, Ronald W. 2008 *Cognitive grammar: A basic introduction*. Oxford: Oxford University Press.

Langacker, Ronald W. 2009 Metonymic grammar. In: Klaus-Uwe Panther, Linda Thornburg and Antonio Barcelona (eds.), *Metonymy and metaphor in grammar*, 45–71. Amsterdam: John Benjamins.

McElhanon, Kenneth A. 2005 From word to scenario: The influence of linguistic theories upon models of translation. *Journal of Translation* 1.3: 29–67.

Nida, Eugene 1964 *Toward a science of translating*. Leiden: Brill.

O'Brien, Sharon (ed.) 2011 *Cognitive explorations of translation*. London: Continuum.

Przybylska, Renata 2002 *Polisemia przyimków polskich w świetle semantyki kognitywnej*. Kraków, Poland: Universitas.

Sewall, Richard B. (ed.) 1963 *Emily Dickinson: A collection of critical essays*. Englewood Cliffs, NJ: Prentice Hall.

Snell-Hornby, Mary 1990 Linguistic transcoding or cultural transfer? A critique of translation theory in Germany. In: Susan Basnett and Andre Lefevere (eds.), *Translation, history and culture*, 79–86. London: Cassell.

Tabakowska, Elżbieta 1993a Articles in translation: An exercise in cognitive linguistics. In: Richard A. Geiger and Brygida Rudzka (eds.), *Conceptualizations and mental processing in language*, 785–800. Berlin: Mouton de Gruyter.

Tabakowska, Elżbieta 1993b *Cognitive linguistics and poetics of translation*. Tübingen, Germany: Gunter Narr.

Tabakowska, Elżbieta 1993c Image as grammar: Some linguistic aspect of translating "The Asian Journal" of Thomas Merton. In: Elżbieta Górska (ed.), *Images from the cognitive scene*, 89–100. Kraków, Poland: Universitas.

Tabakowska, Elżbieta 1996 The linguist and the poet: Nouns and verbs in a Polish translation of Emily Dickinson's poetry. In: Barbara Lewandowska-Tomaszczyk and Martin Thelen (eds.), *Translation and meaning*, 267–282. Maastricht, the Netherlands: Opleiding Tolk-Vertaler.

Tabakowska, Elżbieta 1997 Conditionals as an instance of figure/ground alignment. In: Angeliki Athanasiadou and Rene Dirven (eds.), *On conditionals again*, 273–288. Amsterdam: John Benjamins.

Tabakowska, Elżbieta 2000 Is (cognitive) linguistics of any use for (literary) translation? In: Sonja Tirkkonen-Condit and Riitta Jaaskelainen (eds.), *Tapping and mapping the processes of translation and interpreting. Outlooks on empirical research*, 85–95. Amsterdam: John Benjamins.

Tabakowska, Elżbieta 2004 Point of view in the theory of literature and in linguistics: Grammar or a "logic of reading". In: Barbara Lewandowska-Tomaszczyk and Alina Kwiatkowska (eds.), *Imagery in language*, 693–710. Frankfurt am Main: Peter Lang.

Tabakowska, Elżbieta 2005 Iconicity as a function of point of view. In: Costantino Maeder, Olga Fischer and William Herlofsky (eds.), *Outside-in – inside- out: Iconicity in language and literature 4*, 375–388. Amsterdam: John Benjamins.

Talmy, Leonard 1996 Fictive motion in language and – ception. In: Paul Bloom, Mary A. Peterson, Lynn Nadel and Merrill F. Garrett (eds.), *Language and space*, 211–276. Cambridge, MA: MIT Press.

Talmy, Leonard 2000 *Toward a cognitive semantics*. Vol. 1, *Concept structuring systems*. Cambridge, MA: MIT Press.

Taylor, John 2002 *Cognitive Grammar*. Oxford: Oxford University Press.

Vendler, Zeno 1967 *Linguistics in philosophy*. Ithaca, NY: Cornell University Press.

Vinay, Jean-Paul and Jean Darbelnet [1958] 1995 *Comparative stylistics of French and English: A methodology for translation*. Amsterdam: John Benjamins.

Wójcik-Leese, Elzbieta 2000 Salient ordering of free verse and its translation. *Language and Literature* 9/2: 170–181.

http://www.informaworld.com/translationstudies (accessed June 15, 2009).

http://www.translatum.gr/etexts/translation-theory.htm (accessed August 29, 2011).

Iraide Ibarretxe-Antuñano and Luna Filipović
Lexicalisation patterns and translation*

1 Introduction: Translation Studies and semantic typology

Current approaches to Translation Studies (cf. Munday 2001; Samaniego Fernández 2007; Pym 2009) consider the translator as an intercultural mediator between the source text and the target text. Translations are no longer judged in terms of fidelity to the source text or understood as transfers from a source into a target language; they are considered manipulations, retextualizations conducted by a translator, who determines what is functionally suitable in the target language. In semantic typology, on the other hand, theoretical work on the linguistic organization of motion events has shown that this domain can be described by a limited set of underlying universal patterns, but that it is also construed in different ways in different languages. According to Talmy (1991, 2000), the world's languages can be divided into two main typological groups, verb-framed and satellite-framed, in terms of the way the core feature of a motion event, i.e. path, is expressed linguistically, and in the way languages express the components of a complex event. These lexicalisation differences are directly reflected in the online use of language, and consequently, speakers of verb-framed and satellite-framed languages differ in their rhetorical styles when describing the same motion event. Satellite-framed speakers tend to provide dynamic descriptions of motion events, loaded with expressive details about directionality and Manner of motion, whereas verb-framed speakers are said to provide static descriptions with less details about Manner and directionality (Slobin 1991, 1996). These differences are also present in different degrees even in languages within the same typological group because there is also intra-typological variation (Filipović 2007a, 2008; Ibarretxe-Antuñano 2004, 2009a; Slobin 2004). These findings are especially interesting from the point of view of translation, since translators are the ones in charge of adapting the rhetorical style of source languages onto that of target languages. Based on previous analysis on this area (cf. Cifuentes 2006; Filipović 2007a, 2008; Ibarretxe-Antuñano

---

* This research has been funded by grant FFI2010-14903 from the Spanish Ministry of Economy and Competitiveness. The second author would also like to acknowledge the generous research funding received from the ESRC, Leverhulme Trust and Newton Trust which enabled her to conduct the investigation partly reported in this paper.

2003; Jaka 2009; Slobin 2005, among others), this paper shows the strategies translators follow when adapting texts from languages belonging to different as well as similar lexicalisation patterns, the importance of lexicalisation pattern differences in discourse specific contexts such as witness reports, and their usefulness for translation pedagogy and theory in general.

This paper is organised as follows: the first part briefly describes the main characteristics of the two models at work here, namely, (descriptive) Translation Studies and semantic typology (especially Talmy's lexicalisation patterns). The second part focuses on different case studies on motion events and translation, and summarises different translation strategies followed by translators. The last part draws some conclusions on the mutual benefits of these two frameworks. It is argued that semantic typology (lexicalisation) research can contribute to process-oriented descriptive Translation Studies as well as to applied Translation Studies such as translators training (Holmes [1988] 2000; Toury 1995), while Translation Studies can offer empirical evidence for supporting the validity of these theoretical approaches.

1.1 Translation Studies: Prescriptive versus descriptive

Translation Studies is the area "related to the study of the theory and phenomena of translation" (Munday 2001: 1). It is not a homogeneous discipline and different schools or approaches focus on different aspects and view similar issues from different angles, but in general, there are some areas such as the product of translation, the process of translation, and the role of the translator that every model in translation has to deal with, at least, partially (see Munday 2001 for a review). In general, the study of translation nowadays tends to be characterised as descriptive in opposition to the traditional prescriptive tradition (Samaniego Fernández 2007). The latter were source-oriented; translations had to be as faithful as possible to the source text, they had to reproduce all the meaning and if possible, the form. As a consequence, there were cases which cannot be translated (e.g. metaphors; cf. Dagut 1976; Vinay and Darbelnet 1958), the translation process was always linguistic and the translator was considered a specialist in two linguistic systems. The former, descriptive approach, proposes a radically different perspective. It is goal-oriented, loyalty to the source text is not a necessary condition since translations are seen as manipulations that have to fit in and adapt themselves to the target language. The process of translation is communicative and the translator is an intercultural mediator, "the expert in translation action and whose role is to make sure that the intercultural transfer takes place satisfactorily" and who determines "what is functionally suitable" (Munday 2001: 77).

The models we present in the following section, Talmy's lexicalisation patterns and Slobin's thinking for speaking, clearly align themselves with descriptive Translation Studies; but, perhaps, what these models are really useful for in relation to translation is that (i) they show us that a correct, loyal, and perfect translation is not always the best choice, but that languages, and therefore speakers, favour some constructions over others, not on the basis of their grammaticality, since all of them are grammatical, but on the basis of their rhetorical style, and (ii), from a pedagogical point of view, they provide teachers with linguistic criteria to define in an objective way their intuitions when they affirm that a translation does not sound stylistically natural in the target language. Before we go on describing these two models, let us draw a couple of examples to illustrate what we mean by these "favoured choices".

Imagine a situation where there is man, John, inside a house. Suddenly, somebody calls him out. This other person tells him that he has to go as quickly as possible to his mother's place because she is ill. How would an English speaker describe what John does next? Probably, this speaker would say something similar to (1):

(1) *John rushed out to his mum's place*

The question is now whether this utterance is the only possible choice that English speakers would have to describe this situation. Probably not; there are, of course, other options:

(2) *John went out of the house as quickly as possible and headed towards his mum's place*

(3) *John went out running from his house and went to his mum's place*

(4) *John exited the house running and went to his mum's place*

[...]

All these sentences are grammatically perfect, but an English speaker would most probably not choose (2), (3) or (4). These sentences are fine, but they are not the way an English speaker would usually talk about motion. This type of construction, as discussed later, is more typical of languages such as Spanish (*Juan se fue a toda prisa de su casa y se dirigió a casa de su madre* [sentence 2], *Juan salió de la casa corriendo y fue a casa de su madre* [sentence 4]).

A similar example is the case of the Basque Complete Path construction (Ibarretxe-Antuñano under review). This is the tendency to linguistically express in the same clause both the source and the goal of a translational motion, where

Figure 9.1: Deer scene in Frog Stories (Mayer 1969)

the focus is on the path delimited by source and goal, and not on the source and goal themselves. It can be considered a construction (cf. Goldberg 1995) because it has formal restrictions – it is impossible to insert anything (e.g. adverb) between the source and the goal – and because the construction itself means 'delimited path'. Basque speakers generally use this construction to describe a situation such as that depicted in Figure 9.1 from the Frog Stories.

(5)   *Danak amildegitikan behera   erori   zian ibai batera*
       all.ABS cliff.ABL.LOC   below.ALL fall.PERF aux river one.ALL
       'All of them fell from the cliff down into the river' (Ibarretxe-Antuñano 2004: 328).

The choice is not grammatically constrained, that is, Basque speakers must not use this construction obligatorily; they have other choices: to mention just the source (*amildegitikan* [cliff.ABL.LOC] 'from the cliff'), just the goal (*lurrera* [ground.ALL] 'to the ground') or neither of them. However, they prefer a sentence like that in (5). What is interesting about this construction is that L2 Basque speakers with an excellent command of the language hardly use this construction (Ibarretxe-Antuñano 2011). As in the English case, a choice may be grammatical and correct but it does not really fit into the natives' "favoured" style – what we call below the "rhetorical style" – which is, on our opinion, one of the major contributions that the theory of lexicalisation patterns can make to Translation Studies.

1.2 Semantic typology: Lexicalisation patterns and its discourse application

Talmy (1985, 2000) proposed a semantic typology of languages based on how they map cognitive notions onto words and constructions. This is a particularly beneficial way of contrasting languages because it emphasises the commonality of human linguistic behaviour while providing the necessary basis for teasing the language-specific features apart from the universally shared ones. Talmy discussed the ways in which crucial event components in a universal cognitive domain (e.g. motion) are rendered into different languages. Those lexicalisation patterns (i.e. habitual ways of structuring events in a language) may facilitate the presence of one kind of information over another in a particular language (e.g. Path over Manner of motion). The patterns are then reinforced thorough habitual use, resulting in the preference for omission or inclusion of certain pieces of information in expressions of events. According to Talmy, a motion event has four basic components: *Motion* (presence of motion), *Figure* (the moving object), *Ground* (the reference-point object with respect to which the Figure moves) and *Path* (the course followed by the Figure with the respect to the Ground). A typical example of an expression of a motion event would be: *The ball rolled down the hill*. In this sentence, *the ball* expresses the Figure, *the hill* is the Ground, and the Path is expressed by the particle *down* (termed "satellite" by Talmy). The verb root (*roll*) itself conflates Manner and Motion.

All languages of the world seem to prefer one of the two options, namely expressing Path in the verb or Path out of the verb. This crucial distinction is the basis of Talmy's typology, which divides all the languages into two major groups. Languages that characteristically map the *core schema of the event* onto the verb are *verb-framed languages* and those that do it out of the verb via "satellites" are defined as *satellite-framed languages*.[1] Satellites are defined as "certain immediate constituents of a verb root other than inflections, auxiliaries, or nominal arguments" (Talmy 1985: 102), like prefixes in Slavonic languages (e.g. *u-leteti* meaning 'into-fly' in Serbo-Croatian) or adverbs like "in" as in *He walked in without saying a word*. The representational example of the relevant contrasts in the satellite-framed/verb-framed dichotomy would be the following examples in English and Spanish respectively:

(6) *The man ran out of the house*

(7) El   hombre salió   de la   casa   corriendo
     the man   exited of the   house   running
     'The man exited the house running'

---

1 In the case of the expressions of motion, the core information is that of Path (since motion events are defined as those where a Figure changes location), and it is expressed within the verb itself in verb-framed languages, and via satellites in satellite-framed languages.

In English, a satellite to the verb, *out*, conveys the core information about the Path of the moving Figure, whereas in Spanish it is the verb itself, *salir* 'exit', that conveys this piece of information. Note also that supporting information about Manner of motion is conveyed by the verb in English and by the gerund *corriendo* 'running' in Spanish. These patterns are the most predominant ones in English and Spanish respectively.[2]

Talmy's typology based on these lexicalisation patterns, beyond its implications for semantic typology, seems of crucial importance in neorelativistic theories such as Slobin's (1991, 1996, 1997, 2000, 2004, 2006) *thinking for speaking*. This author suggests that speakers organise their thinking in accordance to the requirements of the on-line linguistic encoding; speakers' attention is "guided" or "directed" by their own languages and therefore, speakers pay attention to certain details that can be easily expressed in their language. In his own words: "'Thinking for speaking' involves picking those characteristics that (a) fit some conceptualisation of the event, and (b) are readily encodable in the language" (Slobin 1997: 435).

In the case of motion events, satellite-framed language speakers due to their own languages' mechanisms (satellites, rich and expressive manner lexicon) would pay attention to certain details or pieces of information that verb-framed speakers would actually neglect or oversee. In a nutshell, Slobin proposes two main differences.

First, satellite-framed narratives contain more information about Manner of motion than those in verb-framed languages. This distinction is reflected in both lexical and combinatorial resources of the two types of languages. English, as a satellite-framed language, has a large and expressive collection of verbs of motion that convey Manner (*walk, run, crawl, fly, clamber, plummet*, etc.), combinable with a large collection of directional satellites (*in, up, to, across*, etc.). They are easy to insert in the construction environment of a motion expression and have higher frequency than directional verbs. In Spanish, a verb-framed language instead, the verbs of inherent directionality (*entrar* 'enter', *bajar* 'descend', *subir* 'ascend', etc.) are the preferred means of expression. Manner verbs are used only in restricted circumstances and the lexicon with regard to Manner verbs is conspicuously less developed in this language (cf. Slobin 1997). These differences in the degree of Manner description have led to the

---

2   It is important to bear in mind that the basis of Talmy's typology is the most *characteristic* expression of a motion event. Consequently, this does not mean that both English and Spanish do not have other choices, but that speakers prefer these constructions when describing a motion event.

proposal of a *Manner salience cline* (Slobin 2004). On the basis of two premises, usage and linguistic resources availability, Slobin argues that languages with large and rich resources for Manner description are prone to be high-manner salient (cf. English), whereas languages with poor resources would be low-manner salient (cf. Spanish). Recent research, however, has shown that the relation between high- or low-manner saliency is not necessarily determined by the type of lexicalisation pattern (verb-framed or satellite-framed) since there are languages such as Basque and Japanese that despite being verb-framed, possess large inventories of motion imitatives (aka ideophones, mimetics, onomatopoeia) (cf. Ibarretxe-Antuñano 2006, 2009b; Sugiyama 2005).

Second, narratives in satellite-framed languages include detailed descriptions of Path, and focus on the dynamics of motion in their rhetorical style, whereas narratives in verb-framed languages contain less detailed Path descriptions, and prefer scene-setting descriptions, leaving trajectories to be inferred from the context. For example, in English, several pieces of information can be attached to one single verb (*the boy ran out of the house, over the fence, down the path, pass the trees, into the cave*), whereas in Spanish, this sentence would require several Path verbs, would probably omit some details and describe landmarks less dynamically (*el chico salió de la casa y tras cruzar la valla, siguió por el camino y terminó en la cueva*, lit. 'the boy exited of the house and after crossing the fence, followed over the path and ended in the cave'). As in the case of the Manner component, the quantity and quality of Path description are not so clear-cut, and there are languages that, no matter which language group they belong to, describe this component in different degrees of detail. Stemming from a study of 24 languages, Ibarretxe-Antuñano (2004, 2009a) also proposes the *Path salience cline*, which cross-cuts the two lexicalisation patterns and classifies languages along a continuum between two ends: high-path to low-path saliency.

Talmy's dichotomy between verb-framed and satellite-framed languages described above has been challenged in recent years. It has received criticisms on several grounds: the complexity and definition of the notion of satellite (Filipović 2007a; Beavers, Levin, and Tham 2010; Croft et al. 2010); the necessity to account for languages that do not fit into this typology and therefore, the creation of other categories such as Slobin's (2004) equipollently-framed languages (see also Zlatev and Yangklang 2004), or Bohnemeyer et al.'s (2007) Type I, II, and III languages; and the existence of intratypological as well as diatopic variation (Berthele 2004, 2006; Cadierno 2004; Filipović 2007a; Hijazo-Gascón 2011; Ibarretxe-Antuñano 2004; Ragnarsdóttir and Strömqvist 2004, among others).

Despite these criticisms, numerous studies have indicated that these typological differences could be relevant to applied domains of linguistics (e.g.

translation, language acquisition [cf. Filipović 2007a, 2007b, 2008; Filipović and Vidaković 2010; Hijazo-Gascón 2011; Hohestein, Eisenberg, and Naigles 2006; Naigles and Terrazas 1998; Slobin 1996, 1997, 2000, 2006] or other related disciplines, such as psycholinguistics [cf. Gennari et al. 2002; Filipović 2010b, 2010c, 2011a; Malt et al. 2003] and forensic linguistics [Filipović 2007b, 2009, 2013]). Our focus at present is on how these typological findings could improve the understanding of what happens in the process of translation from a source language into target language and vice versa. We discuss on how these typological findings could inform research with regard to the process of translation in different contexts and help us account for the reason why some pieces of information may be habitually absent in the original text, but added in translation. A successful transfer of meaning from one linguistic system into another is the main goal in translation and thus preserving semantic content is of prime importance in spite of structural differences. This typological perspective can assist translators and learners of a foreign language by providing insight that may stimulate compensatory strategies, some of which we illustrate in the following section.

2 Motion events, lexicalisation and translation

The first study that applies the theory of lexicalisation patterns to translation is Slobin's paper "Two Ways to Travel: Verbs of Motion in English and Spanish" (1996). Up to that moment, most of Slobin's work had been based on oral narrative data coming from the Frog Stories (Berman and Slobin 1994). However, this author realised that the typological differences he finds in these data are not particular to this type of stimuli or discourse, but that they can be found across different data, for example, novels and their translations. In his 1996 paper, Slobin picks up four English novels and three Spanish novels and their corresponding translations into the other language.[3] The methodology he follows is very simple: first, he selects 80 English motion events and their Spanish translations and 60 Spanish motion events with their English

---

3   The choice of novels did not follow any specific criteria; the only requirement was that these novels had translations in the other language. English novels: Daphne du Maurier's (1938) *Rebecca*, John Fowles' (1969) *The French Lieutenant's Woman*, Doris Lessing's (1952) *A Proper Marriage* and James Michener's (1978) *Chesapeake*. Spanish novels: Isabel Allende's (1982) *La Casa de los Espíritus*, Gabriel García Márquez's (1967) *Cien Años de Soledad*, and Mario Vargas Llosa's (1977) *La Tía Tula y el Escribidor*.

equivalents, and then, he compares translations and examines how much Path and Manner description has been kept in the target text from the source text.

Slobin compares translations in terms of fidelity to Manner and Path-Ground descriptions, and discovers that in both cases, the English source text loses more information in the Spanish target text than the other way round. English to Spanish translators keep 51% and 76% of Manner and Path faithful translation, respectively. Spanish to English translators, on the other hand, maintain 77% for Manner and 92% for Path. With respect to Path translation, Slobin argues that "English translators have an easy task: they almost always follow the original, and sometimes even add a bit. Spanish translators, however, make changes to English trajectories 24 per cent of the time, and of these changes the majority are reductions of the full path-ground depiction" (1996: 210). With respect to Manner translation, he states that "[it] is far more salient in English narratives than in Spanish. Spanish translators omit manner information about half of the time, whereas English translators actually *add* manner to the Spanish original in almost a quarter of their translations" (1996: 212).

Slobin argues that Spanish is less faithful because of lexical and syntactic constraints both at linguistic and discourse level. Spanish tends to add just one piece of Path information to the main motion verb; although this is not a grammatical requirement and a verb can show more than one Path, speakers prefer to keep the tendency of one element per verb, therefore, complex trajectories in English are often broken into smaller clauses headed by a different verb in Spanish as in (8) or, alternatively, as it happens in (9), if the trajectory is obvious and does not add any relevant information to the narrative, translators simply omit the Path information.

(8) a. *Martha walked through the park and along the avenues[. . .]*
 b. *Martha cruzó el parque y paseó a lo largo de las avenidas[. . .]*
 'Martha crossed the park and promenaded along the avenues[. . .]'

(9) a. *He strolled across the room to the door[. . .]*
 b. *Se dirigió a la puerta[. . .]*
 'He went to the door. [. . .]'

In Manner translation, Spanish has less expressive lexical resources than English. This results into certain semantic gaps where the only alternative for the Spanish translator is to add up Manner description by means of adverbials or prepositional phrases to the main verb as in (10).

(10) a. *She rustled out of the room[. . .]*
b. *Salió del cuarto, acompañada del susurro siseante de sus ropas[. . .]*
'She exited from the room, accompanied by the swishing rustle of her clothing, [. . .]'

However, as Slobin points out, this solution provokes a certain unbalance with respect to the English source text. In English, Manner is "given" in the verb at no extra cost, but in Spanish, if it is placed outside the verb, it gives more narrative weight to this semantic component. As a solution, most of the time, Spanish translators omit the translation of Manner as in (11), unless it is relevant for the discourse, in which case they keep it.

(11) a. [. . .]*he bounded up the stairs after her, overtaking her in the bedroom[. . .]*
b. [. . .]*subió tras ella alcanzándola en el dormitorio[. . .]*
'[. . .]he ascended after her, reaching her in the bedroom[. . .]'

Slobin's first study with just two languages, Spanish and English, was then followed by a bigger project with eleven languages; satellite-framed: English (source), Dutch, German, Russian, Serbo-Croatian, and verb-framed: French, Portuguese, Italian, Spanish, Hebrew, Turkish (Slobin 2005). On this occasion, the source text was chapter 6 in Tolkien's 1937 novel *The Hobbit*. It was chosen "because it has been widely translated and is full of vivid motion events" (117). The methodology was the same as in the previous study: pick up motion event descriptions and check how and how much information was translated. This large-scale study corroborates previous findings. Languages in the two groups differ in their Manner salience. Verb-framed languages tend to omit the Manner verb; Slobin compares how languages translate the sentence *Dori climbed out of the tree* and concludes that neither of the six languages in this group actually uses a Manner verb but equivalents to the verb "descend", whereas the satellite-framed languages employ a verb similar to "climb". He also argues that the most striking differences are found in the "vividness" of the Manner verbs. For example, English offers three different lexical items for ascending verbs with Manner: *climb*, *clamber*, and *swarm*. These options are matched in the other four satellite-framed languages but impoverished in verb-framed languages as shown in Table 9.1. There are even cases such as foot motion with one lexical item per satellite-framed language (English *step*, Dutch *dolen*, *zwerven*, *slingeren*, German *wanderen*), but with none in the other typological group.

The results with respect to Path are also as expected. Example (12) and its translations in Table 9.2 illustrate this finding. Verb-framed languages either reduced the number of Path segments (Turkish, Portuguese) or break up the complex description into smaller units by inserting a new verb (French, Hebrew). Satellite-framed languages, especially the Germanic ones, keep faithful to the English source text.

Table 9.1: Ascending verbs with Manner (adapted from Slobin 2005: 125)

	English	Dutch	German	Russian	Serbo-Croatian	
Ascending	Climb	Klimmen	Klettern	Lezt'	Pentrati	
	Clamber	Klauteren	Krabbeln	Karabjat'sja Vzobrat'sja	Peti se	
	French	Portuguese	Spanish	Italian	Hebrew	Turkish
	Grimper	Trepar	Trepar	Arrampicarsi	Tipes	Turmanmak

Table 9.2: Components of Path in example (12) (after Slobin 2005: 122)

Lang	wander	exit	cross	descend
EN	wander on	out of the valley	over its edge	down the slopes beyond
DU	wander further	out of the valley	over the edge	down the slopes lying beyond
GE	march further	out of the valley	down over the slope	down the slope beyond
RU	walk and walk	go up from the valley	wobble across over its edge	start to go down
S-C	stroll further	go out from the valley	over its edge	go down the slope behind it
FR	continue to advance aimlessly	exit from the valley	cross the edge	descend the slope beyond
IT	wander again	out of the valley	cross it	descend down along the slope on the other side
PO	continue advancing	exit from the valley		descend the slope beyond
SP	continue walking	out of the valley	along the edge	then descending the slopes
HE	continue to walk	pass the edge of the valley		descend on the slopes beyond 't
TU		exit from the valley	stroll on its edge	down from the slopes behind it

(12) *He still wandered on, out of the little high valley, over its edge, and down the slopes beyond*

The possibility of using translation for the purpose of language contrasting both within and across different typological groups has been explored by numerous subsequent studies. A bidirectional translation study by Filipović (1999) showed that, although the similarities predicted by the typology are found between the lexicalisation patterns of two languages in the satellite-framed group, English and Serbo-Croatian (e.g. the presence of Manner verbs in motion expressions), a number of differences also seem to emerge.[4] In the Serbo-Croatian translation of the English text the information about Manner is either omitted or is less specific on a significant number of occasions, very much like Spanish in Slobin's findings. In more than one half of the examples of verbalised motion events in the data (40 out of 70 instances), the information about the Manner of motion in Serbo-Croatian has been omitted, simplified (e.g. by using a less complex verb), or expressed in another way, usually by an adverbial (cf. Filipović 1999, 2008, 2010a). For example, *they* rushed *to the top of it* is rendered in translation *as* popeše se *na njegov vrh* which means 'they *climbed* to the top' (omitted: *in a rush*). The translation choices are the result of the impossibility to use an adequate Manner verb in Serbo-Croatian. Manner verbs in English are the most typical and preferred means used in motion expressions and their use is not restricted in any way, whereas the morphological complexity of Serbo-Croatian restricts the use of Manner verbs and their combinability with different prepositions (for further details see Filipović 2007a, 2010a; Filipović and Vidaković 2010). As a result, speakers of Serbo-Croatian cannot use Manner verbs as often as English speakers and the information about the Manner of motion is omitted or simplified in Serbo-Croatian translation compared to the information in the original source (English text). Therefore, Filipović (1999) concludes that certain intratypological contrast plays an important part when it comes to the habitual presence or absence of information in both original text and the translation and this study originally proposed that the typology should be seen as a cline rather than a dichotomy.

---

4 The data from the narratives consist of 70 descriptions of motion events in English, collected from the novel *Animal Farm* (1945) by George Orwell, the translation into Serbo-Croatian by Vera Lebović, 40 descriptions of motion events in Serbo-Croatian from two short stories by Ivo Andrić, *Prokleta avlija* (1954) and *Priča o vezirovom slonu* (1948), and the translation into English by Celia Hawkesworth.

Another piece of work stemming from Slobin's work on lexicalisation patterns and translation is Ibarretxe-Antuñano (2003). This study sets out to investigate the translation of motion events from English into Basque and Spanish using chapter 6 in *The Hobbit* as source of data. Since this novel was not published in Basque at the time, she asked four professional translators to translate the relevant passages. The interest of this study is twofold. On the one hand, it shows that intratypological differences are also a key factor in translation (similarly to Filipović 1999 in satellite-framed languages). In other studies, Ibarretxe-Antuñano (2004) shows that Basque, despite being a verb-framed language and contrary to general assumptions about Path in these languages, is a high-path salient language, because speakers usually offer complex and detailed descriptions of this semantic component. In *The Hobbit*, she finds similar results. For a sentence like that in (12), two of the Basque translations are:

(13) *Bera   oraindik   noraezean   zebilen, goiko   bailara*
     he.ABS   still   where.to.lack.of   walked   top.ADN   valley
     txikitik   kanpo,   bere   mugaz   gain   eta   bestaldeko
     small.ABL   outside   he.GEN   limit.INST   top   and   other.ADN
     aldapan   behera
     slope.LOC below.ALL
     'He was still walking aimlessly, out of the small high valley, over its edge and down the other slope'

(14) *Oraindik   ere   noraezean   jarraitzen zuen,   bailaratxo*
     still   too   where.to.lack.of   continue   AUX   valley-little
     altu   horretatik kanpo,   ertzetik   gora   eta
     high   that.ABL   outside   edge.ABL   above.ALL   and
     urrunago, hegietan   behera
     farther   slope.PL.LOC below.ALL
     'He continued still [walking] aimlessly, out of the high small valley, up and further the edge and down the slopes'

In (13) and (14), Basque translators use only one main verb *ibili* 'walk' and *jarraitu* 'keep on, continue' with all the "exit", "cross" and "descend" trajectories. In (15) and (16), the two other translators offer all the information but reduce the complexity of the path by inserting an verbal form, a participial form of the verb *zeharkatu* 'cross' in (15), and a nominalisation with locative case of the verb *jaitsi* in (16).

(15) *Oinez   jarraitu zuen,   haran txiki eta   garaitik*
    foot.INST continue aux   valley small and   high.ABL
    kanpo,   ertza   zeharkatuta eta   beste aldeko aldapetik
    outside, edge   CROSS.PART and   other side.ADN slope.ABL
    behera
    below.ALL
    'He continued [walking] on foot, out of the small and high valley, the edge crossed and down the other slope'

(16) *Oraindik noraezean   zebilen, goiko   ibar*
    still   where.to.lack.of walked   top.ADN valley
    ttipitik   at,   haren   mugan,   aldapetatik haratago
    small.ABL outside   it.GEN limit.LOC slope.PL.ABL over.there.ALL.ADN
    jaisten
    descend.NOM.LOC
    'He was still walking aimlessly, out of the small high valley, on its edge and descending the slopes beyond'

These four examples demonstrate not only that Basque translations keep Basque rhetorical style, that is, the taste for detailed trajectories, but also that these "favoured" choices, as we called them in Section 2.1, are not grammatical requirements, but speakers' (translators' in this case) rhetorical preferences.

The other interest of this study is that it reformulates Slobin's findings about the behaviour of translators in previous studies in terms of "strategies"[5] and adds up new translation techniques found in her contrastive research. Table 9.3 summarises all the strategies for Manner and Path translation with brief examples. Underlined strategies are Slobin's and the rest are Ibarretxe-Antuñano's. ST is source text (English) and TT target text (Spanish or Basque).

This methodology and the translation strategies found in Slobin (1996) and Ibarretxe-Antuñano (2003) have served as the basis for other studies on lexicalisation patterns and translation in motion events. Cifuentes (2006), for example, examines how English motion events are translated into Spanish in J. K. Rowling's

---

5 The terms "strategy", "technique", "procedure", "method" are controversial in Translation Theory since they have been interpreted differently depending on the author and/or school (see Molina and Hurtado Albir 2002). They sometimes refer to the translation product and some other times, to the translation process; the number of these techniques also varies from author to author. In this paper, we use the word "strategy" theory-free, that is, we do not ascribe to any Translation Theory in particular; it is only a "label" to describe what is going on in the target texts. We discuss this issue further in the conclusions.

Table 9.3: Translation strategies for motion events (adapted from Ibarretxe-Antuñano 2003: 165)

MANNER STRATEGIES	
Strategy M-1	Omission of any Manner information
	e.g. ST *bound up* → TT *subir* 'ascend'
Strategy M-2	Translation of the same type Manner information (verb or separate expression)
	e.g. ST *climb* → TT *trepar* 'wander'
Strategy M-3	Substitution of a Manner of motion verb for a Path verb
	e.g. ST *rustle out* → TT *salir* 'exit'
Strategy M-4	Substitution of a Manner of motion verb for a motion verb (no M-3)
	e.g. ST *creep* → TT *jarraitu* 'continue moving'
Strategy M-5	Substitution of a Manner of motion verb for any verb (no M-3-4)
	e.g. ST *roll* → TT *marruskatu* 'rub'
Strategy M-6	Translation of a portion of Manner information
	e.g. ST *flee* → TT *ziztu bizian ibili* 'walk really fast'
Strategy M-7	Translation of a different type of Manner of motion
	e.g. ST *swing* → TT *jauzi* 'jump'
PATH STRATEGIES	
Strategy P-1	Omission of some Path element
	e.g. example 9
Strategy P-2	Insertion of a new motion verb, usually a Path verb
	e.g. example 8; Table 9.2
Strategy P-3	Translation of all Path information
	e.g. example 13

(2003) *Harry Potter and the Order of Phoenix*. On the basis of 114 motion events in each language, she selects some of the translation strategies (M-1, M-2, M-6, M-7) in Table 9.3 and concludes that translators tend to first omit Manner (36.46%), and second, to include all Manner information (31.25%), then to translate Manner partially (12.50%) and, finally only rarely to change it for a different type (9.27%). With respect to Path strategies, she observes that strategy P-3 (all information) is profusely used (51.61%) but always in combination with strategy P-2 (insertion of a new verb), and that strategy P-1 (omission) is also widely attested (41.93%). Cifuentes (2006: 88) also proposes two more strategies that for the sake of clarity we rename P-4 and ME-1; these are only found once:

Strategy P-4   Inclusion of different Paths
e.g. ST *soar up and down the pitch* → TT *volar por el campo* 'fly over the pitch'

Strategy ME-1   Omission of the whole motion event
              e.g. TT *travel from Harry [. . .] to Seamus* → ST nothing

Jaka (2009) is another similar study that analyses S. T. Coleridge's (1798) *The Rime of the Ancient Mariner* and its translation to Basque. Her analysis supports Ibarretxe-Antuñano's (2003, 2004) insights about Basque motion events and their differences with prototypical verb-framed languages as far as Path and Manner are concerned both in narratives and translations. However, this piece of work is especially interesting because Jaka not only confirms the above-mentioned strategies, but also adds up to the list of strategies more techniques that we properly rename here as follows:

Strategy P-5   Substitution of a Path verb for a Manner verb
              e.g. ST *go down* → TT *murgildu* 'plunge, dive'
Strategy P-6   Omission of a Path verb (but not Path info)
              e.g. ST *followeth the ship as it returned northward* → TT *untziari jarraitu zion ipar alderantza bidean* 'followed the ship on its way to the North'
Strategy P-7   Substitution of a Path verb for any non-motion verb
              e.g. ST *Sun rises* → TT *Eguzkiak argitu* 'the Sun shines'
Strategy P-8   Insertion of new Path information
              e.g. ST *be belated* → TT *berandu ailegatu* 'arrive late'

Jaka also describes translation strategies for neuter motion events. In the previous literature, the focus has always been on Path and Manner verbs, but this option is also worthwhile. She considers four strategies:

Strategy N-1   Translation of a neuter verb with a neuter verb
              e.g. ST *go* → TT *joan* 'go'
Strategy N-2   Substitution of a neuter verb for a Manner verb
              e.g. ST *move* → TT *bultzatu* 'push'
Strategy N-3   Substitution of a neuter verb for a Path verb
              e.g. ST *move* → TT *abiatu* 'set off, head for'
Strategy N-4   Substitution of a neuter verb for any non-motion verb
              e.g. ST *go* → TT *aldatu* 'change'

Another set of related studies are those that combine lexicalisation patterns in translation with the acquisition of a second language. In some cases, motion event translations are used as a tool to discover patterns of acquisition. De Knop and Gallez (2011), for instance, investigate the acquisition of German by

French native speakers. Their tests are based on translation tasks – their subjects have to translate different sets of sentences (motion, location, complex particle verbs, non-motion V+path satellite) – and later, they analyse their results on the basis of Manner and Path. As happened in translation, they conclude that French speakers learning German often omit Manner in their translations and have problems with the acquisition of constructions with satellites. Berthaud and Antonijević (2011) is another study that examines the acquisition of English and French by native speakers of both languages. In their work, they devise an experiment where participants (advanced and upper-intermediate learners, bilinguals, and translators) are asked to produce sentences for images depicting motion events in their L2 and then to translate them into their L1. Their results show that English L2 learners made less errors than French L2 learners, who have problems with prepositions and use latinate verbs to compensate for their lack of vocabulary. They also argue that in the case of translators, French translators are trained to accommodate to satellite-framed as well as verb-framed patterns, they are more aware of the typological differences than English translators.

In relation to translation training, an interesting study is Cerda (2010). This author studies how professional translators studying for their specialization in interpreting deal with the translation of 16 Spanish fragments from Daniel Belma's (1961) *Los túneles morados* into English. These translators are all Chilean Spanish native speakers with a C1 level in English. The author concludes that subjects use satellite-framed constructions correctly (Manner verbs, complex structures) in those cases where motion verbs are very common and frequent in normal discourse, but that these structures, especially, the use of satellites, is limited in less known motion verbs. He also revises Slobin (2005) and Ibarretxe-Antuñano's (2003) strategies and argues that subjects use a combination of all of them. Although he does not offer further insights about the possible application of these results to translation teaching, he points out that these strategies and his results with these interpreting students can serve as a basis for future teaching methods.

The list of studies discussed above offer a number of strategies that can explain what the translator does when dealing with motion events. What is important about these strategies is not their number – we have seen that almost every author refines them or adds a new one – but the regularities in the behaviour of translators. Translators consistently prefer some strategies over others. Satellite-framed to verb-framed language translators, unless the discourse context requires it, tend to avoid complex Path descriptions, add Path verbs, and omit Manner information. Verb-framed to satellite-framed translators, on the other hand, behave quite the opposite; they add Manner information even if it is not present and compress Path information. We have also argued that the intratypological variation that exists within these two lexicalisation patterns can be also seen in translation; Basque favours long and detailed descriptions of Path and this trait clearly shows up in translations from *The Hobbit*. Above all, what we have shown in this section is that all these strategies are not a matter of linguistic behaviour, that is, a simple exchange of words from one language onto the other that looks for the most suitable equivalence. They reflect the rhetorical or narrative style of the target language, and consequently, they can reveal patterns of language and conceptual construal. From an applied linguistics perspective, this is crucial, since it has consequences for translation training (and second language acquisition), but as we will show in the following section, this is vital in certain areas such as forensic linguistics, especially witness interviews.

3 Expressing and translating motion events in witness interviews

3.1 Data and methodology

As already mentioned, Dan Slobin (1996, 1997, 2000, 2003, 2006) has discussed the effects that the relevant typological differences between English and Spanish have in different contexts, such as translation, thinking-for-speaking, etc. The difference in lexicalisation is particularly salient in boundary-crossing contexts (cf. Aske 1989; Slobin 1996, 1997). When a non-boundary-crossing situation is to be expressed, Spanish (like other Romance languages) does use Manner verb + directional particle combination, which is the pattern typical of satellite-framed languages:

(17) a. *They walked slowly through the streets, from the house to the school*
      b. *Caminaron por las calles lentamente, desde la casa hasta la escuela*

However, if boundary-crossing is to be expressed, in Romance languages one cannot use Manner verb + directional particle (cf. Slobin 1997: 438), which is illustrated in the following examples:

(17) c. *He ran out of the house, across the street and into the park*
      d. *Salió de la casa corriendo, cruzó la calle corriendo y entró en el parque corriendo*
          'He exited the house running, crossed the street running and entered the park running'

In (17c) only one verb is used in English, while Spanish speakers and translators have to use three verbs in the same situation (17d). It is conspicuous that all three verbs in (17d) encode Path, and that the Manner component has to be repeated after each directional verb. Another alternative is to put the Manner gerund at the beginning of the expression as in (17e):

(17) e. *Corriendo, salió de la casa, cruzó la calle y entró en el parque*
 'Running, he exited the house, crossed the street and entered the park'

A translator has to make choices in fitting one language to another. By choosing (17d) as a translation for the English expression in (17c), a translator would have foregrounded Manner, which had not been done in the original. Moreover, the repetition of *corriendo* 'running' with all three directional verbs would be stylistically intolerable. The structure in (17e) is also problematic because this would mean that a large number of sentences in Spanish translation would have to begin with a gerund (which normally does not happen in that language) and perhaps, on other occasions, include more than one gerund in the same sentence, since one verbalised motion event in English may often contain elaborate information about different kinds of Manner. This would overburden the structure of expression in Spanish and sound most unnatural in a continuous narrative. In fact, what Slobin (1995, 1997) has shown is that habitually, in situations when expressions such as the English one in (17c) are to be translated, the information on Manner would most likely be omitted altogether. Slobin (1996: 199) states further that the diversity of English verb + satellite is impressive and in most cases (51%), the information about Manner is omitted from Spanish translation of English texts (Slobin 1997).

The findings reported in Slobin (1996, 1997, 2000) provided the incentive to explore the relevant parameters in the context of verbal interactions between police and witnesses, where the consequences could be potentially more profound, reaching beyond the text itself. The role of language in witnesses' accounts of events has been examined before from a number of angles. Ours is a typological one, and it has been discussed originally in Filipović (2007).

Filipović (2007b) used a database of 123 files of transcribed police interviews with witnesses and suspects. The length of the files varies, ranging from approximately 20 to 120 pages, comprising over 74 000 words. They were collected in a number of courts in the counties of San Francisco and San Jose, California, USA. Filipović (2007b) reported the scarcity of Manner detail in accounts of motion events in Spanish in the novel context of police witness interviews. One of the main findings is that in original Spanish texts the number of Manner verbs per motion event compared to that of Path verbs stands in the relation: 21% vs. 79%. The difference in the quantity of Manner vs. Path verbs becomes more conspicuous if we take into consideration that the events described are frequently those referring to very dynamic situations of muggings, robberies, domestic violence, manslaughter, etc., where one could expect a variety of Manners of motion. When translating from Spanish into English, interpreters opt for *run* when in the original Spanish text the verb used is *pasar* 'pass', or *saltar del coche* 'jump out of the car' instead of the expression given in Spanish *bajarse del coche* 'get out of the car'. Out of the 457 motion verbs used in the data, only 5 types (*caminar* 'walk', *correr* 'run', *bailar* 'dance', *brincar* 'skip', *saltar* 'jump') and 96 tokens of Manner verbs were found, opposed to 8 types (*irse* 'go', *venir* 'come', *entrar* 'enter', *salir* 'exit', *bajar* 'go down', *subir* 'go up', *pasar* 'pass', *cruzar* 'cross') and 361 tokens of directional verbs. Directional verbs are used freely and equally frequently in boundary-crossing and non-boundary crossing situations. Information on Manner in general (i.e. verbs and gerunds) is mainly present in non-boundary-crossing situations, while it is conspicuously absent from expressions of boundary-crossing. Out of 96 Manner tokens, boundary-crossing has 5 tokens (Manner gerunds), non-boundary-crossing – 72 tokens (Manner verbs + Manner gerunds), *salir corriendo* phrase – 19 tokens.

For example, even in highly dynamic cases of sexual harassment and knife attack information on Manner is conspicuously absent throughout the description of events:

(18)   *Me salí de la oficina y me fui. Y él se fue atrás de mí, se fue, pero él se fue para allá y yo me vine para allá*
       'I got out of the office and I left. And he went after me, he left, but he went over there and I came over there.'

(19)   *[. . .]y yo le caí atrás, lo vi que traía la, la, la navaja y le caí atrás y cuando le caí atrás, muchos le caímos atrás para agarrar al que agredió el muchacho [. . .]*
       '[. . .]and I took off after him, I saw that he had the, the, the knife and I took off after him and when I went after him a lot of us went after him to grab the guy who had attacked the guy [. . .]'

While these accounts sound natural in Spanish, the absence of Manner verbs sounds very unnatural in English. This is why in the process of interpreting the information about the Manner of motion can be spontaneously added since it is the most natural way to lexicalise motion events in English, as in the following example:

(20) Pero[. . .] salió   por la   puerta detrás
      but[. . .]   exited.3sg   via the door   back
      Literal translation: 'But [. . .] he went out through the back door'
      Transcript translation: 'But he [. . .] ran out via the back door'

The dynamicity of the situation from which the example (20) was taken induced the interpreter to add Manner to describe a chase of the suspect even though the witness did not mention it explicitly in Spanish. The consequence of this is the possibility to impede the identification of a suspect or his whereabouts since the suspect could have entered running but exited via the back door walking in order to avoid suspicion. In the case of pattern clashing such as this between English and Spanish, it may be useful to explicitly encourage speakers of languages like Spanish to provide information about Manner during interrogation. The descriptions of the two situations in (18) and (19) also seem to lack dynamicity and intensity, which undoubtedly accompanied the reported events. We turn to that aspect in the next section in more detail.

Filipović (2007b) also notices that consecutive interpreting in particular (i.e. re-telling the witness's narrative in larger chunks) contains more additional Manner information compared to the original testimonies in Spanish. Such occurrences are possibly due to the *narrative* or *rhetorical style* (cf. Slobin 1991, 1996, 1997, 2000) that underlies the accounts of events in English, favouring the more dynamic construction of events in the narrative as opposed to the more static scene-setting in Spanish. In other words, Spanish texts locate protagonists at scenes but do not specify how the locations were reached, whereas in English it is continuous motion that is habitually described (i.e. how a location was reached). This difference in narrative style was noticed by Slobin (1996, 1997, 2000) in the context of literary texts and elicited narratives based on a picture story, as well as by Barbara Tversky (personal communication), following an analysis of scripts for Latin American soap operas. This difference was ascribed to typological contrasts between lexicalisation patterns in the two languages. For example, the most frequent construction in the Spanish descriptions was *se metió, me metí*, literally meaning 'he put himself, I put myself (somewhere)', but rarely specify how the location was reached. This narrative style would sound extremely unnatural if exercised in English, and as a result, dynamic descriptions of motion are used, frequently involving Manner verbs. If we just imagine an account of a very dynamic motion event in English, about a hundred pages long, containing plenty of directional verbs but no mention of the Manner of motion, it would seem a very odd account indeed. In Spanish, it is the most natural option.

3.2 Dynamicity in translation

In this section we discuss the way typological differences have further consequences for the understanding of events described in both original and the translation. Filipović (2011b) argues that people's judgments with regard to how they conceptualise the intensity and dynamicity of events can be affected by factors such as presence vs. absence of Manner detail in the original and the translation. For that purpose, an experimental translation study was carried out (Filipović 2011b). There were 30 participants in this experiment, 20 monolinguals (10 Spanish and 10 English, 5 male and 5 female participants in each group, mean age 21 for English and 26 for Spanish) and 10 Spanish/English bilingual interpreters (again, 5 male and 5 female participants, mean age 24). The material for this study was a selection of 8 sentences taken from an online newspaper article available in both English and Spanish (The NYPD Murder of Antony Baez, Revolutionary Worker 962, June 21, 1998). The original descriptions and quoted speakers were given by Latin American speakers of Spanish and the English translation of the same statements was provided by the newspaper in its on-line edition in English. The speakers were asked to judge how violent the events described were on the scale 1–10 (1=the weakest, 10=the strongest). Bilingual speakers were also asked to provide their own translation of the sentences either from English into Spanish or from Spanish into English and to judge the strength of violence described in the language they were translating from. Speakers were encouraged to use the whole scale, including points between two round numbers. In total, there were scalar 15 responses regarding the English translation and 15 regarding the Spanish original.

There was a significant difference in the rating of violence based on the language in which the description was available. The mean rating for the descriptions in Spanish was 4.7 by monolingual speakers and 5.0 by the bilinguals. The ratings for the descriptions given in English were 7.4 by monolinguals and 6.9 by bilinguals. The difference in the responses between monolingual and bilingual speakers was not significant, but the difference between languages was highly significant ($p < 0.05$). What this indicates is that the speakers who were reading about the events in English rated the violence described much higher than those who read about it in Spanish. And when we look at the descriptions in question, we can understand more clearly why that was so. For instance, we noticed additions of Manner in the translation from Spanish into English, as in (OT: Original text; TT: Translated text; BT: Back translation):

(21) a. OT: *Luego me **metió** en el radiopatrulla*
Lit. 'then me put.in.3sg in the police car'
b. TT: *He **threw** me in his car*

(22) a. OT: *Me **tiró** al suelo*
Lit. 'me threw.3sg against the floor'
b. TT: *He **slammed** me down to the ground*

(23) a. OT: *Empezó a **tirarme** por las esposas*
Lit. '(he) started pulling me by the handcuffs'
b. TT: *He started **jerking** me back and forth by the handcuffs*

The bilinguals who translated the English text back into Spanish occasionally used Manner verbs that illustrate the start contrast between what the Spanish original text says and the imagery created by the Spanish back translation as a result of the English official translation. For example:

(24) a. OT: *Luego me metió en el radiopatrula*
Lit. 'then me put.in.3sg in the police car'
b. TT *He threw me in his car*
c. BT: *Me tiró en su coche*
Lit. 'me threw.3sg in his car'

Another important detail to be highlighted is the omission of Manner by bilingual participants when translating from English into Spanish. This is evident in the following example:

(25) a. OT: *Otros empezaron a salir de la corte llorando y gritando de ira*
Lit. 'others started to exit of the court crying and yelling of anger'
b. TT: *Others came pouring out of the courtroom, crying and yelling in anger*
c. BT: *Otros iban saliendo y gritando enfadados*
Lit. 'others went exiting and yelling angry'

Another aspect in the contrast between English and Spanish is very important for the process of translation. Namely, when describing motion, Spanish speakers cannot use prepositions to signal the change of location since the prepositions is Spanish, unlike those in English, are directional, not locational. For example (see Filipović 2007b), the suspect questioned in the following excerpt is saying that he did not push the victim *on* the bed but that still does not have to mean that he did not push her *onto* the bed (Q-question; T-translation; A-answer):

(26)   a. Q: *Did you push her **onto** the bed?*
        b. T: *Y tú la empujaste **sobre** la cama?*
           Lit. 'And you her pushed.3sg on the bed'
        c. A: *No. **Sobre** la cama no la toque*
           Lit. 'no. on the bed no her touched.3sg'
        d. T: *No. I did not touch her **on** the bed*

The translation into English contains the preposition *sobre* 'on', which cannot be used to signal change of location as in English. Even though English has the distinction on vs. onto, with dynamic verbs of motion such as *jump* it is possible that both *on* and *onto*, and *in* and *into* can be used interchangeably (Compare: *jump in/into the river*). In the experimental data there was an example where this issue becomes salient again. Consider the following example:

(27)   a. OT: *Fue entonces que Livoti se **lanzó contra** David*
           Lit. 'was then that Livoti himself threw.3sg against David'
        b. TT: *That's when Livoti **jumped on** David*
        c. BT(S): *Eso fue cuando Livoti **se lanzó sobre** David*
           Lit. 'this was when Livoti himself threw on David'
        d. BT(E): *It was then that Livoti **attacked** David*

What transpires from the Spanish original is that the moving figure (*Livoti*) launched himself against David, but we do not know precisely in what manner. The official translation says that he *jumped on David*. In the experimental data, the bilingual participants chose to translate this particular example as *attack* in English while the experimental translation into Spanish contained the preposition *sobre* as a direct equivalent of the English *on*. However, we do not know whether Livoti was on David and in addition the Manner of motion (*jumped*) was present in the English version while absent in the account of the same event in the Spanish text. This induced the understanding of the event in the English description to be understood as more violent that what it appears to be if described in Spanish. Moreover, the use of preposition *sobre* as a result of the translation from the English *on* makes this description of attack more violent in the experimental translation into Spanish than in the original Spanish text.

To sum up, this study based on a limited sample of motion expressions and their translation illustrated the extent to which speakers can understand events differently based on the language in which they get to hear about them. And this is how we find out about events in courtroom or how we get our knowledge about most events in life except those that we witness ourselves. It is therefore essential that we keep alert about the language differences that may affect our judgment, especially in contexts where certain aspects of meaning can be crucial for our judgments about events and their participants. We have to say that without any doubt the event described was most tragic and unfortunate, regardless of language used to talk about it by witnesses and participants. However, it is crucial to understand that language can add or detract to how we view events, which is of central importance in the cases where dispassionate judgment and reliance solely on meaning is required, like witness interviews. In this case the reporting happened in an article with an agenda, namely to raise public awareness about alleged racism, abuse of power and excessive use of force. Thus it is important to highlight the need for responsible reporting events and translating reports in journalism on the whole.

4 Conclusions

This paper has shown that Talmy's theory of lexicalisation patterns and Slobin's thinking for speaking are useful for current Descriptive Translation Studies. Motion events are not easy to translate. In fact, they are always mentioned in translation books as one of the difficult areas for translators, especially between languages that belong to a different typological group. Vinay and Darbelnet (1958: 105 [1995: 103]), for instance, already notice this difficulty for English-French translation: "le resultat est marquee en anglais para la particule [. . .] occupant dans la phrase la même place que la locution adverbial qué en français indique la modalité de l'action. Cette modalité est rendue en anglais par le verbe lui même, alors que le française indique le resultat" [In English the result is marked by the particle [. . .] in the same position as the adverbial expression which in French indicates the mode of action]. They name this process the *chasse-croisé* pattern (*interchange* in English), a linguistic device that refers to a double grammatical transposition.

However, what we have argued here is that these translations are not just a matter of searching for word or construction equivalents. Finding the appropriate equivalent lexical item or grammatical structure does not explain the whole translation process and the decisions that translators, mostly unconsciously, take when they are producing the target text. It is a matter of the interaction between language and cognition. Following Slobin's thinking for speaking theory, we have proposed that these translations are guided by the narrative or rhetorical style of each language, which in turn is motivated by the linguistic choices available in each language. In general, we have seen that verb-framed translators, guided by the restricted Manner vocabulary in their languages, tend to avoid Manner information in the target texts unless the context requires it, but that even in these cases, the information they provide is poorer, less expressive than that in the source text. Satellite-framed translators, on the other hand, just do the opposite. They need more vivid and expressive Manner information, and consequently, they add it up. However, we have also seen that there are differences within languages that belong to the same typological group. Basque, for instance, has more resources for the description of Path, and unlike languages such as Spanish, Hebrew or French, Basque prefers elaborated and complex descriptions of this semantic component. It is only natural then that translators, as intercultural mediators, follow this trait and reflect it in their translations. By the same token, Serbo-Croatian has restrictions that prevent native speakers from using Manner verbs without restrictions. Those speakers are obliged to use Path verbs and express Manner in an adjunct when they describe change of location (as in *The man exited the room limping* instead of *The man limped out of the room*), the lexicalisation pattern more alike that of Spanish.

To keep these narrative styles is fundamental if translators want to maintain both the meaning and the style of the source text, but this is even more crucial in certain contexts where the choice of one piece of information, the omission or the adding of a word becomes crucial. One such as context is witness reports. We have seen that the general traits described for verb-framed and satellite-framed (narrative) translators show up in the translation of witnesses' reports. However, the consequences of not appropriately translating one element can cause the imprisonment, or even the death sentence, of the witness in question.

In sum, these models support the idea that an absolutely correct, loyal, and perfect translation (i) is not what translators usually do (nor should they be obliged to), and (ii) such translation would not always be the best choice, since translators can favour one construction over another, not on the basis of their grammaticality, since they are all grammatically correct, but on the basis of their rhetorical or narrative style.

The studies that we have discussed in this paper are only the tip of the iceberg. There is still a lot to be done in this area. For instance, the list of languages could be expanded. So far, most of the languages are relatively "close" or at least they share a common cultural background. Data from distant genetic, geographical and typological languages will surely bring more food for thought in this field. Another research path could be to examine languages from the same lexicalisation pattern. Most of these studies contrast a satellite-framed against a verb-framed language. However, as shown in the literature, there are differences within languages that belong to the same typological group. Languages describe the semantic components in different degrees of granularity (as shown in Basque with Path or Serbo-Croatian with Manner), and this is reflected in translation. This is even more striking within languages that belong to the same genetic group. On many occasions, languages within the same family, since they share many linguistic characteristics at all levels (morphosyntax, semantics, phonetics) are believed to be similar as far as their descriptions of motion events are concerned, and therefore, they should be "easy" to translate. However, this assumption is not right. Hijazo-Gascón (2011) in his study of motion events in three Romance languages (French, Italian, and Spanish) finds significant differences in the way speakers deal with motion descriptions. Italian speakers, for example, describe Path in more detail than the other two languages, and French speakers are the ones who omit Manner information more systematically. These results are crucial and useful for translation; future studies can shed some light on these intratypological translation differences that are sometimes, due to the superficial similarities among related languages, overseen in translation.

Another line of future research could be the design of translation training methods that would include the insights of these theories in their methodologies (see, for instance, Rojo 2009). These would help future translators to be aware not only of their different structures, but also of the importance of the narrative styles of languages. The application could be also fruitful in forensic linguistics (Filipović 2007b, 2009, 2013).

In this paper, the discussion is built around motion events only; however, both the insights from lexicalisation research and translation could be applied to other semantic domains (e.g. causation, see Filipović 2007b, 2013). This would benefit both fields since results could confirm or not the theory of lexicalisation patterns, and translation data would add more support to the basic assumption that we are dealing with issues beyond the superficial form that these concepts take in every language, that is, that we are dealing with both language and cognition. So far, there are only a bunch of studies devoted to this goal, to study lexicalisation and translation. Rojo and Valenzuela (2001, 2005), for instance, analyse saying verbs and sensory perception verbs in English novels and their translations into Spanish, and Cifuentes (2006) studies emanation events in English and Spanish. However, the possibilities are endless and the benefits enormous. We hope that future researchers would pick up this line of investigation and corroborate this promising future that we foresee for the study of lexicalisation patterns and translation.

References

Aske, Jon 1989 Path predicates in English and Spanish: A closer look. *Proceedings of the Fifteenth Annual Meeting of the Berkeley Linguistics Society* 15: 1–14.

Beavers, John, Beth Levin and Shiao Wei Tham 2010 The typology of motion expressions revisited. *Journal of Linguistics* 44: 183–316.

Berman, Ruth, and Dan I. Slobin (eds.) 1994 *Relating events in narrative. A Cross Linguistic Developmental study*. Hillsdale, NJ: Lawrence Erlbaum.

Berthaud, Sarah and Stanislava Antonijević 2011 Path and manner of motion: translational equivalents and second language acquisition. Paper presented at the 4th International Conference of the French Association of Cognitive Linguistics, Lyon, France, May 24–27, 2011.

Berthele, Raphael 2004 The typology of motion and posture verbs: A variationist account. In: Bernd Kortmann (ed.), *Dialectology meets typology*, 93–126. Berlin: Mouton de Gruyter.

Berthele, Raphael 2006 *Ort und Weg. Eine vergleichende Untersuchung der sprachlichen Raumreferenz in Varietäten des Deutschen, Rätorromanischen und Französichen*. Berlin: Mouton de Gruyter.

Bohnemeyer, Jürgen, Nick Enfield, James Essegbey, Iraide Ibarretxe-Antuñano, Sotaro Kita, Friederike Lüpke and Felix K. Ameka 2007 Principles of event segmentation in language: The case of motion events. *Language* 83.3: 495–532.

Cadierno, Teresa 2004 Expressing motion events in a second language: A cognitive typological perspective. In: Michel Achard and Susanne Niemeier (eds.), *Cognitive linguistics, second language acquisition, and foreign language teaching*, 13–49. Berlin: Mouton de Gruyter.

Cerda, Juan Pablo 2010 *Estrategias utilizadas en la traducción inversa español-inglés de verbos de movimiento: un estudio en lingüística cognitiva*. Unpublished master's thesis, Universidad de Concepción, Chile.

Cifuentes, Paula 2006 *La expresión de los dominios de movimiento y visión en inglés y en español desde la perspectiva de la lingüística cognitiva*. MA Thesis, Departamento de Filología Inglesa, Universidad de Murcia, Spain.

Croft, William, Jóhanna Barðdal, Willem Hollmann, Violeta Sotirova and Chiaki Taoka 2010 Revising Talmy's typological classification of complex constructions. In: Hans C. Boas (ed.), *Contrastive studies in construction grammar*, 201–236. Amsterdam: John Benjamins.

Dagut, Menachem. B. 1976 Can metaphor be translated? *Babel: International Journal of Translation* 22.1: 21–33.

De Knop, Sabine and Françoise Gallez 2011 Manner of motion: A privileged dimension of German expressions. Paper presented at the 11th International Cognitive Linguistics Conference, Xi'an, China, July 11–17, 2011.

Filipović, Luna 1999 *Language-specific expression of motion and its use in narrative texts*. MPhil dissertation, University of Cambridge, England.

Filipović, Luna 2007a *Talking about motion: A crosslinguistic investigation of lexicalisation patterns*. Amsterdam: John Benjamins.

Filipović, Luna 2007b Language as a witness: Insights from cognitive linguistics. *Speech, Language and the Law* 14.2: 245–267.

Filipović, Luna 2008 Typology in action: Applying insights from typological contrasts. *International Journal of Applied Linguistics* 18.1: 42–61.

Filipović Luna 2009 Motion events in semantic typology and eyewitness interviews. *Language and Linguistics Compass* 3.1: 300–313.

Filipović, Luna 2010a The importance of being a prefix. In: Victoria Hasko and Renee Perelmutter (eds.), *New approaches to Slavic verbs of motion*, 247–266. Amsterdam: John Benjamins.
Filipović, Luna 2010b Thinking and speaking about motion: Universal vs. language-specific effects. In: Giovanna Marotta, Alessandro Lenci, Linda Meini and Francesco Rovai (eds.), *Space in language*, 235–243. Pisa, Italy: University of Pisa Press.
Filipović, Luna 2010c Typology meets witness narratives and memory: Theory and practice entwined in cognitive linguistics. In: Elżbieta Tabakowska, Michał Choiński and Łukasz Wiraszka (eds.), *Cognitive linguistics in action: Theory to application and back*, 269–291. Berlin: Mouton de Gruyter.
Filipović, Luna 2011a Speaking and remembering in one or two languages: Bilingual vs. monolingual lexicalization and memory for motion events. *International Journal of Bilingualism* 15.4: 466–485.
Filipović, Luna 2011b *Bilingual witness report and translation: Final research report*. Manuscript, University of Cambridge.
Filipović, Luna 2013 The role of language in legal contexts: A forensic cross-linguistic viewpoint. In: Michael Freeman and Fiona Smith (eds.) *Law and Language: Current Legal Issues (15)*, 328–343. Oxford: OUP.
Filipović, Luna and Ivana Vidaković 2010 Typology in the L2 classroom: Second language acquisition from a typological perspective. In: Martin Pütz and Laura Sicola (eds.), *Inside the learner's mind: Cognitive processing in second language acquisition*, 269–291. Amsterdam: John Benjamins.
Gennari, Silvia P., Steven A. Sloman, Barbara C. Malt and W. Tecumseh Fitch 2002 Motion events in language and cognition. *Cognition* 83: 49–79.
Goldberg, Adele E. 1995 *Constructions: A construction grammar approach to argument structure*. Chicago: University of Chicago Press.
Hijazo-Gascón, Alberto 2011 *La expresión de eventos de movimiento y su adquisición en segundas lenguas*. PhD dissertation, Departamento de Lingüística General e Hispánica, Universidad de Zaragoza, Spain.
Hohestein, Jill, Ann Eisenberg and Letitia Naigles 2006 Is he floating across or crossing afloat? Cross-influence in L1 and L2 in Spanish-English bilingual adults. *Bilingualism: Language and Cognition* 9: 249–261.
Holmes, James S. [1988] 2000 The name and nature of translation studies. In: Lawrence Venuti (ed.), *The translation studies reader*, 172–185. London: Routledge.
Ibarretxe-Antuñano, Iraide 2003 What translation tells us about motion: A contrastive study of typologically different languages. *International Journal of English Studies* 3.2: 153–178.
Ibarretxe-Antuñano, Iraide 2004 Language typologies in our language use: The case of Basque motion events in adult oral narratives. *Cognitive Linguistics* 15.3: 317–349.
Ibarretxe-Antuñano, Iraide 2006 *Sound symbolism and motion in Basque*. Munich: Lincom Europa.
Ibarretxe-Antuñano, Iraide 2009a Path salience in motion events. In: Jiansheng Guo, Nancy Budwig, Susan Ervin-Tripp, Keiko Nakamura and Şeyda Özçalışkan (eds.), *Crosslinguistic approaches to the psychology of language: Research in the tradition of Dan Isaac Slobin*, 403–414. New York: Psychology Press.
Ibarretxe-Antuñano, Iraide 2009b Lexicalisation patterns and sound symbolism in Basque. In: Javier Valenzuela, Ana Rojo and Cristina Soriano (eds.), *Trends in cognitive linguistics: Theoretical and applied models*, 239–254. Hamburg: Peter Lang.

Ibarretxe-Antuñano, Iraide 2011 Aportaciones de la tipología semántica a la lingüística vasco-románica. *Oihenart. Cuadernos de Lengua y Literatura* 26: 299–315.

Ibarretxe-Antuñano, Iraide under review Going beyond motion events typology: The case of Basque as a verb-framed language. *Folia Lingvistica*.

Jaka, Aiora 2009 Mugimenduzko ekintzak ingelesez eta euskaraz, Sarrionandiaren itzulpen baten azterketatik abiatuta. *Uztaro* 69: 53–76.

Malt, Barbara C., Stephen A. Sloman, Meiyi Shi and Yuan Wang 2003 Universality and language specificity in object naming. *Journal of Memory and Language* 49.1: 20–42.

Mayer, Mercer 1969 *Frog, where are you?* New York: Dial Press.

Molina, Lucía and Amparo Hurtado Albir 2002 Translation techniques revisited: A dynamic and functionalist approach. *Meta* 47.4: 498–512.

Munday, Jeremy 2001 *Introducing translation studies: Theories and applications.* London: Routledge.

Naigles, Letitia and Paula Terrazas 1998 Motion verb generalizations in English and Spanish: Influences of language and syntax. *Psychological Science* 9: 363–369.

Pym, Anthony 2009 *Exploring translation theories.* London: Routledge.

Ragnarsdóttir, Hrafnhildur and Sven Strömqvist 2004 Time, space and manner in Icelandic and Swedish. In: Sven Strömqvist and Ludo Verhoeven (eds.), *Relating events in narrative: Typological and contextual perspectives*, 113–141. Hillsdale, NJ: Erlbaum.

Rojo, Ana 2009 *Step by step: A course in contrastive linguistics and translation.* Bern: Peter Lang.

Rojo, Ana and Javier Valenzuela 2001 How to say things with words: Ways of saying in English and Spanish. *Meta* 46.3: 467–477.

Rojo, Ana and Javier Valenzuela 2005 Verbs of sensory perception in English and Spanish. *Languages in Contrast* 5.2: 219–243.

Samaniego Fernández, Eva 2007 El impacto de la Lingüística Cognitiva en los Estudios de Traducción. In: Pedro Fuertes Olivera (ed.), *Problemas lingüísticos en la traducción especializada*, 119–154. Valladolid, Spain: Servicio de Publicaciones.

Slobin, Dan I. 1991 Learning to think for speaking: Native language, cognition, and rhetorical style. *Pragmatics* 1: 7–26.

Slobin, Dan I. 1996 Two ways to travel: Verbs of motion in English and Spanish. In: Masayoshi Shibatani and Sandra A. Thompson (eds.), *Grammatical constructions: Their form and meaning*, 195–317. Oxford: Clarendon Press.

Slobin, Dan I. 1997 Mind, code, and text. In: Joan Bybee, John Haiman and Sandra A. Thompson (eds.), *Essays on language function and language type: Dedicated to T. Givón*, 437–467. Amsterdam: John Benjamins.

Slobin, Dan I. 2000 Verbalized events: A dynamic approach to linguistic relativity and determinism. In: Susanne Niemeier and René Dirven (eds.), *Evidence for linguistic relativity*, 107–138. Berlin: Mouton de Gruyter.

Slobin, Dan I. 2003 Language and thought online: cognitive consequences of linguistic relativity. In: Dedre Gentner and Susan Goldin-Meadow (eds.), *Language in mind: Advances in the study of language and thought*, 157–192. Cambridge, MA: MIT Press.

Slobin, Dan I. 2004 The many ways to search for a frog. In: Sven Strömqvist and Ludo Verhoeven (eds.), *Relating events in narrative: Typological and contextual perspectives*, 219–257. Hillsdale, NJ: Erlbaum.

Slobin, Dan I. 2005 Relating narrative events in translation. In: Dorin Diskin Ravid and Hava Bat-Zeev Shyldkrot (eds.), *Perspectives on language and language development: Essays in honor of Ruth A. Berman*, 115–129. Dordrecht, the Netherlands: Kluwer.

Slobin, Dan I. 2006 What makes manner of motion salient? Explorations in linguistic typology, discourse, and cognition. In: Maya Hickmann and Stéphane Robert (eds.), *Space in languages: Linguistic systems and cognitive categories*, 59–81. Amsterdam: John Benjamins.

Sugiyama, Yukiko 2005 Not all verb-framed languages are created equal: The case of Japanese. *Proceedings of the Thirty-First Annual Meeting of the Berkeley Linguistics Society* 31: 299–310.

Talmy, Leonard 1985 Lexicalisation patterns: Semantic structure in lexical forms. In: Tim Shopen (ed.), *Language typology and semantic description*. Vol. 3, *Grammatical categories and the lexicon*, 36–149. Cambridge: Cambridge University Press.

Talmy, Leonard 1991 Path to realization: A typology of event conflation. *Proceedings of the Seventeenth Annual Meeting of the Berkeley Linguistics Society* 17: 480–519.

Talmy, Leonard 2000 *Toward a cognitive semantics*. Cambridge, MA: MIT Press.

Toury, Gideon 1995 *Descriptive translation studies – and beyond*. Amsterdam: John Benjamins.

Vinay, Jean Paul and Jean Darbelnet 1958 *Stylistique comparée du français et de l'anglais: Méthode de traduction*. Paris: Didier. [Eng. transl. *Comparative stylistics of French and English: A methodology for translation*. 1995. Amsterdam: John Benjamins.]

Zlatev, Jordan and Peeperat Yangklang 2004 A third way to travel: The place of Thai in motion event typology. In: Sven Strömqvist and Ludo Verhoeven (eds.), *Relating events in narrative: Typological and contextual perspectives*, 159–190. Hillsdale, NJ: Erlbaum.

Ana Rojo and Javier Valenzuela
Constructing meaning in translation: The role of constructions in translation problems*

1 Introduction

It is now widely acknowledged that one of the reasons for the failure of linguistic approaches to the study of translation has been their excessive emphasis on form (Bassnett and Lefevere 1990; Gentzler 2001; Snell-Hornby 1990). As the focus progressively moved away towards the pragmatic and cultural context, this failure was partially redeemed by emphasizing the role of the audience and the cultural factors involved in the translation process (Hatim and Mason 1990; Nida [1964] 2004; Toury 1995; Vermeer [1989] 2004). But the niche carved for cultural aspects in linguistic theories was still not wide or deep enough to meet the expectations and needs of the "cultural and experimental turn" which Translation Studies underwent in the 1980s and 1990s (Baker 1993, 1995; Bassnett 1980; Jääskeläinen 1989; Kiraly 1997; Kurz 1994; Lefevere 1992; Venuti 1995). The boom of corpus linguistics in the 1990s temporarily managed to bridge the gap under the initial euphoria generated by studies based on the analysis of real translation data. However, the real flaw of corpus approaches to translation soon came to the surface, revealing a patent need for explanations of the translation process based on a sound theoretical background. At present, the general inability of linguistic approaches to account for the translation process from a cognitive point of view has turned the attention of translation theorists to other disciplines in cognitive science, such as bilingualism studies, psychology or neurology (Diamond and Shreve 2010; Hatzidaki, this volume; Moser-Mercer 2010; Stamenov, Gerganov and Popivanov 2010). Such an interdisciplinary approach is indeed profiling the future of Translation Studies as a field which is still striving to find its own space among the rest of cognitive science disciplines. But the role that disciplines such as psycholinguistics or neurology play in Translation Studies does not preclude the contribution that linguistics can still make to the description and explanation of certain language-related phenomena in translation. Linguistics has still much to offer to translation, but the success of a linguistic approach depends on its ability to enrich the

---

* This research has been funded by grant FFI2010-14903 from the Spanish Ministry of Economy and Competitiveness.

cognitive explanations which are currently demanded by contemporary Translation Studies.

This paper starts from the assumption that the generalization and cognitive commitments of Cognitive Linguistics (cf. Lakoff 1990) bring this linguistic approach closer to meeting the demands of Translation Studies than any other linguistic approach. Moreover, Cognitive Linguistics (CL, henceforth) and translation also find a common cause in foregrounding the centrality of meaning. Translation is about communicating meaning. Independently of less central modes of translation, the most basic definition of translation posits that engaging in translation involves deciphering the meaning from a source text and recoding it into a target text using a different linguistic code. The final aim of translation is thus that of recreating the process of meaning construction undergone by the audience of the source text, in order to activate a similar process in the audience of the translated text. Thus, if any linguistic theory has something to contribute to Translation Studies must be one in which meaning acquires a central role, and one in which language is naturally linked to cognitive processes. And this is where CL and translation find a common cause which makes their relationship hold great promise. CL explanations of language are essentially meaning-based. Moreover, the fact that meaning in CL can be ultimately explained in terms of the cognitive processes that are involved in its interpretation provides a link between linguistic material and cognition which is essential for translation. If we assume that the final goal of translation is to bring as close as possible the activation patterns undergone by the audiences of the source and the target text, then teasing apart the factors that participate in this process of meaning construction is going to be an essential task in order to understand how this process is carried out. And it is precisely in explaining these factors (linguistic or otherwise) that play a role in the activation of meaning where CL can be of any use for translation. CL can help us describe the features that are involved in this meaning construction process, providing a natural way to connect linguistic material to other informational sources, such as contextual constraints or world knowledge, and integrate them in the cognitive processes of the human communicator.

2 Linguistic and semantic equivalence meet in the notion of construction

Equivalence is, beyond all doubt, one of the most debated notions in Translation Studies (see also Halverson, this volume). Part of its controversial character comes from the reluctance to accept the inescapability of a concept which has gone beyond the frontiers of Translation Studies (Eco 2001; Rushdie 1992). The notion of equivalence has unavoidably trespassed onto related fields, where it has been widely incorporated in any issue requiring cross-linguistic comparison (e.g. bilingualism [Harris and Sherwood 1978], philosophy [Derrida [1982] 1985]; anthropology [Rubel and Rosman 2003]). But part of its controversial nature also arises from its linguistic origins. The notion of equivalence was born into linguistic theories of translation which focused on the level of isolated linguistic units and adopted equivalence as a suitable instrument to compare TT units with ST ones (Catford 1965; Vázquez-Ayora 1977; Vinay and Darbelnet [1958] 1972). At the time, translation theorists welcomed a notion which provided them with an easy method to establish a list of translation strategies or procedures based on the comparison between translated and original text. But in their attempts to create an exhaustive inventory of procedures to rule translation behavior, they were unknowingly helping to reinforce the secondary status of an activity which was subordinated to the original text. Translation norms had to be unavoidably established in relation to an original text which set the standard of the comparison. Being thus yoked to the level of isolated linguistic units and blamed for the minor status of translations, equivalence became a stigmatized notion in Translation Studies.

When the idea of dynamic equivalence came on stage, the notion of equivalence was somehow partially redeemed. The notion of dynamic equivalence brought about the importance of meaning over form and insisted on the weight that the function of a given linguistic element played for a given audience (Nida [1964] 2004; Nida and Taber [1969] 1982). From that point onwards, the focus of attention moved from language form to meaning. Later developments of the notion of equivalence, such as functional and pragmatic equivalence (e.g. House 1977; Nord 1997; Reiss [1977] 1989; Vermeer [1989] 2004), also moved in that direction, aiming at widening the scope of the term beyond the level of words and sentences to the level of the text and its impact on a given audience.

But disregarding the label assigned to the concept, the evolution of the notion of equivalence has been inexorably guided by one of the central dilemmas in translation, i.e. the choice between form and meaning. Most of the problems associated to the notion of equivalence lie, precisely, in the attempts to rule out one of the components of this form-meaning dichotomy, instead of conceiving them as the two ends of a translational continuum (cf. Bassnett 1980). By moving away from linguistic form, translation theorists have provided us with many central insights about the cultural and situational factors which surround the translation act. But, at the same time, by overlooking any language level below the text, important linguistic insights may be lost. Setting the focus on language form has also allowed translation theorists to identify a set of useful translation procedures and strategies which can help translators automatize specific translation behaviors.

In this sense, the present paper argues that the notion of construction may be a suitable meeting point for linguistic and semantic equivalence. The pairing of form and meaning implied in the notion of construction provides a way to explain translation problems below the level of the text without focusing predominantly on form. Explaining, for instance, the problems involved in translating an English resultative sentence, such as *He drank the pub dry*, into Spanish from a merely grammatical point of view would involve a complex set of grammatical transpositions, which translators may decide to follow or not depending on the constraints imposed by the textual and the situational context. However, considering the resultative as a construction whereby somebody does something (usually in a particular manner) which causes something else to be in a certain state, and taking into account that this semantic construction is associated to a specific grammatical form in English (i.e. *Subject + Verb + Direct object + Adjective*), helps us explain that translators, forced by the non-existence of an identical construction in Spanish, have to resort to various strategies which aim to reproduce the meaning in the TL at the expense of the linguistic form. The linguistic conventions which link a particular meaning to a certain linguistic form in a given language may be different in another language. For this point of view, the question should be, first, "does the same pairing of form and meaning exist in the target language?" and then "are the strategies translators use predictable in any way in cases where a similar construction does not exist (or rather, are they subject to the translator's arbitrariness)?"

This work aims to illustrate the problems Spanish translators face when dealing with the lack of equivalence of some types of English resultative sentences into Spanish. To this purpose, we will use eye-movements as evidence for the cognitive effort involved in the translation of this type of sentences. Moreover, we will also identify the strategies employed by Spanish translators to render this type of resultative sentences into Spanish. We aim to demonstrate that the pairing of form and meaning proposed by the notion of construction nicely fits translational aims, and that linguistics, in this case, Cognitive Linguistics, still has much to say about translation. The focus on meaning proposed by cognitive linguists provides translation theorists with a suitable point for linguistic and semantic equivalence to meet, finally, in the notion of construction postulated by Cognitive Grammar. Before presenting our study in Section 5, we will introduce the notion of construction paying special attention to crosslinguistic issues (Section 3) and then elaborate on the problems that arise in the cases of constructional mismatch between two languages (Section 4). Final conclusions of the paper are offered in Section 6.

3 Constructional equivalence

In Construction Grammar (e.g. Goldberg 1995, 2006) the basic unit of linguistic organization is the "construction". A "construction" is defined as any pairing of form and meaning, which can range from simple structures, such as morphemes (*-s*) or lexemes (*cat*), to more abstract and complex syntactic configurations, including intermediate structures combining free variables with lexically specified items, such as the constructions "*What's X doing Y?*" in English (Kay and Fillmore 1999) or "*¡Qué N más Adj!* lit. '*What N more Adj!*'" in Spanish. Regardless of their level of syntactic complexity, most of these constructions share a weak compositionality, that is, their meaning does not derive directly from the sum of their individual components, but from the global pairing of form and meaning.[1]

Constructions are further away from universality than other notions; in fact, much crosslinguistic divergence can be found across constructions, depending on the mechanisms exploited by the different languages. For instance, case information about *who did what to whom* can be expressed either morphologically, as in Latin, or syntactically, as in English. It is precisely by showing this way of relating wide formal differences to a common semantic background that the notion of construction becomes particularly useful for translators.

A great amount of work has already been carried out on constructions. The usefulness of a constructional approach has been demonstrated in linguistic analyses of many different languages (cf. http://www.constructiongrammar. org), crosslinguistic contrastive studies (Boas 2010), studies of first language acquisition (Tomasello 2003), applications to second language learning and teaching (De Knop and De Rycker 2008), and even computational applications (Steels 2011). Additionally, there are a number of studies which have investigated the psychological reality of constructions and their role in linguistic processing. For instance, Kaschak and Glenberg (2000) carried out an experiment in

---

[1] In Goldberg (1995), the issue of compositionality was seen as central in order to achieve the status of "construction", which was only attributed to form-meaning configurations which could not be predicted from other units in the linguistic system. In Goldberg (2006) this criterion was widened, and now fully compositional, predictable units can be assigned the status of construction as long as psycholinguistic measures and features such as frequency suggest that they are indeed stored as units.

which they demonstrated that when subjects are given a novel verb, as in the sentence *He crutched her*, they tend to provide an interpretation of its meaning based on the overall construction. Thus, in the previous sentence, their subjects tended to interpret *crutched* as a verb in a transitive construction in which someone hit someone else, while a different constructional context (e.g. *She crutched out of the building*) would elicit a completely different interpretation (namely, that of "motion by means of"). Bencini and Goldberg (2000) also designed a sorting experiment with native speakers of English in order to validate the psychological existence of constructions. In their experiment they found that when asked to sort sentences according to semantic similarity, subjects preferred to use the meaning supplied by the construction instead of that supplied by the sentence verb. This experiment has been replicated with L2 speakers in languages such as Chinese (Liang 2002), German (Gries and Wulff 2005) or Spanish (Valenzuela and Rojo 2008b), all of them providing results which also point to the existence of constructions. Also, Eddington and Ruiz de Mendoza (2010) used a grammaticality judgment priming task as experimental paradigm with the same objective. They designed pairs of sentences with a similar syntactic structure but illustrating a different construction (e.g. *Susan and John kissed* [reciprocal] vs. *Susan and John studied* [non-reciprocal]) and analyzed how accurately subjects judged the grammaticality of a sentence after reading sentences with the same construction (same form, same meaning) or with a different one (same form, different meaning). Their results showed that target sentences primed by sentences with the same constructional template were responded to faster and more accurately than in the syntactically similar condition. Valenzuela and Rojo (2008a) used a slightly different experimental paradigm with Spanish subjects, measuring the subjects' reaction time to a sentence understanding task. They analyzed how fast subjects understood a sentence after reading sentences with the same construction or with a different one. Their results showed that Spanish subjects responded faster to sentences primed by the same constructional templates.

But the effects of constructional equivalence or non-equivalence (i.e. the existence of similar constructions in two languages or the lack of it) for translation processes have not been investigated so far. The present paper attempts to research this matter on the belief that this is a fruitful issue for both CL and translation. Constructions are key elements in the organization and distribution of meaning over the different linguistic elements, being able to convey subtle variations in meaning (cf. *rob* vs. *steal* in Goldberg 1995). By using one or another construction in a given language, we are then able to highlight or background different bits of information in a quite subtle and graded fashion. These subtle informational differences are of vital importance for translators who are struggling to achieve semantic accuracy.

The function of a given construction should also be taken into account in translation. Take, for example, the case of the passive voice in English and Spanish. In English, syntax is rigid and there is fixed word order; thus, in order to highlight the object of a transitive event (or to hide the agent of the action), a special construction has to be used, i.e. the passive construction (e.g. *The cake was eaten by John*). On the contrary, Spanish has a freer word order and objects can be moved around without needing to resort to a passive construction (which does nevertheless exist, but is used to a lesser extent): e.g. *El pastel se lo comió Juan* – 'John ate the cake', lit. 'the cake, MIDDLE[2] it ate John'. Thus, being aware of the role that constructions play in a given example can help translators decide on the most adequate way to convey a given meaning in a different language.

4 Constructional mismatch

Things can go worse when two languages do not share a construction. In that case, translators are forced to re-distribute the information, and exact equivalence in terms of information highlighting and background (and thus, instructions for meaning construction to the receiver) will most probably not be achieved. Let us illustrate our point by looking at some constructions in English and their equivalents in Spanish. When the construction exists in both languages, translators only have to use the corresponding target language equivalent. This is the case of a number of constructions which can be found in both English and Spanish, such as the (roughly equivalent) transitive construction, the intransitive one or the *What's X doing Y* construction.

Unfortunately, there are many cases which are far more complicated, for which no equivalent is readily available for translators. Examples where translators have to deal with some sort of constructional mismatch between English and Spanish are found in the translation of constructions such as the English *Way*-construction (e.g. *She slept her way to the top*; cf. Jackendoff 1990; Goldberg 1995), or the Spanish Reduplicated Topicalization Construction (e.g. *Lejos, lejos no queda, pero no puedes ir andando* – 'it is not really far, but you can't go on foot' – lit. 'far far not is, but not can-you go walking'; cf. Narbona 2000; Valenzuela, Hilferty, and Garachana 2005). These constructions do not have exact replicas in the other language and are thus difficult to translate, forcing translators to resort to different strategies in order to solve the constructional mismatch.

---

2 For a detailed review of the middle voice in Spanish, see Maldonado (1992, 2009)

But besides this type of complex constructions, there are other, apparently simpler constructions, which can also be found to illustrate this lack of constructional equivalence. In this paper we focus on the English resultative construction (e.g. *He hammered the metal flat*; cf. Goldberg 1995; Levin and Rappaport Hovav 1995; Goldberg and Jackendoff 2004) as a type of construction which illustrates the problems translators have to face in order to render it into Spanish. In this construction we find a subject (*He*) who does something to an object (*the metal*) in such a way (*hammered*) that the object ends up in a given state (*flat*). Considering that Spanish lacks a construction with exactly the same form as the English one,[3] the reconstruction of the same meaning in Spanish requires the use of different strategies, depending on the particular context. In this sense, there are two different strategies that can be identified when translating the resultative construction into Spanish. In those cases, such as in the example just mentioned, in which Spanish lacks an equivalent manner verb and the adjective indicating the result cannot easily be transformed into a verb, translators would probably express the manner of the action outside the verb, in a complement (*golpeó el metal* **con un martillo** – 'he pounded on the metal **with a hammer**') and would indicate the result by means of a structure such as *hasta que* (*hasta que quedó plano* – 'until it was flat'). The second strategy applies to those cases where the adjective which expresses the result state of the object *can* be easily transformed into a verb, allowing the translator to express the manner involved in the English verb by means of a Spanish adverbial or other verb complement. This would be the case in the translation of a sentence such as *He pushed the door open* as *Abrió la puerta empujándola* – 'he opened the door by pushing it', where the English adjective *open* is translated as the Spanish verb *abrir*.

One of the most widely researched cases of constructional mismatch is that arising from the difference in lexicalization patterns found between satellite-framed languages, such as English, and verb-framed languages, such as Spanish (Talmy 2000). The work by Dan Slobin (Berman and Slobin 1994; Slobin 1996, 1997, 2005) has illustrated that these differences in lexicalization patterns are one of the key factors explaining certain frequent cases of omission or addition of information when translating Manner of motion and Path of motion between English and Spanish. Thus, Slobin (1996) (see also Ibarretxe-Antuñano

---

[3] It is not completely exact to say that there are absolutely no examples of resultative constructions in Spanish; they are, however, much less frequent, and limited to some isolated examples (e.g. Barrero-Vodal 1992; Mendívil-Giró 2003). Additionally, this should not interfere with the experiment carried out in the present work, since we have carefully chosen our English resultative examples so that they have no possible counterpart in a similar Spanish form.

and Filipović, this volume) showed that when translating into Spanish an example such as *Mrs Tranter **rustled forward***, translators tend to omit the Manner of motion incorporated in the English construction, using, instead, a verb that incorporates the Path of motion, as in *Mrs Tranter **se adelantó*** 'Mrs Tranter moved forward'. In the same way, when translating into English a Spanish path verb construction, such as [. . .] *llegamos al pasillo de la entrada* [. . .] 'we arrived to the entrance corridor', translators sometimes incorporate Manner of motion into the English verb, as in [. . .] *we finally **fought** our way to the exit* [. . .]. This evidence shows that lexicalization patterns color translators' construals, which are influenced by the attentional patterns prevalent in their cultures.

5 Looking at constructional mismatch empirically: An eye-tracking study

Eye-tracking techniques have been applied both to theoretically-oriented studies (e.g. cognitive science and psychology), and to more applied areas (e.g. marketing research and advertising, medical applications, human-computer interaction, web usability, etc; Duchowski [2002] and Richardson and Spivey [2004] provide a review of eye-tracking applications). In psycholinguistics, eye-tracking has been mostly used in studies of syntactic processing and reading (a review of psycholinguistic applications can be found in Rayner 1998 or in Richardson, Dale, and Spivey 2007).

For translation researchers, eye-tracking provides a useful methodology which overcomes many of the disadvantages of other methods, such as those involving the verbalization of the translation process (e.g. Think-Aloud Protocols or TAPs are recordings in which participants think aloud as they are performing a translation; cf. Jääskeläinen 2002; Bernardini 2001). By applying eye-tracking to the investigation of the translation process, researchers have found a reliable method to measure cognitive effort by analyzing the eye-movement patterns of translators. It should be remarked that eye-movements are unconscious and provide objective measurements; they offer clues about the thought processes of translators as they are carrying out their task: which possibilities they are entertaining, which words they are taking into account for their translations, or which are causing problems, how they are they re-organizing the discourse units, etc. One of the major difficulties involved in researching translation is related to the high complexity of the process and the problems in isolating variables which can be unquestionably related to specific factors of that process. Eye-tracking allows researchers to solve some of these problems by focusing on eye movements and pupil dilation changes as indicators of cognitive effort. Moreover, since the application of an eye-tracker does not require the subjects' manipulation of any program or equipment, eye-tracking can be easily combined with other methodologies. For instance, using the information elicited by the eye-movements of translators as they are carrying out their task with the use of Think-Aloud Protocols or key-logging programs[4] would allow researchers to relate eye movements to pauses, repetitions, deletions or any other indicators of problems and cognitive effort recorded in the subjects' verbalization of their own process or their manipulation of a computer keyboard.

Most of the empirical studies on the translation process assume nowadays that combining retrospection with eye-tracking recordings and key logging constitutes a promising methodology to research translation processes (cf. Alves, Pagano, and da Silva 2009). Some of these methods have already been employed in translation to research the role of different aspects involved in the translation process. Some of the aspects investigated include the effect of translation directionality on the translation process (Pavlović and Jensen 2009), the difference between novices and experts regarding text segmentation (Dragsted 2005), coordination of reading and writing processes (Dragsted and Hansen 2008; Dragsted 2010), time consumption and translation behavior (Dragsted, Hansen, and Sørensen 2009), the ability to manage uncertainty and deal with problem-solving while translating (Angelone 2010), the processing difficulties involved in the translation of metaphor (Sjørup 2011), the effect of time pressure on translation (de Rooze 2003; Jensen 1999, 2000; Jensen and Jakobsen 2000; Sharmin et al. 2008), differences between reading for comprehension and reading for translation (Jakobsen and Jensen 2008), differences in the distribution of visual attention between source and target texts (Sharmin et al. 2008), the effect of context on word comprehension (Rydning and Lachaud 2010), the way translators interact with Translation Memory tools (O'Brien 2008) or the effect of controlled language on readability (O'Brien 2010). These methods have also been applied to research aspects of more specialized types of translation, such as the processing effort experienced when viewing subtitles (Caffrey 2009) or to locate relevant visual information which should be included in audio-descriptions for the visually impaired (Chmiel et al. 2010). In addition, there are a few experiments which illustrate the integration of translation process research and the cognitive sciences by combining eye-tracking and ERPs to research bilingual processing (e.g. Gerganov, Hristova, and Stamenov 2009;

---

4 *Translog* is an example of a keystroke logging program which allows researchers to record the translator's typing production. The method helps to locate problems in the translation process by measuring speed and pauses

Stamenov, Gerganov, and Popivanov 2010). They have focused on the effects of priming during the translation of cognates (e.g. "*rico*-rich") and non-cognates (e.g. "*mesa*-table") to help translators find "shortcuts" to the target language.

Eye-tracking also shows a huge potential for researching the effect of specific linguistic issues on the translator's cognitive effort during a certain translation task. In this sense, the work by Shreve, Lacruz, and Angelone (2010) on the effect of L1 syntax on translation is particularly relevant for our study. They researched the effect of increasing syntactic complexity on the translators' eye movements when carrying out a sight-translation task. Although their results were not conclusive, perhaps due to a problem in the task design, their data suggested that sight translation was sensitive to syntactic manipulation and that the processing of complex syntax demanded higher cognitive effort than that of non-complex syntax. This work makes an interesting and challenging move towards the application of eye-tracking to research the role of certain linguistic issues on the translation process by analyzing their effect on the translator's cognitive effort.

The present work also takes a step forward in this direction by applying eye-tracking to investigate the processing effort involved in translating language-specific constructions into a TL not having such constructions. The aim is to use the eye-movement patterns of Spanish subjects when translating a non-existing construction as evidence for the cognitive effort involved in the use of different translation strategies. The initial hypothesis which sustains our work is that constructional mismatch should cause problems in translation, and that these problems should be reflected in two related aspects: the eye-movement patterns of Spanish translators and the translation strategies used when being forced to choose a different lexicalization pattern in Spanish

5.1 Subjects

Twelve native speakers of Spanish volunteered to take part in our study. Out of these initial participants, we selected the eight subjects with the highest quality eye tracking data, i.e. the data where the gaze-to-word mappings were the most precise. There were three males and five females. All the females had corrected vision and wore contact lenses; the three males had normal vision. They were all teachers of translation at the University of Murcia (Spain), and thus they were highly proficient in English and had a high academic command of Spanish. Three of them had professional translation and interpreting experience, defined here as translation and interpreting work which generates at least 70% of annual income over a minimum period of three months. Three other subjects also worked occasionally as professional translators.

5.2 Stimuli

Twelve short texts were designed containing two different constructions with (basically) the same words:

A. One Resultative construction (e.g. *he hammered the handle straight*)
B. One Non-resultative or Predicative construction (e.g. *he hammered the handle until it was straight*)

The constructions were defined as the areas of interest to measure the subjects' eye movements and establish the differences across the two constructions. The full list of stimuli used can be seen in Appendix 1.

5.3 Procedure

Data were collected using an ASL6000 eye-tracker. Eye movements were analyzed with the eye tracking software *Eyenal* 2.63. Texts were projected on a big screen. White font was used over black background to avoid any reduction in pupil size caused by the reflection of the white background. Subjects were told to translate at sight, trying to avoid any head movement. Calibrations were performed before recording each stimulus. To avoid possible order effects, the order of appearance of the construction in the text (Resultative vs. Predicative) was counterbalanced across subjects and texts.

5.4 Parameters of analysis

Four different measures were calculated for each participant: number of fixations, total gaze time, number of backtracks, and pupil dilation changes. All of them were assumed to be indicative of cognitive effort (cf. Pavlovic and Jensen 2009).

Eye fixations, that is, the short stops that eyes make at specific points when reading a text, have been reported to reflect the subjects' visual attention; the fact that a word is fixated at a particular time indicates that it is also being cognitively processed at the same time (Dragsted 2010: 47). In our case, we computed how many fixations subjects made in the areas of interest corresponding to the resultative and the non-resultative constructions.

Total gaze time refers to the total amount of time subjects spent looking at a given construction. To calculate the total gaze time for each construction, we summed up the durations of the different fixations made in the areas of interest of the two constructions under analysis.

The number of regressive fixations or backtracks has also been considered to indicate greater processing effort (Shreve, Lacruz, and Angelone 2010: 71). To calculate the number of backtracks, we computed how many regressive fixations subjects made in resultative vs. non-resultative constructions.

Changes in pupil dilation have also been reported to be indicative of effortful processing effort (Beatty 1982; Hyona, Tommola, and Alaja 1995; Kahneman and Beatty 1966; Piquado, Isaacowitz, and Wingfield 2010). Accordingly, we used the data provided by the eye-tracking software *Eyenal* on the size of the pupil to calculate the number of changes in pupil dilation for each construction.

5.5 Hypotheses

As indicated earlier on, the initial hypothesis of our work was that the problems caused by constructional mismatch in translation would resort in effortful cognitive processing, which would be reflected both in the translators' eye movement patterns and their choice of translation strategies. This general hypothesis has been refined by posing three more specific working hypotheses, which assume that:

Hypothesis 1: Translating the resultative constructions will be more demanding in terms of cognitive effort than translating the predicative constructions.

Hypothesis 2: Using a translation strategy that involves syntactic transposition (e.g. transforming the English adjective which indicates the result state of the construction into a verb in Spanish) will demand higher cognitive effort than a more literal translation strategy (e.g. translating the English verb using an equivalent verb in Spanish).

Hypothesis 3: Using a translation strategy which involves the inclusion of manner information will involve higher cognitive effort than omitting manner.

5.6 Results

The analysis of our data has been organized in three sections which coincide with the hypotheses postulated in the study.

5.6.1 Hypothesis 1

Our first hypothesis postulated that the translation of the resultative constructions would impose higher demands in terms of cognitive effort than the translation of the predicative constructions. In order to test this hypothesis, both constructions were compared using the four parameter of analysis previously established.

Regarding the number of fixations, we started by identifying the specific fixations which belonged to the construction under analysis. An example where the text has already been mapped onto the eye movements and the fixations have been identified is shown in Figure 10.1 below. The line depicts the trajectory of the eye and individual fixations are marked by a number and represented as dots, with greater size indicating longer duration. In the example shown in Figure 10.1, the subject produced ten fixations (from 17 to 26) when translating the resultative construction *She brushed the carpet clean*.

As Figure 10.2 shows below, subjects made less fixations for the predicative construction (mean number of fixations: 9.23) as compared to the resultative one (mean number: 9.81). Once the number of fixations was scaled according

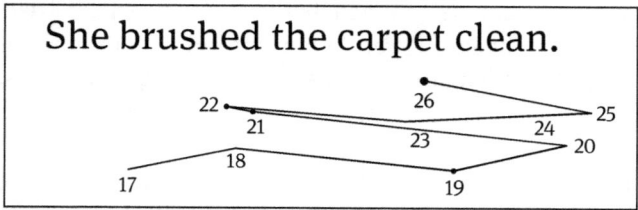

Figure 10.1: Eye fixations and eye movements for a resultative construction

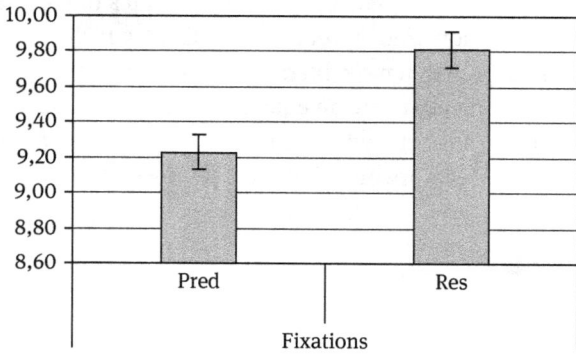

Figure 10.2: Mean number of fixations for the predicative vs. the resultative construction

Table 10.1: Fixation number and duration for the resultative example in Figure 10.1

Fix. Num	17	18	19	20	21	22	23	24	25
Fix. Dur	0.12	0.17	0.08	0.08	0.15	0.2	0.45	0.17	0.18

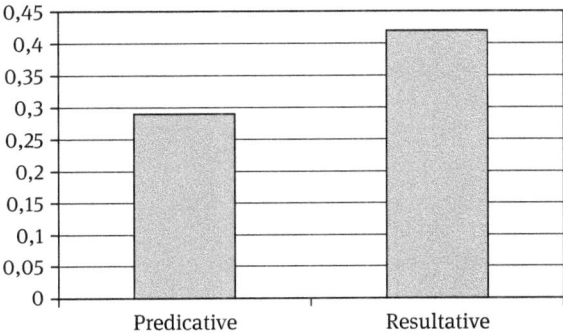

Figure 10.3: Mean gaze time (per word) for the predicative vs. the resultative construction

to the mean number of words in both conditions (since, typically, predicative versions were always longer than resultative ones), this difference was found to be significant in a one-way ANOVA test (F(1,15) = 58.07, $p < 0.005$).

In order to calculate the total gaze time spent in each construction, the durations of all the fixations involved for a specific construction were first added up and then the mean was calculated for each condition. Table 10.1 above exemplifies the number of fixations and their durations for the resultative construction illustrated in Figure 10.1. Once the mean gaze time was scaled according to the mean number of words in each condition, the difference between both types of constructions in terms of total gaze time was once more found to be statistically significant (F(1,15)=8.86, $p < 0.05$), as shown in Figure 10.3 above.

Regarding the analysis of backtracks, eye movements were mapped onto a graph in such a way that motion forward was represented vertically bottom-up; thus, in these graphs, downward lines represented backtracks in terms of eye movements along a text. For instance, Figures 10.4 and 10.5 below illustrate the backtracks made for the resultative (Hor Pos R on the left) and the predicative (Hor Pos P on the right) versions of the same stimulus. Figure 10.4 shows five backtracks for the resultative construction while Figure 10.5 shows no backtrack for the predicative version of the same stimulus.

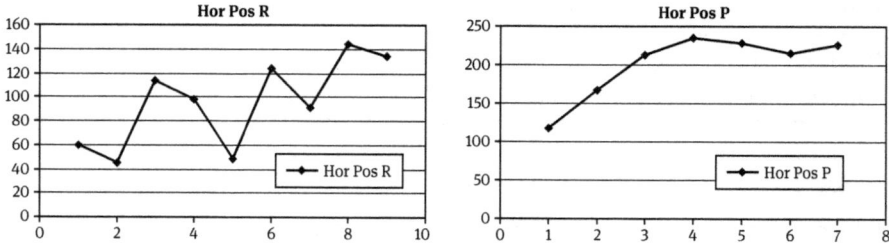

Figures 10.4 and 10.5: Backtracks for the resultative vs. the predicative versions of the same stimulus

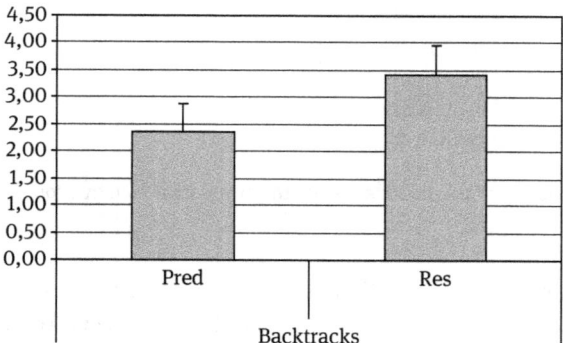

Figure 10.6: Mean backtracks for the predicative vs. the resultative construction

Again, subjects made less backtracks for the predicative construction (mean number of backtracks: 2.35) as compared to the resultative one (mean number of backtracks: 3.42) as seen in Figure 10.6. This difference between both conditions was also found to be statistically significant in a one-way ANOVA test, $F(1,15) = 13.064$, $p < 0.005$.

Regarding changes in pupil diameter, we mapped them on a graph. This time a change in pupil diameter was indicated by vertical change in the Y-axis of the graph. Thus, Figure 10.7 below shows five changes in pupil size for the resultative construction, since it displays five changes in the direction of the graph (changes are counted from the second fixation onwards). On the contrary, Figure 10.8 shows only three changes for the predicative version of the same stimulus.

As seen in Figure 10.9 below, the mean pupil changes was found to be higher for the resultative (3.60) vs. the predicative (2.65) construction. This difference was found to approach near significance in a one-way ANOVA test ($F(1,15)=3.8$, $p = 0.069$).

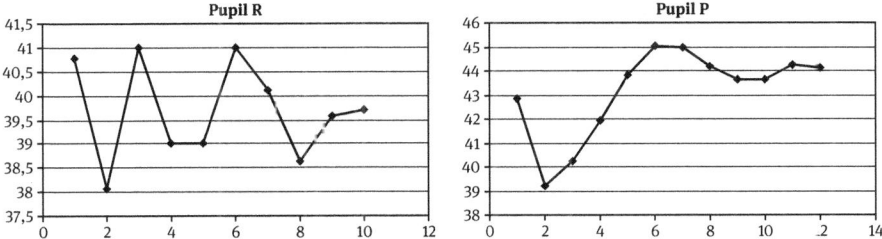

Figure 10.7 and 10.8: Changes in pupil diameter for the resultative vs. the predicative versions of the same stimulus

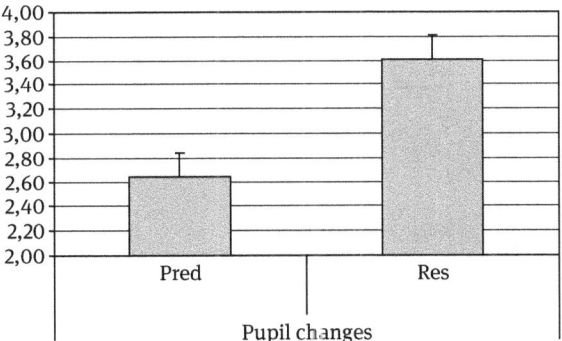

Figure 10.9: Mean pupil changes for the predicative vs. the resultative construction

5.6.2 Hypothesis 2

Our second hypothesis proposed that using a translation strategy involving syntactic transposition would demand higher cognitive effort than a non-transposing translation strategy. In order to test this hypothesis, we identified the two strategies most commonly used by our subjects, which were, Adj-to-verb transposition (i.e. transforming the English adjective indicating the result state of the construction into a verb in Spanish) and Verb-to-verb translation (i.e. translating the English verb by an equivalent verb in Spanish).

These two strategies were compared in terms of the four parameters of analysis which we have been previously identified as indicative of effortful cognitive processing. As the figures below show, our analysis revealed that Verb-to-verb translation was harder for all the parameters than Adj-to-verb transposition: 1,70 vs. 2,12 for mean gaze time (Figure 10.10), 6,91 vs. 9,71 for mean number of fixations (Figure 10.11) and 2,59 vs. 3,13 for mean number of backtracks

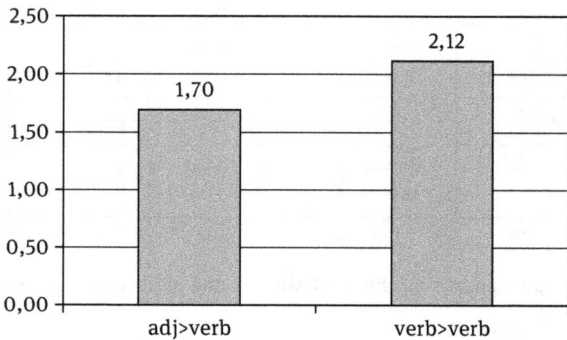

Figure 10.10: Mean gaze time for adj>verb vs. verb>verb

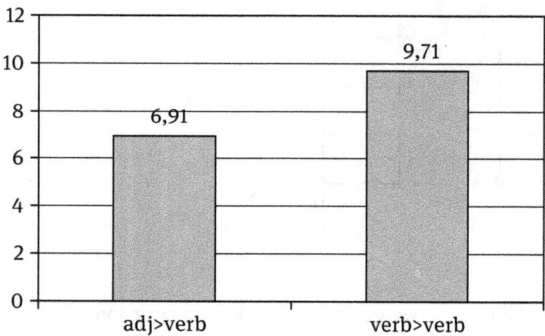

Figure 10.11: Mean number of fixations for adj>verb vs. verb>verb

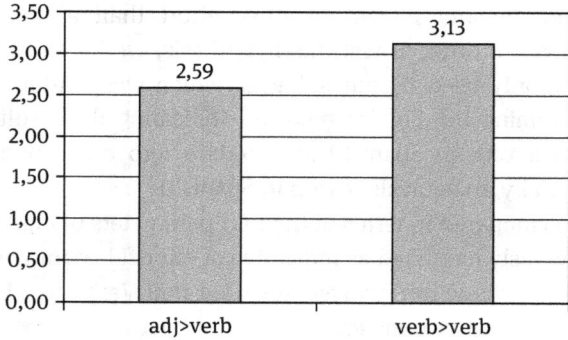

Figure 10.12: Mean number of backtracks for adj>verb vs. verb>verb

(Figure 10.12). The only exception was the mean for pupil dilation changes, which was similar, although slightly lower, for Verb-to-verb translation (3,25 vs. 3,22, as shown in Figure 10.13 below).

5.6.3 Hypothesis 3

Our third hypothesis assumed that using a translation strategy which included manner information would involve higher cognitive effort than one omitting manner. To test this hypothesis, we compared the cognitive cost of including or excluding manner across each strategy using our four parameters of analysis. As shown in Table 10.2 below, when using the strategy of Adj-to-verb transposition the mean measures for the four parameters were lower when manner was included. On the contrary, when using the Verb-to-verb strategy, the mean measures were lower when manner was excluded, with the only exception of total gaze time, which was slightly lower when manner was included.

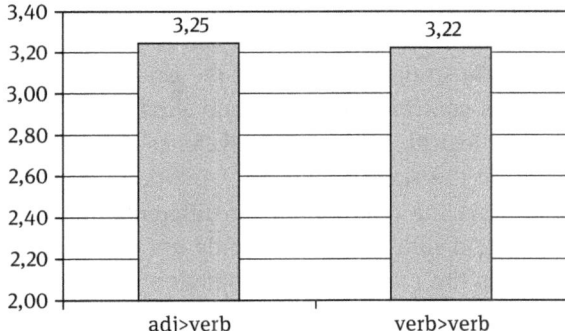

Figure 10.13: Mean pupil changes for adj>verb vs. verb>verb

Table 10.2: Mean measures for the inclusion or exclusion of manner across the different strategies

	Gaze time	Fixations	Backtracks	Pupil changes
Adj>Verb +Manner	1.96	8.69	3.19	3.22
Adj>Verb – Manner	2.39	8.80	3.60	4.00
Verb>Verb +Manner	3.00	11.40	3.55	4.30
Verb>Verb – Manner	3.18	9.00	3.00	3.00

5.7 Discussion

The analysis of our results will also be discussed following the three hypotheses previously formulated.

5.7.1 Hypothesis 1

The results verified our first hypothesis. The fact that a statistically significant difference was found between the processing of resultative vs. predicative constructions, with mean measures higher for the former case in all four parameters analyzed, indicates that translating the resultative version was harder. Such an enhanced difficulty can only be due to the lack of an equivalent construction in the target language. It should be added that this fact, in and of itself, could be taken as a proof of the psycholinguistic existence of the notion of construction (thus adding to the work previously mentioned in Section 3, e.g. Bencini and Goldberg 2000; Goldberg and Bencini 2005; Gries and Wulff 2005; or Valenzuela and Rojo 2008b, among others). Thus, it is seen here how the same group of words is processed in two very different ways, depending on the syntactic configuration into which they are inserted. Since we are comparing basically the very same words (*hammer the handle straight* vs. *hammer the handle until it is straight*), any translation difficulties contributed by the individual items, such as problems derived by possible lexical semantic equivalence mismatches between both languages, should be the same in the two conditions in which these words appear. Considering that the only parameter differentiating both cases is the grammatical construction into which the words are inserted, we are forced to acknowledge that it is the constructional configuration which is causing the extra cognitive effort. Thus, it is the non-existence of a given constructional template which can be shown to be direct cause of a difference in processing, proving in this way the psycholinguistic role that constructions play in an online linguistic processing task.

5.7.2 Hypothesis 2

Our results revealed that Adj-to-verb transposition was easier in terms of cognitive effort than Verb-to-verb translation. Therefore, these results did not verify the second hypothesis postulated in this work, which assumed that the use of a strategy involving syntactic transposition would be harder than a strategy based on literal translation. A possible explanation for these results could be that the "default" strategy acquired by our translation teachers is Adj-to-verb transposition, and only in those cases where problems are found, the translator resorts to a second option. Thus, our subjects opt for Adj-to-verb translation in those cases where English adjectives are easy to transform into Spanish verbs. In our case, this is what happens with the English adjective *open,* which has an easily available verb in Spanish (*abrir*), or the adjectives *awake* (Spanish verb *despertar*) or *clean* (cf Spanish *limpiar*). On the contrary, in those cases where the adjectives are difficult to transform into verbs, our subjects have to resort to a second option, Verb-to-verb translation. This strategy is used in some examples where the meaning of the English adjective is incorporated into the verb, as in the cases of the phrase *fry crispy* being translated as *dorar* (lit. 'to make golden') or *slap red* as *enrojecer* (lit. 'to redden'). There is another case, that of the English adjective *curly,* which could elicit an available Spanish verb, *rizar* (lit. 'to curl'). However, in that case, the manner encoded in the English verb (*to perm*) is difficult to translate into Spanish (rather, it results in an awkward translation). Thus, one possible explanation for the differences in processing shown by the eye-movement patterns found could be that translators use Adj-to-verb transposition as a default strategy and try out other alternatives only when this strategy runs into problems.

5.7.3 Hypothesis 3

Finally, our results confirmed our third hypothesis only partially. The hypothesis predicted that using a translation strategy involving the inclusion of manner information would involve higher cognitive effort than one omitting manner. However, our data revealed that this is not what happened in most cases. The results of our study thus seem to indicate that subjects are aware of manner information most of the time: when such information can be easily rendered into Spanish, then the translation process unfolds smoothly and the cognitive cost is lower (as happened in the case of Adj-to-verb transposition). However, when a viable solution cannot be found, the cost of cognitive processing increases (as was mostly the case for those examples involving the use of a Verb-to-verb translation strategy). This explanation receives further support when listening to the translations provided by the participants coupled to their eye-movements; participants typically produced a pause in their oral translation while their eyes looked at the relevant lexical items as if looking for a possible translation, and moved on after some milliseconds without providing any specification, only once they gave up on finding a suitable translation that would make manner information explicit.

6 Conclusion

Theories of translation have an extremely harsh task to accomplish. If a theory of language has to explain the whole process of meaning construction in both the production and comprehension directions, a theory of translation has to duplicate the task, since there are two different linguistic and cultural codes involved. The particularly complex nature of the translation task has been in fact one of main reasons for the shortcomings of approaches which have focused exclusively on linguistic factors. Recent advances in translation theory have demonstrated that a comprehensive explanation of translation should account for the complexity of the cognitive processes which mediate translation (cf. Halverson 2010, this volume; Muñoz Martín 2010, this volume; Shreve and Angelone 2010). Such an explanation necessarily involves seeking for help in other disciplines, applying data-gathering methods and incorporating findings from related disciplines such as psychology, bilingualism studies or neurology. But leaving linguistics out of this picture would be as much of a mistake as considering that language models can explain the whole translation process on their own. Determining the extent to which linguistics can contribute to any translation theory involves finding the right balance between considering language the key to solve all the translation problems and acknowledging its role as one of the central factors which take part in the translation process.

The fact that language is the working tool of translators and one of the main factors in the translation process is the reason why a theory of language has still a lot to contribute to translation. In this paper, we have argued that Cognitive Linguistics can be particularly useful for translation because of its emphasis on placing meaning in the focus of its theorizing, explaining how meaning is activated from linguistic input and identifying the different factors which play a role in such a process. More specifically, we have focused on the notion of construction as a one of the pivotal factors in the process of meaning activation, and have outlined some of the possible implications that the notion of constructional equivalence may have for the study of the translation process. We hope to have demonstrated that a constructional mismatch between two languages, such as the case of the resultative construction in English and Spanish, results in higher cognitive effort, forcing translators to use alternative strategies which will also be, to a great extent, determined by the grammatical makeup of both languages.

At the same time, we hope that this study will serve to provide further evidence on the existence of constructions, using translation as a suggestive and challenging testing field for linguistics. But beyond our specific and more immediate goals, this paper aims to have demonstrated that, despite the theoretical and methodological prejudices of the past, the future of both disciplines has found in cognition a common place where linguistics and translation still have a lot to contribute to each other.

References

Alves, Fabio, Adriana Pagano and Igor da Silva 2009 A new window on translator's cognitive activity: Methodological issues in the combined use of eye-tracking, key logging and retrospective protocols. In: M. Mees Inger, Fabio Alves and Susanne Göpferich (eds.), *Methodology, technology and innovation in translation process research: A tribute to Arnt Lykke Jakobsen*, 267–292. (*Copenhagen Studies in Language 38*) Copenhagen: Samfundslitteratur.
Angelone, Erik 2010 Uncertainty management and metacognitive problem solving. In: M. Shreve Gregory and Erik Angelone (eds.), *Translation and cognition*, 17–40. Amsterdam: John Benjamins.
Baker, Mona 1993 Corpus linguistics and translation studies: Implications and applications. In: Mona Baker, Francis Gill and Elena Tognini-Bonelli (eds.), *Text and technology: In honour of John Sinclair*, 233–250. Amsterdam: John Benjamins.
Baker, Mona 1995 Corpora in translation studies: An overview and suggestions for future research. *Target* 7.2: 223–243.
Barrero-Vodal, Albert 1992 El resultativo en el español actual: Interrelaciones entre tiempo, modo de acción y aspecto verbal. In: Albert Barrera Vidal, Manfred Raupach, and Ekkehard Zofgen (eds.), *Grammatica Vivat: Konzepte, Beschreibungen und Analysen zum Thema "Fremdsprachengrammatik"*, 69–75. Tübingen, Germany: Gunter Narr.
Bassnett, Susan 1980 *Translation studies*. New York: Methuen.
Bassnett, Susan and André Lefevere (eds.) 1990 *Translation, history and culture*. London: Routledge.
Beatty, Jackson 1982 Task-evoked pupillary responses, processing load, and the structure of processing resources. *Psychological Bulletin* 91: 276–292.
Bencini, Giulia M. L. and Adele E. Goldberg 2000 The contribution of argument structure constructions to sentence meaning. *Journal of Memory and Language* 43.4: 640–651.
Berman, Ruth A. and Dan I. Slobin 1994 *Relating events in narrative: A cross-linguistic developmental study*. Hillsdale, NJ: Lawrence Erlbaum Associates.
Bernardini, Silvia 2001 Think-aloud protocols in translation research: Achievements, limits, future prospects. *Target* 13.2 241–263.
Boas, Hans C. 2010 (ed.) *Contrastive Studies in Construction Grammar*. Amsterdam: John Benjamins.
Caffrey, Colm 2009 *Relevant abuse? Investigating the effects of an abusive subtitling procedure on the perception of TV anime using eye tracker and questionnaire*. PhD dissertation, Dublin City University, Ireland.
Catford, John C. 1965 *A linguistic theory of translation: An essay on applied linguistics*. London: Oxford University Press.
Chmiel, Agnieszka, Iwona Mazur, Elena Di Giovanni, Anna Vilaró and Pilar Orero 2010 Visual perception by sighted viewers and its reflection in audio description: A work-in-progress report on an international eye-tracking study. Paper presented at ScreenIT: The Changing Face of Audiovisual Translation, Forlí, Italy, October 20–22, 2010.

De Knop, Sabine and Teun De Rycker (eds.) 2008 *Cognitive approaches to pedagogical grammar*. Berlin: Mouton de Gruyter.

De Rooze, Bart 2003 *La traducción, contra reloj: consecuencias de la presión por falta de tiempo en el proceso de traducción*. PhD dissertation, University of Granada, Spain.

Derrida, Jacques [1982] 1985 *The ear of the other: Otobiography, transference, translation: Texts and discussions with Jacques Derrida*. Translated by P. Kamuf. New York: Schocken Books.

Diamond, Bruce J. and Gregory M. Shreve 2010 Neural and physiological correlates of translation and interpreting in the bilingual brain. In: Gregroy M. Shreve and Erik Angelone (eds.), 289–321. Amsterdam: John Benjamins.

Dragsted, Barbara 2005 Segmentation in translation – differences across levels of expertise and difficulty. *Target* 17.1: 49–70.

Dragsted, Barbara 2010 Coordination of reading and writing processes. In: Gregory M. Shreve and Erik Angelone (eds.), *Translation and cognition*, 41–62. Amsterdam: John Benjamins.

Dragsted, Barbara and Inge G. Hansen 2008 Comprehension and production in translation: A pilot study on segmentation and the coordination of reading and writing processes. In: Susanne Göpferich, Arnt L. Jakobsen and Inger M. Mees (eds.), *Looking at eyes: Eye tracking studies of reading and translation processing*, 9–29. (*Copenhagen Studies in Language 36.*) Copenhagen: Samfundslitteratur.

Dragsted, Barbara, Inge Hansen and Henrik Selsøe Sørensen 2009 Experts exposed. In: Inger M. Mees, Fabio Alves and Susanne Göpferich (eds.), *Methodology, technology and innovation in translation process research: A tribute to Arnt Lykke Jakobsen*, 293–318. (*Copenhagen Studies in Language 38.*) Copenhagen: Samfundslitteratur.

Duchowski, Andrew T. 2002 A breadth-first survey of eye tracking applications. *Behavior Research Methods, Instruments, & Computers* (BRMIC) 34.4: 455–470.

Eco, Umberto 2001 *Experiences in translation*. Toronto: University of Toronto Press.

Eddington, David and Francisco J. Ruiz de Mendoza 2010 Argument constructions and language processing: Evidence from a priming experiment and pedagogical implications. In: Sabine De Knop, Frank Boers, and Antoon De Rycker (eds.), *Fostering language teaching efficiency through cognitive linguistics*, 213–238. Berlin: Mouton de Gruyter.

Gentzler, Edwin 2001 *Contemporary translation theories*. London: Routledge.

Gerganov, Alexander, Marina Hristova and Maxim Stamenov 2009 Bilingual processing of ambiguous nouns with cognate and non-cognate meanings: Evidence from synchronous recording of eye movements and EEG. Paper presented at Eye-to-IT Conference on Translation Processes, Copenhagen, Denmark, April 28–29, 2009.

Goldberg, Adele E. 1995 *Constructions: A construction grammar approach to argument structure*. Chicago: University of Chicago Press.

Goldberg, Adele E. 2006 *Constructions at work: The nature of generalization in language*. Oxford: Oxford University Press

Goldberg, Adele E. and Giulia Bencini 2005 Support from processing for a constructional approach to grammar. In: Andrea E. Tyler, Mari Takada, Yiyoung Kim and Diana Marinova (eds.), *Language in use: Cognitive and discourse perspectives on language and language learning*, 3–18. Washington, DC: Georgetown University Press.

Goldberg, Adele E. and Ray Jackendoff 2004 The English resultative as a family of constructions. *Language* 80.3: 532–568.

Gries, Stefan and Stefanie Wulff. 2005 Do foreign language learners also have constructions? Evidence from priming, sorting and corpora. *Annual Review of Cognitive Linguistics* 3: 182–200.

Halverson, Sandra 2010 Cognitive translation studies: Development in theory and method. In: Gregory M. Shreve and Eric Angelone (eds.), *Translation and cognition*, 349–370. Amsterdam: John Benjamins.

Harris, Brian and Bianca Sherwood 1978 Translating as an innate skill. In: David Gerver and Wallace Sinaiko (eds.), *Language, interpretation and communication*, 155–170. New York: Plenum Press.

Hatim, Basil and Ian Mason 1990 *Discourse and the translator*. London: Longman.

House, Juliane 1977 *A model for translation quality assessment*. Tübingen, Germany: Gunter Narr.

Hyona, Jukka, Jorma Tommola and Anna-Mari Alaja 1995 Pupil dilation as a measure of processing load in simultaneous interpretation and other language tasks. *Quarterly Journal of Experimental Psychology* 48A: 598–612.

Jääskeläinen, Rita 1989 Translation assignment in professional vs. non-professional translation: A think-aloud protocol study In: Candace Séguinot (ed.), *The translation process*, 87–98. Toronto: York University.

Jackendoff, Ray 1990 *Semantic structures*. Cambridge, MA: MIT Press.

Jakobsen, Arnt Lykke and Kristian T. H. Jensen 2008 Eye movement behaviour across four different types of reading tasks. In: Susanne Göpferich, Arnt L. Jakobsen and Inger M.Mees (eds.), *Looking at eyes: Eye tracking studies of reading and translation processing*, 103–124. (Copenhagen Studies in Language 36.) Copenhagen: Samfundslitteratur.

Jensen, Astrid 1999 Time pressure in translation. In: Gyde Hansen (ed.), *Probing the process in translation: Methods and results*, 103–119. Copenhagen: Samfundslitteratur.

Jensen, Astrid 2000 *The effects of time on cognitive processes and strategies in translation*. PhD dissertation, Copenhagen Business School.

Jensen, Astrid and Arnt Lykke Jakobsen 2000 Translating under time pressure: An empirical investigation of problem-solving activity and translation strategies by non-professional and professional translators. In: Andrew Chesterman, Natividad Gallardo San Salvador and Yves Gambier (eds.), *Translation in context: Selected contributions from the EST Congress, Granada 1998*, 105–116. Amsterdam: John Benjamins.

Kahneman, Daniel and Jackson Beatty 1966 Pupil diameter and load on memory. *Science* 154.756: 1583–1585.

Kaschak, Michael P. and Arthur M. Glenberg 2000 Constructing meaning: The role of affordances and grammatical constructions in sentence comprehension. *Journal of Memory and Language* 43.3: 508–529.

Kay, Paul and Charles J. Fillmore 1999 Grammatical constructions and linguistic generalizations: The What's X doing Y? construction. *Language* 57: 1–33.

Kiraly, Donald C. 1997 Think-aloud protocols and the construction of a professional translator self-concept. In: Joseph H. Danks, Gregory M. Shreve, Stephen B. Fountain and Michael K. McBeath (eds.), *Cognitive processes in translation and interpreting*, 137–160. Thousand Oaks, CA: Sage.

Kurz, Ernst-Nobert 1994 A look into the "black blox" – EEG probability mapping during mental simultaneous interpreting. In: Mary Snell-Hornby, Franz Pöchhacker and Klaus Kaindl (eds.), *Translation studies: An interdiscipline*, 199–207. Amsterdam: John Benjamins.

Lakoff, George 1990 The invariance hypothesis: Is abstract reason based on image-schemas? *Cognitive Linguistics* 1: 39–74.

Lefevere, André 1992 *Translation/history/culture: A sourcebook*. London: Routledge.

Levin, Beth and Malka Rappaport Hovav 1995 *Unaccusativity: At the syntax–lexical semantics interface*. Cambridge, MA: MIT Press.

Liang, John 2002 How do Chinese EFL learners construct sentence meaning: Verb-centered or construction-based? Master's thesis, Guangdong University of Foreign Studies.
Maldonado, Ricardo 1992 *Middle voice: The case of Spanish se*. PhD dissertation, University of California, San Diego.
Maldonado, Ricardo 2009 Middle as a basic voice system. In: Lilian Guerrero, Sergio Ibáñez and Valeria Belloro (eds.), *Studies in role and reference grammar*, 69–109. Mexico D.F., Mexico: Instituto de Investigaciones Filológicas, UNAM.
Mendívil-Giró, Jose Luis 2003 Construcciones resultativas y Gramática Universal. *Revista Española de Lingüística* 33.1: 1–28.
Moser-Mercer, Barbara 2010 The search for neuro-physiological correlates of expertise in interpreting. In: Gregroy M. Shreve and Erik Angelone (eds.), 263–287. Amsterdam: John Benjamins.
Muñoz Martín, Ricardo 2010 On paradigms and cognitive translatology. In: Gregory M. Shreve and Eric Angelone (eds.), *Translation and cognition*, 169–188. Amsterdam: John Benjamins.
Narbona, Antonio 2000 Sintaxis coloquial. In: Manuel Alvar (ed.), *Introducción a la lingüística española*, 463–478. Barcelona: Ariel Lingüística.
Nida, Eugene A. [1964] 2004 Principles of correspondence. In: Laurence Venuti (ed.), *The translation studies reader*, 153–167. London: Routledge.
Nida, Eugene A. and Charles R. Taber [1969] 1982 *The theory and practice of translation*. Leiden: Brill.
Nord, Christiane 1997 *Translating as a purposeful activity: Functionalist approaches explained*. Manchester: St. Jerome.
O'Brien, Sharon 2008 Processing fuzzy matches in translation memory tools: An eye-tracking analysis. In: Susanne Göpferich, Arnt L. Jakobsen and Inger M.Mees (eds.), *Looking at eyes: Eye tracking studies of reading and translation processing*, 79–102. (Copenhagen Studies in Language 36.) Copenhagen: Samfundslitteratur.
O'Brien, Sharon 2010 Controlled language and readability. In: Gregory M. Shreve and Erik Angelone (eds.), *Translation and cognition*, 143–165. Amsterdam: John Benjamins.
Pavlović, Nataša and Kristian Jensen 2009 Eye tracking translation directionality. In: Anthony Pym and Alexander Perekrestenko (eds.), *Translation research projects 2*, 93–109. Tarragona, Spain: Intercultural Studies Group.
Piquado, Tepring, Derek M. Isaacowitz and Arthur Wingfield 2010 Pupillometry as a measure of cognitive effort in younger and older adults. *Psychophysiology* 47.3: 560–569.
Rayner, Keith 1998 Eye movements in reading and information processing: 20 years of research. *Psychological Bulletin* 124: 372–422.
Reiss, Katharina [1977] 1989 Text types, translation types and translation assessment. In: Andrew Chesterman (ed.), *Readings in translation theory*, 105–115. Helsinki: Oy Finn Lectura Ab.
Richardson, Daniel C., Rick Dale and Michael J. Spivey 2007 Eye movements in language and cognition: A brief introduction. In: Mónica Gonzalez-Marquez, Seana Coulson, Irene Mittelberg and Michael Spivey (eds.), *Methods in cognitive linguistics*, 323–344. Amsterdam: John Benjamins.
Richardson, Daniel C. and Michael J. Spivey 2004 Eye tracking: Research areas and applications. In: Gary Wnek and Gary Bowlin (eds.), *Encyclopedia of biomaterials and biomedical engineering*, 573–582. New York: Marcel Dekker.
Rubel, Paula G. and Abraham Rosman 2003 Introduction: Translation and anthropology. In: Paula G. Rubel and Abraham Rosman (eds.), *Translating cultures: Perspectives on translation and anthropology*, 1–22. Oxford: Berg.

Rushdie, Salman 1992 *Imaginary homelands: Essays and criticism 1981–1991*. London Granta Books.
Rydning, Antin Fougner and Christian Michael Lachaud 2010 The reformulation challenge in translation: Context reduces polysemy during comprehension, but multiplies creativity during production. In: Gregory M. Shreve and Erik Angelone (eds.), *Translation and cognition*, 85–108. Amsterdam: John Benjamins.
Sharmin, Selina, Oleg Spakov, Kari-Jouko Räihä and Arnt Lykke Jakobsen 2008 Where on the screen do translation students look when translating, and for how long? In: Susanne Göpferich, Arnt L. Jakobsen and Inger M. Mees (eds.), *Looking at eyes: Eye tracking studies of reading and translation processing*, 31–52. *(Copenhagen Studies in Language 36.)* Copenhagen: Samfundslitteratur.
Shreve, Gregory M. and Erik Angelone (eds.) 2010 *Translation and cognition*. Amsterdam: John Benjamins.
Shreve, Gregory M., Isabel Lacruz, and Erik Angelone 2010 Cognitive effort, syntactic disruption, and visual interference in a sight translation task. In: Gregory M. Shreve and Erik Angelone (eds.), *Translation and cognition*, 63–84. Amsterdam: John Benjamins.
Sjørup, Anette C. 2011 Cognitive effort in metaphor translation: An eye-tracking study. In: Sharon O'Brien (ed.), *Cognitive explorations of translation*, 197–214. London: Continuum.
Slobin, Dan I. 1996 Two ways to travel: Verbs of motion in English and Spanish. In: Masayoshi Shibatani and Sandra A. Thompson (eds.), *Grammatical constructions: Their form and meaning*, 195–219. Oxford: Clarendon.
Slobin, Dan I. 1997 Mind, code, and text. In: Joan Bybee, John Haiman and Sandra A. Thompson (eds.), *Essays on language function and language type: Dedicated to T. Givón*, 437–467. Amsterdam: John Benjamins.
Slobin, Dan I. 2005 Relating narrative events in translation. In: Dorin Diskin Ravid and Hava Bat-Zeev Shyldkrot (eds.), *Perspectives on language and language development: Essays in honor of Ruth A. Berman*, 115–129. Dordrecht, the Netherlands: Kluwer.
Snell-Hornby, Mary 1990 Linguistic transcoding or cultural transfer: A critique of translation theory in Germany. In: Susan Bassnett and André Lefevere (eds.), *Translation, history and culture*, 79–86. London: Routledge.
Stamenov, Maxim I., Alexander Gerganov and Ivo D. Popivanov 2010 Prompting cognates in the bilingual lexicon: Optimizing access during translation. In: Gregory M. Shreve and Erik Angelone (eds.), *Translation and cognition*, 323–348. Amsterdam: John Benjamins.
Steel, Luc (ed.) 2011 *Design Patterns in Fluid Construction Grammar*. Amsterdam: John Benjamins.
Talmy, Leonard 2000 *Toward a cognitive semantics*. Vol. 2, *Typology and process in concept structuring*. Cambridge, MA: MIT Press.
Tomasello, Michael 2003 *Constructing a language: A usage-based theory of language acquisition*. Cambridge, MA: Harvard University Press.
Toury, Gideon 1995 *Descriptive translation studies – and beyond*. Amsterdam: John Benjamins.
Valenzuela, Javier, Joseph Hilferty and Mar Garachana 2005 On the reality of grammatical constructions. *Annual Review of Cognitive Linguistics* 3: 201–215.
Valenzuela, Javier and Ana Rojo 2008a Constructional priming in Spanish: A self-paced reading task experiment. Paper presented at the Sixth International Conference of AELCO/SCOLA, Castellón, Spain, October 22–24, 2008.

Valenzuela, Javier and Ana Rojo 2008b What can language learners tell us about constructions? In: Sabine De Knop and Teun De Rycker (eds.), *Cognitive approaches to pedagogical grammar*, 197–230. Berlin: Mouton de Gruyter.
Vázquez-Ayora, Gerardo 1977 *Introducción a la traductología*. Washington, DC: Georgetown University Press.
Venuti, Lawrence 1995 *The translator's invisibility: A history of translation*. London: Routledge.
Vermeer, Hans J. [1989] 2004 Skopos and commission in translational action. In: Lawrence Venuti (ed.), *The translation studies reader*, 227–238. London: Routledge.
Vinay, Paul and Jean Darbelnet [1958] 1972 *Stylistique compare du français et de l'anglais: méthode de traduction*. Paris: Didier. [Translated and edited by Juan C. Sager and Marie-Josée Hamel (1995) as *Comparative stylistics of French and English: A methodology for translation*. Amsterdam: John Benjamins].

Appendix 1 Resultative constructions used as stimuli

1. Cut a frog open
2. Hammer the handle straight
3. Shake me awake
4. Shoot the bear dead
5. Push the door open
6. Brush the carpet clean
7. Perm my hair curly
8. Slap his cheek red
9. Fry the chicken crispy
10. Talk yourself hoarse
11. Laugh yourself stupid
12. Freeze the water solid

Part IV: **Culture and translation**

Enrique Bernárdez
A cognitive view on the role of culture in translation

1 Introduction

It can be asserted that translation is necessarily linked to culture. However, the real meaning of that assertion is far from clear: what does it mean "to be linked to culture"? What is culture? Where in translation is culture? Quite frequently, things are rather obvious: such an apparently straightforward word as the Chinese 心 xīn, basically glossed as 'heart', is in fact an extremely complex cultural concept, and choosing a correspondence for translation in any other language leaves out the largest part of its rich cultural background.[1] The number of similar examples that could be cited for any other language is practically limitless. In a framework which can be termed as "cognitive" as that of Anna Wierzbicka's crosscultural and cross-semantic studies (Wierzbicka [1991] 2003, 1997), many examples of the cultural uniqueness of words and concepts have been advanced. Wierzbicka's "key cultural words" bear the implication that certain concepts and their corresponding words are very difficult, even impossible to translate, i.e. to "take over" to a different language+culture, as they are idiosyncratic and frequently exclusive of an individual culture. Cultural words in translation have been the object of much theoretical research and practical reflection. It might seem, however, that the problem of translation of such culturally laden words may be incorrectly posed sometimes.

Braz (2006: 202) introduces the problem as it is usually faced in translation:

> Bien que ce terme [*saudade*] puisse désigner la même chose que les termes qui le traduisent, constituant un point commun avec chacun de ces concepts, il faut reconnaître qu'il ne signifie pas la même chose. Sa complexité sémantique ayant exigé la fixation d'un seul mot dans la langue source, l'acte de traduction se confronte à une polysémie telle que le concept de *saudade* devient insaisissable dans la langue cible puisqu'il signifie toujours

---

[1] The large (over 2,000 pages) Spanish Dictionary of Chinese (Mateos, Otegui, and Arrizabalaga 1977: 379) gives the following main meanings of the word *xīn*; among them: (i) heart (one of the five viscera; the main one, seen as seat of the spirit and of thought [. . .]); (ii) the realm of the intimate; (iii) intelligence; reflection, attention; thinking, idea; (iv) soul; internal disposition; feelings, humour; will, intention; conscience, morality; centre; stomach. González España (in Lu 2010: 47), following Zhang (1984: 18; quoted in Lu 2010) points out that it is also understood as "creativity" and that it shows how separating the mind from the body is unthinkable in traditional Chinese culture.

plus que ce qu'il désigne. À partir de cette *intransposabilité*, la question se pose de savoir comment rendre sans perte ce qui ne peut être saisi en entier.

[Even if this term can designate the same thing as the terms used to translate it, thus having a point in common with such notions, it is necessary to recognise that it does not mean the same thing. Its semantic complexity having required the creation of a single word in the source language, the act of translation faces such a polysemy that the notion of *saudade* becomes non comprehensible in the target language because it always means more than what it designates. This *impossibility of transposition* leads to the question of how to translate without any loss what cannot be comprehended in its entirety.][2]

But then he shows that the problem is not so much linguistic as cultural: the problem is not so much finding an adequate word to render the "difficult one", but to "transmettre une réalité dans une culture qui n'est pas celle de la langue source" [transmit a reality in a culture different to that of the source language] (op. cit. 118). Thus,

[. . .] traduire la *saudade* par les différents termes étudiés suggère que la traduction privilégie la langue cible, autrement dit, elle se donne pour visée d'exprimer le contenu comme s'il était pensé dans la langue cible: traduire, c'est alors ramener l'autre au même, tenter de supprimer l'étrangeté culturelle.

[[. . .] translating the *saudade* through the different terms analysed suggests that translation privileges the target language, in other words, it sets itself the aim of expressing the content as if it had been thought in the target language: translating is then bringing down the other to the self, trying to suppress cultural strangeness.]

That is, the problem with such words is not finding a more or less adequate equivalent in another language, but transmitting their cultural content. And, ultimately, the result will be what others (Brems 2010) have called "cultural castration" of the original, be it a whole work (as in Brems' example), a reference, or a word, that is a concept and a certain culturally preferred segment of reality.

Summing up, cultural words are not primarily words, i.e. linguistic elements, but *concepts or notions specific of an individual culture.*

2 (Conceptual) metaphor, culture, and translation

The role of culture in translation is also obvious in the domain of conceptual metaphors, a domain quite frequently and deeply practiced in the framework of

---

[2] All translations by the author unless the contrary is stated.

Cognitive Linguistics (see, e.g. Schäffner 2004; cfr. Dobrzyńska 1995 for a different but fairly coincidental approach). However, while it is generally accepted that most metaphors incorporate a substantial cultural content – perhaps with the exception of the so-called "primary metaphors"[3] – they still tend to be treated as primarily conceptual. In the area of Translation Studies, the following possibilities are usually mentioned: (i) if a metaphor is common to both the Source and the Target languages, it should be kept – if necessary with the corresponding linguistic change, as in English TIME IS MONEY corresponding to Spanish EL TIEMPO ES ORO ('time is gold'). (ii) If there is no equivalent metaphor translators can (a) choose a different but relatively similar one in the T(arget) L(anguage), or (b) use a non-metaphoric expression, but also (c) adapt the S (ource) L metaphor, i.e. keep the metaphorical form whenever it can be easily understood by the reader. But note that this refers to *the existence, not the real conditions* in which they are or may be used.

Sometimes, the metaphor obtained in (c) gets integrated in the TL as a new metaphor which can be further used in new situations. But this metaphor-borrowing can show, as is so frequently the case with borrowing in general, the deep cultural implications of metaphors. A single example will suffice to show this process: the Arabic metaphor X IS THE MOTHER OF (ALL) Y, meaning "X is the most important of all Y" became famous and was widely reproduced as a consequence of the impact on the media of Saddam Hussein's reference to *the mother of all battles*. This new metaphor is now of relatively current use – although most of the time with a humorous implication only. But if we take another instance of the same metaphor in Arabic, this time a well-established one, *?umm al-qurā*, 'the mother of cities', the Western reader will probably be at odds with its interpretation: Does it refer to the "most important of all towns" and, if thus be the case, in which sense is a city to be viewed as more important than any other? And more importantly, which city can it refer to?

---

3 This universality is however doubtful. The proposed primary metaphor CAUSES ARE FORCES would be contradicted by languages as Navajo and Samoan, partially also in Spanish, where the concept of "cause" is mainly expressed in terms of movement along a path (Bernárdez 2001). Similarly, the universal character of some conceptualisations of time is extremely doubtful, as such conceptualisation seems to depend first and foremost on cultural principles and criteria (Sinha et al. 2012; Pinxten and de Munter 2006; Pinxten 1995). Similar doubts have arisen for instance on the cultural determination of such "primary metaphors" as KNOWING IS SEEING. In some languages, the main metaphor would be HEARING IS KNOWING, for instance (see Ibarretxe-Antuñano 2008). Icelandic is a case in point, as it uses both metaphors, the one based on hearing being of more frequent use than the rarer KNOWING IS SEEING. In accordance with the two levels identifiable in Icelandic culture, a double metaphor is used.

Most Western readers would be unable to identify Mecca, because they do not share the significance of Mecca in historical, religious and cultural terms. So, the metaphor has been borrowed in linguistic terms and with a certain meaning but *deprived of its cultural integrity and, consequently, of its full meaning*. This is a risk for every intercultural analysis of metaphor or in any analysis of metaphor at large. Of course, if we keep the metaphor in translation, "the mother of cities", it will be misunderstood by most readers and only seldom will it be correctly identified as Mecca. Thus, even if the metaphor does exist in Western cultures, its value is quite different. It has to be said that *value* is used here in the sense of Bartmiński (2009: 39; see also Zinken 2004) as "that which in the light of language and culture people consider precious. [. . .] Thus my understanding of values is that of folk philosophy". Value can also be understood in the framework of Rossi Landi's theory of the linguistic market (1968; see also Bernárdez 2008; Ponzio 2008).

The notion of value is of exceptional importance, also for translation. Apparently, English *crusade* and Arabic *ṣalībīya* mean the same, as they have the same referent. But the values could not be more different: in English extremely positive, in Arabic extremely negative, threatening (see Maalouf 1983). Translating *crusade* as *ṣalībīya* will certainly bring about quite a different reaction among Arabs than among Westerners. Something similar happens with such a nowadays frequent term as *Al-Qā'ida* which in English and other languages has no specific meaning but is an extremely important cultural word – and concept – in Arabic, not limited to being the name of a terrorist macro-organisation (Miller 2008). In English, that term has a negative value, whereas in the Arab world the term itself is positive, even if the organisation it can refer to is rejected and negatively viewed.

2.1 Non equivalence of (apparently) equivalent metaphors

This lack of cultural correspondence is also patent in the comparison of "equivalent" metaphors among cultures: Two metaphors may seem linguistically and even conceptually similar and equivalent, but their deep cultural value can be altogether different. This is especially noticeable in some analyses operating at a conceptual level with no consideration of the *individual* cultural components of metaphor. For instance, Sweetser (1995: 589) analyses, among other things, the mapping of the sun onto a male divinity and the moon onto a female one in Greek mythology.[4] One of the main points in this mapping is introduced

---

[4] The paper does not explicitly state that its tenets may be limited to Greek mythology. It ignores the frequent cases of female sun-divinities as e.g. Amaterasu in Japanese mythology,

as follows: "Primary, more powerful=Male; Secondary, less powerful=Female"; in spite of its having been elicited on the basis of Ancient Greek mythology, the author (589) posits the present-day validity of the mapping: "[. . .] We certainly still retain the connection between the male/female contrast and a primary/secondary opposition, which allowed the sun/moon contrast to be mapped onto male and female". The sun (strong) is expected to be a male divinity while the moon (less strong) is associated with femininity; the sun's rays can thus be seen as metaphoric images of the male penis (591): "And Eros' arrows may well be an image metaphor for his penis (we may note that the female deity of sexuality, Aphrodite, is not an archer like the male Eros)". As Pagán Cánovas (2008, 2011) first showed, this interpretation does not fit with the real facts of Ancient Greek mythology, as poets like Pindar depicted Aphrodite as the "lady of sharpest arrows" and a similar expression can also be found in Euripides' *Medea* (lines 632–633):

(1) μήποτ᾽, ὦ δέσποιν᾽, ἐπ᾽ ἐμοὶ χρυσέων τόξων ἐφείης ἱμέρῳ χρίσασ᾽ ἄφυκτον οἰστόν
Never, O never, lady mine, discharge at me from thy golden bow a shaft invincible, in passion's venom dipped.

We can add, among many other possible examples, the Roman poet, Lucretius, who writes in his *De rerum natura* (IV 1278–1279):

(2) *Nec divinitus inter dum Venerisque sagittis deteriore fit [. . .]*
[. . .] one who gets a stroke from Venus' shafts [. . .]

That is, the analysis of a fragment of Greek mythology and its correspondence with present-day metaphoric understanding of the same phenomena is wrong, as the author does not consider the *whole* cultural framework where the common metaphors are supposed to work: The cultural bases for the Greek metaphors concerning arrows, illness, and love, have to be seen as different from their contemporary Western counterparts. Even if the aim of the article, viz. to show that "linguistic structure is a part of culture, and linguistic metaphorical usages are based on broader cultural cognitive structures" (592) is totally

---

but also among the Indo-Europeans, as the Germanic pair formed by the Feminine *Só.* = Sun and the Masculine *Máne* = Moon. We shall not enter into the many errors concerning the interpretation of male and female divinities in this paper.

justified, the article itself fails because it does not pay due attention to the particularities of culture, i.e. not to culture in general, even supposedly "universal" terms, but to the particular, concrete, historical elements of Ancient Greek culture on the one hand and to contemporary Western culture on the other.

This means that translating any elements of these Greek metaphors into a modern Western language assuming Sweetser's interpretation will not usually achieve an acceptable degree of equivalence, as most of the culture involved will be different and the TL readers' interpretation will be radically different from that of SL speakers or of people knowledgeable in Ancient Greek culture and mythology.

We can assume that something similar will apply whenever metaphor is involved. And not only metaphor, the same is true for metonymy and simile. For instance, in Musil's *Der Mann ohne Eigenschaften* (654), a girl's eye blinking is compared to "the rapid fire of a Browning" (Bernárdez 2009: 66); this simile can be understood if the reader knows *Browning* refers to a machine gun. But the cultural value of *Browning* in the period before the First World War, where the action is supposed to take place, is quite different from the cultural value of machine guns in present culture: whereas in the early 20th c. a machine gun was probably the most modern instrument of war, its existence, forms, use, etc. are common knowledge nowadays, although most people do not really know how they work (which means by the way that Musil's simile requires his contemporary readers to be more knowledgeable than present-day ones). The cultural value of machine guns could be very high in 1911, practically nil in 2011.

Something similar happens with metonymy. Let us just recall the (in)famous example, *The ham sandwich has left without paying* and its innumerable variants. A first problem is that it simply does not seem feasible in most other languages. How could one translate that metonymy into Spanish, for instance? Of course there is the literal translation *El sandwich de jamón se ha ido sin pagar*; but it will sound extremely odd, in most cases inacceptable, except in a rather humorous interpretation where the real sandwich is seen walking. The "normal" translation would include no metonymy: *El del sandwich de jamón se ha ido sin pagar* ('the one with the ham sandwich has left without paying'). We have been able to find only one European language where this metonymic construction seems to be in use. In Modern Greek, in fact, the following seems to be fully acceptable: *το κοτόπουλο α λα κρεμ θέλει να πληρώσει* ('the chicken à la crème [= the person who ordered chicken à la crème] wants to pay') (Andropoulou Panagiota and Zeljko 2011: 18).

It seems to be especially frequent in such contexts as fast food restaurants in Greece.⁵

If that metonymy, and many similar ones are cognitively possible (and there is no doubt they are) but not normally acceptable in many languages, where does the reason for such unacceptability arise from? Probably, from some cultural conditioning which does not allow reference on such a base: no reference could then be made to a human being on the basis of something that is not an integral, usually inseparable part of his/her body, mind, or personality. This could explain (perhaps) that Spanish is ready to accept metonymies of the type *el gran cerebro ha salido de la sala* ('the great brain has left the room') or *el rostro más bonito de España ha salido* ('the most beautiful face in Spain has left') but not *el abrigo de visón ha salido* ('the mink coat has left') – except in ironic, humorous contexts.

2.2 Figurative language in use

When translating such metaphors, similes or metonymies, much care has to be taken with the cultural values implicated in the expression and, most importantly, its use. The real conditions of use of a metaphor are an essential part of Line and Per Aage Brandt's analysis of the not less (in)famous and much discussed metaphoric expression, *your surgeon is a butcher* (Brandt and Brandt 2005). Although they do not make specific reference to cultural elements in their interpretation, these can be assumed, because every situation of use is necessarily linked to some cultural conditioning: every situation of use is socio-historical *per definitionem*.

Brandt and Brandt do not make any reference to the socio-historical element in metaphor use and interpretation, so let us add a few details about the butcher-metaphor in a historical, cultural and interlinguistic sense. *Your surgeon is a butcher* can be translated into Spanish with the same meaning, if similar semiotic conditions hold: *Tu cirujano es un carnicero*, although some would probably prefer *tu cirujano es un matarife*, 'your surgeon is a slaughterman'.

---

5 One of my referees rightly pointed out that other metonymic expressions are, however, usual. For instance, utterances like *la siete ha pedido la cuenta* ('Table # 7 has asked for their/his/her check'). This is true, but it shows that not any metonymy whatsoever can be used in Spanish to refer to people, the possibilities being quite limited, which is the point I am trying to make here; in the restaurant situation, one can use the LOCATION FOR THE PERSON(S) OCCUPYING THAT LOCATION metonymy, but not FOOD FOR THE PERSON HAVING COMMANDED IT.

But the reason can be not so much the cognitive work of interpretation of a metaphor as the simple access to well-established forms of expression. Let us look up the definition of *butcher* in the *Shorter Oxford Dictionary*

> [ME bocher, boucher, Anglo-Fr. f. OF bochier, bouchier, f. OF., P. boc BUCK. Thus lit. 'dealer in goat's flesh'; cf. It. beccaio, f. becco]
>
> 1. a. One whose trade it is to slaughter large tame animals and sells their flesh; now, occas., a tradesman who deals in meat. b. fig. A 'man of blood'; a brutal murderer 1528. †2. An executioner [. . .] 1494.
>
> [VERB} (1562) 1. To slaughter in the manner of a butcher. 2. To inflict torture upon (1642).

From the end of the 15th century, the word is directly associated to brutality, murder, slaughtering "in the manner of a butcher". In the entry for the same word in the *Collins Cobuild Dictionary*, the following can be found:

> 2. If you call a man a butcher, you mean that he has committed a lot of cruel murders.

We can even go back to Johnson's Dictionary (1843):

> BUTCHER. One that kills animals to sell their flesh. *Sidney*. One delighted with blood. *Locke*.

Similar interpretations of the same word can be found in other languages, such as Spanish, German, or French. The Italian *Garzanti Dictionary* includes the following "figurative and derogatory" meaning of *macellaio* 'butcher': *chirurgo incapace*, i.e. 'very bad surgeon'. The Italian word *macellaio*, in turn, is derived from Latin *macellarius*, itself a loan from Greek μακελλάριος, metonymically derived from a word meaning 'adze, axe', an instrument used by butchers. The word was probably borrowed in order to avoid the very negative meaning already acquired by *carnifex*, the "literal" word for one dealing or working with flesh/meat (*caro/carnis*), which had come to mean nothing less than 'executioner'.

Thus, if we take into consideration the history of words, including their non-literal, figurative usage, and metaphor as part of it, things look different: does the speaker need to carry out a specific "metaphoric interpretation"? It may indeed be enough to know that specific meaning of the word. Of course, this takes us to Bowdle and Gentner's (2005) *Career of Metaphor Theory* and to Steen's (2008) *Paradox of Metaphor*. In a nutshell – and in our own interpretation – a metaphor begins its life or career as a "real metaphor" which asks for a specific form of understanding (in the semiotic conditions sketched by Brandt and Brandt) and ends up as a "fossilised metaphor" which is understood in a direct, non-metaphoric manner and whose metaphoric character is only visible to the analyst – who thus incorrectly gives primacy to the *theoretical reason* as described by Pierre Bourdieu (Bernárdez 2008: 138).

For our purposes in this paper, the following conclusions can be drawn: even linguistically and conceptually equivalent forms of figurative meaning in SL and TL can be dramatically different in the terms of their individual cultures, values and preferences. The existence of a metaphor, simile or metonymy in both languages does not guarantee that they are really equivalent, as their respective degree of cultural conventionalisation can be quite different. Figurative language has to be analysed in its real use, as every translation involves real use in both TL and SL.

3 Culture, language structures, and Natural Translation

On the other hand, one could feel inclined to think that the pervasiveness of culture is only, or mainly, true of the semantic and pragmatic levels or components of language and of complex, mainly written translation, whereas grammar on the one hand and non-regulated forms of translation on the other could be seen as "culture-free". Such would be the case in the so called *natural translation*, which Harris (1977: 1, 2008) defines as "*the translation done in everyday circumstances by bilinguals who have had no special training for it*" (italics in the 2008 original). That is, e.g. translation by "the young children of bilingual families who translate spontaneously from the age of about three. [. . .] However, they may be older; for example, poorly educated immigrants who are learning the language of their new country" (Harris n.d.). Supposedly, children learn to translate in a natural manner in the same way, and at the same time, that they learn their languages in a situation of natural bilingualism. Harris introduces his "first postulate for a new departure in translatology" (1977: 9): all bilinguals can translate (capitals in the original):

> IN ADDITION TO SOME COMPETENCE IN TWO LANGUAGES Li AND Lj, THEY ALL POSSESS A "THIRD COMPETENCE", THAT OF TRANSLATING FROM Li TO Lj AND VICEVERSA. BILINGUALISM IS THEREFORE A TRIPLE, NOT A DOUBLE COMPETENCE; AND THE THIRD COMPETENCE IS BI-DIRECTIONAL.

This view has led to a number of linguistic and psycholinguistic studies for different languages and ethnic groups (see Álvarez de la Fuente 2007; Gómez Hurtado 2007; Harris n.d.; Lozès-Lawani 1994). It has also lead to a nativist view of translation, as this translational competence would be at a pair with language competence at large in a Chomskyan framework. We shall not enter into this topic except in as much as it can have some implications for the role of culture in language and, consequently, in translation.

There is no doubt that bilinguals are able to translate in an effective way without the need of any instruction in translatology or in the methodology of interpreting and at a certain level, natural translators do not seem to be in any way worse than trained translators (Gómez Hurtado 2007). Human history is full of such cases of natural translation which, moreover, still constitute an everyday reality. However, it could be thought that if translation is naturally carried out there could be little room for cultural topics, as natural translation does not ask for specialists in cultural differences: let us recall oral interpretation by natives who had learnt their colonisers' language and proved tremendously useful even if they lacked any significant knowledge of the colonisers' culture. The issue is then whether also at this level, which is the "most purely linguistic one" of all levels of translation and interpretation, culture also plays a role, even when translating metaphors is simply not seen as a problem, a difficulty or just a reality.

3.1 Culture is also present in grammar

Also, the issue of the presence of (identifiable and falsifiable) cultural elements in language, especially in linguistic structures and, still more precisely, syntactic structures, has been a permanent touchstone in linguistic studies. This topic has been the object of much research since the pioneering work reflected in Hymes (1964) (see also Palmer 1994; Bernárdez 2004, 2008) and has enjoyed renewed attention in connection with the revival of interest for the Linguistic Relativity Hypothesis (see Palmer 1994 for a review of some interesting examples) so the comments in this paper will be limited to some very concrete issues only. Enfield (2002a) includes twelve papers on the general topic "explorations in grammar and culture", whereas Levinson (2003) is devoted to cognition and language, but also culture, in the cognition and expression of space. Not to speak of the already mentioned book by Palmer (1994) which devotes much attention to the topic of relationship between grammar and culture.

As Enfield (2002b: 4) writes,

> [g]rammar is thick with cultural meaning. [. . .]. It is intended that "ethnosyntax" – broadly defined as the study of connections between the cultural knowledge, attitudes, and practices of speakers, and the morphosyntactic resources they employ in speech – should encompass [the] diverse range of grammar-culture effects. The field of research asks not just how culture and grammar may be connected, but also how they may be interconstitutive [. . .].

If this is so, we shall have to take culture into account in any kind of translation involving any languages and not only at the lexico-conceptual level. At a level encompassing lexical and grammatical phenomena, Yang (2008) studies the phenomenon frequently termed "grammatical metaphor" and its different ways of functioning in English and Chinese. He draws some conclusions from this work in connection with translation (476):

> This study illustrates the distinctions between Chinese and English in creating and deploying metaphorical expressions. [. . .]. [T]he findings of GM comparison in English and Chinese contribute to the translation between the two languages. As an important method of extending meaning potential in a language, GM is critical for the understanding of both the source language and the target language. Thus, successful translation between Chinese and English is partially determined by the correct understanding of GM in the two languages.

Among many other interesting points he raises, the relative frequency of metaphoric expression merits special mention; grammatical metaphors and, in general, "metaphoricity" is higher in English than in Chinese: "It is found that Chinese deploys metaphorical expressions to a lower degree than English" (476). This is a very important point that is extremely seldom the object of discussion and explanation. English, in a higher degree than many or most other languages, seems to be extremely fond of metaphor and metonymy, using them when other languages would prefer a literal form of expression, as we had the opportunity of seeing above in connection with some metonymies. This of course is not a feature of the language as such but certainly a matter of culture. Does this fact have implications for translation? Of course it does. Translation of English metaphoric expressions at the lexical or the grammatical level does not necessarily call for a metaphoric expression in the TL. It is not a matter of saying "if English has this particular metaphor, which metaphor is used in the TL?" but of ascertaining, in the first place, *whether the TL would tend to use a metaphor or a literal form of expression in the particular instance.*

That is, as with so many other things in translation (and in the study of language at large), the first and foremost question, also from a cognitive perspective, is: *how, when and why is it really used?* This is extremely important when a cognitive stance is adopted, as the "temptation" (and unfortunately the habit and the tendency) exists to pay attention only to the cognitive, individual, supposedly universal features of language; this seems to be changing now, as more and more attention is devoted to the social, interpersonal, collective aspects of cognition, and also to the facts of frequency in real use (Kristiansen and Dirven 2008; Frank et al. 2008; Bybee 2010).

3.1.1 A case study: The use of personal pronouns. And an artificial language

Let us consider an example of the pervasiveness of culture in language: the use of personal pronouns. We shall have a look at them in connection with another possible candidate to non-culturally marked grammatical structures: translation into an artificial language as Esperanto. It is known that Esperanto was created by L. Zamenhoff and was – and still is – expected to be a universally usable and acceptable language without the implications, also political and cultural, of the natural languages. Of course Esperanto was very much based on a few Western European languages but could be expected to be free from their cultural implications. Let us see if this is really the case in the tiny fragment chosen.

We shall take as the original (SL) text, President Obama's *Inaugural Lecture* and its translations to a number of languages in the official web page of the U.S. Government.[6] The Esperanto version has been taken from a different source, however.[7] We shall limit ourselves to one single clause from the very beginning of the speech which in the original English version includes three personal pronouns and/or possessives.

(3)   *I thank President Bush for his service to our nation* [. . .]

The Esperanto translation follows the original closely:

(4)   Mi   dankas   al   Prezidento Bush pro   lia   servo
      I   thank   [to]   President   Bush for   his   service
      al   nia   lando
      to   our   country

Three pronouns corresponding to those used in the SL appear in this fragment: *mi* is the 1st person singular pronoun, the subject of the verb "to thank", *lia* is the 3rd person sg. possessive, *nia* the 1st person pl. possessive. The same can be found throughout the text: in Esperanto, in fact, pronouns are pervasive, a feature typical of most European languages – among others – but essentially absent from, say, most Asian languages. For a Chinese, Japanese or Indonesian reader, in fact, Esperanto texts "sound European" and the "personalised" character of this translation strikes them as European: the cultural-linguistic clash

---

6   http://www.america.gov/st/usgenglish/2009/January/20090120130302abretnuh0.2991602.html.
7   http://www.gutenberg.org/files/28971/28971-h/28971-h.htm.

would be the same as with the original English text: Esperanto does not neutralise the cultural character associated to the extended use of personal pronouns and other forms of personal reference in English and other Western language.

Let us then take three more translations. The official Russian version of the U.S. Government is:

(5) **Я** благодарен президенту Бушу за **его** олужение нашей стране
 Ja blagodaren prezidentu Bušu za **ego** slušenie
 I thank president Bush for **his** service
 našej strane
 to.**our**country[8]

The same pronouns are found in Russian as in English; they are marked in **bold** here. This could perhaps be expected, as they are linguistically and culturally close languages. Let us go on to a culturally and linguistically farther situated language: Arabic.[9]

(6) wa-**ʔaqdumu** ʔaššukra li-r-raʔīsa Bush ʕalā
 and-**I**.give the.thanks to-the-president Bush for
 kidamāti**hi** li-bilādi**nā**
 service-**his** to-country.**our**

In this translation no free personal pronouns appear, morphological affixes being used throughout. All three references are kept, however: ʔa [. . .] u for the 1st person of the imperfective (present) tense. Reference is made to Bush by means of the possessive suffix in kidamāti**hi** 'his service', and instead of the first person plural possessive an affix is also used: li-bilādi**nā** 'to our country'. This could be understood in terms of a downgrading or demotion of personal expression, in such a way that "full" pronouns clearly tend to be avoided (see Bernárdez 1997 for a model of deagentivisation, a similar process for the downplaying of the active role of individuals; Bernárdez 2007 for an example of personal agents-avoidance in Icelandic). However, this is also a typological grammatical feature of Arabic, and no culturally significant consequences can be drawn

---

[8] http://www.america.gov/st/usg-russian/2009/January/20090121085901abretnuhC.7421228.html.
[9] http://www.america.gov/st/usg-arabic/2009/January/20090120171001ssissirdileΔ.272097e-02.html.

from it only. Let us then say that, due its grammatical structure Arabic does not use any personal pronouns or possessives in this clause. However, they could have been used but only if special emphasis were to be given to the personal elements in the corresponding instances.

What about Chinese? This is the official translation:[10]

(7) 我感谢布什总统对国家的贡献
wǒ gǎnxiè Bùshé zǒngtǒng duì guójiāde gòngxiàn
I thank Bush president for country-of service

Only one personal pronoun is here used, in accordance to the usual type of expression in Chinese: the first person *wǒ* referring to Obama. Let us remember there is no personal inflexion in Chinese. It is a matter of grammatical typology, of course, but probably one of "grammatical culture" too: personal reference is usually kept to a minimum in Eastern and Southeastern Asian and Oceanic languages, a fact that has also been the object of research, especially in the East. Thus, Suzuki ([1973] 2001: ch. 6) shows how the introduction of the grammatical category "personal pronoun" in Japanese grammars is a consequence of Western grammatical practice, not a "fact" of Japanese. He writes ([1973] 2001: 112):

> It is true that as a rule when a person speaks in English he calls himself "I" and his hearer "you," barring exceptional cases. However, things are completely different in Japanese. For example, in Japan today, when a father talks to his children at home, he very often refers to himself as *Otōsan* 'Father' or *Papa*. He would normally say *Otōsan no iu koto o kiki-nasai* 'Listen to Father' instead of *Boku/Watashi no iu koto o kiki-nasai* 'Listen to me' [. . .]

He further talks of the infrequent use of such supposed "pronouns":

> present-day Japanese first- and second-person personal pronouns, considered more numerous that those of European languages, are actually not used very much. Not only that, there is a definite tendency to avoid their use as often as possible and to carry on conversations using some other words to designate speaker and addressee. (115–116)

This may seem a purely typological feature of Japanese, with no special relation to culture. However, the same phenomenon exists in many other languages in a vast, linguistically varied, geographical area. Samoan, for instance, prefers not to express the agent (in the ergative case), and very frequently the object (in

---

[10] http://www.america.gov/st/usg-chinese/2009/January/20090120132232abretnuh0.422497.html.

the absolutive) is also left out too (Mosel and Hovdhaugen 1992: 700–704). There exists a clear preference toward the avoidance of explicit transitive expressions. This has been connected to cultural factors (Duranti and Ochs 1990). Mosel and Hovdhaugen (1992: 704) offer the following (linguistic) conclusion:

> All A arguments and the S arguments of predicates expressing temporary states of affairs are dispensable without any grammatical restrictions, whereas O can only be omitted if the participant in question has been explicitly referred to in the preceding context.

Similarly in Indonesian (Mintz 1994), Cambodian (Smyth 1995) and Lao (Enfield 2007), it seems to be an issue ultimately analysable in the terms of face and politeness (Brown and Levinson 1987; Bargiela-Chiappini 2003), i.e. a pragmatic issue. But pragmatic issues are undeniably and directly linked to culture. As Field (1998) showed, Navajo prefers to build directives in the future tense or in the imperfective, as it lacks an imperative. This is explained in terms of a particular cultural view of politeness and the notion of face; more precisely, negative politeness: instead of doing something in a polite way, something different is done. In this case, instead of using words like *please* or similar polite expressions, a different strategy is used: uttering something in the future does not imply that it will necessarily happen. Using the imperfective means that the conversation partner might usually do what is uttered. It is just up to the listener to decide whether s/he will carry out the indicated action in the benefit of the speaker. Similarly, Indonesian prefers "inverse-voice" forms instead of an imperative:

(8) *di-beli   buku*
    INV-buy book
    'a book [someone] buys'

is preferred to

(9) *mem-beli   buku*
    TRANS-buy book
    'you/I/he etc buy a book; buy a book!'

Where do these examples lead to? Both topics are clearly related from a cultural point of view, and they have similar implications for translation, be it "natural" or not. In these – and many other – languages, the full expression of personal pronouns is avoided whenever possible. This goes together with the avoidance of expression of personal agents and frequently also addressees. A sentence may not need to establish any clear personal references, and personal pronouns may – or have to, or tend to – be absent. Two main reasons may be at play: (i) as a consequence of the particular forms adopted by the notions of face and politeness in individual cultures, and their corresponding values, marking in a clear way the persons involved in an activity may seem inappropriate; (ii) for much the same reasons, the use of the personal pronouns is very restricted and can even be a taboo in certain circumstances; these personal pronouns may include socially and culturally marked combinations of features, e.g. in Indonesian, a special "2nd person pronoun" – if we insist in terming it "personal pronoun" – is used only in reference to an elderly lady of higher social class than the speaker who has made her pilgrimage to Mecca; in Japanese *boku* 'I' can only be used among equals in informal situations and exclusively by males.

That the situation is completely different from that in the Western languages can be easily seen: first, Suzuki comments on how grammarians introduced the category of Personal Pronouns in Japanese grammars in order to follow a western trend ([1973] 2001: 111–112). He writes that he has spoken out against the "European" analysis of pronouns as applied to Japanese, arguing that

> the classification of *watakushi/anata, boku/kimi*, etc., as personal pronouns was the result of blindly accepting analyses derived from the studies of other languages [. . .] which are structurally different from Japanese [. . .]. Such classification is highly vulnerable to error, and I contend that it is in fact wrong, since it is incongruent with the linguistic facts in Japanese. (112)

In a recent paper, Chan (2009) shows the process of integration of some new 3rd person pronouns in Chinese directly under the influence of English; specifically, *through translations from English*. Lacking genders, Chinese had – and has – a single third person pronoun, *tā*, plural *tāmen* (respectively 他/ 他們). The character includes the "key" 人 'human being' as the left-most element in the *tā* pronoun. In order to assimilate Chinese to the gender categories of English personal pronouns, a feminine and a neuter were created, and the original one, which was completely gender-less, was re-interpreted as a masculine. Thus, 他/ 他們 came to be used to translate English *he* and *they* (in this case, including a masculine feature alien to the English pronoun). For English *she*, a new key was used: the one referring to female beings, 女, although the pronunciation is exactly the same, but the writing is now different: 她/她們. The same holds for the neuter *it*, now written as 它/ 它們 or 牠 / 牠們.

Translation, then, gave birth to distinctions that had did not exist before and are valid only for the written language. More than translation, however, it was the cultural conveniences of the translator, who viewed gender differences as essential, that lead to this peculiar development. Also other aspects of western grammars were introduced into Chinese in order to "Europeanize" the language. Chan (2009: 1) mentions such innovations as "the lengthening and complication of sentences due to the increased use of pronominal modifiers, embedded structures, passive voice, and conjunctions". One could say that, seeing Chinese so culturally alien to the western languages, translators tried to approximate it to their own "civilised language structures" (these words are not Chan's), at the same time erasing certain linguistic and cultural features of the TL, i.e. Chinese. In the long run, these changes through translation from a SL can indeed alter the grammar of the TL in a permanent way.

The essential question is this: what can the translator do if there is a culture-based or culture-laden grammatically based difference in SL and TL? This question is not frequently asked, as the sociocultural character of some linguistic phenomena is simply left out of the picture, as something belonging to the idiosyncrasy of languages. Thus, the Japanese, Chinese, Cambodian, Samoan or Indonesian lack of personal pronouns and, even more, their preference for not marking transitive actors in a clear way is simply left aside by translators, as keeping it in the TL would bring about a form of expression felt to be too alien to the readers of the TL.[11] The absence of pronouns in contemporary Chinese is simply defined as "colloquial" by Ramírez Bellerín (2004: 119–120), and he draws no cultural conclusions from his very well done review of the history of such pronouns. By the way, the mere fact that in Chinese, as in Japanese and other languages, the personal pronouns are relatively recent, points to their dependence on historical, sociocultural development. Enfield (2007) offers an in-depth analysis of this and related topics from a typological, cognitive and linguistic stance.

We can offer no solution to the translation difficulties posed by the facts just examined. Our aim here is just to introduce the problems and call attention to them. It is clear that at the level of the lexicon much care has to be taken because different words imply different cultural contents; the same is not usually the case when grammatical phenomena are dealt with. Our opinion is that the translator has to be very conscious of their cultural implications and act "accordingly" (although we have to confess that we do not know exactly what "accordingly" might mean in this context). Translators usually take great care not to "betray" the cultural elements in the SL, but this only seldom

---

11 Venuti (1995) speaks of the invisibility of the translator, especially in Anglo-American culture: in order to avoid cultural clash, translations are frequently "disguised" as if they were originally English, also by avoiding any visible reference to a translator, and the contents are expected to be subjected to some kind of cultural "anglicisation".

extends to such culture-laden elements we have – much too briefly – sketched here. If one translates these languages providing all the information left out in the original text (who exactly did what, for instance), can that translation be equivalent to the original? Probably yes, but it may be betraying some important elements of the TL culture.

4 The levelling out of cultural elements

As has been said above, in Cognitive Linguistics the tendency exists to see everything in cognitive, individual terms only, with no reference to culture. The differences we have analysed could therefore be seen as differences in conceptualisation and, in principle, such differences need not be respected. This can lead to a "globalisation" of language – as in the case of the new gender-marked Chinese pronouns – and, if they are in fact not only or primarily cognitive, but essentially cultural, it leads to the levelling out of cultural distinctions and to very much feared globalisation of culture or, as Warnier (2003) prefers to term it, the *mondialisation* of culture, where cultural idiosyncrasy could disappear in favour of some dominant culture (he is not unduly pessimistic, however; he writes "l'humanité est une machine à créer de la difference" [humanity is machine for the creation of difference], 103). Or it can lead to *cultural castration*: Brems (2010: 232) shows how Paul de Man

> weakens the political stance of the novel by tampering with its style. By translating this Dutch novel into French, De Man not only performs a "cultural castration": loosening the ties between language and national character De Pillecyn [the author of the novel. EB] thought to be crucial. [. . .]. But De Man also performs a stylistic castration, loosening the ties between the content and the form of the original novel, working together towards a totalitarian discourse.

De Pillecyn was, on the other hand, extremely conscious of the cultural differences between French and Dutch and it is in this sense that he refers to castration (*ontmanning*); the following is an excerpt from an article he published in the Flemish Newspaper *Het Laatste Nieuws*, June 3, 1942:

> Omdat de taal de uitspraak is van de ziel. [. . .] wij voelen des te beter hoe onze taal, de uitspreekbaarheid van onzen geest en van ons gemoed, en dus van onze kultuur, aan ons volksbestaan verbonden is. [. . .] Het is een kwestie van kultureele vruchtbaarheid of kultureele ontmanning.

> [Because the language is the expression of the soul [. . .] we feel all the better how our language, the expressiveness of our mind and our heart, and hence of our culture, is linked to our people. [. . .] It is a matter of cultural fertility or cultural castration. (In Brems 2010: 231).]

The topic, however, is far from understood. Scalise Sugiyama (2003) studies the effect of the Tiv translation of Shakespeare's *Hamlet* and tends to demote the importance of the effects of cultural differences, as the psychological values of the original are still recognisable and understood – more exactly, felt – by a Tiv audience, in spite of the vast cultural differences. Scalise Sugiyama sees that possibility as the essential similarity of all human minds.

Even if Scalise Sugiyama's theoretical approach – adaptationism, also called evolutionary psychology – is very debatable indeed, her results clearly merit further attention. We can feel moved by a Chinese story, for instance, even if we are unable to understand the many cultural implications in it. But of course, is what we understand the same that any Chinese person would capture? Certainly not. This type of equivalence should have to be researched in detail, something we cannot do here.

5 Cultural domains, not "culture"

A last topic that will be analysed here is the extent or scope of "culture". From what has been said, it should be clear by now that one cannot refer to "culture" as it were a single, unitary, systematic, self-contained domain. There can exist Chinese, English, German, Japanese etc. cultures. But only particular cultural domains that may be seen as integrating what we incorrectly term "X culture". Bourdieu's view of culture as sets of *habitus* shared by a number of individuals can serve as a basis for this distinction. We cannot expect all the Chinese to share all the *habitus* that can be recognised theoretically as part of "Chinese culture". These *habitus* belong to different domains and it is these smaller-scale domains that have to be the object of our research.

Differences in everything cultural are everywhere, even in places where they might seem improbable. This could be expected to be the case of translating the classical Yiddish writer, Sholem Aleychem into Hebrew (Waldinger 2006) or African French literature into African languages (Yetunde 2008). Although Waldinger's paper is interested in the history of Sholem Aleychem's translations, the problem of the cultural, contextual divergences is clearly seen in its pages. Yiddish and Hebrew are both Jewish languages and both belong to Jewish culture in very wide terms; but they represent particular varieties of that Jewish "macro-culture". Translation has therefore to face problems derived from those cultural differences. As to Yetunde's paper, it emphasises certain linguistic+cultural differences between the French-African novelist Ahmadou Kourouma, himself a Malinke from Ivory Coast, and the translation of his novel in the Yoruba spoken in Nigeria. Both countries and languages are in the Northern Part of the Gulf of

Guinea and both belong to what is frequently called "Western African Culture". In spite of the many commonalities that indeed exist, translation is far from straightforward, also from the cultural and cultural-linguistic points of view.

5.1 Problems in translating particular cultural domains

Let us take a very short poem by the American poet, Randall Jarrell.

(10) *The Death of the Ball Turret Gunner*
From my mother's sleep I fell into the State,
And I hunched in its belly till my wet fur froze.
Six miles from earth, loosed from its dream of life,
I woke to black flak and the nightmare fighters.
When I died they washed me out of the turret with a hose.

An adequate understanding implies the knowledge of a very small part of 20th c. American culture: the vocabulary and language of war in the air; more precisely, the structure and missions of heavy bombers during World War II. Without that cultural knowledge, the second line *I hunched in its belly till my wet fur froze* would not be understandable, nor could the last one be adequately interpreted. What is a *ball turret*? How were "life" and "death" within one of them? Why is the verb *hunch* used? Why is a hose needed on a dead man in a ball turret? If understanding is being able to create a mental image of what happened, can an average reader understand the text? And if this poem were translated into another language?

This poem was translated into Spanish in the following way in the web page [poemaseningles. blogspot.com/2005_07_01_archive.html]

(11) *La muerte del artillero de la cúpula blindada*
Desde el sueño de mi madre caí en el Estado,
y me encorvé en su vientre hasta que mi mojada piel se heló.
A seis millas de tierra, separado de su sueño de vida,
me desperté ante una negra barrera antiaérea y la pesadilla de los cazas.
Cuando morí me lavaron de la torreta con una manguera.

Obviously, the second line has not been understood and the last line does not have any clear meaning. Also the title is wrong: a *ball turret* is not a *cúpula blindada* ('armoured turret'). The translator failed to know that a ball turret is a round machine-gun turret under the *belly* of a bomber plane, whose gunner, necessarily of small size, has to crouch, hunch inside it because there is very little room: in a way he was just like a fetus inside his mother's womb. If he is killed there, as was frequently the case, by German 20 mm, even 30 mm shells, he would be literally torn to fragments and a hose would be the best instrument to clean the remains of the turret and recover the gunner's pieces.

The translator has to understand the cultural domain reflected in this poem and in the SL, and then use words and expressions that might allow readers to acquire and/or recover that particular domain in their own TL. The interpretation would also be different. In the original, *hunch* and *belly* serve to make a blend of *mother* and *bomber plane*: the gunner hunches in the plane's belly as he hunched in his mother's belly many years ago. But the gunner's heavy clothes froze – something that does not belong to the mother's space, but the bomber's. If the translator is not "fluent" in the cultural domain at work here, translation will be impossible.

6 Conclusions

We have tried to introduce a number of points which may integrate a coherent theory of culture-in-language and its implications for translation. The following points have been seen as especially significant.

Cultural elements are everywhere in language and translators have to be very conscious of it; they exist at every level, from words (but also phonemes) to whole texts. It is not a matter of whether culture has or does not have any presence in a certain linguistic element, but to what degree is culture visible and identifiable in any element. Also metaphor, metonymy and other "rhetoric figures" or "cognitive operations" have to be primarily approached as cultural, even when dealing with supposedly universal concepts such as "primary metaphors". It can be said that the cultural character of everything in language should work as the default case and that the absence of anything cultural has to be seen as hypothetical and a non-cultural explanation should be tried before defining anything as culture-free or universal.

It may be expected that cultural and historical differences exist among languages in apparently similar metaphorical mappings; these differences can vary quite widely but, among other things, the *sociocultural values* assigned to the mappings may vary, as well as the degree of *fossilization* of metaphors. Also metaphors may include whole cultural domains whose scope and extent may differ significantly among languages, in such a way that in L_i metaphor (or metonymy, etc.) X affects only one tiny domain, whereas the corresponding metaphor in L_j may affect a much larger one. This is of extreme significance for translation. Also the frequency of a certain metaphor in different languages may differ greatly: for any two languages, *metaphor use* in general, or in individual metaphorical mappings, can be completely different.

A basic point to be taken into account is the integrity of the (literal or figurative) sense of words, metaphors etc., in the *conditions of real use*. Isolated words, metaphors etc. cannot be analysed if real insights into their cultural component are to be found. A part of the meaning of a word or metaphor cannot be used as if it were "its whole" meaning: differences will probably be somewhere in the fringes. Also culture is to be found in use, in interaction, not in abstract, ideal cognitive constructs. Bourdieu's *Practical Reason* has to have primacy on *Theoretical Reason*; i.e. real use must always be given preference over the interests of the theory one is trying to develop or justify.

Cultural elements are also visible in grammatical structures *in use*, secondarily in their paradigmatic forms. Although nowadays it may seem impossible to say which elements in grammar are most liable to show cultural elements or bases, research shows that culture may reach much farther than was thought.

Finally, culture must not been seen as a single general, overall, unitary reality but as a set of sets of *habitus*, i.e. of forms acting in practice. Different cultural domains have to be distinguished and it is within these domains that translators have to take their decisions. Translators have to be very conscious of the pervasiveness of culture, even in areas frequently considered to be free of it. They will have to take their translation decisions in this overall belief of the constant present of culture. In a cognitive approach to language and translation the importance of this view cannot be underestimated.

Putting language in direct relation to cognition without the intermediary of culture can lead to unsolvable problems. Núñez and Sweetser (2006) analyse the "culture-specific" Aymara conceptualisation of time as "future is behind, past is in front". Even if this interpretation were right, the problem arises of why has such a "culture-specific" form of conceptualisation come into being. Nothing at all is said in this respect, and the cultural specificity of this feature in Aymara culture is not explained in any way. Maybe an analysis of Aymara culture, which is not carried out in the paper, could help us, also by putting it in relation with other "culture-specific" conceptualisations. Pinxten (1995) did precisely that for the conceptualisation of time among the Navajo: he studied a number of elements of culture, their linguistic representations, and from them got to the conceptualisation; something similar is done by Hurtado de Mendoza (2002) for Quechua, where temporal expressions are similar to those of Aymara; both languages, moreover, are spoken in adjacent, partially coincident areas. It is a pity works like these (and many others in the same tenor) were not taken into account when writing Núñez and Sweetser (2006).

From the translatological point of view, the main teaching we might draw is that in areas such as metaphor, metonymy, conceptualisation of more or less complex concepts, etc., the translator has to be on the alert: even if a metaphor seems to exist in both the source and the target languages, its scope and cultural value can be radically different. And in cases as the one just mentioned, may be translating from Aymara into Spanish – or from Navajo into English, Chinese or whatever – requires that attention be paid to the cultural bases of the conceptualisation of time and its significance in the text; that is, such conceptualsation can be one of those elements in the source language which simply cannot be ignored. Assuming *a priori* the universality of processes, concepts, etc., is a serious danger for translators.

References

Alexandropoulou Panagiota, Duygo F. Taştan and Ana Zeljko 2011 *Metaphors*. Manuscript, Universidad Complutense, Madrid.
Álvarez de la Fuente, Esther 2007 *Análisis lingüístico de la traducción natural: datos de producción de dos niños gemelos bilingües inglés/español*. PhD dissertation, Universidad de Valladolid, Spain.
Bargiela-Chiappini, Francesca 2003 Face and politeness: New (insights) for old (concepts). *Journal of Pragmatics* 35: 1453–1469.
Bartmiński, Jerzy 2009 *Aspects of cognitive ethnolinguistics*. Edited by J. Zinken, translated by A. Głaz. London: Equinox.
Bernárdez, Enrique 1997 A partial synergetic model of deagentivisation. *Journal of Quantitative Linguistics* 4: 53–66.
Bernárdez, Enrique 2001 Cultural determination of cause-effect: On a possible folk model of causation. *Círculo de Lingüística Aplicada a la Comunicación* 6. Available at: http://independientemente/info/circulo/no6/bernardez.pdf.
Bernárdez, Enrique 2004 Intimate enemies? On the relations between language and culture. In: Augusto S. da Silva, Amadeo Torres and Miguel Gonçalves (eds.), *Linguagem, Cultura e Cognição: Estudos de Linguística Cognitiva*, Vol. 1, 21–46. Coimbra, Portugal: Almedina.
Bernárdez, Enrique 2007 The UNCONSCIOUS, IRRESPONSIBLE CONSTRUCTION in Modern Icelandic. In Chris S. Butler, Raquel Hidalgo Downing and Julia Lavid (eds.), *Functional perspectives on grammar and discourse*, 149–164. Amsterdam: John Benjamins.
Bernárdez, Enrique 2008 *El lenguaje como cultura*. Madrid: Alianza.
Bernárdez, Enrique 2009 Comparaciones explícitas con wie en *Der Mann ohne Eigenschaften* de Robert Musil. Una aproximación cognitiva. *Cuadernos de Filología Alemana* Anejo I: 57–71.
Bowdle, Brian F. and Dedre Gentner 2005 The career of metaphor. *Psychological Review* 112.1: 193–216.
Brandt, Line and Per Aage Brandt 2005 Making sense of a blend: A cognitive-semiotic approach to metaphor. *Annual Review of Cognitive Linguistics* 3: 216–249.
Braz, Adelino 2006 L'intraduisible en question: l'étude de la *saudade*. *Revue des Littératures de l'Union Européenne* 4: 101–121.

Brems, Elke 2010 A case of "cultural castration"? Paul de Man's translation of *De Soldaat Johan* by Filip de Pillecyn. *Target* 22.2: 212–236.
Brown, Penelope and Stephen Levinson 1987 *Politeness: Some universals in language usage.* Cambridge: Cambridge University Press.
Bybee, Joan 2010 *Language, use and cognition.* Cambridge: Cambridge University Press.
Chan Ho-yan, Clara 2009 Third person pronouns in indigenous Chinese texts and translated Chinese texts: The westernization of modern written Chinese. *New Voices in Translation Studies* 5: 1–15.
Dizionario Garzanti della lingua italiana. 1969 Milan, Italy: Garzanti.
Dobrzyńska, Teresa 1995 Translating metaphor: Problems of meaning. *Journal of Pragmatics* 24: 595–604.
Duranti, Alessandro and Elinor Ochs 1990 Genitive constructions and agency in Samoan discourse. *Studies in Language* 14: 1–23.
Enfield, Nick J. (ed.) 2002a *Ethnosyntax: Explorations in grammar and culture.* Oxford: Oxford University Press.
Enfield, Nick J. 2002b Ethnosyntax: Introduction. In: Nick Enfield (ed.), *Ethnosyntax: Explorations in grammar and culture*, 3–30. Oxford: Oxford University Press.
Enfield, Nick J. 2007 Meanings of the unmarked: How "default" person reference does more than just refer. In: Nick Enfield and Tanya Stivers (eds.), *Person reference in interaction: Linguistic, cultural, and social perspectives*, 97–120. Cambridge: Cambridge University Press.
Euripides *Medea* 431 b.C. *Medea.* Available at: http://www.mikrosapoplous.gr/eyripedes/medea/medeax3.htm632-633. English translation by E. P. Coleridge, available at: http://ancienthistory.about.com/gi/o.htm?zi=1/XJ&zTi=1&sdn=ancienthistory&cdn=education&tm=15&f=00&tt=14&bt=0&bts=0&zu=http%3A//classics.mit.edu/Euripides/medea.html.
Field, Margaret 1998 Politeness and indirection in Navajo directives. *Southwest Journal of Linguistics* 17.2: 23–33.
Frank, Roslyn M., René Dirven, Tom Ziemke and Enrique Bernárdez (eds.) 2008 *Body, language and mind.* Vol. 2, *Sociocultural situatedness.* Berlin: Mouton de Gruyter.
Gómez Hurtado, M. Isabel 2007 Traducir: ¿capacidad innata o destreza adquirible? *Quaderns. Revista de traducció* 14: 139–153.
Harris, Brian 1977 The importance of natural translation. *Working Papers on Translatology 2.* Ottawa, ON: University of Ottawa Press.
Harris, Brian 2008 *An annotated chronological bibliography of a century of natural translation studies. 1908–2008.* Manuscript, Universidad de Valladolid, Spain.
Harris, Brian n.d. *Brian Harris on native translation.* Available at: http://www.translationadvisor.com/native-translation.html.
Hurtado de Mendoza S., William 2002 *Pragmática de la cultura y la lengua quechua.* Quito, Ecuador: Abya Yala.
Hymes, Dell H. (ed.) 1964 *Language in culture and society: A reader in linguistics and anthropology.* New York: Harper and Row.
Ibarretxe-Antuñano, Iraide 2008 Vision metaphors for the intellect: Are they really crosslinguistic? *Atlantis. Journal of the Spanish Association of Anglo-American Studies* 30.1: 15–33.
Johnson, Samuel [1843] 1994 *Dictionary of the English Language.* Edited by Alexander Chalmers. London: Studio Editions.

Kristiansen, Gitte and René Dirven (eds.) 2008 *Cognitive sociolinguistics: Language variation, cultural models, social systems*. Berlin: Mouton de Gruyter.
Levinson, Stephen C. 2003 *Space in language and cognition: Explorations in cognitive diversity*. Cambridge: Cambridge University Press.
Lozès-Lawani, Christiane 1994 *La traduction naturelle chez des enfants Fon de la République de Bénin*. Master's Thesis in Translation, Université d'Ottawa.
Lucretius *De rerum natura* 1st century b.C. Available at: http://www.intratext.com/IXT/LAT0019/. English translation by W. E. Leonard, available at: http://onlinebooks.library.upern.edu/webbin/gutbook/lookup?num=785.
Lu Ji 2010 *Wen Fu. Prosopoema del arte de la escritura*. Bilingual edition of Pilar González España. Madrid: Cátedra.
Maalouf, Amin 1983 *Les croisades vues par les Arabes*. Paris: Éditions Jean-Claude Lattès.
Mateos, Fernando, Miguel Otegui and Ignacio Arrizabalaga 1977 *Diccionario español de la lengua china*. Madrid: Espasa-Calpe.
Miller, Flagg 2008 Al-Qaṣida as a "pragmatic base": Contributions of area studies to sociolinguistics. *Language and Communication* 28: 386–408.
Mintz, Malcolm W. 1994 *A student's grammar of Malay and Indonesian*. Singapore: EFB Publishers.
Mosel, Ulrike and Even Hovdhaugen 1992 *Samoan reference grammar*. Oslo: Scandinavian University Press.
Núñez, Rafael E. and Eve Sweetser 2006 With the future behind them: Convergent evidence from Aymara language and gesture in the crosslinguistic comparison of spatial construals of time. *Cognitive Science* 30 1–49.
Oluwafisan, Yetunde 2008 Translating francophone African literature into an African language: An experience. *Babel: International Journal of Translation* 54.1: 59–68.
Pagán Cánovas, Cristóbal 2008 The arrows of love: A family of blending networks for love causation in poetry. Paper presented at the 6th AELCO/SCOLA Conference, Castelón, Spain, October 22–24, 2006.
Pagán Cánovas, Cristóbal 2011 The genesis of the arrows of love: Diachronic conceptual integration in Greek mythology. *American Journal of Philology* 132.4: 553–579.
Palmer, Gary B. 1994 *Towards a theory of cultural linguistics*. Austin: University of Texas Press.
Pinxten, Rik 1995 Comparing time and temporality in cultures. *Cultural Dynamics* 7: 233–252.
Pinxten, Rik and Koenraad de Munter 2006 *De Culturele Eeuw* [The cultural century]. Antwerp, Belgium: Houtekiet.
Ponzio, Augusto 2008 *Linguaggio, lavoro e mercato globale. Rileggendo Rossi-Landi*. Milan, Italy: Mimesis.
Ramírez Bellerín, Laureano 2004 *Manual de traducción chino-castellano*. Barcelona: Gedisa.
Rossi-Landi, Ferruccio 1968 *Il linguaggio come lavoro e come mercato*. Milan, Italy: Bompiani.
Scalise Sugiyama, Michelle 2003 Cultural variation is part of human nature: Literary universals, context-sensitivity, and "Shakespeare in the bush". *Human Nature* 14.4: 383–396
Schäffner, Christina 2004 Metaphor and translation: Some implications of a cognitive approach. *Journal of Pragmatics* 36: 1253–1269.
Sinha, Vera da Silva, Chris Sinha, Wany Sampaio and Jörg Zinken 2012 Event-based intervals in an Amazonian culture. In: Luna Filipović and Kasia M. Jaszczolt (eds.), *Space and Time across languages and cultures*. Vol. 2, *Language, culture and cognition*, 15–35. Amsterdam: John Benjamins.
Smyth, David 1995 *Colloquial Cambodian*. London: Routledge.

Steen, Gerard 2008 The paradox of metaphor: Why we need a three-dimensional model of metaphor. *Metaphor and Symbol* 23: 213–241.
Suzuki, Takao [1973] 2001 *Words in context: A Japanese perspective on language and culture*. Translated by Akira Miura. Tokyo: Kodansha.
Sweetser, Eve 1995 Metaphor, mythology, and everyday language. *Journal of Pragmatics* 24: 585–593.
Venuti, Lawrence 1995 *The translator's invisibility*. London: Routledge.
Waldinger, Albert 2006 Sholem Aleichem in Tel Aviv: Classic Yiddish fiction in Hebrew. *Babel: International Journal of Translation* 52.2: 101–123.
Warnier, Jean-Pierre 2003 *La mondialisation de la culture*. New edition. Paris: Éditions La Découverte.
Wierzbicka, Anna [1991] 2003 *Cross-cultural pragmatics: The semantics of human interaction*. Berlin: Mouton de Gruyter.
Wierzbicka, Anna 1997 *Understanding cultures through their key words: English, Russian, Polish, German, Japanese*. New York: Oxford University Press.
Yang, Yanning 2008 Typological interpretation of differences between Chinese and English in grammatical metaphor. *Language Sciences* 30: 450–478.
Zhang Huaijin 1984 *Wen fu yizhu* (Comments and notes to Wen Fu). Beijing: Beijing Chubanshe.
Zinken, Jörg 2004 Metaphors, stereotypes, and the linguistic picture of the world: Impulses from the Ethnolinguistic School of Lublin. *Metaphorik.de* 7: 115–136.

Farzad Sharifian and Maryam Jamarani
Cultural conceptualisations and translating political discourse

1 Introduction

The political events of the last three decades in Iran have attracted significant attention from the international media. Issues of interest have included the 1979 Islamic Revolution, the subsequent engagement of the country in the eight-year war with Iraq, and more recently the nuclear issue, particularly the allegation from the West that Iran is developing potential "weapons of mass destruction" (e.g. Cordesman and Seitz 2006).

In early October 2008 the Australian prime minister, Kevin Rudd, called for the Iranian president, Mahmoud Ahmadinejad, to be brought before the International Court of Justice to face charges of "inciting genocide" for his comments against Israel. In fact, as argued by Sharifian (2009) the information on which the Australian prime minister based this call was mostly an artefact of mistranslation. This example shows how the role of language and specifically the translation from Persian to English and vice versa can play a critical role in geopolitical relations. In fact, as maintained by Schäffner, "any political action is prepared, accompanied, controlled, and influenced by language" (2001b: 201).

Some politicians (most recently the Russian foreign minister) have speculated that the escalating tensions between the West and Iran over the latter's nuclear program is likely to lead to "jihad", a "clash of civilizations", "World War III" or a "Nuclear Holocaust". Beeman (2005) strongly maintains that the conflict between Iran and the US is largely a result of the two countries demonizing each other through political discourse. He maintains that "the mode of communication [between Iran and the US], which is of a mutual demonization nature, is endemic to the 'cultural dynamics' of the relations between the two nations" (Beeman 2005: xii).

Politics involves clarifying as well as obscuring the concepts that are central to political discourse (Arnold 2005). Often politicians engage in lengthy debates about what they actually meant by their statements. That language can be used vaguely enough to create room for alternative interpretations seems to be convenient for politicians. The issue becomes more complicated when political statements from non-English languages are reported in English-based international media (Cohen 2001). Political expressions translated into English lose their socio-cultural "baggage", taking on new connotations that are relevant to the English speaking world's doctrines and traditions (Cohen 1997) but which may have been absent in the source language.

This chapter seeks to highlight some of the complexities involved in translating key concepts in international politics. By examining how concepts such as *"concession"*, *"compromise"* and *"jihad"* may be rendered into Persian, the chapter shows how these culturally constructed concepts take their meaning from the socio-political contexts in which they are used. It is also argued how semantic shift or expansion associated with these terms over a period of time can be socio-politically motivated. The chapter further touches upon the politics and translation of metaphor in international politics.

2 Cultural Linguistics and (translating) political discourse

The role of language in international negotiation cannot be overestimated. The process of negotiation largely involves clarifying certain concepts and coming to a consensus over the understanding and use of certain terms. Cohen observes that:

> When negotiation takes place across languages and cultures the scope for misunderstanding increases. So much of negotiation involves arguments about words and concepts that it cannot be assumed that language is secondary and all that "really" counts is the "objective" issues at stake. (Cohen 2001: 67)

The above observation calls for an approach to the analysis of political discourse that is grounded in a close examination of words and concepts from both a linguistic and a cultural perspective. This lies at the heart of *Cultural Linguistics* (Palmer 1996; Sharifian 2011, 2012), an interdisciplinary area that draws on the analytical tools of several disciplines including Cognitive Linguistics and cognitive anthropology. Cultural Linguistics shares with Cognitive Linguistics the premise that language is grounded in human conceptualisation, but it places a particular emphasis on the *cultural* nature of conceptualisations. In line with cognitive anthropology, Cultural Linguistics views culture as primarily a cognitive phenomenon (e.g. D'Andrade 1995; Holland and Quinn 1987; Kronenfeld 2011).

The main analytical notions employed by a majority of cognitive linguists are "schema", "category" and "conceptual metaphor/metonymy". Cognitive anthropologists, on the other hand, have been exploring human cultural systems using the notions of "cultural schema" and "cultural model". Cultural Linguistics employs the analytical tools of these two disciplines and then extends its theoretical basis within the framework of language and cultural cognition (Sharifian 2011). Cultural Linguistics explores features of human languages as an index to underlying cultural schemas, categories, and metaphors, collectively referred to as *cultural conceptualisations* (Sharifian 2003, 2011).

Cultural conceptualisations are not fixed templates for guiding thought and behaviour but rather are constantly negotiated across time and space among the members of the relevant cultural group. A good example is the development of the word *jihad* in the Iranian conceptualisation, which we will elaborate on later in this chapter.

One area in which Cultural Linguistics can make significant contributions is political discourse analysis including the translation of political discourse. When people attempt to translate from one language into another, such as for the purpose of international negotiation (see also Baker 2006; Cohen 1997; Hatim and Mason 1990), they are very likely to be rendering cultural conceptualisations associated with one language to those associated with another. In other words, if languages encode the ways in which their speakers conceptualise their experiences, which are largely cultural in nature, then the process of translation will find it hard to avoid rendering sets of words in ways that capture different conceptualisations of experience (see Avruch and Wang 2005). As Cohen (2001: 69) states, "Words and their translations are not just interchangeable labels denoting some given, immutable feature of the world but keys opening the door on to different *configurations* of the world" [emphasis added]. It is worth noting that words, as well as the conceptualisations that they instantiate, may also take on connotations from the socio-political environments in which they are used. That is, apart from the effect of culture on our conceptualisations of experiences, which are captured by the semantic and pragmatic aspects of human languages, words may also be influenced by the socio-political contexts in which they are employed. In the following sections we present an analysis of some key words in international politics from a cultural linguistic perspective.

3 Concession and compromise

Two words pivotal to international negotiation are *concession* and *compromise*. Cohen notes that "compromise and concession are inseparable from negotiating in the English-speaking world" and argues that equivalents for these terms are absent in Arabic, Persian and Turkish (2001: 81). However, in supporting his contention he mainly focuses on Arabic and Turkish. In this section we will briefly examine the recent trends in the use of these concepts in English in the context of international negotiation and will then present an analysis of attempts to translate these terms into Persian.

The *Oxford Advanced Learner's Dictionary* defines *concession* as "something that you allow or do, or allow to have, in order to end an argument or to make a situation less difficult". The following statement gives an example of the usage of the word *concession* in this sense:

(1) *The Left has made great concessions: abandoning any semblance of seeking abortion on demand, acceding to all sorts of limits on abortion rights in the 37 years since /Roe v. Wade/ became law*[1]

It should be noted that in contemporary English the conceptualisation captured by the word *concession* provides a culturally constructed *schema* which places an individual, or a party, in control of affairs and gives them the authority to grant certain rights to others, even when this action could be construed as detrimental to their cause, a sign of weakness, or even a loss for their side. If, however, the authority or frame of reference for the course of action proposed is believed to derive from a divine source, then any degree of *concession* may be conceptualised as "morally untenable" or even "sacrilege".

The *Aryanpour English-Persian Dictionary*, which is one of the most reliable bilingual dictionaries, translates *concession* into Persian as *emtiâz* 'advantage', *emtiâz-e enhesâri* 'exclusive advantage' and *e'tâ* 'grant, donate'. The following are examples of how these words may be used in Persian:

(2) *In   moâmeleh   barâyeh   ânha   yek   emtiâz*
    This   deal   for   them   one   advantage
    mahsoub-mishavad
    counts
    'This deal counts as an advantage for them'

(3) *Ou   zamin-hâ-yeh khod   râ   beh   mardom*
    S/he   land-PL-POSS   his/her   DO.marker to   people
    e'tâ kard
    grant.PAST
    'S/he granted/donated his/her to people'

Clearly the definition of *concession* provided by the *Oxford Advanced Learner's Dictionary* is not reflected in its entirety in the Persian translations. Rather,

---

[1] http://www.usnews.com/blogs/erbe/2009/05/18/liberals-have-made-abortion-concessions-now-conservatives-must-give-ground-too.html "Liberals Have Made Abortion Concessions, Now Conservatives Must Give Ground Too." By Bonnie Erbe, posted on May 18 2009.

the renderings in Persian suggest 'granting an advantage' without providing any rationalization for the action such as is found in English, 'to end an argument or to make a situation less difficult'. It might be suggested that the solution to the absence of a translation equivalent is to translate the word *concession* into a sentence. However, the very core conceptualisation that is captured by the English word *concession* would appear negative in contexts where the basis for the action is predetermined by religious precepts. Thus, no matter whether one translates terms such as *concession* into Persian as a single word, a paraphrase or a sentence, they would still be negatively construed if what one is allowing another party or person to have or to do would be in conflict with one's religious beliefs.

Turning to the case of *compromise*, the *Merriam-Webster Dictionary* defines the term as:

n. 1a: settlement of differences by arbitration or by consent reached by mutual concessions
b: something intermediate between or blending qualities of two different things

2: a concession to something derogatory or prejudicial
<a compromise of principles> v. transitive senses

1 obsolete: to bind by mutual agreement

2: to adjust or settle by mutual concessions

3a: to expose to suspicion, discredit, or mischief
b: to reveal or expose to an unauthorized person and especially to an enemy
<confidential information was compromised>
c: to cause the impairment of <a compromised immune system>
<a seriously compromised patient> v. intransitive senses

1a: to come to agreement by mutual concession
b: to find or follow away between extremes

2: to make a shameful or disreputable concession
<wouldn't compromise with their principle>

The word *compromise* is translated by the *Aryanpour Dictionary* into Persian as *tarâzi* 'balance', *mosâleheh* 'settlement', *tavâfogh* 'agreement' and *tasvieh kardan* 'to clear (e.g. an account)'. It can be seen that the Persian translations mainly capture the 'settlement' and 'agreement' components of *compromise* without implying the intended mutual concession outcome. The rendering of *compromise* into *tasvieh kardan* 'to clear' does not seem to correspond to any of the senses of the English word *compromise*. The verb *tasvieh kardan* in Persian, usually used in the phrase *hesâb tasvieh kardan* (a: to settle account, b: to revenge), implies a sense of 'cutting a relation/negotiation process' and/or 'revenge', particularly when it is used in conflict situations.

The argument here needs to move beyond the problem of a language not having a particular word or concept. The real issue is how the conceptualisation indexed by a word is perceived by the speakers of the language in a particular context. As previously shown, when the moral principles guiding a specific course of action are rooted in an absolute belief system, such as that of religion, then any "giving up" maybe construed as "turning one's back" on the belief system in question. In particular, when a government is guided by a shared belief that its motivations are divinely grounded, it would seem only natural for any decision made by government officials to reflect the underlying religious component that is the basis for moral principles. Therefore, any *concession* in such a context may be construed as "deviation" from divine prescription.

It is noteworthy that the meanings associated with the contemporary usage of the word *compromise* in American English range from a rather positive one to ones that are, from the Western perspective, clearly negative. However, the *Oxford English Dictionary* (first and second editions) provides seven major meanings for *compromise* as a noun, out of which only the last one carries a negative valence in Western varieties of English. This is where *compromise* is defined as "a putting in peril or hazard, endangering, exposure to risk or suspicion". The other meanings generally suggest mutual concession without implying that the act could incur any negative consequences, as interpreted from a Western secular perspective. These definitions appear to recognize the rights of both parties involved in a situation as having equal value.

The results of a comparison between the above mentioned entries in the *Oxford English Dictionary* and those in the current version of the *Merriam-Webster Online Dictionary* suggest that there has been a semantic extension of the meanings associated with *compromise* in the direction of negative realisations. Also, a comparison of the entry for *compromise* in the third edition of the *Oxford Advanced Learner's Dictionary* with that of the seventh edition reveals that the latter has an additional meaning of "compromise (on sth.): to do something that is against your principles or does not reach the standards that you have set". This is clearly a negative meaning, which is absent in the earlier version of the dictionary. The positive connotations of *compromise* hearken back to the secular foundations of the Western democracies, linking to the beliefs promulgated by nineteenth century classical liberalism, a view that elevated the status of the individual and promoted the notion of contractual relations between "free agents", commerce, etc.

Similarly, a close analysis of the use of the term *compromise* in recent years in the context of global political debates reveals that the term has increasingly been applied with a negative connotation. Even the *Dictionary of Diplomacy*'s definition of *compromise* as "an agreement reached by negotiation in which each party surrenders a portion of its preferred outcome" (Berridge and James 2003: 47), implies a rather negative sense in that it is predicated on the charged notion of "surrender". An online article entitled "Ex-President Bill Wants to Clean Up the Word 'Compromise'" reports on a speech delivered by Bill Clinton touching upon the Middle East peace process. The article reports:

> Clinton's most passionate moment by far came as he urged those involved in the process to stop considering the word "compromise" a dirty word. His words seemed to be directed more towards the Palestinians than the Israelis. (Atia 2002)

However, it seems that the US government itself has continued to construe the meaning of the word *compromise* in the negative sense of 'backing down' and 'giving in'. This is evident in many websites in which George Bush and other US government officials are quoted, for example, as saying: *the US will not compromise on Iraqi weapons inspections*; *the US will not compromise its long-term plans*; or *the US will not compromise on the sanctions issue*. It seems that this narrow construal has rather "contaminated" the earlier understanding of the "spirit of compromise".

In general, the direction of meaning change in the case of *compromise*, from a rather positive to a negative notion, reflects a shift in the discourse style of many governments as they move away from conceptualising the basis of their actions as secular-political, towards a religious-based morality. This is for instance reflected in Bush's reference to divine missions in his political discourse.

An interesting observation in regard to the word *compromise* is its recent use in the English version of the position statements made by some Iranian government officials. This is despite the fact that earlier in this section it was stated that Persian does not have a complete equivalent for *compromise*. A Google search for the English phrase *Iran will not compromise* yielded many pages in which the exact phrase was used. Most of these websites reported on Iran's position in the context of developing nuclear technology. The following are examples of this usage:

(4) *Iran will not compromise on nuclear know-how*

(5) *Iran will not compromise its right to pursue a peaceful nuclear program*

(6) *Iran will not compromise on its right to nuclear technology*

(7) *Iran will not compromise over its legitimate rights including access to peaceful nuclear technology*

The use of the English word *compromise* by the Iranian government appears to be a recent development. The term seems to have been adopted by Iranian government officials, or their interpreters, in response to the use of the term by Western governments. In the usages by the Iranian government officials, the word *compromise* appears to have been used as a translation of concepts such as *sâzesh* 'put up with', *dast bardâshtan* 'cease' (lit. 'take its hand from') or *aghab neshini kardan* 'to withdraw from a position', because in the government reports that are released in Persian, the government officials usually use these phrases in the context of dealing with US proposals, such as the following:

(8) Irân   az   hoghugheh teknolozhi-e hasteyi-e khod
    Iran   from rights   technology   nuclear   its
    dast   bar.nakhâhad.dâsht
    hand   will.not.take (meaning: not cease)
    'Iran will not give up its nuclear-technology rights'

Such statements are now increasingly being translated as "Iran will not compromise (on) its nuclear technology". In general, the observations made so far in this chapter reveal how terms that capture culturally constructed conceptualisations can take on special signification when aligned to socio-political as well as religious influences.

4 Jihad

Jihad is probably the most discussed term in current debates in international negotiation and international politics. The *Merriam-Webster Online Dictionary* (http://www.m-w.com/) defines the term as follows:

> **1**: a holy war waged on behalf of Islam as a religious duty; also: a personal struggle in devotion to Islam especially involving spiritual discipline.
>
> **2**: a crusade for a principle or belief

Fisher (2008: 534) defines *jihad* as "the Muslims struggle against the inner forces that prevent God-realization and the utter barriers to establishment of divine order". In terms of etymology, the term *jihad* is a borrowing from Arabic into English, and also into Persian. *Jihad* in its original Arabic sense of the word means 'struggle', 'effort', 'to strive', 'to exert', 'to fight', depending on the context. In the West, the word is generally translated in a military context and is often understood to mean 'holy war'. The Quran does call for *jihad* as a military struggle on behalf of Islam. But the Quran also refers to *jihad* as an internal, individual, spiritual struggle toward self-improvement, and intellectual effort. It is said that Prophet Muhammad termed the armed-struggle version of holy war *the little jihad*, but considered the spiritual aspect of *Jihad* which aim at moral and spiritual cleansing as *the great jihad* (Fisher 2008).

The conceptualisations underlying the word *jihad* in Islam are very complex and fall beyond the scope of this chapter (cf. Bonney 2004). As an indication of this complexity, a Google search for the English phrase *the word jihad* yielded 794 pages in which the complete phrase was used. In this section, however, we would like to briefly elaborate on the development of the usage of this term in Persian starting with the period before the 1979 Islamic Revolution in Iran, and continuing to the present day.

Prior to the Revolution, the term *jihad*, which is pronounced as *jahâd* in Persian, was employed by the pioneers of the Revolution to remind people that overthrowing the Pahlavi's regime was a jihad, or a holy action, and therefore every Muslim in the country had the duty to take part in it. The Pahlavi's regime was viewed as a threat to Islam, due to its Western orientation, and thus it was every Muslim's religious obligation to join the revolutionaries in replacing that regime with an Islamic government.

After the revolution, the Islamic government began a semantic shift in the usage of the word *jihad*. It was Imam Khomeini, the leader of the Revolution, who first used the term *jahâd -e sâzandegi* 'jihad of construction' in 1979 in a message in which he invited the people of Iran to cooperate in reconstructing the country after the Revolution. In 1983, Imam Khomeini and the Islamic Parliament formed a ministry with the title of *vezârat-e jahâd-e sâzandegi* 'Ministry of Jihad of Construction' to "address poverty through rural development and construction and agricultural growth and self-sufficiency".[2] During the Iran-Iraq War this Ministry took on a set of responsibilities dealing with military aid such as: "constructing strategic bridges, floating bridges, floating vehicles, submarines, freeways for armoured vehicles, and special vehicles for use in marshy fields". One of the fundamental objectives in the establishment of this Ministry was set out as follows:

> To move towards the country's independence and self-sufficiency and to improve social and economic conditions of villages and nomadic regions by developing agriculture,

---

[2] http://www.nti.org/eresearch/profiles/Iran/Biological/23052370.html (accessed in 2010 but the page no longer exists)

animal husbandry, rural industries, and through reconstructing ruins in collaboration with governmental administrative bodies and participation of people from all walks of life. (Jihad Striving for Development)

Thus, it can be seen that the word *jahâd* in Persian was extended after the revolution to include the type of "striving" associated with construction and development. With the Ministry of Jihad of Construction's active involvement in the Iran-Iraq War, however, the term started to be used in association with military operations, but not necessarily with a negative valence. The activities of this organization during that period are reflected in the Ministry's achievement list below:

- *Jihad-e-Sazandegi* used to collect the people's aids [meaning aid from the public], send them to war fronts, and distribute them in battle fields.
- *Jihad-e-Sazandegi* took active part in all the phases of military operations, and played a major role in gaining victory, stabilising and protecting the military positions.
- Moreover, *Jihad-e-Sazandegi* designed and carried out very important and strategic projects in the field of army. (Jihad Striving for Development)

In 1990, the Iranian government decided to transfer some of the responsibilities of the Ministry of Jihad of Construction to *vezârat-e keshâvarzi* 'the Ministry of Agriculture'. The Ministry of Jihad of Construction was now responsible for issues related to "conservation, rehabilitation, expansion, and exploitation of natural resources (forests, rangelands, and fisheries), watershed management, improvement of rural industries, and rural water-supply" (Jihad Striving for Development). Some seven years later the Ministry of Jihad of Construction was incorporated into the Ministry of Agriculture, and the new Ministry was labelled *the Ministry of Jihad of Agriculture.*

Both the termination of war and the incorporation of the Ministry of Jihad of Construction into the Ministry of Agriculture re-established the meaning of the word *jihad* as 'striving' for development and construction, and directed its connotation away from those associated with the military. Associated with these terms was the use of phrases such as *jahâd-e tose'e* 'Jihad of development/ expansion', which reinforced the constructive sense of the word. With the initiation of the Iranian Cultural Revolution (1980–87), the term *jahâd-e dâneshgâhi* 'jihad of the university/tertiary education' was also coined to refer to the campaign to free tertiary educational institutions from Western influence and gain academic independence for Iran.

Thus it is clear that the conceptualisations associated with the word *jahâd* in Persian have been varied depending on the contexts in which they have been used. It is also clear how government agendas as well as the socio-political conditions of the country have influenced the way in which the term has been utilised. Overall, within Iran, the term *jahâd*, in its contemporary usage, is associated with conceptualisations that embody notions such as construction, development, expansion, campaign and striving, and do not evoke connotations of 'war' or 'destruction'. This is in marked contrast with Western conceptualisation which associate it with civil destruction and war. This takes on significant importance since some Internet blogs use this term in the context of current position statements made by the Iranian politicians, such as the following:

(9) *Iran's jihad against Israel*
    Last week, it was the Iranian hostage terrorist, now President of Iran, Ahmadinejad, who called for the total destruction of Israel[3]

The analysis of Ahmadinejad's speech presented later in this chapter does not reveal any proclamation of *jihad* on the part of Iran. Thus, the inclusion of the word *jihad* in this article's title is misleading.

Various attempts have been made to translate the term *jahâd* into English. For example, some have consistently translated it as 'crusade', such as 'Academic Crusade' for *jahâd-e dâneshgâhi* 'Jihad of the university/tertiary education', or 'agriculture crusade' for *jahâd-e keshâvarzi* 'Jihad of agriculture'. Other translations of the word include 'holy war' such as in 'University holy war' for *jahâd-e daneshgâhi* 'Jihad of the University' and 'corps' such as 'Construction corps' for *jahâd-e sâzandegi* 'construction jihad'. All these translations appear to be based on Persian-English bilingual dictionaries. An interesting point here is that in some cases the title of the *vezârat-e Jahâd-e keshâvarzi* 'Ministry of Jihad of Construction' is abbreviated to 'the Ministry of Jihad'. For instance, this phrase was used to describe the affiliation of an academic at an international conference. It will be left to the readers of this chapter to imagine the aims and activities that many Western readers might attribute to 'the Ministry of Jihad', given the Western perception of the term, particularly in light of the current discourse concerning the "war on terror".

In a sense, the use of *jihad* can be viewed as intrinsically metaphorical, because over time its meaning has been regularly extended into new domains. As a result of the analogical juncture inherent in this conceptual mapping or structural alignment, i.e. mapping from the domain of WAR to CONSTRUCTION,

---

[3] http://moonagewebdream.blogs.com/stormscounterterrorism/2005/11/iransjihadaga.html (Broken link)

activities encountered in both domains end up being viewed as religious obligations; one involves fighting against the infidel and the other against poverty, etc. That is, the religious fervour that is associated with the concept of *jihad*, for example to refer to a holy war, is mapped here onto domains such as CONSTRUCTION elevating them to holy causes. Thus participation in the *jihad* of construction is understood as one's religious duty. At the same time the word *jihad* is increasingly brought into play in international political discourse as a metaphor for any perceived or presumed warning or threat made by a political leader of an Islamic state. Yet, because of its intrinsic religious sense, a president is not in a position to announce *jihad*, nor is it proclaimed implicitly, for such a declaration would need to be issued by a religious leader and in explicit terms. It should be clear from this rather brief discussion on *jihad* that, given the intensely negative connotations this concept tends to have in the English-speaking world, its use as a figure of speech in international political discourse is likely to provoke risky misunderstandings.

5 Metaphors of conflict

The role of conceptual processes such as metaphor and metonymy (e.g. Lakoff and Johnson 1980) in political discourse has been extensively explored by cognitive linguists as well as political scientists. What has become clear from these studies is that political metaphors are often rooted in certain underlying ideologies and cultural models (Dirven, Frank, and Ilie 2001; Dirven, Frank, and Pütz 2003). These conceptual devices are by no means incidental to political discourse but rather serve to establish or legitimize a given perspective.

George Bush, for example, repeatedly used metaphors, either novel or conventional, in his speeches about the Iranian government's nuclear technology. In one of his press conferences, Bush used the metaphorical expression of *house cleaning* in relation to Iran's nuclear program and stated that *these people need to keep their house clean*. In this metaphor, nuclear technology is conceptualised as DIRT, which needs to be removed from the house, the house here being the country. It is difficult to disagree with the statement that *one's house needs to be kept clean* and the use of the *clean house* metaphor appears to give the US president the legitimate position, of exhorting others to perform a socially desirable act. In other words, Bush's statement positions Iran very negatively, as having *dirt*, while positioning himself, or the US government, very positively, as those who put pressure on the Iranian government to *clean Iran's house*. However, Iran construes its nuclear program not in the negative sense of "dirt" but as "technology" and "energy", both of which have positive connotations.

A recent trend in the use of metaphor is to appeal to those who have religious values. An example of this in Western terms is George Bush's calling Iran, Iraq and North Korea *the axis of evil*. On the other hand, the Iranian government has in recent decades employed the metaphor of *Great Satan* to refer to the US government. In the case of the *clean house* Bush's metaphor disguises its religious basis by employing the rhetoric of cleanliness but the one employed by the Iranian government reflects a direct religious focus.

A very prominent post-revolutionary metaphor used by the Iranian officials is POLITICAL CONFLICT AS PHYSICAL ATTACK. Here, the image of "physical attack" is metaphorically mapped onto the domain of "political conflict". The leader of the Revolution, Ayatollah Khomeini, brought this metaphor into play upon his arrival in Tehran by saying *man tooyeh dahan-e in dolat mizanam* I will punch this [Pahlavi-appointed] government in the mouth'. Since then this metaphor has also been used in relation to Iran's position against the USA. It has been very common to hear position statements in which the phrase *mosht-e mohkami bar dahân-e Amrika* 'a strong punch to the mouth of the US' has been used by the Iranian media and officials. Later in this chapter, we will come back to this metaphorical statement and elaborate on how it has often been translated verbatim into English, and has resulted in a great deal of political controversy between Iran and the US.

6 Figurative language and the socio-cultural load of the words

While traditionally figurative language has largely been studied as a property of literary language, it is, in fact, fundamental to all forms of language and thought (e.g. Lakoff and Johnson 1980). As Chandler (2002: 124–125) puts it, "we may think of figurative language as most obviously a feature of poetry and more generally 'literary' writing, but there is more metaphor on the street corner than in Shakespeare". The motivation for the use of figurative language ranges from ease of conceptualisation to manipulation of thought. There is widespread recognition that figurative language is to a large extent socio-culturally constructed. The intended meaning may draw on socio-cultural knowledge that is more or less shared only by the members of a particular speech community and cultural group. Even within a society, different social and regional dialects develop their own figurative language and, consequently, people from outside the speech community often miss the nuances of meaning that are associated with the use of local figures of speech. One of the areas in which the use of figurative language presents both risks and rewards for speakers is political discourse.

Chandler (2002: 124) maintains that "the conventions of figurative language constitute a rhetorical code, and understanding this code is part of what it means to be a member of the culture in which it is employed". In today's international arena where the figurative use of language by politicians is immediately rendered into other languages, the socio-cultural nature of figurative language gives rise to the possibility of cross-cultural misunderstandings, which may potentially cause significant damage to international relationships.

Since figurative language is largely socio-culturally constructed it presents a significant locus for misinterpretation or even manipulation when it enters the realm of international politics.

7 Figurative language and political discourse

Metaphor and figurative language usage is a major field of interest in Cognitive Linguistics, and within the field metaphor in political discourse has been investigated extensively. While the term "political discourse" has been interpreted variously as encompassing most forms of human interaction (see Chilton 2004), or restricted to political rhetoric, particular attention has been paid by scholars to products of the discourse of politics – for example, speeches, election campaigns, public statements, and the reporting of political activity in the media.

Over the years, particular themes have emerged. In the 1980s, for instance, the political arguments for "nuclear proliferation and development" came under much scrutiny. More recently attention has been drawn to the political activities of the Bush administration, including responses to the events of September 11, 2001, the preparations and argument for going to war and their historical precedents, and world reactions to these events. Approaches to this topic have been many and varied. Bergen (2003), for instance, analyses political cartoons published in the week after the 2001 attack, exploring the roles played by conceptual blending, conceptual metaphor, and cultural models. In addition, analyses have demonstrated the dominance of the familial metaphor, e.g. GOVERNMENT AS PARENT, in American politics (e.g. Lakoff 1995; Iyengar 2005) and also that of sports and warfare, e.g. WAR AS SPORT, although these common themes are not restricted to America (Cibulskiene 2002; Howe 1988; Rosati 2000). Other studies have been conducted on the use of specific metaphors in times of war or crisis, for instance, George Bush, Sr.'s choice of metaphor during the first Persian Gulf War (Bates 2004), as for example his use of the phrase *smoking guns* associated with the search for the existence of *weapons of mass destruction* in Iraq (Billig and MacMillan 2005), and Roland Paris' (2002) discussion of Kosovo.

The Cold War and the discourse surrounding the European Union (and the European Community) have also been subject to much analysis (e.g. Chilton and Ilyin 1993; Chilton 1996).

The role of metaphor has also come under investigation from other perspectives. In his re-evaluation of Hobbes' criticism of rhetoric, Musolff (2006: 22) reiterates Hobbes' argument calling for a "critical attitude towards seemingly unproblematic analogies that lead to dangerous conclusions". In other words, we need to be alert to the use of metaphor in politics to deceive, gloss over an issue, or obscure the complexity of an issue.[4] The critical review (Arnold 2005) of Metaphorical World Politics (Beer and De Landtsheer 2004) which draws attention to both the constitutive power of metaphor and the need for more detailed studies into the politics of metaphor, highlights the need to continue investigating into the role that metaphor plays in discourse. Indeed, Anderson (2002) calls, albeit cautiously, for metaphors to be considered causal.

Iyengar's (2005) criticism of Lakoff's *Don't Think of an Elephant!* (an extract from Lakoff's (1996) *Moral Politics*) highlights a recent development in metaphor research, namely the importance of "framing", and of those doing the framing, in political discourse (see also Arnold 2005). The concept of "frame" as used by Lakoff here is very close to the concept of "schema". "Framing" here refers to use of a particular word to evoke a particular schema. An example here would be the use of *tax relief*, which evokes a schema associated with "relief", implying an affliction that needs to be relieved. Here then *tax* is framed as an affliction.

The mass media plays a major role in political discourse, both in terms of framing and in terms of "mediating", that is, shaping, pounding, distorting and/or constraining, the message for the audience (e.g. Shoemaker and Reese 1996). Whatever core value system a politician may have wanted to elicit, this is, inevitably, mediated (to whatever end) before it reaches the target audience. This theme is also discussed by Ekström (2001), who investigates the "mediatisation of politics".

The growth of Translation Studies, and the compilation of bilingual and multilingual corpora, have also led to a greater awareness of the importance of translation in political discourse. Schäffner's latest study (2004) calls for interdisciplinary cooperation between Political Discourse Analysis and Translation Studies, offering several convincing examples from data in the German-English bilingual corpus, and also highlighting the implications for political discourse of the translator's choices and strategies, whether personally or institutionally imposed, on the final text.

---

4   For a detailed, critical analysis of Hobbes, see Chilton 1996.

While much of the focus of English-speaking linguistic studies of figurative language has been directed on the US, attention has also been drawn to Europe, and the European Union (see especially the corpus studies undertaken by Mihas 2005; Musolff 2006; Schäffner 1997, 2001a). Comparatively little literature, however, has been produced specifically about the use of metaphor in other parts of the world.

The frequent use of figurative language by Iranian government officials presents a challenge for the English speaking reporters and commentators (Sharifian 2009). For instance, from the time of the Islamic Revolution in 1979, a recurring set of metaphors, including *Emrikâye jahân-khâr* 'The world-eater America', has been used by the Iranian leadership to refer to the United States. In other words, US invasion is conceptualised as "eating", which reflects the underlying conceptual metaphor of COUNTRY/NATION IS A PERSON/DEMON/ANIMAL. In the following section we present an analysis of several cases of the use of figurative language in Iranian political discourse, to show how transposing a Persian metaphor onto an English metaphor has led to a conceptual shift. We will first explore how figures of speech used in the discourse of Iranian politicians are socio-culturally and historically constructed, and then how such figurative language has been rendered in English. In doing so, we aim to shed more light on how inadequate translation of figurative language from Persian to English risks significant misunderstandings.

8 Figurative language in Iranian political discourse

The political events of the last three decades in Iran have attracted significant attention from the international media.[5] These include the 1979 Islamic Revolution, the subsequent engagement of the country in the eight-year war with Iraq and more recently the nuclear issue – the development of so-called *weapons of mass destruction*. Due to the Iranian government's strong opposition to the West, to name just one reason, Western politicians and media have been following closely the unfolding of political events inside Iran, and as part of that attention, the discourse of Iranian politicians has come under increasing scrutiny by foreign governments and the media.

---

5   Information on the history of US-Iran relations may prove helpful as a preamble to a better understanding of this section. One possible internet source is: http://en.wikipedia.org/wiki/UnitedStates-Iranrelations

As mentioned above, an area that has presented a challenge for the non-Iranian media is the frequent use of figurative language by Iranian government officials. For example, from the beginning of the Islamic Revolution of Iran in 1979, its leaders have drawn on a recurring set of metaphors to refer to the United States, including the following:

(10) Emrikâye[6] jahân-khâr
      America   world-eater
      'The world eater America'

(11) Emrikâye   jenâyatkâr
      America   criminal
      'The criminal America'

(12) Sheitân   bozorg
      Satan   big
      'The big Satan'

The negative force of the metaphors in question is directed toward what are viewed as military acts of aggression on the part of the US. For instance, US invasion of other countries is conceptualised as "eating" in (10) and "committing a crime" in (11). These conceptualisations reflect an underlying conceptual metaphor of COUNTRY/NATION IS A PERSON/DEMON/ANIMAL. The case of (12), on the other hand, reveals a metaphor drawn from the domain of religion; a rhetorical feature of persuasion that has become more prevalent in Iranian political discourse since the Islamic revolution.

It should be noted that US government officials have not been passive recipients of such metaphors, for they have also used equivalent metaphors to label the Iranian government. Perhaps the most well-known is the expression *axis of evil* that George W. Bush first used in a speech in 2002 to refer to Iran, Iraq, and North Korea. This metaphor combines Reagan's famous reference to the former Soviet Union as an *evil empire* with a barely veiled reference to the three Axis Powers of WWII. It is a one-to-one, country-to-country mapping of Iran, Iraq, and North Korea onto Germany, Italy, and the Empire of Japan. The metaphor brings together, albeit indirectly, in a single succinct phrase references to the most formidable enemies that the US faced during the 20th century. Making

---

6 The symbol *â* represents a low back unrounded vowel close to the *a* in the English word *father*.

reference to the word *evil* brings on stage a biblical scenario of "good" versus "evil". Iran has also been said to "harbour" terrorists.[7] Such figurative devices, by all parties, are by no means incidental to political discourse, but rather establish or constitute a privileged perspective. The following sections present an analysis of several cases of international media reports drawing on Iranian political discourse that include the use of figurative language, or figurative devices.

8.1 Israel should be wiped off the map

In a recent case Ahmadinejad was quoted as saying, "Israel was dying and the people in the Middle East would destroy it if given the chance"[8] (Reuters, UK, May 14, 2008). In fact, the original version of this statement in Persian by Ahmadinejad would be more accurately translated as "The Zionist regime is dying. The nations in the region hate this criminal and fake regime and if they see the smallest chance, they will root out this fake regime". Here the phrase *risheh kandan* (literally: 'pulling out its root') *in regim-e ja'ali* (literally: 'this fake regime'), which should be translated as 'would root out this fake regime', is in fact mistranslated as 'would destroy it', where in the sentence "it" would refer to "Israel". Also, it should be added that usually the use of the word *mantagheh* 'region' in Persian, as it appears in the above-mentioned translation, as used in relation to Israel, also refers to other countries like Palestine, Jordon, and Lebanon but does not indicate the whole of the Middle East. It is obvious that such cases of mistranslation/misrepresentation carry serious potential for creating or intensifying misunderstanding and could result in diplomatic/military conflicts, which could lead to colossal damage to the nations, societies, and people involved.

Since 2005, the Iranian president, Mahmoud Ahmadinejad, has constantly been quoted as having said, "Israel must be wiped off the map"[9] or "Israel must be wiped off the face of the earth".[10] The section in question of Mahmoud

---

[7] http://www.voanews.com/uspolicy/archive/2003-08/a-2003-08-11-4-1.cfm (accessed in 2010 but the page no longer exists)
[8] http://uk.reuters.com/article/worldNews/idUKHOS43245220080514 'Iran's Ahmadinejad says Israel "dying"' by Fredrik Dahl, posted on May 14 2008.
[9] http://www.telegraph.co.uk/news/main.jhtml?xml=/news/2005/10/27/wiran27.xml 'Four ways to act against Ahmadinejad.' by Joshua Rozenberg, posted on February 15 2007.
[10] http://www.guardian.co.uk/iran/story/0,12858,1601413,00.html 'Israel should be wiped off map, says Iran's president.' By Ewen MacAskill and Chris MaGreal, posted on October 27 2005.

Ahmadinejad's speech is reproduced below. It includes his original statement in Persian with the authors' literal glossing of it into English.

(13) Va   emâm-e   aziz   mâ   farmudand   ke   in
     and   Imam   dear   our   said-polite.form   that   this
     rezhim-e   eshghâlgar-e ghods   bâyad az   safhe-ye
     Regime   occupying-of Qods   has.to from   page-of
     ruzegâr   mahv-gardad
     history/time disappear

'And our dear Imam said that this occupying regime of Qosd has to be disappeared from the pages of the history'

In the above excerpt Ahmadinejad was, in fact, quoting Ayatollah Khomeni, the leader of the Islamic Revolution of Iran, rather than making a personal statement. Also it is clear that in Persian the statement refers explicitly to the regime, that is, to the current political leadership of Israel, and not to the country of Israel. This shift of focus in the translation reflects a conceptualisation of REGIME AS THE NATION/COUNTRY. In a sense the translation here presupposes that Ahmadinejad does in fact equate the regime with the nation/state. Whether this is true or not is irrelevant to the discussion in this chapter.

Also, it is noteworthy that *history* and *time* do not have the spatial reference that is captured by *map* or *face of the earth*. That is, they refer to time and not space. In this metaphor, disappearance of a regime does not seem to automatically entail the meaning of 'wiping a country off the map', which seems to imply destroying the whole nation as a physical entity. Interpreted in the context of discourse raising fears about Iran's development of nuclear weapons, such translations are very likely to trigger terrifying images. It is to be noted that whether or not this is Ahmadinejad's intention is another issue; the point in question here is the translation of political discourse and the conceptual links and shifts that occur in this process.

It is noteworthy that the seminar in which Ahmadinejad delivered his speech was titled *jahân-e beduneh sahyunism* 'the world without Zionism'. This suggests that the focus of the conference was on the ideology, reflected in the suffix *-ism*, rather than the country. However, during his speech his main focus was on the Zionist regime and this suggests a conceptualisation of REGIME AS IDEOLOGY. This is clearly reflected in another part of the same speech where he makes an analogy between a world without Zionism and Iran without the former Pahlavi regime. He states that just as the Iranian people managed to change the Iranian regime, the world could exist without Zionism.

Based on the same speech, Ahmadinejad has been quoted as referring to Israel as "a stain". The use of this phrase appears in the following examples from different media channels and web pages:

(14) *Very Soon, This Stain of Disgrace [i.e. Israel] Will Vanish from the Center of the Islamic World*[11]

(15) *[The Iranian president] has called Israel "a stain" on Islam that must be erased*[12]

(16) *Very soon, Israel, this stain of disgrace, will be purged from the center of the Islamic world*[13]

(17) *Ahmadinejad described Israel as "a stain of shame that has sullied the purity of Islam", and promised that it would be "cleansed very soon"*[14]

(18) *The new wave of attacks in Palestine will erase this stain from the face of Islam*[15]

(19) *And that the State of Israel had become a tumor or a "stain" on the "face of the Islamic world" and should be removed or "wiped off"*[16]

However, the original text from Ahmadinejad's speech in which he was referring to a recent event in Palestine as "sobering waves", and "the wave of spirituality" is glossed in (20) below. As we saw before his expressions have been translated as "waves of attack" in (18) above. This seems to be more than a mere translation; it is rather an interpretation of Ahmadinejad's figurative language.

---

[11] http://www.defenddemocracy.org/researchtopics/researchtopicsshow.htm?docid=312615&attribid=7684 'Iran's Call For Israel to "Be Wiped Off the Map" – Responses.' By Jonathan L. Snow, posted on October 28 2005.
[12] http://www.campus-watch.org/article/id/2571 'Just How Far Did They Go, Those Words Against Israel?' by Ethan Bronner, posted on June 11 2006.
[13] http://www.telospress.com/main/index.php?mainpage=newsarticle&articleid=144 'Confronting Anti-Semitism—But How.' By Matthias Küntzel, posted in Fall 2006.
[14] http://www.freemuslims.org/news/article.php?article=1028 (accessed in 2010 but the page no longer exists)
[15] http://www.opendemocracy.net/debates/article.jsp?id=3&debateId=128&articleId=2974 (accessed in 2010 but the page no longer exists)
[16] http://www.antiwar.com/prather/?articleid=8458 'When pigs fly.' By Gordon Prather, posted on January 28 2006.

(20) | Man | tardid | na-dâram | moj-e | jadidi | ke | dar |
| --- | --- | --- | --- | --- | --- | --- |
| I | doubt | not-have | wave-of | new | that | in |
| felestin-e | aziz | be | râh-oftâdeh, | mojeh | | |
| Palestine | dear | has | started | wave | | |
| bidâri | ke | emruz | dar | donyâ-ye | eslâm | hast va |
| alertness | that | today | in | world-of | Islam | is and |
| moj-e | manaviati | ke | sartâsareh | donyâ-ye | | |
| wave-of | spirituality | that | across | world-of | | |
| eslâm râ | farâ-gerefteh | be-zudi | in | lakey-e | | |
| Islam | has.spread | soon | this | stain-of | | |
| Nang râ | az | dâmâne | donyâ-ye | eslâm | pâk | |
| disgrace | from | skirt | world-of | Islam | clean | |
| khâhad | kard, | va | in | shodani-st | | |
| will | do | and | this | possible-is | | |

'I do not have doubts that the new wave that has started in dear Palestine, the wave of alertness which is in the world of Islam today, and a wave of spirituality that has spread across the world on Islam will soon clean this stain of disgrace from the skirt of the world of Islam, and this is possible'.

Also, the antecedent for "this stain of disgrace" is "the regime occupying Qods" (i.e. the Zionist regime), which appears in the preceding sentence in the original text, rather than "the State of Israel" as the reports quoted in (13–18) entail. The translation again reflects conceptualisation of REGIME AS THE NATION/COUNTRY/STATE.

In the case of (18) above, the Persian expression has even been rendered as 'tumour'; no doubt everyone would associate 'tumour' with 'removal', whereas Ahmadinejad's expression of *pâk khâhad kard* 'will clean' in the context of his speech can most probably be synonymous to the dissolution of USSR in 1991. However, rendering the expression as 'removal' seems to be a move to a whole new conceptual field, that is, 'illness', 'deadly disease' and the semantic prototype of 'cancer'. Also, contrary to the translations of his speech, Ahmadinejad does not seem to have either "mandated" or "promised" the removal of the stain.

Another phenomenon in this context is a blending that is produced by conflating the two previous sections on 'stain' and 'map', as in the following excerpt taken from the Internet[17] which is presented as a direct quote from the same speech:

---

17 http://antichomsky.blogspot.com/2005/10/shocker-out-of-iran.html 'A shocker out of Iran'. By Benjamin Kerstein, posted on October 27 2005.

(21) *The esteemed president said: "Israel is a humiliating stain that must be erased off the map. There is no doubt that the new wave of attacks in Palestine will soon erase this stain from the face of the Islamic world"*

It is clear that this example is a gloss consisting of a selection and juxtaposition of words from Ahmadinejad's speech, presented as a direct quote. Here the 'stain' and 'off the map' have been merged into one sentence while the meaning of the original expression *the waves in Palestine* has been militarised by the addition of 'attacks'. It should be reiterated that the analysis presented here is not an examination of Ahmadinejad's political position but a comparison of what he has been quoted as having said, and what he actually said.

8.2 To inflict US with "harm and pain"

In March 2006, Western media such as the *Telegraph Newspaper* (UK) announced an Iranian threat against the US, as follows:

(22) *Tehran threatens to inflict "harm and pain" on US over the nuclear row. Iran issued a chilling threat to inflict "harm and pain" on America yesterday as it headed for confrontation at the United Nations Security Council over its suspected nuclear weapons programme*[18]

Upon further reading it becomes clear that the statement was originally issued in English and not in Persian, by Ali Asghar Soltanieh, the Iranian ambassador to the IAEA. The use of the expression "chilling threat" suggests that the statement by the Iranian official was interpreted as Iran threatening to attack the US, perhaps alluding even to a nuclear confrontation, given the fact that at the time Iran was allegedly developing "weapons of mass destruction". Very soon many Western media outlets announced the news, as in the following headlines:

(23) *Iran Threatens "Harm and Pain" to U. S.*[19]

(24) *Tehran warns Washington of "harm and pain"*[20]

---

[18] http://www.telegraph.co.uk/news/main.jhtml?xml=/news/2006/03/09/wiran09.xml 'Teheran threatens to inflict 'harm and pain' on US over nuclear row.' By Anton La Guardia, posted on March 9 2006.
[19] http://www.cbsnews.com/stories/2006/03/08/world/main1381121.shtml 'Iran Threatens 'Harm And Pain' To U.S.', posted on February 11 2009.
[20] http://www.ft.com/cms/s/6d715dcc-af11-11da-b04a-0000779e2340.html (Available only to registered users)

The original English message from the Iranian official is as follows:

(25) *The United States has the power to cause harm and pain, but the United States is also susceptible to harm and pain. So if that is the path that the US wishes to choose, let the ball roll*[21]

It is first of all noteworthy that attributing what the Iranian official has said about *Tehran* and *Iran* is a case of employing the following related metaphors:

A. A GOVERNMENT OFFICIAL IS THE GOVERNMENT
B. THE CAPITAL CITY IS THE GOVERNMENT
C. THE COUNTRY IS THE GOVERNMENT
D. THUS, A GOVERNMENT OFFICIAL IS THE COUNTRY
E. THE COUNTRY IS A PERSON

Metaphors (A) to (D) are reflected in the fact that the Iranian government official appeared as *Iran* and *Tehran* in the news headlines quoted above. Also (E) is reflected in conceptualising "country" or "capital" as an entity that is capable of "threatening", "warning", and even "saying" something, all of which are very common conceptualisations in political discourse.

Also, it appears that it is the "susceptibility of the US to harm and pain" and the phrase *let the ball roll*, which had led to interpretations of "threat" against the US. The verbatim translation of this expression into Persian does not appear to lead to a common expression in current use. The closest expressions in Persian would be *zarar va ziân* meaning 'sustain a loss' and *dard va ranj* (lit., 'pain and suffering') literally meaning 'suffering and hardship'.

The Persian translation of the Iranian official's statement as it appeared in *Etelâât* newspaper reads as follows:

(26) Âmricâ   ghodrat-e lâzeme barâye sadame-zadan
     America   strength-of needed for   harm
     va   ijâd   dard   dârad, amâ in   keshvar   mostaede
     and   create   pain   has   but this   country   susceptible
     sadame-khorda va   dard   keshidan ast va   agar
     to.be.harmed and   pain   suffer   is and   if
     âmricâ be   donbâle   in   masir   ast pas   bogzârim
     America is   after   this   direction is then   let's

---

21 http://www.cbsnews.com/stories/2006/03/08/world/main1381121.shtml 'Iran Threatens 'Harm And Pain' To U.S.', posted on February 11 2009.

tâ	in charkh	be	hamin	ravâl	becharkhad
that	this wheel	as	it	is	turn

'America has the strength to harm and create pain. But this country is susceptible to be harmed and suffer pain, as well. And if America is after this direction, then let's allow this wheel to turn as it is'

As mentioned above, the rendering of "harm and pain" into Persian (i.e. *Sadameh zadan va dard keshidan*) does not appear as a common Persian expression, and it is highly likely that the Iranian official was responding to a statement by the US ambassador to the United Nations, John R. Bolton, who warned Iran of *painful consequences*, in relation to a threat to withdraw oil.[22] It should be added here that *let the ball roll* in English means 'let something start happening', but the above Persian translation suggests 'keep things as they are'.

The issue of "harm and pain" did not end here, for the media made every effort to find out exactly what the Iranian official meant by these words. Eventually when he was questioned about the precise meaning of his words, he replied as follows:

(27) QUESTION: *What do you mean by harm and pain?*
 ANSWER: *We are not going to act, our reaction would depend on the action. Then we will decide after careful study.*[23]

It can be seen that on this occasion, *harm* and *pain* are associated with *act*, which may be interpreted as "military act". But the Iranian official adds, after a few other questions, that:

(28) *The important thing is we have no intention of confrontation. Two parties are needed for any conflict. We are determined to settle this peacefully and welcome any gesture. We are warning and advising the other side to not escalate this situation*

The above quote does not suggest any direct threat of a military attack. In fact, one website makes reference to an interpretation held by some diplomats which is as follows:

---

22 http://www.washingtonpost.com/wp-dyn/content/article/2006/03/05/AR2006030500992.html 'Iran Renews Threat to Withhold Oil.' By Karl Vick, posted on March 6 2006.

23 http://www.comeclean.org.uk/articles.php?articleID=176 (accessed in 2010 but the page no longer exists).

(29) *Diplomats accredited to the meeting and in contact with the Iranians said the statement [harm and pain] could be a veiled threat to use oil as an economic weapon*[24]

Here, *oil* enters the domain of figurative language as OIL AS WEAPON, which can inflict *harm* and *pain*. It has even become common to use the expression oil *weapon*.[25]

8.3 US deserves a punch in the mouth

It seems the conflicts that resulted from the rise to power of the Islamic Government in Iran in 1979 have created a context that allows most position statements made by government officials from either the US or Iran to be interpreted as "threats" and reported to their respective publics as such. A Google search with the English phrase *Iran punch in the mouth* resulted in numerous web pages, most of which quote Iranian government officials. Such verbal translations of idiomatic phrases may result in misunderstandings, even where there is goodwill involved in political negotiations. For example, the rendering of *mosht-e mohkami bar dahân-e Amrika* as 'a punch in the mouth of America' may suggest an aggressive action, particularly a retaliatory military one, when interpreted from a Western perspective. From the Iranian perspective, however, this expression, as we will see later in this chapter, can simply indicate a negative response, such as turning down a proposal. This kind of potential misinterpretation may become much more critical in the contemporary context of Iran's development of nuclear technology, which is referred to by the West as the development of a "weapon". The following quote is from a website, which shows how the punch in the mouth metaphor is used in the context of Iran's nuclear technology:

(30) *The spiritual leader of Iran, Ayatollah Ali Khamenei, is warning the US to stay out of his country's business and, in particular, its nuclear program, which is set to resume this week*
Speaking on a tour of southeast Iran, Khamenei called the US arrogant and rude, and said the country "deserved a punch in the mouth". He also said Iran's presidential elections in June would not make any difference to its

---

[24] http://www.breitbart.com/news/2006/03/08/D8G7JAPG1.html (accessed in 2010 but the page no longer exists)
[25] http://www.iranian.ws/irannews/publish/article16643.shtml (accessed in 2010 but the page no longer exists)

nuclear policy. Khamenei said it was not up to the US to decide which countries needed nuclear technology (WorldNetDaily).

It is clear that, in such contexts, from a Western perspective *the punch in the mouth* can be stretched to mean the possibility of "military action using weapons of mass destruction".

As previously mentioned, this Persian expression has been a common figure of speech in Iranian political and ordinary discourse for some time and is used to foreshadow a very different set of meanings, namely, resistance and refusal to co-operate on Iran's part (Sharifian 2007). The expression *punch in the mouth* entered the Iranian political discourse when Ayatollah Khomeini returned to Iran from exile in February 1979. Upon his arrival he delivered a speech where he made the following statement:

(31) Man   tuye   dahan-e   in   dolat   mizanam, man
      I   to   mouth-of   this government hit   I
      khodam   dolat   tashkil-midaham
      myself   government establish
      'I hit this government in the mouth. I myself establish a government'

By this statement, the leader of the revolution meant that he would not recognise the government of the time (Shapour Bakhtiar's government)[26] as legitimate, and that he would establish his own government. Thus, the implied meaning of *punch in the mouth* was 'not recognise as legitimate', 'not cooperate with', and of course it has the added implication of an attempt to overthrow the existing government, one that is therefore viewed as illegitimate. However, in time this expression became a standard metaphor in Iranian political discourse where it acquired meanings ranging from 'resistance' to 'rejection (of a proposal)'. This is, for example, reflected in the following quote from an Iranian paint company owner, found on a webpage:

(32) *Last year a company run by a friend of mine produced a mural listing a number of goods produced in Israel and saying: "By boycotting these products, let's give a punch in the mouth to Israel"*[27]

---

[26] http://lcweb2.loc.gov/frd/cs/irtoc.html 'A country Study: Iran', accessed on January 5 2013.
[27] http://www.guardian.co.uk/iran/story/0,,1705211,00.html "The Mural maze." By Robert Tait, posted on February 8 2006.

It can be seen that boycotting a product is here viewed as "giving a punch in the mouth" to Israel. Another revealing example that surfaced as Mahmoud Ahmadinejad was taking office after winning the election in 2005 is the following from the GlobalSecurity.org website:

(33) *Ahmadinejad's supporters said he "will punch in the mouth" all those who advocate relations with the United States. Rafsanjani had said in campaign interviews that he would seek to improve Iran's troubled relationship with the United States. Ahmadinejad represents a younger generation whose formative experience was the Iran-Iraq War*[28]

Here the supporters of Mr Ahmadinejad used the expression *punch in the mouth* to suggest that he would refuse to establish relationships with the US, a position which would not impress his predecessors who were open to developing relationships with the US. Thus, overall, it should be clear that *punch in the mouth* has become a common figure of speech in Iranian political discourse, referring to any form of resistance, disagreement, rejection, etc., and that it does not imply any concrete act of physical violence.

In May 2005, the international media reported a quote from Ayatollah Khamenei, the Iranian supreme leader, as follows:

(34) *Iran issues nuclear warning to US*
Speaking on a tour of south-east Iran, Ayatollah Khamenei said the US was arrogant, rude and deserved a punch in the mouth. He also said Iran's presidential elections in June would not make any difference to its nuclear policy. The US has expressed fears Iran is trying to build nuclear weapons

(35) *Enrichment warning*
Ayatollah Khamenei said it was not up to the US to decide which countries needed nuclear technology. He also warned that Iran's forthcoming presidential elections were nothing to do with the Americans. No president would dare violate the country's national interests because the people would not allow it, he said.

---

28 http://www.globalsecurity.org/military/world/iran/ahmadinejad.htm 'Mahmoud Ahmadinejad', accessed on January 5 2013.

> *His comments came as Iran warned on Saturday it might resume suspended enrichment-related activities next week in defiance of an agreement that is underpinning nuclear talks with Europe. Iran is concerned that negotiations are dragging on too long and has proposed a phased resumption of its nuclear activities.*[29]

As can be seen, the expression *deserved a punch in the mouth* is viewed by the BBC as a warning of a possible nuclear attack against the US, as reflected in the headline the newspaper report. This interpretation is likely to have been based on the conceptualisation of NUCLEAR ATTACK AS INDIVIDUAL PHYSICAL CONFLICT. That is, if a nuclear attack is conceptualised as individual physical conflict then it follows that a punch in the mouth implies military action. Again, given the circumstances around the issue of Iran's so-called "nuclear weapons", this background frame implying a potential military conflict makes it easy and convenient to establish the links that are needed to interpret a "punch in the mouth" as a "nuclear warning". This is evident in the following quote from the War on Jihad website:

(36) *Speaking on a tour of southeast Iran, Khamenei said the US "deserved a punch in the mouth." From where does this brashness come? It comes from Iran's plans to launch an Electro-Magnetic Pulse Nuclear war against the USA and Europe, crippling the West in the War on terror*[30]

In the context of Khamenei's use of this expression as directed against the US, it seems to suggest resisting interference by the US. The official website of the Khamenei contains an excerpt from the speech where he first used the expression *punch in the mouth* (*bar dahân-e oo* [US] *mosht mikubim*, literal meaning: 'to mouth-of him/her punch hit'). That section is translated into English as follows:

(37) *U.S. officials are so shameless and impudent as to say that Iran does not need nuclear energy! This matter is none of their business! They have no right to say that the Iranian nation should not make use of nuclear energy*[31]

---

29 http://news.bbc.co.uk/2/hi/middleeast/4503915.stm (accessed in 2010 but the page no longer exists)
30 http://www.waronjihad.com/4thmay2005.html 'Scenarios for Regime Change in Iran', posted on May 4 2005 http://www.khamenei.ir/EN/Speech/detail.jsp?id=20050501B (accessed in 2010 but the page no longer exists)
31 http://www.khamenei.ir/EN/Speech/detail.jsp?id=20050501B

It can be seen that on the website the expression *punch in the mouth* has not been literally translated into English, and it is clear that this section does not include any explicit statement about nuclear threats. Khamenei's speech explicitly concerns the US's interference in Iran's affairs, specifically, Iran's attempts to produce nuclear energy. It does not discuss or overtly imply launching an attack against the US.

Finally, it should be noted that the observations made in this chapter suggest that word meanings respond to and are shaped by concrete socio-political and cultural factors more or less immediately, especially in our age of instant communication. A change in meaning, for example, the introduction of a new term or idiom, that once might have taken a century to spread through a speech community, can now be accomplished in a month. The last two decades have witnessed exemplary cases where socio-political factors and agendas have motivated an accelerated shift, or extension, in the meanings of words such as "terrorism", "war" and "weapon". The role of speechwriters in this context should also be acknowledged as they often are under pressure to exploit language to forward hidden agendas including perhaps serving certain economic agents (see, for example, Gelderman 1997).

9 Concluding remarks

In this chapter we made an attempt to explore some of the complexities involved in translating several terms that are commonly found in the discourse of international politics from the perspective of Cultural Linguistics The analysis of selected cases reveals how the cultural and socio-political circumstances in which certain terms are contextualised may lead to a semantic shift or semantic extension. In other words, the specific cultural and socio-political contexts in which a word is repeatedly brought into play will have implications for how it is eventually interpreted.

We have also tried to shed some light on how rendering the concepts commonly encountered in the discourse of international politics, translating them from one language into another, may involve a shift in the ideological as well as the socio-political underpinnings of the concepts, since they are contextualised in different ways and, therefore, have different histories. We saw how language, and meanings in particular, are influenced by the commitments of the agencies that employ them as well as by the more macro-level contexts in which they are used. In today's increasingly globalised and mediatised world where the destinies of nations are intertwined and repeatedly woven together by means of this international political discourse, it is obvious that extreme caution needs to be exercised when translating and interpreting figurative language from one language to another. Of course, this statement assumes that the goal of those involved in this process is not to deliberately manipulate language in order to distort the picture and justify certain actions. If international politics is aimed at reconciliation, greater attention needs to be paid to the role of language and conceptualisation, particularly in the negotiating processes implicit in efforts at conflict resolution and related current debates around the world. Translators and interpreters can contribute very considerably to international negotiation by unpacking some of the underlying complexities that characterise the use of key concepts in this crucial domain.

Of particular importance here is the process of "re-contextualisation" and therefore the reformulation of meaning brought about by the media (whether by conscious manipulation, unconscious complicities or plain mistakes on the part of the media outlets).

The analyses presented in this chapter aim at developing the following position: since language is socio-culturally and politically situated, the use and translation of figurative language in international political discourse may entail considerable risks or produce substantial rewards, depending on the context of translation. The analyses also highlight the significant contribution that Cultural Linguistics can make to political discourse analysis. Political discourse is not culture-free. In fact, political discourse, in particular its use of conceptual metaphors, is largely culturally constructed. Cultural Linguistics, with its potential for a close examination of the grounding of language in culture, offers a very fitting approach to the exploration of political discourse. We hope the insights presented in this chapter will encourage further research in the area of political discourse analysis from the perspective of this discipline.

Finally, we would like to make it clear that the analyses presented in this chapter are not intended to support a political stance. The chapter does not explore the intentions of the Iranian politicians; it is rather an attempt to underline the importance of a careful linguistic and conceptual analysis when discussing the use/misuse of figurative language in international political discourse. It is obvious that the case of Iran is just one example and, although a pressing one, it is not particularly exceptional. Given the significance of the consequences that may derive from such ill-informed translations, similar socio-culturally situated studies of other languages appear to be absolutely essential.

References

Anderson, Richard D., Jr. 2002 *The causal power of metaphor in politics*. Available at: http://www.polisci.ucla.edu/faculty/anderson/MetaphorsCauses.htm.

Arnold, Samantha 2005 Politics disguised: Disguising politics. *International Studies Review* 7: 636–638.
Aryanpour English-Persian Dictionary. Available at: http://www.aryanpour.com/.
Atia, Tarek 2002 Ex-president Bill wants to clean up the word "compromise". *Cairolive.com*, January 19. Available at: http://www.cairolive.com/newcairolive/dispatch/clinton.html.
Avruch, Kevin and Zheng Wang 2005 Culture, apology, and international negotiation: The case of the Sino-U.S. "spy plane" crisis. *International Negotiation* 10: 337–353.
Baker, Mona 2006 *Translation and conflict: A narrative account.* New York: Routledge
Bates, Benjamin R. 2004 Audiences, metaphors, and the Persian Gulf War. *Communications Studies* 55.3: 447–463.
Beeman, William O. 2005 *The "Great Satan" versus the "Mad Mullas": How the United States and Iran demonize each other.* Westport, CT: Praeger/Greenwood.
Beer, Francis A. and Christl De Landtsheer 2004 *Metaphorical world politics.* East Lansing: Michigan State University Press.
Bergen, Benjamin 2003 To awaken a sleeping giant: Cognition and culture in September 11 political cartoons. In: Michel Achard and Suzanne Kemmer (eds.), *Language, culture, and mind*, 23–36. Stanford, CA: CSLI Publications.
Berridge, Geoff R., and Alan James 2003 *A Dictionary of Diplomacy.* 2nd ed. New York: Palgrave Macmillan.
Billig, Michael and Katie MacMillen 2005 Metaphor, idiom and ideology: The search for "no smoking guns" across time. *Discourse and Society* 16.4: 459–480.
Bonney, Richard 2004 *Jihad: From Qur'an to Bin Laden.* New York: Palgrave Macmillan.
Chandler, Daniel 2002 *Semiotics. The basics.* London: Routledge.
Chilton, Paul A. 2004 *Analysing Political Discourse: Theory and Practice.* London: Routledge.
Chilton, Paul A. 1996 *Security metaphors: Cold War discourse from containment to common house.* New York: Peter Lang
Chilton, Paul A. and Mikhail Ilyin 1993 Metaphor in political discourse: The case of the "common European House". *Discourse and Society* 4.1: 7–31.
Cibulskiene, Jurga 2002 The metaphorization of election as war in the 2001 general election campaign of Great Britain. *Respectus Philologicus* 2.7. Available at: http://filologija.vukhf.lt/2-7/cibulskiene.htm.
Cohen, Raymond 1997 *Negotiating across cultures.* Washington, DC: U.S. Institute for Peace.
Cohen, Raymond 2001 Language and negotiation: A Middle East lexicon. In: Jovan Kurbalija and Hannah Slavik (eds.), *Language and diplomacy*, 67–92. Malta: DiploProjects. Available at: http://www.diplomacy.edu/Books/language_and_diplomacy/texts/pdf/cohen.pdf.
Cordesman, Anthony H and Adam C. Seitz 2006 *Iran's weapons of mass destruction.* Washington, DC: Centre for International and Strategies Studies.
D'Andrade, Roy 1995 *The development of cognitive anthropology.* Cambridge: Cambridge University Press.
Dirven, Rene, Roslyn M. Frank and Cornelia Ilie (eds.) 2001 *Language and ideology.* Vol. 2, *Cognitive descriptive approaches.* Amsterdam: John Benjamins.
Dirven, Rene, Roslyn Frank and Martin Pütz (eds.) 2003 *Cognitive models in language and thought.* Berlin: Mouton de Gruyter.
Ekström, Mats 2001 Politicians interviewed on television news. *Discourse and Society* 12.5: 563–584.
Fisher, Mary Pat 2008 *Living religions.* 7th edition. Upper Saddle River, New Jersey: Pearson Education.

Gelderman, Carol 1997 *All the presidents' words: The bully pulpit and the creation of the virtual presidency*. New York: Walker.
Hatim, Basil and Ian Mason 1990 *Discourse and the translator*. London: Longman.
Holland, Dorothy and Naomi Quinn (eds.) 1987 *Cultural models in language and thought*. Cambridge: Cambridge University Press.
Howe, Nicholas 1988 Metaphor in contemporary American political discourse. *Metaphor and Symbolic Activity* 3.2: 87–104.
Iyengar, Shanto 2005 Speaking of values: The framing of American politics. *The Forum* 3.3, Article 7. Available at: http://www.bepress.com/forum/vol3/iss3/art7.
Jihad. *Merriam-Webster Online Dictionary*. Available at: http://www.m-w.com/.
Jihad Striving for Development and Construction. Available at: http://www.netiran.com/?fn=artd(2499).
Kronenfeld, David 2011 *A companion to cognitive anthropology*. Oxford: Wiley-Blackwell.
Lakoff, George 1995 Metaphor, morality, and politics, or, why conservatives have left liberals in the dust. *Social Research* 62.2: 177–213.
Lakoff, George 1996 *Moral politics: What conservatives know that liberals don't*. Chicago: University of Chicago Press.
Lakoff, George and Mark Johnson 1980 *Metaphors we live by*. Chicago: University of Chicago Press.
Mihas, Elena 2005 Non-literal language in political discourse. In: *LSO Working Papers in Linguistics 5: Proceedings of WIGL 2005*, 124–159. Available at: http://ling.wisc.edu/lso/wpl/5.1/LSOWP5.1-10-Mihas.pdf.
Musolff, Andreas 2006 Metaphor scenarios in public discourse. *Metaphor and Symbol* 21.1: 23–38.
Oxford English Dictionary 1933 1st edition. Oxford: Clarendon Press.
Oxford English Dictionary 1989 2nd edition. New York: Oxford University Press.
Oxford Advanced Learner's Dictionary 1974 3rd edition. Oxford: Oxford University Press.
Oxford Advanced Learner's Dictionary 2005 7th edition. Oxford: Oxford University Press.
Palmer, Gary B. 1996 *Toward a theory of cultural linguistics*. Austin: University of Texas Press.
Paris, Ronald 2002 Kosovo and the metaphor war. *Political Science Quarterly* 117.3: 423–450.
Rosati, Jerel A. 2000 The power of human cognition in the study of world politics. *The International Studies Review* 2.3: 45–75.
Schäffner, Christina 1997 Metaphor and interdisciplinary analysis. *Journal of Area Studies* 11: 57–72.
Schäffner, Christina 2001a Attitudes towards Europe – mediated by translation. In: Andreas Musolff, Colin Good, Petra Points and Ruth Wittlinger (eds.), *Attitudes towards Europe: Language in the unification process*, 201–217. Aldershot, UK: Ashgate.
Schäffner, Christina 2001b Editorial: Political speeches and discourse analysis. *Current Issues in Language and Society* 3.3: 201–204.
Schäffner, Christina 2004 Political discourse analysis from the point of view of translation studies. *Journal of Language and Politics* 3.1: 117–150.
Sharifian, Farzad 2003 On cultural conceptualisations. *Journal of Cognition and Culture* 3.3: 187–207.
Sharifian, Farzad 2007 Politics and/of translation: Case studies between English and Persian. *Journal of Intercultural Studies* 28.4: 413–424.
Sharifian, Farzad 2009 Figurative language in international political discourse: The case of Iran. *Journal of Language and Politics* 8.3: 416–432.

Sharifian, Farzad 2011 *Cultural conceptualisations and language: Theoretical framework and applications*. Amsterdam: John Benjamins.
Sharifian, Farzad 2012 Cultural linguistics. In: Carol A. Chapelle (ed.), *The encyclopaedia of applied linguistics*, 1–6. Oxford: Wiley-Blackwell.
Shoemaker, Pamela J. and Stephen S. Reese 1996 *Mediating the message: Theories of influence on mass media content*. New York: Longman.
WorldNetDaily. *Ayatollah warns U.S. needs punch in mouth*. Available at http://www.wnd.com/2005/05/30111/#KEuSfbbqQruxBKRY.99

Part V: **Beyond translation**

Michele I. Feist
Experimental lexical semantics at the crossroads between languages*

"Each language lays down its own boundaries within the amorphous 'thought-mass' and stresses different factors in it in different arrangements, puts the centers of gravity in different places and gives them different emphases." (Hjelmslev 1961)

1 Introduction

The job of a translator involves the extraction of meaning from a source language text and the recreation of equivalent meaning in the target language (Bell 1991; Hu 2003; McElhanon 2005; Newmark 2003; *inter alia*). When rendering meaning in the target language, the translator may seek translation equivalents – forms in the two languages that are used to communicate the same or similar meaning.

Central to the enterprise of translation are, thus, the issues of meaning and equivalence. In the broadest sense, translation involves the identification of meaning within a source language text and the recreation of that meaning in the target language. Yet the "snag" in this transfer, as noted by Newmark (2003: 55–56), "is in the concept of meaning", made more difficult by the fact that "bilingual dictionaries are almost devoid of definitions" (Werner 1994: 114), opting, instead, for the presentation of potential translation equivalents with little detailed explanation of their differences. Trickier still, as underscored by the ideal of equivalence, the identification and analysis of meaning for the task of translation is two-fold, requiring engagement with meaning within both the source language and the target language. Furthermore, in order to establish equivalence, the meanings must be compared, with the aim of minimizing differences.

The importance of translation equivalents to the job of the translator is undeniable. Translation involves the "obligation to find 'equivalents' which

---

* I am grateful to Ana Rojo and to an anonymous reviewer for their comments on an earlier version of this chapter, and to Melissa Bowerman and Eric Pederson for the use of their Topological Relations Picture Series.

'preserve' features of the original" (Bell 1991: 6), with the aim to use these equivalents to reproduce linguistic features of the original as accurately as possible. However, Bell (1991: 6) notes, "the contrasting forms convey meanings which cannot but fail to coincide totally". For this reason, as Werner (1995) has demonstrated, translation is not a one-to-one mapping. Rather, he argues, each sentence in a source language text will correspond to multiple potential translation equivalents in the target language. As a result, the equivalents sought by translators are variable, and their appropriateness may be contextually determined rather than linguistically pre-determined (cf. Hu 2003), placing the burden of determining the nature of equivalence directly on the translator.

Consistent with the subjective nature of the translator's identification of meaning and evaluation of equivalence, Hu (2003: 113) reinterprets the translator's job as "to uncover as much of the cognitive reality as possible and relay it to the reader of the target-language text". Noting that, in language production, a speaker or writer structures a scene for linguistic expression and incorporates a particular perspective (Langacker 1987), Hu (2003) argues that the analysis of meaning involves a construal of the source-language text's imagery. The translator's task, then, becomes to reconstruct the "representation of reality conceived by [the] author" of the source-language text (Hu 2003: 113).

In this paper, I will investigate issues of meaning and equivalence with respect to spatial relational terms. First, I will discuss the particular problems raised by spatial relational terms in cross-linguistic perspective. Because this domain is pervasive in human communication, virtually every translator will need to translate terms from this domain, making it imperative that translators learn to successfully overcome the problem of inequivalencies in translation in this domain. I will then outline the contributions of experimental work in lexical semantics to our understanding of similarity and variation in this domain, with a particular emphasis on the ways in which insights from experimental lexical semantics may redefine the criteria for meaning and equivalence and ease the translator's task of "uncover[ing] as much of the cognitive reality as possible".

2 The problem of space

As many who have studied a second language can attest, spatial relational terms are among the most difficult to learn to control (Jarvis and Odlin 2000; Tanehashi 2005) and thus present particular problems for the translator (Trujillo 1995). Looking cross-linguistically at spatial terms, the sources of this difficulty become evident, as subtle differences between the meanings of potential translation equivalents are the rule, rather than the exception.

One way in which languages differ is in the number of spatial terms available to label spatial configurations, with distinctions in one language neutralized in the categorization system of a second. For example, as Landau and Jackendoff (1993) have observed, the categories of spatial configurations labeled by English *in* and *on* are typically not distinguished in Spanish, as the Spanish spatial term *en* is applicable to both. Conversely, the category of configurations typically labeled with *on* in English may be divided into three categories in Dutch, corresponding to *op*, *aan*, and *om* (Gentner and Bowerman 2009).

Even in cases where two languages do not differ in the number of spatial terms that may apply to a particular range of configurations, differences have been noted in the ways in which the configurations are grouped in the spatial reference systems of the languages. For instance, English marks a distinction between an apple *in* a bowl and a handle *on* a pan, but does not mark a distinction between a handle *on* a pan and a cup *on* a table. In contrast, Finnish marks a distinction between the latter two configurations (using the inessive case for the handle *on* the pan and the adessive case for the cup *on* the table), but does not mark a distinction between an apple *in* a bowl and a handle *on* a pan (both of which would receive inessive case) (Bowerman 1996b).

Relatedly, in some cases the distinctions marked in one language are simply left unmarked in another, precluding the identification of an optimal translation equivalent. As a case in point, Korean, unlike English, marks a distinction between configurations involving a tight fit between two entities and configurations involving a loose fit (Bowerman and Choi 2001; Choi and Bowerman 1991).

In addition, cross-linguistic differences in the labeling of individual spatial configurations may indicate subtle differences in conceptualization, rather than merely being idiosyncrasies that must be noted on a case-by-case basis. For instance, one might expect that flat geographic expanses, such as deserts and meadows, would occur with the same spatial term when used as a reference object for a spatial relation. While this is the case in English (*in* the meadow; *in* the desert) and in Polish (*na* lace 'on meadow'; *na* pustyni 'on desert'), this parallelism does not hold in Russian (*na* lugu 'on meadow'; *v* pustyne 'in desert') (examples from Cienki 1989), indicating that the manner in which a language conceptualizes one reference object, and, thus, categorizes spatial configurations involving that reference object, may not predict how it will conceptualize other, seemingly similar reference objects, and categorize spatial configurations involving them.

The cross-linguistic variation evident in spatial language presents a special set of challenges for translators, who must go beyond simple characterizations of spatial meaning in order to appreciate the limits on the overlap in the range of application of the spatial relational terms in the source and target languages. Further, in the face of variations in meaning overlap, the translator must make a judgment regarding how much overlap in meaning is necessary for two words to be comparable, or "translation equivalents".

In recent years, the semantics of spatial terms have received considerable empirical attention, both from a semantic typological point of view (e.g. Bowerman 1996a; Bowerman and Choi 2001; Feist 2000, 2008b, 2010; Levinson, Meira, and the Language and Cognition Group 2003) and from a psycholinguistic perspective (e.g. Coventry and Garrod 2004; Feist 2000, 2010; Feist and Gentner 2003). These studies have shed light on the nature of cross-linguistic variation in spatial meaning, in addition to clarifying the meanings of individual spatial relational terms, making them an invaluable resource for the translator who seeks a deeper understanding of the situations in which two words may or may not be considered translation equivalents.

3 Experimental insights into the lexical semantics of space

Empirical research on the semantics of spatial relational terms suggests that their meanings are complex, and that their appropriate use may be both variable across languages and extremely sensitive to contextual factors. As reviewed above, spatial terms vary across languages not only in the distinctions that they lexicalize along a given dimension, both in number (e.g. the differences between Spanish, English, and Dutch noted above) and in kind (e.g. the above-noted differences between English and Finnish), but also in the dimensions that are important to their meanings (e.g. English support and contact vs. Korean tight-fit and loose-fit [Bowerman and Choi 2001; Choi and Bowerman 1991]).

Controlled experimental studies of spatial relational meaning provide a closer look into the complexity of meaning of spatial relational terms. The resulting characterizations of the meanings of the terms under study have afforded a detailed look inside the semantics of spatial relational terms. In addition, studies that use a single set of pictures in their examination of spatial meanings in multiple languages provide a vivid example of the failures of equivalency in the meanings of spatial relational terms across languages.

Studies on the semantic typology of spatial language (e.g. Feist 2000, 2008b, 2010; Levinson, Meira, and the Language and Cognition Group 2003; Levinson and Wilkins 2006; see also Wälchli 2010) have likewise helped to illuminate both the cross-linguistic variation in spatial semantics and the constraints on that variation. In these studies, speakers of multiple languages provide descriptions of a single set of pictured spatial relations, thus providing a concrete comparison of the ranges of application of the spatial terms across the languages sampled. The findings from these studies serve to underscore the care which translators need take to work with words in this domain, while at the same time presenting a model on which to base translation decisions.

3.1 A closer look at meaning: Experimental insights in single languages

In recent years, experimental investigations of the semantics of English spatial prepositions have built upon earlier theoretical work in lexical semantics, demonstrating that speakers are influenced in their choice of spatial term by multiple attributes of the scenes they are describing. Among these attributes are aspects of the geometry of the entities and the geometric relation between them (Coventry and Prat-Sala 2001; Coventry, Prat-Sala, and Richards 2001; Feist 2000, 2002, 2010; Feist and Gentner 2003), functional considerations (Carlson-Radvansky, Covey, and Lattanzi 1999; Coventry, Carmichael, and Garrod 1994; Coventry and Prat-Sala 2001; Feist 2000, 2002; Feist and Gentner 2003), and qualitative information regarding the physics of the interaction, including the presence of a support relation and the ability of the reference object to constrain the location of the located object (Bowerman and Choi 2001. Feist 2000, 2005, 2008b; Feist and Gentner 2003).

As a case in point, Feist (2000, 2010; Feist and Gentner 2003) created a set of pictures to be used to examine the complex interacting influences on English speakers' choice between *in* and *on*. In order to best examine the influence of any factor or set of factors, it is important to avoid varying as many other attributes of the scenes being used as possible. Thus, the pictures used in this study were simple pictures, each depicting one object whose location was to be described (either a firefly or a coin) and one reference object (either a human hand or an ambiguous dishlike object). The manipulation of the animacy of the objects in the pictures allowed an investigation of the influence on preposition choice of animacy, with its concomitant effects on inferences regarding the stability of the scene. In order to investigate the effects of the geometry of the reference object, the set included pictures of each reference object at three different levels of concavity, with the curvature of the two objects matched at each concavity. Finally, because functional information is frequently carried by the noun used to label an object (cf. Labov 1973), participants were told that the dishlike object was one of: *dish, plate, bowl, rock,* and *slab*; whereas *dish, plate,* and *bowl* all describe functional artifacts which vary in the strength of their prototypicality as containers, *rock* and *slab* name entities with no specific functional association.

The entire set of pictures was presented to native English-speaking volunteers who were asked to choose between *in* and *on* to describe the location of the firefly or coin with respect to the reference object (the hand or the dishlike object). An examination of the pattern of responses could thus reveal which, if any, of the factors manipulated in the pictures (and, in the case of the functional noun labels, in the sentences accompanying them) play a role in the use of the prepositions *in* and *on* in English. The results showed evidence that each of the factors influenced English speakers' choice. As predicted, English speakers are more likely to choose *in* if the reference object is more concave, conforming to the geometric relation of inclusion, which is frequently implicated in representations of the meaning of *in* (cf. Herskovits 1986; Miller and Johnson-Laird 1976; Talmy 1983; Tyler and Evans 2003). Similarly, English speakers are more likely to use *in* if the reference object is named with a label typically used for containers, a function typically associated with *in* (cf. Coventry and Garrod 2004; Vandeloise 1991, 1994). Finally, English speakers were influenced by the animacy of the objects, preferring to use *in* if the reference object was animate rather than inanimate, and if the located object was inanimate rather than animate. These preferences suggest that the applicability of *in* may be related to the stability of the configuration (Feist 2008a; see also Feist 2008b). Taken together, these results demonstrate the multi-componential nature of the meanings of the English prepositions *in* and *on*.

A practical consequence of this complexity of meaning is that there are multiple dimensions along which the meanings of two terms must be aligned in order for their meanings to be equivalent. Deviations along a subset of the dimensions would result in subtle differences in meaning. As evidenced by the great amount of semantic variation observed in spatial relational meanings across languages, alignment along the multiple dimensions of spatial meaning does not frequently occur. Rather, spatial relational meanings across languages tend to align imperfectly, displaying many subtle variations.

3.2 Questioning equivalency: Experimental insights across languages

Building on the work of Feist (2000), Tanehashi (2005) asked whether the factors that influence English speakers' use of *in* and *on* would similarly influence Japanese speakers' use of the closest translation equivalents for these terms, *naka* and *ue* (Young and Nakajima-Okano 1984). Furthermore, she asked whether these influences would appear in the use of the English terms by native Japanese learners of English as a second language.

Tanehashi (2005) presented her participants with a simplified version of Feist's (2000) study, in which concavity and animacy were both manipulated, but function was held constant, with all participants told that the inanimate reference object was a dish. As in the native English data of Feist (2000), Tanehashi (2005) found that concavity of the reference object influenced participants' choice of a spatial term, with *naka* chosen more frequently for the more concave reference objects than for the less concave ones. In addition, she found that participants chose *naka* more frequently when the reference object was a hand than when it was a dish, echoing the English data.

Despite these similarities, Tanehashi (2005) found evidence that the distinction between Japanese *naka* and *ue* differs from the corresponding distinction between English *in* and *on*. First, unlike the patterns in Feist's (2000) English data, Tanehashi's (2005) Japanese data did not show evidence for an effect of the animacy of the located object on the choice between *naka* and *ue*. Second, the rate at which Japanese speakers chose *naka* was consistently lower than the rate at which native speakers of English chose *in*, with English choices reflecting a balance between *in* and *on* across the pictures in the experiment set, and Japanese choices demonstrating an overall preference for *ue* across the same set of situations. Taken together, these results begin to illuminate the nature of the incomplete overlap between these translation equivalent spatial terms.

Particularly revealing, Tanehashi (2005) also examined preposition choice across the same set of situations for native Japanese-speaking learners of English as a second language, all of whom were majoring in English at a university in Japan. As in the native English data and the native Japanese data, Tanehashi (2005) observed that concavity influenced the use of *in* and *on* by Japanese learners of English, with more frequent choices of *in* as the concavity of the reference object increased. Similarly, choices of *in* were once again more prevalent if the reference object was the hand than if it was the dish, indicating an influence of animacy of the reference object.

As with the Japanese results for *naka* and *ue*, however, the usage of *in* and *on* by native speakers of Japanese differed from that of native speakers of English. Strikingly, the noted asymmetry whereby *ue* was preferred to *naka* across the picture set was echoed in the Japanese speakers' use of *in* and *on*, with *on* preferred to *in* across the picture set. Similarly, while there was an effect of the animacy of the reference object in all three data sets, the effect is markedly greater for the native English speakers than for the native Japanese speakers, whether they were tested in Japanese or in English. Finally, the effect of the animacy of the located object observed in the responses of the native English speakers was absent in both the Japanese language responses and the English responses provided by native speakers of Japanese. Tanehashi (2005: 43) concludes from these results that "it appears that the effects for the use of '*naka-ni*' and '*ue-ni*',[1] and the use of 'in' and 'on' by JNS [Japanese native speaker; MF] participants, were much more similar than those for the use of 'in' and 'on' by ENS [English native speaker; MF] counterparts".

This set of results demonstrates two important points. First, the comparison of the data on the use of *in* and *on* by native speakers of English and on the use of their translation equivalent counterparts *naka* and *ue* by native speakers of Japanese demonstrates both the overlap and the limits on that overlap between the translation equivalents. Second, the comparison of the data on the use of *in* and *on* by native speakers of Japanese with the other two sets of responses illuminates the extent to which the terms studied are thought to be equivalent by second language learners and the pitfalls associated with that assumption.

The quality of a translation suffers when the translator chooses a target-language term whose meaning differs within the context from that of the source-language term. In this particularly tricky domain, translation may be enriched by a greater awareness of the limits of equivalency and of the multicomponential nature of meaning. Because the meanings of spatial relational terms draw on multiple semantic components, the meanings of potential translation equivalents may align along some, but not all, dimensions, resulting in subtle but important differences in meaning.

3.3 The semantic typology of space

While theoretical investigations into cross-linguistic differences in the meanings of spatial relational terms have been revealing, the true nature of the meaning overlap between spatial terms across languages is impossible without data revealing the referential ranges of the terms under study. With these patterns laid out, it is possible to more directly compare the range of situations for which translation equivalents may be applicable, and to predicate the choice of translation for a particular term on the specifics of the situation in which it has been used.

Studies of the semantic typology of spatial terms have begun to provide this kind of data (e.g. Feist 2000, 2008b, 2010; Levinson, Meira, and the Language and Cognition Group 2003; see also Levinson and Wilkins 2006; Wälchli 2010). In these studies, participants are asked to describe a set of pictures

---

[1] The Japanese particle *ni* marks the locative and is used in combination with the more content-bearing spatial nouns (Feist 2008b).

representing a range of spatial situations. The patterns of application of the terms used by the participants may then be compared, revealing similarities and differences in the use of the terms across the languages sampled.

In one such study, Feist (2000, 2010), building on the pioneering work of Bowerman and Pederson (1992, 1996), presented a series of twenty-nine line drawings to speakers of sixteen languages (representing nine language families) (see Table 13.1). These pictures, drawn largely from Melissa Bowerman and Eric Pederson's Topological Relations Picture Series (Bowerman and Pederson 1992, 1996; Gentner and Bowerman 2009; Levinson, Meira, and the Language and Cognition Group 2003), each depicted one object colored yellow, whose location was to be described, and a second object in black and white, which served as a reference object. For each picture, participants were asked to describe the location of the yellow object with respect to the other object, in a way that they would consider natural and comfortable if talking to a fellow speaker of their native language (for details of the pictures used, see Feist 2000). The resultant database of descriptions can be subjected to a variety of analyses, each of which uniquely contributes to our understanding of meaning within and across languages. I will briefly describe three analyses, illustrating for each the contribution it may make to the theory and practice of translation.

Table 13.1: The language sample[2]

Language	Genetic affiliation
Polish	Indo-European, Slavic, West, Lechitic
Russian	Indo-European, Slavic, East
Croatian	Indo-European, Slavic, South, Western
German	Indo-European, Germanic, West, Continental, High
Swedish	Indo-European, Germanic, North, East Scandinavian
Italian	Indo-European, Italic, Romance, Italo-Western, Italo-Romance
French	Indo-European, Italic, Romance, Italo-Western, Western, Gallo-Romance, North
Hindi	Indo-European, Indo-Iranian, Indo-Aryan, Central zone, Western Hindi, Hindustani
Hebrew	Afro-Asiatic, Semitic, Central, South, Canaanite

(Continued)

---

2 Languages designated with * before their name were only represented in the study reported in Feist (2008b).

Table 13.1: The language sample (*Continued*)

Language	Genetic affiliation
Hungarian	Uralic, Finno-Ugric, Ugric, Hungarian
Cantonese	Sino-Tibetan, Chinese
Telegu	Dravidian, South-Central, Telugu
Turkish	Altaic, Turkic, Southern, Turkish
Tagalog	Austronesian, Malayo-Polynesian, Western Malayo-Polynesian, Meso Philippine, Central Philippine, Tagalog
Japanese	Japanese, Japanese
Korean	Language Isolate
* Indonesian	Austronesian, Malayo-Polynesian, Malayic, Malayan, Local Malay
* Egyptian Arabic	Afro-Asiatic, Semitic, Central, South, Arabic
* Bangla (Bengali)	Indo-European, Indo-Iranian, Indo-Aryan, Eastern zone, Bengali-Assamese
* English (American)	Indo-European, Germanic, West, English
* Thai	Tai-Kadai, Kam-Tai, Be-Tai, Tai-Sek, Tai, Southwestern, East Central, Chiang Saeng
* Mongolian	Altaic, Mongolian, Eastern, Oirat-Khalkha, Khalkha-Buriat, Mongolian Proper
* Vietnamese	Austro-Asiatic, Mon-Khmer, Viet-Muong, Vietnamese
* Mandarin	Sino-Tibetan, Chinese

There is a difference of opinion among scholars as to whether or not Korean is related to Japanese; Korean is also possibly distantly related to Altaic.

For the first analysis, Feist (2000) first coded each picture to indicate whether or not a small set of attributes drawn from theoretical investigations of spatial semantics held true. The coded pictures then served as the basis for characterizing the meanings of the elicited spatial terms. The coded attributes were as follows:

- *a difference in vertical position* (cf. *above, below, over,* and *under*; O'Keefe 1996; Tyler and Evans 2003)
- *contact* (cf. *on*; Cienki 1989; Herskovits 1986; Miller and Johnson-Laird 1976)
- *inclusion* (cf. *in*; Cienki 1989; Herskovits 1986; Miller and Johnson-Laird 1976; Tyler and Evans 2003)
- *support* (cf. *on*; Bowerman and Pederson 1992, 1996; Herskovits 1986; Miller and Johnson-Laird 1976)
- *relative size* (may facilitate other attributes, such as *inclusion* and *support*)

- *a functional relation between the objects* (Coventry, Carmichael, and Garrod 1994; Vandeloise 1991, 1994)
- *control by the reference object* (cf. *in*; Coventry, Carmichael, and Garrod 1994; Coventry and Garrod 2004)
- *animacy* (cf. *in*; Feist 2000; Feist and Gentner 2003)

To examine the range of application of the elicited terms, each term was considered to define a group including all of the pictures which had been described using the term. The grouped pictures were then examined in order to isolate the attribute or attributes that were common to all of the pictures in the group. From this, a characterization was developed for each term as defined by the set of attributes common to the pictures that the term could describe. These characterizations are exemplified by the terms in Table 13.2: for each term, a plus under the attribute indicates that the attribute was present in all pictures described by the term, while a minus indicates that the attribute was absent from all pictures described by the term.

Table 13.2: Representative terms and the attributes characterizing their use

Term	Located object higher than reference object	Contact	Reference object supports located object	Inclusion
üzerinde (Turkish)	+			
ue (Japanese)	+			
nad (Croatian)	+	−		
[upar] (Hindi)	+	−		
sotto (Italian)	−	+		
sous (French)	−	+		
[na] (Russian)		+	+	
[al] (Hebrew)		+	+	
auf (German)		+		
an (German)		+		
i, inne (Swedish)				+
loob (Tagalog)				+
[tʃ] (Cantonese)				−
-da, -ta (Turkish)				
ni (Japanese)				

From this analysis, the following eight classes of spatial meaning were identified, accounting for all sixty-three terms collected:

- located object higher than reference object
- located object higher than reference object, no contact
- located object lower than reference object, with contact
- reference object supports located object, with contact
- contact
- inclusion of located object by reference object
- absence of inclusion of located object by reference object
- general spatial term (no attribute values encoded)

These classes, and the semantic characterizations that led to them, constitute a potentially rich resource for the translator seeking a contextually appropriate match for a source language term. Rather than directly seeking a target language "equivalent" for the source language words, the translator may use the described situation as a mediator between source and target language texts. Drawn from elicited descriptions of viewed spatial scenes, the characterizations provide a means to reconstruct the range of realities for which a given term may be used, after which the translator may match the described situation to a situation within the referential range of the chosen target language term.

While the first analysis provides insight into the meanings of the elicited terms, the characterizations structured by the coded attributes of the pictures remain abstract. A more concrete comparison of the meanings of the elicited terms can be achieved through a Behavioral Profile analysis (Gries 2010). In this type of analysis, each spatial term is characterized by the pattern of speakers' propensities to use the term to describe the pictures in the set – its Behavioral Profile. For example, English *on* is associated with a vector made up of the proportion of speakers who used *on* to describe the first picture, the proportion who used *on* to describe the second picture, the proportion who used *on* to describe the third picture, etc. The Behavioral Profiles of the elicited terms can then be statistically compared – either pairwise, using correlations, or on a larger scale, using hierarchical cluster analysis. The result of the comparison is a set of measures of the similarities amongst the terms in the set.

To apply a Behavioral Profile analysis to the expanded set of spatial terms collected by Feist (2000, 2008b; see Table 13.1 for the list of languages represented), I created a co-occurrence table that included the relative frequency of co-occurrence of each elicited term with each picture; frequency of co-occurrence was defined as the proportion of speakers of the language who had chosen to use the term in their description of the picture. A small excerpt of the co-occurrence table is presented in Table 13.3.

Table 13.3: Excerpt of Behavioral Profile vectors for elicited spatial terms from Feist (2000, 2008b)

Elicited term	Lamp over table	Cloud over mountain	Cup on table	Book on shelf	Cat on mat
Polish *nad*	0.5	0.5	0	0	0
Polish *na*	0	0	1	0.75	0.75
Polish *w*	0	0	0	0	0
Swedish *över*	1	0	0	0	0
Swedish *ovanför*	0	1	0	0	0
Swedish *på*	0	0	1	1	1
Swedish *inne*	0	0	0	0	0
Japanese *ue*	1	1	1	1	1
Japanese *naka*	0	0	0	0	0
English *over*	0.83	0.33	0	0	0
English *above*	0.17	0.67	0	0	0.17
English *on top*	0	0	0.5	0	0
English *on*	0	0	0.5	0.83	0.83
English *in*	0	0	0	0	0

In order to better understand the similarities and differences amongst the elicited terms, I subjected the Behavioral Profiles to a hierarchical clustering analysis. The aim of this analysis is to statistically evaluate the pairwise similarities amongst the Behavioral Profiles (and, hence, the spatial terms), clustering them together with successively decreasing similarity. Thus, Behavioral Profiles clustered together in the smallest clusters will display the greatest similarities, while those that only co-exist within the large clusters will be minimally similar. The clusters are then arrayed in a tree structure, or dendogram, for further examination and analysis. Figure 13.1 shows an excerpt from the dendogram resulting from the hierarchical cluster analysis of the Behavioral Profiles of the 110 spatial relational terms elicited by Feist (2000, 2008b).

The first thing to notice is that the structure in the data set is based on semantic similarities amongst the spatial terms, with terms clustering together based on similarity in their referential ranges. The hierarchical cluster analysis accordingly identified potential translation equivalents, with terms drawn from a single language rarely co-occurring within a lower-level cluster.

In addition, the analysis highlights within-language distinctions made by a subset of the languages sampled. For example, at the far right of the dendogram

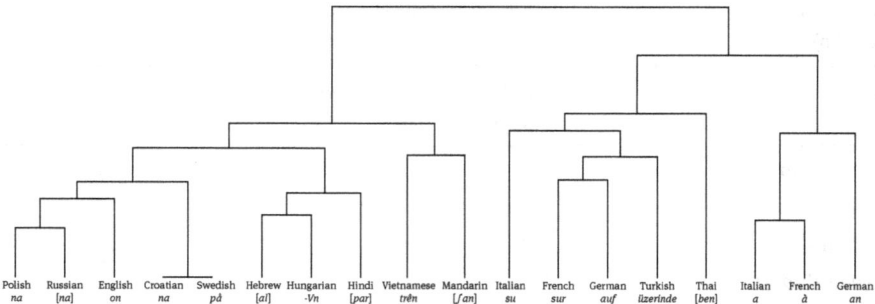

Figure 13.1: Excerpt from the dendogram of the 110 spatial terms collected by Feist (2000, 2008b)

in Figure 13.1 is a cluster including Italian *a*, French *à*, and German *an*; to the left of this cluster, and connected to it one level up in the structure, is a larger one containing Italian *su*, French *sur*, and German *auf*. Farther to the left is a set of clusters which attaches at a still higher level to the clusters containing the Italian, French, and German terms. This clustering indicates that parallel distinctions occur in Italian, French, and German for this data set, but these distinctions are largely absent in the other languages sampled. Thus, in addition to identifying potential translation equivalents, the Behavioral Profile analysis draws attention to subtle semantic distinctions, thereby alerting a translator to potential trouble spots in the search for translation equivalents.

A third way to examine the cross-linguistic usage patterns is through multidimensional scaling (MDS). Like semantic maps (Haspelmath 2003), MDS is useful for the exploration of similarities and dissimilarities in many kinds of typological linguistic data, allowing for probabilistic examinations of large data sets (Croft and Poole 2008; Levinson, Meira, and the Language and Cognition Group 2003; Majid et al. 2004; Wälchli 2010). Based on the assumption that the extent of the overlap in spatial terms used to describe two pictures is indicative of their similarity, Feist (2008b) used MDS to create a similarity space informed by her expanded set of elicited spatial terms (see Table 13.1 for languages represented). The placement of points in this space corresponding to each of the twenty-nine pictures was optimized such that the distances between them were a function of the overlap in the elicited terms that had been used to describe them. Concretely, the fact that an apple *in* a bowl and a handle *on* a pan would be described using separate terms in English would suggest that the two pictures must be located at some distance in similarity space. However, as reviewed above, data from Finnish would provide evidence that this distance may not be too great, as the two pictures would be described with the same spatial term (inessive case). In this way, each term in the data set contributes evidence regarding the similarity and dissimilarity between every pair of pictures in the set. MDS then compiles the complete set of evidence in service of the creation of the completed, optimized similarity space (Figure 13.2).

There is much to be learned from the resultant similarity space. On a global level, the similarity space may suggest universal tendencies within the domain which may be obscured by examining a single language. These universal

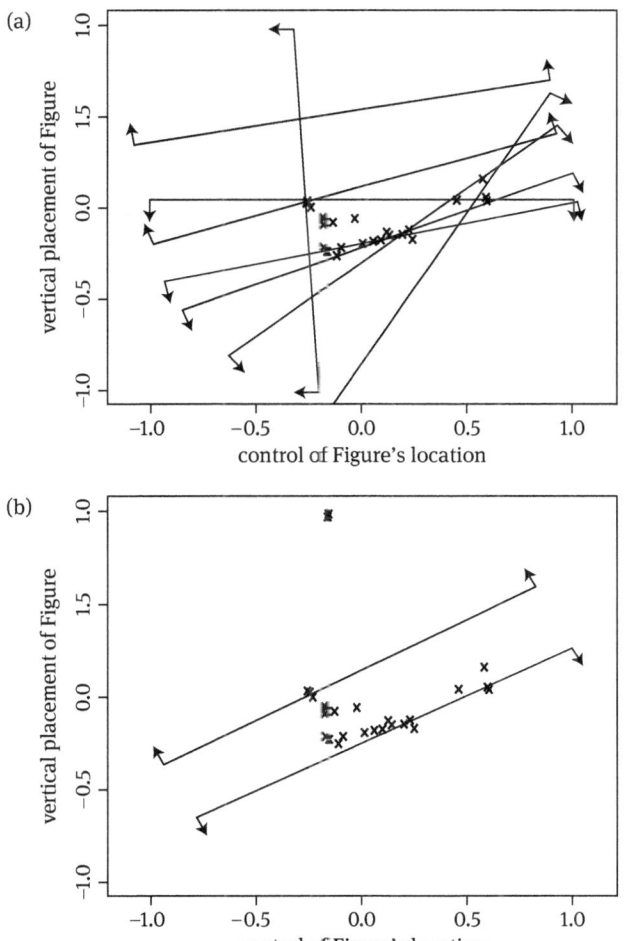

Figure 13.2: MDS plots of the spatial relation similarity space. Each picture in the set is represented by an X. The lines represent spatial terms from English (panel [a]) and Japanese (panel [b]). See text for discussion.

tendencies may emerge as clusters of pictures, suggestive of a semantic similarity which is frequently encoded across languages (Levinson, Meira, and the Language and Cognition Group 2003). Alternatively, universal tendencies may emerge as gradable dimensions of variation along which languages impose lexical categories (Feist 2008b; Wälchli 2010). These dimensions may then represent constraints on cross-linguistic variation in the domain.

On a local level, an MDS solution may be overlaid with "cutting lines" (Croft and Poole 2008) representing the spatial terms. Cutting lines bisect the space, separating those pictures that may be described using the term from those which may not. Arrows on the ends of the lines indicate the portion of the space within which the pictures described by the term defining the cutting line may be found. In plotting the cutting lines for candidate translation equivalents, a translator would have a graphic representation of the overlap in meaning between the terms relative to the set of pictures plotted. In addition, by comparing the sets of cutting lines drawn from two languages, a translator may get an idea of the scope of difference in the spatial semantic systems encoded by the languages in question. For example, Figure 13.2 above presents the similarity space for the spatial relational terms examined by Feist (2008b). In panel (a), the similarity space is overlaid with the cutting lines associated with the eight English spatial terms elicited in the study. Panel (b) shows the same similarity space, overlaid with the two Japanese spatial terms elicited in the study. The difference in the ways in which the two languages subdivide the space is striking, both in the granularity of the divisions, and in the sets of pictures isolated by each term (while the top line on the Japanese graph, corresponding to *ue*, has a near-equivalent in the English graph, the bottom line, corresponding to *naka*, lacks an English match in both placement and slope). Comparison of the placement of cutting lines for different languages allows for a more focused examination of the nature of translation equivalence, and the limits on that equivalence, in attempting to choose a translation for a source language term within a specific context.

Though semantic typological work is still in its infancy, it carries great possibility for deep insights regarding similarities and variation across languages. In addition, in mapping out the extensional ranges of a set of related terms drawn from multiple languages, this method allows for more focused evaluation of similarity and dissimilarity in the meanings of potential translation equivalents.

4 Conclusions

The evaluation of source-language meaning and concomitant reconstruction of that meaning within a target language are central to the task of the translator.

The difficulty of this task lies, in part, in the fact that "[t]here exists no privileged pair of equivalences" (Werner 1995: 4) with the result that all reconstructions within the target language represent subjective choices on the part of the translator.

Hu (2003: 120) has argued that the translator's goal is to create an "experientially equivalent target-language text", but that the actual product "is very much determined by the way the translator construes" the source-language text. In this way, Hu redefines the evaluation of meaning as a cognitive and linguistic analysis of the source-language text. Experimental work in lexical semantics provides a tool with which to conduct such an analysis, grounding the meanings of lexical items in their use across a range of situations. Thus, just as experimental work in lexical semantics has helped to move forward theoretical approaches to word meaning, so could it help to move forward the translator's task of analyzing meaning in the source-language text and mapping that meaning to target-language terms. Furthermore, in addition to illuminating meaning, an experimental approach may allow a direct comparison between the uses of related forms across languages, as demonstrated above, thus facilitating the identification of appropriate translation equivalents.

As demonstrated in this short review, experimental work in lexical semantics makes two potential contributions to the theory and practice of translation. First, this work provides a view of meaning as use, grounding the representation of a term's meaning in speakers' likelihood to use the term to describe a concrete set of situations drawn from the world around them. Second, this body of work provides evidence regarding the degree of equivalence between words of the source language and matched words of the target language. Experimental approaches to meaning provide a foundation for comparing the meanings of terms drawn from multiple languages grounded in concrete choices to use the terms as descriptions of reality. Such evidence is invaluable for the translator seeking target-language words (and contexts) which encode meanings that are the same as, or maximally similar to, the meanings encoded in the source-language text.

Central to the issues of meaning and equivalence in translation is the question of where – and how – a source-language text and a target-language text depart from equivalence. This is a question that cannot be answered without a clearer understanding of the source-language terms and the target-language terms, each considered within the context of their own language (McElhanon 2005). It is here that an experimental approach to lexical semantics really shines, grounding the analysis of meaning squarely in the context of the language system as accessed by the native speaker.

References

Bell, Roger T. 1991 *Translation and translating: Theory and practice*. London: Longman.
Bowerman, Melissa 1996a Learning how to structure space for language: A crosslinguistic perspective. In: Paul Bloom, Mary A. Peterson, Lynn Nadel and Merrill F. Garrett (eds.), *Language and space*, 385–436. Cambridge, MA: MIT Press.
Bowerman, Melissa 1996b The origins of children's spatial semantic categories: Cognitive versus linguistic determinants. In: John J. Gumperz and Stephen C. Levinson (eds.), *Rethinking linguistic relativity*, 145–176. Cambridge, MA: MIT Press.
Bowerman, Melissa and Soonja Choi 2001 Shaping meanings for language: Universal and language specific in the acquisition of spatial semantic categories. In: Melissa Bowerman and Stephen C. Levinson (eds.), *Language acquisition and conceptual development*, 475–511. Cambridge: Cambridge University Press.
Bowerman, Melissa and Eric Pederson 1992 Cross-linguistic perspectives on topological spatial relationships. Paper presented at the 91st Annual Meeting of the American Anthrolopogical Association, San Francisco, CA, December 2–6, 1992.
Bowerman, Melissa and Eric Pederson 1996 *Cross-linguistic perspectives on topological spatial relationships*. Unpublished manuscript.
Carlson-Radvansky, Laura A., Eric S. Covey and Kathleen M. Lattanzi 1999 "What" effects on "where": Functional influences on spatial relations. *Psychological Science* 10: 516–521.
Choi, Soonja and Melissa Bowerman 1991 Learning to express motion events in English and Korean: The influence of language-specific lexicalization patterns. *Cognition* 41: 83–121.
Cienki, Alan J. 1989 *Spatial cognition and the semantics of prepositions in English, Polish, and Russian*. Munich, Germany: Otto Sagner.
Coventry, Kenny R., Richard Carmichael and Simon C. Garrod 1994 Spatial prepositions, object-specific function, and task requirements. *Journal of Semantics* 11: 289–309.
Coventry, Kenny R. and Simon C. Garrod 2004 *Saying, seeing and acting: The psychological semantics of spatial prepositions*. London: Psychology Press.
Coventry, Kenny R. and Merce Prat-Sala 2001 Object-specific function, geometry, and the comprehension of in and on. *European Journal of Cognitive Psychology* 13.4: 509–528.
Coventry, Kenny R., Merce Prat-Sala and Lynn Richards 2001 The interplay between geometry and function in the comprehension of *over, under, above,* and *below*. *Journal of Memory and Language* 44: 376–398.
Croft, William and Keith T. Poole 2008 Inferring universals from grammatical variation: Multidimensional scaling for typological analysis. *Theoretical Linguistics* 34: 1–37.
Feist, Michele I. 2000 *On in and on: An investigation into the linguistic encoding of spatial scenes*. PhD dissertation, Department of Linguistics, Northwestern University, Evanston, IL.
Feist, Michele I. 2002 Geometry, function, and the use of in and on. Paper presented at the Sixth Conference on Conceptual Structure, Discourse, and Language, October 11–14, 2002. Houston, TX. Available at: http://www.ucs.louisiana.edu/~mif8232/feist02.doc.
Feist, Michele I. 2005 In support of in and on. Paper presented at the New Directions in Cognitive Linguistics Conference, Brighton, UK, October 23–25, 2005.
Feist, Michele I. 2008a The changing shape of prepositional meanings. In: Harvey Chan, Heather Jacob and Enkeleida Kapia (eds.), *Proceedings of the 32nd Annual Boston University Conference on Language Development*, 108–119. Somerville, MA: Cascadilla Press.
Feist, Michele I. 2008b Space between languages. *Cognitive Science* 32.7: 1177–1199.

Feist, Michele I. 2010 Inside *in* and *on*: Typological and psycholinguistic perspectives. In: Vyvyan Evans and Paul Chilton (eds.), *Language, cognition and space: The state of the art and new directions*, 95–114. London: Equinox.

Feist, Michele I. and Dedre Gentner 2003 Factors involved in the use of in and on. In: Rick Alterman and David Kirsh (eds.), *Proceedings of the Twenty-Fifth Annual Meeting of the Cognitive Science Society*, 390–395. Mahwah, NJ: Erlbaum.

Gentner, Dedre and Melissa Bowerman 2009 Why some spatial semantic categories are harder to learn than others: The typological prevalence hypothesis. In: Jiansheng Guo, Elena Lieven, Nancy Budwig, Susan Ervin-Tripp, Keiko Nakamura and Şeyda Özçalışkan (eds.), *Crosslinguistic approaches to the psychology of language: Research in the tradition of Dan Isaac Slobin*, 465–480. New York: Psychology Press.

Gries, Stefan Th. 2010 Behavioral profiles: A fine-grained and quantitative approach in corpus-based lexical semantics. *The Mental Lexicon* 5.3: 323–346.

Haspelmath, Martin 2003 The geometry of grammatical meaning: Semantic maps and cross-linguistic comparison. In: Michael Tomasello (ed.), *The new psychology of language*, Vol. 2, 211–242. Mahwah, NJ: Erlbaum.

Herskovits, Annette 1986 *Language and spatial cognition: An interdisciplinary study of the prepositions in English*. Cambridge: Cambridge University Press.

Hjelmslev, Louis 1961 *Prolegomena to a theory of language*. Translated by Francis J. Whitfield. Milwaukee: University of Wisconsin Press.

Hu, Helen Chau 2003 Cognitive-functional considerations in translating. *IRAL: International Review of Applied Linguistics in Language Teaching* 41.2: 107–130.

Jarvis, Scott and Terrence Odlin 2000 Morphological type, spatial reference, and language transfer. *Studies in Second Language Acquisition* 22: 535–556.

Labov, William 1973 The boundaries of words and their meanings. In: Charles-James N. Bailey and Roger W. Shuy (eds.), *New ways of analyzing variation in English*, 340–373. Washington, DC: Georgetown University Press.

Landau, Barbara and Ray Jackendoff 1993 "What" and "where" in spatial language and spatial cognition. *Behavioral and Brain Sciences* 16: 217–265.

Langacker, Ronald W. 1987 *Foundations of cognitive grammar*. Vol. 1, *Theoretical prerequisites*. Stanford, CA: Stanford University Press.

Levinson, Stephen C., Sergio Meira and the Language and Cognition Group 2003 "Natural concepts" in the spatial topological domain – adpositional meanings in crosslinguistic perspective: An exercise in semantic typology. *Language* 79.3: 485–516.

Levinson, Stephen C. and David P. Wilkins (eds.) 2006 *Grammars of space: Explorations of cognitive diversity*. Cambridge: Cambridge University Press.

Majid, Asifa, Miriam van Staden, James S. Boster and Melissa Bowerman 2004 Event categorization: A cross-linguistic perspective. In: Kenneth D. Forbus, Dedre Gentner and Terry Regier (eds.), *Proceedings of the Twenty-Sixth Annual Meeting of the Cognitive Science Society*, 885–890. Mahwah, NJ: Erlbaum.

McElhanon, Kenneth A. 2005 From word to scenario: The influence of linguistic theories upon models of translation. *Journal of Translation* 1.3: 29–67.

Miller, George A. and Philip N. Johnson-Laird 1976 *Language and perception*. Cambridge, MA: Belknap Press.

Newmark, Peter 2003 No global communication without translation. In: Gunilla Anderman and Margaret Rogers (eds.), *Translation today: Trends and perspectives*, 55–67. Clevedon, UK: Multilingual Matters.

O'Keefe, John 1996 The spatial preposition in English, vector grammar, and the cognitive map theory. In: Paul Bloom, Mary A. Peterson, Lynn Nadel and Merrill F. Garrett (eds.), *Language and space*, 277–316. Cambridge, MA: MIT Press.

Talmy, Leonard 1983 How language structures space. In: Herbert Pick and Linda Acredolo (eds.), *Spatial orientation: Theory, research, and application*, 225–282. New York: Plenum Press.

Tanehashi, Nanako 2005 *Cross-linguistic differences and the second language acquisition of spatial terms: The case of English "in" and "on"*. Master's thesis, Nagoya Gakuin University, Nagoya, Japan.

Trujillo, Arturo 1995 Towards a cross-linguistically valid classification of spatial prepositions. *Machine Translation* 10: 93–141.

Tyler, Andrea and Vyvyan Evans 2003 *The semantics of English prepositions*. Cambridge: Cambridge University Press.

Vandeloise, Claude 1991 *Spatial prepositions: A case study from French*. Translated by Anna R. K. Bosch. Chicago: University of Chicago Press.

Vandeloise, Claude 1994 Methodology and analyses of the preposition *in*. *Cognitive Linguistics* 5.2: 157–184.

Wälchli, Bernhard 2010 Similarity semantics and building probabilistic semantic maps from parallel texts. *Linguistic Discovery* 8.1: 331–371.

Werner, Oswald 1994 Ethnography and translation: Issues and challenges. *Sartoniana* 7: 59–135.

Werner, Oswald 1995 Ethnographic translation. Paper presented at the First Conference on Philippino Psychology, University of the Philippines, Quezon City Campus.

Young, John, and Kimiko Nakajima-Okano 1984 *Learn Japanese: New college text*. Vol. 2. Honolulu: University of Hawaii Press.

Anna Hatzidaki
A cognitive approach to translation: The psycholinguistic perspective

1 Introduction

In the introduction of this book, through a comprehensive review of the history of translation and its relationship with linguistics since the 1970s, Ana Rojo and Iraide Ibarretxe-Antuñano outline the stages these two fields have gone through and their interactions up to date. It is rather striking that despite many changes in translation approaches and research directions (e.g. prescriptive; descriptive; cognitive), only recently has a growing body of experimental studies emerged on the process of translation and its theoretical implications (see Shreve and Angelone 2010 for a review). The reason for a delayed interest in experimentally approaching translation may be due to an undervalued view of the interdisciplinary role of Translation Studies and its relevance to other areas of humanities or social sciences. In what follows, we briefly readdress the research methodology that has been employed since the early 1990s to study the process of translation and present new experimental – psycholinguistic methods it has given way to, focusing on the psycholinguistic perspective of the study of translation. That is, how translation has been studied by psycholinguistics and what the latter can tell us about the former. Section 2 contrasts empirical and experimental methodologies used to examine translation and comments on their weaknesses and merits (Subsections 2.1 and 2.2); it also reviews a number of psycholinguistic studies where different approaches to translation have been employed (Subsections 2.2.1 and 2.2.3). Section 3 summarizes how translation has been approached and examined by the field of psycholinguistics to-date, and briefly discusses future directions that encourage a bidirectional relationship between psycholinguistics and Translation Studies.

2 Empirical and experimental methods used to examine translation

2.1 The Think Aloud Protocol

The point of departure is the earliest psychological tool, *Think Aloud Protocol* (TAP), according to which the mental processes that undergo the translation task may be revealed by being explicitly uttered (Lörscher 1991, 1996). Traditionally, the person who is performing a translation is required to say out loud what she is thinking while transferring a text from one language to another. These thoughts may precede or follow any translation act, such as pinpointing translating difficulties; selecting and advising a dictionary; taking notes of likely translation proposals; deleting considered translation alternatives; and so on. In other words, by means of the Think Aloud Protocol, which is often used in combination with video-recording and questionnaires, translation behaviour can be observed and described (by an experimenter who is usually blind to the aim of the study), and is assumed to provide information about a translator's cognitive processing prior to written language production (Krings 1986b, 1987). Subsequently, such information may allow translator theorists and educators to identify successful strategies that can be employed in the classroom as translation teaching methods (Kiraly 1997).

Perhaps Translation Studies have chosen to use the Think Aloud Protocol because that method was previously used to examine the process of writing (Hayes and Flower 1980), and as writing is one of the basic components of the translation procedure, the application of the Think Aloud Protocol might seem to be the most appropriate one. Indeed, as an empirical method, the Think Aloud Protocol can provide interesting information about people's translating tendencies, choices, and problem-solving attitude; for example, it may demonstrate that some (professional or non-professional) translators prefer reading the entire text before starting translating it sentence by sentence; or that some words appear to be better candidates than others depending on each individual's translation experiences; or that not all translators use the same strategies to solve a translation problem such as when dealing with metaphors (see Kiraly 1995; Kussmaul and Tirkkonen-Condit 1995 for reviews). Yet, despite their pedagogical significance, the results of Translation Studies that have employed Think Aloud Protocols should be interpreted with caution when used to address issues of cognitive mechanisms involved in translation, because the Think Aloud Protocol is rather a subjective oriented method, being heavily dependent on the participant's conscious control and the experimenter's personal view of data analysis. Furthermore, on its own, it cannot go far explaining fine cognitive details that modulate the translation process, nor capture the stage of language processing linguistic and extra-linguistic factors may impact on. Hence, as we shall see, more appropriate paradigms, better experimentally controlled methods, and more objective and reliable measures can be used from the field of psycholinguistics to shed light on cognitive processes that underlie translation.

2.2 The advance of experimental techniques: The contribution of Psycholinguistics

Psycholinguistics has developed a wide range of experimental methods borrowed from *Cognitive Psychology* to study the structures of cognition and the mental processes that are involved in various manifestations of language processing, including how people acquire one or more than one language; how language information is organised and represented in the human mind and aspects of it localised in the brain; how comprehension is achieved; and which factors contribute to successful production (Harley 1995). These methods can reveal information about the function (or malfunction) of processing systems (e.g., memory; attention; and so on) that operate both automatically, and thus unconsciously, and of those that are conscious and require effort.

Moreover, psycholinguistic methods are ideal for the study of theoretical concepts of Cognitive Linguistics (e.g. embodiment; influence of language on thought; conceptual organization) and translation (e.g. equivalence; interculturalism; text-typology), and certainly of paramount importance for the investigation of translation practice. Hence, translation can benefit from a psycholinguistic perspective because the latter allows the merging of approaches that tended to consider separately the processing of language as a product and the processing of language as an action (Clark 1992).

The most typical on-line and offline measures used in psycholinguistics are *reaction time* (RT) and *response accuracy*: how much time a participant needs to perform a given task following (computer-based) presentation of the task-stimulus (usually reported in milliseconds), and how well she performs the task (usually reported in percentage of errors committed). These two measures provide important information about knowledge representation (structure) and ease of accessing and processing its components: the simpler the knowledge organization and the easier the processing requirements, the faster and the more accurate the performance. In addition, the combination of the two measures can distinguish between performance due to processing factors and performance due to competence factors; for example, because on-line measures are time-dependent, they may reveal errors that could not be explained in terms of offline measures alone. In other words, a participant may have adequate knowledge of a second language (L2) to perform a word-translation task, yet aspects of it (e.g. contextual environment; attentional demands; memory load) may affect translation speed and overall performance accordingly. Next, before we review studies that have explored translation from a psycholinguistic perspective, we shall briefly explain the process of language production that is relevant to them.

Certain proposals have been put forward to account for how individuals with knowledge of two languages (*bilinguals* from now on) make use of their languages (de Bot 1992; de Bot and Schreuder 1993; Poulisse and Bongaerts 1994). Despite their differences mainly on the issue of how language information is organized at each level of representation (shared or separately for each language), it is generally agreed that there is a common conceptual (or semantic) store where the meaning of words and sentences is organized (see Francis 2005 for a review). There is also agreement on the assumption that this store feeds the activation of multiple semantically-related lexical nodes, as is the case with monolingual speech production. In the case of a bilingual speaker, this multiple activation spreads to both language lexicons since both languages have access to the conceptual store (see de Groot 2002a; Kroll and Dikjstra 2002 for reviews). Most researchers agree that the selected word is the one whose activation exceeds that of other activated words, thus preventing them from being chosen (e.g. La Heij 2005; Roelofs 1998), and it is usually the case that the most activated word is the one that a speaker wishes to produce. Therefore, retrieval of that word is relatively fast and easy.

The process of reading comprehension in bilinguals shares many of the assumptions of the process of language production described in the previous paragraph, in that users of more than one language are sensitive to properties from both language systems regardless of whether a particular context requires use of both languages (Kroll, Sumutka, and Schwartz 2005). For example, there is an abundance of evidence suggesting that morphophonological information from one language may be activated even when reading a text in the other language (see Dijkstra 2005 for a review). Upon presentation of a word, the processor activates letters with similar perceptual features and inhibits unrelated ones; next, lexical items stored in long-term memory that have similar perceptual features as the presented stimulus are activated in both languages, but the non-intended ones are inhibited; successful matching of a string of letters to a word (orthographic representation) ends with the retrieval of a sound (phonological representation) and meaning (semantic representation) that corresponds to the presented word (Dijkstra and van Heuven 2002). Importantly, apart from the involvement of linguistic representations in word recognition, non-linguistic context effects (e.g. participants' expectations and task demands) also play a crucial role in task performance as we shall see. A number of interesting questions can be raised regarding bilingual comprehension and production; for example, what is the mechanism that allows transition from parallel language activation to single-language comprehension or production when both languages of a bilingual are activated? But for current purposes, our focus is on psycholinguistic studies related to the cognitive processes involved in translation.

2.2.1 The role of translation direction in language representation and processing

A question that has attracted the attention of many researchers is how words are mapped onto concepts, and whether translation is achieved on the basis of a common conceptual representation or is based on word-to-word association at lexical level. In a seminal study (1994) – that would instigate a considerable number of follow-up studies – Kroll and Stewart examined the hypothesis that conceptual memory (where semantic features of a word are represented) and lexical memory (where morphological features of a word are represented) are differentially implicated in word translation depending on the direction of translation (see also Kroll et al. 2010 for a recent review). Based on previous findings from translation and picture-naming tasks in the laboratory of Kroll and colleagues, the authors argued that speakers of low proficiency in L2 need to access their L1 first to understand the meaning of an L2 word. That is, when a speaker is presented with a word in L1 to translate in L2, she needs to retrieve that word's meaning from the conceptual store, and then translate that meaning by retrieving a L2 word-form from the L2 lexical store. Hence, bilinguals require more time to translate or name a word from L1 to L2 and are more sensitive to conceptual context than when translating or naming a word from L2 to L1 (Kroll and Sholl 1992). However, as speakers gain proficiency in their L2, dependence on L1 may change gradually and conceptual mediation through L1 may not be necessary (Dufour and Kroll 1995). In the case of L2 to L1 translation or naming, there is direct mapping of lexical items from L2 to L1 because every L2 word is represented in the L1 lexicon, usually also corresponding to the way L2 is learnt (i.e. by word association). Thus, when exposed to a L2 word, bilinguals are much faster translating that word in L1 than vice versa. To summarize the views of Kroll and Stewart (1994), the strength of the links that connect the conceptual and the lexical stores, and consequently the involvement of conceptual and lexical memory, can be modulated depending on language proficiency and translation direction.

To test their hypothesis, Kroll and Stewart conducted a study on *word reading*, *picture naming*, and *word translation*. (Because monolingual experiments are outside of the scope of the present paper, throughout the paper we make reference to bilingual experiments only.) For current purposes, we focus on the findings from Experiment 3 of Kroll and Stewart, where Dutch-English fluent bilinguals[1] were

---

1 We use the convention of naming the native language first and the non-native language second; hence, Dutch-English bilinguals are Dutch native speakers whose second language is English.

used. The important semantic manipulation was the context within which words were presented: either in semantically categorized lists (i.e. lists that contained words from a single semantic category only, such as clothing) or in semantically randomized (i.e. mixed) lists. In the naming task, participants named words in L1 and L2, and in the translation task, participants translated words from L1 to L2, and from L2 to L1. Words were presented on a computer screen, and participants' reaction time and accuracy were measured. The question of interest was whether translations from L1 to L2 (which required concept mediation) would be more affected by the change of semantic context (categorized vs. randomized lists) compared with translations from L2 to L1 (which were assumed to be lexically mediated).

The results showed that the semantic manipulation of context (categorized or randomized) did not affect word naming and translation from L2 to L1, but categorized lists produced longer RTs (interference) in picture naming and translation from L1 to L2. In particular, it took longer to translate words from L1 to L2 in a semantically related (categorized) context than in an unrelated context. However, in both categorized and randomized list conditions, translations from L2 to L1 were faster than translations from L1 to L2. Moreover, the assumption of conceptual mediation in translation from L1 to L2 was further validated when bilinguals participating in the naming and translation tasks received an incidental task: overall, recall was much better for the categorized translation from L1 to L2 than for the randomized translation from L1 to L2. However, in both conditions performance on recall was better for L1-L2 translation direction than for L2-L1 translation direction. Based on these findings, Kroll and Stewart (1994) postulated that the direction of translation between two languages reflects indeed two distinct routes to translation: a conceptual one, from L1 to L2, whereby information about word meaning is primarily used; and a lexical one, from L2 to L1, which is based on word-association, also reflecting well-practiced translation skills.

In a more recent study, Hatzidaki and Pothos (2008) investigated whether previous findings of the involvement of bilingual memory from single-word translation tasks could extend to text translation. The authors employed Greek-English/English-Greek fluent bilinguals (Experiment 1) and French-English/English-French fluent bilinguals (Experiments 2 and 3) who carried out an oral *text translation* task from L1 to L2, and vice versa, followed by a *word recognition* task. Performance on the translation task was assessed according to three typically used textual measures (*coherence, cohesion,* and *accuracy*), which would necessarily implicate semantic and lexical memory. The word recognition task consisted of a list of words that participants were required to read and indicate whether they recognized having seen in the original text they were given to translate. One third of the words from the list had actually appeared in the original text; one third of them had not appeared in the original text; and importantly, one third of them were synonymous words of some words from the original text. Hence, if conceptual memory was more implicated in L1-L2 translation direction, as it was assumed by Kroll and colleagues, the manipulation of the semantic variable of synonymy should have an effect on word recognition, with bilinguals who had participated in L1-L2 translation direction making more false alarms than bilinguals who had participated in L2-L1 translation direction.

The results of the translation task replicated those of Kroll and Stewart (1994), pointing to differential implication of conceptual memory in translation. Participants made more errors in L1-L2 direction than in L2-L1 direction; more errors of sequence of meanings (coherence) were produced in L1-L2 direction than in L2-L1 direction; and more literal translations were produced in L2-L1 direction than in L1-L2 direction. However, the results of the word recognition task – that did not show any difference in recognition accuracy between the two translation directions – suggested that conceptual memory in fluent users of two languages may be employed in a more flexible way than was previously assumed, also depending on the requirements of the task in hand.

2.2.2 Effects of linguistic and extra-linguistic factors in conceptual and lexical access during translation at the *lexical* level

Another finding from psycholinguistic research that shows how word form, meaning, and psycholinguistic factors can affect translation is that certain words are read, comprehended, produced, and translated faster than others. De Groot and colleagues have explained this by arguing that in bilingual memory not all words are represented in the same manner; each concept is represented by several conceptual nodes, and the more similar two concepts are, the more nodes (meaning elements) they have in common. Likewise, the more dissimilar two concepts are, the fewer conceptual nodes they have in common. *Cognates* (words that share most of their morphophonological properties across languages; e.g. *guitar*: in English/*guitarra*: in Spanish), *concrete* words (words that refer to specific entities; e.g. *head*), *high frequency* words (words that are commonly used; e.g. *cat*), and words *high in imageability* (words that can be easily imagined: e.g. *train*) are assumed to have meanings that are similar to their translations. Hence, they should share more of the nodes in conceptual memory and thus be easier to access and more accurate to translate than *non-cognates* (e.g. *dog*: in English/*perro*: in Spanish), *abstract* words (e.g. *freedom*), *low frequency* words (e.g. *snail*), and words *low in imageability* (e.g. *hope*) that are assumed to share less overlapping (e.g. de Groot 1992a, 1992b; de Groot, Dannenburg, and van Hell 1994). Consequently, the similarity of meaning representation that is retrieved for translation equivalents is a function of how much overlapping there is between the concepts that are activated by words in the two languages.

To further examine the factors that can influence conceptual access in bilinguals and their effects in translation production, Tokowicz and Kroll (2007) manipulated the number of translation equivalents of words as well as translation direction. Past research (e.g. de Groot 1992b; de Groot, Dannenburg, and van Hell 1994) has demonstrated that words whose meaning is ambiguous (abstract words) may activate more lexical candidates than words with a clearly defined meaning (concrete words), resulting in slower latency and less accuracy in the former case than in the latter (the so-called *concreteness effect*). We also discussed studies showing that L1-L2 translation direction appears to be more sensitive to semantic manipulations (e.g. Kroll and Stewart 1994). In their study, Tokowicz and Kroll sought to test the hypothesis that the impact of the concreteness effect on translation may also depend on factors other than word ambiguity, such as the differential number of translation equivalents between concrete and abstract words. English-Spanish and Spanish-English fluent bilinguals translated aloud from L1 to L2 and from L2 to L1 (blocked presentation) concrete and abstract words that had either a single (or dominant) translation (Experiment 1), or multiple translations (Experiment 2).

The results of Experiment 1 on translation of words with a single counterpart showed that translation from L1 to L2 was slower and more error-prone than translation from L2 to L1. Interestingly, with regard to translation speed and word ambiguity, there was no difference between concrete and abstract word translation. However, when accuracy was considered, abstract words were found to be more affected than concrete words especially in L1-L2 translation direction. Tokowicz and Kroll (2007) interpreted this as evidence that their participants had learnt more concrete than abstract words in their L2, as showed by the concreteness effect in accuracy. Yet, the absence of a concreteness effect in reaction time suggests that the abstract words they had known – because they had only one translation – were accessed with the same degree of ease and at-similar speed. On the other hand, in Experiment 2, translation of words with one counterpart was faster and more accurate than translation of words with many counterparts. As previously, L1-L2 translation direction was slower and less accurate than L2-L1 translation direction. Translation of abstract words with many counterparts was slower and less accurate than translation of concrete words with many counterparts. However, concrete words with one translation were translated slower but more accurately than abstract words with one translation, revealing a reverse concreteness effect, and showing an interaction between concreteness and ambiguity. Based on these findings, the authors argued that except for the factor of whether a bilingual translates from the L1 to L2 or from the L2 to L1, speed and accuracy of translation performance can also be affected by the ambiguity of a word and the number of translations it has, and that the concreteness effect seems to arise for words with multiple translations only.

Undoubtedly, apart from translation experience, an individual's proficiency in the languages she uses is of paramount importance for successful translation. We saw above that certain psycholinguistic factors can interact with language proficiency in that they may affect the cognitive mechanisms involved in translation from a language one is more competent in (usually the L1) to a language one is less competent in (usually the L2), and vice versa, in different ways. Likewise, age of acquisition (AoA) has been found to affect language processing. For example, monolingual studies have showed that words early acquired in life are processed (e.g. recognised, read, or produced) faster than late acquired words (e.g. Brysbaert, Lange, and van Wijnendaele 2000; Meschyan and Hernandez 2002; Morrison and Ellis 2000). Different accounts have been proposed to explain this advantage (e.g. phonological, semantic, and mapping accounts), but what they all have in common is that they assume qualitative differences in the structure and use of language representations that are formed early as opposed to later in life (see Johnston and Barry 2006 for a review).

Izura and Ellis (2004) investigated how the effect of age of acquisition of L1 and L2 words might be reflected in *translation judgement* and what this may suggest for the underlying cognitive processes involved in this kind of language processing. Spanish-English fluent bilinguals were presented with pairs of words (each in one of the two languages) and were asked to judge whether the words had the same meaning or not. If they thought the two words were counterparts, participants had to press a button on a keypad indicating "yes" and if they thought the two words were not translations of one another they should press a button indicating "no". Half of the word pairs were indeed translations and the other half non-translations. Age of acquisition of the word pairs was manipulated in all possible combinations: early age of acquisition of words in both languages; late age of acquisition of words in both languages; early age of acquisition of the word in L1 but late age of acquisition of the word in L2; and late age of acquisition of the word in L1 but early age of acquisition of the word in L2. The results of the study of Izura and Ellis (2004) that are most relevant for our purposes showed that L2 words were judged faster as being translations of L1 words when L2 words were early than late acquired (Experiments 1 and 3). In other words, age of acquisition of L2 affected the ease with which L2 words were assessed as translations of L1 words. An effect of age of acquisition of L1 was also obtained, with faster translation recognition between word pairs when L1 words were early than late acquired (Experiment 3). In addition, L1 age of acquisition speeded up L2 translation recognition when L1 words were paired with early L2 words but not when L1 words were paired with late L2 words (Experiment 1). To account for the finding that rather L2 age of acquisition seems to drive translation judgment, the authors argued that early acquired words in L2 form special structure representations that map onto L1 words regardless of age of acquisition of L1 words.

2.2.3 Effects of linguistic and extra-linguistic factors in conceptual and lexical access during translation at the *sentential* level

The psycholinguistic studies we have reviewed so far – with the exception of that of Hatzidaki and Pothos (2008) which involved text translation – have looked at cognitive processes underlying language processing in translation at the level of lexical access and representation. However, because translation traditionally involves units larger than a word and words are not processed in isolation, it would be more informative if we also considered studies that have examined how word translation is modulated when words are presented in sentences. In their study (2008), van Hell and de Groot looked at how the *contextual environment* can affect word meaning activation and translation performance. Dutch-English fluent bilinguals were presented with fragments of sentences followed by a target word. Sentences were presented in three conditions: highly constrained context (i.e. the sentence context predicted the target word: *The best cabin of the ship belongs to the [. . .] captain*); low constrained context (i.e. the sentence context did not create a strong bias for the target word: *The handsome man in the white suit is the [. . .] captain*); and target words without context. An equal number of concrete/abstract words and cognates/non-cognates were used as target words at the end or in the middle of these sentences. Participants read each sentence (that remained on a computer screen for a fixed amount of time: Experiment 2, or was presented word-by-word: Experiment 3) and translated the target word either from L1 to L2 or from L2 to L1. Target words without context were simply translated in the other language than the one they were displayed.

To summarize the findings, in both translation directions when the semantic context of a sentence was highly constrained (as opposed to when it was low constrained or no context was available), concreteness and cognate effects were significantly reduced. That is, the semantic (concrete vs. abstract) and morphophonological (cognate vs. non-cognate) nature of the to-be-translated words had little impact on translation performance when those words were considered in a contextual environment that reinforced the activation and retrieval of those words and not of others. The fact that concreteness and cognate effects were strong when the sentence context was not highly constrained also suggests that both linguistic systems of the participants were activated and competing for selection. In addition, translation of abstract non-cognate words (perhaps, the type of words participants found the most difficult to translate) appeared to benefit from the provided high contextual information, resulting in faster translation in high constraint than low constraint or no context condition. Hence, van Hell and de Groot (2008) concluded that semantic contextual information provided in a high constraint sentence can generate predictions that modulate the ease with which upcoming words are processed and, in this case, translated.

A different experimental approach to translation was employed by Macizo and Bajo (2005) who were interested to examine the distinction between *horizontal* (e.g. Gerver 1976) and *vertical* (e.g. Seleskovitch 1976) theories of translation. Namely, whether processing between two languages during translation involves meaning extraction from one language and reformulation of that meaning into the other language on the fly, or whether these two processes take place in a serial manner. The authors hypothesized that if cognitive processes take place during *reading for translation* in parallel, it should impact on participants' working memory performance as opposed to mere *reading for repetition* in the same language. According to the horizontal view, the former type of reading would be more cognitive resource demanding than the latter, because processes such as word recognition, comprehension and partial conversion of meaning from the source language (SL) to the target language (TL) in working memory would take place concurrently. On the other hand, the vertical view would predict no difference between the two types of reading because in both cases the cognitive processes involved would function as a "bottleneck", whereby each process should finish before the next one could take over. To address this issue, Macizo and Bajo examined the performance of Spanish-English professional translators (Experiments 1a and 2a) and highly proficient bilinguals (Experiments 1b and 2b) when reading sentences in their first language (Spanish) to repeat them out loud, and when reading sentences in their first language to translate them orally into their second language (English). Sentences were presented word-by-word on a computer screen and participants were asked to perform each task upon presentation of the entire sentence. Task presentation was blocked. To make sure that participants paid attention to what they read, a sentence verification task followed half of the trials. The difficulty of the tasks (Experiments 1a and 2a) was manipulated by varying lexical ambiguity (an ambiguous word contained in a sentence would have the same spelling across the two languages but different meaning vs. an unambiguous word) and by increasing the working memory load (5 vs. 7 words that would intervene between the ambiguous word and the disambiguating context). In Experiments 1b and 2b, the authors contrasted cognate words (that appeared either at the beginning or at the end of a sentence) with non-cognate words to examine whether both languages are activated concurrently, or whether comprehension in one language precedes reformulation in the other language. In the former case, the nature of the cognate word (similar form and meaning across the two languages) should show facilitation effects in reading for translation, whereas in the latter case, reading in both tasks would be unaffected by this manipulation.

The results of Experiment 1a showed that professional translators were slower and their global comprehension (as indicated by the performance on the sentence verification task) was less accurate in reading for translation of ambiguous sentences when the working memory load was high than when it was low. In reading for repetition, no difference was obtained between ambiguous and unambiguous words or between high and low working memory load. In Experiment 1b, fluent bilinguals yielded the same lexical effects as professional translators, with the exception that their global comprehension was less affected by the difficulty and working memory load manipulations, and they were faster overall. Macizo and Bajo (2005) argued that the surprising direction of different performance between the two groups concerning translation speed and global comprehension might be due to variability within the professional translators' group, or due to a different method of language processing used by the translators. Namely, translators might be used to processing larger language chunks than bilinguals, thus making reading for translation more cognitive resource demanding for the former than the latter group. Experiments 2a and 2b showed that reading for translation was faster for cognates than non-cognates in both groups of participants when a cognate appeared at the end than at the beginning of a sentence. In addition, both professional translators and fluent bilinguals showed that the manipulation of word type (cognate vs. non-cognate) had no effect on reading for repetition. As in the previous two experiments, bilinguals performed faster than translators overall. Based on these findings the authors argued that the cognate facilitation effect was evidence that lexical representations of the TL were partially accessed during reading in the SL, and that the late cognate effect suggested that the TL was activated late in the reading process. Taken together, the results of the psycholinguistic approach to this study provided support for horizontal views of translation.

The studies mentioned so far have showed that language processing during translation may be influenced by various linguistic and extra-linguistic factors, such as the semantic and morphophonological properties of the words in the source language as well as the lexical properties of their translation equivalents in the target language; the context the to-be-translated words appear in (i.e. how words interact with each other and whether they facilitate or impede the translation process); whether the direction of translation is from one's first language to one's second language and vice versa; one's level of proficiency in a second language as well as the age of second language acquisition; and whether reading is used for translation or not. The occurrence and size of these effects have been assessed by statistically analyzing the results of directly observable measures of translation behaviour such as reaction time and accuracy.

2.2.4 What brain activity can tell us about cognitive processes involved in translation

Apart from behavioural measures, psycholinguistics has also combined the use of experimental methods with measures of brain activity (borrowed from *Cognitive Neuroscience*), such as functional magnetic resonance imaging (fMRI) and event-related potentials (ERPs) to investigate language processing. In this way we can obtain valuable information about the impact of linguistic and extra-linguistic factors on cognitive processes that is not directly observable, nor under participants' conscious control. The fMRI technique is used to measure how the brain responds to a stimulus by looking at the neural activity that is showed through increase of blood flow detected by a brain scan (see Bookheimer 2002 for a review on fMRI use in language processing). The ERP technique records electrical brain activity at the surface of the scalp (through electrodes embedded in an elastic cap) as a response to a given stimulus (see Kaan 2007 for a review on ERP use in monolingual and bilingual language processing). The two techniques differ with respect to the information they can provide as far as localization and duration of brain activity is concerned. For example, the fMRI technique provides better spatial resolution (at single-cell level) than the ERP technique, but the ERP technique provides better temporal resolution (on a millisecond-by-millisecond basis) than the fMRI technique; hence, they should be considered as complimentary techniques.

Application of the functional magnetic resonance imaging technique in translation can be seen for example in the study of Lehtonen et al. (2005). The authors examined the neural correlates of Finish-Norwegian fluent bilinguals when translating silently from L1 to L2 visually presented sentences (*translation task*), and when deciding whether the L2 sentence that followed was indeed the correct translation they had in their mind of the L1 sentence they were previously presented with (*control task*). To indicate their responses to the control task, participants pressed a "yes" or "no" button on a keypad that was attached to their chest. The authors additionally manipulated the complexity of the sentences in both tasks (same vs. different word order across the two languages). Hence, half of the sentences were followed by a correct probe and were split into same vs. different word order, and the other half were followed by an incorrect probe and were split into same vs. different word order. Neural activity during these conditions was contrasted against the resting state baseline, and behavioural data (reaction time and accuracy) were also collected.

The results of the behavioural data showed that the translation task took overall longer to perform than the control task, and it was more error-prone than the latter. Both tasks yielded longer reaction times for sentences that had the same word order across the two languages than for sentences whose word order needed to change when translated from one language to the other; however, the manipulation of syntactic complexity did not have an effect on error rates in either task. The results of the analysis of the fMRI data showed that the only significant effect was yielded by the contrast between the translation sentences and the control sentences, which elicited activations in the left inferior frontal cortex in Brodmann's area 47 and in the lateral segment of the globus pallidus (basal ganglia). Hence, the findings from this study – which are supported both by behavioural and brain scan data – suggest that sentence translation is more laborious than sentence translation verification. Interestingly, behavioural responses were not reflected in corresponding brain activation in the manipulation of the syntactic variable of word order. To account for this finding, Lehtonen et al. (2005) argued that perhaps repetition of word-order change during the experiment might have cancelled out any syntactic effects in brain activation. The authors also explained the counterintuitive finding of longer reaction time for same than different word order sentences by arguing that the former contained double adjectives that modified a noun, thus taxing more working memory than the latter. The reported brain correlate of left inferior frontal cortex in Brodmann's area 47 is known to participate in the executive control process of semantic retrieval, and fits well with what is assumed about the participation of semantic memory in L1-L2 translation direction (see previously reviewed studies). Activation of basal ganglia is observed in tasks that require monitoring of task-relevant information and inhibition of task-irrelevant information and language competition.

Finally, the study of Elston-Güttler, Gunter, and Kotz (2005) is another example that shows how brain activity in users of two languages is modulated by psycholinguistic factors such as "global language" context. In particular, the authors were interested in examining how the processing system deals with adjustments that are required when bilinguals change language settings (i.e. from using one language in a given context to using another language in a different context). German-English fluent bilinguals were instructed to read silently sentences that appeared on a computer screen in their L2 (English). The experimental manipulation involved *interlingual homographs* (or else, *faux amis*), that is, words that share morphological properties across languages but have a different meaning (e.g. *gift*: 'poison' in German; 'present' in English). Participants would read a sentence such as *The woman gave her friend a pretty gift* or *The woman gave her friend a pretty shell* and as many more filler sentences (i.e. sentences that did not carry any experimental manipulation) followed by a target word that was a translation of the German meaning of the prime word (e.g. *poison*) or a pseudoword (i.e. a string of letters that sounded like a word, but was not a word). Upon presentation of the target word, participants were required to perform a lexical decision task by pressing one button if the target word was a word and a different button if the target word was a non-word. Importantly, prior to reading the experimental sentences, half of the participants were presented with a short film in German and the other half with the same film narrated in English. Joint measures of reaction time, accuracy, and event-related potentials were used.

The manipulation of related (*gift-poison*) vs. unrelated condition (*shell-poison*) as a function of the language contextual environment that was created by the presentation of a film in participants' L1 or L2 showed the following significant effects: when the film was presented in participants' L1 (German) and the sentences that followed involved as a prime an interlingual homograph, participants were faster at deciding that the target word *poison* in L2 (English) was a word as opposed to when the sentences that followed involved un unrelated prime. In other words, both L1 and L2 lexical items' meanings were activated during the course of the experiment. This effect lasted only through the first half of the experiment (i.e. during the first 15 min). Accuracy was high overall, with fewer errors produced in the related than the unrelated condition. To summarize the main results of the ERP components, analysis of the 150- to 250-ms time window showed an N200 effect when the German film preceded the experimental session in the related as opposed to the unrelated condition. The N200 component, also found in other similar studies (e.g. Elston-Güttler, Paulmann, and Kotz 2005), is taken to be an indicator of word access and/or orthographic processing as well as an indicator of cognitive control across two languages. Hence, in this case the N200 suggested that L1 was active during L2 processing. Analysis of the 300- to 500-ms time window showed a significant N400 priming effect mainly in the first half of the experiment: the related condition was easier to process than the unrelated one, thus resulting in larger negative amplitude for the unrelated than for the related condition. The N400 component is linked to semantic integration and its occurrence here with regard to the semantic relatedness manipulation indicates that there was L1 semantic activation during L2 processing. Hence, both the behavioural and neuropsychological data of this study suggested that the contextual environment can influence language activation, with semantic properties of one language (here L1) affecting word recognition in another language (here L2).

3 Conclusion and discussion for future directions

The present article aimed at providing a brief overview of a variety of experimental methods and techniques that the field of psycholinguistics has used to study the cognitive underpinnings of translation. In doing so, we hope we have demonstrated that theoretical questions that concern both Cognitive Linguistics and translation have been thoroughly examined and their assumptions tested in a number of different language pairs and conditions. It is important to note that the rational and aims of the majority of studies from current psycholinguistic research suggest that translation *per se* has been used so far rather as a tool to better understand the workings of the human mind during language processing, as well as identify those variables that affect language representation and use. In other words, most psycholinguistic work that has been conducted employing a translation task aimed at contributing to the field of psycholinguistics and Cognitive Linguistics, and not that of Translation Studies. In support of this argument for example comes the fact that most studies reported in psycholinguistics literature that have used a translation task involved oral and not written translation (although a reason why this may be is that the execution of motor operations involved in writing can vary considerably among writers, hence not offering an easily controlled environment for experimental research); the majority of psycholinguistic studies on translation usually employ bilingual speakers and not translation students or translation professionals; and most of these studies investigate translation at the lexical level (i.e. processing of words out of context) and not translation at the textual level. Finally, psycholinguistic research usually investigates psycholinguistic theories to inform psycholinguistic models, and very little mention is made to translation theories.

However, recent advances in the domain of research in Translation Studies (Shreve and Angelone 2010), whereby psycholinguistic methods are used to shed light on the process of translation, show that the direction of the relationship between psycholinguistics and Translation Studies can be bidirectional, and that both sciences can benefit from each other. To put it another way, translation is not only an adequate research field that offers ample opportunities to investigate Cognitive Linguistics postulates and test psycholinguistic assumptions, but also fairly ideal to explore from a psycholinguistic perspective to enrich the field of Translation Studies itself. Translation theory assumptions that concern for example *translation units, textual pragmatics* and *equivalence, text register*, and so on, can be tested and enriched through a variety of psycholinguistic ways, covering different dimensions not yet understood in their entirety. Moreover, by means of well-established psycholinguistic paradigms the translator's "black box" may become accessible and the existence of processes speculated until now clearly defined. Also, questions intuitively addressed until recently – such as whether highly fluent bilinguals (i.e. speakers who have a good command of two languages) are able to perform a translation equally successfully as trained translators – are now pursued experimentally by means of a psycholinguistic approach (e.g. Rydning and Lachaud 2010). In addition, availability and combination of a variety of online and off-line measures can be used to inform us about the time-course and locus of the effects of linguistic and extra-linguistic factors on cognitive processes involved in translation. For example, with the application of the method of *eye-tracking* in well-designed experiments (see Rayner 1998 for a comprehensive review), we are now able to monitor a participant's eye-movement behaviour and associate it with her translation behaviour (see for example Shreve, Lacruz, and Angelone 2010 for evidence from eye movements and keystroke logging); in this way we can overcome difficulties and eliminate confounds, previously reported in studies where the Think Aloud Protocol was used to extract information during translation processing. Different translation methods (e.g. "free" vs. "word-for-word" translation), in different translation contexts (e.g. figurative vs. literal language), employing different groups of bilinguals and translators (students or professionals), can be – and some of them are already – experimentally investigated and their findings applied to the field of Translation Studies to educate future translators.

Hence, it becomes clear that an interdisciplinary approach to translation is critical and much needed to advance our knowledge of this exciting faculty called language and its relationship to the human mind, as well as of both translation theory and practice, particularly nowadays that we have the means to do so.

References

Bookheimer, Susan 2002 Functional MRI of language: New approaches to understanding the cortical organization of semantic processing. *Annual Review of Neuroscience* 25: 151–188.
Brysbaert, Marc, Marielle Lange and Ilse van Wijnendaele 2000 The effects of age of acquisition and frequency of occurrence in visual word recognition: Further evidence from Dutch. *European Journal of Cognitive Psychology* 12: 65–85.

Clark, Herbert H. 1992 *Arenas of language use*. Chicago: University of Chicago Press.
De Bot, Kees 1992 A bilingual production model: Levelt's speaking model adapted. *Applied Linguistics* 13: 1–24.
De Bot, Kees and Robert Schreuder 1993 Word production and the bilingual lexicon. In Robert Schreuder and Bert Weltens (eds.), *The bilingual lexicon*, 191–214. Amsterdam: John Benjamins.
de Groot, Annette M. B. 1992a Bilingual lexical representation: A closer look at conceptual representation. In: Ram Frost and Leonard Katz (eds.), *Orthography, phonology, morphology, and meaning*, 389–412. Amsterdam: Elsevier Science.
de Groot, Annette M. B. 1992b Determinants of word translation. *Journal of Experimental Psychology: Learning, Memory, and Cognition* 18: 1001–1018.
de Groot, Annette M. B., Lucia Dannenburg and Janet G. Van Hell 1994 Forward and backward word translation by bilinguals. *Journal of Memory and Language* 33: 600–629.
Dijkstra, Ton 2005 Bilingual visual word recognition and lexical access. In: Judith F. Kroll and Annette M. B. de Groot (eds.), *Handbook of bilingualism: Psycholinguistic approaches*, 179–201. New York: Oxford University Press.
Dijkstra, Ton and Walter J. B. van Heuven 2002 The architecture of the bilingual word recognition system: From identification to decision. *Bilingualism: Language and Cognition* 5: 175–197.
Dufour, Robert and Judith F. Kroll 1995 Matching words to concepts in two languages: A test of the concept mediation model of bilingual representation. *Memory and Cognition* 23: 166–180.
Elston-Güttler, Kerrie E., Thomas C. Gunter and Sonja A. Kotz 2005 Zooming into L2: Global language context and adjustment affect processing of interlingual homographs in sentences. *Cognitive Brain Research* 25: 57–70.
Elston-Güttler, Kerrie E., Silke A. Paulmann and Sonja A. Kotz 2005 Who's in control? Proficiency and L1 influence on L2 processing. *Journal of Cognitive Neuroscience* 17: 1593–1610.
Francis Wendy S 2005 Bilingual semantic and conceptual representation. In: Judith F. Kroll and Annette M.B. De Groot (eds.), *Handbook of bilingualism: Psycholinguistic approaches*, 251–268. New York: Oxford University Press
Gerver, David 1976 Empirical studies of simultaneous interpretation: A review and a model. In: Richard W. Brislin (ed.), *Translation: Applications and research*, 165–207. New York: Gardiner.
Harley, Trevor 1995 *The psychology of language: From data to theory*. New York: Psychology Press.
Hatzidaki, Anna and Emmanuel M. Pothos 2008 Bilingual language representation and cognitive processes in translation. *Applied Psycholinguistics* 29: 125–150.
Hayes, John R. and Linda S. Flower 1980 Identifying the organisation of writing processes. In: Lee W. Gregg and Erwin R. Sternberg (eds.), *Cognitive processes in writing*, 3–30. Hillsdale, NJ: Erlbaum.
Izura, Cristina and Andrew W. Ellis 2004 Age of acquisition effects in translation judgement tasks. *Journal of Memory and Language* 50: 165–181.
Johnston, Robert A. and Chris Barry 2006 Age of acquisition and lexical processing. *Visual Cognition* 13: 789–845.
Kaan, Edith 2007 Event-related potentials and language processing: A brief overview. *Language and Linguistics Compass* 1: 571–591.
Kiraly, Donald C. 1995 *Pathways to translation: Pedagogy and process translation studies*. Kent, OH: Kent State University Press.

Kiraly, Donald C. 1997 Think-aloud protocols and the construction of a professional translator self-concept. In: Joseph H. Danks, Gregory M. Shreve, Stephen B. Fountain and Michael K. McBeath (eds.), *Cognitive processes in translation and interpreting*, 137–160. Thousand Oaks, CA: Sage.

Krings, Hans P. 1986b Translation problems and translation strategies of advanced German learners of French (L2). In: Juliane House and Shoshana Blum-Kulka (eds.), *Interlingual and intercultural communication*, 263–276. Tubingen: Narr.

Krings, Hans P. 1987 The use of introspective data in translation. In: Claus Færch and Gabriele Kasper (eds.), *Introspection in second language research*, 159–176. Clevedon, UK Multilingual Matters.

Kroll, Judith. F. and Ton Dijkstra 2002 The bilingual lexicon. In: Robert Kaplan (ed.), *Handbook of applied linguistics*, 301–321. New York: Oxford University Press.

Kroll, Judith F. and Alexandra Sholl 1992 Lexical and conceptual memory in fluent and nonfluent bilinguals. In: Richard Harris (ed.), *Cognitive processing in* bilinguals, 191–204. (Advances in Psychology 83.) Amsterdam: Elsevier.

Kroll, Judith F. and Erika Stewart 1994 Category interference in translation and picture naming: Evidence for asymmetric connections between bilingual memory representations. *Journal of Memory and Language* 33 149–174.

Kroll, Judith F., Bianca M. Sumutka and Ana I. Schwartz 2005 A cognitive view of the bilingual lexicon: Reading and speaking words in two languages. *International Journal of Bilingualism* 9: 27–48.

Kroll, Judith F., Janet G. van Hell, Natasha Tokowicz and David W. Green 2010 The Revised Hierarchical Model: A critical review and assessment. *Bilingualism: Language and Cognition* 13: 373–381.

Kussmaul, Paul and Sonja Tirkkonen-Condit 1995 Think-aloud protocol analysis in translation studies. *TTR: Traduction, Terminologie, Rédaction* 8: 177–199.

La Heij, Wido 2005 Selection processes in monolingual and bilingual lexical access. In: Judith F. Kroll and Annette M. de Groot (eds.), *Handbook of bilingualism: Psycholinguistic approaches*, 289–307. New York: Oxford University Press.

Lehtonen, Minna H., Matti Laine, Jussi Niemi, Tormod Thomsen, Victor A. Vorobyev and Kenneth Hugdahl 2005 Brain correlates of sentence translation in Finnish-Norwegian bilinguals. *NeuroReport* 16: 607–610.

Lörscher, Wolfgang 1991 *Translation performance, translation process, and translation strategies: A psycholinguistic investigation*. Tübingen, Germany: Gunter Narr.

Lörscher, Wolfgang 1996 A psycholinguistic analysis of translation processes. *Meta* 41 26–32.

Macizo, Pedro and Teresa M. Bajo 2005 Reading for repetition and reading for translation: Do they involve the same processes? *Cognition* 99: 1–34.

Meschyan, Gayane and Arturo Hernandez 2002 Age of acquisition and word frequency: Determinants of object-naming speed and accuracy. *Memory and Cognition* 30: 262–269.

Morrison, Catriona M. and Andrew W. Ellis 2000 Real age of acquisition effects in word naming and lexical decision. *British Journal of Psychology* 91: 167–180.

Poulisse, Nanda and Theo Bongaerts 1994 First language use in second language production. *Applied Linguistics* 15: 36–57.

Rayner, Keith 1998 Eye movements in reading and information processing: 20 years of research. *Psychological Bulletin* 85: 618–660.

Roelofs, Ardi 1998 Lemma selection without inhibition of languages in bilingual speakers. *Bilingualism: Language and Cognition* 1: 94–95.

Rydning, Antin F. and Christian Lachaud 2010 The reformulation challenge in translation: Context reduces polysemy during comprehension, but multiplies creativity during production. In: Gregory M. Shreve and Erik Angelone (eds.), *Translation and cognition*, 85–108. Amsterdam: John Benjamins.

Seleskovitch, Danica 1976 Interpretation: A psychological approach to translating. In: Richard W. Brislin (ed.), *Translation: Applications and research*, 92–116. New York: Gardner.

Shreve, Gregory M. and Erik Angelone (eds.) 2010 *Translation and cognition*. Amsterdam: John Benjamins.

Shreve, Gregory M., Isabel Lacruz and Erik Angelone 2010 Cognitive effort, syntactic disruption, and visual interference in a sight translation task. In: Gregory M. Shreve and Erik Angelone (eds.), *Translation and cognition*, 63–84. Amsterdam: John Benjamins.

Tokowicz, Natasha and Judith F. Kroll 2007 Number of meanings and concreteness: Consequences of ambiguity within and across languages. *Language and Cognitive Processes* 22: 727–779.

van Hell, Janet G. and Annette M. B. de Groot 2008 Sentence context modulates visual word recognition and translation in bilinguals. *Acta Psychologica* 128: 431–451.

Author and Subject Index

active zone, 204, 208–210, 212, 218
adequacy, 5, 14, 188, 189
Al-Hasnawi, Ali, 168, 169, 173
Angelone, Eric, 292, 395, 410
animal grinding, 220, 222
Atkins, B.T.S., 132

Bajo, Teresa M., 405–406
Baker, Mona, vii, 38, 49, 50, 232
Barcelona Sánchez, Antonio, 171, 200
Barsalou, Lawrence, D., 101, 113
behavioral profile, 386–388
Bell, Roger T., 376
Bernárdez, Enrique, 16, 23, 169, 312, 318, 325
bilingualism, 25, 34, 39, 41, 52, 65, 285, 304, 321
– bilinguals, 79
– bilingual representation, 39
Boas, Hans C., 17, 23, 24, 82, 108, 125, 132–137, 287
Bourdieu, Pierre, 321, 331, 334
Bowerman, Melissa, 377, 383
Brandt, Line, 319
Brandt, Per Aage, 319
Braz, Adelino, 314
Brdar, Mario, 17, 22, 24, 84, 199, 223
Brdar-Szabó, Rita, 17, 22, 24, 84, 199, 223
Brems, Elke, 314, 330
Bruner, Jerome, 100

categorization, 12, 76, 106
– category, 12, 76, 106, 342
Catford, John C., 4, 42, 47
Centre for Research and Innovation on Translation and Translation Technology, 55
Chesterman, Andrew, 35, 45–47, 50, 52, 77, 190
Chilton, Paul A., 353
Choi, Soonja, 377, 378
cluster analysis, 386–388
Cognitive Grammar, 8, 10, 16, 22–24
Cognitive Linguistics, 10–13, 18, 38, 64, 76, 169, 304, 315, 330, 397, 410
– Corpus-based Cognitive Linguistics, 56–58

cognitive, cognition, 313, 317, 322, 323, 333, 334
– cognitive commitment, 11, 76
– cognitive domain, 12
– cognitive abilities, 11, 12
– cognitive processes, 398, 403–405
– cognitive routines, 232, 233
– distributed cognition, 114, 115
– situated cognition, 38, 81, 100, 105, 111
compound, 203, 220, 222, 223
connectionism, 104–106, 108
construal, 8, 20, 34, 36, 37, 47, 48, 37, 175, 202, 233, 234–245
Construction Grammar, 12, 23, 137, 289
construction, 14, 24, 253, 254, 284, 286, 288
– constructional mismatch, 289–291, 293, 295, 304
– predicative construction, 294–299, 302
– resultative construction, 286, 290, 294–298, 302
contextualized interpretation, 36, 37
contrastive linguistics, 4
coordination of reading and writing processes, 56, 292
creativity, 174, 176, 189, 313
Croft, William, 22, 34–36, 38, 48, 171, 202, 203
Cruse, D. Alan, 22, 34–38, 48, 171, 203, 204
culture, cultural, 11, 14, 23, 75, 82, 149, 169, 230, 313–319, 321–335, 340
– cultural conceptualizations, 16
– cultural linguistics, 340
– cultural script, 151
– cultural turn, 5, 7, 9, 230

Dagut, Menachem, B., 22, 161–165, 252
Darbelnet, Jean, 4, 23, 48, 232, 252 275
de Groot, Annette, 398, 401–402, 404–405
Delabastita, Dirk, 59, 60
Dewell, Robert, 111, 116
Dickins, James, 166, 173
Dragsted, Barbara, 55, 115, 292

embodied, 11, 36, 53, 168, 230
- embodied cognition, 111–113
- embodied realism, 60–62
Enfield, Nick, 322, 329
equivalence, 4–8, 10, 13, 18, 20, 24, 42–45, 52, 89, 103, 191, 192, 229, 284–288, 290, 302, 304, 316, 318, 331
- constructional equivalence, 287, 288, 290, 304
- dynamic equivalence, 5, 285
- linguistic equivalence, 284, 286
- pragmatic equivalence, 285
- semantic equivalence, 284–286, 302
experimental methods, 55, 57
- event-related potentials or ERPs, 222, 407
- experiments, 267, 272, 379–382
- eye-tracking, 291, 292, 293
- functional magnetic resonance imaging or fMRIs, 407
- key-logging programs, 9, 292
- multi-dimensional scaling, 388–390
- priming, 288, 293
- Think-Aloud Protocols or TAPs, 9, 291, 292, 395–396, 411
- Translog, 9, 54, 292
eye-to-IT project, 55, 56

facet(ization), 203, 204, 209, 210, 211, 213, 220, 223
Fauconnier, Gilles, 12, 86, 230, 244, 262
Feist, Michelle I., 18, 21, 24, 375, 379–381
Filipović, Luna, 17, 23, 24, 26, 87, 141, 251, 257, 262, 269, 272, 274, 291
Fillmore, Charles, 8, 81, 82, 108, 109, 126
focal adjustments, 233
foregrounding, 8
form, see form and meaning
frame, 8, 12, 14, 17, 23, 108–110, 126
- culture-specific frame, 149
- frame element, 127
- Frame Semantics, 76, 126
- FrameNet, 128
- hierarchy of semantic frames, 144
- universal frame 149
- semantic frame 126, 132, 135

García Yebra, Valentín, 4
Glenberg, Arthur M., 111, 287
Golberg, Adele, E., 24, 254, 287–290, 302
gravitational pull hypothesis, 51
Gries, Stephan, 386

habitus (Bourdieu), 331, 334
Halverson, Sandra, L., 15, 23, 25, 33, 45, 48, 50, 51, 64, 75–78, 80, 90, 175, 284, 304
Harnad, Stevan, 101, 102
Harris, Brian, 75, 78, 80, 321
Hatzidaki, Anna, 18, 21, 25, 87, 283, 395, 400, 404
Hendriks-Jansen, Horst, 102, 105
Hermans, Theo, 6, 33
Hierarchical Model, 40
Hilpert, Martin, 223
Holland, Dorothy, 340
Holmes, James S., 6, 54, 160
Holz-Mänttäri, Justa, 5, 81, 113–114
House, Juliane, 5, 85
Hu, Helen Chau, 376, 391
Hymes, Dell, H., 322

Ibarretxe-Antuñano, Iraide, 3, 17, 23, 24, 26, 87, 88, 141, 220, 251–254, 257, 263–267, 290, 315, 395
idealised cognitive model (ICM), 12, 212, 220
imagery, 8, 80, 232, 237, 241
imagination, 12
intercultural mediator, 13, 252
interlingual representation, 137
Iran, 339

Jamarani, Maryam, 15, 16, 22, 339
Jarvis, Scott, 39, 41, 44, 51, 53
Johnson, Mark, 11, 34, 60, 169, 350

kicktionary 147
Kintsch, Walter, 101
Kiraly, Donald C., 115, 396
Kövecses, Zoltán, 169, 202, 207, 212, 214, 221
Kroll, Judith F., 398–402
Kussmaul, Paul, 8, 105, 110, 189, 231, 396

Lakoff, George, 12, 34, 60, 75, 80, 84, 169, 350
Langacker, Ronald W., 8, 34, 35, 37, 39, 45, 59, 82, 87, 113, 202, 204, 231–234, 236, 243
language
- figurative language, 319, 352
- first language (L1), 40, 51, 172, 267, 287, 293, 401, 405
- football language, 148
- second language (l2), 25, 38, 40, 172, 254, 266, 267, 287, 401, 405
- spatial language, 376 ff
- Target Language (TL), 314, 315, 323, 335
language processing, 396–397, 406–407, 410
lexical
- experimental Lexical Semantics, 24
- lexical entry, 129
- lexical unit, 128
lexicalisation pattern 17, 141, 255, 271, 290
- satellite-framed, 141, 143, 255, 256
- verb-framed, 141, 143, 255, 256

Maalej, Zouhair, 173, 174, 208
Macizo, Pedro, 405–406
Mandelblit, Nili, 81, 171, 173, 206
Manner, 256, 259, 260, 262, 265, 270, 273
- Manner salience cline, 257
Marco, Josep, 46, 47
Martín de León, Celia, 15, 23, 25, 75, 81, 99, 103
meaning, 6, 7, 11, 14, 36, 39, 60, 82, 84, 90, 100–115, 126, 151, 169, 230, 231, 252, 258, 276, 284, 366, 375, 398, 401, 406
- conceptual meaning, 20, 220
- encyclopaedic meaning, 11, 20, 23
- experiential meaning, 7
- figurative meaning, 77, 179, 181, 208, 321
- form and meaning, 11, 14, 16, 232, 285–287, 406
- linguistic meaning, 11, 20, 23, 35, 81, 84, 111
- literal meaning, 172, 177, 193
- objectivist meaning, 7
- meaning as use, 391
- schematic meaning, 111, 232

mental simulation, 113, 114
mental space, 12
metaphor, 3, 10, 12, 14–16, 21, 22, 76, 199–203, 205–208, 212, 213, 215, 219, 220, 224, 314, 315, 316–323, 333–335, 340
- career of Metaphor Theory, 320
- metaphors of conflict, 350
- metaphor translation/translation of metaphor, 16, 161 ff
- novel metaphor, 22, 175 ff
- WAR AS SPORT, 352
metonymy, 10, 12, 14, 21, 22, 199–210, 212–224, 318, 319, 321, 323, 333, 335, 340
- complex metonymy, 223–224
- logical metonymy, 220, 221
- metonymic chain, 223
- metonymic source, 200, 202
- metonymic target, 200, 203
- metonymic vehicle, 203
- metonymization, 203
- multi-level metonymy, 223
- regular metonymy, 220, 221
- typology of metonymies, 207, 208, 224
motion event, 255
Muñoz Martín, Ricardo, 15, 24, 25, 56, 75, 79, 109, 304

Natural Semantic Metalanguage 151
Newmark, Peter, 161, 166, 199, 212, 375
Nida, Eugene, A., 4, 103, 229, 285
Nord, Christiane, 5, 38, 168, 285
null instantiation 131

Olohan, Maeve, 76, 85

PACTE group, 56
Pagán Cánovas, Cristóbal 317
Palmer, Gary B., 322, 340
Panther, Klaus-Uwe, 200, 203, 217–218
Paradis, Carita, 202
parallel lexicon fragment 132–135, 137, 139
Path, 256, 257, 259, 261, 263, 265
- Path salience cline, 257
Pavlenko, Aneta, 39–41, 44, 51, 53
Pederson, Eric, 383

perspective 233, 235–237, 243–246
politeness, 327, 328
political discourse, 172, 339 ff
– Iranian political discourse, 354
– Political Discourse Analysis, 353
polysemy, 39, 138, 145, 208, 213, 214, 220, 221
Pothos, Emmanuel N., 400, 404
Practical Reason (Bourdieu), 334
prepositions, 88, 239, 262, 267, 273, 379 ff
Pym, Anthony, 33–35, 38, 42–44, 50, 52, 54
– prototype, 12, 51, 63, 106–112
– prototype semantics, 76
prototype theory, 105–108
psycholinguistics, 18, 258, 291, 395–397, 407, 410
purport, 36

Quinn, Naomi, 340

Radden, Günter, 200, 202, 212, 214, 221
re-contextualisation, 368
retextualization, 13, 251
rhetorical style, 23, 251, 253, 254, 257, 264, 268, 271, 276
Risku, Hanne, 75, 80, 90, 107, 115
Rojo, Ana, 3, 8, 15, 16, 21, 24, 39, 83, 109, 149, 213, 277, 283, 288, 289, 395
Rosch, Eleanor, 12, 76–78, 106, 107
Ruiz de Mendoza Ibañez, Francisco, 200, 223

saliency, 87
Samaniego Fernández, Eva, 15, 20, 21, 23, 159, 174, 252
Schäffner, Christina, 20, 22, 162, 165, 168, 172, 188, 353
schema, 82, 104, 116, 168, 172, 255, 340, 342, 353
– mimetic schema, 116
semantic maps, 388
semantic typology, 254, 378–379, 382–390
Sharifian, Farzad, 15, 16, 22, 339, 340, 341 363, 364
shifts, 6, 20, 23, 42, 46–49, 52–54, 90, 174, 188, 190, 234, 243, 357
Shreve, Gregory M., 78, 79, 284, 293, 395, 410

simile, 166, 246, 318, 319, 321
Slobin, Dan I., 17, 26, 86, 141, 251, 253, 256–271, 290
Snell-Hornby, Mary, 8, 78, 82, 83, 109, 164, 165, 170, 230
specificity, 23, 35, 87, 170, 233, 234, 239–241, 334
Sperber, Dan, 8, 76
Stewart, Erika, 399–401
suffixation, 222, 223
sujet parlant, 236, 240, 242, 245
Sweetser, Eve C., 176, 316, 318, 334
symbol grounding, 15, 101–105, 108, 111

Tabakowska, Elżbieta, 8, 15, 16, 23, 53, 76, 77, 80, 229, 237, 246
Talmy, Leonard, 17, 25, 87–89, 141, 231, 234, 235, 251, 253–258
Tanehashi, Nanako, 380, 381
Theoretical Reason (Bourdieu), 321, 334
thinking for speaking, 17, 86, 87, 253, 256, 268, 275, 276
Thornburg, Linda, 217, 218
Tirkkonen-Condit, Sonja, 50, 81–82, 171, 396
Toury, Gideon, 6, 43, 45, 50, 63, 159, 161, 163 166, 175, 177, 178, 186, 188, 191
trajector-landmark alignment, 235, 242
transfer, 13, 20, 103, 161, 165, 184, 252, 258
Translation Studies, vii, 6–10, 18–21, 25, 34, 42, 49, 53, 54, 59, 62, 159, 160, 190, 192, 193, 231, 252, 283, 285, 315, 353, 396, 410
translation
– cognates vs non-cognates translation, 293, 401, 404–406
– Cognitive Translation Hypothesis, 173, 206
– defining 'translation', 62–64
– effects of syntax on translation, 293
– features of translation, 50–52
– literary vs. non-literary translation, 6, 8, 230
– methodology or research methods in translation, 291–293
– natural translation, 78, 321, 322
– problem solving, 6, 8, 190, 292, 396
– reading for translation, 292, 405, 406
– text segmentation, 292

- time pressure, 56, 107, 163, 292
- translatability, 22, 80, 160, 162–168, 170, 176
- translation direction, translation directionality, 25, 87, 292, 399–404
- translation equivalent 133, 138, 140, 143, 145, 150, 199, 375–376
- Translation Memory Tools, 292
- translation procedures, 4, 6, 46 159, 162, 166, 167, 179, 191, 286
- translation process, 5, 15, 81, 103, 114, 138, 143, 167,169, 230, 252, 284, 291, 292, 304, cognitive effort in translation process, 16, 55, 286, 291–304
- translation shift 6, 20, 46–49, 52, 90, 160, 175, 172, 174, 184, 186, 192, 234, 235
- translation strategies, 9, 10, 26, 83, 264–266, 285, 287, 289, 290, 293, 295, 301, 304
- literal translation, 295, 302
- syntactic transposition, 295, 299, 301–303
- translation training, 17, 81, 84, 116, 267, 268, 277
- translation universals, 25, 49–52, 64, 85–87
- translational act, 13, 35–37, 45, 48, 54
- translational norms, 6, 7, 20, 61, 160, 163, 170, 174, 190, 191, 285
- translationese, 87
- zero translation, 144
translation approaches
- Cognitive Translation Theory, 4, 13, 18, 25
- Cognitive Translatology, 84 ff
- cognitive approach/perspective, vii, 7, 8, 20, 35, 168–172, 190
- corpus-based approaches, 49, 54, 55, 57, 58
- descriptive Translation Studies or approaches, 4, 6, 7, 15, 20, 33, 35, 59, 61, 190, 191, 252

- function-based approaches, 5
- interdisciplinary approach, xi, 18, 283, 411
- Manipulation School, 6
- Polysystem Theory, 6
- prescriptive Translation Studies or approaches, 4, 6, 7, 252, 162, 165, 190
- sociocultural approaches, 6
- text-based approaches, 4, 5
Tymoczko, Maria, 9, 34, 45, 52, 60, 62–64, 66, 77

usage-based, 11, 20, 89

Valenzuela, Javier, 15, 16, 21, 24, 38, 277, 283, 288, 289, 302
value, 60, 151, 175, 169, 316, 318, 319, 321, 328, 331, 333, 335
Van den Broek, Raymond, 162–167
van Hell, Janet G., 402, 404–405
Van Leuven-Zwart, Kitty M., 6, 47
Vázquez-Ayora, Gerardo, 4, 285
Vermeer, Hans J., 5, 81, 82, 106, 107, 110
viewing arrangement, 87, 233, 235, 245
Vinay, Jean-Paul, 4, 23, 48, 232, 252, 275

Western
- languages/cultures, 315–318, 324–329, 332
- media, 354, 360
Wierzbicka, Anna, 125, 151, 152, 153, 313
Wilson, Deirdre, 8, 76
witness reports, 269, 276
Witte, Heidrun, 82, 106, 107, 110
WordNet 132

Yang, Yanning, 323your surgeon is a butcher, 319–320

Zlatev, Jordan, 89, 103–105, 114

Language Index

Arabic, 173, 315, 316, 325, 326, 341, 346
– Egyptian, 384
– Tunisian, 208
Aymara, 334, 335

Bangla, 384
Basque, 254, 257, 263, 264, 266, 268

Cambodian, 327, 329
Chinese, 132, 206, 288, 313, 323, 324, 326, 328–330
– Cantonese, 384, 385
– Mandarin, 206, 384
Croatian, 208, 212–217, 219, 222–224, 383, 385

Dutch, 260, 330, 377, 388, 399, 404

English, 49, 125, 127, 132–134, 136, 140–148, 150, 151, 174, 176, 178, 192, 208, 213, 215–218, 221–223, 231, 237-ff, 256, 258, 259, 262, 263, 267, 271, 272, 286–290, 293, 295, 299, 302, 304, 315, 316, 323–326, 330, 329, 331, 335, 342, 346, 349, 354, 362, 377–381, 384, 386, 387, 388, 390, 399–405, 409
Esperanto, 324, 325

Finnish, 147, 377, 378, 388, 407
French, 137, 147, 221, 260, 267, 320, 330, 331, 383, 385, 388, 400

German, 132–136, 139–143, 147, 148, 150, 152, 208, 213, 217, 220, 222, 260, 267, 288, 383, 385, 388, 409
Greek, Ancient, 316–318, 320
Greek, Modern, 318, 400

Hebrew, 132, 137, 260, 331, 383, 385
Hindi, 383, 385
Hungarian, 208, 213, 215, 218, 222, 384

Icelandic, 315, 325
Indonesian, 324, 327–329, 384
Italian, 260, 320, 383, 385, 388

Japanese, 132, 137, 140, 141, 257, 316, 324, 326, 328, 331, 380, 381, 382, 384, 385, 387, 390

Korean, 377, 384

Latin, 287, 320

Malagasy, 86
Mapundungun, 86
Mongolian, 384

Navajo, 315, 327, 334, 335
Norwegian, 49, 58, 64, 407

Persian, 340–350, 356, 361
Polish, 237-ff, 377, 383, 387
Portuguese, 260
– Brazilian, 144–147

Russian, 260, 325, 383, 385

Samoan, 315, 326, 329
Serbo-Croatian, 260, 262
Spanish, 137, 141, 142, 176, 178, 160, 186, 192, 256, 258, 259, 263, 265, 267, 269, 272, 286–290, 293, 295, 299, 302–304, 315, 318–320, 332, 335, 378, 401–403, 405
Swedish, 49, 383, 385, 387

Tagalog, 384, 385
Telegu, 384
Thai, 384
Turkish, 260, 341, 384, 385

Vietnamese, 384

Yiddish, 331